INSIDE TIME

*A Chassidic Perspective on
the Jewish Calendar*

VOLUME ONE

TIME AND ITS CYCLES

Inside Time
Volume One: Time and Its Cycles

First Edition — 2015

Published by
Meaningful Life Center
ISBN 978-1-886587-52-6

© Meaningful Life Center 2015

INSIDE TIME

*A Chassidic Perspective on
the Jewish Calendar*

VOLUME ONE

TIME AND ITS CYCLES

Based on the works of the Lubavitcher Rebbe
Adapted by Yanki Tauber

Publication of this book
was made possible
through the generosity
of
Kevin Bermeister and family

Lovingly dedicated
in memory of
Avraham Chaim ben Ze'ev—Allan Bermeister

Niftar 18 Elul 5774

INTRODUCTION

$\mathcal{F}$ or the mystic it is the first creation, for the physicist it is a fourth dimension, for the marathon runner it is a hurdle to surmount. But for most of us, time is simply a faceless tyrant—an indomitable force that drives us from a receding past, through a fleeting present, toward an ever-elusive future.

The Torah offers a more intimate experience of time, empowering us to delve beyond its homogeneous expanse to engage a terrain of great diversity. A terrain marked by a weekly cycle of creative workdays and Shabbat rest; with the annual landmarks of Rosh Hashanah awe, Passover freedom, Chanukah light, and Purim joy; with designated hours and minutes for the daily prayers, lighting Shabbat candles, or conducting the *havdalah* ritual. Through these and a host of other time-specific observances, the very entity "time" becomes another object of our life's mission of developing G-d's creation, as we reach within time to uncover its multifaceted nature and actualize its particular potentials.

Inside Time is a three-book series exploring the soul of time as defined by the Torah and as illuminated by chassidic teaching, particularly by the teachings of the Lubavitcher Rebbe, Rabbi Menachem Mendel Schneerson, of blessed memory. The three volumes of this series contain 113 essays grouped into 25 chapters. Volume I (chapters 1–7) includes essays on the essence and origins of time, and on the time-cycles that define the trajectories of our lives—the day, the week, the month, the year, the 19-year cycle of the Jewish calendar, etc. Volumes II and III explore the particular time-qualities that are brought into focus by the festivals and special dates of the Jewish year: Volume II (chapters 8–16) discusses the inner significance of Rosh Hashanah, Yom Kippur and the "ten days of *teshuvah*," Sukkot, Shemini Atzeret and Simchat Torah, Chanukah,

INTRODUCTION   III

Tu BiShevat, and Purim, as well as the unique characteristics of the
months of *Cheshvan* and *Tevet*; and Volume III (chapters 17–25)
contains the chapters on *Nissan*, Passover, the *omer* count, Pesach
Sheini, Lag BaOmer, Shavuot, the "three weeks" and Tishah B'Av,
and *Elul*. A detailed table of contents for all three volumes follows
this introduction on pages VI–XXI.

Each of the 25 chapters in the series includes a number of essays on the primary themes and observances of the time element it
covers. Each chapter also has a short introductory overview of the
history, laws, and customs of the particular festival or time-period,
and a summary of the concepts explored in each of its essays.

A listing of the sources for each of the essays, referencing the
talks and published works of the Rebbe on which it is based, appears at the end of Vol. III (pp. 318–323). A glossary of Hebrew, Aramaic, and Yiddish terms, as well as an index of topics for all three
volumes, is also appended to the end of Vol. III (pp. 360–382).

The essays that comprise *Inside Time* were first published between 1992 and 1999 in *Week In Review*, a weekly publication that
presented the Rebbe's teachings to a contemporary audience.[1]
Each of these essays was originally composed as a self-contained
entity, and was preserved as such in these volumes; thus, while the
various essays in a chapter combine to provide chassidism's "inside"
view of a particular time-element or festival, each essay can also be
perused independently of the others. The reader will therefore encounter certain basic concepts explained more than once in these
books, as necessary components of the essays in which they appear.

---

1   For a discussion on the nature of the Rebbe's teachings and the manner
    in which they have been adapted for the *Week In Review*, see the intro-
    ductions to our two previous compilations of *Week In Review* essays:
    Beyond the Letter of the Law (Meaningful Life Center, 2012), and *The
    Inside Story* (Vaad Hanochos Hatmimim, 1997; an expanded, five-vol-
    ume edition of *The Inside Story* is scheduled for publication in 2016).

It is important to note that the essays in this collection are adaptations, rather than direct translations, of the Rebbe's writings and talks. So while the brilliance and profundity of the concepts they introduce and expound are the Rebbe's alone, the essays must be viewed as no more than my own subjective and limited interpretation of the Rebbe's teachings.

I am greatly indebted to those whose guidance, critique, and assistance have aided me in the writing of these essays for the *Week In Review* and in their compilation and editing for this collection: Simon Jacobson, Ben-Zion Rader, Rochel Chana Schilder Riven, Alex Heppenheimer, Ya'akovah Weber, and Gani Goodman. Batsheva Levinson and Shimon Gorkin did wonders with the design and layout; Batsheva also produced the artwork for the book covers and the chapter frontpieces.

I also wish to express my love and gratitude to my partner in life, Riki, and our three wonderful children, Leah, Chany, and Racheli, for their unqualified and unending support through the long and challenging road of bringing this, and my other writing projects, to fruition.

I conclude with the Talmud's "Prayer for the Student":

> *May it be Your will, L-rd my G-d and G-d of my ancestors, that I should not harbor any animosity toward my colleagues, nor should they toward me. That we shall not profane the sacred nor sanctify the profane. That You bless me with a good heart, a meek soul, and a humble spirit. That You grant us our portion in Your Torah with those who do Your will. That You rebuild Your home and city, speedily in our day.*

Yanki Tauber
Nissan 5775 (March 2015)

A Note to the Reader

Throughout this book, "G-d" is written with a hyphen instead of an "o." According to Torah law, the divine name is sacred, and great care must be taken to accord it proper care and reverence. For this reason, it is best to avoid writing or printing the word "G-d" in its full spelling in all but the most recognizably sacred books (e.g., a Bible or prayer book), lest it be unwittingly defaced or treated irreverently.

May this also serve to remind us that even as we discuss G-d and His influence upon our lives, He is above and beyond all our words; that even as we are enjoined, by the Almighty Himself, to seek Him with our thought, speech, and deeds, He transcends all human effort to name and describe His reality.

VI

CONTENTS

VOLUME I: TIME AND ITS CYCLES

CHAPTER I: ON THE ESSENCE OF TIME I

Essay 1: **The Evolution of Time**........................ 3

Time as the essence of the cosmic *seder hishtalshelut*—of process, sequence, and duration. Why G-d desired a time-bound world, and why the Creator also incorporated supra-time elements and experiences within it.

Essay 2: **The First Creation**............................. 20

Time as the first creation, and therefore the "object" of the first *mitzvah* commanded to the people of Israel. The human input into the makeup of time.

Essay 3: **The Now**.. 3 I

The doctrine of "perpetual creation." The significance of the fact that G-d deliberately creates each individual instant of time, imparting to each moment its particular function.

Essay 4: **Appointments in Time**................................ 3 8

The Torah's concept of *mo'adim* ("appointed times") and *mikra'ei kodesh* ("callings of holiness"). Two visions of time: one sequential, providing us with a linear calendar; and the other conceptual, in which every moment of time has its own "Passover," "Rosh Hashanah," etc.

Essay 5: **Routine and Occasion**................................ 46

How our experience of time generates these two modes of consciousness; and how we employ them both, as well as transcend the distinction between them, in our service of G-d.

Essay 6: **Masculine Moment, Feminine Time**.............. 5 0

The concept of "time-related *mitzvot*," and why women are exempt from them. Woman as time incarnate.

VII

CHAPTER II: THE DAY 57
Darkness and Light

Essay 1: **Garments for the Soul** 60
Why do we live our life in the form of time-segments, rather than as
an unbroken continuum? The concept, put forth by the *Zohar*, that our
days are the most primary "garments" of our soul.

Essay 2: **Evening and Morning** 64
Which comes first: evening or morning? Is life a journey from darkness into light, or is it the movement of light into darkness? Indeed it is
both, as our lives incorporate the dual domains of matter and of spirit.

Essay 3: **The Threshold** 70
The *Modeh Ani* prayer as the connecting point between sleep (supra-
conscious faith) and waking (conscious faith).

CHAPTER III: THE WEEK AND SHABBAT 73
The Cycle of Creation

Essay 1: **The Seventh Element** 77
If time equals motion and change, how are Shabbat and the seventh
millennium—whose essence is "rest"—part of time? Time as a circle:
Shabbat is the center point, and the six days are its outer surface.

Essay 2: **The World of Thought** 89
Three modes of creation—divine speech, divine thought, and the "subconscious" of G-d—and the corresponding realities they generate: the
workday, Shabbat, and the age of Moshiach.

Essay 3: **A Private World** 95
The prohibition against "transferring from domain to domain" as the
essence of Shabbat.

Essay 4: **Bread from Heaven** 106
Shabbat and the manna. The Jew's perspective on *parnassah* (earning
a living).

Essay 5: **Havdalah** 119

Differentiation as the essence of morality. The double paradox of *havdalah*: meaningful difference imposed on intrinsic synonymy, and differentiation for the sake of connection.

Essay 6: **The Eighth Dimension** 127

Beyond the "seven" of nature. The *shemittah* and jubilee cycles

Essay 7: **Twilight** 139

The unique moment of "the eve of Shabbat at twilight" in the six days of creation and on the historical scale.

CHAPTER IV: THE MONTH 149
Renewal

Essay 1: **The Sixteenth Increment** 151

The Jewish people's identification with the lunar cycle. The paradox that the closer the moon is to its source of light, the less visible it is to the earthly observer.

Essay 2: **G-d on the Moon** 160

The cosmic and personal significance of the "diminution of the moon" on the fourth day of creation. Sun and moon as the model for the giver/recipient relationships that drive our existence.

Essay 3: **Locating the Moon** 167

The making of the Jewish calendar through the "consecration of the month." Two elements which lie at the heart of this—and every— *mitzvah*: logical calculation, and absolute confirmation.

Essay 4: **The Monthly Bridge** 175

Shabbat Mevarchim as a juncture between two time-qualities in which one "blesses" the other.

CONTENTS   IX

CHAPTER V: THE YEAR AND THE SEASONS 179
Change and Repetition

Essay 1: **A Seasoned Life**.............................. 181
The year as an encapsulation of all phases and stages of life.

Essay 2: **A Rising Mist**................................. 184
The "season of the sun" and the "season of rains" as two basic modalities of life: divinely granted, and self-generated.

Essay 3: **Agricultural Man**............................ 190
Why the festivals are attuned to the agricultural seasons.

CHAPTER VI: THE LEAP YEAR 193
The Synthesis of Solar and Lunar Time

Essay 1: **Jewish Time**.................................. 195
The sun and moon as paradigms of consistency and flux; the Jewish calendar as the ongoing endeavor to integrate the two.

Essay 2: **A Complete Year**............................ 203
The spiritual and the material aspects of the Jewish year. "Dark matter" as a source of light.

CHAPTER VII: CONFLUENCE 207
Junctures in Time

Essay 1: **Three Times Three**.......................... 210
The uniqueness of a year in which Rosh Hashanah falls on Thursday and Friday, making for a triad of holiness that opens the year. The history and spiritual significance of the "additional festival day of the Diaspora."

Essay 2: **Shammai's Shabbat**......................... 219
Rosh Chodesh ("head of the month") of the month of *Elul* falling on Shabbat and Sunday. The goal, the process, and their integration.

Essay 3: **The Hard Life**..................................225
"Living with the times" via the weekly Torah reading. The lessons of
the Torah portions of *Matot* and *Masei*, their union, and their connection with the time of year in which they are read.

VOLUME II:
ROSH HASHANAH TO PURIM

CHAPTER VIII: ROSH HASHANAH I
Commitment, Memory, and Deed

Essay 1: **The Neurology of Time**..................................5
Rosh Hashanah as the "head" of the year.

Essay 2: **The Man in Man**..................................8
Rosh Hashanah as the birthday of man. Man's role in creation. Man
as a "miniature universe," and the four kingdoms (mineral, vegetable,
animal, and human) within the human being.

Essay 3: **To Will a World**..................................17
Rosh Hashanah as the "coronation" of G-d as king. The cosmic slumber that befalls the entirety of creation on the eve of Rosh Hashanah,
and its arousal through our sounding of the *shofar*.

Essay 4: **A Glass of Milk**..................................25
Asking G-d for our material needs on Rosh Hashanah. Chanah's prayer.

CHAPTER IX:
YOM KIPPUR AND THE TEN DAYS OF TESHUVAH 33
Repentance, Transcendence, Quintessence

Essay 1: **The 120-Day Version of the Human Story**.......37
The historical roots of Yom Kippur as the day on which G-d forgave
us the sin of the Golden Calf and gave us the Second Tablets. G-d's
"awesome plot on the children of man" in making us susceptible to evil.

CONTENTS   XI

Essay 2: **Sin in Four Dimensions**......................44
The dynamics of *teshuvah* ("repentance" and "return").

Essay 3: **Moment**...........................57
Why the most potent time of the year lasts a mere 26 hours, and the
most powerful human deed takes but a moment to achieve.

Essay 4: **Ketoret**............................59
The offering of *ketoret* ("incense") in the "Holy of Holies" as the climax of the Yom Kippur service in the Holy Temple. *Teshuvah* as an
approach to life that not only rectifies sinful or negative deeds but liberates our every endeavor from the limitations of time.

Essay 5: **Day One**.............................65
The "ten days of *teshuvah*" and their relationship to Rosh Hashanah
and Yom Kippur. Yom Kippur as the "one of the year" whose essence
supplies, but also supersedes, the concept of *teshuvah*.

Essay 6: **Reverse Biology**......................72
The deeper significance of fasting on Yom Kippur.

CHAPTER X: SUKKOT 77
Revelation, Unity, Joy

Essay 1: **The Easy Mitzvah**......................81
Dwelling in the *sukkah*. *Sukkah* as the *mitzvah* that embraces the totality of the person.

Essay 2: **The Four Mysteries of King Solomon**.............86
The "four kinds" taken on Sukkot and the paradoxical truths they
express.

Essay 3: **The Taste of Water**.......................95
Joy as a quality of Sukkot. The spiritual significance of the "pouring
of the water" ritual, and of the water-drawing festivities in the Holy
Temple.

Essay 4: **Unity in Three Dimensions**............................106
Unity as a quality of Sukkot. The various degrees of unity achieved by the three *mitzvot* of Sukkot—joy, the four kinds, and *sukkah*.

Essay 5: **One Twig and One Leaf**................................114
The significance of the willow, both as one of the "four kinds" and as the particular *mitzvah* of "*aravah*" on the seventh day of Sukkot.

CHAPTER XI:
SHEMINI ATZERET AND SIMCHAT TORAH 125
Culmination and Integration

Essay 1: **Essence**..129
The concept of *atzeret* ("retention" and "absorption"). Internalizing the unity of Sukkot.

Essay 2: **Daughters Near and Far**................................135
Why we celebrate our bond with the Torah on Shemini Atzeret rather than on Shavuot. The parallels and differences between the "*atzeret* of Sukkot" and the "*atzeret* of Passover."

Essay 3: **Scrolled**...148
Dancing with the Torah on Simchat Torah.

Essay 4: **Intuition**...151
The special joy of *hakafot*.

CHAPTER XII: CHESHVAN 155
The Ordinary Life

Essay 1: **The Last Jew**......................................157
Returning to the daily grind. Making a "dwelling for G-d in the lower realms." The significance of the seventh day of *Cheshvan*.

CONTENTS   XIII

CHAPTER XIII: CHANUKAH 163
Light, Purity, and Spirituality

Essay 1: **The Transparent Body** 167
Chanukah as the most spiritual of the festivals.

Essay 2: **Nightlight** 173
Light as the essence of our mission in life. The light-related *mitzvot*—the lights of the Holy Temple, of Shabbat, and of Chanukah—as a progression of light through time and space.

Essay 3: **The Lamp** 180
The components of the lamp—oil, wick, and flame—and their corresponding elements in the life of man.

Essay 4: **The Mudswamps of Hella** 184
The essence of "*Yavan*" (Greece) as a noxious brew of materialism (earth) and intellect (water), combated through the suprarational self-sacrifice of Chanukah.

Essay 5: **The Miracle** 188
Why the festival of Chanukah was established only on "the next year." The challenge of transforming a momentary flash of heroism into a permanent state of being.

Essay 6: **Compromise** 190
The unnecessary miracle of Chanukah. The connection between Chanukah and education (*chinuch*).

Essay 7: **The Towering Servant** 193
The *shamash* (servant candle) and its place in the *menorah*.

Essay 8: **Accumulating Lights** 194
The meaning behind the debate between the House of Shammai and the House of Hillel regarding the number of candles to be lit each night of Chanukah. The significance of *Zot Chanukah* ("This is Chanukah"), the eighth day of Chanukah.

CHAPTER XIV: TEVET 205
Winter

> *Essay 1*: **Spirit and Substance**.. 207
> The talmudic adage that the month of *Tevet* is a time when "a body de-
> rives pleasure from a body," and its application in the marriage-bond
> between G-d and Israel.

CHAPTER XV: TU BISHEVAT 215
The New Year for Trees

> *Essay 1*: **Of Trees and Men**.. 217
> The various components of the tree—roots, body, fruit, and seeds—in
> the life of man.

> *Essay 2*: **Fruit for Thought**... 221
> The spiritual and psychological significance of the "seven kinds":
> wheat, barley, grapes, figs, pomegranates, olives, and dates.

CHAPTER XVI: PURIM 229
Nature, Physicality, Choice

> *Essay 1*: **Oil and Wine**.. 233
> The difference between Chanukah (oil, innerness, spirituality) and Pu-
> rim (wine, externality, physicality).

> *Essay 2*: **Esther's Story**... 235
> The two "versions" of Purim—the spiritual holiday proposed by Mor-
> dechai, and physical festival propagated by Esther.

> *Essay 3*: **A Roll of Dice**... 240
> The deeper significance of the "casting of lots" that gives Purim its
> name. The parallels and differences between Purim and Yom Kippur
> ("a day like Purim").

> *Essay 4*: **The Thousand-Year Difference**........................ 247
> Purim as the second "giving of the Torah."

CONTENTS   XV

Essay 5: **A Feast and a Fast**............................254
Purim as a lesson on the proper perspective on the "garments of nature."

Essay 6: **A Singular People**............................259
Four aspects of the uniqueness of the Jewish people as seen through
the lens of Purim: "light" (Torah), "happiness" (the festivals), "joy"
(circumcision), and "prestige" (*tefilin*).

Essay 7: **The Purim Drunk**............................266
Four levels of joy; the *mitzvah* to get drunk on Purim.

Essay 8: **The Beginning and the End**............................272
The "Minor Purim" of *Adar* I. Awe and joy as the two poles of the "way
of life" for the Jew.

VOLUME III: PASSOVER TO ELUL

CHAPTER XVII: NISSAN I
The Miraculous Month

Essay 1: **Our Other Head**............................4
The month of *Nissan* as the year's other "Rosh Hashanah."

Essay 2: **The Coiled Spring**............................13
The spiritual significance of the season of spring, and its connection
with the Exodus.

Essay 3: **The Great Shabbat**............................15
The significance of the miracle of *Shabbat HaGadol*, and why its date
of commemoration is set according to the day of the week rather than
the day of the month.

XVI INSIDE TIME

CHAPTER XVIII: PASSOVER 23
Freedom, Faith, and Nationhood

Essay 1: **Endless Lives** 28

If the goal of the Exodus was the covenant at Sinai with its multitude of restrictions on human life, why is Passover the festival of freedom?

Essay 2: **Midnight** 34

Why the Exodus took place at midnight. The two *mitzvot* by which the people of Israel "deserved" their redemption—the Passover offering and circumcision.

Essay 3: **The Festival of the Child** 42

The child as the personification of freedom. The "Four Sons" of the *Haggadah*, and the elusive fifth child of our day.

Essay 4: **Hillel's Paradox** 47

To be or to belong? The role of the Passover offering in our birth as a people, and the ever-present dichotomy between individual and communal identity.

Essay 5: **Bread of Faith** 53

The three matzot and the four cups of wine of the *seder*. Simple faith vs. understanding and appreciation.

Essay 6: **A Speck of Flour** 62

The all-out prohibition against leaven on Passover. The progression from the "barley offering" of the second day of Passover to the "two loaves" offering of Shavuot. The custom to eat matzah *sheruyah* ("wetted matzah") on the eighth day of Passover.

Essay 7: **The Vegetarian Era** 71

The significance of the "great wealth" the people of Israel took out of Egypt. The three staples of the *seder*—the Passover offering, matzah, and *maror*—in the Jew's approach to materiality.

Essay 8: **The Muddy Path** 80

The deeper significance of the "Splitting of the Sea" on the seventh day of Passover. Two paths through the "sea" of our internal hidden worlds.

CONTENTS   XVII

Essay 9: **Miriam's Song**...86
The womanly strain in the "Song at the Sea," and the woman's role in
the redemption from Egypt and the future redemption

Essay 10: **Passovering Time**...91
Remembrance and anticipation; the eighth day of Passover and its
connection with the messianic redemption

CHAPTER XIX: THE COUNTING OF THE OMER 95
Growth and Self-Refinement

Essay 1: **The Journey**..98
The history and significance of the *omer* count. The "days" and "weeks"
in the journey from Exodus to Sinai as a collusion between the sublimity of the goal and the mortality of the journeyer.

Essay 2: **Accumulative Time**..109
What happens to time when we count it? Instead of "running out," it
accumulates.

Essay 3: **A Month of Mitzvot**...111
The specialness of the month of *Iyar* in that each of its 29 days has its
own *mitzvah*.

CHAPTER XX: PESACH SHEINI 113
Second Chance

Essay 1: **The Distant Road**...115
The differences between the first and second Passovers as the difference between the orderly and compartmentalized life of the righteous
person, and the frenzied and inclusive life of the "returnee."

Essay 2: **The Missing Complaint**....................................126
The cry and demand, "Why shall we be deprived?"; our right and duty
to protest G-d's imposition of the state of *galut* (exile) and His diminishing of His presence in our lives.

XVIII   INSIDE TIME

CHAPTER XXI: LAG BAOMER 129
The Mystic Dimension

> *Essay 1*: **24,000 Plus One**................................... 132
> Rabbi Akiva's disciples and Rabbi Shimon bar Yochai; reconciling love
> with truth.
>
> *Essay 2*: **Long-Range Missile**.......................... 138
> The custom of playing with bow-and-arrow on Lag BaOmer; the mys-
> tical "inner soul" of Torah—reaching inward to fly outward.
>
> *Essay 3*: **The Many and the Few**..................... 144
> Rabbi Shimon bar Yochai's approach of "Torah is one's sole occupa-
> tion" and its relevance to otherwise occupied lives.

CHAPTER XXII: SHAVUOT 151
Law, Truth, and Peace

> *Essay 1*: **Doing Nothing**................................. 155
> The first six days of *Sivan* and the series of preparations for receiving
> the Torah. Torah as the divine wisdom and will, requiring an absolute
> *bittul* (self-abnegation) on the part of its student.
>
> *Essay 2*: **Truth**... 162
> Relative and absolute truth. The deeper significance of Rav Yosef's
> statement, "Were it not for this day (Shavuot), how many Yosefs are
> there in the marketplace!"
>
> *Essay 3*: **Peace**.. 166
> Torah as the harmonizing force in a diverse and fragmented world.
> The connection of Torah with the number "3."
>
> *Essay 4*: **Law**.. 170
> The "limitations" imposed by Torah on human behavior as the ulti-
> mate liberators of human potential.

Essay 5: **The Breakthrough**.............................171

The giving of the Torah at Sinai as the revocation of the "decree" that had separated the supernal and the earthly. The concept of a *cheftza snel kedushah*, a physical object made holy through its actualization of a divine desire and command.

Essay 6: **Real Estate**.............................177

The legal battle between Moses and the angels when Moses came to bring the Torah "down from heaven." The transformation of Torah from a spiritual manifesto into the instrument of our development of the physical world into a "dwelling" for G-d.

Essay 7: **The Mathematics of Marriage**.............................187

Torah as the vehicle of relationship between G-d and man; as a collaboration of divine revelation and human intellect.

Essay 8: **The Three Names of Shavuot**.............................193

The three names of Shavuot—"The Time of the Giving of Our Torah," "The Festival of Weeks," and "The Day of the First Fruits"—as they describe the Torah's influence upon our behavior, character, and environment.

Essay 9: **The Phantom Days of Shavuot**.............................201

The "substitute days" of Shavuot (*Sivan* 7–12). Why Shavuot has no special *mitzvah*. The concept of a "chosen people."

CHAPTER XXIII:
THE THREE WEEKS AND TISHAH B'AV 207
Exile and Redemption

Essay 1: **The Pinch**.............................212

The deeper reason why the three weeks from *Tammuz* 17 to *Av* 9 are referred to as *bein ha'metzarim*, "between the strictures."

Essay 2: **Good Grief**.............................214

The difference between *merirut*, constructive grief, and *atzvut*, destructive grief.

Essay 3: **Postponed**.............................215

The essence of the fast day as "a day of goodwill before G-d."

Essay 4: **Difficult Days** 220

The making and worship of the Golden Calf on *Tammuz* 16 and 17. The two related events of the Torah's translation into Greek, and the temporary triumph of Shammai's stringent approach to Torah law.

Essay 5: **Shabbat of Vision** 234

Rabbi Levi Yitzchak of Berdichev's metaphor for the "Shabbat of Vision" that precedes the Fast of *Av* 9.

Essay 6: **The Subterranean Temple** 239

Our 3,000-year journey, along the "hidden, convoluted tunnels" built by King Solomon in the Holy Temple.

Essay 7: **The Legalities of Destruction** 244

Was G-d's destruction of the Holy Temple a violation of Torah law? The Ninth of *Av* as the birthday of Moshiach. The practice of "calculating deadlines" for Moshiach's arrival.

Essay 8: **The Intimate Estrangement** 253

The "three weeks of rebuke" and the "seven weeks of consolation" as the mind and heart of our relationship with G-d. The meaning of an enigmatic passage in the Talmud describing the destruction of the Holy Temple as a most intimate moment in the marriage of G-d and Israel.

Essay 9: **Regret** 262

The meaning of the talmudic statement that G-d "regrets" the creation of *galut* (exile). The "split personality" of the Jew in exile.

Essay 10: **Cholent** 268

With all the benefits of *galut*, we still cry: Enough already!

CHAPTER XIV: THE 15TH OF AV 273
Love and Rebirth

Essay 1: **The Day of the Breaking of the Ax** 275

The mystery of *Av* 15: What is the significance of five relatively minor historical events that occurred on this day, and why do they signify it as our "greatest festival"?

CONTENTS   XXI

Essay 2: **The Dancing Maidens of Jerusalem**..............285

The three types of prospective brides who danced in the vineyards on
Av 15—the "beautiful," those of "good lineage," and the "ugly"—and
their counterparts in the Jew's love of G-d.

Essay 3: **No and Yes**....................................291

The Sinaitic and messianic phases of our marriage to G-d. The correlation between Torah's positive and negative laws and the positive/
negative architecture of our binary world.

CHAPTER XXV: ELUL 295

Compassion and Introspection

Essay 1: **A Haven in Time**...............................298

The month of *Elul* as a "city of refuge." The spiritual meaning of "unintentional murder."

Essay 2: **Month of the Bride**............................301

Elul's astral sign of "virgin" and how it relates to the dynamics of the
cosmic marriage of G-d and Israel.

Essay 3: **The King in the Field**.........................304

The month of *Elul* as a time when "the King is in the field." The relationship between the 39 forbidden labors of Shabbat and the 39 constructive acts of the building of the *mishkan* ("sanctuary"), and why
these are categorized primarily as "the order of bread-making." *Elul* as
a month of "spiritual workdays."

ADDENDA 315

The Jewish Calendar (Infographic).......................316

Sources...318

Glossary..324

Index...360

CHAPTER ONE

On the Essence of Time

What is time? Why does it exist? Is our time-bound world just one of many possible worlds the Creator might have made, or is there a deeper purpose to the temporality and flux that define our existence? How does living in time affect our consciousness and our vision of reality? These are the questions explored in the first essay in this chapter, *The Evolution of Time*.

Our relationship with time, however, is not a one-way street. As *The First Creation* describes, even as time molds and shapes our lives, we mold and shape time. *The Now* examines the esoteric idea of "perpetual creation" and its practical application as a tool for optimal utilization of time. *Appointments in Time* explores the unique relationship between time and the "*mo'adim*," the special dates on the Jewish calendar. In *Routine and Occasion*, we take a closer look at these two mind-constructs which our experience of time generates in us.

The closing essay in this chapter, *Masculine Moment, Feminine Time,* explores the different ways in which Torah law defines a man's relationship with time as opposed to a woman's, and how these relate to the feminine and masculine aspects of time.

In addition to the six essays that comprise this chapter, the following essays also touch upon the essential nature of time: *The Seventh Element* (pp. 77–88); *The Neurology of Time* (in vol. 2 of this series, pp. 5–7); and *Midnight* (vol. 3, pp. 34–41)

THE EVOLUTION OF TIME

The world was created with ten divine utterances. Could it not have been created with a single utterance?
Ethics of the Fathers 5:1

G-d certainly could have generated the whole of creation without any process at all, instantaneously creating the world He desired. But then, one of two things would be the case. Either every phenomenon would be a visible act of G-d, leaving no room for free choice. Or else the world would have no traceable link to its Creator at all. This is why G-d created the world through the "ten utterances," each of which is reflected in some aspect of the nature of our existence, so that they stand as a ladder by which we ascend to appreciate the Master of All.
Akeidat Yitzchak, Bereishit 3

For thousands of years, information traveled no faster than its human bearer. Beyond the range of the human ear and eye, man could communicate with his fellows only as speedily as the swiftest means he could devise to physically carry a person (or animal) across the miles which separated them.

But a century and a half ago, the very concept of communication underwent a radical transformation: Man learned to translate words into pulses of energy surging through a wire. Then radio waves were discovered and exploited, even further freeing the flow of information from the limitations imposed by physical distance. Ideas and data could now be transmitted across vast distances in virtually no time at all.

The new communication technologies yielded a vast array of tools which man—imbued by his Creator with the capacity to freely choose between good and evil—could utilize to the betterment of himself and his world, or to their detriment. But no less significant is the way these discoveries changed our very perception of the reality we inhabit. For the first time in our history, we experienced timelessness.

As physical beings, we inhabit a world defined by "spacetime"— a virtual grid in whose context all objects and events are assigned a "place" which defines their relationship with each other, and also separates them by placing an X amount of "distance" between them. Bridging this distance "takes time": To get from event A to event B, one must first pass through the seconds or centuries which separate them, one at a time; for object A to exert an influence upon object B, it must first surmount the millimeters or miles which separate them, one at a time. In other words, getting from point A to point B is a *process*—a sequence of actions occurring one after the other.

Such was our experience of reality before the advent of electronic communication. But with the invention of the telegraph, telephone, and radio, the transfer of information became instantaneous. No longer did it take any longer to communicate across the globe than across the room. No longer was time an indomitable factor in linking two points on earth, regardless of the distance between them.

Of course, it does take time for radio waves to pass through space; ultimately, our world is no less physical (i.e., no less defined by the parameters of time and space) than it was two centuries ago. But the fact that we *experience* a link across distances in no perceptible duration of time represents a breakthrough not only in the way we live but also in the way we think. Perhaps we, living today, cannot appreciate how incredible the notion of instantaneous communication was to the mind of pre-telegraph man. We do know, however, that despite the fact that we never actually supersede time, the concept of "timelessness" has become part and parcel of our idea and experience of reality.

Paradoxically, our newly-acquired capacity to experience timelessness has also deepened our awareness of the timeliness of our lives. As long as we lived wholly within time, we could not attain a true appreciation of what time is. Would we know that "light" exists and be able to study its characteristics if we never experienced darkness? Would we be aware of the phenomenon of "life" if never confronted by its deterioration and departure? To know a thing and appreciate its qualities and potentials we must first surpass its limits, at least in the realm of the mind.

A MEANINGFUL WORLD

Why is time necessary? And why is it important that we should understand what time is? Of course, we cannot even imagine what a truly timeless reality would be like. (Would everything happen at once? Or would things not "happen" at all, only "be"?) But no matter: If G-d would have created a timeless world, that would have been the only comprehensible form of existence, and we would have had no idea of what "time" might be. So is time just one of many possible ways to make our world "work"? Or is there a deeper reason for this particular formulation of reality?

Conversely, we might ask: Having been placed within a time-bound reality, why have we been granted the ability to try its limits and advance to the threshold of timelessness? Is this just so that we should better appreciate the significance of time? Or is there some deeper reason why our time-contextualized lives must also include a glimpse of a reality beyond time's boundaries?

The Torah's opening chapter describes the creation of the world as a series of divine communications. ("G-d said, 'There shall be light!' and there was light... G-d said, 'The earth shall sprout forth vegetation...' and it was so.") In other words, with His every creation, G-d is communicating something to us. A tree is not just a food-making machine—it is an insight into the nature of productivity.[1] The sun and the moon are not just celestial light fixtures—they are a metaphor for the giver/recipient dynamic that pervades our existence.[2] In addition to its "functional" purpose, every component of our world is G-d's way of telling us something about Himself and His relationship with us.

The same is true of time, which can be said to be the first and most basic creation:[3] The phenomenon of time plays a crucial role in our relationship with G-d. For time is the essence of the *seder hishtalshelut*, the "order of evolution" which G-d employed in His creation of the world in order to facilitate our quest for connection with our Creator and Source.

---

1   See *Of Trees and Men,* in vol. 2 of this series, pp 217–220.
2   See *G-d on the Moon,* on pp. 160–166 below.
3   See below. Also see *The First Creation,* on pp. 20–30.

The "Order of Evolution"

What is the *seder hishtalshelut*? The teachings of kabbalah describe the physical universe as the last in a chain of numerous "worlds." We all recognize the existence of realities more abstract than that which frames the physical world: We speak of "the world of ideas," the "world of emotions," or the "spiritual world" of the believer and the mystic. The created reality, say the kabbalists, consists of a multitude of such worlds, each the product and outgrowth of the more abstract and spiritual world which precedes it, thus forming an "order of evolution."

In other words, G-d began His work of creation by creating all existences in their most sublime and spiritual form. He then proceeded to cause them to evolve and metamorphose, in many steps and stages, into successively more concrete forms, ultimately producing our physical world—the "lowliest" and most tangible embodiment of these realities.

Hence, the many worlds of creation are all mirror-images of each other, each containing the same array of elements and creations, and differing only in the degree of substance and tactility they impose on them. For example, physical water is the end product of a series of more spiritual creations, such as the emotion of love and the divine attribute of *chesed* ("benevolence"); physical earth is the material incarnation of a string of creations that includes concepts such as "femininity" and "receptiveness," and originates in the divine attribute of *malchut* ("sovereignty"). And so it is with every object, phenomenon, and concept in existence: Each exists on the many levels of the *seder hishtalshelut*, ranging from its most ethereal state to its most corporeal form.

With each descending step of the *seder hishtalshelut*, the creation not only becomes more tangible and substantial, it also grows more distant from its Creator and Source. For although spiritual entities are also "creations" (i.e., realities distinct from the reality of their Creator), they are transparent existences that reveal the higher reality from which they stem and which they serve.[4] But the more "substantial" a thing becomes, the less it exhibits its divine essence and function. A physical object exudes immanence; its very mass proclaims "I am," belying the truth that it exists in order to serve a higher end. The more "presence" a thing possesses, the more it asserts its own self and the more it obscures its Creator and the purpose for which He created it.

Yet this was G-d's objective in creation: that there should exist a world that obscures the truth of its Creator, and that the human being, out of his or her own free will (which only such a disconnected world could allow), should choose to overcome the concealment this world entails and direct its resources to serve the fulfillment of the divine will. So G-d evolved a chain of successively more substantial and self-absorbed realities, culminating in a world so corporeal that we must toil greatly to uncover and develop, in ourselves and in our environment, a sense of spiritual direction and purpose.

This, explains chassidic master Rabbi Dov Ber of Mezheritch, is the significance of the divine name *Sha-dai*, which our sages interpret as an acronym for the phrase *she'amar le'olamo dai*—"He who said to His world: Enough!"[5] Had G-d proceeded any further with the *seder hishtalshelut*, it would have passed the point of no

---

4 This is even true of the more "spiritual" or abstract elements of our physical reality. For example, an idea implies and reflects the mind which conceived it; the existence of light indicates its source and serves to express its qualities. Certainly such is the case with the truly spiritual creations of the higher worlds of the "chain"—creations that are devoid of any and all vestiges of selfhood and exist solely to express and serve the omnipotence and majesty of their Creator.

5 Talmud, *Chagigah* 12a.

ON THE ESSENCE OF TIME (1)   9

return. Had G-d caused His creation to descend a single increment
lower in terms of selfhood and corporeality; had He smothered
even that faint glimmer of spirituality which the material mantle
of our world allows to seep through; had our lives and consciousness been even more cut off from their Source—it would have
been impossible for us to overcome the spiritual darkness of such a
world. So G-d said "Enough!", halting the *seder hishtalshelut* when
creation reached the degree of substantiality represented by our
physical world.

SPIRITUAL TIME

Not only the contents of our physical world, but also its defining
parameters—space and time—are "end-of-the-line" products of
the *seder hishtalshelut*.

We know space as the three dimensions—as the context within
which physical objects are positioned in spatial relation to each
other (above, below, behind, etc.). But there is also a conceptual
space: We speak of "higher" and "lower" planes of reality; we describe ideas as "deep" or "shallow." So spiritual entities also occupy a "space" which defines their position in relation to each other,
and in relation to the world they occupy. Common thinking is
that these "conceptual space" characterizations are merely mental
projections of physical phenomena in an attempt by our physical
minds to contemplate and discuss metaphysical abstractions. The
truth, say the kabbalists, is the very opposite: Space originates as
a wholly spiritual phenomenon, and then "descends" through the
seder hishtalshelut to evolve into increasingly more concrete forms.
Thus physical space derives from "conceptual space," which in turn
evolves from an even more abstract form of space, and so on. The

higher we ascend the chain of *hishtalshelut*, the more abstract and ethereal is the space of that particular "world."

Time, too, exists on many levels, as it evolves from its most spiritual form all the way down to "our" physical time. What we experience as a one-way time arrow through the tenses of past, present, and future is but the last and most concrete incarnation of the element or phenomenon of time. As it descends through the *seder hishtalshelut*, time is expressed in many forms: It is the essence of motion, causation, and change; it underlies the pulse of life, the processional nature of reason, and the pendulum of feeling.

While physical time is chronological—its "past" occurs before its "future"—spiritual time is not so limited. By way of example, let us consider the nature of the "time" which defines the world of logic. The logical concepts A (1+1=2) and B (2-1=1) occupy different positions in the timeline of this world, as A precedes B in logical sequence (because one plus one equals two, *therefore* two minus one equals one). But the fact that B "follows" A does not mean that there is a point in time at which A exists and B does not. They are both always existent, even as the "first" causes the "second." Or, to take an example from the world of emotion: feeling A may cause feeling B (e.g., a feeling of reverence and awe toward a great and magnificent being produces a yearning to approach this being and be touched by its greatness), but the possessor of these two feelings always had them both; they developed simultaneously in his heart, although the "first" (the awe) is the root and cause of the "second" (the craving to come close). In other words, spiritual realities such as ideas and feelings also exist within "time," yet theirs is a more abstract, spiritual form of time, transcending the "one at a time" and "one-way travel" limitations of physical time.[6]

---

6   In the words of Shaloh (Rabbi Isaiah Horowitz, 1560–1630), citing the great kabbalist Rabbi Moshe Cordovero (1522–1570): When discussing

ON THE ESSENCE OF TIME (1)

The *seder hishtalshelut* itself is a function of spiritual time: The very concept of an "order" and an "evolution" presumes a reality governed by cause and effect. Of course, the evolution of creation from spirit to matter did not "take time" in the commonplace sense of the word—G-d did not have to "wait" for the successive phases and stages of the *seder hishtalshelut* to yield the material world He wanted. In terms of physical time, the creation of the physical world—G-d's desired end-result of the creation process—was instantaneous. But on the conceptual level, "time" is the framework within which the many levels of the created reality unfold.

Thus time may be regarded as the "first" creation. Since creation is a process in which a series of worlds evolve one from (and thus "after") the other, it is an event which "takes time"—at least in the most abstract sense of the term. On the other hand, G-d's act of creation did not take place "in" time, which would imply that there already was something (i.e., the phenomenon of time) that wasn't created by G-d! This means that time came into being as an integral part of the very concept "creation" (which is itself a created entity).

In other words, time exists because G-d desired that creation should constitute a *process*—a chain of worlds extending from heaven to earth, each the product of its "predecessor." Without time (on

---

the different stages in G-d's emanation of worlds and spheres of reality, we need to bear in mind an important distinction between our physical world and the higher, spiritual realms. In a physical, time-bounded world, change and progression mean that the previous state no longer prevails. Wool becomes yarn, yarn becomes cloth, cloth becomes a coat; the person now has a coat, but the sheep is left bereft of its wool. Not so with a spiritual evolution, where all stages exist simultaneously, each on its own plane. There is no change of mind in the Creator, G-d forbid, nor a "before" and "after" in the temporal sense, but rather a hierarchy of realities which derive from and impact each other.

the most abstract level) there could not be a *seder hishtalshelut*;[7] and without time (on the physical level), we, who can only relate to spiritual concepts as abstractions of their counterparts in our physical reality, could not conceive of, much less contemplate, the "order of evolution" linking the Creator's most sublime works to our own world.

THE THREE THOUSAND METAPHORS OF SOLOMON

Of course, G-d did not need all this. He could have created the physical world in a truly instantaneous manner—not only in terms of physical time but in the conceptual sense as well, without passing through the stages of the *seder hishtalshelut*. So why create an entire chain of universes populated by spiritual versions of our reality, just so that our world should congeal into being as its lowest link? Why not just create the physical reality as it is, since this was the objective of His creation?

In any act of creation or development, the method which yields instantaneous results usually represents the most direct and convenient approach—as far as the creator or developer is concerned. But what about those at the receiving end? How is such an approach—as opposed to a phased, evolutionary process—reflected in the nature of the end-product? How does it affect its utility for those for whom it is intended? Let us examine a particular case in which both these options are available to one who seeks to "create" something.

---

7 Spiritual space is also a prerequisite to a *seder hishtalshelut*, since it defines the relationship between the higher, more sublime level of existence at the "top" of the chain and the chain's "lower" links. But time will always precede space as necessary to the very concept of process.

ON THE ESSENCE OF TIME (1)

A teacher wishes to convey to his pupil a concept whose profundity and abstraction far exceed the capacity of the pupil's mind. So the teacher must create a new reality in the mind of the pupil, implanting within it a knowledge which not only had never existed there before but which is, in essence, beyond anything the pupil's mind is capable of attaining on its own. But how to articulate a concept to someone who has no understanding of the terms and "language" which apply to it? The teacher decides to use a parable.

What is a parable? We are told that King Solomon "grew wiser than all men... and he spoke three thousand parables."[8] At first glance, this seems to describe a versatility of imagination rather than a depth of wisdom. The parable, however, is not just an innovative or entertaining way to convey an idea: It is the translation of a concept into a lower level of intellectual discourse. In the parable, concepts which can generally be discussed in terms comprehensible only to the most refined and abstract minds are rendered as objects and events which are part of a lesser mind's "world" and life experience.

In other words, the teacher "lowers" and coarsens the concept, articulating it in terms to which the pupil's mind can relate. But once it has been imbibed by the pupil in this guise, the pupil can then proceed to strip it of its metaphoric garments. Once the idea has been implanted in the pupil's mind in a form which is comprehensible to him, the door has been opened for him to begin to relate to the deeper significance buried within it.

But what if the parable itself is too profound and abstract for the pupil's mind? The teacher will then clothe this parable in an even "lowlier" parable, spinning a tale which employs even more commonplace objects and events to make its point. Thus the

---

8   I Kings 5:11–12.

concept will be "smuggled" into the mind of the pupil coated in two metaphoric layers. Having imbibed the concept in this double guise, the pupil can now proceed to strip it of its outermost layer and comprehend the more abstract parable. This achieved, his mind will be ripe for a further abstraction, and the pupil will realize that what he has understood is also just a metaphor for an even loftier and more abstract dimension of the concept.

The teacher may thus subject the idea he wishes to convey to many levels of embodiment, shrouding it with layer upon layer of metaphor and palpability. The objective: to create a series of stepping stones, neither of which is too far from the next, to accommodate the pupil's intellectual stride, which would lead the pupil deeper and deeper into the concept. Ultimately, it would enable the pupil to gain entrance into its innermost kernel of significance, no matter how far removed he was from it at the onset of his quest.

Now we can understand the significance of King Solomon's three thousand parables. These are not three thousand parallel alternatives for the articulation of a concept in a story, but three thousand *successive* metaphorizations, each clothing its predecessor with yet another layer of tangibility, lowering it yet another level in order to address yet a coarser mind, for which the previous parable is still too abstract to digest. The greatness of King Solomon's wisdom lay in that he could take the most sublime of thoughts and successfully articulate them to a mind so removed from his own that it took a parable of a parable of a parable—three thousand times over—to translate it into this mind's terms.

So our teacher, who wishes to impart to his pupil a concept that, by its very nature, will represent a new and unprecedented reality in the pupil's mind, embarks on an involved and laborious process of *hishtalshelut*. He begins with his own knowledge of the concept in its abstract purity and proceeds to vest it in slightly more concrete and tangible terms. He then repeats the process time and again, imposing layer upon layer of crudity and embodiment upon it, until it has descended and metamorphosed into a thought which belongs to the pupil's intellectual world.

But why bother? Why not simply relate the concept to the pupil as it exists in his, the teacher's, mind? Because were he to do so, his words would be absolutely meaningless to the pupil. The teacher may be espousing the most profound words of wisdom to ever reach the pupil's ears, but to the pupil it would be pure gibberish. The pupil may record his master's words; he may review them and learn to repeat them verbatim; he may even, if he keeps at it long enough, convince himself that he understands them. But, in truth, he has not gained an iota of insight into their significance.

Certainly, G-d could have created our physical reality in an "instantaneous" manner, without bothering with a *seder hishtalshelut*. But where would that leave *us*? We and our world would exist, but would we be capable of any insight into the significance of our existence? We could be *told* about our mission in life and our relationship with our Creator, but could we possibly understand it?

G-d wanted our lives to be a parable (of a parable of a parable of a parable) of a higher reality. He wanted that the world we occupy should be but the outermost layer of successively more abstract and spiritual realities, each but a single leap of insight from the one within it, so that beginning with our comprehension of our own reality, we may ascend, step by step, in our understanding of what and why we are and from where we come.

THE LIMITATIONS OF HISHTALSHELUT

This explains the necessity for the *seder hishtalshelut*. This is why the essence of time—the very phenomena of "process," "cause and effect," and "evolution"—was created: so that our physical existence should not be an island in the void of the incomprehensible, but a connected link in a chain of worlds leading to its sublime origins in the creative energy of G-d. And because we experience time on our, physical level, we can relate to the concept of a *seder hishtalshelut* in "spiritual time," and retrace the process of creation by climbing the links of this cosmic chain to gain increasingly deeper insight into the dynamics of creation and our Creator's involvement in our reality.

All this, however, is only one side of the story. The *seder hishtalshelut* is crucial to our mission in life, which insists that we not only serve G-d but also strive to comprehend our relationship with Him. But the *hishtalshelut* is not only a link, it is also a screen. Were our relationship with the Almighty to be confined to the channel offered by the *hishtalshelut*, it would mean that we have no direct connection with the infinite and utterly undefinable reality of our Creator and the true essence and function of our own existence. It would mean that we can relate to these truths only via the many garments in which G-d has shrouded Himself in order to make Himself and His creation comprehensible to us.

On the one hand, our lives are governed by the ordered and rational process of *hishtalshelut*. On the other hand, however, we are empowered to transcend it. For G-d has also granted us the ability to touch base with the very essence of our life, with a "timeless" essence which transcends reason, order, and the process of creation itself.

Let us return to the teacher and pupil. If you recall, the teacher is in the midst of expounding a parable (the last and most external of a string of parables) which will encapsulate the concept, but will also conceal it and convey only the greatly constrained and coarsened version which the pupil is capable of comprehending. Yet the

ON THE ESSENCE OF TIME (1)   17

teacher also wants to somehow allow his pupil a glimpse of the real
thing, to accord him a true if fleeting vision of the concept in all its
sublime purity. He wants the pupil to know that this is not where
it's at, to appreciate the extent of what lies buried within. Because
although the "multi-parable" approach presents the pupil with the
tools to rise to a full and comprehensive understanding of the concept, it is not free of its own pitfalls. There is a danger as well: the
danger that the pupil will get bogged down in the parable itself
(or in its second, third, or fourth abstraction), and fail to carry it
through to its ultimate significance; the danger that he will come
to mistake a shallow and external version of his master's teaching
for the end of his intellectual quest.

So in the course of his delivery the teacher will allow a word, a
gesture, an inflection to escape the parable's rigid constraints. He
will allow a glimmer of unconstrained wisdom to flicker through
the many metaphoric veils which enclose the pure concept within.
This "glimmer" may be incomprehensible to the pupil (in the conventional, logical sense), but it will impress upon him an appreciation of the depth of the concept within the parable .⁹

---

9   This concept also has a parallel in Torah law (*halachah*). On Shabbat,
     it is forbidden to transfer an object from a private to a public domain
     or *vice versa*. However, there exists the option of making an *eiruv*, a
     halachic procedure (involving the fashioning of an enclosure around
     the area and the creation of a common meal area) which "combines"
     a courtyard, street, or even an entire city into a single private domain,
     thereby allowing the transfer of objects from home to home within
     the *eiruv* area. The law states that in the case that an *eiruv* is made for
     an entire city, one section of the city must be left outside of the *eiruv*'s
     boundaries; this, so that "there be the recognition that it is forbidden
     to carry on Shabbat, and that only the *eiruv* has permitted it within
     a certain area." Were the *eiruv* to include the entire city, the danger

THE WINDOW

The same applies to our probing of our world to gain insight into the divine reality which underlies it. The physical existence is a "parable" offering a link to the truth of its Creator; but it also obscures that truth. So unless one is guided by a transcendent vision of the essence and purpose of creation, there is the danger that these "garments" may distort or even eclipse what they were created to express and reveal.

Therefore, G-d did not evolve an "airtight" *seder hishtalshelut*. Even as He projected His creative powers via its successive phases and worlds, He allowed a pinpoint of His infinite light to penetrate this multilevel edifice from end to end. Even as He set up a step-by-step plan for us to proceed in our life's task of comprehending, refining, and sanctifying our existence, He also provided us with a window through which to glimpse the underlying reality which transcends it all.

In our experience of physical time, pulses of energy, moving at the speed of light, generate the effect of timeless communications in our daily lives. The same is true of our spiritual lives: Even as G-d relates to us via the *seder hishtalshelut*, which dictates that our experience of Him be filtered through a chain of intellectual,

---

would exist that, in time, the entire concept of this most fundamental aspect of Shabbat rest will be forgotten by its populace.

In other words, a secondary or superimposed reality has been created by the *eiruv*. Although it is a valid reality, sanctioned by Torah law, it is important to retain the awareness of a deeper, more underlying reality: the nature of the holiness of Shabbat, an important expression of which is the fact that one should not transfer an object from domain to domain. So a breach is created in the *eiruv* reality, to serve as a window through which one may behold and experience the deeper Shabbat reality.

emotional, and spiritual processes, He also granted us moments of direct and unfiltered contact with Himself—moments of "instantaneous" connection that transcend the order of creation.

THE
FIRST
CREATION

"In the beginning" means in the beginning of time — that is, the first indivisible moment, as time did not exist prior to it.

Sforno to Genesis 1:1

"In the beginning G-d created the heavens and the earth." A significant part of the earth's population would recognize this as the opening verse of the Bible. But in the view of a number of the biblical commentaries, these words, as written above, are a mistranslation of the original Hebrew.

The precise meaning of the Torah's first word, *bereishit*, is not "in the beginning" (that would be *barishonah* or *ba'techilah*), but "in the beginning of." How, then, are we to read the Torah's first sentence? *In the beginning of* what?

The commentaries offer various interpretations. Rashi[1] suggests that the Torah's first three verses might be read as a single sentence: "In the beginning of G-d's creation of the heavens and the earth, when the earth was chaotic and void... G-d said, 'There shall be light,' and there was light." Sforno[2] interprets *bereishit* as "In the beginning of time." *Bereishit* is the very first moment of time, a moment without a past; nothing preceded this moment, since with this moment G-d created time itself.

---

1   Rabbi Shlomo Yitzchaki, 1040–1105, author of the primary commentary on the Torah.

2   Rabbi Ovadiah Sforno, c. 1475–1550.

ON THE ESSENCE OF TIME (2)   21

In other words, while time is itself a creation—a most basic principle of the Jewish faith is that every reality was created by G-d—it is the first and most primary of creations. Indeed, "creation" (*beriah*, in the Hebrew), which means bringing something into being out of a prior state of nonexistence, implies a "before" and "after." So to say that G-d created anything is also to say that He first (or simultaneously) created time. To say, "In the beginning G-d created..." is also to say, "G-d created the beginning."

Rabbi Saadiah Gaon (c. 882–942) applies this concept to resolve a philosophical problem regarding G-d's creation of the world. Since G-d is eternal and unchanging,[3] we obviously cannot say that He "matured" to a certain state or had a certain idea "grow on Him." So why did He create the world only when He did? Why not one year, a hundred years, or a billion years earlier, since whatever reasons He had for creation were certainly just as valid then? But this question, explains Rabbi Saadiah Gaon, is a *non sequitur*. Time is itself part of G-d's creation. We cannot ask why the world was not created earlier, since there is no stretch of time that can be termed "before" creation.[4]

THE FIRST MITZVAH

Time's status as the first creation sheds light on another point raised by the commentaries on the first verse of the book of Genesis. In his commentary on this verse, Rashi quotes the Midrash:

---

3   As in Malachi 3:6: "I, G-d, have not changed."

4   *Emunot ve-Deiot* 1; Rabbi Saadiah Gaon's commentary on Torah (Ratzavi) 1:1. Also see Rabbi Schneur Zalman of Liadi, *Siddur Im D'ach, Shaar ha-Keriat Shema.*

       Of course, the universe was "preceded" by a state of nonexistence—at a certain point, G-d desired to create a world. This "point," however,

The Torah ought to have begun with, "This month shall be to you the head of months..."[5] which is the first mitzvah *commanded to the people of Israel. Why does it begin "In the beginning of..."?*

Torah means "law" and "instruction." The function of the Torah is instruct us on the laws of life, which it does via the 613 *mitzvot* (divine commandments) it addresses to the people of Israel. But the first such *mitzvah* appears in the 12th chapter of Exodus, where G-d commands the *mitzvah* of *kiddush hachodesh* — the "sanctification of the new month" and the setting of the Jewish calendar. Why, asks the Midrash, does the Torah devote the first of its five books, and a good part of the second, to things other than its primary purpose? Certainly, there are many lessons to be learned from the Torah's accounts of the creation of the universe, the history of mankind, and the lives of the founding fathers and mothers of the people of Israel. But would it not be more appropriate for the Torah to *begin* with G-d's direct instructions to us?[6]

The Midrash goes on to explain the Torah's reason for opening with its account of the creation — namely, to establish the eternal

---

is not a point in time, but a point in the divine will. G-d, in essence, is above the desire for a world, yet He desired that He have this desire. In relation to this desire, the world exists; in relation to the divine essence which transcends this desire, it is utter nothingness. This is the "before" and "after" of the creation of "the beginning." But in terms of physical time, the very first moment of time is also the first moment of creation. Also see *The Evolution of Time*, the section called "Spiritual Time," on pp. 9–12 above.

5   Exodus 12:2.

6   Indeed, many events and laws appear in the Torah not in the order in which they occurred or were instructed, but in sequences dictated by other priorities. Hence the rule: "There is no earlier and later in Torah" (see *The Missing Complaint* in vol. 3 of this series, pp. 126–128).

right of the people of Israel to the Holy Land.[7] But the rule is that "a question in Torah is also Torah." When a Torah idea is proposed as a hypothesis, this expresses a Torah truth, also if the hypothesis is "rejected" in favor of a different approach. This means that, in effect, the Torah has two beginnings: the actual, textual beginning of the opening verse of Genesis ("In the beginning G-d created..."); and "the first *mitzvah* to be commanded the Jewish people," in the 12th chapter of Exodus, which is the Torah's ought-to-have-begun beginning.

Furthermore, there obviously exists an essential connection between the "first creation" and the "first *mitzvah*," as each represents, in its own way, the beginning of the Torah.

To better understand this connection, we first need to explain why the *mitzvah* of *kiddush hachodesh* was our first *mitzvah*. Obviously, the setting of the Jewish calendar has a far-reaching influence

---

7   In the words of the Midrash, as quoted by Rashi: "So that if the nations of the world say to the people of Israel, 'You are thieves, for having conquered the lands of the seven nations,' they would reply to them: 'The entire world is G-d's ; G-d created it, and G-d grants it to whomever He desires. It was G-d's will to give it to them, and it was G-d's will to take it from them and give it to us.'" (*Midrash Tanchuma, Bereishit Rabbah*, and Rashi to Genesis 1:1).

   Maharal (Rabbi Judah Lowe, 1520–1609) explains that the observance of most of the *mitzvot*—and the ideal fulfillment of every *mitzvah*—can be achieved only in the Holy Land, making the Jewish claim to the Land of Israel a perquisite for the entire Torah. Chassidic teaching takes this a step further, explaining that in the conceptual-spiritual sense, "conquering and settling the lands of the seven nations"—i.e., transforming mundane earth into a "holy land" by utilizing its resources to serve G-d—is the essence of what we accomplish with every *mitzvah* we do.

   Another perspective on the foundational nature of the Torah's opening verse is contained in the following essay, *The Now* (pp. 31–37).

on many other *mitzvot*: It determines when we will sound the *shofar*, when we will fast and atone for our sins, when we will conduct the Passover *seder*, and a host of other time-specific observances. But it would seem that there are a number of other, no less fundamental *mitzvot*. What of the *mitzvah* to know and believe in the existence of G-d, which is indeed listed first in Maimonides' enumeration of the *mitzvot*? Or the *mitzvah* to "love your fellow as yourself," of which the talmudic sage Hillel said, "This is the entire Torah; the rest is commentary"? Or the study of Torah, which the Talmud regards as "the equivalent of all the *mitzvot*"? In what sense is the *mitzvah* of setting the calendar the first of the 613 divine commandments which define our mission in life?

MAN AND THING

There are two basic aspects to a *mitzvah*: its relationship to the person performing it, and its relationship to the materials and resources with which it is performed. In talmudic terminology, there is the *gavra* ("person" element) of the *mitzvah*, and the *cheftza* ("object") of the *mitzvah*.

Every *mitzvah* action, by virtue of its being the fulfillment of a divine command, creates a link between the person doing the *mitzvah* and the One who commanded it; indeed, the word *mitzvah* means both "commandment" and "connection." In particular, each of the 613 *mitzvot* has its own specific effect on the mind, character, and habits of the person. An act of charity contributes not only to the fulfillment of the needs of the recipient, but also to the making of a more sensitive and caring giver; putting on *tefilin* reminds its wearer of his special relationship with G-d and of his duty to commit his mind and heart to serve Him; eating matzah on Passover makes tactual the experience of the Exodus

ON THE ESSENCE OF TIME (2)

and increases the eater's awareness of the gift and responsibilities of freedom; studying Torah inculcates the mind of its student with the divine wisdom. It is of this "personal" aspect of the *mitzvah* that our sages speak when they say, "The Torah was given to refine the human being."[8]

In addition, a *mitzvah* has a profound effect on the physical resources with which it is performed—the animal hide in the *tefilin*, the woolen threads of the *tzitzit*, the branches covering the *sukkah*. The act of *mitzvah* refines and sanctifies these physical substances, transforming them into "objects of holiness"—things whose form and utility express their subservience to the divine will.

On the face of it, it would seem that a *mitzvah's* effect on its "person" is far more significant than its effect on its "object." The person doing the *mitzvah* is perceptibly changed. Our sages note that "habit becomes second nature"[9]—even a formal, routine action, with little or no conscious awareness of its significance, has an effect upon the mindset and character of the actor. On the other hand, it would seem that nothing really "happens" to the object of the *mitzvah*, which remains a mute piece of matter. So what does it mean when we say that a thing with which a *mitzvah* is performed is "refined," "sanctified," and "transformed"? In what sense is pair of *tefilin* "holier" than an ordinary piece of leather?

THE OBJECT

Common wisdom has it that the more abstract a thing is, the loftier and more worthy it is. Thus, it is generally agreed that the ethereal is grander than the real, that idea is greater (more "ideal") than

---

8   *Midrash Rabbah, Bereishit* 44:1.
9   *Tanya*, chapter 14.

fact, that the spiritual is holier (i.e., closer to G-d) than the physical. Indeed, our sages refer to the physical world as the "lowliest" of G-d's creations.[10]

Why is it that greater tangibility renders a thing lowlier and less divine? The chassidic masters explain the un-G-dliness of the physical as due to its self-centeredness. "I am," proclaims the physical thing. "If you wish to search for a deeper meaning to my existence, be my guest. But as far as I am concerned, I have no need for significance or definition beyond the self-contained fact of my existence."

This is in direct conflict with the cardinal law of reality, which is the truth that "There is none else besides Him"[11]—that G-d is the only true existence, and that everything "else" is *not* "besides Him," but an extension and expression of His reality.

The first step in resolving this contradiction is to impose function and purpose on a physical substance. For example: When wood, wire, and ivory are formed into a piano, the result is an "object"—i.e., matter with a manifest objective. Rather than simply saying "I am," a piano states: "There is more to me than the fact of physical matter of a certain quantity and shape. Everything about me speaks of other, more transcendent realities. I convey the fact that there is music; that there are people who compose, play, and listen to music; that there are craftsmen who assemble instruments to serve this end. My existence is a result of, a testimony to, and serves these truths."

But this elevation from material to object is only a transcendence of a limited sort. True, a piano (or a book, or a hammer) bespeaks ideas and endeavors beyond its own brute substantiality; but are these ideas and endeavors more G-dly? Are they less

---

10   *Midrash Tanchuma, Nasso* 16; et al.

11   Deuteronomy 4:35.

ON THE ESSENCE OF TIME (2)

in conflict with the truth that "There is none else besides Him"? Perhaps. Perhaps the music being played on the piano expresses a yearning for something beyond mere existence; perhaps it elevates its listeners an increment above the animal self and its needs and wants, and suggests to the listeners a higher purpose to life. But not necessarily. Music can also be an expression of the ego and its most base aspirations, in which case its "spirituality" is nothing more than an idealization of the very fallacy we are striving to transcend.

But when a physical substance is formed and used as the object of a *mitzvah*, it becomes a vessel and instrument of the divine. The "I am" of the physical now becomes, "I am nothing on my own; I exist to serve my Creator."

TIME AS MATERIAL

In this way, the 613 *mitzvot* of the Torah transform the physical world into what the Midrash calls "a dwelling for G-d"[12] — an abode which houses and serves the divine truth. For every physical thing, force, and phenomenon can be utilized to fulfill a divine command: brute matter (the animal hide of *tefilin*, the wool of *tzitzit*, the coin or banknote given as charity), the human body (the brain that studies Torah, the lips that pray, the feet that run to help a fellow in need), physical light (Shabbat and Chanukah lights), and the very essence of physicality — time and space themselves.

Every *mitzvah* is a physical action — hence, an action transpiring in time and space. So every *mitzvah* utilizes a certain area of both time and space as component parts of its "object," thereby

---

12 *Midrash Tanchuma,* op. cit.

sanctifying them as instruments of the divine will. Thus our sages have said that it is preferable to perform many "smaller" *mitzvah* actions instead of one "big" *mitzvah*. A common application of this principle is the *pushka*, or "charity box," which is a prominent feature of the Jewish home. Every day, one drops a few coins in the box; when the box fills, its contents are given to charity. In terms of the objective to aid the needy, nothing is gained by giving $1 a day over 100 days rather than giving $100 in a lump sum; but in terms of the *mitzvah's* effect on the person and the physical world, more acts of charity means more refining influences upon the person, and more utilizations of time in fulfillment of a divine command.

Rabbi Israel Baal Shem Tov[13] takes this a step further, saying that it is preferable to perform two *mitzvot* on two different days than to do two such actions on a single day. For in this way, two different time units (the "day" being an integral component of time)[14] are refined and elevated through their participation in an act of *mitzvah*.[15]

Man-Made Time

Torah law distinguishes two levels in a thing's utilization by a *mitzvah*: as an "object of a *mitzvah*," or as an "instrument of a *mitzvah*." A *mitzvah's* "object" is the thing or substance with which the *mitzvah* is actually performed, such as the leather boxes which the Jew binds on his head and arm as *tefilin*. A *mitzvah's* "instruments" are the resources which facilitate and enable the *mitzvah's* performance, such as the tools which fashion a piece of leather into

---

13 1698–1760; founder of the chassidic movement.

14 See *Garments for the Soul*, on pp. 60–63 below.

15 See *Tzavaat HaRivash*, pg. 1.

ON THE ESSENCE OF TIME (2)   29

tefilin or the food which provides a person putting on the *tefilin* with the energy to bind them on himself.

Time fills an auxiliary, "instrumental" role in the performance of every *mitzvah*. There is one *mitzvah*, however, in which time is the primary "object"—the resource which is actually shaped and formed in conformity with the divine will. This is the *mitzvah* of *kiddush hachodesh*, "sanctification of the new month."

The Jewish calendar is punctuated with numerous "callings of holiness"[16]—the festivals and special days designated by the Torah as possessing special spiritual qualities. These are more than "commemorations" of historical events: The very substance of the time occupied by Passover is imbued with the quality of freedom, that of Sukkot with joy, of Shavuot with the revelation at Sinai, of Rosh Hashanah with G-d's annual resumption of His sovereignty over the universe, of Yom Kippur with *teshuvah*—the capacity to access the very quintessence of one's soul and its bond to G-d. And so it is with every festival and special day on the Jewish calendar: each has its unique "holiness" and divine quality woven into the very fabric of its time for us to "call forth" and actualize by observing the *mitzvot* of the day.

One would think that the spiritual character of time is fixed, established by the Creator when time itself was formed. Indeed, such is the case with the weekly Shabbat, which G-d "blessed" and "sanctified" by resting from His work of creation, thereby establishing the seven-day work/rest cycle which defines our week.[17] But with regard to the annual cycle of the festivals, G-d desired that these should be sanctified by human beings. The *mitzvah* of *kiddush hachodesh* is that *we* should fix the calendar based on monthly

---

16   Leviticus 23:4; see *Appointments in Time,* on pp. 38–45 below.

17   Genesis 2:1–3.

sightings of the new moon and on our calculations of the lunar and solar cycles,[18] and that these sightings and calculations should determine which day will be a Yom Kippur, which days will comprise the festival of Passover, and so on. The Torah goes so far as to state that even if those entrusted with the task of making these calculations err, it is their "mistaken" conclusions which create the holiness and specialness of the festivals.[19]

This is the "first *mitzvah* commanded to the Jewish people." Knowledge of G-d, Torah study, charity, and acts of kindness might be more fundamental in terms of the effects of the *mitzvot* upon the person; but in terms of the transformation and sanctification of the universe achieved by the *mitzvot*, the "sanctification of the month" is the *mitzvah* whose "object" is the most basic element of the physical creation.

---

18   See *Locating the Moon* on pp. 167–174 below.

19   Talmud, *Rosh Hashanah* 25a, after Leviticus 23:2. This difference between the Shabbat and the festivals is reflected in the special blessings of these days. The Shabbat *kiddush* concludes with the words, "Blessed are You G-d, who sanctifies the Shabbat," attesting to the fact that the Creator imbued the seventh day with its special qualities. Whereas the *kiddush* for the festivals closes, "...Who sanctifies Israel and the times"—which the Talmud (*Berachot* 49a) reads as, "Who sanctifies Israel, who sanctify the times."

ON THE ESSENCE OF TIME (3)

THE
NOW

The Baal Shem Tov taught that the letters
of the "ten utterances" by which the world
was created during the six days of creation
stand firmly forever within all creations, and
are continually invested within them, to give
them life and existence. For if these letters
were to depart even for one instant, G-d for-
bid, and return to their source, all would be-
come naught and absolute nothingness, and
it would be as if they had never existed at all,
exactly as before the divine utterance...

Tanya, Shaar HaYichud VehaEmunah, Ch. 1

$\mathcal{T}$ he Hebrew word *bara*, "created," specifically implies the
creation of "something from nothing."[1] Accordingly, Maimonides explains the significance of the Torah's opening statement, "In the beginning G-d created the heavens and the earth."
Since the world was created out of a prior state of absolute nothingness, G-d is not just the maker of the world, but also its primal
cause and source. When someone fashions an object out of preex-
isting materials, that object may then assume an existence of its
own, and no longer be dependent on its maker. The carpenter may
die, but the cabinet he built will continue to exist. Not so the

---

[1]   According to Rabbi Saadiah Gaon, Maimonides, Radak, Sforno, and
many others.

created reality, which derives its very existence from G-d, and thus remains perpetually dependent on its Creator to supply it with existence.[2]

The mystical teachings of kabbalah take this a step further: Not only is the entirety of creation perpetually dependent on G-d for its existence, but G-d in fact actively creates the world anew every moment of time.

> *A common perception is that G-d's creation of the world was a one-time occurrence, after which the world exists on its own; that while G-d has the power to intervene whenever and however He chooses, as long as G-d does not choose to do so, the world runs on the energy and the capabilities imparted to it at the time of its creation.*
>
> *In truth, G-d is constantly creating the world, continually forcing it out of absolute nothingness into existence and life. Should this flow of vitality cease for even an instant, G-d forbid, all would revert to nothingness. As we say in the daily prayers, "Who in his goodness renews each day, constantly, the first act of creation."*
>
> *This is the meaning of the verse, "Know today, and take it to your heart, that G-d is the G-d in the heavens above and upon the earth below; there is none else."[3] The meaning of this is not that there is no other G-d, for that is a given, and is already stated by the verse, "G-d is one."[4] Rather, it means that there is no other existence besides G-d, for without him there is nothing.[5]*

---

2   *Guide for the Perplexed*, 1:69; *Mishneh Torah*, Laws of the Fundamentals of Torah, 1:1–3.

3   Deuteronomy 4:39.

4   Ibid., 6:4.

5   Shaloh, *Asarah Maamarot, Maamar* 1, 40b-41a (citing *Pardes Rimonim*, 6:8).

ON THE ESSENCE OF TIME (3)   33

The founder of chassidism, Rabbi Israel Baal Shem Tov, makes this principle a central doctrine of his teachings. In the chassidic classic, *Tanya*, Rabbi Schneur Zalman of Liadi (1745–1812) expounds on this doctrine, explaining that the idea that G-d is perpetually creating the world is an extension of the above-stated principle that the world was created *ex nihilo* ("out of nothingness"). For when we appreciate that the initial state of reality is utter nothingness, we understand that existence is a contrived state, which must constantly be imposed by a higher force.[6]

THE GOODNESS OF THE MOMENT

These are, of course, fascinating ideas: To think that our world—which, to our five senses, seems so solid and contiguous—is actually pulsating from existence to nothingness, and back again, every fraction of time! But aside from stimulating our minds and inspiring our mystic wonder, does it make any real difference to us in our daily lives? What are the practical ramifications of the truth that G-d is creating the world anew every moment of time?

Often, as we journey through life and grapple with its myriad challenges, we experience moments of hopelessness and despair. At these times, we seem incapable of seeing any good in ourselves or in a fellow human being, nor of discerning any redeeming purpose in the dilemma or circumstance in which we find ourselves.

But the doctrine of perpetual creation means that at every point in time, the world is the way it is only because G-d actively chooses to so create it. So in truth, there can be no "hopeless" situations, no "meaningless" moments. For this very moment, with all its attendant circumstances, was just now brought into existence

---

6   *Tanya, Shaar HaYichud VehaEmunah* 1–3.

out of absolute nothingness by a purposeful Creator who is the ultimate source of good.

LIVING IN THE NOW

An appreciation of G-d's perpetual creation of reality also means that our attitude toward time, and the manner in which we experience it and utilize it, undergoes a radical transformation.

An often heard lament is that we never really "have" any time. The past is irretrievably past, and the future is forever one elusive step ahead of us. As for the present—isn't the very notion of a "present" an illusion, since any given moment already was or has yet to be? And if all that we have is either in the past or in the future, does this not mean that we don't ever have anything?

But when we appreciate the truth that G-d is perpetually engaged in the act of creation—that every moment of time, the Creator chooses to bring the entirety of existence, including the entire past and the entire future,[7] into being out of utter nothingness —this means that nothing is more real and more accessible than

---

7　This is the meaning of the statement by Rabbi Schneur Zalman of Liadi (quoted at the beginning of this essay) that if G-d were to cease, for even one instant, his active creation of the world, "all would become naught and absolute nothingness, and it would be *as if they had never existed at all, exactly as before the divine utterance...*" If the world would simply cease to exist, but would still have existed in the past, then it would still not be "exactly as before the divine utterance." But in truth, everything, including time itself—that is, the entire past and the entire future—is constantly being created anew. Should G-d not choose to create the present moment, not only would it not exist, but nothing would ever have existed in the past as well. (See *Three Times Three*, the section called "Condensed Time," on pp. 212–214 below.)

ON THE ESSENCE OF TIME (3) 35

the present moment. Time, indeed creation itself, is wholly concentrated in the here and now.

The Lubavitcher Rebbe once demonstrated this attitude and approach at a *farbrengen* (chassidic gathering) with his followers.

The occasion was the 20th anniversary of the Rebbe's leadership in January of 1970, and thousands of visitors from all parts of the globe gathered in the Rebbe's New York headquarters to celebrate. Among those attending the gathering was a group of vistors who were scheduled to return to their homes in Israel later that evening. As the gathering progressed, the departure time of the Israeli group's flight neared. Noticing their anxious glances at the clock, the Rebbe smiled and told the following story:

"It was in the darkest days of the Communists' attempt to uproot the Jewish faith in Soviet Russia. My father-in-law,[8] who headed the underground network dedicated to keeping Judaism alive, was being watched constantly by the NKVD[9] and was followed wherever he went. We all knew that it was only a matter of time before they would pounce on their prey.[10]

"Late one night, I entered my father-in-law's study in his Leningrad apartment. For several hours, he had been receiving people in *yechidut*,[11] a physically and spiritually draining task for a *rebbe*. In another half-hour or so, he was scheduled to leave for the train station, where he was to catch a train to Moscow for a meeting

---

8   The sixth Lubavitcher Rebbe, Rabbi Yosef Yitzchak Schneerson, 1880–1950.

9   Secret police, forerunners of the KGB.

10   In 1927, Rabbi Yosef Yitzchak was in fact arrested and sentenced to death, G-d forbid. It was only by the force of international pressure that his sentence was commuted to exile, following which he was freed entirely and allowed to leave the country.

11   Private audience, in which a chassid seeks his Rebbe's counsel and blessing in all that troubles his life and ails his soul.

with a foreign businessman for the purpose of acquiring funds to support his work. Needless to say, to meet with a foreign citizen, a 'capitalist' at that, and especially for the above purposes, was extremely dangerous; in those days, many forfeited their lives for a fraction of such 'crimes.'

"To my great surprise, I found my father-in-law working calmly at his desk, arranging his papers, as if it were the middle of an ordinary workday. There was no sign of the strain of several hours of listening to people's most personal and painful dilemmas, and no sign of the fact that in another half-hour he would be leaving for the station on his dangerous mission.

"I could not contain myself and asked him: 'I know that Chabad chassidism is predicated on the principle that "the mind rules the heart."[12] I know what sort of education you received and how you were trained in self-sacrifice for the Jewish people and for Judaism. But to such an extent? That you could sit at your desk at a time like this, as if there were nothing else on your schedule?'

"In response, my father-in-law told me about the great sage, the Rashba.[13] The Rashba would give three in-depth classes in Torah each day. In addition, he wrote thousands of responsa to queries on Torah law. He was also a practicing physician who devoted many hours each day to healing the sick. And he would also find time for a daily stroll.

"This, said my father-in-law, is what is called 'success with time.' We cannot make our days longer, nor can we add additional hours to our nights. But we can maximize our usage of time by regarding each segment of time as a world of its own. When we devote a portion of time—whether it is an hour, a day, or a minute—to a

---

12 See *Tanya*, chapter 12.
13 Rabbi Shlomo ben Aderet of Barcelona, c. 1235–1310.

ON THE ESSENCE OF TIME (3)   37

certain task, we should be totally invested in what we are doing, as if there exists nothing else in the world.

"When the Rashba gave a class, this was his sole occupation. When he wrote his legal responsa, the task had his undivided attention and commitment. When he was treating a patient, there existed nothing else in the world. And when he went on his daily stroll, it was a *leisurely* stroll, for the minutes he devoted to it belonged to it entirely.

"I know you have a plane to catch," concluded the Rebbe. "Perhaps you still have to pack your suitcases and say your goodbyes. But look at it this way. G-d creates the world anew in every microsecond of time. The El Al plane that will carry you to the Holy Land has not been created yet! Kennedy Airport, where you have to be in less than an hour, does not yet exist. At the moment that it will be of use to you, G-d will create it for you. A moment before that, it does not exist for you. This moment has its own purpose. Use it fully."

APPOINTMENTS IN TIME

These are the appointed times (mo'adim) of G-d, callings of holiness, which you shall call in their appointed time...

Leviticus 23:4

A king was traveling with his child through the wilderness. And when a king travels, his entire entourage travels along: ministers, guards, attendants, and servants, all at the ready to serve their master and carry out his will.

Suddenly, the procession ground to a halt. The king's child had a request. "Water," said the crown prince. "I want water."

The king convened his cabinet to address the crisis. "My son is thirsty," he said to his ministers. "But how is water to be obtained in the wilderness?"

After much deliberation, two proposals were laid before the throne. "I shall dispatch my ten ablest horsemen on my ten fastest steeds," proposed the commander of the royal cavalry. "They will ride to the nearest settlement and fill their waterskins. Within the hour, there will be water for the prince."

"I shall put my men and equipment to the task," proposed the chief of the royal engineering corps. "They will erect a derrick and sink a well right here, on the very spot at which we have stopped. Before the day is out, there will be water for the prince."

The king opted for the latter proposal, and soon the royal engineers were boring a well through the desert sand and rock. Toward

ON THE ESSENCE OF TIME (4)   39

evening they reached a vein of water and the prince's thirst was quenched.

"Why," asked the prince of his father, after he had drunk his fill, "did you trouble your men to dig a well in the desert? After all, we have the means to obtain water far more quickly and easily."

"Indeed, my son," replied the king, "such is our situation today. But perhaps one day, many years in the future, you will again be traveling this way. Perhaps you will be alone, without the power and privilege you now enjoy. Then, the well we dug today will be here to quench your thirst."

"But father," said the prince, "in many years, the sands of time will have refilled the well, stopping its water and erasing its very memory!"

"My son," said the king, "you have spoken with wisdom and foresight. This, then, is what we will do. We will mark the site of this well on our maps, and preserve our maps from the ravages of time. If you know the exact spot at which this well has been sunk, you will be able to reopen it with a minimum of effort and toil.

"This we shall do at every encampment of our journey," resolved the king. "We shall dig wells and mark their places on our map. We shall record the particular characteristics of each well and the method by which it can be reopened. So whenever, and under whatever circumstances, you will travel this route, you will be able to obtain the water that will sustain you on your journey."

TIME AS TERRAIN

The Torah refers to the festivals of the Jewish calendar as *mo'adim*, "appointed times,"[1] and as *mikra'ei kodesh*, "callings of

---

1   The Hebrew word *mo'ed* means a specific point or area of time that

holiness."[2] "These are G-d's appointed times," reads the introductory verse to the Torah's listing of the festivals in the book of Leviticus, "callings of holiness, which you shall call in their appointed times."[3]

A festival is an appointment with the past, an encounter with an event and phenomenon in our history. It is an opportunity to "call" forth the particular "holiness" of the day, to tap the spiritual resources it holds.

Each of the festivals marks a point in our journey through time at which our Heavenly Father, accompanying us in our first steps as a people, supplied us with the resources that nurture our spiritual lives. On Passover, we were granted the gift of freedom; on Shavuot, G-d revealed Himself to us at Mount Sinai and gave us His Torah, the embodiment of His wisdom and will and our charter as His "kingdom of priests and a holy people"; Rosh Hashanah is the day on which G-d first became King; on Yom Kippur, G-d

---

possesses a particular quality or which serves a certain purpose. The word also means "conference" or "meeting." A third meaning of *mo'ed* is "designation." A rough English equivalent that includes all three meanings of *mo'ed* would be "appointment": a point in time that has been designated to serve as the venue for an encounter toward the achievement of a certain end.

2   Like its English equivalent, the Hebrew verb *kara*, "call," means both to call something in the sense of naming and identifying it ("They called him Jacob"), as well as to summon and bring forth ("I called him into the room"). In the most basic meaning of the phrase, a festival is a "calling of holiness" in the sense that the *bet din* (court of Torah law) is empowered to set the calendar and identify a certain day or days as "Yom Kippur," "Passover," etc. (see the essays *The First Creation*, pp. 20–30, and *Locating the Moon*, pp. 167–174, in this volume). On a deeper level, this alludes to the significance of the festivals as days possessing certain spiritual potentials which we "call forth" through the particular observances of the day.

3   Leviticus 23:2.

forgave our first and most terrible betrayal as His people, the sin of the Golden Calf, granting us the gift of *teshuvah*—the capacity to rectify and transform a deficient past; Sukkot commemorates the time that we were sheltered and unified by the divine "clouds of glory" in our journey through the desert toward our Promised Land; the miracle of Chanukah marks the salvation of the Jewish soul—the triumph of light and purity over darkness and adulteration; the miracle of Purim, the salvation of the Jewish body and the specialness and chosenness of our physical selves; and so with all the festivals and special dates and periods on our calendar.

But these were not one-time gifts from above. Freedom, wisdom, commitment, joy, illumination, peace, etc., are constant needs of the soul, the spiritual nutrients that sustain her in her journey through life. Like the king in the above parable, G-d sunk "wells" at various points in the terrain of time, to serve as perpetual sources of these blessings. As we travel through the year—the year being a microcosm of the entire universe of time—we encounter the festivals, each marking the location of a well of nurture for our souls.

G-d also provided us with a map of these wells—a calendar denoting their locations in our journey through time. The map also comes with instructions on how to "reopen" each well and access its waters: Sounding the *shofar* on Rosh Hashanah will regenerate the divine coronation that transpired on the first Rosh Hashanah when Adam crowned G-d as king of the universe; eating matzah evokes the freedom of Passover; kindling the Chanukah lights recreates the miracle of Chanukah. And so it is with every such "appointment" on our calendar: each comes supplied with its own *mitzvot* and observances—the tools that open the well and unleash the flow of its waters.

MAIMONIDES ON TIME

Time is a terrain. But time is also an organism.

An organism is comprised of numerous cells, which in turn form a diversity of tissues, organs, and limbs, each with its distinct composition and function, which together form its body. Yet each and every cell of the organism contains, encoded within it, the make-up of the entire organism.

The same is true of time. Time, as a whole, embodies the multi-faceted scene of life. But each individual cell of time also embodies its entire expanse. For in calling freedom, refinement, wisdom, awe, unity, or joy into a specific point in time, we also imbue time's very essence with these qualities. And since every moment of time is an outgrowth of its essence, every moment ultimately reflects them all. In the words of Rabbi Israel Baal Shem Tov, "The essence of a thing, when you grasp a part of it, you grasp it all."[4]

These two dimensions of time—the varied landscape of the calendar, and the quintessential all-inclusiveness of each "cell" and moment—are reflected in the different ways in which the laws and practices of the festivals are recounted in the Torah and in the writings of our sages.

The 23rd chapter of Leviticus, known as *parashat hamo'adim* (the "Chapter of the Appointed Times"), which instructs our sanctification of time, follows the order of the Jewish calendar. Beginning with the weekly Shabbat, it proceeds to relate the observances of Passover, the counting of the *omer*, Shavuot, Rosh Hashanah, Yom Kippur, Sukkot, and Shemini Atzeret. This is also the order followed by Maimonides in his *Book of Mitzvot* and (with a few exceptions) by the Mishnah's *Order of Mo'ed*.[5]

---

4   *Keter Shem Tov*, addendum, section 116.

5   See Maimonides' *Introduction to the Mishnah*. In the Jewish calendar,

ON THE ESSENCE OF TIME (4)   43

But in his monumental codification of the entire body of Torah law, the *Mishneh Torah*, Maimonides takes a different approach. The third of its fourteen books, *The Book of Times*, specifies the laws of Jewish time according to a logical-qualitative order rather than a chronological one. Maimonides, too, begins with the laws of Shabbat; but he does so not only because of its dominant place in the calendar, but also because "its laws are the strictest of them all... and because its commandment relates to the creation of the world and is a cornerstone of the faith of the Torah..."[6]

Maimonides then follows with the laws of Yom Kippur, the holiest of the festivals, followed by the "laws of *yom tov* rest"—the less stringent laws that pertain equally to all other festivals. Next come the specific festival and time-related observances, again in the order of their importance and centrality to the Jewish faith: the laws of leaven and matzah on Passover, *shofar* (on Rosh Hashanah), *sukkah* and *lulav* (on Sukkot), the giving of the half-*shekel* on the first of *Adar*, the laws of *Rosh Chodesh* (the new month) and of the fast days, and concluding with the two rabbinic festivals, Chanukah and Purim.

Maimonides wishes to emphasize the deeper effect of our "calling holiness" into time. If we view time as a sequence of moments and days, each to be imbued with its specific quality and calling, then the logical order of laws of time is indeed that of the calendar: We journey through the year, implementing and experiencing each time-quality at its appointed season. But if we relate to the quintessence of time, then its every moment encapsulates its entirety. Every moment has its Shabbat element, its Yom Kippur,

---

the first of *Nissan* is considered "the beginning of the year for the festivals" (Talmud, *Rosh Hashanah* 2a). See *Our Other Head* in vol. 3 of this series, pp. 4–12.

6   From the *Maggid Mishneh*'s introduction to the *Book of Times*.

its Purim. Every moment is pregnant with tranquility, joy, liberty, and every other feature of Jewish time. On this level, the sequence of calendar time is less relevant than the nature and priority of these qualities.

NAME AND QUOTE

This is why Maimonides names the book in his *Mishneh Torah* which deals with the festivals and special days of the calendar *Sefer Zemanim* ("The Book of Times"), rather than adapting the biblical *Mo'ed* ("Appointed Times") chosen by the Mishnah. While the Torah's list in Leviticus and the Mishnah's order of tractates relate to the festivals as rises and peaks in a journey through time, Maimonides touches on the all-inclusiveness of time — on the way that its every particle ultimately possesses the many features of the collective whole.

This also explains the quote with which Maimonides prefaces *The Book of Times*. Maimonides begins each of the *Mishneh Torah's* fourteen books with a quote from the Torah — a verse that reflects his conception of the area of Torah law covered by each book. For *The Book of Times*, he chose Psalms 119:111: "Your testimonies[7] I have taken as a heritage always, for they are the rejoicing of my

---

7   The *mitzvot* fall under three general categories: a) "Laws" (*mishpatim*), whose logic and imperative are self-evident, such as charity, the prohibitions against murder and theft, etc. b) "Statutes" (*chukim*) — suprarational decrees, such as the kosher dietary laws, laws of ritual purity, etc. c) "Testimonials" (*eidut*) — *mitzvot* that serve a symbolic and commemorative function, such as the festival observances. While the human mind might not necessarily have conceived of them on its own, it can appreciate the need for symbols and commemorative customs to keep a concept alive in a people's consciousness and behavior.

ON THE ESSENCE OF TIME (4)   45

heart." At first glance, the verse seems inappropriate, even antithetical, to the contents of this book. If *The Book of Times* deals with time-specific *mitzvot* (in Maimonides' own words, "I will include in it all the *mitzvot* that apply to specific times"), how can these be categorized as testimonials that are a heritage to us *always*? Indeed, this verse seems more appropriate for the preceding book, *The Book of Love*, of which Maimonides writes, "I will include in it all the constant *mitzvot*, which we have been commanded so that we should love G-d and remember Him always, such as the reading of the *Shema*, prayer, *tefilin*,... circumcision..."[8]

But Maimonides wishes to emphasize that our time-specific experiences and achievements are not confined to their specific points of the calendar. On the contrary: Because they are time-related, time becomes the conduit that extends them to our every moment. Because they impact the one element which pervades every corner of our existence, they become a perpetual presence in our lives.

---

8   Introduction to *Mishneh Torah*. There are those who explain the verse's connection with the book to be in its latter half, "for they are the rejoicing of my heart"—a reference to the festivals which are "the seasons of our rejoicing." But this relates only to the festivals of Passover, Shavuot, and Sukkot; not to Shabbat, *Rosh Hashanah*, Yom Kippur, *Rosh Chodesh*, and the fast days. In any case, why choose a verse whose first half expresses the very opposite of the nature of the book's contents?

ROUTINE AND OCCASION

*My offering, My bread for My fire, My sweet
savor, you shall observe to offer Me in its appointed time... two [offerings] each day, a
regular offering...*   Numbers 28:2–3

*L*iving in time has this effect on our psyche: We are indifferent to the usual and attracted to the unusual. One
might argue that it is the routine things in life—the regular intake
and expulsion of breath, our daily meals, our home life, our jobs—
that are most crucial to our existence, while the "special" things
are of lesser import. One might so argue, but to little avail. Our
nature dictates that the occasionality of an event makes it "an occasion," while an event's regular occurrence drains it of interest
and significance.

It is in recognition of this feature of our nature that the Torah
delegates various aspects of our relationship with G-d to *mo'adim*, or "appointed times."[1] We are enjoined to sustain a perpetual
awareness of the Creator;[2] yet one day a week is designated as the
particular time in which "to remember ... that the world has a Creator" and to "establish in our hearts the belief in the creation of

---

1   See previous essay, *Appointments in Time* (pp. 38–45).
2   Knowledge of G-d is one of the six "perpetual commandments" bind-
    ing upon the Jew at all times (Foreword to *Sefer HaChinuch*).

ON THE ESSENCE OF TIME (5)   47

the world by G-d in six days."[3] We are commanded to "Remember the day that you went out of Egypt, all the days of your life"[4]; yet the once-a-year festival of Passover is appointed as the occasion to dwell upon and internalize the gift of freedom. And so it is with the other *mo'adim* of the Jewish calendar. If these are to be "special" days whose message and import make a lasting impression upon our souls, they must be occasional days—departures from the routine of our lives.

Our sages go so far as to say: "One who recites *hallel* every day commits blasphemy."[5] *Hallel* is a prayer of praise and thanks to G-d for the miracles He performs for us, which is recited on festivals and other designated days. But are we not enjoined to thank G-d "for the miracles You perform for us every day"?[6] Why reserve *hallel* for the days which commemorate the Exodus from Egypt or the miracle of the oil that burned for eight days? Is not every heartbeat no less a miracle, and no less cause for recognition and gratitude?

But to recite *hallel* every day is akin to not reciting it at all. Certainly, our routine lives should be imbued with an awareness of our indebtedness to our Creator—to this end the Jew prays three times a day, morning, afternoon, and evening. But the entire point of *hallel* is that, in addition to our daily prayers, we devote certain occasions to a special appreciation of G-d's miracles—a specialness which would inevitably be diluted if the recitation of *hallel* were to be made a daily routine.

---

3   Nachmanides on Exodus 20:8; *Sefer HaChinuch*, Positive Commandment 31.

4   Deuteronomy 16:3.

5   Talmud, *Shabbat* 118b.

6   From the thrice-daily *amidah* prayer.

BEYOND NATURE

In this and numerous other ways, the Torah encourages us to employ our inborn characteristics and inclinations in the quest for a holier and more G-dly life. But the Torah also calls for more. G-d desires more than the optimal exploitation of human nature; He also desires that we transcend our natural selves in our relationship with Him.

The Torah provides us with "routines" (such as the twice-daily reading of the *Shema*) designed to make our relationship with G-d an integral part of our daily lives, as well as with "appointed times" to lend it prominence and distinction. At the same time, however, the Torah also urges us to transcend these categorizations, to impart a sense of specialness and occasion also to the regular rhythms of life.

This is reflected in the manner in which the Torah introduces the laws of the daily *korbanot* (animal and meal offerings) brought in the Holy Temple. The communal *korbanot* fall into two general categories: the regular offerings (*temidim*) brought each day; and the additional offerings (*musafim*) brought on special occasions — Shabbat, *Rosh Chodesh*, the festivals, etc. The same "regular offerings" were brought each day; the "additional offerings" varied in accordance with the occasion, reflecting the nature and characteristics of their appointed times.

As a rule, the Torah uses the term *mo'ed* ("appointed time") to refer to those special days of the calendar imbued by the Creator of time with unique spiritual resources and potentials (the tranquility of Shabbat, the freedom of Passover, the joy of Sukkot, etc.). However, in introducing the laws of the daily offerings, the Torah states: "My *korban*, My fire-offering, My sweet savor, you

ON THE ESSENCE OF TIME (5)   49

shall observe to offer Me in its appointed time."[7] Rashi, in his
commentary to this verse, notes this unusual application of the
term *mo'ed*, and remarks: "The 'appointed time' of the regular offerings is every day."

The service of *korbanot*—or in its present-day incarnation, the
"service of the heart" of daily prayer—represents man's endeavor to
refine and elevate his natural self and bring himself close to G-d.
This "service" is one of the "three pillars" of creation; in the words
of the Talmud's *Ethics of the Fathers*, "The world stands on three
things: Torah, service, and acts of kindness."[8]

In referring to times for daily offerings in the Holy Temple as
mo'adim, the Torah is alluding to the need to go beyond the habits
and instincts of the natural self in our relationship with G-d. Our
nature dictates that the "occasions" in our lives are touched with
a special vitality and enthusiasm, and we exploit this trait in our
seasonal celebrations of the various aspect of our relationship with
G-d. But we should also endeavor to make "every day an appointed time"—to evoke in ourselves a sense of wonder and specialness
in the most routine aspects of our daily existence.

Indeed, the very concept of "monotony" and "ordinariness" is
an illusion, resulting from our inability to see beyond the limitations of human nature. In truth, distinction is not a factor of a
thing's difference from other things, but an inherent quality of the
thing itself. In truth, every moment of life is a distinct creation
of G-d, embodying a unique, special, and indispensable potential
which cannot be duplicated by any other moment.[9]

---

7   Numbers 28:2.
8   *Ethics of the Fathers* 1:2. See *Kuzari* 2:26; *Siddur im D'ach*, 33b-c.
9   See *The Now* on pp. 31–37 above.

MASCULINE MOMENT, FEMININE TIME

It is written, "Your sovereignty is the sovereignty of all worlds, and your rulership is in every generation and generation."[1] *The "worlds" are the reality of space, and "generations" are the reality of time; both of which derive from the divine attribute of* malchut *("sovereignty").*

Torah Ohr, Mikeitz 37a

𝔐 uch of Jewish life is lived by the clock and the calendar. There are set times of the day for prayer, for the reading of the *Shema*, and for the beginning and conclusion of the Shabbat. There are specific days of the year designated for sounding the *shofar*, eating matzah, counting the *omer*, or dwelling in the *sukkah*. The *halachic* (Torah law) term for these observances is *mitzvot she-ha'zeman gerama*—"commandments promted by the time."

Yet, fully half of our number are exempted, in principle, from this aspect of Jewish life. According to Torah law, the Jewish woman is absolved from virtually all time-specific *mitzvot*.[2] To be sure,

---

[1] Psalms 145:13.

[2] The exemption of women from time-specific *mitzvot* applies only to the *mitzvot asei*, or "positive commandments," not to the *mitzvot lo taaseh*, or "prohibitions." Thus, a woman is equally obligated to observe time-specific *mitzvot* that include a *mitzvah lo taaseh,* such as resting on Shabbat or fasting on Yom Kippur. In addition, there are certain positive commandments to which the Torah specifically obligates the Jewish woman, such as the active observances of Shabbat (*kiddush*, etc.) and eating matzah on the first night of Passover. For a

ON THE ESSENCE OF TIME (6)   51

a woman can (and many do) observe these *mitzvot*,[3] but the very
fact that she is not obligated to do so implies that they are not intrinsic to her mission in life. Why, indeed, does the Torah de-em-
phasize the Jewish woman's role in the sanctification of time?

TWO COMMUNICATIONS

The 19th chapter of Exodus recounts how G-d sent Moses to tell
the Jewish people to ready themselves to receive the Torah:

> *G-d called to him from the mountain, saying: "So you*
> *shall say to the house of Jacob, and you shall pronounce*
> *to the children of Israel..."*

The Midrash *Mechilta* comments on the repetitive language in this
verse, and explains that these were in fact two communications:

> *"The house of Jacob" are the women; "the children of Isra-*
> *el" are the men... Relate the [Torah's] general principles*
> *to the women, and pronounce the exacting particulars to*
> *the men.*

The entire community of Israel was given the same Torah. But the
fact that this was preceded by two separate communications, one
to the women and another to the men, implies a basic distinction
between the women's reception of Torah and that of the men. The
sages are telling us that men and women differ not only biologi-
cally and psychologically, but also spiritually, having been charged

---

full treatment of a woman's obligations under Torah law, see *Encyclopedia Talmudit*, vol. 2, pp. 242–257.

3   With the few notable exceptions (e.g., putting on *tefilin*) proscribed by
law or custom (see Ibid., pp. 250–251).

and empowered by their Creator with two distinct roles in mankind's overall mission in life. Hence the *mitzvot* commanded only
to men, and the *mitzvot* specific to women.

This is not to say that each of us relates to only half a Torah. For
as the teachings of kabbalah relate, man and woman are two halves
of a single soul, separated at birth and reunited through marriage.
So each individual soul is charged with the implementation of the
entire Torah: its masculine element, acting through a male body,
to carry out the Torah's masculine commandments; and its feminine element, vested in a female body, to realize the Torah's feminine goals. In the words of master kabbalist Rabbi Isaac Luria,[4]
"When the male performs a *mitzvah* [commanded specifically to
men], there is no need for the woman to do it on her own, since
she is included in his performance of the *mitzvah*... This is the
deeper significance of what our sages have said,[5] 'A man's wife is
as his own body.'"

PARTICULAR MAN

What does this division of roles entail? Man and woman are both
multifaceted and complex creatures, and no single thesis can
summarize the many ways in which they complement and fulfill
each other. Ultimately, we can only say that G-d, who created the
human soul and halved it between two separate bodies and lives,
has ordained for each a program for life that is consistent with
its strengths and potentials. The Torah, however, does provide a

---

4   The "Holy Ari," 1534–1572. The quote is from the Ari's *Likutei Torah*,
    Bereishit 15a. Also see *Zohar* 1:91b, 3:7b, 3:109b, and 3:296a; Genesis
    1:27 and *Midrash Rabbah*, ad loc.; and Talmud, *Sotah* 2a.
5   Talmud, *Menachot* 93a.

number of clues that illuminate certain aspects of the male and female roles.

One such insight can be found in the above-cited Midrash, where Moses is told to relate the "general principles" of the Torah to the women and its "exacting particulars" to the men. The woman relates to the essence, the all-inclusive, in Torah. The man relates to the detail, the specific law, the particular application.

This distinction is also seen in the role of the father and mother in determining the identity of their child. According to Torah law, it is the mother who determines the Jewishness of the child. If the mother is Jewish, so too, is the child; if the mother is not, neither is the child, no matter how much Jewish blood there is in its parentage. On the other hand, regarding the particulars of the child's Jewishness—his tribal identity,[6] or his classification as a "Kohen," "Levite," or "Israelite"—the child takes after the father.

Another expression of this difference is that the man is the one with the more "intellectual" relationship with Torah—it is to him that the commandment "study it day and night"[7] is directed. The woman, on the other hand, imbibes the Torah at its suprarational root with her faith and receptiveness. She is naturally one with the truth of G-d, whereas the particular-minded man apprehends the divine truth by dissecting and analyzing it.

---

6   The people of Israel comprise twelve *shevatim*, or "tribes," descendant from the twelve sons of Jacob. A Jew's tribal identity determines his share in the Holy Land as well as his role in Jewish life.

7   Joshua 1:8. See Talmud, *Kidushin* 29b; *Shulchan Aruch, Yoreh De'ah* 246:6.

WOMEN FIRST

This also explains why, when preparing the people of Israel to receive the Torah, Moses was sent first to the women.

The Torah's revelation to mankind unfolded from the general to the particular, from the supra-spatial point of concept to the breadth and depth of thought and law. Originally, we received the Torah from G-d in the form of a single divine utterance, which encapsulated all Ten Commandments.[8] Then, we heard the two basic precepts of the Torah, "I am the L-rd your G-d," which embodies all the positive commandments (*mitzvot assei)*, and "You shall have no other gods," from which all prohibitions (*mitzvot lo taasseh*) derive.[9] These were followed by the communication, through Moses, of the other eight Commandments, and G-d's inscription of the Ten Commandments on the Two Tablets. For the next forty years, Moses taught the people of Israel the particulars of Torah, which he transcribed, by divine dictation, in the Written Torah (the Five Books of Moses); but the Written Torah, with its 613 *mitzvot*, is only a detailing of the principles embodied in the "Engraved Torah" of the Ten Commandments.[10] Nor did the extrapolation of Torah end with Moses: thirty-five generations of interpretation and application produced the Mishnah, and a further 300 years of analyzing the Mishnah gave us the Talmud. Indeed, it is a process that continues to this very day, as the many streams of Torah—*halachah, aggadah, kabbalah, chakirah* (Jewish philosophy), *mussar*, and *chassidut*—continue to flow from the wellspring of Sinai, an ever-expanding mass of wisdom and law, every word of

---

8   *Mechilta* on Exodus 20:1.
9   Talmud, *Makot* 24a; *Tanya*, ch. 20.
10   Rashi, Exodus 24:12.

which is encapsulated in the single utterance of the original divine communication.[11]

So when G-d sent Moses to prepare the Jewish people to receive the Torah, He sent him first to the women. First, the Torah must be received as is, free of talmudic *pilpul*, free of philosophical theorizing, free of mystical experience—free of everything save the unequivocal identification with its truth. Go first to the Jewish woman, said G-d to Moses, for she is the prime conduit of this first step in the communication of My truth to humanity. Then, go to the men and instruct them of the details; it is they who shall play the pivotal role in the second stage—the application of Torah to the particulars of man's external experience of his world.

TIME AND MOMENT

Now we can understand the different emphases that the Torah places on men's and women's respective roles in the sanctification of time.

The detail-oriented spiritual life of the male is a *process*—a sequential string of particulars in which each item is dealt with on its own terms and fitted into context with the others. In time, his is the domain of the year, the month, the week, the day, the hour. So it is the man whom the Torah charges to imbue these time-particulars with holiness, to develop their individual natures and potential.

But while man is of the moment, woman is time incarnate. In the language of kabbalah, woman is *malchut* ("sovereignty"), which is the source of time and space.[12] So the woman relates to

---

11 Jerusalem Talmud, *Pe'ah* 2:4.

12 See *Ohr Hatorah, Bamidbar* vol. 4, *Pinchas* 1191–1203.

the essence of time, to the pure potential for change and flux as it transcends the particulars of quantified time. Therefore, the *mitzvot* assigned to her are primarily "time-neutral," relating to the whole of life rather than the specific segments defined by calendar and clock.

CHAPTER TWO

The Day
Darkness and Light

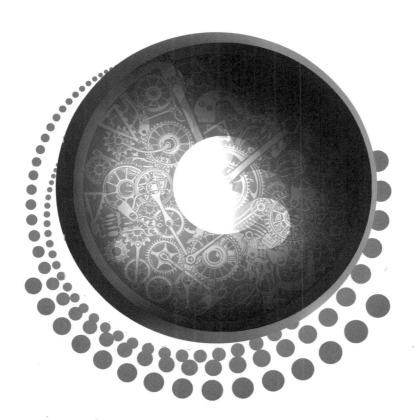

In our first chapter, we explored the essence and nature of time itself. In the next six chapters, we will examine the various cycles and systems by which we quantify time—the day, the week, the month, and the year—and the ways in which these cycles converge and interact with each other.

One possible way of viewing these time-cycles is to see them as purely technical impositions, necessitated by the business of everyday life. How else would we schedule a dentist appointment, calculate an employee's pay, or plot a long-term project? As we shall see, however, the Torah has a very different conception of these time-cycles, seeing them as integral to the nature of time and to the implementation of our mission in life. In the same way that time itself plays an important role in the forging of the human consciousness and the manner in which we live our lives, so too do the divisions of our lives into days, weeks, months, years, etc. Each of these time-cycles generates a particular set of characteristics within our psyche, and equips us with a particular set of tools with which to develop our inner selves, our relationships with our fellows, and the world in which we live.

Our current chapter deals with the time-component that has the most visible impact on our daily lives: the 24-hour cycle of day and night. Its first essay, *Garments for the Soul,* addresses the essential question:

Why should our lives be lived as "segments" rather than as an unbroken continuum? Does not the fragmentation of life into numerous periods of productive wakefulness, separated from each other by periods of sleep and inactivity, constitute a colossal waste of our most precious resource—time?

The second essay, *Evening and Morning*, discovers two distinct cycles within the day itself: the night-day cycle, and the day-night cycle. Is life a journey from darkness into light, or is it the movement of light into darkness? Indeed it is both, in keeping with the bilateral nature of the human being as an amalgam of matter and spirit.

The third essay in this chapter, *The Threshold*, focuses on a distinct point in the daily cycle: our moment of waking, which serves as the bridge between our supraconscious nocturnal self and our rational daytime identity.

GARMENTS FOR THE SOUL

Each and every day has its task to accomplish.
Zohar 3:94b

Sleep is one-sixtieth part of death.
Talmud, Berachot 57a

he first chapter of Genesis describes G-d's creation of the sun, moon, and other heavenly bodies:

> *And G-d said: "There shall be luminaries in the firmament of the heavens, to divide between day and night. And they shall be for signs, and for seasons, and for days and years.*
> *"And they shall be for luminaries in the sky of the heavens, to give light upon the earth." And it was so.*[1]

A close reading of these two verses yields an astonishing insight into the purpose for which these astral bodies were created. The natural assumption would be that the primary function of the sun, moon, and stars is to yield light, and the fact that they are used to measure and categorize time is secondary. But the Torah first describes their function to serve "for signs and for seasons and for days and years," and only after that speaks of their role as sources of illumination.[2]

---

[1] Genesis 1:14–15.
[2] *Chafetz Chaim al HaTorah* to Genesis 1:14.

THE DAY (1)   61

Indeed, the teachings of kabbalah convey that the cycles and divisions by which we measure and categorize time—the day, week, month, year, etc.—are not artificial impositions, but were woven into the very fabric of time by its Creator, who desired that these time-units be an integral part of our experience of time.

The most basic of these time-units is the day. The physiology of the human being dictates that our lives consist of periods of wakefulness interposed by periods of sleep. Complementing this cycle is the 24-hour day, which consists of periods of daylight separated by periods of night. This daily interruption of the stream of conscious and productive life, and the resultant segmentation of our lives into "days," creates the most basic of the frameworks by which we arrange our lives and profoundly influences the manner in which we pursue our goals and accomplishments.

Indeed, we are taught: "Each and every day has its task to accomplish." In the same way that every individual is unique and irreplaceable, each day of that individual's life was created to serve a distinct purpose, and imbued with the distinct potentials to accomplish it.

In the words of the *Zohar*:

> *When a person is born, all his days are already in existence, and they await that he should fill them with good deeds. If he is righteous, his days become garments of glory in which his soul is clothed. Thus it is said of Abraham that he was "old and coming in days."[3] For Abraham merited to arrive at the end of his life fully vested in his days, and his soul did not lack even one of its garments.*

---

3   Genesis 24:1.

Another passage in the *Zohar* comments on the Torah's description of the end of Jacob's life:

> *Why does it say that "the days of Israel[4] came near to dying"? Would it not have been more correct to say that the day of his dying came near?*
>
> *Because when G-d desires to return a person's soul to Himself, all the days which that person lived in this world are gathered up to be counted and accounted for. Fortunate is the man whose days can approach G-d without shame, and for whom not a single day is rejected and found unworthy.[5]*

Time is the most primary of all the resources we have been given to develop and sanctify. Thus, the days of our lives—the day being the most basic time unit—are the ultimate receptacles ("garments") for our life achievements.[6]

A REFRESHING DEATH

The Talmud declares that, "In all that G-d created in His world, He did not create a single thing in vain."[7] This begs the question: Why did G-d create this cycle of darkness and light, night and day, sleep and wakefulness? Isn't it a colossal waste of human potential?

Imagine that we did not need to sleep in order to remain conscious and productive. Instead of restarting our lives each morning,

---

4   Another name for Jacob—see Genesis 35:10.

5   *Zohar* 1:224a-b, 1:129a, and 1:221b; also see *Responsa of Rashba*, no. 423.

6   See *The First Creation* on pp. 20-30 above, specifically the teaching from the Baal Shem Tov cited on p. 28

7   Talmud, *Shabbat* 77b.

our entire creative life would span a single continuum. Would this not enable us to utilize our talents and resources more efficiently? This is aside from the fact that slumbered time is arguably our most wasted resource, with tens of billions of human life-hours slept away each day.

But the night-day cycle gives us something immeasurably more valuable: the gift of a tomorrow. If we didn't sleep, our every thought and action would be an outgrowth of all our previous thoughts and deeds. There would be no new beginnings in our lives, for the very concept of a "new beginning" would be utterly foreign to us.

The fact that we live our life as distinct days means that we have the capacity to not only improve but also transcend ourselves. Each morning, we are granted the opportunity to open a new chapter in life that is neither predicted nor constrained by what we did and were until now. The "minor death" of sleep empowers us to build a new, recreated self every morning of our lives.

EVENING AND MORNING

And it was evening and it was morning, one day.   Genesis 1:5

"irst came darkness, then light," says the Talmud,[1] summarizing what is perhaps the most basic law of life.

So it was when the world came into being. As related in the opening verses of the Torah, G-d first created a dark and chaotic world and only afterward introduced light into the darkness by decree of His creating word:

> *The earth was chaotic and void, with darkness on the face of the depths...*
> *And G-d said, "Let there be light," and there was light...*
> *And G-d called the light "day" and the darkness He called "night." And it was evening and it was morning, one day.*[2]

So too it is with every individual life. We enter the world in the dark: ignorant, uncomprehending, barely aware of our surroundings. Then begins the slow process of learning to recognize the world in which we live, comprehending its significance, and ultimately, generating our own light to illuminate and enlighten it.[3]

---

1   *Shabbat* 77b.
2   Genesis 1:2–5.
3   See Talmud, *Nidah* 30b; and *Likutei Torah, Shelach* 44a.

Even the Torah, G-d's blueprint for creation and His guide to life on earth, follows this pattern of "first darkness, then light." The Torah consists of two basic components: the "Written Torah" (the "Five Books of Moses"), and the "Oral Torah"—a system of laws, rules, and interpretative techniques given to Moses and handed down through the generations. The Written Torah contains the whole of the divine communication to man; but much of it is hidden, implicit within an extra word, a turn of phrase, or a comparison between two other laws. So the Torah, as G-d communicated it and Moses transcribed it, is a closed book; it is only by a lengthy and arduous process of study and exegesis that its life-illuminating wisdom can be deciphered.

G-d could just as easily have created a light-flooded world, had us emerge from the womb as mature and informed beings, and given us a Torah in which everything is explicitly spelled out. But he desired a world in which "first comes darkness, then light"—a world in which order is preceded by chaos, knowledge by ignorance, and achievement by toil and struggle.

The Natural and the Holy

When G-d created time, He embedded the law of "darkness first" into the structure of time's most basic component—the day. In the words of the creation narrative cited above, "It was evening and it was morning, one day." Each day of our lives is conceived in the womb of darkness, chaos, and strife, before emerging into the light of day.

The Jewish calendar follows suit: the calendar day begins at nightfall and ends with the following nightfall. Thus, the weekly Shabbat begins on Friday evening and ends on Saturday evening. The same applies to the festivals of the Jewish calendar, the counting of the *omer*, the observance of *yahrtzeit* (anniversary of the passing of a parent or relative), and so on.

There is, however, an exception to this rule: The service in the Holy Temple followed a dawn-to-dawn day. In the words of the Talmud, "While in the natural world day follows the night, in all matters pertaining to *kodoshim* ('sacred things') night follows the day."[4]

This is because the reality we inhabit consists of two parallel worlds. There is the natural, material world; and there is the sacred, spiritual world. In our own lives, we engage with spiritual and holy things, as well as with the imperfect and the mundane. Not only are these two worlds populated by different elements and events, they even run on different calendars, as the very process of time runs differently in each. In the natural-material world, day follows night; and in the sacred-spiritual world, night follows day.

With our holy pursuits, our starting point is "day." These are already luminous and perfected, and our task is to build upon and develop their holiness and specialness, and then, to further extend them so that they illuminate the hitherto unlit "night." On the other hand, dealing with the material world is a struggle from the bottom up. This is a dark world, for it shrouds and conceals the truth of its Creator. Here we must begin—as did the created existence—with the night, groping through the darkness as we strive toward dawn and day.

THE DUALITY OF PRAYER

There is one area of our lives which straddles both universes: the activity and experience of prayer.

---

4   Talmud, *Chulin* 83a

THE DAY (2)   67

Three times a day we address G-d in prayer: morning, afternoon,
and evening. Or is it evening, morning, and afternoon? When
does the day begin in regard to prayer? An examination of the laws
and history of prayer seems to say: both.

For example, the talmudic tractate of *Berachot* begins by recounting the laws of the evening recitation of the *Shema*, followed
by the rules which govern the morning *Shema*. It also quotes King
David, "Evening, morning, and afternoon, I speak forth and yearn,
and He hears my voice,"[5] as the model for the daily schedule of
prayer, indicating that it is of a "night first" nature. But in the
fourth chapter of *Berachot*, it discusses the morning prayers first,
then the afternoon prayers, and the evening prayers last. And on
another occasion it states that the three daily prayers correspond
to the morning, afternoon, and evening services in the Temple.

We are also taught that "Abraham instituted the morning prayer,
Isaac instituted the afternoon prayer, and Jacob instituted the evening prayer"—again indicating a night-follows-day sequence.[6]

Indeed, prayer is both a spiritual activity for the soul and a
pragmatic part of physical life. When Maimonides traces the biblical origins of prayer, he quotes two sources:

> *It is a positive commandment to pray each day. As it is
> written, "You shall serve the L-rd your G-d [and He will
> bless your bread and your water] (Exodus 23:25)." We
> have it by tradition that this "service" is prayer, as it is
> written "To serve Him with all your hearts [and with all
> your souls] (Deuteronomy 11:13)." Said our sages: "What
> is the service of the heart? This is prayer."[7]*

---

5   Psalms 55:18.
6   Talmud, *Berachot* 2a, 31a, and 26a-b.
7   *Mishneh Torah, Laws of Prayer* 1:1.

The obvious question is: Why quote the first verse (from Exodus), if in any case we need to quote the second verse (from Deuteronomy) to establish that the "service" of which the Torah speaks is the service of prayer? Why couldn't Maimonides simply say, "It is a positive commandment to pray each day, as it is written, 'To serve Him with all your hearts'"?

But Maimonides wishes to emphasize that prayer cannot be defined only as an outpouring of heart and soul, or as the quest of the spirit of man to cleave to its Creator (as indicated by the verse in Deuteronomy). First and foremost, prayer is a person turning to G-d for his or her daily bread and water (as per the verse in Exodus). Prayer is our acknowledgement that G-d is not only the focus of our spiritual life, but the provider and sustainer of our physical existence.

There is, of course, the spiritual side of prayer. "The pious would meditate for an hour," say our sages, "and only then would they pray."[8] "They would seclude themselves and direct their minds until they had totally divested themselves of the physical and reached a supremacy of the spirit of reason, so that they attained a state close to that of prophecy."[9] They "bound their souls to the Master of All, in an overpowering state of awe and love and true attachment."[10] Obviously, bread and water was not what was on their minds. But this is the "service of the heart" aspect of prayer, which—as presented in the above-quote from Maimonides—comes after prayer has been defined as requesting one's material needs from the Almighty.

The purpose of life is not only for the soul to soar to yet greater attachment to G-d, but to illuminate the "darkness" of the

---

8   Talmud, *Berachot* 30b.
9   *Tur, Orach Chaim* 98.
10 Rabbi Schneur Zalman of Liadi's *Hilchot Talmud Torah* 4:5.

physical world. So we begin by battling the greatest lie of the natural world: the contention that it is a person's ability, toil, and "luck" which earn him his livelihood. Three times a day we ask G-d for our bread and water, affirming our belief that it is G-d who grants life and existence to every being, every millisecond of time.

FUTURE DAY

"It was evening and it was morning, one day." In natural time, night leads to day; in sacred time, day expands into night. But regardless of how evening and morning are ordered, they comprise "one day"—a single, integral unit of time.

Indeed, in the "World to Come," the future world that is the culminating state of creation, "night will be as luminous as day."[11] Night and day are but two faces of the same entity—the one is the means to the other's end, the process to its product. While the process is still underway, the two seem worlds apart: the night dark where the day is bright, obscure where it is lucid, trying where it is tranquil. But when the process reaches its culmination, the night will be revealed as an integral part of the day's harmony and luminescence.

---

11   Psalms 139:12.

THE THRESHOLD

No impurity in the world can contaminate the
Modeh Ani of a Jew. HaYom Yom, Shevat 11

Our first conscious act of the day is to avow our indebtedness and gratitude to our Creator, acknowledging that it is G-d who grants us life and being every moment of our existence. As soon as we wake from sleep, before getting out of bed or even washing our hands,[1] we recite the *Modeh Ani* prayer:

> *I offer thanks to You, O living and everlasting King, for having restored my soul within me; great is Your faithfulness.*

The ideas contained in the ostensibly simple lines of *Modeh Ani* fill many a chapter in the legal, philosophical, and mystical works of Torah. They touch upon the omnipresence and all-pervasiveness of G-d; on the principle of "perpetual creation" (G-d's constant infusion of vitality and existence into the world, without which it would revert to utter nothingness); on the laws governing the return of a *pikadon* (an object entrusted to one's care); and on the

---

[1] The *Modeh Ani* prayer does not contain any of the names of G-d, referring to Him instead as the "living and everlasting King." It is for this reason that we may recite it before washing our hands in the morning, when it is forbidden to say any "words of holiness." Chassidic teaching explains that this does not mean that *Modeh Ani* is less a communication with G-d than the other, "holier" prayers. On the contrary: It addresses the very essence of G-d, which transcends all divine "names" and descriptions — including the concept of, and the conditions required for, "holiness."

kabbalistic concept of *sefirat hamalchut* (the divine attribute of "sovereignty").[2] So why is the *Modeh Ani* said immediately upon waking, with a mind still groggy from sleep? Would it not have been more appropriate to precede it with a period of study and contemplation of these concepts?

The Nocturnal Mind

The physiology of our bodies and the rhythm of the astral clocks partition our lives into conscious and supraconscious domains. During our waking hours, our conscious mind assumes control of our thoughts and actions, screening, filtering, and interpreting the stimuli that flow to it, and issuing commands and instructions to the body. But at night, when we sleep, the "command-center" shifts to a deeper, darker place within our psyche—a place where fantasy supersedes logic, sense supplants thought, and awareness is replaced by a more elemental form of knowing. Hard facts become pliant, absurdities become tenable, in this nocturnal world.

There are certain truths, however, that are unaffected by these fluctuations of knowledge and awareness. Our faith in G-d, His centrality to our existence, the depth of our commitment to Him— we know these things utterly and absolutely, and we know them at all times and in all states of consciousness.[3]

Wakefulness and sleep only affect the external activity of the intellect: What we know with the very core of our being, we know no less when plunged into the deepest recesses of slumber. On the contrary: when awake, we must wade through the presuppositions

---

2   See the Rebbe's essay, *On the Essence of Chassidus* (Kehot, 1978).

3   See the section titled "The Guilt-Offering" in the essay *Sin in Four Dimensions*, in vol. 2 of this series, pp. 46–48

and polemics of an intellect shackled to the "realities" of the physical state in order to arrive at these truths; asleep, our mind is loosened from its subjective moorings and we enjoy a closer and deeper (albeit less conscious) awareness of our innermost convictions.

The *Modeh Ani* prayer exploits a most unique moment of our day: the moment that lies at the threshold of wakefulness, the moment that straddles the conscious and supraconscious domains of our day.

There are other moments, other prayers in the course of our day, which take full advantage of our powers of intellect and reasoning. These prayers indeed follow lengthy and profound meditations upon their content and significance. But each morning, as we move from the liberating hours of sleep to a day of conscious thought, a unique opportunity presents itself: the opportunity to express to the conscious mind a truth that inhabits our deepest selves, and declare it to the awaiting day.

In our moment of waking, we cross from dream to reality—a reality that actualizes the dream, but which also coarsens its purity. This is the moment in which to give expression to all that we know and sense about our connection with our Creator. For though our knowledge at this moment may be primitive and unformed by the standards of daytime reality, it comes from a place in us that will no longer be accessible when we have ventured further into this realm of conscious knowledge and feeling. Only by expressing it now, on the threshold between supraconscious awareness and conscious knowledge, can we carry over from the perfection and purity of our supraconscious selves into the tactual reality of our conscious lives.

CHAPTER THREE

The Week and Shabbat
The Cycle of Creation

The seven-day week is the only one of the major time-systems not predicated on any observable natural cycle. Indeed, *Kuzari* (the classic 11th-century Jewish philosophical work by Rabbi Judah HaLevi) sees this phenomenon as a proof to G-d's creation of the world: The Torah relates how G-d created the world in six days and sanctified the seventh as a day of rest; the fact that so many diverse cultures follow a seven-day week indicates that they are all descendant from the first man, Adam, who transmitted this tradition to his children.

The cosmic week comes in a number of forms. Most prominent, of course, is the seven-day cycle of work and rest which constitutes our perpetual reenactment of the divine cycle of creation. But there is also a seven-year "sabbatical" cycle mandated by the Torah governing the cultivation of land, the suspension of debts, and the release of indentured servants. The sabbatical cycle is itself part of a greater 50-year cycle, in which seven sabbatical cycles are capped by a "jubilee" year. Finally, the Talmud states that the whole of human endeavor consists of six millennia of work and achievement, culminating in a seventh millennium that is "wholly Shabbat and rest for life everlasting." Each of these "weeks" follows the same 6/1 paradigm: six "days" of work, toil, and achievement, which culminate in, and are empowered by, a seventh "day" of rest and tranquility.

The first essay in this chapter, *The Seventh Element*, examines the relationship of the seven-day cycle of creation with the substance of time itself. If the essence of time is motion and change, how can "rest" be a component of time? The answer lies in the particular geometric "shape" of the weekly cycle, as described in the teachings of kabbalah and elaborated on by the chassidic masters.

The next three essays explore the practical, spiritual, and mystical significance of the weekly day of rest. *A World of Thought* addresses the question: If G-d ceases His work of creation on the seventh day, how do we exist? *A Private World* analyzes a dialogue between the talmudic sage Rabbi Akiva and a Roman ruler, that illuminates the different mode of existence into which the Shabbat observer enters for 25-plus hours each week. *Bread from Heaven* discusses the unique perspective on earning a living which the Torah imparts to us, and the role of Shabbat in sustaining and validating that vision.

The fifth essay in this chapter, *Havdalah*, examines the significance of the ritual which separates the Shabbat from the rest of the week, and the manner in which our capacity for "differentiation" is at the core of a moral existence as well as our ability to introduce sanctity and G-dliness into our lives.

The next two essays look beyond the seven-day cycle to the greater, overriding goal that defines it, transcends it, and pervades it. In *The Eighth Dimension*, the biblical jubilee year in its various forms serves as a model for the different ways in which that ultimate goal informs and vitalizes our everyday progression within the cosmic cycle of seven. *Twilight* identifies a place within the cycle where turmoil and tranquility overlap, lending insight to the unique time in history that we occupy as the world transitions from *galut* (exile and spiritual displacement) to redemption.

Also see the essay, *The King in the Field,* in vol. 3 of this series, pp. 304–313.

THE SEVENTH ELEMENT

*For everything there is a time and season... A
time for war, and a time for peace.*

Ecclesiastes 3:1, 8

We seem to be forever waging war. Most blatant are the actual wars fought with armed troops and increasingly sophisticated weaponry. We also wage wars against crime, bigotry, disease, and addiction. Even when there isn't an enemy or a negative phenomenon to challenge us, we pit ourselves against the prevalent reality: In school, in the workplace, or in the social arena, we are constantly fighting our way to the top, forever combating obstacles in our quest toward greater success. Embedded in our psyche is the unceasing drive to make more of ourselves, to reach beyond yesterday's attainments. Man is forever at war with the past.

The state of perpetual struggle seems innate to the very nature of existence. Wherever we turn, we encounter turmoil. The solar system spins like a top; the galaxies simmer and revolve. The earth's core is aboil, its atmosphere storms, its oceans churn. Physical life is sustained by movement—the throb of the heart, the contraction and expansion of the lungs. Seemingly "inanimate" matter is a cauldron of motion on the nuclear, atomic, and subatomic levels. Motion means change, and every change is a struggle—the struggle to vanquish the status quo and supplant it with a new reality.

The primary culprit in this unending strife is the phenomenon of time. Time is what gives us a past to reject, a present with which not to suffice, a future toward which to strive. Time is the mother of motion, change, and struggle; time is the canvas upon which all battles of life are etched. It would seem that as long as we exist in time, as long as our lives are defined by its pulse and flux, the battle of life will rage on.

Can we transcend time? A timeless existence would be free of motion and strife. But would it allow for challenge, improvement, and progression?

THE ORIGINAL WEEK

In Exodus 20:11 (the fourth of the Ten Commandments), we read:

> *Six days G-d made the heavens, the earth, the sea, and all that is in them; and He rested on the seventh day.*[1]

The plain meaning of this verse is that G-d created the world *in* six days; but the actual wording is, "six days G-d made..." The teachings of kabbalah explain that, on a deeper level, the Torah is saying that the created reality consists of "six days."

The whole of creation, kabbalah teaches, is comprised of six basic spiritual elements—*chesed, gevurah, tiferet, netzach, hod,* and *yesod* (roughly: benevolence, power, beauty, ambition, devotion, and bonding)—deriving from six corresponding divine attributes (*sefirot*) which the Creator chose to invest in His creation of our reality.

---

1   Also in Exodus 31:17.

THE WEEK AND SHABBAT (1)   79

G-d's creation of the universe spanned six days, each of which was
the conduit for a new class of creations particular to the nature
of that day. The attribute of *chesed*, with its "giving" or "bestow-
ing" nature, defines the creation of the first day, light. The "firma-
ment"—the barrier separating the material from the spiritual—
created on the second day, is a product of the divine forces of "constraint" and "judgment," in keeping with the attribute of *gevurah*.
And so with each of the six days of creation.

A seventh element, *malchut* (sovereignty), is embodied by
Shabbat. Shabbat is part of the cycle of creation, yet stands apart
from it, since—as will be explored below—the nature of what was
brought into being on the seventh day is of a different order of
existence than the creations of the other six days.

What is true of creation as a whole, is also true of the particular creation called "time." Time, like the universe it underlies, was
created in seven days because it possesses seven distinct qualities:
On each day of creation, another dimension of time was brought
into being. *Chesed*-time was created on the first day, *gevurah*-time
on the second day, and so on. It was not until "G-d concluded, on
the seventh day, the works which He had made"[2] that the seven
primary components of time were completed and fixed in place as
a seven-day cycle.

In the Holy Tongue, Sunday is called *yom rishon*, "first day,"
Monday is *yom sheini,* "second day," and so on. This is not merely
a reference to the first week of time, in which Sunday was the first
day ever and Monday the second. Each and every Sunday is a "first
day"—the first of a new time cycle which repeats, from the beginning, the seven qualities of time.

---

2   Genesis 2:2.

The Creation of Rest

What is the nature of the seventh day, and how does it differ from the other six? Are there six or seven days of creation?

On the latter point, the Torah's account of creation seems to take *both* positions. Genesis 2:2 declares:

> *G-d concluded on the seventh day the works He had made; and He rested on the seventh day from all the works He had made.*

The latter part of this verse implies that the work of creation was concluded before the seventh day; whereas the first part of the verse indicates that G-d completed the work of creation *on* the seventh day. The sages explain: "What was the world lacking? Rest. When Shabbat came, rest came."[3] On Shabbat G-d created rest — the final and culminating element of creation.

Time, too, was also almost complete on the eve of the first Shabbat, lacking only the element of rest. With the creation of Shabbat-time — time possessing the quality of rest — the cycle of time was closed.

Can "rest" be considered a characteristic of time? Is not time the very antithesis of rest?

But that is precisely the point. Shabbat represents an area in time that transcends time's own basic definition. Time, though synonymous with motion and change, also includes the potential for permanence and tranquility.

The Torah defines the weekday aspect of our lives as "going out to war on your enemies."[4] But regarding Shabbat it proclaims: "Remain each man in his place; no man shall go out of his place on the

---

3   Rashi on verse.
4   Deuteronomy 21:10; *Likutei Torah, Ki Teitzei* 35c; et al.

THE WEEK AND SHABBAT (1)   81

day of Shabbat."[5] If our mission in life is to "go out"—to vanquish
the negative, to perfect the imperfect, to extend oneself beyond
the limitations of one's presently defined self—it also includes the
capacity for rest, for settling down, for the tranquility of finding
one's true "I" and place. Life includes not only the challenge of
getting there, but also the fulfillment of being there.

"Six days a week you shall labor," commands the Torah, "and
you shall do all your work; the seventh day is Shabbat to G-d"[6] But
how can a person do "*all*" your work" in six days? Even to conclude
"all your work" in the course of a lifetime is no small feat! But on
Shabbat, explain the sages, "all your work is done."[7] Shabbat is not
only a break in the toil of life; it is a taste of its ultimate completion and realization.

On Shabbat, we cease to struggle with the world not because
the task of perfecting it is "on hold," but because on Shabbat the
world *is* perfect: we relate to what is perfect and unchanging in
it. We cease to battle darkness not merely to recoup our strength
for the next onslaught, but because there is no darkness—the
light which we have created through our positive deeds, obscured
during the week by the veil of mundanity which envelopes our
workday lives, is now perceptible to our more rarefied selves.

This better explains why each Sunday is indeed a "first day."
Shabbat is a venture into the realm of timelessness that lies beyond
the struggles that characterize our weekday lives. Following each
Shabbat, we return to a time-bound existence. Time, in the sense
of motion and flux, begins anew.

Shabbat not only provides us a weekly respite from the turmoil
of life, it also has a profound effect on the entire week. If, in our

---

5   Exodus 16:29.
6   Ibid., 20:9–10.
7   *Mechilta* on verse.

daily lives, we experience not only the drive for achievement but also satisfaction over what has been achieved; if we have the ability not only to vanquish the challenges which the world throws up against us but also to transform these challenges into allies; if our life is not only an ongoing quest but also a series of attainments—it is because Shabbat radiates its essence to the other six components of time.

THE GEOMETRY OF TIME

The paradox of Shabbat—a point in time that transcends the very definition of time, yet exerts its influence throughout time's expanse—has an analogy in geometry, which measures and quantifies the properties of space.

(Time and space are closely related; indeed, modern physics is wont to combine the two as "spacetime," with time functioning as a fourth dimension for physical phenomena. While time is the more abstract of the two, many of the characteristics of space are attributed to time as well. We speak of a "point" in time, a "stretch" of time, time "cycles," even of the "condensation" or "fanning out" of time.[8] Thus, many of time's complexities can be better understood when we apply the spatial models of geometry to our conception of time.)

The analogy for the cosmic week is the circle, long considered the most perfect of spatial shapes. The primary features of the circle are: a) the *center*, the point from which the circle's area extends

---

8   See *Derech Mitzvotecha*, 59a: "In the chambers of *yetzirah* (a spiritual world which precedes our physical universe in the 'chain of evolution' from spirit to matter which G-d employed in His creation), fifteen years (of 'our' time) are included in a single glance."

THE WEEK AND SHABBAT (1)   83

uniformly in all directions; b) the *radius*, which is the distance
from the circle's center to its outer limit; and c) the *circumference*,
the circle's outer rim, which contains the area of the circle within
it. The circumference is approximately six times the length of the
radius.[9] This is true of all circles, regardless of size: The greater the
radius, the greater the area of the circle, and thus the greater the
circumference that encloses this area; but the proportion always
remains the same—each additional inch (or yard or mile) of radius will translate into (slightly more than) six additional inches (or
yards or miles) of circumference.

The geometric point possesses no area; as such, it would seem
to hardly qualify as a component of space. In fact, the very opposite is true: The point is the most basic component of all geometric
forms—every line is defined by the points that mark its beginning,
end, center, convergence with other lines, etc.; and every area is
defined by the lines that frame it. Indeed, it is precisely because

---

9   While the exact figure cannot be expressed in numbers, mathemati-
    cians have determined that the ratio of a circle's circumference to its
    diameter (a circle's diameter is its width from end to end, or a line
    exactly double its radius) is an endless string of numbers that begins
    3.14... (represented by the symbol π). According to this, the circum-
    ference of a circle is within a hundredth part of 6.28 times its radius.
    For purposes of Torah law, the Talmud (*Eruvin* 13b) rules that "[a cir-
    cle] whose circumference is three *tefachim*, has a width of one *tefach*."
    Maimonides, in his *Commentary on the Mishnah* (*Eruvin* 1:3) explains:
    "Know, that the ratio of a circle's diameter to its circumference is not
    known and can never be expressed absolutely. This lack of knowledge
    is not due to our [ignorance]... for this thing is, in essence, unknow-
    able. It can, however, be known approximately... the closest figure [that
    has been arrived at] is approximately three and one seventh. Since the
    exact figure cannot be known, [the Talmud] adopts a round figure, rul-
    ing that, regarding all measurements required by the Torah, that which
    has a circumference of three *tefachim*, has a diameter of one *tefach*."

the point possesses no area itself that it can define and quantify the areas that relate to it.

This is exemplified by the circle's center. A "mere" point, the center occupies none of the circle's area, but the center is what makes the circle a circle. The radius extends from it, the diameter turns on it, the circumference is drawn in relation to it—virtually every feature and characteristic of the circle is derived from the point upon which it is centered.

To understand the week—the seven-day cycle which the Creator stamped into the very fabric of time—we can envision it as a circle. The center of the circle is Shabbat. The exterior surface of this circle (its "circumference"), generated by multiplying the distance from the center six-fold, are the six workdays—days that are tracts of time, expanses of progression and change, each characterized by another of the six time-qualities of the six *sefirot*. Shabbat is a timeless point in time, an island of tranquility in a sea of flux. Yet despite—indeed, because of—its "timelessness," Shabbat is the axis upon which the week turns.[10]

For Shabbat is the day that embodies the purpose and end-goal of time—the objective of all the work, development, and change in our restless existence. On Shabbat, our efforts of the past six workdays yield a holier and more G-dly world, a world brought that much closer to the harmonious perfection that G-d imbued in creation and charged us to develop. One day a week, we penetrate below the whirling perimeter of time to experience its tranquil core. And it is this weekly taste of tranquil perfection that supplies us with the vision and fortitude to grapple with and transform the

---

10   In kabbalistic terms, Shabbat is the quality of *malchut*, which "possesses no qualities of its own," yet is the focus and end-goal of the other six qualities (*Zohar* 1:249b; *Eitz Chaim* 6:5 and 8:5).

THE WEEK AND SHABBAT (1)   85

still imperfect world we return to during the six workdays of the coming week.

Shabbat, then, is both the source and the goal of the six days of "conventional" time that form the circumference of the weekly cycle. It is the very essence of time, precisely because it is devoid of the motion and flux which characterize time—in the same way that the area of the circle derives from and is defined by its center-point, precisely because the center is devoid of any area of its own.

With the spatial circle, the greater the radius, the greater the circumference. The same is true of the circle of time. The further we depart from its timeless center, the more "body" time has: the more turbulent it is, the more at odds with the "Shabbat" at its core. But no matter how great the surface flux of our life, it is inexorably bound to the tranquil axis, deriving from it and tending toward it. Ultimately, even the most tumultuous periods of our lives are generated by its quintessential purpose and serve its harmonious end.

THE MILLENNIAL SHABBAT

The seven-day week is a microcosm of a far greater time span. The Talmud teaches that the entirety of history is also a "week" comprised of six "workday" millennia and a seventh millennium of rest—the era of Moshiach.[11] Thus, the weekly Shabbat is but a foretaste of "the day that is wholly Shabbat and rest, for life everlasting"[12]

---

11 Talmud *Sanhedrin* 97a; Nachmanides' commentary on Genesis 2:3. See the essay *Twilight*, section titled "The Cosmic Week," pp. 142–144 below.

12 *Grace after Meals*, addendum for Shabbat.

On the weekly level, Shabbat is a day on which we experience the perfection that has been achieved through our efforts of the past six days to develop and refine our world. On the cosmic level, the era of Moshiach is when the combined attainments of all generations of history will be realized; when every positive deed, word, and thought of the six millennia of human endeavor will result in a truly tranquil world—a world free of discord and strife, a world suffused with the wisdom, goodness, and perfection of its Creator.

INWARD TIME

We have explained that "rest," seemingly the antithesis of time, is the essence and goal of time. Yet Shabbat is also a *day* in time. Even the messianic age is an era in time—a seventh millennium of history. Obviously, then, these are not static states of existence, but arenas for progression and achievement. How is this compatible with the fact that their essential nature is rest and tranquility?

On the most basic level we might explain that, indeed, both the workweek and the weekly Shabbat, both the six millennia of history and the era of Moshiach, are times for advancement and progression, and that the difference lies in the *manner* in which this is achieved. Our workweek challenges include dealing with outright evil and negativity, so progress inevitably involves struggle. On Shabbat, however, and to an even greater extent, in the age of Moshiach, advancement and progression mean the tranquil graduation from good to better, the attainment of greater heights within the infinite realm of good itself.

If today we fight to eliminate war and hatred, in the era of Moshiach, when "they shall beat their swords into plowshares,"[13]

---

13   Isaiah 2:4.

THE WEEK AND SHABBAT (1)   87

the pursuit of peace will mean finding deeper and more meaningful ways for people to fuse their differences into a symphonious whole. If today we struggle to defeat illness, the "medicine" of the seventh millennium will concern itself with the further perfection of good health and the enhancement of the bond between body and soul. If today we battle ignorance, in the era when "the world shall be filled with the knowledge of G-d as the waters cover the sea,"[14] the quest for wisdom will be for greater and greater degrees of insight into the infinite truth of truths.

Nevertheless, this does not fully answer the question. For any change, any departure from a previous state, is ultimately a battle and struggle, albeit a far more subtle battle and struggle than the conquest of evil. Again we ask: How can any form of progress be defined as a state of rest?

But progress may have two directions: outward and inward. The equation of progress with struggle, of graduation with change, is valid when we speak of "going out of our place," of reaching beyond what we are in order to make more of ourselves. But there is also progress that is an inward journey, a journey to uncover deeper dimensions to our own being.

On such an inward journey, each successive station is not a "change," but the very opposite of change: It is a state that is *more* consistent with who and what we truly are. It is rest in the truest sense. Not rest as lack of movement, but rest as a settling into one's quintessential place and identity.

For "G-d created man in His image"[15] to reflect His own goodness and perfection. In the "workday" phases of our existence, the veil of corporeality that shrouds our world and encases our souls

---

14   Ibid., 11:9.

15   Genesis 1:26.

causes us to live a life that is at odds with our true identity and essence. So the betterment of ourselves and our world is a *struggle*, a battle to change reality (or rather, what to our perception is reality) into something which is (again, to our perception) beyond us. But in truth, this "reality" is a distortion of our true selves, while the elusive "beyond" is our true self.

When six millennia of struggle and achievement will come to fruition, when six millennia of battling darkness will reveal the light within, we will experience an era "that is wholly Shabbat and rest." This will not be a golden age of retirement for humanity, for the potential within us is as infinite as the divine perfection it reflects. But the direction of progress will be reversed: The conflict-ridden, outward-bound quest for change will be revealed as the serene, inward-bound encounter with self.

This reversal of the flow of time is not confined to the seventh millennium. Every Shabbat is a taste of this future time, and a provider of its tranquility to the entire week. While yet in the midst of the war of life, we are empowered to experience moments of true rest. Even as we struggle to transcend the imperfections of a more external self, we can touch base with the goodness and perfection that lies at the core of each and every one of us.

THE WORLD OF THOUGHT

Regarding the time of the Redemption, G-d
says: My heart does not reveal it to my mouth.

Talmud, Sanhedrin 99a;

Zohar Chadash, Bereishit 8a

he Torah, "speaking in the language of men,"[1] describes the divine act of creation as an act of speech: G-d said, "There shall be light,"[2] "The earth shall sprout greenery,"[3] and so on, and the various elements of existence came into being.

Chassidic teaching takes this a step further: The world *is* the speech of G-d. The divine utterances of Genesis are not merely mediums or forces which bring the creations into existence, but are the very essence of their being. What we perceive as a stone, a living creature, or a physical law is, in truth, the divine communication that it should be.

Why speech? Why is "and G-d said" the appropriate metaphor to borrow from human experience to describe what happened at creation? Because despite its apparent formidability, our world can hardly be said to exist at all. Is what we experience as "reality" in fact real? Yes and no, say the chassidic masters. On the one hand, it is wholly dependent upon its Creator, every fraction of time, for

---

1   Talmud, *Berachot* 31b, et al.

2   Genesis 1:3.

3   Ibid., v. 11.

being and life.[4] As one chassidic thinker put it, if G-d no longer wished that our world should exist, G-d forbid, He need not destroy it; the moment He ceases to will it into being, it no longer is. A "reality" of such dependence and subjectivity hardly qualifies as an existence in its own right—all it is, is the expression of another, infinitely greater being's desire that it should be.

On the other hand, our world is imbued with a sense of selfhood and distinctiveness of being. Although the fact that we sense our own existence and that of our environment to be real does not prove anything (for all we know, our sense of existence may be an illusion), the Torah gives credence to this reality. It states: "In the beginning G-d created the heavens and the earth."[5] It also tells us that G-d created the world with a purpose in mind—that He desires that we improve and perfect it through our good deeds (*mitzvot*), and that we refrain from other deeds which corrupt His creation. Furthermore, the sense of self which we experience is an integral part of this purpose: G-d specifically wanted a world which would perceive itself as a reality apart from its Creator, and that this "lowly realm" should choose to develop itself as a "dwelling for G-d"—an environment receptive and hospitable to His reality.[6] Illusion or not, creation's self-definition as a distinct reality has a truth to it, a validity granted it by its Creator.

To express the paradoxical nature of creation's reality, the Torah borrows the term "speech" from human experience. The human being creates on three basic levels: thought, speech, and action. Were the Torah to say that G-d "made" a world, this would imply a creation as disconnected from its creator as the products of man's physical actions are from theirs: a person builds a building, paints

---

4   See *The Now* on pp. 31–37 above.
5   Genesis 1:1.
6   *Midrash Tanchuma, Nasso* 16; *Tanya*, ch. 36.

a picture, or writes a book, and his creation is now a distinct and independent existence, even possessing a "life" of its own. On the other hand, to describe reality as a divine "thought" would imply that it exists only within its Creator's reality. Speech, however, describes an existence which, on the one hand, is distinct from its source, yet on the other, is utterly dependent upon it and possesses no reality other than that dependence.

When a person speaks, he creates something which extends beyond his own existence. The thought which he had conceived, and which, up until now, has existed only within his mind, is now translated into words which "leave" his person to attain a separateness from their creator. Nevertheless, they are utterly dependent upon him for existence: The moment he ceases to speak, the entity we refer to as his "speech" no longer exists. In other words, their existence can only be defined in terms of his ongoing involvement to create them.

So it is with our world. G-d desires that it exist, and that it constitute a reality which is (at least in its own perception) distinct from His own. On the other hand, the world has no independent existence; it possesses no reality other than G-d's constant involvement to create and sustain it. In other words, G-d did not make a world—He spoke it.

RETREATING INTO THOUGHT

A person may articulate a thought to himself and "create" no further; but every word or act of his is also a thought, conceived first in the mind and then given an existence distinct from himself, as words or actions.

The same is true of G-d's creation: The "spoken" world we inhabit represents the "lowliest" and most external layer of His creation, and is preceded by a higher, more intimate version of creation—a reality which may be described as "G-d's thought." When we say that this thought reality "precedes" our conventional speech reality, this is not to say that it precedes it in physical time —physical time is itself a product of G-d's creation. Rather, it is the selfsame world we inhabit, yet on an "earlier" (i.e., closer to its source) plane of awareness and self-definition. This is a world which sees itself not as an entity distinct from its Creator, but as a concept within the divine mind—as something wholly subsumed within the divine reality.

This describes the state of creation on the weekly Shabbat. For six days a week we live in the "spoken world" generated by the divine utterances of Genesis. But for one day each week, we enter a higher plane of awareness, as our world recedes from its spoken state to the realm of divine thought. As the Torah relates in its account of creation, for six days G-d spoke the world, projecting His concept of creation into the "separate" reality we know. On the seventh day He ceased to speak. He did not, however, cease to create; were He to do so, the world would have ceased to exist. Rather, He withdrew from the externalization of speech and confined Himself to the internal creation of thought. He continued to articulate our world, not as something "outside" of himself but as a self-contained conceptualization of His vision of creation.

The seven days of creation are an ongoing cycle. Every Shabbat, G-d withdraws from His more external mode of creation, elevating our world to the level of divine thought. On Shabbat we still live in the very same world we inhabit during the other six days of the week; but on Shabbat the "I am" of our world is muted, its illusion of distinctiveness more transparent. On this day, man can more readily transcend the disconnectedness of the material reality and experience a union and identification with his essence and source.

THE SUBCONSCIOUS OF G-D

Within the realm of thought itself are many levels of definition and tangibility.

Conscious thought is closest to the outward projection of speech. It, too, is composed of images and words. Although expressed in a language more abstract and nebulous than that of speech (a single fleeting thought may take hours to articulate verbally and may contain many nuances of understanding which are not translatable into spoken words), it has a language nonetheless, and is thus a "world" comprised of definitive entities. While a person's conscious thoughts do not exist outside of himself, they occupy a distinct place within his mind.

If we apply this metaphor to the divine thought-reality of Shabbat, we might say that on Shabbat we enter a state of being that might be described as G-d's "conscious thought": a realm that is "within" the divine reality but whose union and identification with its source is not absolute. It is a distinct creation, albeit a wholly internal one.

Thus, Shabbat is only a "taste" of a higher reality—a reality that can only be described as the "subconscious thought" of G-d.

Subconscious thought has no language, no definition, no parameters—nothing to distinguish it from the mind which contains it. The definitive thoughts to which it gives birth seem to spring out of nowhere—from the essence of the mind itself. We know that they must already "exist" in some earlier, more sublime state—in what we, in "the language of men," call "subconscious thoughts." Yet these form no identifiable part of the conceiver's mind, but are seamlessly woven into the very fabric of its essence.

The Torah tells us that at the very beginnings of creation, "the spirit of G-d hovered" above a still vacant and formless world.[7] This "spirit of G-d," say our sages, is the spirit of Moshiach[8] — G-d's primordial "subconscious" conception of creation.

This is the significance of the statement by our sages regarding the time of the future redemption: "The divine heart does not reveal to the divine mouth." Once again, we are employing "the language of men" to describe a divine reality. In our experience, the subconscious is a realm where there are ideas and feelings so deeply known and felt, some integrally one with our core self, that they cannot be articulated even to our own conscious mind. That is the only metaphor we have for a world that is utterly one with its Creator.

The era of Moshiach is therefore described as a time of "absolute and eternal Shabbat."[9] For if on Shabbat our world is elevated to the realm of divine conscious thought, the era of Moshiach is a time when we will inhabit the "subconscious" of G-d. Again, it is our world, the same world we live in today, different not in substance but in awareness. Its self-perception is not that of the external world of "speech," nor even that of the subsumed but still distinct world of "conscious thought," but one of seamless unity with its Conceiver and Creator.

Yet it is this most intimate heart of G-d that will become our everyday experience and reality, when we complete our task to make our lives and world a "dwelling for G-d."

---

7   Genesis 1:2.

8   *Midrash Rabbah* on verse.

9   From the Shabbat addendum to the *Grace after Meals*.

A PRIVATE WORLD

There are thirty-nine primary types of work forbidden on Shabbat: sowing, plowing, reaping... and taking out an object from domain to domain.
Talmud, Shabbat 73a

he Midrash records the following exchange between the Roman governor Turnus Rufus and Rabbi Akiva:

> *Said Turnus Rufus to Rabbi Akiva: "If G-d honors the Shabbat, then He should not blow winds on it, He should not cause rain to fall on it, He should not cause the grass to grow on it!"*
>
> *Replied Rabbi Akiva: "If two people live in one courtyard, unless they both contribute to an* eiruv, *would they be permitted to carry in the yard? But if one person lives in a courtyard, he has free reign in the entire yard. The same is true of G-d: Since there is no other authority besides Him, since the entire world is His, He has free reign in the entire world."*[1]

On the face of it, Rabbi Akiva's reply does not seem to truly answer the Roman's question. While it is true that a person is permitted

---

1   *Midrash Rabbah, Bereishit* 11:5.

to move things from place to place within a "private domain" on Shabbat, regarding all the other forms of forbidden labor, there is no difference between such a domain and some other place. For example, it is no less a violation of the Shabbat to water an enclosed garden than it is to water an open field. So if G-d's "causing rain to fall" could be regarded as a violation of Shabbat, why would the fact that the entire world is His exclusive domain make this activity any more "permissible" for Him?

The Eiruv

In his reply, Rabbi Akiva mentions the law of *eiruv*. What is the relevance of this law to the discussion on hand?

On Shabbat, it is forbidden to transfer an object from a "private domain" to a "public domain," or vice versa. A "private domain" is an enclosed area, such as a home or a fenced yard; a "public domain" is an open public thoroughfare, such as a street or plaza.

The laws of Shabbat also define another category: areas that are technically a "private domain" but whose function resembles that of a "public domain." For example, an enclosed courtyard shared by several homes, or the lobby and hallways of an apartment building. Here, too, it is forbidden (by rabbinical ordinance) to transfer articles between "domains." It is such a domain that Rabbi Akiva is referring to when he speaks of "two people living in one courtyard."

There is, however, a procedure which makes it permissible to borrow a cup of sugar from the neighbor down the hall on Shabbat, or to take along a house key or baby carriage on a stroll to the park. This procedure, whose detailed laws take up an entire tractate in the Talmud, is called *eiruv*.

How is an *eiruv* made? First of all, if the area is not already enclosed, it must be physically defined as a singular entity; a wire running along the tops of poles will transform a street, a neighborhood, even an entire city, into a "private domain." Then, something must be done to deal with its resemblance to a "public domain." This is achieved by taking a loaf of bread, designating it as the common property of all the residents of the enclosed area, and keeping it in one of the homes or apartments. Because they all have a (potential) meal awaiting them in one place, the residents of this "domain" are now legally considered a single household. Hence the term *eiruv*, which means "combining" or "intermixing": The various sub-domains in this physically enclosed area have been integrated into a single "private" province.

What exactly is an *eiruv*? Is it a legal gimmick formulated by some ingenious talmudic lawyer? Are we "outsmarting" G-d? If the divine law intended that we should *not* carry from domain to domain, why are we devising ways of "getting off on a technicality"?

But the *eiruv* is no mere loophole. Not only does Torah law sanction its use, but it declares that "It is a *mitzvah* to pursue [the arrangement of] both a courtyard *eiruv* and one for the street."[2] Indeed, on a deeper level, the effecting of an *eiruv* relates to the very essence and function of Shabbat.

WORK DEFINED

"For six days shall work be done," commands the Torah, "but the seventh day shall be to you a holy day, a sabbath of rest to G-d."[3] But what, exactly, constitutes "work"? The Hebrew word employed by the Torah, *melachah*, actually means "creative work." Thus, writing a single word is a *melachah*, while dragging a heavy

---

2   *Shulchan Aruch, Orach Chaim* 395.

3   *Exodus* 35:2.

sofa from one end of the room to the other is not. Specifically, the Talmud enumerates thirty-nine categories of "creative work" that are forbidden on Shabbat, such as "sowing," "baking," "tanning hides," "weaving," "writing," "building," "igniting a fire," and the like.[4]

This is in keeping with the function that the Torah attributes to Shabbat: "It is an eternal sign between Me and the children of Israel, that six days G-d made the heavens and the earth, and on the seventh day He rested and He was refreshed."[5] Obviously, G-d did not sweat and toil to create the world, and the "rest" and "refreshment" He experienced on the seventh day were not relief from exertion. Rather, for six days G-d created, and on the seventh day He ceased to create. So when we attest to G-d's creation of the universe by emulating G-d's work/rest cycle in our own lives, the "work" we cease from on the seventh day of the week is defined not by the degree of physical effort it extracts from us, but by its creativity.

It is also siginificant that the 39 types of creative work forbidden on Shabbat are the same 39 creative actions that were employed in the construction of the *mishkan*, the "dwelling for G-d"[6] that the people of Israel constructed in the Sinai Desert, which the Torah describes immediately following its commandment not to perform work on Shabbat. For six days we engage in creative involvement with the world, laboring to transform it into a home for G-d. Shabbat, however, is a day of disengagement from the material, and cessation of all physically transformative activity.

---

4   Talmud, *Shabbat* 73a.
5   Exodus 31:17.
6   Exodus 25:8, as per *Midrash Tanchuma, Nasso* 16, and *Tanya*, ch. 36.

THE WEEK AND SHABBAT (3)

This difference between Shabbat and the other days of the week is expressed not only in what we do or do not do on Shabbat, but also in the way we do the things that we do.

A prime example is the manner in which we regard physical pleasure on Shabbat. During the week, we seek to remake our physical drives and resources into a "sanctuary" that serves and expresses the divine. For example, when we eat, we do so with the intention of utilizing the energy we derive from the food to serve G-d. In this way, the material substance of the food and the physical act of eating are transformed into the acumen of the mind studying the divine wisdom in Torah, into the fervor of prayer, into the energy expended in helping the needy; transformed, that is, into an instrument of the divine will. Eating for no purpose other than for the sake of physical pleasure is not a constructive, much less a holy, act. Instead of sublimating the material, it has the very opposite effect—it sinks the person deeper into the morass of self, even further distancing him, and the material environment he occupies, from their divine purpose and function.

Such is our approach to material life for the first six days of the week. On Shabbat, however, pleasure for the sake of pleasure is a *mitzvah*, a fulfillment of G-d's will. There is no need for the physical to be developed and transformed into something that serves a "higher" purpose. Deriving pleasure from the material world is itself an act of holiness, a way of experiencing and bringing to light the divine nature of G-d's creation.

In other words, during the week, we struggle to *change* the world—to divest it of its corporeality and direct it toward a higher goal. But on Shabbat we cease from the effort to transform the material reality; instead, we relate to the world as it is, to the divine essence implicit in our existence.

What happens on Shabbat to effect this drastic change in how we relate to the world? To understand this, we must again look at the nature of G-d's "work" and "rest" in the seven days of creation.

PROJECTION AND WITHDRAWAL

Chassidic teaching[7] likens G-d's "rest" on Shabbat to what an artist experiences upon the completion of a work of art. While he labors, the artist's prowess and vitality are invested in his work; he may actually feel drained of the energy that is flowing from his own soul into his creation. But when he completes his work, this tremendous projection of mind and talent ceases; he now experiences the "return" of his creative powers and their re-inclusion into his own being.

The same may be applied to G-d. For six days of the week (*every* week, for creation is an ongoing cycle of divine involvement with our existence to grant it being and life) G-d projects His creative powers into our existence. On Shabbat, G-d ceases this outward flow, withdrawing back into Himself. This concept is alluded to by the Hebrew word *vayinafash* ("and He was refreshed") in the verse quoted above ("six days G-d made the heavens and the earth, and the seventh day He rested and He was refreshed"). *Vayinafash* means "his soul returned to him."[8]

There is, however, an important difference between G-d's withdrawal and that of our hypothetical artist. When the artist pulls back his creative powers, he leaves the completed work behind — his creation is now an entity wholly separate from himself, no

---

7   *Torah Ohr, Beshalach* 65c.

8   See Rashi's commentary on Exodus 31:17. The word *shabbat* is also related to the Hebrew word for "return."

THE WEEK AND SHABBAT (3)

longer dependent upon his involvement. When G-d withdraws, He takes His work back with Him. For while the artist's work is the result of his projection, G-d's work is the projection itself. G-d does not take pre-existing materials and work His creative energy upon them; what we experience as reality *is* G-d's creative energy.

In other words, when the Torah tells us that "G-d said, 'Let there be light,' and there was light," this does not mean that G-d's words caused something else—the thing we call light—to come into being. It means that what we experience as light is actually the divine words "Let there be light." By describing creation as G-d's "speech," the Torah is giving us its definition of reality. Speech is the projection of one's ideas outside of oneself (as opposed to thought, which is a wholly internal articulation). What is the world? The world is G-d speaking—G-d's continuous outward projection of His creative powers.

At least, that's what the world is for six days a week. On Shabbat, G-d withdraws this projection back into an uncommunicating self. The world is no longer divine speech but divine thought. It is no longer an existence "outside" of G-d.[9]

This is why the world is "holier" on Shabbat. Were G-d's work to be "left behind" when He withdraws His creative energies, then the very opposite would be the case—the world would now be further removed from G-d. But Shabbat is not G-d's withdrawal *from* creation, but G-d's withdrawal *of* creation. Shabbat is a "holy" day because, on Shabbat, the created existence is reabsorbed within its divine source.

Hence the difference in how we relate to physical reality in the course of the week. For the first six days of the week, we labor to *change* the world into a "dwelling for G-d." True, the world is

---

9   See previous essay, *The World of Thought* on pp. 89–94.

not an existence separate from G-d, and it is certainly not independent of Him—all it is, is His spoken words. Nevertheless, G-d relates to the created existence as an *outward* projection of His creative powers, and this is what allows the world to perceive itself as something outside of the divine reality. So for six days we struggle to divest the world of the illusion and delusion of selfhood. We seek to demonstrate how things do not exist for their own sake, but to serve a higher truth.

On Shabbat, however, G-d ceases to speak the world. He now thinks it, relating to it as something that is wholly subsumed within His reality. In our own lives, our focus shifts accordingly: Instead of seeking to change the world, we seek to reveal how the world, as it is, is one with its Creator.

TRANSFER AND TRANSFORMATION

In light of the above, we can understand the deeper significance of the *melachah* of transferring things between "private" and "public" domains.

At first glance, the *melachah* of "transferring from domain to domain" on Shabbat—the last on the Talmud's list—hardly seems to qualify as a *melachah*. The other 38 categories of work are all tangibly creative endeavors: activities which visibly change something in a constructive manner. But the change effected by transferring an object from domain to domain is far more subtle—all that one has changed is the thing's place. Or, to put it another way, there has been no actual change in the thing, only a change in the thing's potential: Its potential use, originally private, has now been made public (or vice versa).

THE WEEK AND SHABBAT (3) 103

For this reason, the sages of the Talmud refer to "transferring" as a "weak *melachah*."[10] Nevertheless, the very first laws to be discussed in the talmudic tractate *Shabbat* are the laws which define the various "domains" and the prohibition of transferring objects between them. For in truth, the prohibition to transfer from domain to domain lies at the very heart of what Shabbat is all about.

When we look at the world during the first six days of the week, we see two distinct "domains." On the one hand, there are the objects and resources which we have enlisted to serve G-d, thereby transforming them into a "dwelling" for Him—His own "private domain" where everything submits to His singular reality. On the other hand, we have the "street," the world "out there"—a "public," pluralistic domain which regards itself as separate, or even independent, from its divine source.

Six days a week, it is indeed our duty to "transfer from domain to domain." We strive to transfer things from the "public domain" into that sacred corner of our lives that is consecrated as G-d's private realm (e.g., a coin given to charity, a piece of animal hide made into *tefilin*). We also seek to transfer from this "private domain" out into the "street," to instill its holiness into the still "public" areas of the material existence (e.g., running a business in accordance with the ethics of Torah).

On Shabbat, however, there is only one reality: creation as the private domain of G-d. And the entire point of Shabbat is to express this truth in our daily lives. Any attempt to transform reality—even for the sake of serving G-d—is a violation of Shabbat, for it means that one is dealing with the world as if it were something outside of G-d.

---

10   See *Tosafot* on Talmud, *Shabbat* 96b and *Eruvin* 17b.

In other words, *all* of the 39 *melachot* are, in essence, a form of the prohibition to "transfer from domain to domain" on Shabbat. By doing creative work on Shabbat, a person perpetuates the notion of a "public" world on this divinely private day.[11]

On a deeper level, it is the law of the *eiruv*, rather than the laws pertaining to truly public domains, which expresses the essence of Shabbat. For even during the six workdays of the week, there is no such thing as a truly public domain—only a private domain which *appears* as a public domain. Ultimately, there is no corner of the existence that is outside of the exclusive province of G-d; only areas in which the surface reality obscures this truth. Thus it can be said that our world is comparable to the essentially private but seemingly public "courtyard," in which it is forbidden to carry things about on Shabbat without an *eiruv*.

This explains Rabbi Akiva's reply to Turnus Rufus. Certainly G-d observes the weekly day of rest: On Shabbat He ceases to speak the world, thereby altering the very nature of reality. But while we inhabit a "multi-occupant courtyard" which has the appearance of a public domain, and in which it is therefore forbidden to "transfer" on Shabbat, G-d is the exclusive occupant of His courtyard. From His perspective, there is no such thing as a public domain, or even a public-seeming domain. So for Him, effecting changes *within* our world does not violate the Shabbat. Everything He "moves about" in our world is a movement within His exclusive domain; any "change" wrought by Him in our world on Shabbat

---

11 This is the deeper significance of the Hebrew term *chilul Shabbat*, "desecration of the Shabbat." The root *chalal* ("desecrate") also means "void" or "hollow": By doing work on Shabbat, one injects a bubble of emptiness into G-d's private domain, creating—in the realm of his own perception and behavior—an area that is devoid of G-d's all-pervading reality.

THE WEEK AND SHABBAT (3)   105

is neither a "transformation" nor a "transfer," since the entirety of existence is now wholly absorbed within His all-inclusive reality.

EFFECTING THE EIRUV

The ultimate function of Shabbat is to establish an *eiruv* in our "multi-occupant courtyard": to integrate the diverse forces and realities of our world as a singular, harmonious expression of the divine truth; to make the exclusivity of G-d's dominion as real in our lives as it is from G-d's own perspective.

Our present-day experience of Shabbat is only a "taste" of the era of Moshiach—"the day that is wholly Shabbat and rest for life everlasting."[12] Each Shabbat, we assume a mode of being that reveals the innate "privacy" of G-d's world. But this is mostly a reality manifest only in our individual lives and communities; the world without still shows a face of plurality and disconnection from its source. For while it is Shabbat in the weekly cycle, we are still in the six "workday" millennia of history.

With the advent of the seventh millennium, "The world will be filled with the knowledge of G-d as the waters cover the sea,"[13] readily perceiving itself as wholly subsumed within the divine reality.

---

12   Shabbat addendum to *Grace after Meals*.
13   Isaiah 11:9.

BREAD FROM HEAVEN

G-d will bless you in all that you will do.

Deuteronomy 14:29

Seven weeks after their Exodus from Egypt, the entire people of Israel stood at the foot of Mount Sinai and heard the Ten Commandments proclaimed by G-d. The fourth of these commandments (Exodus 20:8–11) establishes Shabbat as one of the fundamental observances of Judaism. Yet the first laws of Shabbat observance to be specified in the Torah appear several chapters earlier, in Exodus 16, in connection with an event that transpired three weeks before the revelation at Sinai. This is the chapter known as "The Section of the Manna" (*parashat ha-man*), which tells the story of the miraculous "bread from heaven" that sustained the people of Israel during their 40-year journey in the desert:

> *And G-d said to Moses: "Here I will rain down for you bread from the heavens. And the people will go out and gather the portion of each day on its day; in order that I shall test them if they will follow My teaching or not.*
>
> *"And it will be on the sixth day, that they shall prepare that which they bring; and it will be double of that which they gather each day."*
>
> *…In the morning, there was a layer of dew around the camp. And the layer of dew lifted; and here upon the face*

THE WEEK AND SHABBAT (4)

of the desert was a fine grainy substance, fine as frost upon the earth.

And the children of Israel saw it, and they said to each other, "It is manna," as they did not know what it was. And Moses said to them, "It is the bread which G-d has given you to eat.

"This is the thing which G-d has commanded: Gather of it, each according to his eating-capacity, an omer *for each head, according to the number of persons, each for those in his tent you shall take."*

And the children of Israel did so. And they gathered, both the one who gathered much and the one who gathered little. And they measured it with an omer, *and whoever gathered much did not have more, and whoever gathered little did not have less; each one, according to his eating-capacity they gathered.*

And Moses said to them: "Let no man leave over any of it until morning." And they did not listen to Moses; and people left over from it until the morning, and it bred worms and became putrid; and Moses was angry with them...

And it was on the sixth day that they gathered a double portion of bread, two omer *for each one. And all the leaders of the community came and told Moses.*

And he said to them: "This is what G-d spoke: Tomorrow is a rest day, a holy Shabbat unto G-d. Bake that which you would bake, and cook that which you would cook, and what is left over, put away for yourselves as a safekeeping until the morning." And they put it away until morning, as Moses had commanded; and it did not become putrid, and no worm was in it.

And Moses said: "Eat it today, as today is a Shabbat unto G-d; today you will not find it in the field. Six days you shall gather it; on the seventh day is Shabbat, there will not be on it."

And it was on the seventh day that some of the people went out to gather, and they did not find. And G-d said to Moses: "Till when will you refuse to observe My commandments and My teachings?

"See that G-d has given you the Sabbath; therefore, on the sixth day He gives you bread for two days. Let each man remain in his place; let no man leave his place on the seventh day." And the people rested on the seventh day...

And Moses said: "This is the thing that G-d commanded. A fill of an omer *of it shall be preserved for your generations, in order that they should see the bread which I fed you in the desert when I took you out of the land of Egypt..."*

Nothing in Torah is coincidental. The fact that the Torah chooses the story of the manna as the background against which to begin spelling out the guidelines for Shabbat observance means that Shabbat and manna are interrelated. Indeed, one of the very first things we are told about Shabbat, back in Genesis 2:3, is that "G-d blessed the seventh day and sanctified it," which the Midrash interprets as follows: "He blessed it with manna and sanctified it with manna."[1] This link is also expressed in a ruling by Rabbi Saadiah Gaon: If a group of Jews find themselves in the situation that they

---

[1] I.e., G-d sanctified the Shabbat in that no manna fell on the holy day of rest, and blessed the Shabbat in that a double portion was provided on Friday in its honor. *Midrash Rabbah, Bereishit* 11:2; Rashi to Genesis 2:3.

THE WEEK AND SHABBAT (4)   109

do not know which Torah-section is to be read on a certain Shabbat, they should read "The Section of the Manna," as it pertains to Shabbat in general.[2]

THE SHABBAT MEALS

The link between Shabbat and manna is even more pronounced in regard to the Shabbat meals. The practice of eating three meals in the course of Shabbat is derived from Exodus 16:25, where the word "today" appears three times regarding the eating of the manna on Shabbat.[3] The two *challah* loaves that grace the Shabbat table commemorate the double portion of manna that was provided each Friday in honor of the Shabbat. We spread a cloth under the *challot* and drape another cloth over them, for such was the manner in which we received the manna: protected, below and above, by layers of dew. And the obligation to honor the Shabbat by preparing delicious food in advance of the holy day is derived from the verses describing the preparations for that first manna-nourished Shabbat: "On the sixth day, they shall prepare that which they bring... Tomorrow is a rest day, a holy Shabbat unto G-d. Bake that which you would bake, and cook that which you would cook..."[4]

The very word "Shabbat" evokes the image of a richly laid table, the glint of candlelight on silver, the aroma of chicken soup mingling with stewing *cholent*. Torah law enjoins us to honor the most spiritual of days with fine clothes and tableware and to delight in

---

2   Quoted in *Sefer Ha'itim, Laws of Shabbat Blessings and Pleasure*, 184.

3   "Eat it today, as today is a Shabbat unto G-d; today you will not find it in the field."

4   Talmud, *Shabbat* 117b; *Shulchan Aruch HaRav, Laws of Shabbat*, 271:17 and 274:1–2

it with meat and wine.[5] We know of Jews who scrimped and saved the entire week, who pawned the only things of value in their homes, to buy wine, *challah*, fish, and meat for the Shabbat meals.

There is even a law in the *Shulchan Aruch* (Code of Jewish Law) which legislates the extent to which one may go, and ought to go, in the endeavor to provide for the Shabbat meals:

> *The more one spends on the Shabbat, preparing more numerous and superior dishes, the better—as long as it is within his means. This also includes one who does not have money to spend but has possessions to pawn—he should borrow against them for his Shabbat expenses, and the Almighty will provide him with the means to repay. It is regarding such a case that our sages have said: "G-d says: Borrow on My account, and I will repay..."[6] However, one who has nothing to pawn is under no obligation to*

---

5   "You shall call unto the Shabbat, pleasure; to the holy day of G-d, honored" (Isaiah 58:13). *Halachah* (Torah law) defines the obligation to pleasure and honor the Shabbat to include: (a) eating three festive meals, the first two of which should include at least two cooked dishes; (b) including in these meals warm food, fish, meat, and wine (unless they cause a person discomfort rather than pleasure); (c) lighting candles at the place where the meals are eaten; (d) singing of songs in honor of the Shabbat (*zemirot*) at the Shabbat table; (e) sleep; (f) marital relations; (g) washing and grooming the body before Shabbat; (h) cleaning the house for Shabbat; (i) dressing in freshly cleaned and pressed festive clothes; (j) setting the Shabbat table in a beautiful and luxurious manner; (k) setting aside of all weekday worries from one's mind (*Shulchan Aruch HaRav, Laws of Shabbat*, 242:1-2, 7, and 11; 260:1; 262; 263:1; 280:1; 281:1-2; 306:1).

6   Talmud, *Beitzah* 15b. The Talmud (ibid.) also states: "A person's sustenance for the year is allotted him on Rosh Hashanah, except for what he spends on Shabbat and the festivals; here, the more he spends, the more is repaid to him."

THE WEEK AND SHABBAT (4)   111

*spend beyond his means. Therefore, he should not borrow
on the account that G-d will repay, since in such a case the
above "guarantee" would not apply.*[7]

In these lines, the *Shulchan Aruch* expresses a profound truth
about the relationship between Shabbat and the workweek, and
about man's material involvements in general.

Let us examine this law more closely. Why this difference between one who has something of value to borrow against and one
who does not? In any case, the pawned object will not be sold to
purchase food for Shabbat—G-d Himself guarantees that "I will
repay." Certainly, the *Shulchan Aruch* is not suggesting that we
need an alternate source of funds "just in case" G-d doesn't make
good on His promise! The pawning of an object, then, is a mere
formality: G-d will provide the money to repay the loan. Nevertheless, without this "formality," no loan should be taken out,
since in such a case G-d does not commit Himself to provide for
one's Shabbat needs.

But this is the Jew's approach to earning a living in general. The
Jew believes that his sustenance comes from G-d, that "a person's
sustenance for the year is alloted him [by G-d] on Rosh Hashanah,"[8] and no amount of effort and ingenuity on his part will increase it in the slightest. Why, then, work for a living at all? Why

---

7   *Shulchan Aruch HaRav, Laws of Shabbat,* 242:3. See *Tosafot* commen-
    tary and the *Glosses on the Rosh* on Talmud, *Beitzah* 15b.

8   Talmud, *Beitzah* 15b. Rosh Hashanah, the first day of the Jewish year,
    is the day that G-d decides the fate of every creature. "On Rosh Hasha-
    nah it is inscribed, and on Yom Kippur it is sealed... who shall live and
    who shall die... who shall enjoy tranquility and who shall be afflicted
    with suffering, who shall grow rich and who shall be impoverished,
    who shall be humiliated and who shall rise" (from the *musaf* prayer of
    Rosh Hashanah and Yom Kippur).

need the laborer toil, the artisan create, and the businessman deal if, in any case, G-d will supply them with what they have been assigned on Rosh Hashanah? Because G-d commanded us to fashion a "vessel" through which He then promises to channel His blessings. In the words of the Torah, "G-d will bless you in all that you will do."[9] Our workday efforts, then, are nothing more than a formality, a natural "front" for a supernatural process. *G-d* provides our needs, without regard to such natural criteria as a person's expertise, capital, and enterprise. On the other hand, G-d insists on this formality, promising the bestowal of his blessing only when man creates the vessel enabled by his natural talents and resources.

THE ECONOMICS OF FAITH

At first glance, it may seem that there is little *practical* difference between the Torah's approach and the conventional approach that "my power and my physical might have generated this fortune."[10] Both agree that to earn a living one must utilize, to the utmost, the natural tools at one's disposal, whether this is because these natural tools actually generate one's income or because they are needed as a "vessel" to receive a unilateral gift from Above. In truth, however, these two approaches result in radically different behaviors in work, business, and money management.

What happens, for example, when a struggling shopkeeper is faced with the dilemma of whether to open his establishment on Shabbat? Conventional wisdom will dictate that more business hours will generate more income, positing that the shopkeeper must choose between his religious beliefs and his financial

---

9 Deuteronomy 15:18, as per *Sifri*.
10 Ibid., 8:17.

THE WEEK AND SHABBAT (4)   113

betterment. On the other hand, one who knows that his shop, and all the time and toil invested in it, is only a channel for G-d's blessing, understands the folly of expanding the channel in a manner that violates the will of the supernal provider. This would be comparable to reducing the fuel supply of a power plant in order to allocate funds for the construction of additional power lines, in the hope that this would increase the net output of the plant. Certainly, it is important to put up power lines; without them, the energy produced by the plant will not reach its intended destination. But simply pulling more lines from the plant will not generate more power, especially if such activity is to the detriment of the power's source. Thus, to violate the Shabbat (or any divine command, such as the prohibitions against stealing, lying, withholding payment from one's employees or debtors, dealing in merchandise that causes physical or moral harm to its consumers, etc.) to increase one's income is not only detrimental to one's spiritual health—it's also bad business sense.

Another marked difference between these two approaches is how a person views his contributions to charity. From the conventional perspective, money given to charity represents a reduction in one's financial resources. A person may still be moved to give out of compassion, duty, or guilt, but he will weigh each dollar against the sacrifice it involves, against what he is giving up in order to give. On the other hand, to a person who believes that G-d's blessing is the ultimate and only source of wealth, charity is an investment. Indeed, to give to charity is far more effective an investment than any business initiative: The latter only serves to construct the channel (the nature of which in no way determines how much will be funneled through it), while the former stimulates the source, as per the divine promise/command, "Tithe, so that you may prosper."[11] To such a person, it is also obvious that he will not "save" anything by disregarding the divine imperative to aid a fellow in need.[12]

Finally, these two approaches differ in the extent of their devotion to the building of a career or business. True, both concur that the natural effort must be made, that one must utilize, to the utmost, the tools at one's disposal to earn a living. But what exactly does "utilizing to the utmost" mean? To the person who sees his career or business as the *source* of his income, "the utmost" is an open-ended parameter: the greater one's efforts, the greater one's success, or, at least, the greater one's chances for success. Eight daily hours become 10, become 12, become 14. Second and third jobs are assumed to cover all possibilities. Plans and anxieties invade every waking and non-waking thought.

On the other hand, when a person sees his career or business as nothing more than a formality—as a vessel constructed at G-d's behest—"the utmost" is the utmost that G-d requires. Anything beyond that is a waste of time and effort. And what G-d requires is that we create a natural framework that would suffice as the

---

11   Ibid., 14:22 as per Talmud, *Shabbat* 119a.

12   The Talmud (*Bava Batra* 10a) relates the following story: One year, Rabbi Jochanan ben Zakkai repeatedly pressured his nephews, two wealthy businessmen, to contribute to charity. In the course of the year they gave, at his prodding, 683 dinars. The day before Yom Kippur they were arrested on a libelous charge of tax evasion and thrown into prison. Rabbi Jochanan assured them that the matter would be settled with 17 dinars. "How do you know?" they asked him. "In the beginning of the year," he told them, "it was revealed to me in a dream that it has been decreed that you will sustain a loss of 700 dinars. This is why I pressured you to contribute to charity, so that the money you give should supplant your ordained loss. The amount you gave comes to 17 dinars less than 700, so this is the sum that you will now have to forfeit."

THE WEEK AND SHABBAT (4)   115

receptacle for our most basic needs. Should He desire to grant us more than our most basic needs, He will do so—*within that framework*. Going to greater lengths will not increase the chances of this happening; on the contrary, it can only decrease them, by impinging on those pursuits and activities (prayer, Torah study, observance of *mitzvot*) that relate directly to the source of all blessing.[13]

THE PRECEDENT

Shabbat is the day "from which all other days are blessed."[14] On Shabbat we are granted, in the potential, all the spiritual and material blessings that the Almighty has chosen to impart to us in the course of the following week.[15] So although Shabbat is a day utterly free of all material cares—a day on which we are to consider "all our work as done"[16]—it is also the day that establishes the precedent as to how we are to approach our workday endeavors.

Thus, on Shabbat we delight in food, drink, and fine clothes. On a weekday evening, such feasting would border on the hedonistic; on Shabbat, however, the pleasure derived from meat and wine is a holy pleasure, a pleasure that elevates its material embodiment instead of entangling the indulger in its corporeal trappings. This sublimation of the material establishes a precedent: Now, when we enter the workday world—a world in which the mundane remains mundane—the memory of Shabbat empowers us to harness it to serve a higher, G-dly end.

---

13   See *Derech Mitzvotecha*, p. 214.
14   *Zohar* 3:63b and 3:88a; also see *Ohr Hatorah, Beshalach*, pp. 638–639.
15   *Zohar* 3:88a.
16   Exodus 20:9; see Rashi's commentary on this verse.

And to procure our Shabbat pleasures, we enter a consciousness in which our faith in G-d's provision takes no account of our financial prospects. *Borrow on My account, and I will repay!* Pawn the family heirloom to finance a meal! On any other day of the week, such behavior would be nothing less than reckless; when it comes to providing for Shabbat, however, we are establishing a precedent. Now, when we enter the workday world—a world in which we must be more cautious in our borrowing—we carry this mindset with us: It is G-d who provides, regardless of and despite the economic prospects of the "vessel" we create to receive His blessing, and regardless of and despite the effort we invest in this vessel beyond the requirements mandated by the supernal provider Himself.

On the other hand, even for Shabbat there must be the formality of a conventional economic context in which the loan is acquired. Although we have not the slightest doubt that the Almighty, not the mortgaged collateral, will pay for our feast, we must still create the vessel. For such is the nature of the precedent that we are establishing.

THE 40-YEAR SHABBAT

The manna is to Jewish history what Shabbat is to the workweek: a precedent.

What greater exemplar can there be of the principle that G-d is the sole provider of sustenance? The manna was nourishment that literally descended from heaven. No matter how much effort a person invested in obtaining it—no matter how much manna he gathered—he ended up with his precise nutritional needs for a single day: no more, no less. It was forbidden to set aside manna from one day to the next; those who attempted to do so found that

THE WEEK AND SHABBAT (4) 117

their "savings" had spoiled. The manna trained the first generation of Jews to complete dependence and utter reliance upon G-d for their daily bread.

On the other hand, the manna was not a direct, unilateral infusion of vitality from the supernal source of life into the body: One had to *do* something to obtain it. "For the righteous," says the Talmud, "it came down on their doorstep. The average man had to go out and gather it. The wicked had to venture far to find it... For the righteous, it was bread. For the average man it was cakes of dough. The wicked had to mill it or pound it in a mortar."[17] While the natural "vessel" that one needed to create differed from individual to individual (determined by one's relationship with the Divine Provider), even the righteous had to step out of their tents, pick up the manna, eat it and digest it. For—as in the weekly case of Shabbat—the precedent had to include an element of "channel building."

The manna came to impart a dual lesson to the consciousness of a nation. No matter what you do, bread comes from Heaven; on the other hand, although the nurturing of man is a daily miracle, the miracle can be received only via a vessel of earthly construction.[18]

---

17 Talmud, *Yoma* 75, derived from Exodus 16:4 and Numbers 11:7-8.

18 Thus, the Torah uses the idiom "rain" to describe the manna's descent from heaven ("Here I will rain down bread to you from the heavens"). Rain descends from above, but only because first "a mist rises from the earth" (Genesis 2:6); rain is therefore a metaphor for a bestowal from Above that must be stimulated by human initiative from below. However, the manna is also associated with dew ("In the morning there was a layer of dew around the camp... and here upon the face of the desert was a fine grainy substance...") which denotes an utterly unilateral initiative from Above. In the words of the Talmud (*Taanit* 2b-3a), rain may be withheld (in punishment for wrongdoing), whereas dew is never withheld. For the manna embodies both these truths: the recognition that we generate nothing on our own and are sustained solely by the Almighty; and the imperative to create a vessel "below"

Indeed, the blessing we recite after each meal ("Blessed are you G-d... Who nourishes the entire world with His goodness, with grace, with kindness, and with compassion...") is the very same blessing composed by Moses in gratitude for the manna. Ultimately, the bread we eat—bread we purchase with money earned through our respective professions; bread that is sown, reaped, milled, kneaded, and baked—is no less "bread from Heaven" than the manna consumed by our ancestors. Our challenge is to recognize what was obvious to a generation who daily saw their daily bread descending from the heavens.

---

to evoke and receive the divine blessing (*Likutei Torah*, *Haazinu* 73a–c and 74a–76a; also see *A Rising Mist* on pp. 184–189).

THE WEEK AND SHABBAT (5)   119

HAVDALAH

To differentiate between the pure and the impure; between the animal that may be eaten and the animal that may not be eaten.

Leviticus 11:47

In the Jewish home, the close of the Shabbat is marked with a special ceremony, called *havdalah* ("differentiation"). Over a brimming cup of wine, to the multi-flamed light of a braided candle and the smell of aromatic spices, we recite:

> *Blessed are You, L-rd our G-d... Who differentiates between the holy and the mundane, between light and darkness, between Israel and the nations, between the seventh day and the six days of work...*

Differentiation is at the heart of what we call "morality." If theft and adultery are wrong, it is only because there is a real difference between "mine" and "yours," and between the wedded and the unwedded state. If ceasing work on Shabbat and eating matzah on Passover are meaningful deeds, this is only because Shabbat is truly different from Friday, and matzah is truly different from leavened bread. If there is meaning and purpose to our actions, there must be true significance to the differences between things.

"Differentiation," however, also implies a sameness to the things being differentiated. If Shabbat and Sunday looked, smelled, and tasted differently to our physical senses, there would be no need to actively differentiate between them. Indeed, when the Torah employs the verb "to differentiate" (*lehavdil*), it is to distinguish between things that are essentially similar. A case in point is the concluding verse of Leviticus 11, the chapter which lays down the kosher dietary laws. The verse reads: "To differentiate between the pure and the impure; between the animal that may be eaten and the animal that may not be eaten," regarding which our sages remark:

> *Need this be said regarding the difference between a donkey and a cow? …Rather, this is to tell us to differentiate between the animal which had half its windpipe cut [during the slaughtering] and the animal which had most of its windpipe cut…*[1] *Need this be said regarding the difference between a wild ass and a deer? Rather, this is to tell us to differentiate between an animal in which there developed a defect yet remains fit to be eaten and an animal in which there developed a defect which renders it unfit to be eaten.*[2]

In other words, "differentiation," or *havdalah* in the Hebrew, requires the ability to look at two similar things and appreciate that, despite their rudimentary similarity, they are to be differentiated and held apart. In the words of our sages, "If there is no *daat* (discriminating intelligence), how can there be *havdalah*?"[3]

Things as Words

The capacity to "differentiate," as we have noted, is the basis for any moral vision of life. Chassidic teaching takes this a step further,

---

1   According to the laws of *shechitah* (ritual slaughter), if a majority of the windpipe is not severed in an uninterrupted motion of the slaughterer's knife, the animal is rendered *tereifah* and unfit for consumption.
2   Rashi on verse, citing *Torat Kohanim*.
3   Jerusalem Talmud, *Berachot* 5:2.

THE WEEK AND SHABBAT (5)   121

demonstrating how the concept of *havdalah* is the essence of the created existence, of what we call "reality."

An axiom of the Jewish faith is that G-d is infinite—"without beginning and without end."[4] This raises the problem, addressed by all major Jewish philosophers, of how our world could possibly exist, since a truly infinite being precludes the existence of anything other than itself.[5] Indeed, the Torah asserts that "There is nothing else besides Him."[6] But what about ourselves, our world, our "reality"? Are these not existences "besides Him"?

In the chassidic classic *Tanya*, Rabbi Schneur Zalman of Liadi lays the groundwork for a resolution of this problem by defining the created reality as "divine speech." In the first chapter of Genesis, G-d's creation of the world is described as a series of (ten) utterances. Citing teachings from the Midrash, from the kabbalist Rabbi Isaac Luria, and from chassidism's founder Rabbi Israel Baal Shem Tov, Rabbi Schneur Zalman deduces that these divine utterances are not merely the cause of these existences—they *are* these existences. What we experience as "light" is but the embodiment of the divine utterance "There shall be light"; what we experience as a "tree" is but the embodiment of the divine utterance "The earth shall sprout vegetation"; and so on.

So the created reality is not, in truth, "something else besides Him," any more than our spoken words are things distinct of ourselves. Speaking is a creative act; but when we speak we are not creating anything that is "other" than ourselves—we are giving vocal form to our own ideas, feelings, and desires. In describing G-d's

---

4   *Adon Olam* prayer, based on Maimonides' "Thirteen Principles."
5   For if something other than the infinite being exists, this means that there is some area, some realm of reality, to which the infinite being does not extend, meaning that it is not truly infinite.
6   Deuteronomy 4:35.

creation of the world as a series of divine utterances, the Torah wishes to convey the idea that the world is not something distinct of its Creator, but His "spoken words"—His articulation of concepts and potentials which are an integral part of His being.[7]

The implications of such a conception of ourselves and our world—of reality as divine speech—are numerous and manifold. One of these implications is the realization that the differences between things are secondary to a primary sameness that embraces them all. A language might include millions of words, but these are all variations on a handful of consonants and vowels. On a more basic level, these consonants and vowels are just variations on how a minute expulsion of breath is bounced off the speaker's vocal cords, tongue, palate, teeth, and lips.

A tree might seem very different from a ray of light, as might a fish from a star. But each of these objects is, in essence, the same thing: a divine word, an articulation of divine will. In origin, they share a singular essence; their differentiation occurs at a later stage, as they pass through the divine "mouth" that imparts to them their respective forms and characteristics.

Thus the Torah relates how, on the first day of creation, G-d "differentiated between light and darkness."[8] What two entities can be more different from each other than are light and darkness? What "differentiation" is necessary between such obviously different phenomena? But light and darkness are both creations of G-d; both are divine words—formulations of the same surge of divine will. Their distinction is the product of a divine act of *havdalah*, of a deliberate differentiation between two essentially synonymous realities. Indeed, a closer reading of the first chapter of Genesis

---

7 *Tanya, Shaar HaYichud VehaEmunah*, chs. 1–3. See *The World of Thought* on pp. 89–94 above.

8 Genesis 1:4.

THE WEEK AND SHABBAT (5)   123

shows that a series of differentiations (between the spirit and matter, land and sea, night and day, male and female, etc.) is at the
heart of the creation process.[9]

DAAT

In light of this, we can better understand the above-quoted talmudic dictum regarding the connection between *daat* and *havdalah*. The Talmud is discussing the fact that in the evening prayers
recited after the close of Shabbat, the text of the *havdalah* prayer
is inserted in the prayer which begins: "You grant *daat* to man,
and teach the human understanding; grant us, from You, wisdom,
understanding, and knowledge..."[10] The reason for this placement,
says the Talmud, is that "If there is no *daat*, how can there be
havdalah?"

On the most basic level, the Talmud is saying that an act of
havdalah requires the discriminating intelligence of *daat*. On
a deeper level, it is saying that *havdalah* is possible only because
"*You* grant *daat* to man"—only because G-d Himself grants us the
capacity to differentiate between various elements of His creation.

For if the world is divine speech, if all created things are essentially the same, how can we differentiate between them? And if we
do differentiate, what significance can there be to our differentiation? We might discern "light" and "darkness"; we might identify
certain things as "holy" and others as "mundane"; we might des-
ignate the first six days of the week for material achievement and
its seventh day for spiritual rest. But if all of these are, in essence,
divine words, what significance is there to our differentiations?

---

9   E.g., Genesis 1:6–7, 1:9–10, 1:14 &18, and 2:21–23.
10   Fourth benediction of the *amidah* prayer.

But G-d wanted a moral world—a world in which the deeds of man are purposeful and meaningful. So He imparted variety, diversity, and distinction to His creation, decreeing that the differences between things should possess import and significance. His act of creation was an act of *havdalah*, of differentiating between essentially similar entities. And He granted the human being a mind capable of appreciating the paradox of *havdalah*—the paradox of meaningful difference imposed upon intrinsic synonymy—thereby empowering us to implement, through our awareness and our actions, the differentiations He decreed in His world.

THE SECOND PARADOX

Havdalah carries another paradox: that its ultimate function is to join and unite the very things it comes to differentiate.

The Torah commands us to "remember" and to "keep" the day of Shabbat—to distinguish it, in mind, word, and deed, from the six days of work.[11] Yet Shabbat is integrally bound to the other days of the week. It is the culmination of our weekday endeavors, the day on which all that we labored for and achieved in the preceding six days "ascends on high," attaining its most complete and perfect realization.[12] And Shabbat is the day "from which all days are blessed"[13]—the source of the fortitude and energy that drives our efforts of the workweek that follows it.

We are told to preserve our uniqueness as Jews—to safeguard the delineation "between Israel and the nations." Yet the people of

---

11   Exodus 20:8; Deuteronomy 5:12; see *Mishneh Torah, Laws of Shabbat* 29:1.

12   *Ohr HaTorah, Bereishit* 42b ff. and 508a ff.

13   *Zohar* 3:63b and 88a.

THE WEEK AND SHABBAT (5)   125

Israel are designated to serve as "a light unto the nations,"[14] as the
conveyers of the ethos and ideals of Torah to all inhabitants of the
earth.

We are instructed to "differentiate between the holy and the
mundane"—to embrace what is sacred and G-dly in our lives while
exercising wariness and restraint in the material aspects of life.[15] At
the same time, we are told that "the purpose of man's creation, and
of the creation of all worlds, spiritual and material" is "to make for
G-d a dwelling place in the lowly realms"[16]—to involve our everyday material pursuits in the quest to know and serve G-d, thereby
making Him "at home" in the lowliest, most mundane stratum of
creation.

For it is only through our awareness and enforcement of the
boundaries within creation that these objectives can be achieved.
Only if Shabbat is preserved in its distinctiveness and transcendence can it elevate and empower the other six days of the week.
Only in their uniqueness as G-d's chosen people does the nation
of Israel have anything of true value to offer the peoples of the
world. Only when our spiritual life is kept inviolably apart from
the coarsening influence of the material can it in turn sanctify the
material by enlisting it to serve its spiritual aims.

Havdalah is the substance of our daily lives, as every hour
and moment confronts us with the challenge to define and

---

14   Isaiah 42:6.
15   "Sanctify yourself [by abstaining also from] that which is permissible
     to you" (Talmud, *Yevamot* 20a, explaining Leviticus 19:2; see Nachma-
     nides on Leviticus 19:2); "A person should eat and drink only what is
     necessary for the health of his body... not all that the palate desires"
     (*Mishneh Torah, Laws of Character Traits* 3:2); "What is forbidden, one
     must not; what is permitted, one need not" (Rabbi Schneur Zalman of
     Liadi, cited in *Hayom Yom*, 25 *Adar* II).
16   *Midrash Tanchuma, Nasso* 16; *Tanya*, ch. 36.

differentiate—to distinguish between right and wrong, between holy and mundane. But these delineations are merely a means to an end, a process springing from a primordial unity and leading toward a future synthesis.

In origin and essence, all is one. But an even deeper unity is achieved when differentiations and demarcations are imposed upon the primordial oneness, and its component parts are each given a distinct role in creation's symphonious expression of the goodness and perfection of its Creator.

THE WEEK AND SHABBAT (6)   127

THE
EIGHTH
DIMENSION

The harp of the messianic age has eight strings.

Talmud, Erchin 13a

𝔍 he number "seven" figures prominently in our reckoning
and experience of time. Most familiar, of course, is the seven-day work/rest cycle that comprises our week, in reenactment of
the original seven days of creation when "six days, G-d made the
heavens and the earth... and on the seventh day He rested."[1] Each
Shabbat thus completes a full revolution of time's original cycle,
following which we start anew from *yom rishon*, "the first day"—as
"Sunday" is called in the Holy Tongue.

This is why many Jewish life cycle observances are seven-day
affairs. Two seven-day festivals frame our year—Passover, which
runs from the 15th to the 21st of *Nissan*;[2] and Sukkot, occurring exactly six months later, on *Tishrei* 15–21. A marriage is celebrated for
a full week of *sheva berachot* ("seven blessings"); and the death of
a loved one, G-d forbid, is mourned for seven (*shivah*) days.[3] Thus
the freedom of Passover, the joy of Sukkot, the bond of marriage,

---

1   Exodus 20:11, et al.
2   Outside of the Holy Land, an additional, eighth day of Passover is ob-
     served as a rabbinical ordinance—see "The Dividend of Doubt" on pp.
     214–217 below, in the essay *Three Times Three*.
3   Also: the seven "clean days" of the *niddah* (menstruating woman); the
     seven-day "training" (*shiv'at yemei milluim*) of the Sanctuary (see be-
     low); the seven-day purification period from ritual impurity, and nu-
     merous others.

and the coming to terms with loss are assimilated in all seven dimensions of created time.

Our years, too, follow the cycle of creation: six "workday" years culminate in a sabbatical year of *shemittah* ("suspension"). As the Torah instructs:

> *Six years you shall sow your field, and six years you shall prune your vineyard and gather its fruit. And the seventh year shall be a sabbath of rest for the land, a sabbath for G-d...* [4]

In the Land of Israel, all agricultural work is suspended in the seventh year, and the land's produce is declared free for the taking for all. Also suspended during the *shemittah* year are all private debts and the terms of servitude of indentured servants.

Finally, our sages describe the whole of human history as a seven-millennia "week," consisting of six thousand years of human labor in developing G-d's world and a seventh millennium "that is wholly Shabbat and rest, for life everlasting" [5] — the era of Moshiach. [6]

The teachings of kabbalah explain that the seven days of Creation embody the seven *sefirot* (divine attributes) which G-d emanated from Himself to define and characterize His relationship with our existence. [7] So seven is not only the elemental number of time, but of every created thing and of the created reality as a whole. This is especially true of the human being, who was created "in the image of G-d": [8] The human character is comprised of seven

---

4   Leviticus 25:3–4.

5   Shabbat addendum to *Grace after Meals.*

6   Talmud, *Sanhedrin* 97a; Nachmanides on Genesis 2:3.

7   See *The Seventh Element,* on pp. 77–88 above.

8   Genesis 1:27.

THE WEEK AND SHABBAT (6)   129

drives (love, restraint, harmony, ambition, devotion, bonding, and sovereignty), mirroring the seven "attributes" which G-d assumed as creator of the universe.

MATTER AND SPIRIT

Each of the seven units of the "week" embodies the particular characteristics of its respective *sefirah*. But in more general terms, the cycle consists of two primary phases: "mundanity" (*chol*) and "holiness" (*kedushah*). Six days of mundane labor are followed by a day of spiritual rest; six years of working the earth, by a year of "suspension" and disengagement from the material; six millennia devoted to struggling with and developing the physical world, by a seventh millennium in which "the sole occupation of the entire world will be the knowledge of G-d."[9]

The Torah's word for "holy," *kadosh*, literally means "removed" and "apart." Its names for the seventh day, *shabbat*, and for the seventh year, *shemittah*, respectively mean "cessation" and "suspension." For holiness requires complete disengagement from all material involvements. In order to experience the holiness and spirituality of Shabbat, we must cease all material labor; in order to touch base with the holiness of the land in the *shemittah* year, we must suspend all physical work upon its soil and all claims of ownership on its produce; in order to experience the divine goodness and perfection of our world in the age of Moshiach, we must first achieve a state in which "there is no jealousy and no competition" over its material wealth.[10]

---

9   *Mishneh Torah, Laws of Kings* 12:5.

10 Ibid. This is not to say that Shabbat has no effect upon the rest of the week, that the *shemittah* year does not profoundly influence the

Yet despite their transcendent nature, the seventh day, year, and millennium are constituent parts of the cycles of creation. Materiality and spirituality might differ greatly—to the point, even, of mutual exclusivity—yet both are part of "nature": Both are governed by the framework of laws which define the created reality.

Indeed, the very fact that "holiness" demands the cessation and suspension of all things mundane, indicates that it, too, has its limits. It means that just as there exists a physical nature which defines and delimits the scope of physical things and forces, so too does the realm of the spiritual have its "nature"—its own set of laws which define what it is and what it is not, where it can exist and where it cannot, and how, and in what manner, it can make itself felt beyond its inviolate boundaries. So while the concept of "transcendence" seems the antithesis of definition, transcendence is itself a definition, for it defines—and thus confines—itself as beyond and distinct from the finite and the material.

This offers insight into a key passage in the Torah's account of creation. In Genesis 2:2 we read: "And G-d concluded on the seventh day the work that He had done." This seems to contradict the second part of that very verse, which reads: "And He rested on the seventh day from all the work that He had done." If the work of creation was concluded *on* the seventh day, then the seventh day was one of the days of creation; but if the seventh day is the day on

---

farmer's relationship with his land during the other six years of the cycle, or that the age of Moshiach is divorced from the "workday" generations of history. On the contrary: The primary function of these "Sabbaths" is to provide spiritual vision, fortitude, and purpose to the "mundane" periods of their cycle. But in order to do so, they must be kept distinct and apart. It is only when the boundaries between the holy and the mundane are strictly enforced that we can experience holiness in our lives, and then extend its vision and influence to our mundane endeavors. See previous essay, *Havdalah* (pp. 119–126).

THE WEEK AND SHABBAT (6)   131

which G-d rested "from all the work that He had done," there were
only six days of creation, and a seventh day of *Shabbat*—*cessation*
from work.

Our sages explain: "What was the world lacking? Rest. When
Shabbat came, rest came."[11] Rest—transcendence and spirituality—is itself a creation. Though removed from the nature of the
material, it is part of a greater "nature"—the nature of the created reality, which includes the realm of the spiritual as well as the
realm of the material.[12]

EIGHT

If the number "seven" defines the natural reality, "eight" represents
that which is higher than nature, that which lies beyond the circle
of creation.

"Seven" includes both matter and spirit, both mundanity and
holiness, both involvement and transcendence, but as separate,
distinct components of the cycle of creation. The seventh dimension will exert its influence on the other six, but only in a transcendent way—as a spiritual, other-worldly reality that will never be
truly internalized and integrated within the system. In contrast,
"eight" represents the introduction of a reality that is beyond all
nature and definition, including the definition "transcendence."
This "eighth dimension" (if we can call it a "dimension") has no
limitations at all: It transcends and pervades, being beyond nature
yet also fully present within it, being equally beyond matter and
spirit, and equally within them.

---

11   Rashi on Genesis 2:2.
12   See *The Seventh Element* on pp. 77–88 above.

Thus, the covenant of circumcision, which binds the Jew to G-d in a bond that supersedes all nature and convention even as it pervades every nook and cranny of life, is entered into on the eighth day of life.[13] The Sanctuary,[14] whose role was to make the infinite reality of G-d an "indwelling" presence in the physical world, was inaugurated "on the eighth day"[15] following a seven-day "training" period. The festival of Shemini Atzeret ("eighth day of retention"), whose function is to internalize the transcendent "encompassing light" of the *sukkah*, occurs on the "eighth day" that follows Sukkot's seven days.[16] Seven *shemittah* cycles are followed by a "jubilee" year characterized by "liberty" (i.e., freedom from all bounds) rather than just "suspension." And the messianic seventh millennium of history will be followed by the supra-historical "World to Come" (*olam haba*), in which the divine reality will unite with the created reality in ways that we, who currently inhabit a world in which "finite" and "infinite" are mutually exclusive, cannot even speculate upon. In the words of the Talmud, "All prophets prophesied only regarding the days of Moshiach; regarding the World to Come, 'No eye can behold it, O G-d, save Yours.'"[17]

---

13 Genesis 17:12; Leviticus 12:3. According to *Keli Yakar*, this is the deeper reason why, if the eighth day following the birth of a child falls on Shabbat, the circumcision is performed on that day, despite the commandment of Shabbat rest; as the supranatural "eight" of *brit milah* supercedes the natural "seven" of Shabbat, the seventh day of the cycle of creation (*Keli Yakar* to Leviticus 9:1).

14 *Mishkan*—the portable "Tabernacle" built by the children of Israel to accompany them in their journeys in the desert, which was the forerunner of the Holy Temple.

15 Leviticus 9:1.

16 See Chapter XI of this collection, "Shemini Atzeret and Simchat Torah" (vol. 2, pp. 125–153).

17 Isaiah 64:3; Talmud, *Berachot* 34b.

FIFTY

The "eights" in our lives come in two forms: eight and fifty.

For example, the two seven-day festivals, Sukkot and Passover, each culminate in an *atzeret*—a one-day "festival of retention" whose function is to internalize the festival's achievements. But while the *atzeret* of Sukkot immediately follows the festival, in effect constituting its "eighth day," the *atzeret* of Passover is the festival of Shavuot, observed fifty days after Passover, culminating a forty-nine-day (seven times seven) "counting of the *omer*."

For each of the seven components of the natural system has a "natural system" of its own—its own seven-phased cycle of immanence and transcendence, making a total of forty-nine elements and phases in the cycle of nature.[18] Thus, "fifty" is an "eight" which follows a thoroughly detailed development of the seven dimensions of nature in all of its forty-nine sub-dimensions. Shavuot, the *atzeret* of Passover, is such an "eight": Our exodus from Egypt marked the onset of a forty-nine-day process in which we refined and perfected the forty-nine drives and impulses of our souls, thereby liberating ourselves from the "forty-nine gates of impurity," to which we sank in the course of our enslavement to the most debased society in the history of mankind, and entering into the "forty-nine gates of understanding" of awareness of and commitment to G-d. This 49-day process (reexperienced each year with our seven-week "counting of the *omer*") culminated in the revelation at Sinai on Shavuot, when we were granted the Torah—the divine "fiftieth dimension" which supersedes and integrates all forty-nine dimensions of creation.

Another "eight" that comes in the form of "fifty" is *yovel*, the "jubilee" year. As the Torah instructs,

---

18   See *A Speck of Flour* in vol. 3 of this series, pp. 62–70.

You shall count for yourself seven sabbaths of years, seven times seven years... [for a a total of] forty-nine years...

And you shall sanctify the fiftieth year, and proclaim liberty throughout the land and to all inhabitants thereof...[19]

Seven seven-year *shemittah* cycles, each culminating in a year of "suspension" and transcendence of the material, are followed by a fiftieth year of "liberty" in which all servants, including those who had sold themselves for lifetime labor, were set free, and all ancestral lands that had been sold reverted to their original owners. The jubilee year represents a state of true freedom in which, rather than just "suspending" the earthliness of the land, we free it of all the restraints of materiality.

Thus, our experience of time (which defines practically everything we do and achieve) comes in various forms and configurations. There are times and situations in which we live our lives completely within the natural cycle of "seven." There are times and circumstances in which we relate to the supranatural "eighth" dimension, but only in a general, abstract way. Finally, there are times and circumstances in which we access an "eight" that is a "fifty"—an "eight" that is experienced in all particulars and subparticulars of our existence.[20]

Three States of Jubilee

The *shemittah/yovel* cycle itself comes in three different forms, as dictated by the variant spiritual climates of different epochs in our history.

---

19 Leviticus 25:8–10.

20 Also see *Daughters Near and Far* in vol. 2, pp. 135–147 of this series.

THE WEEK AND SHABBAT (6)   135

As quoted above, the Torah instructs that the jubilee year is to be proclaimed "throughout the land and to all inhabitants thereof." The Talmud interprets this as a stipulation that the special laws of the fiftieth year are enacted only when the Land of Israel is fully populated by the Jewish people.[21] The only period in our history when this was the case was from the year 2503 from creation (1258 BCE), when the Jewish people under Joshua completed their conquest and settlement of the Holy Land, until they were driven from it by Babylon's armies 836 years later, with the destruction of the First Temple in the year 3339 (422 BCE).

Seventy-six years later, with the partial return of the Jewish people to their land under Ezra (six years after the building of the Second Temple) the *yovel* count resumed—but this time only for the sake of calculating and implementing the sabbatical year seven times in each 50-year period. Since much of the Holy Land was not resettled, and a large part of the Jewish nation remained in exile, the jubilee year could not be observed. Nevertheless, a fiftieth year was counted following each seven *shemittah*-cycles, "so that the sabbatical years should fall at their proper time."[22] In other words, after the seventh sabbatical year on year 49 of Ezra's count, the next seven-year cycle could not begin until after a theoretical jubilee was proclaimed; thus, the next sabbatical year came eight years later (on year 57), *not* seven years later (on year 56).

Upon the Second Temple's destruction in the year 3829 from creation (69 CE), this *yovel* count also ceased. The sabbatical year continues to be observed every seventh year; but because we are in a state of *galut* (exile), deprived of the divine presence that manifested itself in the Holy Temple, we lack even the "theoretical"

---

21 Talmud, *Erchin* 32b.
22 Rashi on Talmud, Erchin 32b.

jubilee of the Second Temple Era. Today (as was the case in the period between the two Temples), our seven-year cycles run consecutively, without the half-century landmark of *yovel*.

THE THREE JUBILEES IN OUR LIVES

What is the significance of the three different ways that, historically, the *mitzvah* of the jubilee was implemented?

Much of our time and energy is spent working toward a goal. Rarely do our efforts yield "instant" results; and when they do, these results are usually shallow and transitory. To achieve something that has any value or permanence takes many steps, each building on the previous, and consumes much effort and time.

In many cases, the goal toward which we are striving is invisible and elusive. We cannot see it, or even fully envision it in our minds. Our efforts are an act of faith, undertaken in the belief that we're doing the right thing, that our toil is creating something great and magnificent, even if it is beyond the horizon of present-day existence.

Sometimes we are privileged to have been granted a vision of the goals toward which we are toiling. We may not experience the actual impact and result of our day-to-day efforts—that is still in the invisible future—yet the big picture is accessible to us, and it informs and encourages every step that we are taking toward our goal.

Finally, there are times when we are not only inspired by the "big picture," but actually merit to experience its realization, stage by stage, as we work toward its fulfillment. We actually see the edifice of our endeavor rising, brick by brick and level by level, and appreciate the manner in which each particular action and accomplishment contributes toward the overall goal.

THE WEEK AND SHABBAT (6)   137

This is the significance of the three different "jubilees" in our history of a people, as applied to the endeavor to refine and transform the forty-nine chambers of our soul.

The ideal model, which defined the lives of our ancestors in the First Temple Era, is one of seven *shemittah*-cycles which yield a fiftieth jubilee year. On the individual level, this means that a person's struggles to "suspend" and transcend the negative in himself are fully experienced as stages in the process of the complete transformation and liberation of his soul.

A lesser state was that of the Second Temple Era, which represented an intermediate state between *galut* and redemption. While a large segment of the Jewish people lived in the Holy Land, they were (with some brief exceptions) under the dominion of other nations. And while the Holy Temple facilitated G-d's presence in their lives, it was a lesser expression of the divine reality than the First Temple.[23] Thus, the *shemittah*-cycles were not of the caliber to produce a full-fledged "liberation." Nevertheless, they were permeated by the vision of perfection that the jubilee year represents, as expressed by the fact that while the *yovel* was not actually observed, it set and defined the *shemittah*-cycles.

But in the more than nineteen centuries since the Holy Temple's destruction, we have been fully engulfed in *galut*: Ours is an existence that obscures all but the faintest glimmer of purpose and direction. Our lives are, by and large, consumed by the struggle with evil; not only are our efforts at self-improvement confined to the narrow, seven-phased cycle of nature, but we also lack even the vision to see and appreciate their place within the context of a liberating jubilee.[24]

---

23 See Talmud, *Yoma* 21b.

24 The differences between these three eras are also reflected in their *halachic* status. Until the destruction of the First Temple, when both

Today, our lives are a seemingly endless chain of *shemittah*-cycles, with nary a jubilee in sight. Yet this "blind" struggle will yield the final and ultimate redemption, when "Moshiach will arise and restore the sovereignty of David to its former glory and power, build the Holy Temple, and gather the dispersed of Israel. In his days, all the laws will be restored: We will offer the sacrifices, and enact the sabbatical and jubilee years as commanded by the Torah."[25] Then, our cycles of seven will yield the ultimate "eight"—the all-embracing perfection of the World to Come.

---

the *shemittah* and *yovel* laws applied, their observance was a biblical imperative (*mitzvah mide'oreita*). Today, when only the *shemittah* is observed, it is only a rabbinical obligation. As for the twilight era of the Second Temple, when *yovel* was calculated but its laws were not applicable, there is a dispute between the two Talmuds: According to the Jerusalem Talmud, the *shemittah* laws were then binding only by rabbinical decree (*Shvi'it* 5:2), while the Babylonian Talmud maintains that then, too, they were mandated by biblical law (as per *Tosafot, Erchin* 32b; Rashi, however, understands also the Babylonian Talmud's view to be that during the Second Temple Era the observance of *shemittah* was by rabbinical decree only).

25 *Mishneh Torah, Laws of Kings*, 11:1.

TWILIGHT

"Today" is the time to do; "tomorrow," to receive the reward.   Talmud, Eruvin 22a

he Talmud (in *Ethics of the Fathers* 5:6) relates:

Ten things were created on the eve of Shabbat at twilight. These are: the mouth of the earth;[1] the mouth of the well;[2] the mouth of the donkey;[3] the rainbow; the manna; the staff;[4] the shamir;[5] and the writing, the inscription, and the tablets [of the Ten Commandments].

"Twilight"—*bein hashemashot* in Hebrew—is a *halachic* (Torah law) term for a time period that marks the transition from day to night and from one calendar day to the next.

According to Torah law, the calendar day runs from nightfall to nightfall;[6] thus, Shabbat begins Friday evening at nightfall and ends at nightfall on Saturday night. "Nightfall" is when the light

---

1. Which swallowed Korach, as related in Numbers 16:32.
2. The "Well of Miriam"—a miraculous stone which provided water to the people of Israel during their wanderings in the desert; see Exodus 17:6 and Numbers 21:16-18.
3. The mouth of Balaam's donkey, which miraculously spoke to him, as related in Numbers 22:28.
4. Moses' staff, with which he performed the miracles of the Exodus—see Exodus 4:17, et al.
5. A worm which split stones for the construction of the Holy Temple in Jerusalem. See Talmud, *Gittin* 68a.
6. As per Genesis 1:5: "And it was evening, and it was morning: one day." See *Evening and Morning* on pp. 64-69, above.

of day has faded to the point that three middle-sized stars are visible in the sky. The halachists calculate this to be the point at which the sun has descended 5.9 degrees below the horizon; this occurs approximately 30 minutes after sunset, depending on the location and the time of year.[7]

Nightfall, however, only marks the point at which the night—and the next calendar day—is certain to have begun. Between sunset and nightfall is a period defined as "twilight," a time-period with laws and rules of its own. The previous day has ended (or perhaps ended), yet the following day has not yet (or perhaps not yet) commenced.[8]

Halachic literature presents three definitions of "twilight":

a) It is a period that is "possibly day, possibly night." According to this definition, the concept of "twilight" is wholly a product of our ignorance of the precise point at which one day ends and the next begins. Nevertheless, our ignorance results in special laws that apply to this period.

b) It is an admixture of day and night; a time-period in which day and night "overlap," so that it possesses both qualities.

c) It is neither day nor night, but an entity of its own which effects the transition from day to night and from one day to the next.[9]

---

7 Twenty-four minutes after sunset on March 22 in the Land of Israel (see *Siddur HaRav, Seder Hachnasat Shabbat*; et al.).

8 The actual duration of "twilight" is a matter of debate between the halachists. According to one opinion, "twilight" is the entire period between sunset and nightfall; according to other opinions, it is a certain time period within this period. Another opinion is that twilight occupies but "the blink of an eye"—a brief moment that intervenes between day and night (see Talmud, *Shabbat* 34b and commentaries; *Siddur HaRav*, op. cit.; *Encyclopedia Talmudit*, vol. 3, s.v. *Bein HaShemashot* [pp. 122–126] and sources cited there).

9 See Talmud, *Shabbat* 34b; *Mishneh Torah, Laws of Eruvin* 1:21; *Ritva, Yoma* 47b; *Mefaaneach Tzefunot*, p. 177–178.

THE MEDIATOR

The above-quoted passage from *Ethics of the Fathers* enumerates ten things that G-d created in the closing moment of the six days of creation, "on the eve of Shabbat, at twilight." But if twilight is a product of our ignorance as to the precise moment at which the day ends, it follows that for G-d, the creator of night and day, there is no "twilight." Obviously, then, the twilight of which the Talmud speaks is an actual entity, a time period that is some sort of intermediary between one day and the next, as in definitions "b" or "c" above.

In truth, "b" and "c" are essentially the same definition. Chassidic teaching explains that an "intermediary"—a thing or force that facilitates a transition from one state to another—must include elements of both states, as well as an overriding element that effects the transition. Thus, a poet who wishes to translate a poem from English into French must possess mastery of both languages; indeed, if the translation is to capture the full power and beauty of the poem, the translator's mastery of the two languages must be greater than what would be required to write such a poem in either language.

Another example of this principle: A child psychologist must be familiar with the world of childhood. A psychologist who counsels adults must have knowledge and insight primarily into the psyche and experiences of adults. But a psychologist counseling adolescents—people who are struggling with the transition from childhood to adulthood—must have intimate knowledge of both worlds, as well as of the unique challenges of their overlaping period.

Each and every day of time was created by G-d for a specific purpose; each possesses qualities and potentials uniquely its own.[10] Thus, the days of our lives do not simply begin where the previous day leaves off. Rather, there is a "gap" between them that must be bridged, a transition that must be effected. Hence the special quality and function of "twilight"—the period that possesses qualities of both days and can thus bridge this gap and facilitate this transition.

This is especially true of the transition from Friday to Shabbat, a transition from work to rest, from achievement to repose, and from flux to tranquility—two states which differ greatly in their function, nature, and very essence.[11]

THE COSMIC WEEK

Our sages tell us that the original week of creation embodies the whole of history, which likewise constitutes a "week": six "workday" millennia, followed by a seventh, sabbatical millennium.

Thus, writes Nachmanides, the first day of creation, which saw the creation of light, embodies the first millennium of history—the millennium of Adam, "the light of the world,"[12] when the world was still saturated with knowledge of its Creator and was sustained by the indiscriminate benevolence of G-d.[13] The second day, on which the Creator distinguished between the spiritual and the physical elements of His creation, yielded a second millennium of judgment and discrimination—as reflected in the Flood which wiped out a corrupt humanity and spared only the righteous Noah and his family. The third day, on which the land emerged

---

10 *Zohar* 3:94b; *Responsa of Rashba*, no. 423; see *Garments for the Soul* on pp. 60–63, above.
11 See *The Seventh Element* on pp. 77–88, above.
12 *Midrash Tanchuma, Noach* 1.
13 Cf. Talmud, *Pesachim* 118a.

from the sea and sprouted forth greenery and fruit-bearing trees, encapsulates the third millennium, in which Abraham began teaching the truth of the One G-d and the Torah was given on Mount Sinai. The fourth day, on which G-d created the sun and the moon, "the two great luminaries: the greater luminary... and the lesser luminary," corresponds to the fourth millennium, in which the first Holy Temple (2928–3338) and the second Holy Temple (3408–3829) in Jerusalem served as the divine abode "from which light emanated to the entire world."[14] The fifth day, the day of fish, birds, and reptiles, unfolded into the lawless and predatory Dark Ages of the fifth millennium.[15] The sixth day, whose early hours saw the creation of the beasts of the land, followed by the creation of man, the apex and purpose of G-d's creation, is our millennium—a millennium marked by strong, forceful empires, whose beastly rule will be followed by the emergence of Moshiach, who leads humanity to the realization the divine purpose in creation and ushers in a seventh millennium of perfect peace and tranquility.

Nachmanides also notes that each thousand-year "day" is preceded by a "twilight"—an overlapping period which, while technically belonging to the previous millennium, contains the beginnings of the next. Thus, Abraham was born 52 years before the third millennium, King Solomon built the First Temple 72 years before the fourth, and so with each millennium.[16]

Therein lies the special significance of the twilight following the sixth day of creation, on which G-d created the ten things enumerated by *Ethics of the Fathers*. For on the macro-historical level, this is the twilight which facilitates the transition from the six millennia of history to the age of Moshiach.

---

14   Jerusalem Talmud, *Berachot* 4:5.

15   240–1240 CE in the secular calendar.

16   Nachmanides' commentary on the Torah, Genesis 2:3.

The significance of this time is of primary relevance to our generation. For it is we, who have entered the final quarter of the sixth millennium,[17] who are living in this most crucial juncture of history—the twilight that translates six thousand years of human toil and achievement into "the day that is wholly Shabbat and rest, for life everlasting."

THE DICHOTOMY

What are the primary qualities of these two epochs, and in what way do they overlap in the twilight era that connects them? One clue can be found in the Talmud's list of the "ten things created on the eve of Shabbat at twilight," particularly in "the writing, the inscription, and the tablets" which served as the medium for the Ten Commandments.

In his parting words to the people of Israel, Moses enjoins: "You shall keep the *mitzvah*, the decrees, and the laws which I command you *today to do them.*"[18] The Talmud interprets this to imply:

"*Today* to do them"—and not to do them tomorrow;

"Today to *do* them"—and tomorrow to receive their reward.[19]

In other words, our present-day world and the World to Come represent two different modes of existence, each exclusive of the other. Our present world is the environment for deed and achievement, but without the possibility to enjoy, or even envision, the true fruits of our labor. On the other hand, the World to Come is a world of ultimate reward, tranquility, and bliss, but one that

---

17 The year 5750 from creation was equivalent to 1989–1990 on the secular calendar.

18 Deuteronomy 7:11.

19 Talmud, *Eruvin* 22a.

THE WEEK AND SHABBAT (7)   145

precludes any further achievement on the part of man. The Talmud goes so far as to quote the verse, "There will come years of which you will say, 'I have no desire in them,'"[20] and to declare: "This refers to the days of the messianic era, in which there is neither merit nor obligation."[21] As one chassidic *rebbe* expressed it, "In the days of Moshiach we will yearn for the hardships and challenges of *galut*."[22]

Intrinsic to our nature is that we derive true satisfaction only from what we achieve in the face of challenge. Yet it is the paradox of life that true satisfaction can be experienced only under conditions of tranquility, and that true challenge can exist only under conditions in which the satisfaction of achievement lies hidden and unknowable beyond the horizon of one's goal.

Hence the delegation of the reward of our deeds to an unknowable "tomorrow," and delegation of achievement to a strife-ridden "today." If the first six "workday" millennia of history were to include more than the merest hint of the satisfaction implicit in our life's work, then its challenges, and thus its achievements, would be greatly diminished. On the other hand, if the seventh millennium were to include the conditions that allow for true achievement, it could not serve as the arena for true satisfaction.

Hence reality consists of two worlds locked into dichotomy by their very natures and their most basic functions. In the words of *Ethics of the Fathers*, "A single moment of *teshuvah*[23] and good

---

20   Ecclesiastes 12:1.

21   Talmud, *Shabbat* 151b.

22   Rabbi Shalom DovBer of Lubavitch (1860–1920), cited in *Hayom Yom*, *Av* 3.

23   "Return." In its narrower sense, *teshuvah* is repentance for sin; in its broader sense, it is the rebounding from negative and challenging experiences to an acme of achievement unattainable under conditions of tranquility and perfection.

deeds in this world is greater than all of the World to Come. And a single moment of bliss in the World to Come is greater than all of this world."[24]

Yet there also exists an environment in which these two worlds overlap, an unique time-period that incorporates both deed and reward, both struggle and tranquility; a twilight that mediates between the six "workdays" of creation and the ultimate Shabbat.

GRAVEN WORDS

How does a person experience tranquility while in the pith of struggle? How can a person enjoy perfection while still grappling with his shortcomings? When he is completely one with what he is doing.

"This is the law of the Torah," proclaims the verse introducing the laws of the Red Heifer.[25] The chassidic masters point out that the word *chukat* ("the law of") used by the verse derives from the word *chakikah*, "engraving"; so the above verse may also be rendered, "this is the engraving of the Torah." Indeed, the Torah was first given to us in the form of Ten Commandments engraved into two tablets of stone.

Chassidic teaching explains that a person's relationship with the truths he bears can be like that of a parchment scroll with the words written upon it, or like that of a stone tablet with the words engraved in it. The scroll, too, serves as a platform and medium for its words, yet the substance of the scroll and the substance of the words remain two distinct entities, however strongly the

---

24 *Ethics of the Fathers* 4:17; see *Beyond the Letter of the Law* (Meaningful Life Center, 2012), "*Essence and Expression*," pp. 196–204.

25 Numbers 19:2.

THE WEEK AND SHABBAT (7)   147

ink might adhere to the parchment. The stone tablet, on the other hand, is one with its message: the words are the stone and the stone is the words. The Torah is telling us that its words should be engraved words rather than written words to us: words that are the very form and substance of our lives, rather than something superimposed upon its surface.[26]

This is the significance of the last three of the ten things created "on the eve of Shabbat, at twilight"—the "writing, the inscription, and the tablets" of the Ten Commandments.[27] On the twilight between the six days of creation and the first Shabbat, G-d bestowed upon us the capacity to not only carry out His blueprint for creation, but to engrave it in our very selves, so that everything we do is in full harmony with who and what we are.

As "tablets" of Torah, we transcend the dichotomy of deed and reward. For when a person is completely one with his path through life, his most arduous climb is a tranquil flight of soul, and his most painful deficiencies are the building blocks of an integral and perfect self. In such a person, the defining line that divides achievement from satisfaction is permeable, allowing for a "twilight" in which the two mutually exclusive worlds are merged.

Today, we stand at this most unique moment of history. At this time of transition, on the threshold between today and tomorrow, as six millennia of human endeavor approach their climax into the tranquil perfection of the eternal Shabbat, we are, in a sense, in possession of both worlds. Let us seize the moment.

---

26 *Torah Ohr, Chukat* 56a.

27 The other things created at this time likewise represent realities that are of a "twilight" quality—realities relating to the transition from our world to the world of Moshiach. See *Beyond the Letter of the Law*, op. cit., "On the Essence of the Instrument," pp. 246-255.

CHAPTER FOUR

The Month
Renewal

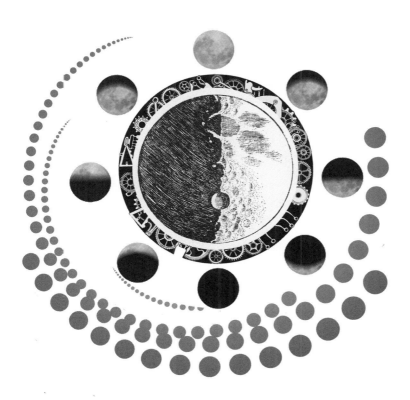

If the week is the primary cycle of creation, the month is the primary component of the Jewish calendar. When the *sanhedrin* (highest court of Torah law) operated in the Holy Land, the Jewish month would be created anew each month by a special process called *kiddush hachodesh* ("consecration of the new month"), which included testimony by witnesses who sighted the new moon. With the exception of Shabbat, all the festivals and special dates of the Jewish calendar derive from the monthly lunar cycle.

The first essay in this chapter, *The Sixteenth Increment*, explores the special relationship between the people of Israel and the moon, and the ways in which the lunar cycle informs our national and individual identities. *G-d on the Moon* delves further into the lunar side to life by analyzing an enigmatic Midrash describing the "diminution of the moon" on the fourth day of creation. *Locating the Moon* examines the process by which the *sanhedrin* consecrates the new month, and applies it as a prototype for all our efforts to bring sanctity into our lives. *The Monthly Bridge* looks at the significance of *Shabbat Mevarchim*—the Shabbat which "blesses" and empowers the month to come.

<small>The nature and significance of the month is also touched upon in our chapter on the Jewish leap year (pp. 193–206 below), and in the essay *Shammai's Shabbat* (pp. 219–224).</small>

THE
SIXTEENTH
INCREMENT

*And Jonathan said to [David]: "Tomorrow is
the new month; and you will be remembered,
for your seat will be vacant."*

I Samuel 20:18

"𝔍he people of Israel count by the moon," declares the Talmud, meaning that in contrast to other nations, who follow a solar-based calendar, the Jewish people mark time with the moon.[1] As the sages of Israel expound, this is because the Jewish people emulate the moon in their character and destiny.[2]

The Jewish calendar is predicated on the lunar month — the 29.5-day cycle in which the moon, as perceived by an earthly observer, completes its revolution around the earth. The beginning of the Jewish month coincides with the birth of a "new moon," and ends when the next new moon marks the start of the next month.[3]

---

[1] Talmud, *Sukkah* 29a.

[2] *Bereishit Rabbah*, 6:3; *Zohar* 1:236b.

[3] Twelve such months add up to a "year" of approximately 354 days. For the manner by which the Jewish calendar reconciles its months with the 365.25-day solar cycle, see *Jewish Time* on pp. 195–202, below.

In contrast to the lunar months of the Jewish calendar, the months of solar-based calendars are wholly artificial, being merely the division of the solar year into twelve more-or-less equal segments. These "months" bear no relation to the lunar cycle or to any other natural phenomenon.

The "new moon" is the night on which the moon is first visible after its monthly disappearance from our nighttime sky. The alignment and movement of the moon in relation to the earth and sun means that, to the earthly observer, the moon passes through "phases" in which it grows and diminishes and, at one point in its cycle, disappears altogether. When the moon is closest to the sun, positioned between the sun and earth, its lighted side—the side illuminated by the sun's light—faces away from the earth, so that it is invisible to us. As it moves away from the sun to orbit the earth, it appears first as a thin crescent of light and continues to grow and fill for the next fifteen days. Midway through its orbit, when it is furthest from the sun, and the earth is between the sun and the moon, the lighted half of the moon is entirely visible on earth, so that it appears as a complete sphere in the sky and bathes our night with the full luminescence of its pacific glow. Then, as the moon continues its orbit of the earth, moving closer to the sun, less and less of it is visible to us; the sphere shrinks by nightly increments to a half-sphere, and then to progressively leaner slivers of light until, at the point of its greatest proximity to the sun, it once more disappears from our view.

The night on which the moon is first visible after its hiatus is the first of the Jewish month (hence the Hebrew word for "month," *chodesh*, from the root *chadash*, "new"). The month consists of 29 or 30 days, until the next "new moon" marks the onset of a new month. The first half of the Jewish month is thus marked by a nightly growing moon, which reaches its full luminescent potential on the night of the 15th; but on the 16th of the month the moon is already diminished, and continues to shrink nightly until a new moon and month are born.[4]

---

4 At the time that the *sanhedrin* (highest court of Torah law) existed, the

THE MONTH (1)   153

A Lunar People

The history of the Jewish people emulates the lunar cycle. In the words of the Midrash:

> As the cycle of the moon is thirty days, so did the sovereign-
> ty of Israel extend for thirty generations from Abraham
> to the destruction of the Holy Temple. And as the moon's
> light begins to shine on the first of the month, growing
> each night until its disk is full on the fifteenth, and then
> declines until the thirtieth night when its light is hidden—
> so, too, was the sovereignty of Israel.
>
> Abraham began to shine; then came Isaac, Jacob, Ju-
> dah, Perez, Hezron, Ram, Aminadab, Nahshon, Salmon,
> Boaz, Obed, Jesse, David, and Solomon; each added to
> the light of his predecessors, until the disk of the moon
> was full in the days of Solomon, the fifteenth generation
> from Abraham, and Israel attained the acme of its glory.
> Then came fifteen generations of decline from Rehoboam
> to Zedekiah, whose eyes were blinded and in whose day
> the Temple was destroyed...[5]

Like the moon, the Jew dips and soars through history, his regressions and defeats but preludes to yet another rebirth, yet another renewal. The story of the moon is the story of a nation, and the

---

onset of a new month was proclaimed each month based on the actual sighting of the new moon—a practice which will be resumed with the coming of Moshiach and the re-establishment of a central Torah authority for all of Israel. Today, our preset calendar is not as exact, with the first of the month falling within a day or two of the new moon's birth (*molad halevanah*).

5   *Midrash Rabbah, Shemot* 15:26.

story of every productive life: lack fuels initiative, setbacks stimulate growth, and one's highest achievements are born out of times of diminution and depreciation.

GOING MOON

In its account of the creation of the world, the Torah speaks of "the two great luminaries" created by G-d "to shed light upon the earth" and set the "signs, times, days, and years" of life on earth. In the very same verse, however, the "two great luminaries" become "the great luminary to rule the day" and the "small luminary to rule the night."[6] The Talmud explains: Initially, the sun and moon were indeed equally great.[7] But the moon objected that "two kings cannot share the same crown." So G-d commanded it: "Go, diminish yourself."[8]

Thus was born the month—the cycle by which the moon's illumination of the earth would be curtailed by the constant changes in its juxtaposition with the source and with the recipient of its light. For two weeks of each month, the moon faithfully fulfills the divine decree, "Go, diminish yourself," steadily reducing itself to the point in which it is completely enveloped in darkness.

---

6   Genesis 1:16.

7   This is usually understood to mean that, originally, the moon was the sun's equal in size and luminosity. On a deeper level it means that—unlike today's world, in which a giver is, by definition, greater than a recipient—in G-d's original creation, the role of recipient was manifestly as great as that of giver, and reflected a "rebounding light" as great as original or "direct light." See the following essay, *G-d on the Moon*, pp. 160–166.

8   Talmud, *Chulin* 60b. See full citation on pp. 160–161 below.

These repeated diminutions are what yield the unique qualities of lunar time. Living with the moon, we learn how darkness can give birth to light and how absence can generate renewed presence. We learn to exploit the momentum of our descents to scale new and unprecedented heights—heights which would never be contemplated in an unvarying "solar" path through life.

On a deeper level, the injunction "Go, diminish yourself" relates to the very essence of our humanity. Man is unique among G-d's creations in that he alone is a *mehalech*, a "goer" or journeyer through life. All other creations, including the loftiest of spiritual beings (and this includes the soul of man prior to its investiture in a physical body) are *omdim*, stationary "standers." A "stander" is not necessarily immobile; indeed, all things possess, to some degree or other, the potential for development and advancement. But all creations move in a "solar" orbit—an orbit defined by pre-ordained limits which they cannot transcend. Only the human being is "lunar," with a trajectory through life that includes both growth and decline, obliteration and rebirth.

For man alone possesses the power of free choice—a power as potent as it is lethal, as infinite as it is constricting. With free choice comes the capacity for utter self-destruction, and the capacity for utter self-transformation. Man has the power to negate everything he is and stands for, and in the next moment, to re-create himself in a new mold and embark on a path that his prior existence could never have anticipated.

"Go, diminish yourself," is the Creator's perpetual injunction to His lunar creation. For it is only by diminishing itself that the human soul can "go." Only by making itself vulnerable to the mortality and pitfalls of the physical state can the soul of man become a "goer," a being with the power to make of itself more than it is.

David's Absence

This is the message implicit in the *haftarah* (reading from the prophets) read in the synagogue when Shabbat falls on the day before *Rosh Chodesh*, as the first of the month is called. The opening verse of this *haftarah* reads: "And Jonathan said to [David]: 'Tomorrow is the new month; and you will be remembered, for your seat will be vacant.'"[9] David has reason to suspect that King Saul wishes him harm, so he plans to avoid the royal palace. Jonathan tells him that his very absence will attract Saul's notice, inducing the king to reveal his intentions toward him.

At first glance, the connection between the *haftarah* and the new month seems merely incidental—the reading begins by relating a conversation that took place on the day before *Rosh Chodesh*, so we read it on the day before *Rosh Chodesh*. But upon closer examination, Jonathan's words to David express the deeper significance of the lunar month, and particularly of the day before *Rosh Chodesh*—the day of the moon's "disappearance." Jonathan tells David that "you will be remembered because your seat will be vacant." The key word in the Hebrew original of this sentence is *pakod*, which is the root of both *ve'nifkadta*, "you will be remembered," and *yipaked*, "will be vacant." Indeed, the two are intertwined: we are remembered when we are missed. Like the vacuum which draws fluid into a syringe, it is the voids and absences of life that compel its greatest achievements and fulfillments.

This is the essence of lunar time, to which the Jew sets the rhythm of his individual and communal life: oblivion as the harbinger of renewal; darkness as the impetus for reborn light.[10]

---

9   I Samuel 20:18

10 The subsequent verses of the *haftarah* also relate to the greater achievements that are spurred by regression—see *Long Range Missile* in vol. 3, pp. 138–143 of this collection.

The Month (1)

The Fifteenth and the Sixteenth

Thus the fifteenth of the Jewish month, the day on which the moon achieves the pinnacle of its luminary potential, marks the high point of that month's particular contribution to Jewish life.

Nissan is the month of redemption, and it is on the first day of *Nissan* that the process of our liberation from Egypt began; but the results of this process were fully manifest only on the 15th of *Nissan*, the day of the Exodus, which we celebrate each year as the festival of Passover and on which we reexperience the divine gift of freedom through the observances and customs of the *seder*. By the same token, the first of *Tishrei* is the day on which we crown G-d as king of the universe, rededicating the entirety of creation to the purpose for which it was created and evoking in G-d the desire to continue to create and sustain it;[11] but the celebration of the divine coronation is eclipsed by days of solemnity and awe which occupy the first part of *Tishrei*, coming to fruition only on the joyous festival of Sukkot which commences on the fifteenth of the month.[12]

The same is true of each of the twelve months of the Jewish year. Each has its own unique import and quality, and each undergoes a cycle of diminution and growth, concealment, and expression, which reaches its climax on the fifteenth of the month. Thus we have the "New Year for Trees" on the 15th of *Shevat*; Purim on the

---

11 See *To Will a World* in vol. 2, pp. 17–24 of this series.

12 This is the deeper significance of the verse (Psalms 81:4, as per Talmud, *Rosh Hashanah* 8a), "Sound the *shofar* on the moon's renewal (*chodesh*), which is concealed until the day of our festival." The *shofar*, whose trumpet-like blast echoes our "coronation" of the Almighty, is sounded on the 1st day of *Tishrei*, the day of the moon's renewal; but like the moon itself, the experience remains "concealed" and largely unexpressed until Sukkot—"the day of our festival"—on the 15th of *Tishrei*.

14th and 15th of *Adar*; and the 15th of *Av*, which the Talmud calls "the greatest festival" on the Jewish calendar.[13]

Yet the sixteenth is greater than the fifteenth.

In Torah, everything is precise and meaningful. So if the fifteenth were truly the apex of the month, it would also be represented by its highest numeric figure. Yet following the fifteenth, we have a day which the Torah refers to as the "sixteenth"—a number *greater* than fifteen. And the numbers continue to climb: seventeen, eighteen, nineteen, and so forth, up to the 29th or the 30th. According to this, the loftiest day of the month is the day on which the light of the moon is completely concealed!

But as we have already noted, the point at which the moon disappears from our earthly view is also the point at which it achieves its greatest proximity to the sun. In other words, there are two perspectives from which the lunar cycle may be viewed: from the perspective of the moon's illumination of the earth, or from the perspective of the moon's relationship with the source of its light, the sun. Viewed from the first perspective, the moon undergoes changes and diminutions, achieving its full luminary potential only after an arduous climb of fifteen days, and then waning to nothingness in the course of the latter half of the month. Viewed from the second perspective, the moon, of course, is never "diminished": It remains the same size throughout its orbit, and the light of the sun bathes its surface at all times.[14] Indeed, the very point at which the moon is completely dark (and thus "nonexistent") to the earthly observer is the apex of the moon's relationship with the

---

13 See *The Day of the Breaking of the Ax* in vol. 3, pp. 275–284 of this series.

14 Except in the case of a lunar eclipse, when the earth comes directly between the sun and moon, and blocks the light of the sun from reaching the moon.

sun—the point at which the sun's illumination of the moon is at its brightest and most intense.

Viewed from the perspective of manifest light, the setbacks of life are points of diminished luminescence and vitality. But when one looks at the deeper significance of these "descents," one recognizes them as points of intensified vitality, points at which we draw closer to our Source to receive the fortitude and impetus to surmount the next challenge and summit of "visible" life.

G-D
ON THE
MOON

More than the giver does for the recipient, the
recipient does for the giver.

Midrash Rabbah, Vayikra 34:10

$\mathcal{I}$ n the first chapter of Genesis, the Torah describes G-d's creation of the sun and moon on the fourth day of creation:

> *And G-d said: "There shall be luminaries in the heavens, to distinguish between day and night; and they shall be for signs, and for times, and for days, and for years. And they shall be luminaries in the heavens to give light upon earth." And it was so.*
>
> *And G-d made the two great luminaries: the great luminary to rule the day, and the small luminary to rule the night…*[1]

The Talmud dwells on the apparent contradiction in the above verses. Are there, in fact, "two great luminaries," or a "great luminary" and a "small luminary"?

The Talmud explains that initially, the sun and the moon were equal in greatness and luminance. But then,

> *The moon said to G-d: "Master of the Universe! Can two kings wear the same crown?"*

---

[1] Genesis 1:14–16.

THE MONTH (2)   161

Said G-d to her: "Go diminish yourself."

Said she to Him: "Master of the world! Because I said a proper thing, I must diminish myself?"

Said He to her: "You may rule both during the day and at night."

Said she to Him: "What advantage is there in that? What does a lamp accomplish at high noon?"

Said He to her: "The people of Israel will calculate their dates and years by you."

Said she to Him: "But the sun, too, shall have a part in that, as they will calculate the seasons by him."

Said G-d: "The righteous will be called by your name—'Jacob the Small,' 'Samuel the Small,' 'David the Small.'"

Still G-d saw that the moon was not appeased. So G-d said: "Offer an atonement for My sake, for My having diminished the moon." This is the significance of what Reish Lakish said: "Why does the he-goat offered on the first of the month differ from the others in that it is specified as 'for G-d'?[2] G-d is saying: "This he-goat shall atone for My diminishing of the moon."[3]

Reading this celestial dialogue, several questions come to mind:

a) How did G-d intend for the "two great luminaries" to "distinguish between day and night" if He made them identical to each other?

b) G-d "diminishes" the moon, apparently as a punishment for her having insisted that she and the sun cannot be equals. But then

---

2   In Deuteronomy 28:15, the Torah adds the clause "for G-d," to the commandment to bring the he-goat sin-offering on the first of the month, which marks the new moon. The clause does not appear in connection with the sin-offerings of the other festivals.

3   Talmud, *Chulin* 60b.

He appeases the moon for her loss. And when the moon is not placated, He offers her one reparation after another. At the end, G-d still feels guilty about the whole affair and commands that every month, as the moon enters a new cycle of rebirth, growth, and diminution, a sacrifice be offered in the Holy Temple in atonement for His deed. On the other hand, He does not restore the moon to her original greatness, so obviously He still feels that her diminishment is warranted. So we still don't know who is in the right in this argument. Did or did not the moon "say a proper thing"?

c) Rereading the verse, "G-d made the two great luminaries: the great luminary to rule the day, and the small luminary to rule the night," we now realize that the Torah is telling us that this was indeed G-d's intention: that there should originally be "two great luminaries," one of which should, at some later point, emerge as the "small luminary." But the prophet Isaiah describes the future perfect world of Moshiach as a time when "the light of the moon will be as the light of the sun"[4]—implying that, on the contrary, the moon's *original* status is the ideal. Or perhaps this was all some grand plot on the part of G-d—to create an impossible situation, have the moon complain, diminish her, and then decree that at the culmination of history, the original state of affairs (now somehow possible and desirable) should be restored?

GIVE AND TAKE

No man is an island, goes the old cliché. But then again, neither is anything else in G-d's world. Every being is inexorably married to its fellows in a series of reciprocal relationships: spirit and matter, male and female, parent and offspring, prey and predator, teacher

---

4   Isaiah 30:26.

THE MONTH (2)

and student, manufacturer and consumer, employer and employee, philanthropist and pauper, and so on.

Sun and moon are the metaphor and prototype for the innumerable give-and-take relationships which form the foundation of life—indeed of existence as we know it. When G-d created the sun and the moon on the fourth day of creation, and tasked the sun to radiate its light and the the moon to receive the light of the sun and reflect it to a darkened earth, He also created the giver/recipient dynamic—the dynamic by which a man inseminates life in the womb of a woman, and the woman conceives it and nurtures it; by which the farmer invests toil and seed in the soil, which the earth absorbs to sprout forth vegetation; by which the rich give to the poor, the pupil learns from the teacher, and the rivers feed the seas.

Indeed, "two kings cannot wear the same crown." For it is only out of the interplay between giver and recipient that new realities are born. Without this give-and-take dynamic, our world would be as static as a museum display; with it, the world becomes vibrant and creative.

One can say that the giver is the "great" element in the relationship, and the recipient the "small." The "suns" of the world are givers by virtue of their superior resources and prowess; its "moons" are recipients due to their lack of whatever it is that they receive. This, however, represents only one perspective on the relationship—that of the giver and the recipient themselves. But what about the designer and creator of their reality? How does the ultimately objective viewer see it?

Seen from G-d's perspective, is there any real difference between the fact that He provides the rich with wealth-generating talents and opportunities, and that He provides the poor with rich men with generous hearts? Both thereby participate in the divine plan that "the world should be built through benevolence,"[5] each in his own way. Is there any qualitative difference between His making the sun a cauldron of energy and His making the moon a "passive" sphere of matter positioned so that it reflects the sun in a certain fashion? Both are thereby enabled to illuminate the earth and generate the rhythmic cycles of life, again each in its own way. From G-d's perspective, they are *all* recipients in that He gives them everything they have, including the capacity to give and/or receive; and they are all givers in the sense that through their partnership with each other, they create the world He desired.

So every sun and every moon in G-d's world is a "great luminary." It is only that the *way* in which they are great luminaries is by forming partnerships in which some of them are great and abundant and others are small and wanting. As far as G-d is concerned, darkness is just another form of light, poverty another form of wealth, imperfection another form of perfection. Yes, He created the sun and the moon to *differentiate* between night and day—to polarize His creation between the givers and the receivers, between illuminators and the reflectors. This, however, is not a differentiation between great and small but between great and great—or rather, between great as great, and small as great.

INFERIORITY COMPLEX

Therein lies the significance of the dialogue between G-d and the moon. The moon's greatness—her capacity to receive—is born of a sense of diminution and insufficiency. So when G-d created two great luminaries, it is the moon who cried—her very nature demanded it—"Wait a minute! We cannot be equals! If we are,

---

5   Psalms 89:3.

where is the differentiation? Where is the creative relationship? Only one of us can give—the other must receive. Only one of us can shine—the other must be dark."

"You are absolutely right," says G-d. "Go diminish yourself."

"But why me?" asks the moon. "Just because I'm the one who spoke up?"

"Yes. That's precisely *why* you spoke up—because you are the recipient. The sun feels perfectly comfortable with his greatness; that's his role—to be great through giving. But you are different. It is you who cannot reconcile herself to a world that consists only of givers; it is you who senses the necessity for a receptive element in My creation."

"But why should I be the lesser one in the relationship?"

"You are 'lesser' only in the reality of your perception. But in essence, you are equals. In fact, you're even superior in certain ways."

"How?"

"When the day ends, the sun drops out of the sky. The night is inaccessible to him. But you are present not only at night when you illuminate the world, but also during the day, when your light is not seen."

"But I'm a *luminary*. If I'm not illuminating, I'm nothing."

"Exactly. That's the difference between you and the sun. He illuminates by illuminating, but you illuminate by virtue of your nothingness, through your passive reception of his light. So when he isn't seen, he isn't there. But you—even when you're nothing, you are present."

"I don't understand."

"Of course you don't. If you did—if you sensed your own greatness—you wouldn't be a recipient."

And so it goes. G-d tells the moon about the unique qualities of lunar time, where, unlike the steady, unfaltering solar cycles, diminution and extinction give rise to rebirth and renewal.[6] He tells her of the great men of history who achieve true greatness by virtue of their humility and perpetual sense of inadequacy.

But the moon persists: "I still feel inferior!"

"Of course you do," says G-d. "Your smallness is the essence of your greatness. If you did not feel inferior, you wouldn't be driven to receive, and would not actualize your greatness. *I* see your greatness, but you cannot—at least not until the ultimate realization of your role. Then, on the day that all the givers and takers in my creation have produced the perfect world I have charged them to create, the true worth of the recipient will come to light.

"I know that all of this is My fault," G-d continues. "I could have created a perfect world, or no world at all. It is because of My desire for an imperfect, self-perfecting world—a world in which giver and recipient unite to create new realities—that the moons I created experience darkness, weakness, and poverty. So I will join you in your plight. From My perspective, you are already great— your potential as good as realized, your future perfection already recognized. Still, I shall enter your world and perspective, and together with you strive for and await redemption. Until that day when 'the light of the moon shall be as the light of the sun,' I, too, will subject myself to the ups and downs of lunar life."

---

6   See the previous essay, *The Sixteenth Increment* on pp. 151–159.

LOCATING THE MOON

G-d spoke to Moses and to Aaron in the land of Egypt, to say: "This new-moon shall be unto you a head of months; it is the first of the months of the year unto you."

Exodus 12:1–2

G-d showed Moses the moon in its renewal, and said to him: "When the moon renews itself, it shall be the first of the month for you."

Moses was having difficulty regarding the birth of the moon, as to what extent it must be seen for the new month to be consecrated. So G-d pointed to the moon in the sky and said to him: "Such as this see, and consecrate."

Rashi, ad loc.

"By the word of two witnesses," rules the Torah, "a thing shall be established."[1] According to Torah law, the testimony of two witnesses constitutes absolute proof. The witnesses must be qualified to testify under Torah law, and in certain cases, their accounts must corroborate under separate cross-examinations; but once their testimony has been validated, it is accepted unequivocally. According to Torah law, evidence "beyond a

---

1   Deuteronomy 19:15.

reasonable doubt" does not suffice to punish a criminal, certify a marriage, or expropriate a single dollar from the possession of its owner; nothing less than absolute proof will do. Yet the Torah instructs us to accept the word of two valid witnesses as absolute proof.

The concept of *eidut* (witnesses' testimony) is thus a suprarational one. In the words of Maimonides, "We are commanded to decide the law by the word of two valid witnesses, although it is possible that they are testifying falsely."[2] Rationally, there is no reason to view a statement by two individuals as established fact; rationally, the word of one hundred witnesses should carry more weight than the word of two; rationally, if we have conflicting testimonies from two pairs of witnesses, we ought to consider which pair is more credible or whose story is more consistent with the circumstantial evidence. But by divine decree, the word of two witnesses is deemed absolutely compelling; one hundred witnesses and all the circumstantial evidence in the world cannot be more compelling.[3]

---

2   *Mishneh Torah, Laws of the Fundamentals of Torah* 7:7.

3   In the case that two witnesses testify one way and another two witnesses—or another hundred—contradict the first pair's testimony, the court is deadlocked: Confronted with two "absolute proofs," it cannot act on either one (see *Mishneh Torah, Laws of Witnesses* 18:3). The only case in which the testimony of two valid and mutually consistent witnesses is discredited is the case of *zimum*, where a second pair of witnesses testify that the first pair could not possibly have witnessed the event they attest to since "they were with us" in a different location at the time they say that they witnessed the event. In this case, the second pair is not contradicting the testimony of the first (they do not claim to know whether the event did or did not take place), but are disqualifying them as witnesses by exposing them as liars.

THE MONTH (3)   169

THE EXCEPTION

There is, however, one area in which the testimony of two witnesses is not enough to "establish a thing" on its own. This concerns the role of witnesses' testimony in setting the Jewish calendar.

The Torah instructs us to base our calendar on the lunar cycle, with the night on which the new moon is first visible marking the start of a new month. The Torah further instructs that each new month be proclaimed and "consecrated" by the *sanhedrin* (highest court of Torah law) after hearing the testimony of at least two witnesses who sighted the new moon. This process is called *kiddush hachodesh*, the "consecration of the new month."[4]

---

4   Since the moon completes its orbit of the earth in 29.5 days, the new moon is first visible either on the 30th or the 31st night after the previous new moon. Thus, a month on the Jewish calendar consists of either 29 or 30 days, with the 30th or the 31st day becoming the *Rosh Chodesh* ("head" or first of the month) of the following month. When the calendar was set each month by the *sanhedrin*, the procedure was as follows: On the 30th day after the previous new moon, the *sanhedrin* would convene and await the appearance of witnesses. If at least two witnesses arrived and testified that they saw the new moon on the previous night, that day would be proclaimed *Rosh Chodesh* — meaning that the previous month had only 29 days. If no witnesses appeared that day, the next day would be proclaimed *Rosh Chodesh*, and the previous month would have had 30 days. (In such a case the *sanhedrin* would not wait for witnesses to appear, since the first occurrence of a [technically visible] new moon will never be later than the 31st night from the previous new moon.) In the case that witnesses arrived on the 30th day but late in the day, this created a unique situation. On *Rosh Chodesh*, special *korbanot* (animal and meal offerings) were offered in the Holy Temple. These had to be offered before the daily afternoon offerings; thus, if witnesses appeared in the late afternoon of the 30th day, after the afternoon offering had been brought, the *korbanot* of *Rosh Chodesh* could no longer be offered. In such a case, the *sanhedrin* would proclaim two days of *Rosh Chodesh*, the first of which would be counted as the 30th day of the

But the judges of the *sanhedrin* are not to rely solely on the witnesses' testimony. They are also instructed to calculate the moon's path through the heavens so that they should know, in advance, when the new moon is scheduled to appear. The implications of this are twofold. On the one hand, this indicates that the need for witnesses is not for lack of a more "efficient" way of determining the night of the new moon's birth (which the *sanhedrin* already knows), but in order to impart to the calendar the divinely-ordained absoluteness that is effected by the institution of *eidut*. On the other hand, the divine mandate granted to two witnesses is not enough—the date of the new month must also be determined by the *sanhedrin*'s astronomic calculations.

In other words, the setting of each new month involves two different—even opposite—dynamics: the suprarational, divinely decreed, "establishing" power of witnesses; and the logical, empirical proof provided by human observation and calculation. Both are important components of the sanctity which the "consecration of the new month" imparts to our experience of time.[5]

---

previous month, while the second day of *Rosh Chodesh* (on which the offerings would be brought) would be the first day of the new month.

    When the conditions of the exile and dispersion of the Jewish people no longer allowed the monthly setting of the calendar by the *sanhedrin*, a preset calendar was established in which each month has a set number of days: *Nissan* always has 30 days, *Iyar* 29, *Sivan* 30, and so on. (The exceptions are two months, *Cheshvan* and *Kislev*, which vary in length: In certain years both have 30 days; in other years, both have 29 days; and in certain years, *Cheshvan* has 29 and *Kislev* 30.) When a month has 29 days, the following month has only one day of *Rosh Chodesh*. When a month has 30 days, our calendar follows the model of a double *Rosh Chodesh*: the 30th day also serves as the first day of *Rosh Chodesh* for the following month, followed by a second day of *Rosh Chodesh* on the first of that month.

5   Thus, the fact that the dispersion of Israel and the disbanding of the

THE MONTH (3)   171

THE FIRST MITZVAH

As discussed in a previous essay, the "consecration of the new month" was the first *mitzvah* commanded to the people of Israel because it sanctifies the most primary element of the physical reality—the element of time.[6]

When two witnesses sight the new moon and testify before the *sanhedrin*, and when the *sanhedrin* calculates the night of the new moon and then use this knowledge, together with the witnesses' testimony, to proclaim a new month, what they are doing is imbuing time with holiness—determining the nature and quality of G-d's involvement in our lives via the medium of time. By declaring a certain day *Rosh Chodesh*, the "Head of the Month" (as the first of the month is referred to in the Torah), they establish that this day shall encapsulate the flow of divine sustenance into creation for the entire month to come.

For this is the deeper significance of *Rosh Chodesh*: a stretch of "compacted time" out of which the month's other 28 or 29 days subsequently emerge. *Rosh Chodesh* is thus a day that is "holier" than the ordinary days to follow: a day closer to the divine source of being and life; a day especially suited for self-improvement and for embarking on new initiatives, since everything done and resolved on this day profoundly affects the entire month it embodies. (This is why *Rosh Chodesh* is called the "head" of the month,

---

sanhedrin has deprived us of the ability to "consecrate the new month" based on monthly sightings by witnesses—leaving us with only the second, logical aspect of this *mitzvah*—means that, today, we lack the ability to fulfill this *mitzvah* in its most complete and optimal manner. Daily we pray for the ingathering of exiles and the restoration of the *sanhedrin* so that we once again merit to fully sanctify our months and years by the formula established by the Torah.

6   See *The First Creation* on pp. 20–30 above.

rather than the "first" or the "beginning" of the month. The head is more than the body's beginning and highest point—it is also its nerve-center, the seat of all its faculties.)

The *mitzvah* of "consecrating the new month" also sanctifies time by establishing which days will serve as the other annual "islands of holiness" in our calendar: which 24-plus hours of the year shall be Yom Kippur, which seven days shall be Passover, and so on.

The Servant and the Calculator

There are two ways in which a person might approach the observance of a *mitzvah*. He might take the "servant of G-d" approach—an approach that, in effect, says: "Let's face it, this is all beyond us, anyway. Who can fathom the divine will? Is there any *reason* why binding *tefilin* on my arm should sanctify the material world any more than tying a scarf around my neck? Is there any reason, even, why giving to the poor is a "good" deed while stealing from the poor is an "evil" act? True, we sense certain deeds to be good and others to be bad. But this is *because* G-d willed it thus. *Why* G-d so desired is something we can never objectively know—we can only accept it as the quintessential truth of our lives. Certainly, we must study and strive to understand His will as He communicated it to us in His Torah. But ultimately, a *mitzvah* is an act of faith, the acceptance of an absolute that lies beyond the reach of our finite minds."

A second approach argues: "How can I possibly marginalize the most vital aspects of my humanity—my thinking and feeling selves—in my observance of the *mitzvot*? If G-d would have wanted me to go about my mission in life as a mindless robot, He would have created me as a mindless robot. If my implementation of the divine will is to truly sanctify my life, it must permeate my

THE MONTH (3)   173

entire being: I must comprehend it, appreciate it, be moved by it, enjoy it—not only do it."

The first *mitzvah* bespeaks the nature of all *mitzvot*. Thus, the process of "consecrating the new month" expressly incorporates both these approaches, as both are integral to the essence and function of the *mitzvah*.

To sanctify the new month, the *sanhedrin* studies the movements of celestial bodies so that they can predict when and where the new moon will make its monthly appearance. This underscores the need to involve our human faculties in our implementation of the *mitzvot*. For if the *mitzvah* is to sanctify the physical reality, it must be effected within and by the physical reality, not imposed upon it as something disconnected from its laws and *modus operandi*. If man is a rational being who charts his way through life by what his senses perceive and what his mind deduces, then his observance of the *mitzvot* must also incorporate these most basic aspects of his being. Otherwise, his implementation of the divine will would remain a "spiritual" endeavor, confined to the ethereal reaches of his soul, with little or no bearing on his everyday existence.

On the other hand, the first *mitzvah* also requires the testimony of two witnesses and the absolute validation that the Torah empowers them to confer on what they testify to. This underscores another dimension to the *mitzvah*: the *mitzvah* as the suprarational will of G-d. While it is important to involve our humanity in our *mitzvah* observance, we must never lose sight of what a *mitzvah* is—a divine institution that transcends the human even as it pervades it.

Therein lies the lesson of *eidut*. By all means, examine your witnesses' credentials; by all means, check and double-check their story. But, beyond a certain point, you must accept their word unequivocally. By all means, make your mission in life *your* journey, *your* quest. But no human investigation can attain the absolute. To achieve truth in your life, you must also surrender to the divine will, the ultimate arbiter and empowerer of truth.[7]

---

7   This is the deeper significance of the fact that, unlike most other *mitzvot*, which the Torah prefaces by the standard "G-d spoke to Moses, saying," the *mitzvah* of consecrating the new month is described (in Exodus 12:1) as having been communicated to both Moses and Aaron. In the cosmic marriage between G-d and Israel, Moses, the communicator of G-d's will to man, is described as the "best man" of the divine groom (*sushvinin d'malka*); Aaron the High Priest, chief representative of the community of Israel in their service of G-d, is described as the "bridesmaid" (*sushvinin d'matrunita*)—the one who escorts the bride Israel to her nuptial union with G-d. Moses thus embodies the bestowal of absolute truth from Above, while Aaron represents the human effort to seek the divine (*Zohar* 1:266a). In its account of the first *mitzvah*, the Torah deems it necessary to emphasize both the human and divine dimensions of the endeavor to sanctify our world.

THE
MONTHLY
BRIDGE

The head of the month of _____ will be on the upcoming _____. May G-d renew it for us, and for all His people the house of Israel, to life and to peace, to happiness and to joy, to salvation and to consolation, and let us say: Amen.

Siddur, text for the "Blessing of the Month"

Viewed from the perspective of Torah, the seemingly homogenous span of time is revealed as a complex, multi-hued mosaic. The hour, the day, the week, the month, the year, the millennium—these are not arbitrary grids imposed on time to make it more "manageable," but demarcations intrinsic to its very nature, each defining an area of time with its own characteristics and qualities.

Thus we learn that the seven days of the week are embodiments of the seven divine attributes which define G-d's involvement with our reality, as established in the original seven days of creation.[1] We also learn that the twelve hours of the day, and the twelve months of the year, correspond to the twelve configurations of the divine name, which serve as channels for various divine energies that

---

[1] As are the seven years of the *shemittah* cycle, the seven *shemittot* of the *yovel* cycle, and the seven millennia of history; see *The Seventh Element* on pp. 77–88 above, and *Twilight* on pp. 139–147 above.

vitalize our existence and shape our lives.[2] The same applies to all time designations employed by the Torah: As G-d's blueprint for creation,[3] the Torah does not merely relegate certain observances and experiences to certain times, but, in doing so, the Torah also describes the nature and structure of time as forged by its Creator.

THE MONTH

The idea that each month of the year is the embodiment of a distinct spiritual quality provides a unique perspective on the Jewish calendar.

The calendar is commonly regarded as an expanse of hundreds of ordinary days "dotted" with festivals and dates of special import. In truth, however, the festivals are not islands of specialness in a sea of vapid time, but expressions of the spiritual character of their respective months. The eight days of Passover represent an intensification of the quality of the month of *Nissan*, the month of redemption; Purim is a one-day eruption of the unbridled joy that characterizes the month of *Adar*; the awe of Rosh Hashanah and Yom Kippur, and the joy and unity experienced on Sukkot, are various elements in the "coronation" of G-d as king of the universe, which is the theme of the month of *Tishrei*; and so on.

In other words, the twelve months of the calendar are twelve time-qualities which flow into each other, each with its unique personality and character. The festivals are the peaks and plateaus of these time-qualities — points at which a particular month's properties achieve a greater intensity and emphasis.

---

2   The Hebrew letters which spell the ineffable name of G-d have twelve possible configurations.

3   *Midrash Rabbah, Bereishit* 1:2.

THE MONTH (4)

THE LINK

The last Shabbat of each month is *Shabbat mevarchim hachodesh*—the "Shabbat that blesses the month." On this Shabbat, a special prayer is recited which names the coming month, identifies the day (or days) of its *Rosh Chodesh*,[4] and beseeches G-d to "renew it... to life and to peace, to gladness and to joy, to deliverance and to consolation."[5] According to chassidic teaching, the "blessing of the month" evokes the flow of sustenance and spiritual energy for the coming month.

Thus, the final days of each month form a juncture in the terrain of time in which two time-qualities overlap. For example, when the *Rosh Chodesh* of the month of *Elul* falls on Tuesday and Wednesday, its *Shabbat Mevarchim* is on the 27th of *Av*. As such, it is an integral part of the month of *Av*, a time-segment whose quality is mourning and consolation—mourning over the destruction of the Holy Temple and the breakdown in our relationship with G-d that this represents, and consolation in the potential for renewal that lies in every regression.[6] On the other hand, it is also the Shabbat that calls forth the qualities of the coming month of *Elul*—a month characterized by divine compassion and intimacy with G-d.[7]

4　Each month begins with either one or two days of *Rosh Chodesh* ("head of the month"). If the previous month had 30 days, then the 30th of the previous month and the first of the new month serve as the new month's *Rosh Chodesh*.

5　It is also customary to announce the exact moment of the *molad ha-levanah* ("birth of the moon") that marks the beginning of the coming month.

6　Thus the 9th of *Av* is both the day of the Temple's destruction and the birthday of Moshiach (see Jerusalem Talmud, *Berachot* 2:4). Also see *The Day of the Breaking of the Ax* in vol. 3 of this series, pp. 275–284

7　See our chapter on *Elul* in vol. 3 of this series, pp. 295–313.

The same is true of every *Shabbat Mevarchim*: Rooted in one month and time-quality, it evokes the time-quality of the following month, stimulating the flow of spiritual energy that saturates the next of the twelve time-segments that comprise the calendar year.

THE LESSON

Therein lies a lesson in how we are to experience and utilize the various time periods of our lives.

Often, we reach a point in our lives at which we are inspired to "turn over a new leaf": to reassess our past, and readjust, or even radically transform, our prior vision and approach to life. All too often, this is accompanied with a break from the past, a disavowal of all prior achievement; it is as if all we have done up to this point must be eradicated to give way to our "new" self.

But as the monthly *Shabbat Mevarchim* teaches us, different and even antithetical qualities of time form a chain in which each link is an outgrowth of its predecessor. Yes, a new year, month, week, day, hour, or moment must always provoke us to a new understanding, a new feeling, a new achievement; the very fact that we have passed from one time frame to another means that we must exploit the new potential implicit in this new environment. At the same time, however, we must appreciate how each new moment is "blessed" by the moment before, which nourishes and enriches its very different neighbor with its own qualities and achievements.

CHAPTER FIVE

The Year and the Seasons

Change and Repetition

The significance of the solar year in Jewish time is the subject of our fifth chapter. Its first essay, *A Seasoned Life,* defines the year as a condensed version of the entire range of experiences and achievements that comprise a lifetime. *A Rising Mist* dwells on the year's division in Torah law and thought into two six-month segments—the "season of the sun" and the "season of rains"—and the manner in which these are reflected in our inner, spiritual calendar. *Agricultural Man* gleans insights from the relationship of the annual cycle of the Jewish festivals to the cycle of agricultural life.

A SEASONED LIFE

Furthermore for all the days of the earth
seed and harvest
and cold and heat
and summer and winter
and day and night
shall not cease.

Genesis 8:22

The year is a microcosm of life. The bud and bloom of youth, the fruitfulness of maturity, the autumn of one's later years, the winter of old age—all find expression in the annual seasons. The year includes mundane workdays and holy *Shabbatot*; masculine solar cycles and feminine lunar orbits;[1] and, of course, the *mo'adim*, the "appointments in time" that the festivals represent, each a fountainhead of its particular quality—freedom on Passover, joy on Sukkot, etc.[2] The year incorporates the full spectrum of human experience; the next year can only repeat its cycles and phases, albeit on the higher elevation of accumulated acumen and achievement.

Hence the Hebrew word for "year," *shanah,* which, paradoxically, means both "change" and "repetition." The year embodies all changes and transitions of life—which each annual cycle repeats. Essentially, we live for one year, and then relive our lives for as

---

[1]   See *Jewish Time* on pp. 195–202 below, and *G-d on the Moon*, pp. 160–166 above.

[2]   See *Appointments in Time* on pp. 38–45 above.

many times as we are enabled. At the same time, this "repetition" is conducted on the higher level to which a year's worth of maturity and achievement have elevated us.[3]

This is the deeper significance of the fact that the *etrog* (citron fruit), which represents the *tzaddik* (perfectly righteous person) among the "four kinds" taken on the festival of Sukkot, is described by the Torah as "the fruit that dwells in its tree from year to year."[4] The perfection of the *tzaddik* is expressed by the fact that he or she is a person who weathers all changes and fluctuations; whose integrity, growth, and connection with his or her source are not compromised by any of life's vacillations.

PERFECT VESSEL

On the last day of his life, Moses says to the children of Israel, "I am one hundred and twenty years old today."[5] The sages comment:

> *Today my days and years were fulfilled; on this day I was born, and on this day I will die... This is to teach us that G-d fulfills the years of the righteous to the day and to the month, as it is written, "I shall fulfill the number of your days."*[6]

Moses was born on the seventh day of the month of *Adar*, and passed away on the same date. This phenomenon repeats itself

---

3   In the words of Rabbi Schneur Zalman of Liadi: "Each year there descends from On High a new and renewed light that has never yet shone, which illuminates... all worlds, supernal and terrestrial" (*Tanya, Igeret HaKodesh* 14).

4   See *The Four Mysteries of King Solomon* in Vol. 2 of this series, pp. 86–94.

5   Deuteronomy 31:2.

6   Exodus 23:26; Talmud, *Rosh Hashanah* 11a; Rashi to Deuteronomy 31:2.

THE YEAR AND THE SEASONS (1)   183

throughout Jewish history, which records a number of righteous
individuals whose date of passing is the same as their birth date.

The world we inhabit has both a spiritual content and a physical vessel. While these are two faces of one reality, not always is
the one a precise mirror of the other. Thus there are many righteous men and women whose lives were "fulfilled" in the spiritual
sense—the potential in each of their days and moments was optimally realized[7]—yet this "fullness" did not find expression in the
calendar dates of their birth and passing. Physically, their final year
on earth was "incomplete." But then there were those great men
and women whose physical life was a perfect reflection of its spiritual content, evidenced in the fact that "G-d fulfills their years to
the day and to the month."

---

7   See *Garments for the Soul* on pp. 60–63, above.

A
RISING
MIST

*And no plant of the field was yet in the earth,
and no herb of the field had yet grown; for
G-d Almighty had not caused it to rain upon
the earth, and there is naught a man to work
the land.*

*And a mist would rise from the earth, and
water the surface of the land.*

Genesis 2:5–6

In the Land of Israel, the rains are confined to the half-year from *Tishrei* to *Nissan* (roughly, October to March). This six-month period is therefore referred to by the Talmud as the "season of rains" (*yemot hageshamim*), while the six months from *Nissan* to *Tishrei* (April to September) are called the "season of the sun" (*yemot hachamah*).

The calendar is more than a measure of time; it is a cycle that charts our inner life and our relationship with our Creator. This spiritual cycle is also comprised of two basic parts—a "season of the sun," and a "season of rains."

SUNLIGHT AND RAIN

Sunlight and rain are both critical to the sustaining of life on earth. Indeed, there is a certain similarity in the manner in which these two sources of nourishment are bestowed upon us—both "rain"

THE YEAR AND THE SEASONS (2)   185

down upon the earth from above, drenching it with energy or
moisture. In both cases, we seem quiescent recipients to a shower-
ing of blessing from the heavens.

But a closer examination reveals a significant difference between them. While sunlight is a unilateral gift from above, rain
originates as moisture which rises from the earth, forms clouds,
and returns as life-giving waters. So the earth is not, in truth, a
passive beneficiary of the rain falling from the heavens; it is she
who generates it in the first place, raising columns of mist from her
oceans and lakes to water the soil of her land masses.

The earth, of course, could not do this on her own. It is the sun
who stimulates the release and ascent of her watery stores; it is the
sun who drives the weather patterns which carry them through the
atmosphere and impel them earthward. In other words, the sun,
ultimately, is the force behind both sunlight and rain. But the sun's
nurture of life on earth takes two forms: a) nourishment which
the earth simply absorbs from her benevolent provider, such as the
sun's light- and warmth-purveying rays; and b) nourishment, such
as rain, which the earth generates herself, with the sun serving as
the catalyst that wakens her potential for self-nurture and assists
in its realization.

All of the above also applies to the "miniature world"[1] that is
the soul of man. Here, too, there is "sunlight" and "rain." Here, too,
the soul is dependent upon her "sun" for both, yet differs in her
relationship with these two purveyors of her nourishment.

Ultimately, everything we possess, including our potential to
initiate and create, is granted us from Above. Yet G-d sustains our
inner lives in two ways: a) with direct and unilateral bestowal of

---

[1]   *Midrash Tanchuma, Pikudei* 3; cf. Ecclesiastes 3:11: "Also the world He
       has placed within their hearts."

enlightenment and experience ("sunlight"); and b) by enabling and assisting us to gravitate upward in our own search for truth and meaning in life, and thereby generate a spiritual nurture of our own making ("rain").

Both divine gifts are crucial to the spiritual life of the soul. On the one hand, we recognize our inherent limitations and deficiencies. We understand that if there is to be anything that is absolute and transcendent in our lives, we must open ourselves to a higher truth—a truth to which we can relate only as a passive recipient, for it is beyond anything we could possibly generate by ourselves.

At the same time, however, human nature dictates that we identify more with what we ourselves have achieved: that something earned is more appreciated than a gift, that an idea independently conceived is more meaningful than a teaching from the greatest master. For an experience to become "real" to us—for it to be grafted into our nature and personality—it must stem from within.

The real or the ideal? Mine or more? We need them both. Indeed, the tension between these two needs is crucial to our growth in all areas—intellectual, emotional, or spiritual.

SEASONS OF THE SOUL

In the cycle of the Jewish year, the six months from *Nissan* to *Tishrei* are the "season of the sun," and the *Tishrei* to *Nissan* months are our "season of rains."

During the "season of the sun," we celebrate and reexperience the great unilateral acts of divine involvement in our destiny: the Exodus on Passover, when G-d descended to Egypt "to take for Himself a nation from the womb of a nation, amidst trials, signs,

THE YEAR AND THE SEASONS (2)   187

wonders, and battles"[2]; the giving of the Torah on Shavuot, when
"G-d came down on Mount Sinai"[3] to grant us His blueprint for
life and our charter as His "kingdom of priests and a holy nation."[4]

The "Season of Rains," on the other hand, is a half-year characterized by human endeavor and initiative. The month of *Tishrei*—
the month of Rosh Hashanah, Yom Kippur, and the ten days of
repentance—is a time of *teshuvah*, of soul-searching and self-improvement. The "season of rains" also contains the two "rabbinical"
festivals of the Jewish year—Chanukah (*Kislev* 25 to *Tevet* 2[5]) and
Purim (*Adar* 14). Unlike the biblical festivals, which were unilaterally commanded by G-d, these are humanly initiated festivals, instituted as *our* response to the milestones in our relationship with
G-d which they commemorate.[6]

Another winter festival is the "New Year of Chassidism" celebrated on the 19th of *Kislev*.[7] The teachings of chassidism emphasize the need for intellectual appreciation and emotional experience in our fulfillment of the *mitzvot* (as opposed to mere

---

2   Deuteronomy 4:34.

3   Exodus 19:20.

4   Ibid., v. 6.

5   Or 3, depending on whether *Kislev* has 29 or 30 days—see further on
    in text.

6   See *Accumulating Lights* in vol. 2, pp. 194–203 of this series.

7   On *Kislev* 19, 5559 (1798), Rabbi Schneur Zalman of Liadi, founder of
    Chabad chassidism, was released from Czarist prison after being ex-
    onerated of charges leveled against him and the chassidic movement.
    Rabbi Schneur Zalman saw these events as a reflection of what was
    transpiring Above—his arrest as the result of a heavenly indictment
    against his revelation of the most intimate secrets of the Torah, and
    his subsequent release as signifying his exoneration in the heavenly
    court and its endorsement of the continued dissemination of chassid-
    ic teaching. *Kislev* 19 therefore marks the "birth" of chassidism—the
    point at which it emerged into the world to grow and develop as an
    integral part of Torah and Jewish life.

mechanical observance of the divine commandments). Chassidism thus belongs to the "rain" area of our spiritual lives—our capacity for involvement and initiative in our relationship with G-d.

Sometimes More, Sometimes Less

The Jewish calendar is based upon the lunar cycle, with the beginning of each month falling within a day or two of the new moon. Since the moon completes its orbit of the earth every 29.5 days, the Jewish month alternates between 29 and 30 days. A thirty-day month is called a *malei* ("full" month), and a twenty-nine-day month is called a *chasser* ("lacking" month).

Generally speaking, the months follow a set pattern: *Nissan* is always "full," *Iyar* always "lacking," *Sivan* "full," *Tammuz* "lacking," and so on. However, two months, the months of *Cheshvan* and *Kislev* (the second and third months after *Tishrei*), have no fixed length: in certain years both are "full," in other years both are "lacking," and in others still, *Cheshvan* is "lacking" and *Kislev* is "full."

In other words, the summer months are fixed and unvarying, while the months of the "season of rains" are subject to changes and fluctuations.

In this, too, our calendar reflects the dynamics of the seasons of the soul. The "sunlight" aspect of our spiritual lives is fixed and unvarying. When we surrender ourselves to higher truth, we also surrender our human frailties and inconsistencies. We surrender to what is infinite, perfect, and unequivocal, and what we receive is likewise infinite, perfect, and unequivocal.

But when we turn to our "rainmaking" self, our initiatives and achievements are subject to the rises and falls of a finite, imperfect self. This is a season with fluctuating months, sometimes "lacking," sometimes "full," reflecting the vacillating nature of everything human.

Therein lies the weakness of our rainy season as well as its strength. By all objective criteria, this is the "lesser" half of our internal cycle, plagued by the instabilities and deficiencies of the human state. But it is also our more flexible half, where a lack might be transformed into a gain and a vulnerability exploited as a source of blessing.

AGRICULTURAL MAN

Three pilgrimage-festivals you shall celebrate for Me each year.

Keep the festival of matzot... at the season of the month of the barley-ripening...

And the festival of the reaping of the first fruits of your work which you sow in the field.

And the harvest festival at the close of the year, when you gather in your work from the field.

Exodus 23:14–16

The Jewish calendar is closely attuned to the agricultural seasons. The Torah instructs that Passover must coincide with the season of *aviv*, which is broadly defined as "spring" but specifically means the season of the ripening of barley.[1] Shavuot is called "the reaping festival," and coincides with the reaping of the staple crop, wheat; and Sukkot is the "harvest festival," celebrated when the grain, which has been drying in the field all summer, is brought into storage.[2] And then there is the "New Year for Trees" on the 15th of the month of *Shevat* (Tu BiShevat), observed as the first tree blossoms emerge from their winter slumber. Indeed, our calendar goes to great lengths to reconcile its lunar-based months with the solar-based seasons.[3]

---

1 Exodus 23:14 and 34:18; Deuteronomy 16:1; see Exodus 9:31.
2 Exodus 23:16.
3 See *Jewish Time,* on pp. 195–202, below.

THE YEAR AND THE SEASONS (3)

Our forefathers, observing these festivals in the Holy Land three thousand years ago, were primarily an agrarian people. Still, even then there was Levi, the tribe of priests and spiritual leaders; there were also the schoolteachers from the tribe of Simeon, the scholars of Issachar, and the seafaring merchants of Zebulun. Today, a very small percentage of us work the land. But the Torah, G-d's blueprint for creation, transcends differences of time and cultural circumstance, and is deeply relevant to all generations and all societies of history. So what does all this mean to those of us who have never planted a seed or gathered a harvest?

But the very experience of life is agrarian. The soul's descent into physical life, like the planting of a seed, is an investment—a precarious investment at that, given the fact that one's capital erodes significantly before returning a profit. The farmer who sows his field knows that he is taking perfectly good grain—grain with which he could feed his family—and casting it into the soil, where it will decompose and rot. But he also knows that the disintegrating seed will stimulate the earth to yield many times the quantity he has "squandered."

The soul, too, is buried in earth—cast into a body of clay with material drives and desires. It is worse for the wear: Its spiritual senses are dulled, its moral rectitude compromised. But the soul's investment within earth and earthiness stimulates it, and the body and the physical environment in which it has been placed, to a far greater "harvest" than what the soul alone could yield.

The human "farm" includes many and varied crops. On Passover we celebrate the ripening of barley—a grain that serves primarily as animal feed. This represents the development of the animalistic nature with which the soul has been saddled upon its descent into the physical state, but whose passion and intensity surpass anything the spiritual soul can muster for its own spiritual ideals. Properly cultivated and directed, the beast in man proves a priceless resource in the soul's quest to deepen and intensify its bond with its Creator.

On Shavuot, wheat, the staple of the human diet, is harvested. This represents the development of the "human" element in man, the soul's own spiritual potential, made more potent and bountiful by the challenge of material life. And so it is with the other agricultural festivals on our calendar, such as the "internalization" of the harvest on Sukkot[4] or the element of "delight" in life represented by Tu BeShevat's fruit blossoms[5]: Each embodies another aspect of the soul's saga as buried seed, sprouting shoot, and gainful harvest.

---

4 See *The Easy Mitzvah* in vol. 2, pp. 81–85 of this series.
5 See *Fruit for Thought* in vol. 2, pp. 221–227 of this series.

CHAPTER SIX

The Leap Year
The Synthesis of Solar and Lunar Time

The lunar cycle, which generates the Jewish month, and the solar cycle, which drives the annual seasons, are asymmetrical. The Jewish "leap year" or *shanah me'uberet* (literally, "pregnant year") is the means by which these two divergent time systems are synthesized.

The deeper significance of this dissonance, and of the manner in which it is bridged in our consciousness and in our daily lives, is the subject of the two essays in this chapter, *Jewish Time* and *A Complete Year*.

JEWISH TIME

He made the moon for its appointed times; the
sun knows its setting. Psalms 104:19

ost of us believe that we have some sort of cohesive approach to life, some consistent way of dealing with the countless decisions, great and small, which face us every day. Yet there is a dichotomy to our very selves which extends to our most basic instincts and drives. Every person will tell you that he or she has a set of inviolable principles, a canon of axiomatic laws which govern his or her life. In the same breath this person will maintain that he or she is a revolutionary at heart, that the old must give way to the new, that one most never become mired in the morass of past convictions; that life is never black and white but a gray mass of uncertainty and so it ought to be, for error is the mother of invention and regret begets rebirth.

Which of these instincts should we cultivate? Should we anchor our lives to a bedrock of moral absolutes and time-tested truths, or seek out what is innovative and creative in our souls? Should we venerate the past or worship the future? Should we cling to our roots or fly with the wind?

THE TIMES OF OUR LIVES

A calendar is more than the way in which we measure and calculate our days: It is how we define and experience time. If you wish to know the soul of a people, study their calendar. It is no coincidence that the very first *mitzvah* given to the Jewish people, commanded to us even before our exodus from Egypt was to make us a nation, specified the formula by which to set the cycles of Jewish time.

How does the Jew categorize time? The primary features of our calendar, as with many other calendars, are the month and the year. But the Jewish calendar also insists that these two time-cycles be determined by two completely different time-markers: the month by the phases of the moon, and the year by the cycle of seasons created by the sun.

The Jewish month (as G-d instructs Moses in Exodus 12:2[1]) commences with the new moon. The moon orbits the earth in slightly more than 29 days, 12 hours and 44 minutes; so the next new moon will be visible 29 or 30 nights later, marking the start of the next month. Hence the Hebrew word for month, *chodesh*, which means "new" or "renewal": The Jewish month is born with the new moon, grows with it, dwindles and ceases with it, and is born anew with its renewal.

The Jewish year, however, must keep pace with the solar seasons. "Keep the month of spring," commands the Torah, "and make [in it] a Passover-festival for G-d."[2] In other words, the Hebrew month of *Nissan*, the 15th of which is the festival of Passover, must also be "the month of spring." This means that the vernal equinox (the point when the sun's center crosses the equator from south to north—March 20 on the Gregorian calendar) must always fall sometime in the month of *Nissan*.

This is more difficult to achieve than it might seem. The annual solar cycle is slightly less than 365.25 days. How can this time

---

1 See Rashi's commentary on verse.
2 Deuteronomy 16:1.

THE LEAP YEAR (1)   197

span be subdivided into months of 29 or 30 days? Twelve lunar months will add up to approximately 354 days (the actual number may be 353, 354, or 355). This leaves us more than 11 days short of a solar year. If the Jewish year were to consist of twelve such months, there would be 34 lunar "years" in the course of only 33 seasonal cycles. The month of *Nissan* would travel backward through the seasons, only occasionally returning to its mandated place as "the month of spring."

How are we to fulfill both these requirements? Should we keep the month and the year as two distinct time-cycles (as we do the 7-day week and 29–30 day month) which run independently of each other? If we did that, a year would consist of twelve months and eleven days; most years would begin and end in the middle of a month. But the Torah specifically instructs otherwise. In Exodus 12:2 — the very same verse from which we derive that the Jewish month is to commence with the birth of the moon — Moses is instructed: "This month (*Nissan*) shall be unto you the head of the months; it shall be unto you the first of the months of the year." As the Talmud points out, the second half of this verse seems entirely superfluous. Why the redundant phrasing? Explains the Talmud: This is to emphasize that our months are to be "the months of the year" — that the year is to consist wholly of complete months.[3]

In other words, the Torah is telling us that each day of our lives is to be contextualized within both lunar and solar frameworks. Furthermore, it is also insisting that we incorporate these two

---

3   Talmud, *Megillah* 5a. Another verse — Numbers 11:20, which speaks of "a month of days" — teaches us that the month should consist of full days, and full days only. Thus, we alternate 29-day and 30-day months, instead of making all months a uniform 29 days, 12 hours and 44 minutes.

disparate cycles into a single calendar, while preserving the integrity of each!

How do we to reconcile the asynchronous rhythms of sun and moon? With what is probably the most complex calendar ever employed by man. The Jewish year follows a 19-year cycle, and comes in six different sizes—353, 354, 355, 383, 384, or 385 days. A month is always 29 or 30 days; but the year consists of either 12 months (years 1, 2, 4, 5, 7, 9, 10, 12, 13, 15, 16, and 18 of the cycle) or 13 months (years 3, 6, 8, 11, 14, 17 and 19). Thus, by the third year of the cycle, when 36 lunar months would have set us back almost 34 days in relation to the annual solar cycle, we add a thirteenth month to the year—thus "safeguarding the month of spring" and ensuring that *Nissan* will not fall before the vernal equinox. Three years later, now some 38 days behind, we repeat the process. Another two years accumulate a deficit of approximately 29 days, so that the thirteenth month of the eighth year actually sets us slightly ahead. And so it goes. At the conclusion of each 19-year cycle, we will always be realigned with the solar year.

Thus, the marriage of sun and moon, so divergent in the paths they cut across the heavens, is actually effected on earth, in our organization and experience of time.[4]

---

4   Today, we work this out according to the preset formula outlined above. When the *sanhedrin* (the highest court of Torah law) functioned in the Holy Land, the human involvement in the reconciliation of solar and lunar time was even more pronounced. The court would hear the testimony of witnesses who had sighted the new moon; they would then proclaim the onset of a new month, and dispatch messengers to all Jewish communities to inform them of the date. They would also calculate the seasons, and proclaim a 13-month leap year as the need arose. Although the *sanhedrin* made use of astronomic calculations in order to corroborate the testimony they heard, Torah law insists that, whenever possible, we employ a "hands on" approach—specifically "consecrating" each new month based on the physical sightings by witnesses,

THE HUMAN UNIVERSE

But why does it have to be so complicated?

If solar and lunar time are so disinclined to concur, why go to such lengths to reconcile them? And if, for whatever reason, it is important that the two cycles should flow in concert, why *are* they so different? Surely the Creator could have set their clocks to a more compatible beat.

And yet, this is the essence of Jewish time: to reconcile this dichotomy, to integrate these opposites.

What is more regular than the fireball of energy that warms and lights our planet each dawn? "As sure as tomorrow's sunrise," goes the telling cliché. In a world plagued by uncertainty, thank G-d there is *something* we can rely on.

If the sun is a paragon of consistency, its nocturnal counterpart is the essence of flux. The moon often arrives only several hours into the night, and is usually only partly there. One or two nights a month it fails to show up altogether. But we cannot but admire the hardy little fellow. How frustrating it must be, when the shifting alignments of your source of light and the planet you are charged to illuminate keeps on compromising your mission! Yet the moon doesn't give up. Time and again it rises from oblivion, nightly growing from its humble sliver of a beginning to luminous fullness—a fullness all the more glorious for its painstaking triumph over deficiency. But then—alas!—perfection, for the moon, is a precarious state. Soon it succumbs to the setbacks and declines of lunar life. Yet it never fails to rebound, to recreate itself from nothing, to again scale the peak of its full luminary potential.

---

and individually setting each leap year (see *Locating the Moon* on pp. 167–174, above).

"Man is a miniature universe."[5] Man, too, possesses both a "solar" and "lunar" self—the capacity for unequivocal commitment, as well as the wax and wane of creativity. And yet, despite the tremendous disparity between the two, we recognize that, ultimately, there is no contradiction. Not only do they both orbit in the same universe, they complement and fulfill each other. At times, the lunar element will lag behind; at times, it will overreach its solar mate; but in the end, they will always converge within a cohesive whole.

Three Examples: Mitzvot, Prayer, and Torah

The duality, twinship, and union of the solar and the lunar paradigms is present in every area of our lives. In this essay, we will apply it to three signature features of Jewish life: the *mitzvot* (divine commandments), prayer, and the study of Torah.

An important principle of Judaism is the immutability of G-d's commandments; in the words of Deuteronomy 4:2: "Do not add to what I command you, neither shall you diminish from it." We do not invent new *mitzvot*, or retire those which the human mind may deem "archaic"; for we know that they represent the will of G-d, and are thus as timeless, as absolute, and as intrinsically unfathomable as their Conceiver. At the same time, with each and every *mitzvah* we create a distinctly personal bond with our Creator. A *mitzvah* is the bridge between man and G-d—an act that creates a relationship between its divine commander and its human implementer—and a relationship, by definition, is bilateral. So we bring our mortal selves to the relationship: our finite comprehension of the *mitzvah*'s significance, our subjective emotional

---

5   *Midrash Tanchuma, Pikudei* 3.

response to it, our innovative ways of enhancing and beautifying the object and the experience of the *mitzvah*.

Thrice daily, we stand before G-d in prayer. We mouth the very same words with which so many others, throughout the generations and across the globe, have addressed the Creator. This inviolable text, composed by our sages and based on the manner in which G-d Himself gave license to human speech to describe and address Him, ensures that our prayers are a communication with G-d rather than a projection of our own fanciful image of what He is or ought to be. But at the same time, prayer is a highly personal dialogue between the individual and his G-d. Thus, there are sections of the prayers devoted to our personal needs, in which we are free to express them in our own words.[6] And the "soul" of prayer — the meditation which precedes it, the emotions which saturate it, the melody which carries it aloft — makes the seemingly static text of prayer an individualized and innovative articulation of our soul's yearning to cleave to her Maker.

The Torah is the suprarational wisdom of G-d. Thus, a basic tenet of the Jewish faith is that "This Torah shall never be changed"[7] and that "Everything that a faithful student will discover has already been given to Moses at Sinai."[8] At the same time, we are charged to "increase the Torah and strengthen it"[9] with our own expositions and extrapolations upon its teachings. For the

---

6   For example, it is forbidden to diverge from the text of the first three and final three sections of the *amidah*, which describe G-d's relationship to us and express our gratitude to Him. But the 13 middle sections are appeals to the Almighty for our personal needs (health, sustenance, etc.), and allow for a personal articulation of specific requests, particularly in the 16th section (*shomei'ah tefilah*).

7   The ninth of Maimonides' "Thirteen Fundamental Principles of Faith."

8   Jerusalem Talmud, *Pe'ah* 2:4.

9   Talmud, *Chulin* 66b.

Almighty desired that His revealed wisdom be the product of a partnership between divine revelation and human genius; that the mortal mind of man be the one to translate and apply His word to His world.[10]

The Jew does not make light of the gulf which separates faithfulness from creativity and tradition from innovation. We know that the dichotomy between sun and moon cannot be reconciled in a year, or two, or ten; indeed, a hasty "solution" will always mean that one or the other has been compromised. The absolutes which underlie and guide our life, and the personal struggles and triumphs which pervade it, are two distinct, even contrary, realms. And yet, as our solar/lunar calendar demonstrates, we can simultaneously inhabit, and ultimately reconcile, both these worlds.

---

10 See *The Mathematics of Marriage* in vol. 3 of this series, pp. 187–192.

A COMPLETE YEAR

There are two paths of the divine light: the path of the direct light, and the path of the rebounding light.   Eitz Chaim 6:6

S etting the Jewish calendar is a complex task, as its two central components derive from two natural cycles which do not easily lend themselves to synchronization. The month derives from the moon's 29.5 day orbit of the earth; the year, from the 365.25-day solar cycle. The problem is that 12 lunar months add up to 354 days—11.25 days short of the solar year.

Most calendars deal with this discrepancy by simply ignoring one or the other of the celestial timekeepers. For example, the Gregorian calendar (which has attained near-universal status) is completely solar-based. Its 365 days are divided into 12 segments of 30 or 31 days, but these "months" have lost all connection with their original association with the moon. There are also calendars (such as the Moslem calendar) which are exclusively lunar-based, with months that are faithfully attuned to the phases of the moon. Twelve such months are regarded as a year, but these "years" bear no relation to the solar cycle (a given date in such a calendar will, in certain years, fall in the midst of summer and, in other years, in the dead of winter).

The Jewish calendar is unique in that it endeavors to reconcile the solar and lunar time-streams. By employing a complex 19-year cycle, in which months alternate between 29 and 30 days and years alternate between 12 and 13 months, the Jewish calendar sets its months by the moon and its years by the sun, incorporating both lunar time and solar time into a single system while preserving the integrity of each.

For the sun and the moon represent the two sides of a dichotomy which characterizes virtually every aspect of our existence—a dichotomy whose differences we must respect and preserve, even as we integrate them into a cohesive approach to life.

LIGHT SOURCE AND REFLECTOR

On previous occasions, we have explored various aspects of the solar/lunar polarity: the contrast between the surety and consistency of tradition on the one hand, and the yen for flux, innovation, and creativity on the other;[1] and the male/female dynamic, which imbues us with the passion to give and bestow on the one hand, and the capacity to accept and receive on the other.[2] In this essay, we will dwell on another aspect of this cosmic duality: the twinship of spirit and matter.

The spiritual and the material are often equated with light and darkness. Indeed, a number of religions and moral-systems regard the spiritual as enlightened, virtuous, and desirable, and the physical-material side of life as belonging to the "forces of darkness." The Torah, however, has a different conception of spirituality and materiality—a conception embodied by the solar/lunar model.

The sun is a luminous body while the moon is a dark lump of matter. Yet both are luminaries.[3] Both serve us as sources of light;

---

1   See previous essay, *Jewish Time*, pp. 195–202.
2   See *G-d on the Moon,* on pp. 160–166, above.
3   See citation from Genesis 1:14–16 on p. 160, above.

the difference is that the sun's light is self-generated, while the moon illuminates by receiving and reflecting the light of the sun.

Spirituality is a direct effusion of divine light. When studying Torah, praying, or performing a *mitzvah*, we are in direct contact with G-d; we are manifestly revealing His truth in the world. But not every thought that we think relates directly to the divine wisdom of the Torah; not every word we utter is a prayer; not every deed we perform is a *mitzvah*. G-d created us as material creatures, compelled to devote a considerable part of our time and energies to the satisfaction of a multitude of material needs. By necessity and design, much of our life is "lunar," comprised of the "dark matter" of non-holy pursuits.

Dark matter, however, need not entail an absence of light. It can be a moon—dark matter serving as a conduit of light. It's all a matter of positioning. The moon is dark matter positioned in such a way as to convey the light of the sun to places to which it cannot flow directly from its source. Placed in the proper context, our material pursuits can serve as facilitators of divine truth to places which, in and of themselves, are not in the "direct line" of spirituality and holiness.

Our lives include both a solar and a lunar track—a course of spiritual achievement as well as a path of material endeavor. These orbits do not run in tandem; at times they clash, giving rise to dissonance and conflict. The simple solution would be to follow a single route, choosing an exclusively solar or exclusively lunar path through life. But the Jewish calendar does not avail itself of the simple solution.

Our calendar insists that we incorporate both systems in our time-trajectory: that we should cultivate a solar self—thoughts and feelings, deeds and endeavors, moments and occasions of consummate holiness and spirituality; and that at the same time we should also develop a lunar personality—a material life which reflects and projects our other, spiritual self. The result is a "complete year" in which lunar and solar time converge.

CHAPTER SEVEN

Confluence
Junctures in Time

"Everything is by divine providence," taught the founder of chassidism, Rabbi Israel Baal Shem Tov. "If a leaf is turned over by a breeze, it is only because this has been specifically ordained by G-d to serve a particular function within the purpose of creation."

"Everything a Jew sees or hears," the Baal Shem Tov also taught, "should serve as a lesson in how to better serve the Creator." The latter teaching is actually a derivative of the first. If every aspect of every event is by divine providence, then the fact that one witnessed it or heard about it must also be of significance.

The Rebbe, who made the doctrine of "specific divine providence" (*hashgachah peratit*) a central pillar of his teachings, would often comment that if such is the case with every worldly event, how much more so is it the case with all that pertains to Torah and Jewish life. Certainly, no phenomenon in this realm can be attributed to chance or happenstance. Rather, it must be examined for the wealth of lessons and insights it can yield.

The Rebbe would regularly apply this principle to the "coincidence" of the various Torah-ordained time systems of which every day and hour is a product. At almost every occasion on which he delivered a public address, the Rebbe would note the particular lessons to be derived from the unique time-juncture created by the specific day of the week, day of the month, proximity to a particular festival or important date in Jewish history, and so on.

This chapter includes three examples from the many hundreds of similar lessons the Rebbe wove.

The essay *Three Times Three* examines the uniqueness of a year in which the two days of Rosh Hashanah fall on Thursday and Friday. It also touches on the phenomenon of "the second festival day of the Diaspora" and the mystical concept of "conical time."

Shammai's Shabbat discusses the case of a two-day *Rosh Chodesh* ("head of the month") for the month of Elul which occurs on Shabbat and Sunday. *The Hard Life* analyzes the connection between the Torah readings *Matot* and *Masei*, and the time of year in which they are read as part of the annual Torah-reading cycle, particularly in the case when the format of the calendar year dictates that these two sections be combined as a single reading.

THREE TIMES THREE

Three times create a chazakah *(legal status quo).*
Talmud, Yevamot 24b

S*hanah*, the Hebrew word for "year," means both "repetition" and "change." Indeed, the Jewish year exemplifies how a faithful repetition of something might also profoundly differ from it.

Each annual journey through the Jewish calendar follows the same roadmap and passes through the same landmarks. Each embarks from a two-day Rosh Hashanah, immerses in the awe of Yom Kippur, enters within the unifying walls of the *sukkah*, dances on Simchat Torah, kindles the lights of Chanukah, is inebriated with joy on Purim, is liberated on Passover, climbs the 49-step "counting of the *omer*" ladder to Shavuot, mourns in the "three weeks," and culminates in the warm embrace of Elul. And yet, how different is each journey from its predecessors! We are a year older, wiser, and holier. What was last year's experience and achievement is this year's norm; now, the challenge is to transcend our last year's self with a more exalted awe, a deeper joy, a more liberated freedom.

Furthermore, the very structure of the Jewish calendar provides us with a different journey each year. The itinerary is the same, the landmarks are affixed to the same points in the roadmap, but there are subtle changes in the terrain. The year might be

CONFLUENCE (1)   211

longer by a month[1] or the month shorter by a day;[2] the Passover
seder, held on a Wednesday night one year, might be conducted on
Shabbat eve on another, and on the night following Shabbat on a
third year, each instance introducing new nuances into our experience of freedom; the grief of Tishah B'Av might be supplanted
by the delight of Shabbat and postponed to the following Sunday;
or the festive meals of Shabbat might be sublimated into fasting
and prayer when the holiest day of the week coincides with Yom
Kippur, the holiest day of the year. Time, for the Jew, is defined by
several incongruent cycles—the weekly cycle set by the seven days
of creation, the monthly cycle set by the phases of the moon, the
annual cycle of the solar seasons—and their ever-varying confer-
ences make for a different calendar each time we repeat the familiar journey through the year.

Triple Header

One example of the unique features a year assumes as a result of its
intersection with the other time-cycles is the case of the year that
opens with a succession of three holy days. This occurs when the
two days of Rosh Hashanah fall on Thursday and Friday, followed
immediately by Shabbat, the weekly day of sacred rest.

In Torah law, a three-time occurrence achieves the status of
chazakah—a "strengthened" or firmly established phenomenon.[3]

---

1   Every two or three years, a thirteenth month is added to the Jewish
    year, in order to keep it in sync with the seasons. See our chapter on
    "The Leap Year" on pp. 193–206, above

2   Most months have a fixed length of either 29 or 30 days. Two months,
    however—*Cheshvan* and *Kislev*—have 29 days in some years and 30
    days in others; see pp. 188 above.

3   Talmud, *Yevamot* 64b; et al.

For example: Since it is considered uncommon behavior for a domesticated beast to attack another animal, this was not an occurrence that the owner might reasonably have foreseen. So if an ox gores another ox, the owner of the attacking ox is absolved from full payment of the damage it inflicted. However, if the ox gores another ox on three different occasions, this becomes the "normal" behavior of this particular beast, and its owner becomes fully responsible for the damage it causes. The ox now has a *chazakah* of violent behavior toward other oxen.

Ordinarily, the holy days in our lives are exceptions to the rule, as opposed to the days devoted to material pursuits, which are the norm. This makes the task of fulfilling the ultimate function of Shabbat and the festivals—which is to carry forth their sanctity and spirituality into the ordinary days of the year—a most difficult and challenging task. We are being called upon to impart an "abnormal" quality to a "normal" day.

But when the year opens with three successive holy days, holiness becomes the norm. A *chazakah* of holiness empowers us to regard the mundane areas of our lives as abnormal, and the sanctity with which we are to imbue them as natural and necessary to our existence.

CONDENSED TIME

The Jewish calendar contains several possibilities for three successive days of holiness (for example: the first two days of Passover can also fall on Thursday and Friday). Yet the particular constellation of two days of Rosh Hashanah followed by Shabbat is unique in several respects.

Firstly, because "Rosh Hashanah" is not merely the year's beginning, but—as a literal translation of the term implies—the "head

CONFLUENCE (1)   213

of the year." This reflects the kabbalistic conception of creation, by which the entirety of time was created by G-d in a single instant; what we experience as "time" is the unfolding of that instant into myriads of particulars, which we then experience as a succession of "moments" aligned one after the other. In other words, G-d did not create the world in one state—its state in the first moment of time—and then allow or compel its development into its state in the next moment, and then the next, and so on; rather, G-d created all states of existence simultaneously. The fact that we relate to these states in terms of "past," "present" and "future" is only because we experience them one at a time, one "after" the other.

This "timeliness," or the fractionalization of creation into so many time-segments, is a feature of our physical world; the higher, more spiritual worlds are less finite, less fragmented. Thus, the *seder hishtalshelut*—the chain of "worlds" that make up the created reality—can be said to resemble a pyramid. At the highest point of the pyramid—the divine act of creation—all of time and history is encapsulated within a single point. At a lower "world" or dimension of reality, the point fans out into seven components (the seven days of creation), each embodying one of the seven millennia of history.[4] In lower worlds, these are further broken down into successively more detailed segments.[5] Finally, in the lowest strata of creation—our physical world—the singular act of creation is broken down into the numerous moments of time that comprise our "reality."

---

4   Cf. Talmud, *Rosh Hashanah* 31a.

5   Thus Rabbi Israel Baal Shem Tov, known for his ability to "ascend" to higher worlds, once forewarned his brother-in-law, Rabbi Gershon Kitever, of an event that was to befall Rabbi Gershon fifteen years later, explaining that he had seen him in the world of *yetzirah*, where many years are encapsulated in a single moment (*Derech Mitzvotecha*, p. 59a).

Nevertheless, we are not completely locked into the moment-bond nature of the physical world. In the calendar He ordained in His Torah, G-d inserted days and moments of higher, more "concentrated" time. Shabbat is not just another day of the week, but a day that encapsulates an entire week in a higher, more spiritual form.[6] The day (or days) of *Rosh Chodesh* ("head of the month") contain the spiritual essence of an entire month. And the forty-eight hours of Rosh Hashanah, the "head of the year," include within them the entire year, in the same way that the head incorporates all of the body's faculties.[7]

This is why everything we do on Rosh Hashanah has a profound effect on the entire year. If we commit ourselves to a certain change in our behavior, it is more easily implemented than if we had made our resolution on any other day. For, in a certain sense, we have already effected this change every day of the year, since they all exist within the "condensed time" of the year's head.

So a *chazakah* of holiness established on Rosh Hashanah is doubly potent, having been established in the days that "head" and encapsulate the entire year.[8]

THE DIVIDEND OF DOUBT

Also unique about the succession of holy days formed when the two days of Rosh Hashanah are followed by Shabbat is the fact

---

6   See section, "The Geometry of Time," in the essay, *The Seventh Element*, on pp. 77–88, above.

7   See *The Neurology of Time* in vol. 2, pp. 5–7 of this series.

8   The third day of this *chazakah* of holiness is also a "Rosh Hashanah" of sorts: As the year's first Shabbat, it encapsulates all the year's *Shabbatot* and, by extension, all of its weekdays (*Pri Eitz Chaim, Shaar Tefilot Rosh Hashanah*, end of chapter 6).

CONFLUENCE (1)   215

that this is the only example of this phenomenon to occur in the Holy Land.

Outside the Land of Israel, the "holy days" of the biblical festivals (Rosh Hashanah, the first day of Sukkot, Shemini Atzeret, the first and last days of Passover, and Shavuot) are all observed for two days. In the Land of Israel, however, only Rosh Hashanah extends for two days, while all other festivals are observed for a single day only.

Historically, this is due to the structure of the Jewish calendar and the process by which its months are set. The Jewish calendar follows the phases of the moon — the night on which the new moon is first visible marks the start of the new month. Originally, the new month was "consecrated" on a month-by-month basis by the *sanhedrin* (highest court of Torah law), based on the testimony of two eyewitnesses who sighted the new moon.[9] Messengers would then be dispatched to all Jewish communities to inform them of the proper date. But the communities outside of the Land of Israel were too distant to receive word of the new month before the festivals. As a result, they fulfilled the laws of each festival for two full days, to ensure that they had observed them on the day mandated by the Torah.

This practice continued until nearly three hundred years after the destruction of the Holy Temple, during which the *sanhedrin* continued to function in the Holy Land under Roman rule. In the year 361 CE, however, Hillel the Second, the then-president of the *sanhedrin*, recognized that the days of the *sanhedrin* were numbered and that soon the dispersion of the Jewish people would reach a point where it would be impossible to maintain contact

---

9   See *The Sixteenth Increment* on pp. 151-159, above; and *Locating the Moon* on pp. 167-174, above.

between all the communities of the Diaspora. He therefore established a calendar system by which the years and months could be calculated in advance. Hillel's *sanhedrin* then "consecrated" all subsequent months until the coming of Moshiach, when the *sanhedrin* will be reestablished.

Today, then, there is no longer any doubt as to the exact date of the biblical festivals. Nevertheless, the practice of observing two days for each festival continues. The circumstances that brought us "the second festival day of the Diaspora"—our distance from the Holy Land, the ignorance and doubt spawned by *galut* (the exile)—were negative, but their yield was decidedly positive: an additional twenty-four hours of holiness and festivity, which we have never relinquished.[10] In the Holy Land, however, only one day is observed, for there the need never arose for the festivals to be observed for more than the requisite day. The single exception is Rosh Hashanah, which, because of its particular place in the calendar, was observed for two days in the Holy Land as well.[11]

So while there are many possibilities for a three-day succession of holy days in the Diaspora—whenever any of its two-day festivals occur in immediate proximity to Shabbat—the only case in which the residents of the Holy Land can enjoy this phenomenon is when Rosh Hashanah falls on Thursday and Friday.[12] Indeed,

---

10 This reflects the very essence of *galut*: a most negative and undesirable state which has yielded the highest achievements of our history as a people.

11 Because Rosh Hashanah is on the first of *Tishrei*—the very day on which the new month is sanctified—the Jews of Israel outside of Jerusalem (and in certain years, even the Jews of Jerusalem and the *sanhedrin* itself) also had to observe the festival for two days, out of doubt (see *Shulchan Aruch HaRav, Orach Chaim,* section 600; *Zohar* 3:231a; Jerusalem Talmud, *Eruvin* 3:9; *Tosefta Rosh Hashanah* 1:10.)

12 The first day of Rosh Hashanah never falls on a Sunday, so there is no

CONFLUENCE (1)   217

on such years the distinction between the Holy Land and the Diaspora is sharply emphasized: When the first day of Rosh Hashanah falls on a Thursday, so does the first day of Sukkot, which occurs exactly two weeks later on the 15th of *Tishrei*, and so does the
festival of Shemini Atzeret, which occurs on the 22nd of *Tishrei*.
Thus, the Diaspora has no less than three three-day continuums of
holiness in a single month, while in the Land of Israel, where the
"holy days" of Sukkot and Shemini Atzeret are observed for one
day only, there is only one such occurrence.

Conical Time

Everything is by divine providence, especially something as integral to the cosmic order as the timing of the festivals. Thus, chassidic teaching explains that underlying the historical and technical
reasons described above, there is a deeper reason for the difference
in how the festivals are observed within the Land of Israel and outside its borders. In essence, the reason for the Diaspora's second
day is that the world outside the Holy Land requires that additional day for the function of the festival to be fulfilled. If a single
day of holiness suffices to provide us with the spiritual fortitude to
elevate and sanctify the "ordinary" days which follow in the Holy
Land—"a land upon which the eyes of G-d are from the beginning
of the year to the year's end"[13]—we require two such days to infuse
holiness into the more mundane lands that lie outside its borders.

(Rabbi Menachem Mendel of Lubavitch[14] compares this phe-

---

possibility for a *chazakah* of holiness formed by Shabbat followed by
two days of Rosh Hashanah.

13   Deuteronomy 11:12.

14   The third Rebbe of Chabad-Lubavitch, the "Tzemach Tzedek,"
1789–1866.

nomenon to the conical nature of a beam of light: The farther it travels from its source, the greater the area over which the light is diffused. Similarly, the holiness that is concentrated in a single day in the Holy Land, the source and epicenter of G-d's provision in the physical world, fills two complete days in more distant lands.[15])

By the same token, whereas a single *chazakah* of holiness suffices to establish the precedent for a sanctified year within the Holy Land, a *chazakah* of *chazakot* is required outside its borders. Thus, when the year begins with three successive days of holiness in the Land of Israel, this phenomenon repeats itself three times in the course of the festivals of the month of *Tishrei* as observed by the communities of the Diaspora.

THE LESSON

Whatever the circumstances in which we might find ourselves, we are granted the necessary tools with which to fulfill our mission in life to elevate the ordinary and sanctify the mundane. If we find ourselves outside of the Holy Land, whether in the geographical or the spiritual sense, we possess the power to "make *this* a Holy Land"[16] — to sanctify our own environment as an abode for holiness.

Furthermore, we are given not only the spiritual resources that the task requires, but also the "vessels" with which to receive them and integrate them into our lives. If our day proves too "narrow" to absorb the holiness slated for it, or if a single *chazakah* proves insufficient to ingrain a new standard, then our holy days are doubled and trebled to accommodate our particular needs.

---

15   *Derech Mitzvotecha*, p. 114a–b.

16   As Rabbi Menachem Mendel of Lubavitch told a follower who desired to move to the Land of Israel.

SHAMMAI'S SHABBAT

It was said of Shammai the Elder that all his days he would eat for Shabbat... But Hillel the Elder had a different approach. He did everything for the sake of Heaven.

Talmud, Beitzah 16a

Our every moment is a product of the various time-currents that have converged to form the particular time-juncture it occupies. At any given moment, it is a certain hour of the day, as well as a certain day of the week; the month is either growing or dwindling with the moon; a certain Torah-section will be read this Shabbat, and a certain festival is approaching or receding; the moment might be replete with mourning, or joy, or repentance, or compassion. We might have have stood in the same day of the same month one year ago, but then it was on a different day of the week, or in a week with a different Torah reading, or in a different year of the *shemittah* cycle. The various time-streams that flow through our lives spin an endless variety of configurations, imparting a distinct significance and lesson to every moment of our lives.

A MONTH WITH TWO HEADS

Let us, by way of example, examine the significance of the particular constellation formed when the two days of the *Rosh Chodesh* ("head of the month") of the month of *Elul* fall on Shabbat and Sunday.

Each month begins with a "head of the month," which serves as the month's beginning and its nerve center. In essence, it is a day that encapsulates a month, just as the head is the source and seat for everything that occurs in the body.[1]

Due to the particular construction of the Jewish calendar, a month's *Rosh Chodesh* might consist of either one or two days. When there are two days of *Rosh Chodesh*, the first is actually the 30th day of the previous month, while the second is the first day of the new month. In such cases, the first day of *Rosh Chodesh* has a dual function, completing the previous month as well as "heading" the coming month.[2]

The month of *Elul*, which always has two days of *Rosh Chodesh*, likewise faces in two directions. As the last month of the year, *Elul* serves as a time for moral and spiritual stocktaking for the closing year, as well as a time of preparation for the coming year. Deemed a time of divine goodwill,[3] the month of *Elul* is uniquely suited for rectifying the failings and consolidating the achievements of the bygone year, as well as for readying ourselves for the "days of awe" of Rosh Hashanah and Yom Kippur.

But *Elul* and its double *Rosh Chodesh* do not exist in a vacuum. Underlying the monthly cycle is the weekly cycle, which, in many ways, is the most basic cycle of created time. As related in the book of Genesis, G-d created the world in six days and rested on the seventh, imprinting this cycle of work and repose into the very fabric of creation. Every Sunday opens a new cycle of human

---

1   See *The Neurology of Time* in vol. 2, pp. 5–7 of this series.

2   See *Locating the Moon* on pp. 167–174 above, specifically footnote 4 there.

3   The month of *Elul* coincides with Moses' third 40 days atop Mount Sinai, during which he procured G-d's wholehearted forgiveness of Israel for their worship of the Golden Calf. See our chapter on "Elul" in vol. 3 of this series, pp. 295–313.

CONFLUENCE (2)   221

achievement, which gathers momentum over the next six days and
culminates in Shabbat, when the week's achievements are "elevated" toward their ultimate fulfillment and objective.

To summarize: "*Elul*" is a month that embraces a year; "*Rosh
Chodesh*" is a day or two that encapsulate a month; "Sunday" represents the beginnings and initiations of human endeavor; "Shabbat," its culminations and realizations. What, then, is the significance of the confluence of these four time-dynamics when a
Shabbat and a Sunday together serve as the *Rosh Chodesh* for the
month of *Elul*?

THE DUALITY

In approaching a task, a relationship, or any other endeavor, we
usually adopt a "staircase" approach. We assess our current station,
taking into account our limits and deficiencies. We then act to
raise ourselves to a place that is more elevated than our starting
point—but not so much elevated from it that it is beyond our
reach. From this point we seek to raise ourselves one more step,
and from that step, to the next. Thus we work our way up from the
bottom, building yesterday's gains into a platform from which to
reach for tomorrow's.

But there are also times when we aim straight for the top. Times
when we shed our "realism," disregard our limitations, transcend
our deficiencies, and focus directly on our ultimate goal. Times
when we experience a surge of faith in our potential to achieve the
head of the staircase, no matter how removed it may be from our
present station.

Each approach has its advantages. The step-by-step approach
might be burdensome and time-consuming, but it allows a person
to achieve full identification with what he or she has achieved. In

the words of the Talmud, "If someone tells you: 'I have not toiled but I have achieved—do not believe him."[4] Even if we think that we have found some sort of "shortcut" to attain our goal without toil, what we will find is an empty gift, as it will never be truly our own. "Nothing comes automatically," goes the chassidic dictum, for at the heart of the chassidic ethos is the demand for *penimiyut*, "internalization"—that everything one does should be fully integrated into one's character and personality.

On the other hand, we also sense, with every fiber of our being, that we are capable of more. We sense that, ultimately, the pull of the earth that holds us to the staircase of measured progress does injustice to our true potential; that there must be some way to free ourselves from this imposition, so that we might leap directly to the full realization of our dreams.

Two Sages

These two approaches to life were personified by the two great talmudic sages, Shammai and Hillel.

The Talmud[5] relates:

> It was said of Shammai the Elder that all his days he would eat for Shabbat. How so? When he came across a prime quality animal, he would buy it and say: "This is for Shabbat." When he found a better one, he would buy the second one for Shabbat and eat the first.
>
> But Hillel the Elder had a different approach. He did everything for the sake of Heaven. [He would say:] "Blessed be G-d, who every day provides us with the day's needs."

---

4 Talmud, *Megillah* 6b.
5 Ibid., *Beitzah* 16a; Rashi, ad loc.

To Shammai, everything was for Shabbat. Everything was oriented toward the goal, to the extent that the process of getting there was wholly absorbed within the goal. Going to the marketplace on Sunday, he thought only of what might be acquired for Shabbat. Eating on Sunday was "for Shabbat"—not to satisfy today's needs, but in order that the better portion be reserved for Shabbat.

Hillel, on the other hand, purchased food on Sunday for Sunday's consumption, on Monday for Monday's consumption, and so on. For Hillel, too, the purpose of it all was for Shabbat, but in order to get to Shabbat, one must first feed one's Sundays and nourish one's Mondays.

We each have a Shammai and a Hillel within us. For man is an amalgamation of matter and spirit, a body coupled with a soul. Of the body it is said, "Dust you are"[6]; of the soul, "Veritably a part of G-d above."[7] Hence the inherent duality in our self-perception and our approach to the endeavors of life. The body's finite nature necessitates the "Sunday approach"—that we begin at the beginning and work our way up the steps and stages of natural progression. The soul's innate perfection is the source of the "Shabbat approach," in which we relate directly to the infinite source and endpoint of all.

SYNTHESIS

But must it be one or the other? In the human being, body and soul fuse to form a dynamic, integrated whole, generating a consciousness in which their respective approaches to life intertwine.

This is the lesson of a year in which the *Rosh Chodesh* of the month of *Elul* falls on Shabbat and Sunday. *Elul*, which sums up

---

6   Genesis 3:19.
7   *Tanya*, ch. 2, after Job 31:2.

the year, is headed by the culminating point of the week as well as by its starting point. The month of *Elul*—and, by extension, the year as a whole—is thus defined as a Shabbat-Sunday reality: a reality that is focused on the ultimate goal and, at the same time, respects and is devoted to the process of getting there.

CONFLUENCE (3)

THE
HARD
LIFE

Just as the olive yields its oil only when pressed,
so do the people of Israel yield their potential
for teshuvah *through the oppression of exile.*

Midrash Rabbah, Shemot 36:1

The people of Israel were exiled amongst the
nations only so that converts might be added
to them.

Talmud, Pesachim 87b.

"One should live with the times," said chassidic master Rabbi Schneur Zalman of Liadi to his disciples, and explained his meaning: A person should derive guidance and inspiration from the weekly Torah reading.

Every week, another *parashah* ("chapter" or "section"; pl. *parashiot*) of the Torah is publicly read in the synagogue, in an annual cycle which is completed on the festival of Simchat Torah.[8] The weekly *parashah*, Rabbi Schneur Zalman was saying, is the soul of the week in which it is read, the spiritual warp and woof of

---

8   The weekly *parashah* is read in full on Shabbat morning, and in part on Mondays, Thursdays and (the previous) Shabbat afternoon. An old chassidic custom, publicized and propagated by the sixth Lubavitcher Rebbe, Rabbi Yosef Yitzchak Schneerson (1880-1950), is to study a part of the weekly *parashah*, together with Rashi's commentary, each day, so that one completes the entire *parashah* in the course of the week.

its time-weave. By following the *parashah*'s dictates and directives, we attune our lives to the inner essence of the particular stretch of time in which we find ourselves.

"Living with the times" assumes an added dimension when two *parashiot* are joined to form a single reading. Because the number of Shabbat readings varies from year to year,[1] there are eight such potential "pairs" among the Torah's fifty-four *parashiot*. This creates a situation in which the different—and at times, even contrasting—lessons of two *parashiot* combine into a unified "directive of the week" for their joint week.[2]

In addition, the weekly *parashah* bears an integral relationship with the other time-landmarks with which it intersects. The fact that a *parashah* is read in a certain month, or in proximity to a certain festival, imparts a distinct context and an additional facet to the lessons with which it instructs our "living with the times."

In the words of the 16th-century sage and mystic, Shaloh:[3]

> *The three parashiot of* Vayeishev, Mikeitz, *and* Vayigash, *which relate the story of Joseph and his brothers... are always read (in the annual Torah-reading cycle) before,*

---

[1] The Jewish calendar year varies in length from as few as 353 to as many as 385 days (see *Jewish Time* on pp. 195–202, above). Furthermore, when Shabbat coincides with a festival, the festival reading, rather than the weekly *parashah*, is read. So depending on the length of the year and the arrangement of its festival days vis-à-vis the days of the week, a year may contain anywhere from 46 to 54 readings in its annual Torah-reading cycle.

[2] Each *parashah* is divided into seven readings (called *aliyot*), for the seven individuals who are called up to read from the Torah. On those weeks when a joint *parashah* is read, the fourth *aliyah* begins in the first *parashah* and ends in the second, emphasizing the fact that the two *parashiot* now constitute a single *parashah*.

[3] Rabbi Isaiah Horowitz, 1560–1630.

during or immediately after the festival of Chanukah. Since "to everything is its season, and a time for every purpose,"[4] certainly the arrangement of the festivals of the year, which are the "appointed times of G-d,"[5] as well as of the festivals and fasts instituted by the sages, all have a special connection to the Torah readings in whose weeks they fall, as everything is masterminded by G-d.[6]

By way of example, we might look at two contiguous *parashiot*—*Matot* (Numbers 30:2–32:42) and *Masei* (Numbers 33:1–36:13). We will examine their individual lessons, but also note that, in certain years, they combine to form a single Torah reading and jointly instruct a single week. We will also note that these two *parashiot* are always read during the "three weeks"—the twenty-one-day period from *Tammuz* 17 to *Av* 9 when we mourn the destruction of the Holy Temple and the onset of the centuries-long *galut* (exile and spiritual displacement) from which we have yet to emerge.[7]

TWO STATES OF THE JEW

Hardness is one of those qualities which we are forever seeking to acquire and to rid ourselves of at the same time. There is more than a hint of censure when we describe a particular individual as a "tough" person, but no small measure of admiration as well. We denounce, in ourselves and others, behavior that is obstinate and unyielding, but also agree on how important it is to have the

---

4   Ecclesiastes 3:1.

5   Leviticus 23:4.

6   Shaloh, introduction to *Parashat Vayeishev*.

7   See our chapter on "The Three Weeks and Tishah B'Av" in vol. 3 of this series, pp. 207–271.

"backbone" to stand one's ground and not be swayed from one's principles.

Indeed, our journey through life requires firmness as well as flexibility, hardiness as well as pliancy. There are times and situations which necessitate, as our sages put it, to "be yielding as a reed, not hard as a cedar";[8] yet there are also times and situations when we are called upon to employ every iota of obstinacy we can muster to resist all that threatens our integrity and seeks to deter us from our mission in life. In the words of chassidic master Rabbi Simcha Bunim of Peshischa: "A person should have two pockets in his coat. In one pocket he should keep the verse,[9] 'I am but dust and ashes.' His second pocket should contain the talmudic saying,[10] 'A person is commanded to say: For my sake was the world created.'"

This dual approach to life is implied in the Torah's two names for the tribes of Israel. While the people of Israel constitute one entity as G-d's "singular nation,"[11] they are comprised of twelve distinct tribes, each of which contributes its unique character and capabilities to our national mission. Thus, the Torah refers to Israel's tribes as *shevatim*, "branches," or *matot*, "rods," expressing the concept that they are offshoots from a common stem, distinct from each other yet parts of a greater whole.

While *shevet* and *mateh* are both synonyms for "branch," the *shevet* is a pliant, flexible bough, while *mateh* denotes a stiff stick or rod. Therein lies the deeper significance of these two names for the tribes of Israel. On certain occasions the Torah refers to us as "branches," stressing the need for flexibility and tractability in life.

---

8   Talmud, *Taanit* 20b.
9   Genesis 18:27.
10   Talmud, *Sanhedrin* 37a.
11   Ibid., *Berachot* 6a.

In other contexts we are called "rods," underscoring the need for firmness and determination in carrying out our mission as "a holy people"[12] and "a light unto the nations."[13]

The latter point is the lesson of the *parashah* of *Matot*, which opens with the verse, "And Moses spoke to the heads of the tribes..." Here, the tribes are called by the name *matot*—a designation which becomes the name of the *parashah* and the crux of its message. Namely, that there are times in the history of a people when they must employ the fortitude and fixity of the rod to persevere in a hostile and capricious world.

THE STAFF OF EXILE

"Hardness" is an acquired rather than an intrinsic state. While the potential for hardness always exists, it is actualized when a substance is subjected to galvanizing conditions and influences.

This can be seen in the *shevet/mateh* model. As a branch, the *shevet* is supple and yielding, bending to the wind and to every pressing hand. But when it is disconnected from the tree to face the elements as a lone, rootless rod, it stiffens into a *mateh*.

In other words, a *mateh* is a *shevet* hardened by the experience of *galut*. Deprived of tenderizing moisture from its nurturing roots, the latent hardness of the wood asserts itself, transforming the pliant branch into a rigid staff.

Therein lies the connection between the *parashah* of *Matot* and the time of year in which it is read. During the "three weeks", we mourn our exile from our homeland and the removal of G-d's open presence in our lives as it was revealed in the Holy Temple in

---

12 Exodus 19:6.
13 Isaiah 42:6.

Jerusalem. We remember how the *shevatim* of Israel—a people anchored to their roots, vitalized by an undisrupted flow of spiritual nurture through their limbs—were torn from their tree to become a nation of homeless *matot*.

But even as the Torah commands us to mourn the events of the "three weeks", it insists that our mourning be a constructive endeavor, an opportunity to focus on how our state of exile might be exploited to a positive end. Even as we agonize over the rootlessness of *galut*, we must take advantage of the manner in which our disconnection from our natural environment strengthens us and galvanizes us. Even as we weep over the destruction of G-d's home and the absence of His revealed presence in our lives, we must tap the tremendous reserves of faith and fortitude evoked by the challenges of an alien society and environment—reserves which would not have been actualized were we to have remained a nation of *shevatim* undisturbed from their stem.

FORTY-TWO JOURNEYS

But there is more to *galut* than the toughening of the Jewish soul.

Galut is also a journey. A journey is not just a departure from home—it is also, and primarily, an advance toward a destination. Therein lies the difference between a wanderer and a journeyer. The wanderer is escaping or being driven away from someplace, while the journeyer is going *to* someplace. The wanderer is defined by where he is not, by the state and experience of homelessness and what this does to his inner self; the journeyer is defined by the place or places to which he goes and what he achieves there. When the wanderer and the journeyer return home, the wanderer brings back his "hardened" and matured self, while the journeyer brings the treasures procured at the various points of his itinerary.

CONFLUENCE (3)

What are we seeking in our places of exile? What do we bring home with us when we return from our journey to the ends of earth? The Talmud defines the purpose of *galut* as the acquisition of converts. "The people of Israel were exiled amongst the nations," it declares, "only so that converts might be added to them."[14]

These "converts" assume many forms. There are the literal converts—non-Jews who were included in the community of Israel as the result of our contact with the peoples of the world. On another level, there is the more subtle conversion of a pagan world to the monotheistic ethos and ideals of Torah, achieved by our millennia-long sojourn amongst the nations of the world.[15]

The teachings of kabbalah add that the "converts" gained in the course of our *galut* are not only of the human sort, but also include the souls of all creatures and creations with which we have gainfully interacted in the course of our dispersion to all corners of the globe. For every created entity has at its core a "spark of holiness," a pinpoint of divinity that constitutes its "soul"—its function within G-d's overall purpose for creation. Every time we utilize something—be it a physical object or force, an idea, a cultural phenomenon—to serve the Creator, we penetrate its shell of mundanity and realize its divine essence. This, the Talmud is saying, is the

---

14 Talmud, *Pesachim* 87b.

15 In the words of Maimonides, "Moses bequeathed the Torah and the *mitzvot* only to the people of Israel... and to whoever desires to convert from the other nations... but one who does not desire to do so is not compelled to accept the Torah and *mitzvot*. In addition, Moses commanded, in the name of G-d, to compel all inhabitants of the world to accept the *mitzvot* commanded to the children of Noah" (*Mishneh Torah, Laws of Kings* 8:10). The universal Noahide *mitzvot* are: belief in G-d; prohibitions against murder, theft, adultery and incest, blasphemy, and cruelty to animals; and the establishment of a legal and social justice system.

purpose of our *galut*: to redeem the sparks of holiness which lie buried in the most far-flung places and circumstances.

This concept of *galut* is expressed by the second *parashah* of our pair, the section of *Masei* ("journeys"), which chronicles the travels and encampments of the people of Israel in the Sinai desert. The *parashah's* name derives from its opening verses: "These are the journeys of the children of Israel, who went out from the land of Egypt... And they journeyed from Raamses... and they camped at Sukkot. They journeyed from Sukkot, and camped at Eitam..." *Masei* goes on to list the 42 journeys which comprised Israel's travels from Egypt to Mount Sinai to the Holy Land.

The commentaries explain that these "journeys" are the forerunners and prototypes for the historical saga of Israel, as we advance through "the desert of the nations"[16] (as the prophet Ezekiel refers to the *galut*) to our ultimate "entry into the Land" in the age of Moshiach.[17]

It is significant that the Torah refers to our ancestors' travels as "journeys" in the plural—a plurality that is preserved in the name of the *parashah*. If the purpose of *galut* were to lie solely in its rootlessness and what this brings out in the Jewish soul, then it should be defined as a "wandering" rather than a "journey"; and if its purpose were to lie exclusively in its ultimate "entry into the Holy Land" at *galut's* end, then our sojourn in the "desert of the nations" should be regarded as a single journey, not a series of journeys. The fact that the Torah considers *galut* to be *Masei*, "journeys," means that the purpose of *galut* is to be found also, and primarily, in the places to which it brings us, so that each of its travels is a journey and each of its "encampments" is a destination.

---

16   Ezekiel 20:35.

17   Rabbeinu Bechayei and *Ohr HaChaim* on Numbers 33:1.

CONFLUENCE (3)

INTEGRATION

Both *Matot* and *Masei* are *parashiot* read during the "three weeks"—both are lessons on *galut*. On the face of it, however, they seem to be different, even conflicting, insights into the nature and purpose of our exile. *Matot* instructs us on how the purpose of *galut* is to evoke in us the steadfastness and *immobility* of the branch-turned-rod. *Masei*, on the other hand, regards *galut* as a journey—as movement, change, and transformation.

Indeed, we know that virtually everything in our existence is multifaceted; that life is the endeavor to navigate, rather than to eliminate, its paradoxes. If "sticking to your principles" and "changing the world" seem to be conflicting goals, so be it; we nevertheless pursue them both, exercising our judgment and sensitivity as to which of these objectives should be emphasized in a given circumstance. So one week we dwell on the *Matot* aspect of *galut*, regarding the challenges of its alien environment as something to resist and repel, thereby strengthening our resistance and hardening our inner resolve. The next week we focus on the *Masei* approach to exile, exploring the ways in which our interaction with our *galut* environment serves to elevate it and transform it into a holier and more G-dly place.

But what happens when *Matot* and *Masei* unite into a single Torah-reading? Then the "directive of the week" is to integrate them both into a single approach to *galut*. "Living with the times" in such a week means discovering how your interaction with a hostile environment is not a challenge to your values and convictions, but their strengthening and their affirmation. It means discovering how your toughness and intractability in your faith is not a hindrance to achievement and creativity, but actually an aid in your endeavor to transform the corner of the world to which you have been dispatched, on the mission to build a home for G-d.

INSIDE TIME

*A Chassidic Perspective on
the Jewish Calendar*

VOLUME TWO

ROSH HASHANAH TO PURIM

Inside Time
Volume Two: Rosh Hashanah to Purim

First Edition — 2015

Published by
Meaningful Life Center
ISBN 978-1-886587-52-6

© Meaningful Life Center 2015

INSIDE TIME

*A Chassidic Perspective on
the Jewish Calendar*

VOLUME TWO

ROSH HASHANAH TO PURIM

Based on the works of the Lubavitcher Rebbe
Adapted by Yanki Tauber

Publication of this book
was made possible
through the generosity
of
Kevin Bermeister and family

Lovingly dedicated
in memory of
Avraham Chaim ben Ze'ev — Allan Bermeister

Niftar 18 Elul 5774

II

CONTENTS*

VOLUME II:
ROSH HASHANAH TO PURIM

CHAPTER VIII: ROSH HASHANAH I
Commitment, Memory, and Deed

> *Essay 1:* **The Neurology of Time**.....................................5
> Rosh Hashanah as the "head" of the year.

> *Essay 2:* **The Man in Man**...8
> Rosh Hashanah as the birthday of man. Man's role in creation. Man
> as a "miniature universe," and the four kingdoms (mineral, vegetable,
> animal, and human) within the human being.

> *Essay 3:* **To Will a World**...17
> Rosh Hashanah as the "coronation" of G-d as king. The cosmic slum-
> ber that befalls the entirety of creation on the eve of Rosh Hashanah,
> and its arousal through our sounding of the *shofar*.

> *Essay 4:* **A Glass of Milk**..25
> Asking G-d for our material needs on Rosh Hashanah. Chanah's prayer.

CHAPTER IX:
YOM KIPPUR AND THE TEN DAYS OF TESHUVAH 33
Repentance, Transcendence, Quintessence

> *Essay 1:* **The 120-Day Version of the Human Story**.......37
> The historical roots of Yom Kippur as the day on which G-d forgave
> us the sin of the Golden Calf and gave us the Second Tablets. G-d's
> "awesome plot on the children of man" in making us susceptible to evil.

---

* A full Table of Contents of the chapters and essays for all three volumes of *Inside Time* is provided at the beginning of Volume I. Sources,
glossary, and index for all three volumes are provided at the end of
Volume III.

Essay 2: **Sin in Four Dimensions**......................44
The dynamics of *teshuvah* ("repentance" and "return").

Essay 3: **Moment**...57
Why the most potent time of the year lasts a mere 26 hours, and the most powerful human deed takes but a moment to achieve.

Essay 4: **Ketoret**...59
The offering of *ketoret* ("incense") in the "Holy of Holies" as the climax of the Yom Kippur service in the Holy Temple. *Teshuvah* as an approach to life that not only rectifies sinful or negative deeds but liberates our every endeavor from the limitations of time.

Essay 5: **Day One**.......................................65
The "ten days of *teshuvah*" and their relationship to Rosh Hashanah and Yom Kippur. Yom Kippur as the "one of the year" whose essence supplies, but also supersedes, the concept of *teshuvah*.

Essay 6: **Reverse Biology**...............................72
The deeper significance of fasting on Yom Kippur.

CHAPTER X: SUKKOT 77
Revelation, Unity, Joy

Essay 1: **The Easy Mitzvah**.............................81
Dwelling in the *sukkah*. Sukkah as the *mitzvah* that embraces the totality on the person.

Essay 2: **The Four Mysteries of King Solomon**..............86
The "four kinds" taken of Sukkot and the paradoxical truths they express.

Essay 3: **The Taste of Water**...........................95
Joy as a quality of Sukkot. The spiritual significance of the "pouring of the water" ritual, and of the water-drawing festivities in the Holy Temple.

Essay 4: **Unity in Three Dimensions**............106

Unity as a quality of Sukkot. The various degrees of unity achieved by the three *mitzvot* of Sukkot—joy, the four kinds, and *sukkah*.

Essay 5: **One Twig and One Leaf**............114

The significance of the willow, both as one of the "four kinds" and as the particular *mitzvah* of "*aravah*" on the seventh day of Sukkot.

CHAPTER XI:
SHEMINI ATZERET AND SIMCHAT TORAH 125

Culmination and Integration

Essay 1: **Essence**............129

The concept of *atzeret* ("retention" and "absorption"). Internalizing the unity of Sukkot.

Essay 2: **Daughters Near and Far**............135

Why we celebrate our bond with the Torah on Shemini Atzeret rather than on Shavuot. The parallels and differences between the "*atzeret* of Sukkot" and the "*atzeret* of Passover."

Essay 3: **Scrolled**............148

Dancing with the Torah on Simchat Torah.

Essay 4: **Intuition**............151

The special joy of *hakafot*.

CHAPTER XII: CHESHVAN 155

The Ordinary Life

Essay 1: **The Last Jew**............157

Returning to the daily grind. Making a "dwelling for G-d in the lower realms." The significance of the seventh day of *Cheshvan*.

CONTENTS   V

CHAPTER XIII: CHANUKAH 163
Light, Purity, and Spirituality

Essay 1: The Transparent Body 167
Chanukah as the most spiritual of the festivals.

Essay 2: Nightlight 173
Light as the essence of our mission in life. The light-related *mitzvot*—the lights of the Holy Temple, of Shabbat, and of Chanukah—as a progression of light through time and space.

Essay 3: The Lamp 180
The components of the lamp—oil, wick, and flame—and their corresponding elements in the life of man.

Essay 4: The Mudswamps of Hella 184
The essence of "*Yavan*" (Greece) as a noxious brew of materialism (earth) and intellect (water), combated through the suprarational self-sacrifice of Chanukah.

Essay 5: The Miracle 188
Why the festival of Chanukah was established only on "the next year." The challenge of transforming a momentary flash of heroism into a permanent state of being.

Essay 6: Compromise 190
The unnecessary miracle of Chanukah. The connection between Chanukah and education (*chinuch*).

Essay 7: The Towering Servant 193
The *shamash* (servant candle) and its place in the *menorah*.

Essay 8: Accumulating Lights 194
The meaning behind the debate between the House of Shammai and the House of Hillel regarding the number of candles to be lit each night of Chanukah. The significance of *Zot Chanukah* ("This is Chanukah"), the eighth day of Chanukah.

VI   INSIDE TIME

CHAPTER XIV: TEVET 205
Winter

> *Essay 1*: **Spirit and Substance**.................................... 207
> The talmudic adage that the month of *Tevet* is a time when "a body de-
> rives pleasure from a body," and its application in the marriage-bond
> between G-d and Israel.

CHAPTER XV: TU BISHEVAT 215
The New Year for Trees

> *Essay 1*: **Of Trees and Men**... 217
> The various components of the tree—roots, body, fruit, and seeds—in
> the life of man.

> *Essay 2*: **Fruit for Thought**.. 221
> The spiritual and psychological significance of the "seven kinds":
> wheat, barley, grapes, figs, pomegranates, olives, and dates.

CHAPTER XVI: PURIM 229
Nature, Physicality, Choice

> *Essay 1*: **Oil and Wine**.. 233
> The difference between Chanukah (oil, innerness, spirituality) and Pu-
> rim (wine, externality, physicality).

> *Essay 2*: **Esther's Story**.. 235
> The two "versions" of Purim—the spiritual holiday proposed by Mor-
> dechai, and physical festival propagated by Esther.

> *Essay 3*: **A Roll of Dice**.. 240
> The deeper significance of the "casting of lots" that gives Purim its
> name. The parallels and differences between Purim and Yom Kippur
> ("a day like Purim").

> *Essay 4*: **The Thousand-Year Difference**....................... 247
> Purim as the second "giving of the Torah."

CONTENTS

Essay 5: **A Feast and a Fast**.................................... 254
Purim as a lesson on the proper perspective on the "garments of nature."

Essay 6: **A Singular People**.................................... 259
Four aspects of the uniqueness of the Jewish people as seen through the lens of Purim: "light" (Torah), "happiness" (the festivals), "joy" (circumcision), and "prestige" (*tefilin*).

Essay 7: **The Purim Drunk**.................................... 266
Four levels of joy; the *mitzvah* to get drunk on Purim.

Essay 8: **The Beginning and the End**........................... 272
The "Minor Purim" of *Adar* I. Awe and joy as the two poles of the "way of life" for the Jew.

CHAPTER EIGHT

Rosh Hashanah

Commitment, Memory, and Deed

Tishrei 1 & 2

Rosh Hashanah, observed on the first and second days of the Jewish year (*Tishrei* 1 and 2), is unique among the festivals of the Jewish calendar. Unlike the other festivals, which mark a particular event in Jewish history and the Jewish experience, Rosh Hashanah is the anniversary of a universal event: the creation of the first man and woman and their first actions toward the realization of mankind's role in G-d's world.

Accordingly, Rosh Hashanah is the festival that emphasizes the universal, rather than the distinctly Jewish, aspect of our mission in life. On Rosh Hashanah we proclaim G-d sovereign of the universe and dedicate ourselves to the goal that "Every object shall know that You have made it, and every creature shall understand that You have created it, and every thing that has the breath of life in its nostrils shall proclaim: G-d, the G-d of Israel, is king, and His sovereignty rules over all." The *shofar*, the ram's horn sounded on Rosh Hashanah, represents the trumpet blast of a people's coronation of their king.

The cry of the *shofar* is also a call to repentance. For Rosh Hashanah is also the anniversary of man's first sin and his repentance thereof; it is thus the first of the "ten days of repentance" which culminate in Yom Kippur, the Day of Atonement.

Another function of the *shofar* is to recall the *akeidah*, the "binding of Isaac" which occurred on this date, in which a ram took Isaac's place as an offering to G-d. We evoke Abraham's readiness to sacrifice his son, and plead that the merit of this deed should stand by us as we pray for a year of life, health, and prosperity. For Rosh Hashanah is the day on which the deeds of man are weighed and his sustenance for the year allotted by the supernal Judge and Provider.

These themes are expressed in the special prayers of the day, which include a section on "sovereignty"; a section on G-d's "remembrance" of all creations on this day; and a section called "*shofarot*," on the various aspects of the central *mitzvah* of the day, the sounding of the *shofar*. Each section is followed by ten soundings of the *shofar*. (Altogether, the *shofar* is sounded 100 times in the course of the Rosh Hashanah service.)

Rosh Hashanah customs include eating a piece of apple dipped in honey, to symbolize our desire for a "sweet year"; wishing one another, "May you be inscribed and sealed for a good year"; and reciting *tashlich*, a special prayer said near a body of water (an ocean, river, pond, etc.) in evocation of the verse, "cast their sins into the depths of the sea" (Michah 7:19).

Rosh Hashanah means "the head of the year." The implications of the year having a "head" (as opposed to merely a beginning) is the subject of the first essay in our chapter on Rosh Hashanah, *The Neurology of Time*.

3

The second essay of this chapter, *The Man in Man*, discusses the significance of Rosh Hashanah as the birthday of mankind, and the role of man in creation. *To Will a World* explores the kabbalistic idea that every Rosh Hashanah the universe reverts to its primordial, pre-human state, and the divine will for creation must be reawakened through the sound of the *shofar*. Our closing essay, *A Glass of Milk*, addresses the apparent dichotomy between Rosh Hashanah serving as the day of the divine "coronation," and the fact that we avail ourselves of this most sublime moment to request our mundane, everyday needs from G-d.

See also the following essays: *Day One*, on pp. 65–71 below; and *Our Other Head* in vol. 3 of this series, pp. 4–12.

ROSH HASHANAH (1)

THE NEUROLOGY OF TIME

On Rosh Hashanah it is inscribed, and on Yom Kippur it is sealed: how many shall pass on, and how many shall be born; who shall live, and who shall die... who shall rest, and who shall wander... who shall be impoverished, and who shall be enriched; who shall fall, and who shall rise...

From the Musaf prayer for Rosh Hashanah

"*I*t's all in the head," is a fairly accurate description of every man's reality. If you stub your toe and cry out in pain, it is only because the event has been detected by your brain and your brain has so chosen to so react to the experience. Everything you sense, know, and feel relates to the universe between your ears; any action you take is first conceived, considered, and executed inside the head.

And whatever occurs within the head has a profound effect upon the external person: An injury to the brain, G-d forbid, or the alteration of its chemical constitution, will affect the function and behavior of the entire body. Neurologists have even learned to evoke certain external responses, or improve the function of a certain faculty, by stimulating the corresponding area of the brain.

What is true of the human being is also true of another of G-d's creations: time. Time, too, has a body and a brain, a persona and a mind.

We are accustomed to regarding time as a string of segments: second follows second, hour follows hour, Monday follows Sunday. Special days — Shabbat, Rosh Hashanah, Passover — each have their place in the sequence of days and months mapped out by our calendar, preceded and followed by the "ordinary" days that separate them. This, however, is a most perfunctory perception of time, just as a description of the human body in purely physical terms — hair, skin, bone, blood, flesh, sinew, and brain tissue classified solely by their spatial juxtaposition to each other — is a most superficial vision of man.

Time is a complex organism whose various organs and faculties interact with each other, each fulfilling its individual function and imparting its effect upon the whole. G-d created the whole of time — every age, millennium, century, year, and second of it — as a single, multifaceted body. It is only that we, finite and temporal creatures that we are, encounter its "limbs," "organs," and "cells" one at a time, regarding the past as passed because we have passed through it, and the future as yet to be because we have yet to experience it.

Just as time, as a whole, constitutes an integral organism, so it is with the various time-bodies designed by the Creator of time as distinct components of the universal time-body: the day, the week, the month, the year, etc. Each of these has its own "head," a neurological center which generates, processes, and controls the stimuli and experiences of its "body."

So if we learn to be sensitive to the structure of time, we can transcend the sequential timeline of our lives. If, upon entering the "head" of a particular time-body, we imbue it with a certain quality and stimulate its potential in a certain way, we can profoundly affect the days and experiences of that entire time-body, whether they lie in our "future" or our "past."

FORTY-EIGHT HOURS

The two days of Rosh Hashanah—the name literally means "head of the year"—are 48 hours that embody an entire year.

On Rosh Hashanah we recommit ourselves to our mission in life, reiterating Adam's crowning of G-d as king of the universe,[1] a commitment that becomes the foundation for our service of G-d throughout the year. Rosh Hashanah also commences the "ten days of *teshuvah*" which culminate in Yom Kippur—days especially suited for soul-searching and undertaking new initiatives, since resolutions made on these "neurological" days of the year are far more effective: Having stimulated the brain, the body readily follows suit. On Rosh Hashanah, we also pray for life, health, and sustenance for the year to come; for, in the words of the *u'netaneh tokef* prayer, Rosh Hashanah is the day on which "all inhabitants of the world pass before Him as a flock of sheep," and it is decreed in the heavenly court, "who shall live, and who shall die... who shall be impoverished, and who shall be enriched; who shall fall, and who shall rise."

It's all in the head. On Rosh Hashanah we enter into the mind of the year; our every thought, word, and deed on this day resonates throughout its entire body.[2]

---

[1] See citation from *Zohar* on p. 10, and the next two essays in in this chapter, *The Man in Man* (pp. 8–16), and *To Will a World* (pp. 17–24).

[2] Other "heads" of time include Shabbat, the nerve-center of the weekly cycle, which both sublimates the past week's endeavors and empowers those of the following week; and the monthly mind of *Rosh Chodesh* ("head of the month"), every moment of which has a profound influence on the entire month.

THE
MAN IN
MAN

The human being is a miniature universe.

Midrash Tanchuma, Pikudei 3

"This day is the beginning of Your works," reads a key passage in the Rosh Hashanah prayers, "a remembrance of the first day." In fact, Rosh Hashanah marks not the beginning of G-d's creation of the universe, but His creation of man. The anniversary of the first day of creation is the 25th of the Hebrew month of *Elul*. *Tishrei* 1, the date observed as Rosh Hashanah, is the sixth day of creation, the day on which the first man and woman, Adam and Eve, were created.

Nevertheless, we say of Rosh Hashanah, *Zeh hayom techilat maasecha*—This day is the beginning of Your works. *This* day, because although man is the last of the creations in terms of chronological order, he is first among them in terms of function and purpose.[1] For man alone possesses the one quality that gives meaning and purpose to G-d's creation.

FREE AGENT

Without man, the universe is a mere machine. Every mineral, plant, and animal behaves in accordance with an ironclad set of

---

[1]   In the words of Psalm 139 (attributed to Adam), verse 5: "First and last, You created me."

ROSH HASHANAH (2)

laws dictated by its inborn nature, and has neither the inclination nor the ability to behave otherwise. Only man reflects his Creator in that he possesses free choice. Only man can will and act contrary to his nature; only man can make of himself something other than what he is, transcending the very parameters of the self into which he was born.

So only man's deeds have true significance. The industry of the ant or the faithfulness of the dove are no more "moral" than the cruelty of the cat or the deviousness of the snake. The majesty of a snow-capped Alp is no more virtuous than the stench of a putrefying swamp. For their "positive" or "negative" traits are solely the result of the manner in which they have been formed and programmed by their Creator. But when man acts virtuously, rising above his instinctive selfishness to serve his Creator; or when he acts unvirtuously, corrupting his nature in a manner that no animal or object ever would or could, and then repents of his evil and even converts it into a force for good—something of true significance has occurred. Man has broken free of the programmed universe G-d created, and has expanded it in ways that its implicit potential could not have generated or anticipated. The human being has, in the words of our sages, become "a partner with G-d in creation."[2]

The other, non-human elements of creation achieve fulfillment through the human being, when the human being involves them in the performance of a *mitzvah*—an act that fulfills a divine command. For example, the person who writes a check to charity has many participants in his deed: the paper and ink of his check, the natural resources and forces he has enlisted to earn the money he is giving, even the mountain out of which was quarried the marble

---

2   Talmud, *Shabbat* 10a and 119b.

in the facade of the bank which processes his check. These and innumerable other morally neutral elements have been elevated to inclusion in a creative, transcendent, human act, thereby realizing the purpose of their creation.

This is why Rosh Hashanah is the "beginning of Your works." On this day, the first human being opened his eyes, beheld himself and his world, and chose to dedicate them both to the service of his Creator. His first act was to involve all of creation in his submission to G-d. In the words of the *Zohar*,

> *When Adam stood up on his feet, he saw that all creatures feared him and followed him as servants do their master. He then said to them: "You and I both, 'Come, let us worship and bow down, let us kneel before G-d our maker.'"*[3]

Every Rosh Hashanah, we repeat Adam's call. We intensify our awareness of our Creator, reiterate our acceptance of His sovereignty, and rally all our resources for the task of making Him a tangible presence in our lives. As we proclaim in a central passage of the Rosh Hashanah prayers:

> *Our G-d and G-d of our fathers: Reign over the entire world in Your glory... And every object shall know that You have made it, and every creature shall understand that You have created it, and every thing that has the breath of life in its nostrils shall proclaim: G-d, the G-d of Israel, is king, and His sovereignty rules over all.*

Thus the "head of the year" coincides not with the first day of creation, on which G-d brought time, space, and matter into being; or with its third day, on which He created life; or with its fourth

---

3   Psalms 95:6; *Zohar* 1:221b.

ROSH HASHANAH (2)

day, on which He created creatures of instinct and feeling; but with the day on which G-d made man "in His image, after His likeness,"[4] imparting to him the divine capacity to will, choose, and create. For this is the day on which the purpose of every component of G-d's creation—mineral, vegetable, animal, and human— began its actualization, in the deeds of the first man and woman.[5]

"Ko" and "Zeh"

The difference between these two first days—the beginning of the physical creation on *Elul* 25, and the beginning of man's implementation of creation's purpose on Rosh Hashanah—is expressed in the difference between two Hebrew words associated with these dates: *zeh* ("this") and *ko* ("so" and "like this").

Zeh implies a clear a clear and direct association with its object. When the Torah tells us that our forefathers, upon their miraculous crossing of the Red Sea, proclaimed *Zeh Keili*, "This is my G-d," our sages interpret this to imply that it was "like one who points with his finger and says 'This!'"[6]

In contrast, the word *ko*, which means "like this," implies a more ambiguous reference. The Midrash sees the difference between *zeh* and *ko* as indicative of superiority of the prophecy of

---

4   Genesis 1:26.

5   In addition to being the day of man's willing acceptance of the divine sovereignty, the first Rosh Hashanah was also the day on which man first transgressed the divine will and then repented for his deed, introducing the concept of *teshuvah* into the world—the distinctly human capacity to rebound from a negative experience and utilize the momentum of the "return" to fuel a deeper, more passionate bond with G-d (see the first three essays of the following chapter, "Yom Kippur and the Ten Days of *Teshuvah*").

6   Exodus 15:2; *Midrash Rabbah*, Shemot 23:14.

Moses over that of other prophets: "All prophets prophesied with *ko*," beginning their prophesies with the proclamation, *Ko amar Hashem*, "So said G-d...", since, as a rule, a prophet receives his communication from the Almighty by way of allusion and metaphor. Only Moses, to whom G-d spoke "mouth to mouth, manifestly, and not in riddles," was able to say *Zeh hadavar asher tzivah Hashem*—This is the thing which G-d has commanded.[7]

Ko is also the date of the beginning of creation. In the Holy Tongue, the letters of the *aleph-bet* also serve as numbers; as a result, every word has a numerical value, and many numbers also form a word. The number 25 spells the word *ko*.

The world created on the 25th of *Elul* is a manifestation of G-dliness. As the psalmist proclaims, "When I see Your heavens, the work of Your fingers, the moon and the stars which You have ordained..."[8] G-d chose to express Himself in His creation, much as the mind and character of an artist can be discerned in his work. But if the pre-Adam world bespeaks its Creator, it does so via a screen of evocation and insinuation. It is a *ko* expression of the divine, an intimation which obscures even as it reveals.

Only in the consciousness and achievements of man can there be a *zeh* revelation of G-dliness. Only in a mind enabled to look beyond the veil of nature and self, only in a will not incorrigibly shackled to instinct and ego, can the divine reality unequivocally reside. Only in our choices and actions can G-d be made real in our world.

With the creation of man on the first of *Tishrei*, the world became more than a *ko* entity, more than an allusion to its Creator. By choosing to subordinate himself to the Almighty, by devoting

---

7 Numbers 12:8 and 30:2; *Sifri* ad loc.

8 Psalms 8:4.

ROSH HASHANAH (2)   13

his mind to seek His truth, his heart to love and fear Him, and his
life to implement His will, man made his soul and world a "dwelling for G-d."[9]

So Rosh Hashanah, the birthday of man and the day of our
annual affirmation of our role in creation, is the day of which we
say: *Zeh hayom techilat maasecha*—This is the day that marks the
true beginning of Your works.

Life as a Mineral

The human being, say our sages, is a universe in miniature. So just
as creation as a whole is comprised of *ko* and *zeh* factors—of the
pre-human world created on *Elul* 25 and the human element introduced on *Tishrei* 1—so it is within the human being.[10] And just as
all elements of the macro-universe fulfill their purpose in creation

---

9   In the words of the sages (*Midrash Tanchuma, Nasso* 16), "G-d desired a
     dwelling in the lower realms (i.e., the physical world)." Rabbi Schneur
     Zalman of Liadi sees this midrashic statement as expressing the divine
     purpose in creation: "This is what man is all about; this is the purpose
     of his creation, and of the creation of all worlds, supernal and ephem-
     eral: that G-d should have this 'dwelling in the lower realms.'" (*Tanya*,
     ch. 36).

10   The *zeh* and *ko* elements in man are alluded to in the above-quoted verse
     from Genesis (1:26), which describes man as having been created both
     in the "image" (*tzelem*) and in the "likeness" (*demut*) of G-d. *Tzelem*,
     commonly translated as "image," actually means "structure" or "con-
     figuration." This refers to the overtly G-dly characteristics of man—
     the spirituality of his soul and his aptitude for the divine. *Demut*, "like-
     ness," refers to the more allusive and elusive elements of man's divine
     image—traits which, though they ultimately reflect his divine essence,
     are shrouded in the guises of his mortal and material self, requiring
     much effort to uncover their true function and direct them toward
     their G-dly ends.

via the deeds of man, so do all strata of the human universe attain fulfillment and realization through its distinctly human element—through the man in man.

Our sages categorize the entirety of creation as consisting of four "worlds" or "kingdoms": the "inanimate" or mineral kingdom; the vegetable kingdom; the animal kingdom; and the "speaker" kingdom—the human being.

Man, too, incorporates these four kingdoms within himself. There are occasions and pursuits in our life in which we resemble the inert mineral. We might be asleep, on vacation, at play, or engaged in any of the other forms of repose and recreation to which we devote a significant portion of our time. Obviously, we are physically alive at these times; we might even be greatly exerting ourselves and employing our keenest faculties. But spiritually, we are an inanimate stone. "Life," in its ultimate sense, is the endeavor to transcend one's present state—to grow and achieve beyond what one is—while the function of our "mineral" pursuits is to sustain rather than produce, to conserve rather than create.

There are also times when we are in our "vegetable" mode—when our focus is on self-growth and self-development. With these activities, we exhibit signs of spiritual life, as opposed to the inertia of our "mineral" hours. Nevertheless, because they are confined to the betterment of self, these represent a limited, "botanical" vitality. We are growing upward, blossoming and bearing fruit; but we remain rooted to the "spot" where nature has planted us.

A more dynamic vitality is exhibited by the "animal" in us—the instincts, passions, and sensitivities by which we relate to others. With our faculties for love, awe, and other emotions, we roam the terrain beyond the narrow spectrum of self, transcending the merely vertical growth of our vegetable element.

But we are more than the sum of our mineral, vegetable, and

animal lives; more than repose, growth, and feeling. The *man* in man is our intellect and our spirituality—our quintessentially human qualities.

With our unique capacity for independent thought and discriminating intelligence, we transcend the self-defined world of instinct and feeling to view ourselves from the outside, and change ourselves accordingly. Thus the intellectual self is truly "alive"—constantly reassessing and redefining its perceptions and sensitivities.

Even more transcendent than the intellect is our spiritual self, the "spark of G-dliness" within us that makes us the apex of G-d's creation. The intellect is "free" and "objective," but only relative to the subjective emotions; ultimately the intellect is defined and confined by the nature and laws of reason. The divine in ourselves, however, knows no bounds, surmounting all constraints and limitations that might inhibit our relationship with our Creator.

When we engage our intellectual and spiritual faculties we are truly our human self. It is in these moments—when we employ our mind to literally recreate ourselves through self-critique and the refinement of our character and behavior, and when we transcend all inhibitions of ego, feeling, and even intellect to serve G-d without restraint or equivocation—that we rise to our role as G-d's partner in creation, as the only one of His creations who possesses the freedom to originate and create.

THE PRIMACY OF MAN

Therein lies the double lesson of Rosh Hashanah, the day that emphasizes the centrality of man in creation.

On the macrocosmic level, Rosh Hashanah teaches us that "Every man is obligated to say: 'The entire world was created to serve me, and I was created to serve my Creator.'"[11]—that our "privilege" to exploit nature's resources to serve our own needs is also a duty and a responsibility, since it is through their contribution to our lives that all elements of creation can rise from the limitations of their "robotic" existence to share in the spirituality and transcendence of a human deed. When we prove equal to this task, we not only rise above our created state but also raise the entire world with us; when we fail to do so, G-d forbid, we not only debase our own humanity, but also drag down with us everything that is a partner to our existence.[12]

The same applies to the microcosmic universe—the four-tiered life of man. Our "mineral," "vegetable," and "animal" endeavors are important, even indispensable, components of our lives; but we must remember that also in this inner world, everything was created "for my sake"—to serve the human in me.

When the goal of our recreational, growth-oriented, and experiential activities is to empower our intellectual and spiritual lives, these "lower" aspects of our existence become incoporated in our transcendental endeavor to remake ourselves, and the world we inhabit, in the divine image imprinted within us; they, too, become *human* endeavors, participants in the realization of the divine potential invested in man.

---

[11] Talmud, *Kidushin* 82b.

[12] According to *Tanya*, there are no morally neutral choices in man's life: Because he has been granted the capacity to rise above his "programmed" existence, his failure to do so is a debasement of his humanity. For an animal to behave as an animal is its nature; for man to confine himself to an animal existence is a corruption of his nature (see *Tanya*, chapters 7 and 8).

ROSH HASHANAH (3)

TO WILL
A WORLD

On the eve of Rosh Hashanah, all things re-
vert to their primordial state. The "inner will"
ascends and is retracted into the divine es-
sence; the worlds are in a state of sleep and
are sustained only by the "outer will." The
service of man on Rosh Hashanah is to re-
build the divine attribute of sovereignty and
reawaken the divine desire, "I shall reign,"
with the sounding of the shofar.

The kabbalistic masters[1]

O ne night a year, the world succumbs to a cosmic slumber.
On the functional level, the sleeper's vital signs plod
on: The sun still rises, winds blow, rains fall, seeds germinate, fruit
ripens. But the consciousness of creation is muted. For its soul of
souls—the "inner will" of the divine desire for creation—has ascended, retreated to a place from where it views its body and life
with a calculated detachment. Only the "outer will"—the most external element of the divine desire—remains to sustain the sleeping body of creation.

And then, a piercing sound rises from the earth and reverberates through the heavens. A sound that wakens the sleeping

---

[1] *Pri Eitz Chaim*, 24:1; *Shaar HaKavanot, D'rushei Rosh Hashanah*; *Tan-*
ya, Igeret HaKodesh 14.

universe, stirring its soul to resume its conscious, willful animation of its material shell.

The cry of the *shofar* resounds. A profound yet utterly simple cry, a note free of the nuances of rational music. A cry that rouses the soul of creation to a renewed commitment to the endeavor of life.

Thus the kabbalists describe the cosmic drama which repeats itself each year, as the world "falls asleep" on the eve of Rosh Hashanah and is "awakened" the following morning by the sound of the *shofar*. Indeed, it is told of certain *tzaddikim* (righteous people) that on the night and morning of Rosh Hashanah they would feel physically weak. So attuned were they to the diminution of divine involvement in the world during this time, that it affected their own souls' investment in their bodies.

What does it mean that the world is asleep? How does our sounding of the *shofar* restore the consciousness and vitality of creation? Why is G-d's inner will withdrawn on Rosh Hashanah eve, and why does G-d's outer will remain behind? What, indeed, is the difference between "inner will" and "outer will"? The Talmud teaches, "As the soul fills the body, so G-d fills the world."[2] So to answer these questions, we must first examine the dynamics of "will" in our own psyche and our own lives.

THE LAYERS OF WILL

Will is the soul of deed. Ultimately, no act is ever performed that is not driven by the engine of volition.

But will is a multilayered thing. There is the outermost layer of will that directly drives our actions. Then there is the deeper

---

2   Talmud, *Berachot* 58a.

ROSH HASHANAH (3)

will that underlies this external will, which, in turn, contains yet a deeper will, which is itself an outgrowth of yet a deeper will, and so on.

Thus, the relationship between will and deed is not static, but subject to changes and fluctuations. At times, the innermost level of will suffuses our actions, enlivening them with the desire and satisfaction that motivate them. Other times, our deeds may be lifeless and lethargic, sustained only by the most superficial aspect of our will.

To illustrate, let us take the example of a person who owns and operates a business. Our businessman does many things in the course of the day—waking at an early hour, commuting to the office, answering the telephone, meeting with potential clients, and so on. On the most basic level, these deeds are driven by the will to do them: He *wants* to get out of bed, he *wants* to drive to work, he *wants* to pick up the receiver—if he didn't want to do these things, he wouldn't do them. But *why* does he want to do these things? Because of an underlying will that the business should survive and prosper. But why does he want his business to survive and prosper? Because it brings him income and prestige—if this were not the case, he would have no desire for a business. Delving deeper, the desire for money and status stem from deeper wants—the desire for food, shelter, and acceptance by his fellows—which, in turn, are outgrowths of the desire, intrinsic to every creature, to continue to exist and propagate its existence.

This does not mean that every time our businessman picks up the telephone he does so because he senses that his very existence depends on it. Indeed, he need not even be convinced that the act will yield a profit, or even that it is crucial to the functioning of his business. Ultimately, however, the act of lifting that telephone receiver "contains" the entirety of the will that drives it, including its deepest cause of causes.

This "inner will" is the soul of our businessman's action, suffusing it with a vitality that reflects how deeply its origins lie in his innermost self. Thus, there is a quality to the way that the owner of a business picks up the phone that shows a desire and commitment deeper than that of the most devoted employee.

ASSESSMENT

There are times, however, when the soul of a deed ascends a notch, to view its body and life with a calculated detachment.

There are times when a person reassesses what he does. Is the business indeed turning a profit? Is it meeting my needs? Is this what I want to do with my life?

His actual involvement with the business continues as before. He continues to get out of bed in the morning, continues to drive to the office, continues to answer the telephone. He continues to "want" to do these things on the most external level of will. But the deeper elements of his will are no longer in it. The business can be said to be "asleep," animated only by the most external layer of its soul.

Then something happens to rekindle our businessman's desire. Perhaps he sees a lucrative figure on the year's balance sheet, or a promising projection for the future. Or a certain deal materializes that embodies everything he loves about his business, everything about it that reaffirms his self-vision and furthers his goals. His deeds, dry and mechanical in his contemplative interim, are reinfused with life and vitality. The business wakes up from its slumber.

King of the Universe

Once a year, the universe enters into a state of suspended animation.

G-d reconsiders His creation. Is it turning a profit? Is it realizing My goals? Do I still desire to invest Myself in the role of "Creator"?

The sun still rises, winds blow, rains fall, seeds germinate, fruit ripens. G-d's desire for a world continues to sustain and drive the universe. But G-d's desire for a world is but the most external layer of the universe's soul.

Why does G-d desire a world? There is a deeper motive beneath this membrane of will, and yet a deeper motive beneath it, and so on. The kabbalistic writings abound with various divine motives for the creation of the world: the desire to express His infinite potential; the desire that He be known by His creations; the desire to bestow goodness; among others. Each of these "motives" relates to another layer of the divine will, describing the soul of the universe as manifested on another level of reality.

At the heart of it all lies the very essence of the divine will to create: G-d created a world because He wanted to be king.

Defining Sovereignty

G-d is all-capable and all-powerful. So it would seem a relatively simple matter for Him to make himself king—all He has to do is create a world, populate it with creatures, and rule over them. But this alone would not make Him a king, at least not in the ultimate sense of the word.

A shepherd who drives a herd of a million sheep is not a king. A tyrant who rules an empire of a billion terrified subjects is not a king. A benevolent patriarch who extends his authority over dozens of his descendants is not a king. A teacher with a thousand devoted disciples is not a king. All these have one thing in common: their subjects are compelled to submit to them. They may be compelled by their reliance on the shepherd's devotion to their needs, by their ruler's power over them, by their filial bond to their father, or by their appreciation of their master's wisdom—the bottom line is that they are compelled. And true sovereignty cannot be compelled.

A true sovereign is one whose subjects *freely choose* to submit to him. Not because they need him, not because they fear his power, not because they love him, not even because they appreciate his greatness, but because they see in him the very embodiment of their core identity, and thus choose him as their sovereign with an act of choice that is free of any and all motives or considerations save for their own truest, quintessential will.

So to become king of the universe, G-d created man—a creature endowed with free choice. G-d created a being that is both the furthest from Him and the closest to Him of all His creation. Furthest from Him in that man is a free and independent being— free even to rebel against his Maker. Closest to Him in that man is a free and independent being—as only G-d is free and independent. In the words of the first man, Adam, "First and last, You created me."[3] G-d created man, "dust from the earth," the lowliest of His creations, and "blew into his nostrils a breath of life" that is the very "image of G-d."[4]

There are many aspects to our relationship with G-d. We relate to G-d as our shepherd, expressing our gratitude for His providence over and sustenance of our lives. We fear and revere Him,

---

3   Psalms 139:5.

4   Genesis 2:7 and 1:27. See Talmud, *Sanhedrin*, 38a.

ever mindful of His majesty and power. We love Him with the boundless love of a child, recognizing our intrinsic bond with our Father in Heaven. We gain a disciple's unique appreciation of his or her master by studying His wisdom, implicit in His creation and revealed to us in His Torah. Each of these relationships realizes another aspect or "layer" in the divine motive for creation, intensifying and enlivening G-d's involvement with His world.

But once a year, "all things revert to their primordial state," as G-d reevaluates the very core of His desire for a world, the underlying "why" of His involvement with us as shepherd, ruler, father, and teacher. Once a year, G-d asks Himself: Why create a world?

THE FIRST CORONATION

The timing of this cosmic audit is not arbitrary: Rosh Hashanah is the day on which G-d's sovereignty of the world was first realized.

Rosh Hashanah is the sixth day of creation, the day on which man was created. G-d had already created the heavens and the earth, the animals and the angels; He already presided over a world that submitted to His rule, over creations who feared and loved Him and appreciated His wisdom. But the world was still in a state of suspended animation; its soul of souls had yet to be evoked. Then G-d created man, the only one of His creations with the freedom to choose or reject his Maker.

Moments later, G-d was king. "When Adam stood up on his feet," the *Zohar* tells us, "he saw that all creatures feared him and followed him as servants do their master. He then said to them: 'You and I both, *Come, let us worship and bow down, let us kneel before G-d, our Maker.*'"[5] When the first man chose G-d as his king,

---

5   *Zohar* 1:221b, citing Psalms 95:6.

the primordial purpose in creation came to fruition, infusing G-d's work with life and vitality.[6]

Every year, "all things revert to their primordial state" as G-d again relates to His creation as He did prior to Adam's crowning Him king. On Rosh Hashanah eve, the divine inner will for creation is retracted and the world is plunged into a state of sleep.

Then, a piercing sound rises from the earth and reverberates through the heavens. The cry of the *shofar* resounds: an utterly simple cry, reflecting not the fear of the subject, not the love of the child, not the sophistication of the student's understanding, but the simple trumpet blast of a people's coronation of their king. A cry that reflects the simplicity of choice—true choice, choice that is free of all external motives and influences.

A cry that rouses the soul of creation to a renewed commitment to and involvement in the endeavor of life.[7]

---

6   G-d's desire for "sovereignty" is also described by our sages as a desire for a "dwelling in the lowly realms"—see next essay, *A Glass of Milk* (pp. 25–31).

7   This conception of Rosh Hashanah as the day of G-d's "coronation" as king of the universe explains a most puzzling paradox in the nature of the day. On the one hand, Rosh Hashanah is when we stand before the supreme king and tremulously accept the "yoke of His sovereignty." On the other hand, it is a festival (*yom tov*), celebrated with feasting and rejoicing—a day on which we are enjoined to "eat sumptuous foods and drink sweet beverages, and send portions to those for whom nothing is prepared, for the day is holy to our L-rd; do not be distressed, for the joy of G-d is your strength" (Nehemiah 8:10).

But such is the nature of a coronation: It is an event that combines trepidation and joy, awe and celebration. For true kingship, as opposed to mere rulership, is a product of the willful submission of a people to their sovereign. So the coronation of a king includes a display of reverence and awe on the part of the people, conveying their submission to the king, as well as the joy that affirms that their submission is willful and desirous. (Cf. *The Beginning and the End*, pp. 272–275.)

ROSH HASHANAH (4)

A GLASS
OF MILK

As she prayed profusely before G-d, Eli ...
thought her a drunkard.

And he said to her: How long will you be
drunken? ...And Chanah replied: No, my
lord... I have poured out my soul before the
face of G-d...

I Samuel 1:12–15

𝔍 he chassid Rabbi Shmuel Munkes was traveling to spend
Rosh Hashanah with his *rebbe*, Rabbi Schneur Zalman of
Liadi, when he was stranded in a small village over Shabbat.

Soon after Shabbat was over, the townspeople retired to an
early bed. Several minutes before midnight, the *shamash* (beadle
of the synagogue) began making his rounds with a lantern in one
hand and a wooden mallet in the other, pounding on the shut-
ters of each home and calling, "Wake up! Wake up! Wake up to
the service of the Creator!" The entire village climbed out of bed,
dressed swiftly, and hurried to the brightly lit synagogue for *selichot*, the solemn prayer that opens the High Holiday season.

In the home of Rabbi Shmuel's host there was much confusion.
The entire family had dressed and gathered at the door, prayer
books in hand, ready to depart for the synagogue; but their prestigious guest had yet to emerge from his room. Finally, the villager
knocked softly on Rabbi Shmuel's door. No response. Slowly he
entered the room. To his amazement, he found the chassid sound
asleep.

"Reb Shmuel, Reb Shmuel," he urged, shaking his guest awake. "Come quickly. *Selichot*."

Rabbi Shmuel's only response was to burrow even more deeply under the covers.

"Hurry, Reb Shmuel," his host persisted. "They're about to begin in the synagogue any moment now."

"Begin what?" asked Rabbi Shmuel, quite obviously annoyed. "It's the middle of the night. Why are you waking me in the middle of the night?"

"What's the matter with you?" cried the villager. "Tonight is *selichot*! A fine Jew you are! Why, if I hadn't woken you, you would have slept through the entire *selichot*!"

"*Selichot*?" asked Rabbi Shmuel. "What is *selichot*?"

Rabbi Shmuel's host was beside himself with incredulity. "Are you making a mockery of me? Don't you know that today was the Shabbat before Rosh Hashanah? Every man, woman, and child of the village is now in the synagogue, trembling with trepidation. Soon the cantor will begin chanting the *selichot* prayers and the entire community will burst into tears, praying and begging G-d to bless them with a good year..."

"So that's what this commotion is all about?" asked Rabbi Shmuel. "You're going to the synagogue to pray? What's so urgent that can't keep until morning? What are you praying for?"

"There's so much to pray for, Reb Shmuel," sighed the villager. "I pray that the cow should give enough milk to keep my children healthy. I pray that the oats should fetch a good price on the market this year, for soon I shall have a daughter to marry off. I pray that my horse should not break a leg, G-d forbid, as happened the year before last..."

"I don't understand," interrupted Rabbi Shmuel. "Since when do grown men wake up in the middle of the night to ask for a bit of milk?"

The Villager Was Right

Rabbi Shmuel Munkes wished to impress upon his host that there is more to preparing for Rosh Hashanah than praying to G-d for one's material needs. Rosh Hashanah is the day on which we proclaim G-d sovereign of the universe and commit ourselves to obey and serve Him. It is a time for *teshuvah*, for repenting for one's sins and failings and resolving never to repeat them. Is this the time to approach G-d with a "shopping list" of our material needs?

And yet, a glance at the Rosh Hashanah prayer book shows that it abounds with requests for life, health, and sustenance. For on Rosh Hashanah, the divine energy that vitalizes all of creation is "renewed" for another year, and every creature is allotted its share of life, happiness, and wealth. The simple villager was right: Rosh Hashanah *is* the time to pray that the cow should give milk and the oats should fetch a good price in the marketplace.

How, indeed, are we to reconcile the loftiness of the day with the mundane subject of a significant part of its prayers?

Indeed, the very concept of prayer carries the same paradox. Prayer is the soul's communion with its Creator, its island of heaven in an otherwise earthbound day. Indeed, the Hebrew word for "prayer," *tefillah*, means "attachment," it being the endeavor to rise above our pedestrian concerns and connect to our divine source. Yet the essence of prayer, the foundation upon which its spiritual edifice rests, is our beseeching the Almighty to provide us with our everyday needs.[1]

The paradox of prayer is magnified when it comes to the prayers of Rosh Hashanah. On Rosh Hashanah, we are not only standing before G-d; we are crowning Him king, pledging to Him the total

---

[1] See *Evening and Morning* in vol. 1 of this series, pp. 64–69.

abnegation of our own self, and all its desires, to His will. What place is there on this day for the very notion of personal need?

A DWELLING BELOW

As discussed at length in our previous Rosh Hashanah essays, only man can make G-d king, for only man possesses the capacity for free choice—without which the very concept of "kingship" is devoid of significance. By freely submitting to the divine sovereignty on Rosh Hashanah, we reawaken His desire to be king and infuse a new vitality into His involvement with the whole of creation.

The divine desire to be king is also described by our sages as a desire for "a dwelling in the lower realms"—a home in the physical world.[2] Why the physical world? Because only in the physical arena does true choice exist. The world of spirit is naturally inclined toward its divine source. Thus, our service of G-d in the spiritual areas of our lives is driven by the natural inclinations of our spiritual selves. On the other hand, when we invite G-d into our physical lives, when we serve Him through physical deeds and with the materials of our physical existence, we are truly *choosing* to submit to Him, for such servitude goes against the very grain of our physical nature.

Thus, one who considers it "unbecoming" to entreat G-d for milk for his children on Rosh Hashanah rejects a most fundamental aspect of the divine sovereignty. Crowning G-d king means accepting Him as sovereign in *all* areas of our lives, including—and primarily—our most mundane needs and requirements. It means acknowledging our utter dependence upon Him not only for our

---

2   *Midrash Tanchuma, Nasso* 16; *Tanya*, chapter 36.

spiritual nurture, but for the piece of bread that sustains our physical existence.

Seen in such a light, our needs are not personal needs, and our requirements are not selfish requirements. Yes, we are requesting food, health, and wealth; but we are requesting them as a subject requests them from his king—as a servant asking his master for the means with which to better serve him. We ask for money to observe the *mitzvah* of charity; for strength to build a *sukkah*; for food to keep body and soul together so that our physical lives may serve as a "dwelling in the lower realms" that houses His presence in our world.

Chanah's Prayer

The *haftarah* (reading from the Prophets) for the first day of Rosh Hashanah tells the story of Chanah, the mother of the prophet Samuel:

Chanah, the childless wife of Elkanah, came to Shiloh (where the Sanctuary stood before King Solomon built the Holy Temple in Jerusalem) to pray for a child.

> *She prayed to G-d, weeping profusely. And she vowed a vow, and said: "O L-rd of hosts, if You will give Your maidservant a man child, I shall dedicate him to G-d all the days of his life…"*

Watching Chanah's prayer was Eli, the High Priest at Shiloh. Eli observed that she

> *prayed profusely before G-d… Only her lips moved; her voice was not heard.*
>
> *Eli thought her a drunkard. And he said to her: "How*

long shall you be drunken! Put away your wine!" Cha-
nah replied: "No, my lord… I have drunk neither wine nor
strong drink. I have poured out my soul before the face of
G-d…"[3]

Eli blessed her that G-d should grant her request. That year, Chanah gave birth to a son, whom she named Samuel. After weaning
him, she fulfilled her vow to dedicate him to the service of G-d by
bringing him to Shiloh, where he was raised by Eli and the priests.
Samuel grew up to become one of the greatest prophets of Israel.

The "prayer of Chanah," as this reading is called, is one of the
fundamental biblical sources for the concept of prayer, and many
of the laws of prayer are derived from it. Indeed, the dialogue between Eli and Chanah touches on the very essence of prayer, and
of prayer on Rosh Hashanah in particular.

Eli's accusation of "drunkenness" can also be understood as a
critique of what he saw as an excessive indulgence in the wants and
desires of the material self on Chanah's part.[4] You are standing in
the most holy place on earth, Eli was implying, in the place where
the divine presence has chosen to dwell. Is this the place to ask
for your personal needs? And if you must ask for them, is this the
place to "pray profusely," with such tenacity and passion?

You misunderstand me, answered Chanah. "I have poured out
my soul before the face of G-d." I am not merely asking for a son; I
am asking for a son that I might "dedicate him to G-d all the days
of his life."

---

3   I Samuel 1:10–15.

4   Indeed, there are several aspects of the story that indicate that Eli
did not think her to be literally drunk (see *Likutei Sichot*, vol. 29, pp.
291–292).

ROSH HASHANAH (4)

Our sages tell us that Samuel was conceived on Rosh Hashanah.[5] G-d's fulfillment of Chanah's prayer on this day encourages us to indeed avail ourselves of the awesome moment of the divine coronation to approach G-d with our requests for our everyday needs. For on this day, our personal needs and our desire to serve our Master are one and the same.

---

5 Rashi, *Megillah* 31a.

CHAPTER NINE

Yom Kippur and the Ten Days of Teshuvah

Repentance, Transcendence, Quintessence

Tishrei 1 to 10

"Seek G-d when He is to be found," proclaims the prophet Isaiah. "Call upon Him when He is near." When is G-d to be found and near? The prophet, say our sages, is speaking of the "ten days of *teshuvah*" that mark the first ten days of the Jewish year.

These ten days, which begin with the two days of Rosh Hashanah (*Tishrei* 1 and 2) are the most solemn of the year: ten days designated for soul-searching, greater diligence in the observance of *mitzvot*, and *teshuvah* (repentance; literally, "return"). G-d is near: more attentive to our prayers, more accepting of our repentance, than on the other days of the year.

The ten days of *teshuvah* culminate in Yom Kippur ("day of atonement"), the day on which terrestrial man most resembles the supernal angel. For close to twenty-six hours, from several minutes before sunset on *Tishrei* 9 to after nightfall on *Tishrei* 10, we abstain from food and drink; nor do we wash or anoint our bodies, wear leather shoes, or engage in marital relations. Garbed in a snow-white *kittel* and *tallit*, we spend the day in the synagogue, where five lengthy prayer services (*maariv*, with its solemn *kol nidrei* service, on the eve of Yom Kippur; and the *shacharit, musaf, minchah* and *ne'ilah* services on Yom Kippur day) and the recitation of Psalms engage our every waking moment.

The day is solemn—the most solemn of the year— yet an undertone of joy suffuses it: a joy that revels in the spirituality of the day and expresses the confidence that G-d will accept our repentance, forgive our sins, and seal our verdict for a year of life, health, and happiness. When the closing *ne'ilah* service climaxes in the resounding cries of "Hear O Israel... G-d is one" and a single blast of the *shofar*, the joy erupts in song, dance, and feasting that make the evening following Yom Kippur a *yom tov* (festival) in its own right.

And that very night, we begin building the *sukkah* in preparation for Sukkot—the seven-day festival that celebrates the achievements of Rosh Hashanah and Yom Kippur, and fully reveals the joy that was overshadowed by the solemnity of these "days of awe."

The first essay of our chapter on "Yom Kippur and the Ten Days of *Teshuvah*" is <u>The 120-Day Version of the Human Story</u>, which describes the historical roots of Yom Kippur. The tenth day of *Tishrei* was the day on which G-d forgave the people of Israel their first and most terrible betrayal—their worship of a golden calf only forty days after entering into their covenant with G-d at Sinai. With His fateful words to Moses, "I have forgiven, as you ask," Yom Kippur was born, inaugurating a fountainhead of *teshuvah* for all generations.

Teshuvah also is the subject of the next four essays of our chapter. <u>Sin in Four Dimensions</u> examines the dynamics of *teshuvah*: How, exactly, is a deleterious deed

35

transformed into a positive force in one's life? <u>Moment</u> touches on the mystery of how the most amazing and transformative of human abilities is achieved in the merest fraction of time. Drawing on its analysis of the Yom Kippur service in the Holy Temple, <u>Ketoret</u> explains how *teshuvah* is not merely an antidote to sin, but a state of being that transforms the nature of our every endeavor.

<u>Day One</u> explores the relationship between the ten days of *teshuvah* and their opening and closing days—Rosh Hashanah and Yom Kippur. We discover that the essence of Yom Kippur, while serving as the source and enabler of *teshuvah*, reaches far beyond the concept of "return."

The prohibition of food and drink on Yom Kippur is the topic of the sixth and final essay in our chapter. <u>Reverse Biology</u> shows how, rather than being a renunciation of the body and its needs, fasting on Yom Kippur actually enhances the bond between body and soul and uncovers the depth and power of our physicality.

See also the following essays: *Daughters Near and Far* (pp. 135–147); *A Roll of Dice* (pp. 240–246); and *The Distant Road* (vol. 3, pp. 115–125).

THE 120-DAY VERSION OF THE HUMAN STORY

Come see the doings of G-d, His fearsome plot
on the children of man.   Psalms 66:5

On the 7th of Sivan, Moses went up onto the
mountain... On the 17th of Tammuz, the
Tablets were broken. On the 18th, he burned
the [golden] calf and judged the transgressors.
On the 19th, he went up for forty days and
pleaded for mercy. On the 1st of Elul, he went
up to receive the second tablets, and was there
for forty days. On the 10th of Tishrei, G-d
restored His goodwill with the Jewish people
gladly and wholeheartedly, saying to Moses,
"I have forgiven, as you ask," and gave Moses
the second tablets.
                        Rashi, Exodus 32:1 and 33:11

$\mathcal{T}$raversing the surface of time, we experience it as a succession of events and experiences. Each era is unique; each year, day, and moment distinct in content and character. But there are also time-vistas of a more inclusive nature. As we often recognize, the story of an individual life may tell the story of a century, and the events of a single generation may embody those of an entire era. Finally, there are stretches in the journey of an individual or a people in which a series of events offers a condensed version of the entire universe of time.

One such potent stretch of time was a 120-day period in the years 2448–9 from Creation (1313 BCE). The events of this period, experienced by the Jewish people soon after their birth as a nation, choreograph the essence of the human story—the basis, the process, and the end-goal of life on earth. The 120 days from *Sivan* 6, 2448 to *Tishrei* 10, 2449 contained it all: the underpinnings of creation, the saga of human struggle, and the ultimate triumph that arises from our imperfections and failings.

THE EVENTS

On[1] Sivan 6, 2448, the entire people of Israel gathered at Mount Sinai to receive the Torah from the Almighty. There, they experienced the revelation of G-d, and heard the Ten Commandments which encapsulate the entire Torah. The following morning Moses ascended the mountain, where he communed with G-d for forty days and forty nights and received the Torah proper, the more detailed rendition of G-d's communication to humanity.

At the end of Moses' (first) forty days on Mount Sinai, G-d gave him two tablets of stone, "the handiwork of G-d," upon which the Ten Commandments were "engraved by the finger of G-d."[2] But in the camp below, the Jewish people were already abandoning their newly made covenant with G-d. Reverting to the paganism

---

1   The sequence of events related below are chronicled in the book of Exodus, chapters 19 and 20, 24:12–18, 32:1–19, and 34:1–2; also see Rashi to Exodus 32:1 and 33:11.

2   Exodus 31:18 and 32:17.

YOM KIPPUR AND THE TEN DAYS OF TESHUVAH (1)   39

of Egypt, they made a calf of gold and, amidst feasting and hedonistic disport, proclaimed it the god of Israel.

> G-d said to Moses: Descend, for your people, whom you have brought up from the land of Egypt, have been corrupted; they have quickly turned from the path that I have commanded them...
>
> And Moses turned and went down from the mountain, with the two tablets of testimony in his hand... And when Moses approached the camp and saw the calf and the dancing... he threw the tablets from his hands and shattered them at the foot of the mountain.[3]

It was the 17th of *Tammuz*.

Moses destroyed the idol and rehabilitated the errant nation. He then returned to Sinai for a second forty days, to plead before G-d for the forgiveness of Israel. G-d acquiesced, and agreed to provide a second set of tablets to replace those which had been broken in the wake of Israel's sin. These tablets, however, were to be not the "handiwork of G-d," but of human construction:

> G-d said to Moses: "Carve yourself two tablets of stone, like the first; and I will inscribe upon them the words that were on the first tablets which you have broken... Come up in the morning to Mount Sinai, and present yourself there to Me on the top of the mountain.[4]

Moses ascended Sinai for his third and final forty days on the mountain on the 1st of *Elul*. G-d had already forgiven Israel's sin, and now a new and invigorated relationship between G-d and His

---

3   Ibid., 32:7–19.
4   Ibid., 34:1–2.

people was to be rebuilt on the ruins of the old. On *Tishrei* 10, we received our second set of the Ten Commandments, inscribed by G-d upon the tablets carved by Moses' hand.

Thus, we have three forty-day periods, and three corresponding states of Torah: the "first tablets," the "broken tablets," and the "second tablets." These embody the foundation of our existence, the challenge of life, and the ultimate achievement of man.

THE PLOT

Our sages point out that the opening verse of the Torah's account of creation, *Bereishit bara Elokim...* ("In the beginning G-d created...") begins with the letter *bet*, the second letter of the Hebrew *aleph-bet*. This is to teach us that there is an *alef* that comes before the *bet* of the created existence; that creation is not an end in itself, but comes to serve a principle which precedes it in sequence and substance.

The pre-Genesis *alef* is the *alef* of "*Anochi Hashem Elokecha...*" ("I Am the L-rd your G-d...") — the first letter of the Ten Commandments. Torah is G-d's "preconception" of what life on earth should be like. The basis and *raison d'être* of creation is that we develop ourselves and our environment toward this ideal.

But G-d wanted more. More than the realization of His original blueprint for existence, more than the falling into place of a pre-programmed perfection. More than a "first tablets" world that is wholly the handiwork of G-d.

A created entity, by definition, has nothing that is truly its own: all the tools, potentials, and possibilities it possesses have been *given* to it by its Creator. But G-d desired that the human experience should yield a profit beyond what is projected — or even

YOM KIPPUR AND THE TEN DAYS OF TESHUVAH (1)   41

warranted—by His initial investment in us. So He created us with the vulnerabilities of the human condition.

G-d created us with the freedom to choose, and thus with the potential for failure. When we act rightly and constructively, we are behaving "according to plan" and realizing the potential invested within us by our Creator. When we choose to act wrongly and destructively, we enter into a state of being that is not part of the plan of Torah—indeed, it is the antithesis of what Torah prescribes. Yet this state of being is the springboard for *teshuvah* ("return")—the power to rise from the ruins of our fall to a new dimension of perfection, one that is beyond the scope of an untarnished life.[5]

Thus chassidic teaching explains G-d's creation of the possibility of evil. This is G-d's "fearsome plot upon the children of man."[6] The soul of man is a spark of G-dliness, inherently and utterly good; in and of itself, it is in no way susceptible to corruption. Its human frailties are nothing less than a contrived plot, imposed upon it in total contrast to its essential nature.

If the "first tablets" are the divine vision of creation, the "broken tablets" are our all-too-familiar world—a world that tolerates imperfection, failure, even outright evil. It is a world whose first tablets have been shattered—a world gone awry of its foundation and its true self, a world wrenched out of sync with its inherent goodness.

The broken tablets are a plot contrived by the Author of existence to allow the possibility for a "second tablets." Every failing, every decline, can be exploited and redirected as a positive force. Every breakdown of the soul's first-tablets-perfection is an

---

5   See next essay, *Sin in Four Dimensions* pp. 44–56.
6   Psalms 66:5. See *Midrash Tanchuma, Vayeishev* 4; Talmud, *Berachot* 31b and Rashi, ad loc.

opportunity for us to "carve for yourself" a second set, in which the divine script is chiseled upon the tablets of human initiative and creation; a second set which includes an entire vista of potentials that were beyond the scope of the first, wholly divine set. In the words of the Midrash:

> G-d said to Moses: "Do not be distressed over the first tablets, which contained only the Ten Commandments. In the second tablets I am giving you also Halachah, Midrash, and aggadah."[7]

"Had Israel not sinned with the golden calf," our sages conclude, "they would have received only the Five Books of Moses and the book of Joshua. As it is written, 'Much wisdom comes through much grief.'"[8]

REMEMBERED AND ENACTED

These 120 days have left a lasting imprint on our experience of time. For the Jewish calendar does more than measure and mark time; in the words of the book of Esther, "These days are remembered and enacted."[9] The festivals and commemorative dates that mark our annual journey through time are opportunities to reenact the events and achievements which they commemorate.[10]

Every Shavuot, we once again experience the revelation at Sinai and our acquisition of the blueprint and foundation of our lives.[11] Every year on the 17th of *Tammuz*, we once again deal with the

---

7   *Midrash Rabbah, Shemot* 46:1
8   Ecclesiastes 1:18; Talmud, *Nedarim* 22b.
9   Esther 9:28.
10 See *Appointments in Time* in vol. 1, pp. 38–45 of this series.
11 See our chapter on "Shavuot" in vol. 3, pp. 151–206 of this series.

YOM KIPPUR AND THE TEN DAYS OF TESHUVAH (1)   43

setbacks and breakdowns epitomized by the events of the day.[12]
The month of *Elul*[13] and the first ten days of *Tishrei*, corresponding to Moses' third 40-day stay on Mount Sinai, are today, as they
were then, days of "goodwill" between G-d and man—days in
which the Almighty is that much more accessible to all who seek
Him.

And Yom Kippur, the holiest and most potent day of the year,
marks the climax of this 120-day saga. Ever since the day that G-d
gave the second tablets to the people of Israel, this day is a fountainhead of *teshuvah*—the source of our capacity to reclaim the
deficiencies of the past as fuel and momentum for the attainment
of new, unprecedented heights; the source of our capacity to exact
a "profit" from G-d's perilous investment in human life.

---

12 The 17th of *Tammuz* is observed as a fast day in commemoration of
    five tragedies that occurred on this day, the first of which is the break-
    ing of the first tablets (Talmud, *Taanit* 26a-b). For more on the signif-
    icance of *Tammuz* 17, see the essay *Difficult Days*, in vol. 3, pp. 220–233
    of this series. Also see our chapter on "The Three Weeks and Tishah
    B'Av" in vol. 3, pp. 207–271.
13 See our chapter on "Elul" in vol. 3, pp. 295–313 of this series.

SIN IN FOUR DIMENSIONS

One who does teshuvah *out of awe, his premeditated sins are rendered as errors.*

One who does teshuvah *out of love, his premeditated sins are rendered as merits.*

Talmud, Yoma 86b

he Midrash recounts the following dialogue on the significance of sin:

> They asked Wisdom: "What is the punishment for the sinner?" Wisdom replied: "Evil pursues sinners" (Proverbs 13:21).
>
> They asked Prophecy: "What is the punishment for the sinner?" Prophecy replied: "The soul that sins, it shall die" (Ezekiel 18:20).
>
> They asked the Torah: "What is the punishment for the sinner?" The Torah replied: He shall bring a guilt-offering, and he shall be forgiven (Leviticus 5).
>
> They asked G-d: "What is the punishment for the sinner?" G-d replied: He shall do teshuvah, *and he shall be forgiven.*[1]

---

1   *Yalkut Shimoni, Tehillim* 702.

YOM KIPPUR AND THE TEN DAYS OF TESHUVAH (2)   45

The Philosophical Perspective

The concept of "reward and punishment" is one of the fundamental principles of Jewish faith.[2] But punishment for wrongdoing, say our sages, is no more G-d's "revenge" than falling to the ground is divine retribution for jumping out the window, or frostbite is G-d's punishment for a barefoot trek in the snow. Just as the Creator established certain laws of cause and effect that define the natural behavior of the physical universe, so, too, did G-d establish a spiritual-moral "nature," by which doing good results in a good and fulfilling life, and doing evil results in negative and strifeful experiences.[3]

This is the philosophical perspective on sin and punishment expressed by King Solomon in the above-quoted verse from Proverbs. "Evil pursues iniquity"—the adverse effects of sin are the natural consequences of acts that run contrary to the Creator's design for life.

The Prophet's View

Prophecy, which is G-d's empowerment of man to cleave to and commune with Him,[4] has a deeper insight into the significance of sin.

The essence of life is connection with G-d. "You who cleave to G-d," says Moses to the people of Israel, at the end of their

---

2   The eleventh principle of Maimonides' "Thirteen Principles of Faith" (*Commentary on the Mishnah*, introduction to *Perek Cheilek*).

3   Shaloh, *Bayit Acharon* 12a; *Shaar HaTeshuvah* (by Rabbi DovBer of Lubavitch), part I, 6c and 50b; *Likutei Biurim* on *Tanya*, vol. 2, p. 129.

4   See ch. 7 of Maimonides' "Eight Chapters" of introduction to his commentary on *Ethics of the Fathers*.

physically and spiritually perilous 40-year journey through the desert, "are all alive today."[5] "Love the L-rd your G-d," he also enjoins them, "for He is your life."[6]

So a transgression is more than a spiritually deleterious deed—it is an act of spiritual suicide. In the words of the prophet Ezekiel, "The soul that sins, it shall die," since to transgress the divine will is to sabotage the channel of vitality that connects the soul to its source. Our sages echo the prophetic perspective on sin when they state: "The wicked, even in their lifetimes, are considered dead... The righteous, even in death, are considered alive."[7]

THE GUILT-OFFERING

The Torah has yet a more penetrating view on the dynamics of transgression. It, too, recognizes that the essence of a person's life is his or her relationship with G-d. But the Torah also perceives the superficiality of evil—the fact that "a person does not sin unless a spirit of insanity enters into him."[8]

The soul of man, which is "veritably a part of G-d above,"[9] "neither desires, nor is able, to separate itself from G-d."[10] It is only our animal self—the material and selfish drives which overlay our G-dly soul—which might, at times, take control of our lives and compel us to act in a manner that is completely at odds with our true self and will.

---

5   Deuteronomy 4:4.
6   Ibid., 30:20.
7   Talmud, *Berachot* 18a-b.
8   Ibid., *Sotah* 3a, based on Numbers 5:12.
9   *Tanya*, ch. 2, after Job 31:2.
10 Rabbi Schneur Zalman of Liadi; cited in *Hayom Yom, Tammuz* 25; *Sefer HaMaamarim* 5751, p. 50; et al.

YOM KIPPUR AND THE TEN DAYS OF TESHUVAH (2)   47

Thus Maimonides writes:

> If the law mandates that a person should grant his wife
> a divorce, and he refuses, a Jewish court, in any time or
> place, may beat him until he says "I am willing" and
> writes the writ of divorce. This is a valid divorce [despite
> the fact that, according to Torah law, a divorce must be
> granted willingly]... Why? Because an act is not consid-
> ered to be "coerced" unless the person has been forced to
> do something to which he is not morally obligated by the
> Torah; for example, one who has been forced to sell or give
> away his property. But one who has been overpowered by
> his evil inclination to negate a mitzvah or to commit a
> transgression, and is forced to do what is right, he is not
> considered "coerced"—on the contrary, it is his evil char-
> acter which has forced him, against his true will, in the
> first place.
>
> Therefore: This individual who refuses to grant a di-
> vorce desires, in truth, to be of Israel, and desires to ob-
> serve all of the commandments and to avoid all of the
> transgressions of the Torah. It is only that his evil inclina-
> tion has overpowered him. So if he is beaten so that his evil
> inclination is weakened, and he says: "I am willing"—he
> has willingly divorced.[11]

Because the Torah perceives the superficiality of sin, it can guide
the transgressor through a process by which he can undo the negative effects of his transgression—a process by which the transgressor recognizes the folly and self-destructiveness of his deed and re-
instates his true, G-dly self as the sovereign of his life. This process

---

11   *Mishneh Torah, Laws of Divorce* 2:20.

culminates with the transgressor's bringing of a *korban* (animal sacrifice) as an offering to G-d, signifying his subjugation of his own animal self to the spark of G-dliness within him.[12]

In this way, the "guilt-offering" achieves atonement for sin. Only the most external self was involved in the transgression in the first place; by renouncing the deed as "animal behavior" and subjugating the beast within to serve the soul's G-dly aims, the transgressor restores the integrity of his relationship with the Almighty.

THE COMMON DENOMINATOR

There is one thing, however, that the philosophical, prophetic, and Torah perspectives on sin have in common: the transgression was, and remains, a negative phenomenon.

"Wisdom" sees it as the harbinger of misfortune in a person's life. "Prophecy" sees it as antithetical to life itself. Torah delves deeper yet, revealing the root cause of sin and providing the key to the transgressor's rehabilitation. But even after the atonement prescribed by the Torah, the transgression itself remains a negative event. Torah itself defines certain deeds as contrary to the divine

---

12 Cf. Talmud, *Sotah* 14a: "[The transgressor] acted like an animal; therefore she should bring an offering of animal-feed." Thus Rabbi Schneur Zalman of Liadi interprets the verse (Leviticus 1:2), "A person who shall offer, from amongst you, an animal-offering to G-d...": Should not the verse have said, "A person, from amongst you, who shall offer..."? But the Torah is stressing that, indeed, the *offering* is to be "from amongst you"—it is the animal in you that you must first subjugate to G-d, if your offering is to be of any significance (*Likutei Torah*, *Vayikra* 2b–d).

YOM KIPPUR AND THE TEN DAYS OF TESHUVAH (2)

will; so nothing in Torah can change the fact that a transgression constitutes a betrayal of the relationship between G-d and man.

As the author of wisdom, the bestower of prophecy, and the commander of Torah, G-d is the source of all three perspectives. But G-d also harbors a fourth vision of sin, a vision that is His alone: sin as the potential for *teshuvah*.

THE FORBIDDEN REALM

The commandments of the Torah categorize the universe into two domains: the permissible and the forbidden. Beef is permissible, pork is forbidden; doing work on the first six days of the week is permissible, to do so on Shabbat is not; the trait of compassion is to be cultivated, and that of haughtiness is to be eliminated.

Chassidic teaching explains that this is more than a list of dos and don'ts; it is also a catalog of realizable and unrealizable potentials. Every created entity possesses a "spark" of divine energy that constitutes its essence and soul—a spark that embodies its function within the divine purpose for creation. When a person utilizes something—be it a physical object or force, a trait or feeling, or a cultural phenomenon—toward a G-dly end, he or she brings to light the divine spark at its core, manifesting and realizing the purpose for which it was created.

While no existence is devoid of such a spark—indeed, nothing can exist without the pinpoint of divinity that imbues it with being and purpose—not every spark can be actualized through our constructive use of the thing in which it is invested. There are certain "impregnable" elements—elements with which the Torah has forbidden our involvement, so that the sparks they contain are inaccessible to us.

For example, one who eats a piece of kosher meat and then uses the energy gained from it to perform a *mitzvah*, thereby "elevates" the spark of divinity that is the essence of the meat, freeing it of its mundane incarnation and raising it to a state of fulfilled spirituality. However, if one would do the same with a piece of nonkosher meat—meat that G-d has forbidden us to consume—no such elevation would take place. Even if that person applied the energy from the nonkosher food to positive and G-dly ends, this would not constitute a realization of the divine purpose in the food's creation, since its consumption was an express violation of the divine will.

This is the deeper significance of the Hebrew terms *assur* and *mutar*, employed by Torah law for the forbidden and the permissible. *Assur*, commonly translated as "forbidden," literally means "bound"; this is the Torah's term for those elements whose sparks it has deemed bound and imprisoned in a shell of negativity and proscription. *Mutar* ("permitted"), which literally means "unbound," is the term for those sparks which the Torah has empowered us to extricate from their mundane embodiment and actively involve in our positive endeavors.

Obviously, the "bound" elements of creation also have a role in the realization of the divine purpose outlined by the Torah. But theirs is a negative role—they exist so that we should achieve a conquest of self by resisting them. There is no Torah-authorized way in which they can *actively* be involved in our development of creation, no way in which they may themselves become part of the "dwelling for G-d"[13] that we are charged to make of our world. Of these elements it is said, "their breaking is their rectification."[14]

---

13 *Midrash Tanchuma, Nasso* 16; *Tanya*, chapter 36.
14 Paraphrase of *Sifra, Shemini* 7; see *Sefer HaMaamarim* 5654, pg. 76.

YOM KIPPUR AND THE TEN DAYS OF TESHUVAH (2)   51

They exist to be rejected and defeated, and it is in their defeat and exclusion from our lives that their *raison d'être* is realized.

THE MAN IN THE DESERT

These are the rules that govern our lives and our service of G-d. One who lives by these rules, establishing them as the supreme authority over his behavior, attains the status of *tzaddik* ("perfectly righteous"). Yet our sages tell us that there is an even higher level of closeness to G-d—that "in the place where *baalei teshuvah* ("returnees"; penitents) stand, absolute *tzaddikim* cannot stand."[15]

The *tzaddik* is one who has made the divine will the very substance of his existence. Everything that becomes part of the *tzaddik's* life—the food he eats, the clothes he wears, the ideas and experiences he garners from his surroundings—is elevated, its "spark" divested of its mundanity and raised to its divine function. And the *tzaddik* confines himself to the permissible elements of creation, never digressing from the boundaries that Torah sets for our involvement with and development of G-d's world.

The *baal teshuvah*, on the other hand, is one who *has* digressed; one who has ventured beyond the realm of the permissible and has absorbed the irredeemable elements of creation into his life. His digression was a wholly negative thing;[16] but having occurred, it holds a unique potential: the potential for *teshuvah*, "return."

Teshuvah is fueled by the utter dejection experienced by one who wakes to the realization that he has destroyed all that is beautiful and sacred in his life; by the pain of one who has cut himself

---

15 Talmud, *Berachot* 34b.
16 Indeed, the Talmud (*Yoma* 85b) warns that one who says, "I shall sin and then repent" is "not given the opportunity to repent."

off from his source of life and well-being; by the alienation felt by one who finds himself without cause or reason to live. *Teshuvah* is man's amazing ability to translate these feeling of worthlessness, alienation, and pain into the drive for rediscovery and renewal.

The *baal teshuvah* is a person lost in the desert whose thirst, amplified a thousand-fold by the barrenness and aridity of his surroundings, drives him to seek water with an intensity that could never have been called forth by the most proficient well-digger; a person whose very abandonment of G-d drives him to seek Him with a passion the most saintly *tzaddik* cannot know. A soul who, having stretched the cord that binds it to its source to excruciating tautness, rebounds with a force that exceeds anything experienced by those who never leave the divine orbit.

In this way, the *baal teshuvah* accomplishes what the most perfect *tzaddik* cannot: He liberates those sparks of divinity imprisoned in the realm of the forbidden. In his soul, the very negativity of these elements—their very contrariness to the divine will—becomes a positive force, an intensifier of his bond with G-d and his drive to do good.[17]

This is *teshuvah*, "return," in its ultimate sense:[18] the reclaiming of the "lost" moments (or days, or years) and energies of a negative past; the restoration of sparks imprisoned in the lowliest realms of creation; the magnified force of a rebounding soul.

---

17   *Tanya*, chapter 7.

18   The Torah's prescription for atonement is also called *teshuvah*, but that is *teshuvah* in the more limited sense of "repentance," as opposed to the ultimate *teshuvah* which transforms the past. Thus the Talmud distinguishes between "*teshuvah* out of awe," through which "premeditated sins are rendered as errors" (i.e., the transgressor's guilt and culpability are annulled while the negativity of the deed remains), and "*teshuvah* out of love," through which "premeditated sins are rendered as merits"—retroactively transformed into a positive force.

YOM KIPPUR AND THE TEN DAYS OF TESHUVAH (2)   53

GOOD AND EVIL

But what of the "bindings" that imprison these sparks? If the *tzaddik* were to employ a forbidden thing toward a positive end, he would fail to elevate it; indeed, the deed would drag him down, distancing him, rather than bringing him closer to the G-d he is presuming to serve. From where derives the *baal teshuvah*'s power to redeem what the Torah has decreed "bound" and irredeemable?

In its commentary on the opening verses of Genesis, the Midrash states:

> *At the onset of the world's creation, G-d beheld the deeds of the righteous and the deeds of the wicked... "And the earth was void and chaotic..."*[19] — *these are the deeds of the wicked. "And G-d said: 'There shall be light'"*[20] — *these are the deeds of the righteous. But I still do not know which of them He desires... Then, when it says, "And G-d saw the light, that it is good,"*[21] *I know that He desires the deeds of the righteous, and does not desire the deeds of the wicked.*[22]

Essentially, what this Midrash is telling us is that the only true definition of "good" or "evil" is that "good" is what G-d desires, and "evil" is what is contrary to His will. The fact that we instinctively sense certain deeds to be good and others to be evil—the fact that certain deeds *are* good and certain deeds *are* evil—is the *result* of G-d having chosen to desire certain deeds from man and to not desire other deeds from man. We cannot, however, speak of good

---

19   Genesis 1:2.
20   Ibid., v. 3.
21   Ibid., v. 4.
22   *Midrash Rabbah*, Bereishit 2:7.

and evil "before" G-d expressly chose the "deeds of the righteous." On this level, where there is nothing to distinguish right from wrong, we cannot presume to know what G-d will desire.

Therein lies the difference between the *tzaddik* and the *baal teshuvah*.

The *tzaddik* relates to G-d through his fulfillment of the divine will expressed in the Torah. Thus, the *tzaddik*'s achievements are defined and regulated by the divine will. When he or she does what G-d has commanded to be done, he or she elevates those elements of creation touched by his or her deeds. But those elements with which the divine will forbids our involvement, are closed to the *tzaddik*.

The *baal teshuvah*, however, relates to G-d Himself, the formulator and professor of this will. Thus, the *baal teshuvah* accesses a divine potential that, by Torah's standards, is inaccessible. Because the *baal teshuvah*'s relationship with G-d is on a level that precedes and supersedes the divine will—a level on which one "still does not know which of them G-d desires"—there are no "bound" elements, nothing to inhibit the actualization of the divine potential in *any* of G-d's creations. So when the *baal teshuvah* sublimates his or her negative deeds and experiences to fuel a yearning and passion for good, he or she brings to light the sparks of G-dliness they hold.

TO BE AND TO BE NOT

What enables the *baal teshuvah* to connect to G-d in such a way? The *tzaddik*'s ability to relate to G-d through the fulfillment of the divine will was granted to each and every one of us when G-d gave us the Torah at Mount Sinai. But what empowers the *baal*

YOM KIPPUR AND THE TEN DAYS OF TESHUVAH (2)

teshuvah to reach the "place where absolute *tzaddikim* cannot stand" and tap the "pre-will" essence of G-d?

The thrust of the *baal teshuvah*'s life is the very opposite of the *tzaddik*'s. The *tzaddik* is good, and the gist of everything he or she does is to amplify that goodness. The *baal teshuvah* had departed from the path of good, and the gist of everything he or she does is to deconstruct and transform what he or she was. In other words, the *tzaddik* is occupied with the development of self, and the *baal teshuvah*, with the negation of self.

Thus, the *tzaddik*'s virtue is also what limits him. True, the *tzaddik*'s development of self is a wholly positive and G-dly endeavor — the *tzaddik* is developing the self that G-d wants him or her to develop, and by developing this self the *tzaddik* becomes one with the will of G-d. But a sense of self is also the greatest handicap to relating to the *essence* of G-d, which tolerates no camouflaging or equivocation of the truth that "there is none else beside Him."[23]

The *baal teshuvah*, on the other hand, is one whose every thought and endeavor is driven by the recognition that he or she must depart from what he or she is in order to come close to G-d. This perpetual abnegation of self allows the *baal teshuvah* to relate to G-d as G-d is, on a level that transcends the specific divine self-projection which G-d formulated as His Torah.

THE FOURTH DIMENSION

This is *G-d*'s perspective on sin: sin as the facilitator of *teshuvah*. "Wisdom," "prophecy," and "Torah"[24] are all part of a reality

---

23 Deuteronomy 4:35.

24 The "Torah" of which we speak here is the Torah of the "first tablets" given on the 6th of *Sivan* (Shavuot). The "second tablets," given on

polarized by good and evil; they can perceive only the damage inflicted by sin, or, at most (as in the case of Torah), the manner by which it might be undone. G-d's reality, however, is wholly and exclusively good. "No evil resides with You," proclaims the Psalmist. In the words of Jeremiah, "From the Supernal One do not stem both evil and good."[25]

From G-d's perspective, there is only the positive essence of transgression—the positive purpose for which G-d created man's susceptibility to evil and man's capacity for sin in the first place.[26] As viewed by its Creator, transgression is the potential for a deeper bond between G-d and man—a bond born out of the transformation of evil into good and failure into achievement.

    Yom Kippur, include (and are the source for) the power of *teshuvah*: In its second incarnation—evoked by Israel's repentance for the sin of the Golden Calf—Torah transcends its basic definition as the divine will, to embrace the "pre-will" essence of G-d (see the previous essay, *The 120-Day Version of the Human Story*, and the essays in our chapter on "Shemini Atzeret and Simchat Torah," pp. 125–153 below).

25 Psalms 5:5; Lamentations 3:38.

26 Thus, the Psalmist calls the negative inclinations of the human heart "G-d's fearsome plot upon the children of man" (Psalms 66:5): G-d creates things which He declares to be contrary to His will (an oxymoronic phenomenon, since the essence of every existence is the divine desire that it exist), and makes man vulnerable to their enticements, so as to set the stage for *teshuvah* (see *Midrash Tanchuma*, Vayeishev 4; Talmud and Rashi, *Berachot* 31b; also see previous essay, *The 120-Day Version of the Human Story*, pp. 37–43, above).

YOM KIPPUR AND THE TEN DAYS OF TESHUVAH (3)

MOMENT

When Elazar ben Durdaia (a notorious sin-
ner) found that all his appeals for assistance
in pleading his case before G-d had been
turned down, he said: "It all depends entirely
on myself." He placed his head between his
knees and wept until his soul departed from
him. A voice from heaven then announced:
"Rabbi Elazar ben Durdaia is destined for life
in the world to come!"

Hearing this, Rabbi [Judah HaNassi]
wept: "There are those who acquire their
world in many years, and there are those who
acquire their world in a single moment."

Talmud, Avodah Zarah 17a

*I*n this world of ours, more is less and less is more.

Quantitatively, the earth is but a tiny speck in a vast universe; in significance, it is the focus of G-d's creation. Of the earth itself, inanimate matter constitutes virtually all of its mass, only a minute fraction of which are living cells. Plant life is more plentiful than animal life, and animals far more numerous than humans. Within the human being, the head, seat of man's most sophisticated faculties, is smaller than the torso or limbs. In a word, the greater the quality, the smaller the quantity.

The same is true of man's most precious resource: time. Quality time — time that is most optimally and fulfillingly utilized — comprises but a quantitative fraction of the time we consume. How many minutes of each day do we spend on truly meaningful things? The bulk of our hours are taken up with earning a living, sleeping, eating, and fulfilling a host of social and other obligations—worthy pursuits them all, but secondary to the purpose of our lives.

The very structure of time, as designed by its Creator, follows the "less is more" model. There are six mundane workdays, leading to a single day of spirit and tranquility. Yom Kippur—the "Sabbath of Sabbaths,"[1] whose twenty-six hours bring us in touch with our deepest, most essential self—occupies less than 0.3 percent of the year. Everything we do takes time, but the greater the quality of our endeavor, the less the quantity of time it consumes.

The most potent of human deeds is *teshuvah*—our ability to rectify and sublimate past wrongdoing by returning to the timeless, inviolable core of self which was never tainted by sin in the first place. And *teshuvah* is the least "time-consuming" of events: the essence of *teshuvah* is a single wrench of self, a single flash of regret and resolve.[2] "There are those who acquire their world in many years," says the Talmud, building it brick by brick with the conventional tools of achievement. Then there are those who acquire their world in "a single moment"[3]—in a single, timeless instant that molds the future and redefines the past.

---

1   Leviticus 16:31, et al.

2   Thus the Talmud (*Kidushin* 49b) rules that "If a man betroths a woman on the condition that he is a *tzaddik* (perfectly righteous person), she is considered as possibly betrothed to him, even if he is an utterly wicked man—for perhaps, at the moment that he betrothed her, he had a thought of *teshuvah*."

3   The Hebrew word the Talmud uses, *shaah*, is a basic term for "time unit," and translates as both "hour" and "moment." The word also means "turn," implying the shift from state to state that is the elementary measure of time and the essence of *teshuvah*.

KETORET

And he shall take a censer-full of burning coals from the altar, and the fill of his hands of finely-ground ketoret; *and he shall bring [these] inside the curtain.*

And he shall place the ketoret *upon the fire before G-d; and the cloud of the incense shall envelop the covering of the [Ark of] Testimony…*   Leviticus 16:12–13

O ur quest to serve our Creator is perpetual and all-consuming, and can be pursued by all people, at all times, and in all places. There was one event, however, that represented the apogee in the human effort to come close to G-d—an event that brought together the holiest day of the year, the holiest person on earth, and the holiest place in the universe. On Yom Kippur, the *kohen gadol* ("high priest") would enter the innermost chamber of the Holy Temple in Jerusalem, the "Holy of Holies," to offer *ketoret* to G-d.

The offering of the *ketoret* was the most prestigious and sacred of the services in the Holy Temple. The *ketoret* was a special blend of eleven herbs and balms whose precise ingredients and manner of preparation were commanded by G-d to Moses.[1] Twice a day, *ketoret* was burned on the "golden altar" that stood in the Temple.[2] On Yom Kippur, in addition to the regular *ketoret* offerings, the

---

1   Exodus 30:34–38; see Talmud, *Keritot* 6a and Jerusalem Talmud, *Yoma* 4:5.
2   Exodus 30:8–9.

kohen gadol would enter the Holy of Holies with a pan of smoldering coals in his right hand and a ladle filled with *ketoret* in his left; there, he would scoop the *ketoret* into his hands, place it over the coals, wait for the chamber to fill with the fragrant smoke of the burning incense, and swiftly back out of the room.[3] The moment marked the climax of the Yom Kippur service in the Holy Temple.

Maimonides describes the function of the *ketoret* as the vanquishing of the unpleasant odors that might otherwise have pervaded the Holy Temple. "Since many animals were slaughtered in the sacred place each day, their flesh butchered and burnt and their intestines cleaned, its smell would doubtless have been like the smell of a slaughterhouse... Therefore G-d commanded that the *ketoret* be burned twice a day, each morning and afternoon, to lend a pleasing fragrance to [the Holy Temple] and to the garments of those who served in it."[4]

Many of the commentaries wonder at the attribution of such a prosaic function to this most sacred ritual. In the words of Rabbeinu Bechayei,[5] "G-d forbid that the great principle and mystery of the *ketoret* should be reduced to this mundane purpose."[6]

Chassidic teaching explains that Maimonides' words carry a significance that extends beyond their superficial sense. The animal sacrifices offered in the Holy Temple represent the person's offering of his own "animal soul"[7] to G-d—the subjugation of his natural instincts and desires to the divine will. This is the deeper

---

3   Leviticus 16:12–13; Talmud, *Yoma* 5:1 (Mishnah).

4   *Guide for the Perplexed* 3:45.

5   Rabbi Bechayei (or Bachya) ibn Chalawah, c. 1255–1340.

6   Bechayei on Torah, Exodus 30:1.

7   As Rabbi Schneur Zalman of Liadi elaborates in his *Tanya*, every person possesses two souls: an "animal soul" that is the essence of his physical self, and a "G-dly soul" that embodies his drive for self-transcendence and union with G-d.

YOM KIPPUR AND THE TEN DAYS OF TESHUVAH (4)   61

significance of the "foul odor" emitted by the sacrifices which the
ketoret came to dispel: The "animal soul" of man, which is the basic
drive, common to every living creature, for self-preservation and
self-enhancement, possesses many positive traits which can be directed toward gainful and holy ends; but it is also the source of
many negative and destructive traits. When a person brings his
animal self to the temple of G-d and offers what is best and finest
in it upon the altar, there is still the "foul odor"—the selfishness,
the brutality, and the materiality of the animal in man—that accompanies the process. Hence the burning of the *ketoret*, which
possessed the unique capability to sublimate the "evil odor" of the
animal soul within its heavenly fragrance.

ESSENCE AND UTILITY

This, however, still does not define the essence of the *ketoret*. For
if the more external parts of the Temple might be susceptible to
the foul odor emitted by the "animal souls" offered there, the
Holy of Holies was a sanctum of unadulterated holiness and perfection. No animal sacrifices were offered there, for this part of
the Temple was exclusively devoted to sheltering the "Ark of Tes-
tament" that held the tablets upon which G-d had inscribed the
Ten Commandments. If the "garments" (i.e., character and behavior[8]) of the ordinary priest might be affected by the negative smell
of the "slaughtered beasts" he handled, this was certainly not the
case with the *kohen gadol*, "the greatest of his brethren"[9] in the
fraternity of divine service. If every day of the year the scent of evil
hovers at the periphery of even the most positive endeavor, Yom

---

8   See *Tanya*, chapters 4 and 6.
9   Leviticus 21:10.

Kippur is a day in which "there is no license for the forces of evil to incriminate."[10] If the *ketoret* was offered by the *kohen gadol* in the Holy of Holies on Yom Kippur, its ultimate function could not be the sublimation of evil.

The sublimation of evil is something that only the *ketoret* can achieve, but this is not the sum of its purpose and function. The word *ketoret* means "bonding." The essence of the *ketoret* is the pristine yearning of the soul of man to cleave to G-d—a yearning that emanates from the innermost sanctum of the soul and is thus free of all constraints and restraints, free of all that inhibits and limits us when we relate to something with the more external aspects of our being.[11]

Its purity and perfection are what give the *ketoret* the power to sweeten the foulest of odors, but dealing with evil is not what it is all about. On the contrary, its highest expression is in the utterly evil-free environment of the Holy of Holies on Yom Kippur.

BRINGING THE PAST IN LINE

Today, the Holy Temple no longer stands in Jerusalem, and the *kohen gadol* enters the Holy of Holies only in our recitation of the account of the Yom Kippur Temple service in the prayers of the holy day and in our vision of a future Yom Kippur in the rebuilt Temple. But the *ketoret* remains a basic component of our service of G-d in general, and of our observance of Yom Kippur in particular. We are speaking of the spiritual *ketoret*, which exists within the human soul as the power of *teshuvah*.

Like the incense that burned in the Holy Temple, the manifest

---

10   Talmud, *Yoma* 20a.
11   Cf. *Zohar* 3:288a.

YOM KIPPUR AND THE TEN DAYS OF TESHUVAH (4)

function of *teshuvah* is to deal with negative and undesirable things. On the day-to-day, practical level, *teshuvah* is "repentance"—a response to wrongdoing, a healing potion for the ills of the soul. But *teshuvah* is also the dominant quality of Yom Kippur, the holiest day of the year. Obviously, there is more to *teshuvah* than the rectification of sin.

The word *teshuvah* means "return": return to pristine beginnings, return to the intrinsic perfection of the soul. For the essence of the soul of man, which is "a spark of G-dliness," is immune to corruption. The inner self of man remains uninvolved in the follies of the ego, untouched by the outer self's enmeshment in the material and the mundane. *Teshuvah* is the return to our true self, the cutting through of all those outer layers of misguided actions and distorted priorities to awaken our true will and desire.

This explains how *teshuvah* achieves atonement for past sins. *Teshuvah* enables the sinner to reconnect with his own inherent goodness, with that part of himself which never sinned in the first place. In a sense, he has now acquired a new self, one with an unblemished past; but this "new self" is really his own true self come to light, while his previous, corrupted "self" was but an external distortion of his true being.

Only *teshuvah* has such power over the past; only *teshuvah* can "undo" a negative deed. But this is only one of the "uses" of the power of return. *Teshuvah* is not only for sinners, but also for the holiest person in the holiest time and the holiest place. For even the perfectly righteous individual needs to be liberated from the limitations of the past.

Even the perfectly righteous individual is limited—limited because of knowledge not yet acquired, insights still not gained, feelings yet to be developed, attainments still unachieved; in a word, limited by time itself and the tyranny of its "one way only" trajectory. As we advance through life, we conquer these limits, gaining wisdom and experience, and refining and perfecting our character. But is our ability to grow and achieve limited to the future only? Is the past a closed frontier?

When we adopt the inward-seeking approach of *teshuvah* in everything we do, we need not leave an imperfect past behind at the waysides of our lives. In a *teshuvah* state, when we learn something new, we uncover the deeper dimension of our self which was always aware of this truth; when we refine a new facet of our personality, we bring to light the timeless perfection of our soul. Never satisfied in merely moving forward, our quest for our own true self remakes the past as well.

DAY ONE

[The sages say:] Yom Kippur atones only for those who repent.

Rabbi [Judah HaNassi] says: Yom Kippur atones whether one repents or one does not repent.
Talmud, Shevuot 13a

On Yom Kippur, the day itself atones... as it is written,[1] "For on this day, it shall atone for you."
Mishneh Torah, Laws of Repentance 1:3

$\mathcal{C}$ iting the prophet Isaiah's call, "Seek G-d when He may be found, call upon Him when He is near," the Talmud says: "These are the ten days between Rosh Hashanah and Yom Kippur."[2] These ten days, called "the ten days of *teshuvah*," are the most solemn days of the year—days designated for soul-searching and return (*teshuvah*) to G-d. G-d is near—more attentive to our prayers, more accepting of our repentance, than on the other days of the year.

But *are* there ten days between Rosh Hashanah and Yom Kippur? Rosh Hashanah occurs on the first and second days of *Tishrei*, while Yom Kippur is on the 10th of that month. Thus, the "ten days of *teshuvah*" would *include* Rosh Hashanah and Yom Kippur. Indeed, *teshuvah* is a dominant theme in the observances and prayers of both festivals.[3] Yet the Talmud, in the above-quoted

---

1 Leviticus 16:30.
2 Isaiah 55:6; Talmud, *Rosh Hashanah* 18a.
3 On Rosh Hashanah there is no confession of sins, nor any mention of

passage and in other places,[4] speaks of "the ten days *between* Rosh Hashanah and Yom Kippur."

Chassidic teaching explains that while Rosh Hashanah and Yom Kippur are themselves days of *teshuvah*, they each embody a principle that goes beyond the concept of "return": the essence of Rosh Hashanah precedes *teshuvah*, while the essence of Yom Kippur supersedes *teshuvah*. Thus, the ten days of *teshuvah* include the days of Rosh Hashanah and Yom Kippur and, at the same time, they are "the ten days between Rosh Hashanah and Yom Kippur."[5]

THE VIRTUE IN SIN

The Torah describes the people of Israel as "the nation close to Him."[6] What does it mean that we are "close" to G-d? There are

---

sin, in the day's prayers. But the theme of *teshuvah* pervades the atmosphere and observances of the day, and one of the basic functions of the *shofar* is to rouse us to repentance (see *Mishneh Torah, Laws of Teshuvah,* 3:4).

4   Cf. Talmud, *Berachot* 12b.

5   Indeed, there is a special quality to those seven of the ten days that are literally "between Rosh Hashanah and Yom Kippur." Master kabbalist Rabbi Isaac Luria (the "Holy Ari," 1534–1572) notes that these seven days will always include one Sunday, one Monday, etc. These seven days, says Ari, correspond to, and are inclusive of, their sister days of the entire year: the Sunday between Rosh Hashanah and Yom Kippur encapsulates all Sundays of the year, the Monday between Rosh Hashanah and Yom Kippur embodies all Mondays of the year, and so on. The Shabbat between Rosh Hashanah and Yom Kippur (called *Shabbat Shuvah,* "the Shabbat of Return") is also the quintessential Shabbat—the Shabbat from which all Shabbats of the year draw their Shabbat-essence.

6   Deuteronomy 4:7; Psalms 148:14.

YOM KIPPUR AND THE TEN DAYS OF TESHUVAH (5)

three fundamental aspects to our relationship with the Almighty and the manner in which it is expressed in our lives.

On the most elementary level, we achieve connection with G-d through our observance of the *mitzvot*, the divine commandments. The *mitzvot* embody the will of G-d; by observing the *mitzvot* and making their fulfillment the substance and aim of our lives, our souls and bodies become vehicles of the divine will, thereby connecting with the One who desired and commanded this action. Indeed, the Hebrew word *mitzvah* means both "commandment" and "connection."

But when a person violates the divine will, G-d forbid, he uncovers an even deeper dimension of his bond with G-d. The connection created by the *mitzvah* is exactly that—a connection *created* between two separate entities. Taken on its own, this connection does not point to any intrinsic bond between the two. In fact, it implies that the natural state of the observer of the *mitzvah* is one of separateness and distinction from G-d—a state which is overcome by the act of the *mitzvah*, which bridges the gulf between the mortal and the divine. But when a person transgresses a divine command, a deeper bond with G-d comes to light. His inner equilibrium is disturbed; his soul finds no peace and is driven to compensate for its devastated identity with material excesses or profane spiritual quests. His transgressions highlight the fact that there is nothing more *unnatural* than a soul estranged from her G-d.

Teshuvah is a soul's experience of the agony of disconnection from its source and its channeling of this agony to drive its return to G-d. Thus, our sages have said that the sins of a *baal teshuvah* ("returnee") are "transformed into merits," and that he or she attains a level of relationship with G-d on which "even the perfectly righteous cannot stand."[7] The transgressions of the *baal teshuvah* become virtues, for the distance and disconnection they created have become the impetus for greater closeness and deeper connection. The *baal teshuvah*'s sins have provoked—and his or her *teshuvah* has actualized—a dimension of the soul's connection to G-d which a perfectly righteous life never touches.

THE "ONE OF THE YEAR"

But there is also a third, even deeper, dimension to our bond with G-d.

The two types of connection discussed above have one thing in common: They both allow for the possibility of disconnection. The *mitzvah* relates to the level on which our finite and mortal nature sets us apart from G-d—a state of affairs which the *mitzvah* comes to overcome. The transgression makes the opposite point (that connection with G-d is the natural state of every soul) with its very dissevering of this connection, *teshuvah* being the consequential effort to restore the natural bond.

Ultimately, however, there is a quintessential bond between the soul and G-d that is immutable. On the deepest level of our being, there can be no disconnection, "natural" or "unnatural."

This underlying oneness with G-d is the root from which the other two levels of connection stem. Every time we do a *mitzvah*, we draw from this quintessential unity with G-d the power to overcome our "natural" apartness and connect to G-d through the fulfillment of His will. Every time we sin and experience the agony of disconnection from G-d, this is but another expression of the fact that, in essence, our soul is one with its Creator. And it is

---

7   Talmud, *Yoma* 86b and *Berachot* 34b.

YOM KIPPUR AND THE TEN DAYS OF TESHUVAH (5)   69

this unity with G-d that empowers us to restore our relationship with G-d—on the level on which our transgressions do affect it—through the process of *teshuvah*.

These, however, are only *expressions* of a deeper truth, glimmers of unity rising to the surface of a life that is perceptively distinct and apart. But one day each year, our quintessential oneness with G-d shines forth in all its glory. This day is Yom Kippur, which the Torah refers to as "the one of the year."[8]

Yom Kippur is more than a day of *teshuvah*. *Teshuvah*, "return," implies that, in the interim, one has been somewhere else; Yom Kippur is a day on which we are empowered to actualize that dimension of our souls whose unity with G-d has never been disturbed in the first place.

Thus, our sages say that on Yom Kippur, "the day itself atones." There is even an opinion, held by Rabbi Judah HaNassi, that "the day itself" atones even for those who do not repent their sins.[9] For on this day, we achieve atonement for our sins not only by

---

8   *Achat bashanah*, in the Hebrew; Leviticus 16:34.

9   See quotations cited at the beginning of this essay. The Talmud (*Shevuot* 13a) cites an even more extreme view, namely that Yom Kippur atones even for one who transgresses the commandments of Yom Kippur itself by doing work or not fasting! In any case, all opinions—including that of the sages who maintain that Yom Kippur atones only for those who repent—agree that on Yom Kippur "the day itself atones," achieving a quality of atonement that cannot be attained at any other time, even with the most fervent *teshuvah*. Where they differ is on the question of how and when this essential quality of the day is actualized. According to "the sages," it can be accessed only through *teshuvah*. According to Rabbi Judah HaNassi, the day itself achieves atonement even without the "catalyst" of *teshuvah*; however, if a person violates the integrity of "the day" itself, he actively prevents its effect upon him. Finally, there is an opinion that states, "No matter what, it is a day of atonement" that reaches to the core of the soul regardless of the person's behavior and conscious will.

exploiting them as an impetus for "return," but also by uncovering that element of self that is never touched by sin at all.

FOUNDATION AND END

During the ten days of *teshuvah*, G-d makes Himself more accessible to us—on all three levels of connection discussed above.

It is a period in which special *mitzvot* are commanded to us (sounding the *shofar* on Rosh Hashanah, fasting on Yom Kippur, etc.), opening unique avenues of connection to G-d via the fulfillment of His will.

It is a period of heightened opportunity for *teshuvah*—a time when our souls are more sensitive to the break from G-d caused by our transgressions, and more driven to "return."

But the foundation and objective of all connection with G-d is the quintessential bond which requires no deed to effect it and which no deed can affect. In the ten days of *teshuvah*, the foundation is laid on Rosh Hashanah and attains its ultimate realization on Yom Kippur.

The defining quality of Rosh Hashanah is that it is the day we crown G-d as king over us. What does it mean that we accept G-d as our "king"? The king-subject metaphor is one of many employed by the Torah to describe our relationship with G-d, which is also referred to in terms of the relationship between husband and wife, shepherd and flock, and master and disciple, among others. The king-subject relationship is unique in that it is not defined by equivocal criteria (love, nurture, intellectual appreciation, etc.), but rather involves the abnegation of the subject's very self to the sovereign. On Rosh Hashanah we relate to G-d as our king, affirming our bond to Him as the very essence of our identity.[10]

---

10   See *To Will a World*, pp. 17–24 above.

YOM KIPPUR AND THE TEN DAYS OF TESHUVAH (5)

Our acceptance of G-d as king is the basis for our other levels of connection with G-d—*mitzvot* and *teshuvah*. The concept of a "divine commandment" has meaning only after one has accepted G-d as the authority over one's life;[11] and a transgression is a transgression (and thus an impetus to *teshuvah*) only because it violates a divine command.

Thus, the ten days of *teshuvah* are defined as the "days *between* Rosh Hashanah and Yom Kippur." They are preceded by "Rosh Hashanah," since our submission to the divine sovereignty is the basis for *teshuvah*—including the *teshuvah* we do on the two days of Rosh Hashanah (which are themselves part of the ten). And they are superseded by "Yom Kippur," since Yom Kippur, in addition to itself being a day of *teshuvah*, is the ultimate realization of the soul's quintessential oneness with G-d—a oneness which *teshuvah* expresses and from which *teshuvah* draws its power, but which transcends the very concept of "return."[12]

---

11   *Mechilta* (on Exodus 20:3) offers the following analogy: "This is comparable to a human king who entered a country. Said his servants to him: 'Make decrees for them!' Said he to them: 'When they accept my sovereignty, I shall make decrees for them; for if they do not accept my sovereignty, they will not accept my decrees.' Thus, G-d said to Israel: 'I am G-d...', and then, 'You shall not have other gods before me...' Meaning: I am the one whose sovereignty you accepted in Egypt... If you accept My sovereignty, you must accept My decrees."

12   More specifically, Rosh Hashanah itself includes all three levels of connection with G-d, as exemplified by the festival's primary feature, the sounding of the *shofar*: *shofar* is a *mitzvah*, an instrument of *teshuvah*, and the trumpet-blast of G-d's coronation as king of the universe. Yom Kippur, too, embodies all three elements: the day's own particular *mitzvot* (fasting, refraining from work, etc.); its designation as a day of *teshuvah* (there is a special quality to the *teshuvah* of Yom Kippur that sets it apart from the *teshuvah* one can achieve in the course of the year, and even from the *teshuvah* of the other of the ten days of *teshuvah*—see *Mishneh Torah, Laws of Teshuvah*, 2:6–7); and the "essence of the day" as the "one of the year."

REVERSE BIOLOGY

In Your abounding compassion, You have given us this fast day of Yom Kippur… A day on which it is forbidden to eat, forbidden to drink… From the Musaf prayer for Yom Kippur

In the World to Come, there is neither eating nor drinking… Talmud, Berachot 17a

The human being consists of a body and a soul—a physical envelope of flesh, blood, sinew, and bone, inhabited and vitalized by a spiritual force described by the chassidic masters as "veritably a part of G-d above."[1]

Common wisdom has it that spirit is loftier than matter, and that the soul is holier (i.e., closer to the Divine) than the body. This conception seems to be borne out by the fact that Yom Kippur, the holiest day of the year—the day on which we attain the height of intimacy with G-d—is ordained by the Torah as a fast day, a day on which we seemingly abandon the body and its needs in order to devote ourselves exclusively to the spiritual activities of repentance and prayer.

In truth, however, a fast day brings about a deeper, rather than a more distant, relationship with the body. When we eat, we are nourished by the food and drink we ingest. On a fast day, vitality comes from the body itself—from energy stored in its cells. In

---

[1] *Tanya*, chapter 2, after Job 31:2.

YOM KIPPUR AND THE TEN DAYS OF TESHUVAH (6)

other words, on less holy days, it is an outside force (the energy in one's food and drink) that keeps body and soul together; on Yom Kippur, the union of body and soul derives from the body itself.

Yom Kippur thus offers a taste of the culminating state of creation known as the "World to Come." The Talmud tells us that "in the World to Come, there is neither eating nor drinking"—a statement that is sometimes understood to imply that in its ultimate and most perfect state, creation is wholly spiritual, devoid of bodies and all things physical.[2] Kabbalistic and chassidic teachings, however, describe the World to Come as a world in which the physical dimension of existence is not abolished, but is preserved and elevated.[3] The fact that there is "neither eating or drinking" in the World to Come is not due to an absence of bodies and physical life, but to the fact that in this future world, "the soul will be nourished by the body" itself, and the symbiosis of matter and spirit that is man will not require any outside sources of nutrition to sustain it.[4]

---

2   See Maimonides' *Mishneh Torah, Laws of Teshuvah* 8:2–3; see, however, Raavad's gloss on *Mishneh Torah*, ad loc.; Rabbi Saadiah Gaon's *Emunot V'Dei'ot*, sections 47 and 49; and Nachmanides' *Shaar HaGemul* (p. 309 in the Chavel edition).

3   *Zohar* 1:114a; *Avodat HaKodesh*, 2:41; Shaloh, introduction to *Beit David*; *Likutei Torah, Tzav* 15c and *Shabbat Shuvah* 65d–66a; *Derech Mitzvotecha*, pp. 28–30.

4   *V'kachah 5637*, section 88; *Yom Tov Shel Rosh Hashanah 5666*, p. 528. In fact, there are talmudic and midrashic passages that imply that there will be eating and drinking in the World to Come (e.g., the "feasts" that G-d will prepare for the righteous). In light of this, the statement that there will be "neither eating nor drinking" might be understood in the sense that the body will not require food or drink for its sustenance, and the consumption of food and drink will be for other purposes (The Rebbe, *Igrot Kodesh*, vol. 2, p. 77).

Two Vehicles

The physical and the spiritual are both creations of G-d. Both were brought into being by the Creator of all out of utter nothingness, and each bears the imprint of its Creator in the particular qualities that define it.

The spiritual, with its intangibility and its transcendence of time and space, reflects the sublimity and infinity of G-d. The spiritual is also naturally egoless, readily acknowledging its subservience to a higher truth.[5] It is these qualities that make the spiritual "holy" and a vehicle of relationship with G-d.

The physical, on the other hand, is tactual, egocentric, and immanent—qualities which brand it "mundane" rather than holy, which mark it as an obfuscation, rather than a manifestation, of the divine truth. For the unequivocal "I am" of the physical belies the truth that "there is none else besides Him"[6]—that G-d is the sole source and end of all existence.

Ultimately, however, everything comes from G-d; every feature of every creation has its source in G-d and serves to reveal His truth. So on a deeper level, the very qualities that make the physical "unholy" are the qualities that make it the most G-dly of G-d's creations. For what is the "I am" of the physical, if not an echo of the unequivocal being of G-d? What is the concreteness of the physical if not an intimation of the absoluteness of His reality? What is the "selfishness" of the physical if not an offshoot, however

---

5   Spiritual entities, such as souls and angels, perceive themselves as vehicles of a divine trait or objective, rather than as beings with an ego and identity of their own, as physical creatures do. The selflessness of the spiritual is also discernible in non-sentient things: a thought or a feeling is always about something else, while a physical object is ostensibly about itself.

6   Deuteronomy 4:35.

remote, of the exclusivity of G-d expressed in the axiom "There is none else besides Him"?

Today, the physical world shows us only its most superficial face, in which the divine characteristics stamped in it are corrupted as a concealment of divine truth rather than its revelation. Today, when the physical object conveys to us "I am," it bespeaks not the reality of G-d but an independent, self-sufficient existence that challenges the divine reality. But in the World to Come, the product of the labor of generations and millennia to make the material world more transparent to its own inner truth, the true face of the physical will come to light.

In the World to Come, the physical will be no less a vehicle of divinity than the spiritual. In fact, in many respects, it will surpass the spiritual as a conveyor of G-dliness. For while the spiritual expresses various divine *characteristics*—G-d's infinity, transcendence, etc.—the physical expresses the *being* of G-d.

Today, the body must look to the soul as its moral guide, as its source of awareness and appreciation of all things divine. But in the World to Come, "the soul will be nourished by the body." The physical body will be a source of divine awareness and identification that is loftier than the soul's own spiritual vision.

Yom Kippur is a taste of this future world of reverse biology. It is thus a day on which we are "sustained by hunger,"[7] deriving our sustenance from the body itself. On this holiest of days, the body becomes a source of life and nurture rather than its recipient.

---

7   Psalms 33:19; see *Likutei Torah, Shir HaShirim* 14b.

CHAPTER TEN

Sukkot

Revelation, Unity, and Joy

Tishrei 15 to 21

For forty years, as our ancestors traversed the Sinai Desert prior to their entry into the Holy Land, miraculous "clouds of glory" surrounded and hovered over them, shielding them from the dangers and discomforts of the desert.

On the festival of Sukkot (*Tishrei* 15–21), we remember G-d's kindness and reaffirm our trust in His providence by dwelling in a *sukkah*—a hut of temporary construction with a roof covering of branches—for the duration of the festival. For seven days and nights, we eat all our meals in the *sukkah* and otherwise regard it as our home.

A second Sukkot observance is the taking of the "four kinds": an *etrog* (citron), a *lulav* (palm frond), three *hadassim* (myrtle twigs), and two *aravot* (willow twigs). On each day of the festival (except Shabbat), we take the four kinds in our hands, recite a blessing over them, and wave them in all six directions: right, left, forward, backward, up, and down. The Midrash tells us that the four kinds represent the various types and personalities that comprise the community of Israel, whose intrinsic unity we emphasize on Sukkot.

Sukkot is also called "the time of our joy." Indeed, a special joy pervades the festival. Nightly "water-drawing" celebrations, reminiscent of the evening-to-dawn festivities held in the Holy Temple in preparation for the drawing of water for use in the festival service, fill the synagogues and streets with song, music, and dance until the wee hours of the morning.

The special joy of Sukkot derives from its location on the calendar on the "full moon" or 15th night of *Tishrei*. "There is no greater joy than the resolution of doubt," says the Talmud. A person might possess all the ingredients of happiness, but if he has no clear vision of how to direct his potential, he cannot experience joy. Sukkot is "the time of our joy" because it is the full revelation of what we have experienced and achieved during the first half of the month of *Tishrei*.

On Rosh Hashanah (*Tishrei* 1 and 2) and Yom Kippur (*Tishrei* 10), we touch base with the quintessence of our souls and of our bond with G-d. In these "days of awe" we crown G-d sovereign of the universe; we actualize the power of *teshuvah* to transform the past and invigorate the future; and we draw forth from Above life, sustenance, and well-being for the year to come. But the trepidation in standing before the divine throne eclipses the joy we would experience if we could fully celebrate the attainments of these days.

On Sukkot, the veil of trepidation recedes and the days of awe are reexperienced as a seven-day feast of joy — a joy that reaches its climax in the festival of Shemini Atzeret/Simchat Torah, which is actually the extension and culmination of the festival of Sukkot.

The first of our essays on Sukkot, *The Easy Mitzvah*, explores the significance of the *sukkah* as our "dwelling" for seven days, and its uniqueness as a prototype for the divine laws of life.

The Four Mysteries of King Solomon is a journey into the heart of the "four kinds," each of which embodies a paradox that baffled the wisest of men. *The Taste of Water* describes the "water-drawing" celebration held on Sukkot in the Holy Temple and its eternal significance to our lives.

Revelation, the harbinger of joy, also elicits unity: the things that separate us from each other belong to the superficialities of life and soon recede when our true self comes to light. *Unity in Three Dimensions* examines the various degrees of unity exhibited by the three primary features of Sukkot: the *sukkah*, the four kinds, and joy.

The fifth and final essay of our chapter, *One Twig and One Leaf*, probes the significance of the *aravah* (willow branch), both in its role as one of the four kinds and as the separate *mitzvah* of "*aravah*" on the seventh day of Sukkot.

THE EASY MITZVAH

How [does one fulfill] the mitzvah *of dwelling in the* sukkah? *One should eat, drink, and live in the* sukkah, *both day and night, as one lives in one's house on the other days of the year: For seven days a person should make his home his temporary dwelling, and his* sukkah *his permanent dwelling.*

Shulchan Aruch, Orach Chaim 639:1

G-d says… "I have one easy mitzvah, *called* sukkah.*"*

Talmud, Avodah Zarah 3a

"$\mathcal{I}$n *sukkot* you shall dwell for seven days," instructs the Torah, "…in order that your generations shall know that I made the children of Israel dwell in *sukkot* when I took them out of the land of Egypt."[1]

Our sages, noting the Torah's use of the verb "to dwell" in the above verses, define the *mitzvah* of *sukkah* as a commandment that, for the duration of the festival of Sukkot (*Tishrei* 15–21), the

---

[1] Leviticus 23:42–43.

sukkah is to become our primary dwelling. Everything ordinarily done in the home should be done in the *sukkah*.[2]

So every autumn, just as the weather is turning inhospitable, we move outdoors. For a full week, we exchange our regular home for a home which leaves us at the mercy of the elements, demonstrating our trust in G-d's providence and protection, as our ancestors did when "following Me in the wilderness, in an uncultivated land."[3]

The Talmud relates that there will come a time when the nations of the world will argue before G-d, "Give us the Torah (as you gave it to the people of Israel) and we will fulfill it." G-d will respond to them: "I have one easy *mitzvah*, called *sukkah*; go and do it." But the moment the weather turns uncomfortable, "they will each kick their *sukkah*, and storm out."[4]

Dwelling in the *sukkah* for seven days is a beautiful and inspiring experience; however, one would hardly describe it as "easy." So why is this *mitzvah* singled out by the Talmud as G-d's "easy *mitzvah*"?

THE COMMANDING CONNECTION

Mitzvah, the Torah's word for the divine precepts which guide and govern every aspect of our lives, from the moment of birth to one's

---

2   Talmud, *Sukkah* 28b; *Mishneh Torah, Laws of Sukkah* 6:5; *Shulchan Aruch, Orach Chaim* 639:1. This also defines when a person is *not* obligated to do something in the *sukkah*: One is not obligated to eat or sleep in the *sukkah* in the case that, under similar conditions, one would not do so in one's own home (Talmud, *Sukkah* 28b; *Shulchan Aruch, Orach Chaim* 639:2 and 5).
3   Jeremiah 2:2.
4   Talmud, *Avodah Zarah* 3a.

SUKKOT (1)

last living breath, has a dual meaning: the word means both "commandment" and "connection."

In commanding us the *mitzvot*, G-d created the means through which we could establish a connection with Him. The hand that distributes charity, the mind that studies the wisdom of Torah, the heart that soars in prayer, even the stomach that digests the matzah eaten on the first night of Passover—all become instruments of the divine will. There are *mitzvot* for each limb, organ, and faculty of man, and *mitzvot* governing every area of life, so that no part of us remains uninvolved in our relationship with our Creator.

Therein lies the uniqueness of the *mitzvah* of *sukkah*. While other *mitzvot* each address a certain aspect of our persona, the *mitzvah* of *sukkah* provides a medium by which the totality of man is engaged in the fulfillment of G-d's will. The entirety of the person enters into and lives in the *sukkah*. "*Sukkah* is the only *mitzvah* into which a person enters with his muddy boots," goes the chassidic saying. For the seven days of Sukkot, the *sukkah* is our *home*—the environment for our every endeavor and activity.

MAN AND TURF

The special distinction of the *mitzvah* of *sukkah* as an all-embracing medium of connection with G-d is best understood in light of the significance of the "home" to the human being.

Our sages point out how deeply rooted is a person's desire for a home. The desire for a home is much more than the need for shelter and security—the satisfaction of these needs alone, without a plot of land to call one's own, does not satisfy the craving for a home. The Talmud goes so far as to say that "One who does not possess a homestead is not a man."[5] The need for a home is intrinsic to the soul of man and a defining aspect of the human state.

Thus, a person's identification with his or her home is not confined to the hours he or she spends within its walls. Also when we are at work, visiting with friends, or taking a stroll in the park, it is as the owner of this particular home that we work, visit, or stroll. Since our very humanity is incomplete without it, it is part and parcel of everything we do.

For the seven days that we make the *sukkah* our home, it comes to form an integral part of our identity. Everything we do, including what we do outside of the *sukkah*, is included in the "connection" with G-d achieved by this *mitzvah*.

EASY AS LIFE

Now we might understand why the *mitzvah* of *sukkah* is G-d's "easy" mitzvah.

A person can approach the fulfillment of G-d's commandments in one of two ways:

a) *As a duty.* Such an individual sees the purpose of his life in the realization of his own personal ambitions. At the same time, he recognizes that G-d is the master of the world and is the one who created him, granted him life, and continues to sustain him in every moment of his existence. So he feels duty-bound to obey G-d's commandments.

b) *As the purpose of his existence.* This individual understands that "I was not created, but to serve my Creator."[6] He recognizes

---

5   Talmud, *Yevamot* 63a, as per *Tosafot*, ad loc., s.v. *She'ein Lecha.*
6   Talmud, *Kidushin* 82b.

SUKKOT (1)

this calling as his true "I" and as the ultimate fulfillment and realization of who and what he is.

If we assume the first approach, and regard the observance of a *mitzvah* as a duty, there will be both "difficult" and "easy" *mitzvot*. We might fulfill them all, perhaps even willingly and joyfully, but some will be more pleasant and inspiring, others more tedious and toilsome. The expenditure of time, effort, or money that a *mitzvah* requires will also affect the degree of difficulty we experience in its fulfillment.

But when we see the fulfillment of the divine will as the very stuff of our life, the concept of a difficult *mitzvah* is nonexistent. All *mitzvot* are "easy," for they do not constitute an imposition on our life—they *are* our life. Indeed, there will be no division between the *mitzvah* and "non-*mitzvah*" areas of our life. When we live to implement G-d's purpose in creation, our entire life—including those activities which are not explicit *mitzvah* acts—becomes a single, seamless quest to connect to our Creator and serve His will.

If all *mitzvot* could be observed in either of the above two ways, there is one *mitzvah* whose terms of observance call for nothing less than the second approach. The *mitzvah* of *sukkah* does not tell us to do something; it tells us to *be* something—a *sukkah*-dweller. The way to observe this *mitzvah* is to make the *sukkah* our home—our environment, our roots, our very identity—for seven days of each year of our life.

And when we apply the model of the *mitzvah* of *sukkah* to our observance of all of G-d's commandments, they, too, assume the all-embracing quality of the *sukkah*. They, too, become as "easy" as life itself.

THE FOUR MYSTERIES OF KING SOLOMON

Three things are wondrous to me, and four I do not know.

Proverbs 30:18

Despite all the wisdom granted to [King] Solomon… he was mystified by the four kinds. As it is written: "Three things are wondrous to me"— these are the Passover offering, matzah, and maror *[eaten at the Passover seder]; "and four I do not know"— these are the four kinds [taken on Sukkot].*

Midrash Rabbah, Vayikra 30:14

On Sukkot, the Torah commands us to take the "four kinds"—the *etrog* (citron), *lulav* (an unopened frond of a date palm), *hadas* (myrtle twig), and *aravah* (willow twig).

As is often the case with the Torah's commandments, the "Written Torah" (the Pentateuch or "Five Books of Moses") conveys this *mitzvah* in a few cryptic words, leaving it to the "Oral Torah" (the traditional interpretation of the Written Torah taught by Moses and handed down through the generations) to decipher their meaning. In the Written Torah, the verse regarding the four kinds reads:

SUKKOT (2)

You shall take for yourselves... the splendid fruit of a tree, fronds of dates, the branch of the thick-leafed tree, and aravot *of the river...*[1]

King Solomon, the Midrash tells us, was mystified by this verse. "Who says that 'the splendid fruit of a tree' is the *etrog*?" he queried. "All fruit trees produce splendid fruit! [As for] 'fronds of dates,' the Torah tells us to take fronds, in the plural... yet we take a *lulav*, the unopened heart of the palm. And who says that 'the branch of the thick-leafed tree' is the myrtle? ...And concerning the '*aravot* of the river'—all trees tend to grow near water."[2]

How, indeed, do we know that "the splendid fruit of a tree, fronds of dates, the branch of the thick-leafed tree, and *aravot* of the river" are the *etrog, lulav*, myrtle, and willow? The Talmud, which summarizes forty generations of the oral tradition of Torah interpretation, identifies the four kinds through a series of homiletic exegeses of the Hebrew words employed by the verse. The clue to the identity of "the splendid fruit of a tree" lies in the word *hadar* ("splendid"), which can also be read as *ha-dar*—"which dwells." The *etrog* is unique in that while other fruits each have a particular season of the year in which they grow, the *etrog* "dwells in its tree all year round," continuing to grow and develop under a variety of climatic conditions.[3]

As for the *lulav*, the Torah indeed writes, "fronds of dates," but the word *kapot* ("fronds of") is spelled without the letter *vav*, meaning that it can also be read *kapat*, "a frond of," in the singular. In addition, the word *kapot* also means "bound," implying that

---

[1]   Leviticus 23:40.
[2]   *Midrash Rabbah*, Vayikra 30:14; *Tanchuma*, Emor 20.
[3]   Talmud, *Sukkot* 35a.

we are to take a closed frond ("the heart of the palm").[4] By these means, the Oral Torah identifies the second of the four kinds as the *lulav*.

There are many "thick-leafed trees" in whose branches "the leaves completely cover the stem"; but the Hebrew word *avot* ("thick") also means "plaited" and "rope-like." Hence the "branch of the thick-leafed tree" (*anaf eitz avot*) is identified as the myrtle twig, whose overlapping leaves grow in knots of three, giving it the appearance of a plaited rope. There is another plant that meets this description—the *hirduf* (*nerium oleander*)—but the Talmud rejects that possibility as inconsistent with the rule that "[the Torah's] ways are ways of pleasantness, and all its pathways are peace"[5] (the *hirduf* is a thorny and poisonous plant).[6]

The *aravot* of the verse are identified as willow branches because of the willow's tendency to grow near water and the elongated shape of its leaves (like a river).[7] Another identifying mark of the *aravah* is that it "grows in brotherhood"—willow bushes tend to grow in close-knit groups (*aravah* is related to the word *achavah*, "brotherhood").[8]

So what was it about the identity of the four kinds that so mystified King Solomon? Surely "the wisest of men"[9] was as proficient in the ways of Torah exegesis as the talmudic sages whose analysis is summarized above. In any case, there are many cryptic passages in the Torah where laws are derived from double meanings and variant spellings of its words. Solomon's dramatic declaration

---

4 Ibid., 29b and 32a.
5 Proverbs 3:17.
6 Talmud, *Sukkot* 32b.
7 Ibid., 33b.
8 See Talmud, *Shabbat* 20a; *Sefer HaMaamarim* 5568, p.447; *Siddur Im D'ach, Shaar HaLulav*, 264d.
9 I Kings 5:11.

SUKKOT (2)   89

regarding the *etrog, lulav,* myrtle, and willow—"[Three are wondrous to me] and four I do not know"—must bode a deeper meaning—a meaning that relates to the inner significance of the four
kinds taken on Sukkot.

FOUR SPECIES OF MAN

The "four kinds," says the Midrash, represent four types of people.

Man's mission in life consists of two basic challenges: learning
and doing; or, as these relate to Jewish life, Torah and *mitzvot.* The
Torah is the vehicle by which we gain knowledge of our Creator
and insight into the essence of life; the *mitzvot,* the divine commandments, are the means by which we build a better and holier
world, developing the physical creation into a "dwelling for G-d."
These two endeavors define the four personalities represented in
the four kinds.

The *etrog,* which has both a delicious taste and a delightful aroma, represents the perfect individual who both learns and achieves.
The *lulav,* being the branch of the date palm, produces fruit that
has a taste but no aroma; this is the prototype of the reclusive
scholar who grows in wisdom but shuns the world of action. The
fragrant but tasteless myrtle is the activist whose profusion of
good deeds consumes all his time and energies. Finally, the tasteless, scentless willow represents the person who neither learns nor
does, actualizing neither his intellectual potential nor his capacity
to improve the world.

On Sukkot, concludes the Midrash, these "four kinds" are "all
bound together in one bundle," each an integral part of the community of G-d.[10]

---

10   *Midrash Rabbah, Vayikra* 30:11.

The Tormented Fruit

In light of this, we can understand the four things that mystified the wisest of men.

If the "splendid fruit" in the four kinds represents the harmony of learning and accomplishment, why is this the fruit that "dwells in its tree all year round"? One would expect such perfection from a fruit maturing in tranquility, in a climate that is singularly attuned to its nature and needs; not from one whose development is agitated by ever-shifting conditions. And yet, time and again we indeed find that the greatest lives are those beset by travail and challenge. History has shown us that the most balanced personalities are forged by the need to deal with changing circumstances and to constantly adapt to new climates and environments.

This, to King Solomon, was one of the great mysteries of life. How does vacillation fuel growth? Why is it that the individual who enjoys a tranquil existence is never as "fragrant" and "delectable" as the one who is battered by the vicissitudes of life?

Pressed Leaves

The *lulav*, too, perplexed the great mind of Solomon. Is not the very nature of intellectual discourse that it produces varied opinions and conclusions? In the words of the Talmud, "Torah scholars sit in numerous groups and study the Torah. One group deems a thing impure, and another deems it pure; one group forbids a deed and another permits it; one group disqualifies something and another renders it fit."[11]

So when the verse speaks of "fronds of dates," we are inclined

---

11 Talmud, *Chagigah* 3b.

SUKKOT (2)

to understand these words in their literal, plural sense. For if the second of the four kinds denotes the Torah scholar—the human mind enfranchised to process the divine wisdom—should it not consist of two palm branches, in keeping with the plural nature of the intellect? Should not their leaves be opened and spread, pointing to the various directions that the rational examination of a concept will take when embarked on by the mind of man?

And yet, the *lulav* commanded by the Torah is a single, closed frond, its leaves fused to a single rod pointing in a single direction. As the above-quoted talmudic passage, about varied opinions resulting from Torah study, concludes: "Should a person then ask: How, then, might I study Torah? But all was received from a single provider." Or, in the words of another talmudic statement, "These and these are both the words of the living G-d."[12]

This was the second of the two mysteries pondered by King Solomon. How do numerous opinions and perspectives of Torah relate to their "single provider"? How can the divine wisdom be funneled through the multifarious world of human reason and remain the singular truth of a singular G-d?

THE PLAITED TWIG

The myrtle in the four kinds represents the "deed" aspect of life—the manner in which we fulfill the purpose of creation with the physical actions of the *mitzvot*, thereby constructing a "dwelling for G-d in the physical world."[13] Thus, the Torah identifies the myrtle by alluding to its "plaited" appearance, given it by the fact that its leaves grow in clumps of three. The number "three" rep-

---

12 Talmud, *Eruvin* 13b.
13 *Midrash Tanchuma*, Nasso 16; *Tanya*, ch. 36.

resents the realm of action, which is the third of the soul's three "garments" or vehicles of expression (thought, speech, and action).[14]

Here lies what is perhaps the most profound mystery of all. How can the finite and mundane physical deed "house" the divine essence? Indeed, the plaited twig that comes to mind when thinking of the physical world is not the fragrant myrtle, but the barbed and poisonous *hirduf*!

Yet it is in the material world that G-d elected to make His home. It is the physical deed to which G-d imparted the ability to serve as man's highest form of connection with Him. Why? To the wisest of men, this was one of the four phenomena to which he could only say: "I do not know it."

A Brotherhood of Trees

The fourth of Solomon's mysteries concerns the willow, a plant with neither fragrance nor taste, representing the person devoid of learning as well as of deeds.

Why is this species counted among the four kinds? The verse itself answers that question by referring to the fourth kind as "*aravot* of the river." The willow might not exhibit any positive qualities, but its roots are embedded in the banks of its ancestral river and are nourished by the waters of its heritage. It, too, is a child of Abraham, Isaac, and Jacob; in its veins, too, course the love and awe of G-d that they bequeathed to all their descendants.

Another hallmark of the willow is that it "grows in brotherhood." This alludes to a unique feature of the human "willow": Taken alone, a person might exhibit not a single positive trait or achievement; but when gathered in a community, the aura of holiness that suffuses each individual soul suddenly comes to light.

---

14 Ibid., chapter 4.

SUKKOT (2)   93

Thus our sages tell us that the divine presence rests upon a gathering of ten individuals (the number that comprises a "community"), even if they are not engaged in the study of Torah or the performance of a *mitzvah*.[15] This is also the significance of the *minyan* (the quorum of ten required to recite certain prayers): Ten individuals gathered together represent a quantum leap in holiness. Ten ignorant boors make a *minyan*, while nine pious scholars do not.

This is what mystified King Solomon about the willow. How does ten times nothing add up to something? If each individual possesses no visible expression of his innate holiness on his own, how does that change when ten of them come together? All trees grow on water, mused the wisest of men; what sets the willows apart, earning them a place among the four kinds? Simply the fact that they grow close together?

IMPOSSIBLE TRUTHS

If we think of these mysteries, they are as enigmatic and elusive as when King Solomon pondered them thirty centuries ago. But we usually don't think of them at all—so deeply are they ingrained in our reality. Despite their logical incomprehensibility, these are obvious and ever-present truths in our lives.

Why do vacillation and hardship fuel growth? How can contradictory ideas embody a singular truth? Why does a simple physical deed elevate us to levels of holiness and G-dliness unequaled by the most transcendent spiritual experience? How are a number of ordinary human beings magically transformed when knit into a community, greatly surpassing the sum of their individual parts?

King Solomon could not explain these mysteries; certainly, we cannot. But we recognize them as axiomatic to our lives, as

---

15   Talmud, *Sanhedrin* 39a; *Tanya*, end of ch. 11.

four cornerstones to our existence that bear the stamp of a Creator within whose infinite being opposites merge and paradoxical truths harmoniously reside.[16]

---

16 The "four kinds" therefore evoked in King Solomon the admission that "I do not know them," while the three *mitzvot* of Passover were only "wondrous to me." What amazed King Solomon about Passover was the fact that an undeserving people—in the words of the Midrash (*Yalkut Reuveni, Shemot* 14:27), "How are these any different from these? These (the Egyptians) are idol-worshippers, and these (the Israelites) are idol-worshippers!"—were given the gifts of faith (matzah), freedom (the Passover offering), and perseverance (*maror*). G-d chose to take us out of Egypt and make us His people solely in the merit of our three ancestors, who embodied these three traits: because of the faith of Abraham (who observed the *mitzvah* of matzah—see *Pesikta Rabbati* on Genesis 18:6), the self-transcendence of Isaac (who ate of the Passover offering—see Rashi on Genesis 27:9), and the perseverance of trouble-worn Jacob (see Genesis 31:40; Talmud, *Shabbat* 89b).

This was indeed wondrous—that G-d should elect a people as His chosen nation by no merit of their own—but it is not illogical. It is an act that transcends reason, but it is not contrary to reason. On the other hand, the four paradoxes embodied by the four kinds of Sukkot are logical impossibilities, prompting King Solomon to not only express wonderment but to proclaim, "I do not know them."

This also reflects the respective positions of Passover and Sukkot in the Jewish calendar. As elaborated in another essay in this series (*Our Other Head*, vol. 3, pp. 4–12), the Jewish year has two "heads" or beginnings: *Nissan*, the month of the Exodus; and *Tishrei*, the month in which the "second tablets" were given to Israel after they repented of the sin of the Golden Calf and were granted a new beginning in their relationship with G-d. *Nissan* represents the divine service of the *tzaddik* (perfectly righteous individual); *Tishrei*, that of the *baal teshuvah* ("returnee" or penitent). The *tzaddik*'s perfection transcends our finite world to relate to the "wondrous" (i.e., suprarational and infinite) light of G-d. The *baal teshuvah*, however, reaches yet higher, relating to the "unknowable" essence of G-d that not only transcends the limits of reason and existence, but is also the singular source for the counterforces and paradoxes that pervade our world (see *Sin in Four Dimensions*, pp. 44–56 above).

SUKKOT (3)   95

THE
TASTE OF
WATER

Draw water with joy, from the wellsprings of
salvation.   Isaiah 12:3

The pouring of the water was held on all sev-
en days [of Sukkot]...

The one who was doing the pouring was
told, "Raise your hands" (so that all could
see him pouring the water on the altar). This
was because... there was once a Sadducee
who spilled the water on his feet, and the en-
tire people pelted him with their etrogim...

Talmud, Sukkah 42b; 48b

When the Holy Temple stood in Jerusalem, the "pouring
of the water" (*nisuch hamayim*) was an important feature of the festival of Sukkot.

Throughout the year, the daily offerings in the Temple were
accompanied by the pouring of wine on the altar; on Sukkot, water was poured in addition to the wine. The drawing of water for
this purpose was preceded by all-night celebrations in the Temple
courtyard, with music-playing Levites, torch-juggling sages, and
huge oil-burning lamps that illuminated the entire city. The singing and dancing went on until daybreak, when a procession would

make its way to the Shiloah Spring which flowed in a valley below the Temple.[1]

> *A golden pitcher, holding three* lugim,[2] *was filled from the Shiloah Spring. When they arrived at the Water Gate,[3] the* shofar *was sounded... [The priest] ascended the ramp [of the altar] and turned to his left... where there were two bowls of silver... with small holes [in their bottom], one wider and the other narrower so that both should empty at the same time;[4] the western one was for the water and the eastern one for wine...*[5]

"For all the days of the water drawing," recalled Rabbi Joshua ben Chanania, "our eyes saw no sleep,"[6] for the nights of Sukkot were devoted to the singing, dancing, and merrymaking in preparation to "draw water with joy."[7] And the Talmud declares: "One who did not see the joy of the water-drawing celebrations, has not seen joy in his life."[8]

---

1   Talmud, *Sukkah* 51a–b.
2   Approximately one liter.
3   One of the gates leading into the courtyard of the Holy Temple, so named because the procession that carried the water for the "pouring of the water" on Sukkot passed through it.
4   Wine, being denser than water, would flow more slowly if the openings were the same size.
5   Talmud, *Sukkah* 48a–b.
6   Ibid., 53a
7   Isaiah 12:3.
8   Talmud, *Sukkah* 51b. Today, until the Holy Temple is restored to us with the coming of Moshiach, we are unable to conduct the water drawing celebration in its original form. Nevertheless, the festivities remain. Night-long singing and dancing, reminiscent of the celebrations held in the Temple courtyard, are held throughout the festival in synagogues and neighborhood streets.
    In fact, there are aspects of these joyous celebrations that are

SUKKOT (3)   97

The Sadducees

There was, however, a segment of the Jewish people that was not party to the joy of the water-drawing celebrations.

The Sadducees were a breakaway Jewish sect who denied the oral tradition received by Moses at Sinai and handed down through the generations, arguing that they had the right to interpret the Torah according to their own understanding. Unlike the pouring of the wine, which is explicitly commanded by the Torah,[9] the pouring of the water on Sukkot is derived by interpretation. In the verses (Numbers 29:19, 29, and 33) where the Torah speaks of the libations to accompany the Sukkot offerings, there are three extra letters; according to the Sinaitic tradition, these letters are combined to form the word *mayim* (water). The Sadducees, who rejected the "Oral Torah," maintained that only wine was to be poured on the altar on Sukkot, as on every day of the year.

During the Second Temple Era, there were times when the Sadducees amassed political power and even gained the High Priesthood—the highest spiritual office in Israel. Thus it came to pass that one Sukkot, the honor of pouring the water on the altar was

---

possible only today, precisely because they cannot be held in the prescribed manner. Due to the prohibition against the use of musical instruments on *yom tov* (the opening and closing days of the festival), the pouring of the water celebrations in the Holy Temple did not begin until the second night of Sukkot. For the same reason, it was not held on Shabbat. Today, however, since our observance is only commemorative, we can celebrate without the instruments. Thus, a negative situation results in an even greater, and deeper, jubilation. We hold celebrations on all nights of Sukkot, including *yom tov* and Shabbat, calling forth from within ourselves a quintessential joy that does not require any mechanical aids to inspire it. (For another example of this phenomenon, see section called "The Dividend of Doubt" in the essay *Three Times Three,* on pp. 214–217 of vol. 1 of this series.)

9   Numbers 15:1–12; et al.

given to a Sadducee priest; but instead of pouring the water into its prescribed bowl in the southwest corner of the altar, this priest spilled it on his feet to demonstrate his opposition to the practice. The assembled crowd expressed its outrage by pelting him with the *etrogim* which, this being Sukkot, they held in their hands.[10]

WATER AND WINE

The deeper, spiritual significance of this event reflects the fact that there are two basic components to man's endeavor to serve his Creator. First, there is what the Talmud calls *kabbalat ol malchut shamayim*, "the acceptance of the yoke of the sovereignty of Heaven." *Kabbalat ol* is the basis and foundation of Torah: Without a recognition of G-d as our master and a commitment to obey His will, the very concept of a *mitzvah* (divine commandment) has no meaning.[11]

But G-d gave us more than a body and a nervous system, which is all we would have required if our purpose in life were only the carrying out of commands with robotic obedience. He created us with a searching mind and a feeling heart, because He desired that these, too, should form an integral part of our relationship with Him.[12]

Thus the Torah states: "See, I have taught you statutes and laws... for this is your wisdom and understanding before the nations"; "You shall know today, and take into your heart, that the

---

10   In those days it was the custom to carry the "four kinds" all day long (see Talmud, *Sukkah* 41b).

11   Talmud, *Berachot* 13a. See *Mechilta* on Exodus 20:3, quoted in footnote 11 on p. 71. above

12   "All that G-d created in His world, He created solely for His glory" (*Ethics of the Fathers* 6:11). Therefore, it cannot be said that serving

L-rd is G-d"; "Know the G-d of your fathers and serve Him with a whole heart and desirous soul"; "You shall love G-d... with all your heart"; "Serve G-d with joy."[13] G-d wants us to know, understand, appreciate, love, desire, and enjoy our mission in life.

In the language of kabbalah and chassidism, these two elements in our service of G-d are referred to as "water" and "wine." Water is tasteless, scentless, and colorless, yet is a most basic requisite of life; thus it represents the intellectually and emotionally vacuous, yet fundamentally crucial, "acceptance of the yoke of the sovereignty of Heaven." Wine, which is pleasing to the eye, nose, and palate, intoxicating to the brain, and exhilarating to the heart, is the sensually gratifying aspect of our divine service: our understanding of the inner significance of the *mitzvot* and the fulfillment and joy we experience in our relationship with G-d.

In light of this, "the joy of the water drawing" seems a contradiction in terms. If water represents the "flavorless," emotionally devoid aspect of our service of G-d, why did the pouring of water upon the altar on Sukkot yield a joy not only greater than that produced by the pouring of wine, but a joy such as was not equaled by any other joy in the world?

THE FULL MOON OF TISHREI

A clue to unraveling the paradox of the "joyous water" of Sukkot might be found in what *halachah* (Torah law) has to say about the taste or non-taste of water.

G-d is a matter of blind obedience while our intellectual and emotional selves exist for other, "secular," purposes.

13 Deuteronomy 4:5–6, 4:39, and 6:5; I Chronicles 28:9; Psalms 100:2; cf. Deuteronomy 28:47.

The law is that "it is forbidden to derive pleasure from this world without a *berachah*"—without a blessing of praise and thanks to G-d.[14] Thus, even the smallest amount of food or drink requires a *berachah*,[15] since, even if the amount consumed is of little nutritional value, the person derives pleasure from its taste. Water, however, has no taste, so it does not require a *berachah* unless "one drinks water out of thirst," in which case, explains the Talmud, a person derives pleasure from this otherwise tasteless liquid.[16]

To a thirsty man, a cup of water is tastier than the most delectable wine. In the spiritual sense, this means that when a soul experiences a "thirst" for G-d—when it recognizes how vital its connection to G-d is for its very existence—the prosaic "water" of commitment is a feast for its senses. To the soul who thirsts for G-d, a self-negating act of *kabbalat ol* is more exhilarating than the most profound page of Talmud, the most sublime kabbalistic secret, the most ecstatic flight of prayer, or the most intense spiritual experience. To such a soul, the "water" it draws from its deepest self to pour onto its altar of service to G-d is a greater source of joy than the flesh and wine offered upon its altar or the incense wafting through its Temple.

And Sukkot is the time when we are most open to experiencing pleasure and joy in the ordinarily prosaic act of "accepting the yoke of the sovereignty of Heaven."

---

14 Rashi and *Tosafot* on *Sukkah* 26b; Rosh on *Berachot* 35a; *Tur, Orach Chaim* 210.

15 In contrast to the *berachah* after eating, which is recited only when a person has been sated by the food.

16 Talmud, *Berachot* 44b–45a; *Tosafot*, ad loc., s.v. *Dechanaktei Umtza*; *Mishneh Torah, Laws of Berachot* 8:1; *Shulchan Aruch* and commentaries, *Orach Chaim* 204:7–8.

SUKKOT (3)   101

Rosh Hashanah, which occurs fifteen days before Sukkot on the
first of *Tishrei*, is our fountainhead of *kabalat ol* for the entire year:
This is the day on which we crown G-d as our king and reiterate
our acceptance of the divine sovereignty.[17] But on Rosh Hashanah,
the joy that the thirsting soul derives from its elemental water is
subdued by the awe that pervades the occasion, as the entirety of
creation trembles in anticipation of the annual renewal of the divine kingship. Sukkot is the celebration of this joy, the revelation
of what was implicit fifteen days earlier on Rosh Hashanah.

This connection between Rosh Hashanah and Sukkot derives
from their respective positions in the month of *Tishrei*. The Jewish calendar is a lunar calendar, in which each month begins on
the night of the new moon, progresses as the moon grows in the
nighttime sky, and reaches its apex on the fifteenth of the month,
the night of the full moon. This is why so many of the festivals and
special days of the Jewish year fall on the fifteenth of the month,
this being the day on which the particular month's special quality is most expressed and manifest. In the month of *Tishrei*, Rosh
Hashanah coincides with the birth of the new moon on the first
of the month, while Sukkot coincides with the full moon on the
15th. Thus, Sukkot is the revelation and manifestation of what was
hidden and concealed on Rosh Hashanah.[18]

This is the meaning of a verse which figures prominently in the
Rosh Hashanah liturgy: "Blow the *shofar* on the new moon, in
concealment to the day of our festival."[19] "Blow the *shofar*," proclaiming our acceptance of the sovereignty of Heaven, "on the new
moon," on Rosh Hashanah; this, however, remains "in conceal-

---

17 See *The Man in Man*, pp. 8–16 above.
18 See *The Sixteenth Increment*, in vol. i, pp. 151–159 of this series; and *The
     Day of the Breaking of the Ax*, in vol. III, pp. 275–284.
19 Psalms 81:4.

ment to [i.e., until] the day of our festival," the festival of Sukkot,[20] when it erupts in a seven-day feast of joy.

Throughout the year, only wine was poured on the altar, since ordinarily, only the savory and aromatic elements of our service of G-d are a source of joy to us. But on Sukkot, when the full import of our *kabalat ol* is revealed to us, the joy we experience in the "water" of life is the greatest joy in the world, surpassing even the joy of its "wine."

ANATOMICAL STATEMENT

The Sadducees, however, opposed the "pouring of the water" on Sukkot.

The Sadducees refused to accept the divinely ordained interpretation of Torah transmitted to Moses at Sinai and handed down through the generations. While recognizing the divine origin of Torah, they regarded it as a series of laws open to personal interpretation — an interpretation dictated solely by the interpreter's understanding and feelings.

In other words, for the Sadducee, there is no true submission to the divine authority. For the Jew who accepts both the Written Torah and the Oral Torah, the basis and end of everything he does is to serve the divine will. The "wine" of his divine service — the intellectual and emotional fulfillment that he experiences in the process — is also part of this end: this, too, is something that G-d desires from him. The Sadducee, on the other hand, sees the "wine" as the end and objective of his observance of the *mitzvot*:

---

20   The term *chag*, "festival," without qualification refers to the festival of Sukkot.

SUKKOT (3)   103

everything he does is subject to his personal understanding and appreciation.

The Sadducee might accept the need for "water" in one's life, but only as an accessory to the wine. He might acknowledge the need for unquestioning obedience to Torah on the part of the masses, for not every man is capable of interpreting these laws himself. He might acknowledge the need for such obedience on the part of even the wisest of men, for no man can expect to understand everything. But the Sadducee will always see such "mindless" and "unfeeling" obedience as a necessity rather than the ideal—the ideal being a fulfillment of Torah based on the observer's understanding and appreciation.

So for the Sadducee, there is no joy in submission to the divine will, no "taste" to the water of commitment. The Sadducee does not *thirst* for this water; if he obeys G-d's laws, it is only as a means to an end—to enable him to savor their intellectual flavor and emotional aroma.

This is why the Sadducee priest poured the water on his *feet*. He was not condemning the phenomenon of "water" in serving G-d; he was regulating it to the feet—to the "foot-soldiers" of the nation, or to the lower extremities of the human form. Water might be necessary in certain individuals and in certain circumstances, but it is hardly the element to grace the altar in the year's most joyous celebration of man's relationship with G-d.

A HAIL OF FRUIT

The people responded by pelting him with their *etrogim*.

The Midrash tells us that the "four kinds" taken on Sukkot—the *etrog* (citron), the *lulav* (palm frond), the *hadas* (myrtle branch), and the *aravah* (willow branch)—represent four types of individuals. The *etrog*, which has both a taste and a fragrant smell, represents the perfect individual who is both knowledgeable in Torah and proficient in the observance of *mitzvot*. The *lulav* is the branch of the date palm, whose fruit has a taste but no smell, representing those accomplished in Torah though less so in regard to the *mitzvot*. The *hadas*—tasteless but aromatic—represents the type who, though lacking in Torah knowledge, has many *mitzvot* to his credit. Finally, the tasteless and scentless *aravah* represents the individual who lacks both Torah and *mitzvot*.[21]

On a deeper level, the four kinds represent four personas within every individual, each with its own domain in our psyche and its appropriate place in our life. In this sense, "Torah" is the intellectual appreciation of the divine wisdom, and "*mitzvot*" are the love and awe of G-d experienced in the observance of the commandments.[22] Thus, the *lulav* is the "intellectual" in us who does not allow feeling to cloud the purity of knowledge and comprehension. The *hadas* is the emotional self, who sets experience as the highest ideal, even at the expense of the intellect. The *etrog* is the force that strives for a synthesis of mind and heart. And the *aravah* is the capacity for acceptance and commitment, for setting aside both intellect and feeling to commit oneself absolutely to a higher ideal.[23]

When the Sadducee priest spilled the water on his feet, the "entire people pelted him with their *etrogim*." We reject what you represent—the people were sayin—not only with the self-negating *aravah* in us, not only with our intellectual or emotional selves,

---

21 *Midrash Rabbah, Vayikra* 30:11.

22 In his *Tanya* (chapter 4), Rabbi Schneur Zalman of Liadi explains that the mind is the tool with which man has been equipped to apprehend the divine wisdom of Torah, while the emotions of the heart are the motivators and facilitators of *mitzvah* observance.

23 See *One Twig and One Leaf* on pp. 114–124 below.

SUKKOT (3)

but also with the synthesis of wisdom and feeling that defines what is highest and most perfect in man. For also—and especially—the *etrog* within us recognizes the water of life as our ultimate source of joy.

UNITY IN THREE DIMENSIONS

In sukkot *you shall dwell for seven days; all citizens of Israel shall dwell in* sukkot.

Leviticus 23:42

It is fitting that all of Israel should dwell in a single sukkah.   Talmud, Sukkah 27b

When is something yours? When you control it? When you have legal and moral right to its use? When it is yours alone, to the exclusion of everyone else? Ownership may mean many things, depending on the individual and social circumstances that define it.

A legal difference between the two major observances of the festival of Sukkot—dwelling in the *sukkah* and acquiring the "four kinds"—is one example of the different possible definitions of ownership. Regarding both these *mitzvot*, the Torah stipulates that the object of the *mitzvah* must be "yours"; but the definition of "yours" varies from *mitzvah* to *mitzvah*.

In the case of the four kinds, the Torah states:

> *You shall take for yourselves on the first day [of the festival] the splendid fruit of a tree* (etrog), *fronds of dates* (lulav), *the branch of the thickly leafed tree* (hadas), *and* aravot *of the brook...* "[1]

---

[1]   Leviticus 23:40.

SUKKOT (4)   107

Our sages explain that the words "You shall take *for yourselves...*" (*lachem*, in the Hebrew) come to teach us that these must be the absolute property of their user. One who uses a stolen *etrog* (or *lulav, hadas,* or *aravah*), or a borrowed *etrog*, or even an *etrog* which he owns in partnership with another person, has not fulfilled the *mitzvah* of taking the four kinds on the first day of Sukkot.[2]

Regarding the *mitzvah* of *sukkah*, the Torah likewise stipulates that "You shall make, for yourself, a festival of *sukkot*."[3] But here, the phrase "for yourself" is more broadly defined. In this case, says the Talmud, the verse comes only to exclude a stolen *sukkah*. A borrowed or partially owned *sukkah* is considered to be sufficiently "yours" to satisfy the *mitzvah*'s requirements.[4]

To support this broader interpretation of ownership being applied in the case of the *sukkah*, the Talmud cites another of the Torah's statements regarding the *mitzvah* of dwelling in the *sukkah*. In Leviticus 23:42 we read: "In *sukkot* you shall dwell for seven days; all citizens of Israel shall dwell in *sukkot*." In this verse, the word *sukkot*, which is the plural of *sukkah*, is spelled without the letter *vav*, which indicates that the word might be understood in the singular. Explains the Talmud: The Torah wishes to imply that the entire nation of Israel may, and ought to, dwell in a single *sukkah*!

---

2   Talmud, *Sukkah* 41b; *Mishneh Torah, Laws of Lulav,* 8:10–11 (see *Maggid Mishneh* on section 11); *Shulchan Aruch, Orach Chaim* 649 and 658. Thus, if a person wishes to accord his fellow the opportunity of observing the *mitzvah* of taking the four kinds with his own set, he must give it to his fellow as a gift, and have his fellow give it back to him as a gift after observing the *mitzvah*.

3   Deuteronomy 16:13.

4   Talmud, *Sukkah* 27b (as per the majority opinion, whose ruling we follow in practice); *Mishneh Torah, Laws of Sukkah,* 5:25; *Shulchan Aruch, Orach Chaim* 637 (see especially the words of *Shulchan Aruch HaRav,* ad loc., section 2).

Aside from stressing the brotherhood and equality of all Jews, this also has the legal implication that a *sukkah* need not be exclusively "yours" in order for you to fulfill the *mitzvah* of dwelling in it. If all Israel may dwell in a single *sukkah*, then the requirement to make it "for yourself" cannot be understood in the narrow sense of exclusive ownership, but in the sense of the right to a thing's use.[5]

Why does the "yours" of the *sukkah*-dweller differ from the "yours" of one engaged in the *mitzvah* of taking the four kinds? Obviously, there is an intrinsic difference between these two Sukkot observances—a difference that extends to the very identity and self-definition of their observer.

THE JOY OF GIVING

Sukkot is the festival that celebrates Jewish unity. Unity is the underlying theme of the festival's three precepts: joy, the taking of the four kinds, and dwelling in the *sukkah*.

All of the festivals are referred to as "occasions for joy" (*moadim lesimchah*); yet the Torah stresses the centrality of joy to the festival of Sukkot more than with any other festival.[6] Thus, only the festival of Sukkot is defined, in our prayers of the day,[7] as *zeman simchateinu*, "the time of our joy" (Passover is subtitled "the time

---

5 This is also the source for another of the *sukkah*'s *halachic* criteria. Torah law sets all sorts of specifications for the *sukkah*'s dimensions: Its ceiling may be no lower than ten *tefachim* (approx. 32 inches) and no higher than 20 *amot* (approx. 31.5 feet); its area must be no less than seven *tefachim* by seven *tefachim*. However, since "It is fitting that all of Israel should dwell in a single *sukkah*," there can be no maximum limit for the length and breadth of the *sukkah*.

6 See *Mishneh Torah, Laws of Lulav*, 8:12.

7 Instituted by the "Great Assembly" in Ezra's time (circa 350 BCE).

SUKKOT (4)   109

of our freedom," and Shavuot, "the time of the giving of our Torah"). Indeed, there is a unique joy associated with Sukkot—a joy
that reaches its height in the nightly "water-drawing" celebration
held during the festival.[8]

And joy, for the Jew, is an exercise in empathy and communal
concern. "You shall rejoice on your festival," enjoins the Torah,
"you, your son, your daughter, your servant, your maid, the Levite, the stranger, the orphan, and the widow..."[9] In the words of
Maimonides:

> *When one eats and drinks, one must also feed the stranger,
> the orphan, the widow, and the other unfortunate paupers.
> One who locks the doors of his courtyard and feasts and
> drinks with his children and wife but does not feed the
> poor and the embittered—this is not the joy of* mitzvah *but
> the joy of his stomach.*[10]

Selfish festivity is divisive, accentuating the differences between
the haves and the have-nots, between the full and empty stom-
achs of society. But the joy of *mitzvah*, joy as defined by Torah,
unites. Master and servant, family man and loner, wealthy man
and pauper, are all united by the giving and compassionate joy of
the Jewish festival.

Nevertheless, even the most generous joy cannot be said to
achieve a "unity" in the ultimate sense of the word. At most, it
introduces a connection between disparate individuals. The pauper remains separated from the rich man by a gulf of status and
economic station, as does the servant from the master and the

---

8   See previous essay, *The Taste of Water*, pp. 95–105.
9   Deuteronomy 16:14.
10   *Mishneh Torah, Laws of the Festivals* 6:18.

stranger from the homesteader. Joyous hearts and giving hands extend across these gulfs, but the division and distance remain.

So to inspire a deeper and truer unity, the Jew acquires the "four kinds" on Sukkot.

TASTE OF KNOWLEDGE AND SCENT OF DEED

The Midrash[11] explains that the four kinds represent four spiritual classes within the community. The *etrog*, which has both a delicious taste and a delightful aroma, represents the perfect individual—one who is both knowledgeable in Torah and replete with good deeds. The *lulav*, whose fruits (dates) have taste but no smell, personifies the learned but deed-deficient individual—the scholar who devotes his life to the pursuit of the divine wisdom but shuns the active sphere of life. The delightful scent and lack of flavor of the *hadas* describe the active but unlearned individual. Finally, the flavorless and scentless *aravah* represents the Jew who lacks all outward expression of his Jewishness.

On Sukkot, the *lulav*, *hadas*, *aravah*, and *etrog* are bound and joined together,[12] reiterating the underlying oneness of a topically diverse people. Whatever may divide the scholarly from the ignorant, and the more observant from the less so, Sukkot is a time when all are held together in the hand of Jewish identity.

So while the joy of Sukkot introduces a unifying give-and-take relationship between various segments of the community of Israel, the mitzvah of the four kinds takes this unity a step further,

---

11 *Midrash Rabbah, Vayikra* 30:12.

12 The *lulav, hadassim,* and *aravot* are actually tied together in a single bundle. But the perfect *tzaddik*, personified by the *etrog*, also bridges his natural distance from the rest during the actual observance of the *mitzvah*, when all four species are held and pressed together.

SUKKOT (4)   111

integrating us into a single entity. By taking the four kinds in hand,
we reiterate that, despite our disparities, we are all one.[13]

---

13 In addition to symbolizing the unity of Israel by being bound
    and held together, each of the four kinds expresses the concept of
    unity in its *halachically* ordained characteristics. The *lulav* is re-
    ferred to by the Torah as *kapot temarim,* "fronds of dates." The He-
    brew word *kapot* ("fronds") can also be read *kafut* ("bound to-
    gether"); from this the Talmud deduces that the *lulav* must
    be an unopened frond whose leaves are still pressed together.
    The *hadas* is referred to by the Torah as *anaf eitz avot,* "the branch of
    the thickly-leafed tree." The word *avot* (thick) also means "rope-like"—
    a reference to the myrtle's tendency to grow its leaves in groups of three
    stemming from the same point (so that it resembles a plaited rope).
    This mark of unity, too, translates into a *halachic* requirement: a myrtle
    twig whose leaves do not grow in this three-in-one pattern is invalid
    for use in the four kinds.

    The *etrog* is called *pri eitz hadar,* "the splendid fruit of a tree." The
    word *hadar* ("splendid"), which can also be read as *ha-dar,* "that which
    dwells," refers to the fact that the *etrog* "dwells in its tree throughout
    the year" and continues to grow and develop all year round. This is a
    unique phenomenon, since most fruits grow only in the course of a
    single season, as their development requires that particular season's set
    of conditions. The *etrog,* however, unites within it the entire array of
    climatic temperaments that prevail throughout the year, incorporating
    them all in its growth process to create a "splendid fruit" that is a har-
    mony of all the currents and flavors that comprise an annum of nature.
    Finally, an identifying mark of the *aravah* is that it grows in close-knit
    groups—in "unity" and "brotherhood" (*achvana:* Talmud, *Shabbat*
    20a; Rashi, ad loc.).

    The *aravah* is unique in that while the other three "kinds" express
    the concept of unity within their own individual form (the *lulav*'s be-
    ing "bound together," the *hadas*' "three-in-one" leaf pattern, and the
    etrog's conglomeration of seasons and conditions), the *aravah* express-
    es a broader unity—a unity that embraces its relationship with its
    fellows. This is because the *aravah*'s "featureless" nature enables it to
    serve as a purer expression of the all-embracing unity of G-d (see fol-
    lowing essay, *One Twig and One Leaf,* pp. 114–124).

The Enveloping Home

Despite our disparities, we are all one. For the disparities remain, as even the unifying four kinds express.

The *lulav* towers above the lot in scholarship and erudition. The *hadas* exudes its scent of good works, while the *aravah* is marked by its obvious ignorance and fruitlessness. The *etrog*, of course, outshines them all with its sublime perfection. Even as they symbolize the unity of the various segments of Israel, the four kinds underscore the differences between them. Indeed, they stress these very differences as the complementary components of one people.

There is, however, yet a higher form of unity that is realized by the festival of Sukkot. This is the unity of the *sukkah* — the unity embodied by the structure worthy of accommodating an entire people within its walls.

"The entire nation of Israel may, and ought to, dwell in a single *sukkah*." For the *sukkah* represents a oneness so deep and all-embracing that all distinctions pale to insignificance before it.

"*Sukkah* is the only *mitzvah* into which a person enters with his muddy boots," goes the chassidic saying, and this expresses the very essence of the *sukkah*. When a person enters a *sukkah*, its walls and roofing encompass him entirely, and equally encompass his entirety. His mind is no more and no less in the *sukkah* than his toes; his heart is simply another occupant of its space, as are his "muddy boots." So when the entire nation of Israel dwells in a single *sukkah*, the unity expressed is one that transcends all differences and distinctions between them.

This is not the unity that is created by our love and compassion for each other. Nor is it the deeper unity that stems from the way in which our individual roles, talents, and strengths complement and fulfill one another, forming the organs and limbs of a single, integrated body. Rather, the *sukkah* brings to light the oneness

SUKKOT (4)   113

implicit in our very beings—the simple and absolute oneness of a
people rooted in the utterly singular oneness of their Creator and
Source.

SELF AND SELVES

This explains the different ways in which our sages interpret the
Torah's requirement of "for yourself" regarding the *mitzvot* of the
four kinds and of *sukkah*. The Jew taking the four kinds is uniting
with his fellows in a manner which preserves—indeed, employs—
his or her identity as an individual. Hence the Torah's use of the
word *lachem*, "for yourselves" (in the plural): In addressing the
people of Israel as they relate to the four kinds, the Torah is speaking to many individuals, each with his or her own unique contribution to the communal whole. In this context, "yours" is something
that is unique to your individual self; a borrowed or jointly owned
object is not "yours."

Regarding the making of a *sukkah*, however, the Torah addresses us in the singular *lecha* ("for yourself"). For the *mitzvah* of *sukkah* touches on the intrinsic unity of Israel—a unity in which we
are all seamlessly one. Here "for yourself" is the singular self of
Israel; as long as your use of a *sukkah* does not violate the integrity
of this unity (as does the use of a stolen *sukkah*), the *sukkah* of your
fellow is no less yours than is your own.

ONE TWIG
AND
ONE LEAF

Rabbi Simon would instruct those making the calculations (to set the calendar): "Bear in mind not to allow the blowing [of the shofar] to fall on Shabbat, nor aravah to fall on Shabbat. If you cannot manage this, allow the blowing to fall on Shabbat, but not aravah."
Jerusalem Talmud, Sukkah 4:1

The simplicity of the simple Jew is of a piece with the utterly simple essence of G-d.
Rabbi Israel Baal Shem Tov

$\mathcal{T}$he term "simple" (*pashut*, in Hebrew) is used in various connotations. When applied to human beings or physical objects, it usually implies a lack or absence of something. A simple man is one who has not been blessed with much intelligence, depth of feeling, or talent; a simple home or car is one that comes without the accoutrements of ornament and luxury. There might be a hint of admiration and longing in our voice when we speak of the "simple soul" or "the simple life," but more than a hint of condescension as well. We are acknowledging that wisdom, sensitivity, talent, beauty, or wealth are not without their drawbacks, but neither are we really considering relinquishing whatever of the above we are fortunate enough to possess for the sake of a "simpler" existence.

SUKKOT (5)

There is, however, another application of the word "simple"—simple as the antonym of "composite." In this sense, a simple thing is something that is pure and singular, as opposed to something that consists of various parts and elements. Thus, G-d is described as "the ultimate simplicity" (*pashut betachalit ha'peshitut*); for, as Maimonides writes, "G-d... is one, and His unity is unlike any other unity in existence. He is not 'one' as in 'one species,' which includes many individuals. Nor is He 'one' as in 'one body,' which includes various parts and dimensions. Rather, [His is] a unity the likes of which there is no other unity in the world."[1]

In our world, we have no model for such a unity, for even the most homogeneous body or entity is a composite of various parts, qualities, and aspects. A physical body possesses, at the very least, both substance and form, and both a beginning and an end (in the spatial as well as durational sense); a metaphysical entity (an idea, a feeling, a soul) possesses the various characteristics that distinguish it from other metaphysical entities. So while a thing might be "one" in the sense that it is a distinct and individual unit, it is a unit comprised of parts and characteristics. G-d, however, is utterly and absolutely one[2]—a "simple unity" (*achdut ha'peshutah*) rather than a composite unity.[3]

---

1   *Mishneh Torah, Laws of the Fundamentals of Torah*, 1:7.
2   Deuteronomy 6:4; the second of the "Thirteen Principles" of the Jewish faith.
3   As Maimonides goes on to explain, the fact that G-d is "one" in the sense that He is a "simple unity" also implies, *a priori*, that He is "one" in the conventional sense—that there is only one G-d, not two or more gods. Two of a kind can exist only if each is limited in space or time (as in two identical tables which exist in two different places or times), or if they somehow differ in nature or composition. Hence, there cannot be two "simple unities," for there is nothing to differentiate the one from the other.

G-d's "simplicity" does not mean that He is devoid of the qualities that make us complex. He is the source of all, and certainly does not lack for anything He imparts to His creations; in the words of the Psalmist, "He who implanted the ear certainly hears; He who formed the eye certainly sees."[4] Rather, it means that unlike every created thing, whose being is the sum of its diverse qualities, G-d's "diverse qualities" are but expressions of His simple perfection. A human being's wisdom is a component of his composite being; G-d's "wisdom" is but our way of saying that His infinite and singular being is utterly perfect and does not lack for whatever it is that makes "wise" a higher state of being than "unwise." Simplicity, as applied to G-d, is not a dearth of qualities, but a perfection so complete that it is featureless, since every conceivable "quality" is but a finite and imperfect formulation of the divine perfection.

And yet, Rabbi Israel Baal Shem Tov draws a parallel between human "simplicity," defined by a lack of learning and spiritual sophistication, and the divine "simplicity." One of the fundamental teachings of the Baal Shem Tov is that "the simplicity of the simple Jew is of a piece with the utterly simple essence of G-d."

WHEN LESS IS MORE

G-d is the source of all. Furthermore, since, as the Torah declares, "There is none else besides Him,"[5] we are all nothing more than extensions of His being. In other words, G-d is the essence of reality, and all "existences" and "creations" are but expressions and manifestations of the divine essence.

We do not expect a blue star to emit red light or for musical

---

4   Psalms 94:9.
5   Deuteronomy 4:35.

genius to express itself in business management. And yet, the utterly simple essence of G-d is manifested via the composite forms that make up creation. The explanation for this lies in the meaning of G-d's "simplicity." As we said, the divine simplicity is not an absence of qualities and characteristics, but, on the contrary, their inclusion within a being that transcends all which defines them and distinguishes them from each other (as the number "infinity"—to use a most inadequate analogy—includes all finite numbers). Creation is the process in which G-d "filters" His infinite simplicity, isolating finite areas within its infinite expanse which solidify as entities that each have a distinct existence and character.

So the multifarious and fractional world we encounter conceals an underlying unity and simplicity—the divine essence that it embodies. The more complex a thing is, the greater the concealment, for the greater its departure from its original simplicity.

Thus we can understand the Baal Shem Tov's statement that "the simplicity of the simple Jew is of a piece with the utterly simple essence of G-d." In truth, all souls (as, ultimately, all existences) are of a piece with the divine essence; but their external complexity conceals this truth. The concealing elements might, in themselves, be positive and constructive forces; they might even bring one closer to G-d, as does an intelligence that explores the divine wisdom, emotions that are attuned to one's relationship with G-d, a talent that is utilized to a G-dly end, and so on. At the same time, however, their complexity obscures the soul's original and quintessential existence as an integral part of the simple essence of G-d.

The simple soul, however, lacks these qualities. By all standards—and here we include the standards set by Torah as to how a soul might realize its relationship with G-d—this is indeed a deficiency. But this deficiency means that its simple essence is less obscured by the complexities of mind, heart, and accomplishment.

The simple Jew has a simple faith in G-d and an unequivocal commitment to Him not observed in his more sophisticated fellows. This is not because scholars and mystics do not possess this faith and commitment, which is intrinsic to every Jewish soul; but because in them, its simplicity is blurred — at times, even contorted — by the sophistication of their understanding and experience of that selfsame simplicity.

THE FOUR KINDS

"And you shall take for yourselves on the first day [of Sukkot]," instructs the Torah, "the splendid fruit of a tree, fronds of dates, the branch of the thickly-leafed tree, and *aravot* of the brook."[6] This is the *mitzvah* of *arba minim*, the "four kinds" — the *etrog* (citron), *lulav* (date frond), *hadas* (myrtle twig), and *aravah* (willow twig) — that the Jew takes in hand each day of the festival of Sukkot.[7]

The "four kinds" represent the various types within the Jewish people. In the words of the Midrash: "Just as the *etrog* has a taste and an aroma, so, too, does Israel include individuals who have Torah [learning] and good deeds... The date (the fruit of the *lulav*) has a taste but does not have an aroma... [representing those] who have Torah but do not have good deeds... The *hadas* has an aroma but not a taste... [representing those] who have good deeds but do not have Torah... The *aravah* has no flavor and no aroma... [representing those] who do not have Torah and do not have good deeds... Says G-d: 'Let them all bond together in one bundle and atone for each other.'"[8]

---

6   Leviticus 23:40.

7   Except on Shabbat—see below.

8   *Midrash Rabbah, Vayikra* 30:11.

On the most basic level, the Midrash is referring to the various levels of Torah knowledge and actual observance of the *mitzvot* among Jews. On a deeper level, the four kinds also describe four categories in a person's *experience* of Torah and *mitzvot*, as defined by their intellectual and emotional capacities. On this level, the *etrog* is one who has been blessed with a "taste," or intellectual appreciation, for Torah, as well as the emotional capacity ("aroma") to experience a love and awe of G-d in his fulfillment of the *mitzvot*[9]; the *lulav* is one who masters Torah but whose observance of *mitzvot* is "dry" and technical; the *hadas* is the fervently active but unlearned Jew; and the *aravah* is the simple Jew, who possesses a simple faith in and commitment to G-d, but has not been blessed with the depth of understanding and sophistication of feeling that enriches the Torah and *mitzvot* of the other three types.

Seen in this light, the concluding words of the Midrash assume a deeper significance. On the face of it, it would seem that it is only the *etrog*, who possesses both "taste" and "smell," who does the "atoning," fulfilling the deficiencies of the other three. But the Midrash describes G-d as saying, "Let them *all*... atone for one another." In other words, every one of the four kinds possesses something that the other three do not. Each has a uniqueness which it introduces to the union of Israel, compensating for its absence in the other three.

The distinctive quality of the *etrog* is obvious: a harmony of thought and deed and of mind and heart which it contributes to the other three. But there is a special value in the *lulav*'s utter devotion to Torah-study even at the expense of the emotional/experiential content of his *mitzvah* observance — a specialness lacking in the other three, including the *etrog*. The same is true of the

---

9   See *Tanya*, chapter 4.

hadas, who devotes all his energies to "the service of the heart" and good deeds.

The special characteristic of the *aravah* is its simplicity. The very virtues of the other three kinds—the understanding of the *lulav,* the feeling of the *hadas,* the across-the-board perfection of the *etrog*—spell their deficiency: a complex life that obscures the divine simplicity. The inclusion of the *aravah* in the group enables *all* its members to appreciate, and perhaps even stimulate, the quintessential simplicity of their own souls.[10]

---

10 The uniqueness of the *aravah* is also expressed in the manner by which it is identified by the Torah.

As discussed at length in a previous essay (*The Four Mysteries of King Solomon,* pp. 86–94), the Written Torah does not explicitly name the four kinds; rather, it leaves it to the Oral Torah to decipher the terms "splendid fruit of a tree," "fronds of dates," "the branch of the thickly-leafed tree," and "*aravot* of the brook."

Yet there is a difference in how the first three items are identified and how the fourth is designated. The words and allusions with which the Written Torah refers to the *etrog, lulav,* and *hadas* not only identify which fruit, or branch, is to be taken, but also set conditions for their qualification to be used in the observance of the *mitzvah.* The *etrog* must be *hadar*—"splendid"—a shriveled or otherwise blemished citron is not fit for use. The verse's use of the word *kapot*—which means both "fronds" and "bound"—to identify the *lulav* also requires it to be a closed frond; if its leaves have begun to spread it is disqualified. The designation of the *hadas* as a branch that is *avot*—meaning "thickly [leafed]" as well as "rope-like"—establishes the requirement that its leaves must cover the stem completely and must grow in knots of three.

On the other hand, the Torah's reference to the fourth "kind" as "*aravot* of the brook" is understood by the Talmud merely as a means to identify the species—it must be of the *type* of willow that is usually found at a river bank; but an *aravah* that grows in a land-locked field is also fit for observing the *mitzvah* of taking the four kinds.

The *etrog, lulav,* and *hadas* define segments of the community of Israel in terms of their expression and actualization of their Jewishness via their knowledge, feelings, and behavior. These have very

SUKKOT (5)

A COMPLICATING ASSOCIATION

In addition to the *aravah* that is taken together with the *lulav*, *hadas*, and *etrog* as the four kinds, there is another Sukkot observance that involves the willow branch. This is the *mitzvah* of *aravah*, observed in the Holy Temple by surrounding the altar with willow branches on Hoshana Rabbah, the seventh day of Sukkot,[11] and which we today commemorate with a special procession in the synagogue with willow twigs on that day.

The two observances are two distinct *mitzvot*, each with its own laws and guidelines. Thus "one cannot fulfill the obligation of '*aravah*' with the *aravah* of the *lulav*."[12] Even the physical requirements of the willow branches are different: For the four kinds, one requires two willow twigs, each with at least three fresh leaves[13];

---

specific guidelines and parameters which determine whether a certain idea, feeling, or action is consistent with the ethos and mores of Torah. Hence, the same words that identify these "kinds" also define the qualities an *etrog*, *lulav*, or *hadas* must possess in order to be "kosher," fit for use.

On the other hand, the defining characteristic of *aravah* is in its "non-quality" of simplicity—in the way that its lack of outward virtues allow the bond with G-d that is the essence of our identity to shine forth in all its purity. Hence, the process of identifying the *aravah* includes no implicit message as to what qualities make a proper *aravah*. The term "*aravot* of the brook" is not a quality; also the *aravah* that grew in an arid field, far from the life-giving waters of Torah and devoid of all outward expression of its Jewishness, is a "kosher" *aravah*, fit for inclusion as a member in the four kinds and able to contribute of its divine simplicity to the entire community of Israel.

11   Talmud, *Sukkah* 45a. In the Holy Temple, the willows were set around the altar every day of the festival; but the primary *mitzvah* of *aravah* is on the seventh day.

12   Ibid., 44b. See Me'iri ad loc.; and *Mishneh Torah, Laws of Lulav* 7:20.

13   *Ibid.* 7:8. Other opinions require an even greater number of leaves— see *Tur* and commentaries, *Orach Chaim* 647.

the *mitzvah* of "*aravah*," however, can be fulfilled with "one twig with one leaf."[14]

Another difference concerns the possibility of these *mitzvot* being deferred because of Shabbat. *Mitzvot* that require the handling of a physical object and special expertise may not be observed on Shabbat, lest a person forget and violate the Shabbat by carrying them from a private to a public domain (except in the Holy Temple, where these *mitzvot* were performed also on Shabbat). Thus, when Rosh Hashanah falls on Shabbat, the *shofar* is not sounded, and on the day of Sukkot that coincides with Shabbat, the four kinds are not taken—even if it is the first day of Sukkot, which is the only day that the Torah explicitly commands us to do so.[15]

The same would apply to the *aravah* of Hoshana Rabbah—if it were possible for the seventh day of Sukkot to fall on Shabbat. This, however, never happens. When the calendar used to be set on a monthly basis by the *sanhedrin* (highest court of Torah law), the judges made sure that Hoshana Rabbah should never fall on Shabbat.[16] The Talmud relates that "Rabbi Simon would instruct those making the calculations: 'Bear in mind not to allow the blowing [of the *shofar*] to fall on Shabbat, nor *aravah* to fall on Shabbat. If you cannot manage this, allow the blowing to fall on Shabbat, but not *aravah*.'"[17] Today, we follow a fixed calendar on which Rosh Hashanah (*Tishrei* 1) and the first day of Sukkot (*Tishrei* 15—two

---

14 Talmud, *Sukkah* 44b.; *Mishneh Torah, Laws of Lulav*, op. cit.. 7:20.

15 As per the verse quoted above from Leviticus 23:40; taking the four kinds on the other six days of Sukkot is only a rabbinical *mitzvah*. See *Mishneh Torah, Laws of* Lulav 7:13-18.

16 After the destruction of the Holy Temple. In the Temple itself, the *mitzvah* of *aravah* was observed on Hoshana Rabbah even if it was Shabbat (Ibid. 7:21-22).

17 Jerusalem Talmud, *Sukkah* 4:1.

SUKKOT (5)   123

dates that always fall on the same day of the week) occasionally coincide with Shabbat, while Hoshana Rabbah never does. This is a
halachic curiosity, in light of the fact that today, in the absence of a
Holy Temple, the *aravah* procession on Hoshana Rabbah is merely
a commemorative custom (*minhag*), while sounding the *shofar* on
Rosh Hashanah and taking the four kinds on the first day of Sukkot are biblical commandments!

As we explained above, the *aravah*'s inclusion in the four kinds
"atones" for the sophistication of the other three by imparting its
simplicity to them. The reverse is also true: Through its bond with
the *etrog, lulav,* and *hadas,* the *aravah* is enriched by their special
qualities.

Therein lies the difference between the *aravah* of the four kinds
and the *aravah* of Hoshana Rabbah. While the enrichment of
the *aravah* is certainly a positive thing—the *aravah* is now more
knowing and feeling in its relationship with G-d—this inevitably
affects its simplicity. The *aravah* becomes less simple, less transparent a window into the divine essence.

Thus we have two *aravot*: the *aravah* of the four kinds, which
enriches and is enriched by the great minds and hearts of Israel;
and the *aravah* of Hoshana Rabbah, whose crystalline simplicity
we zealously preserve, lest it be clouded in the slightest degree, if
only by association with its sophisticated brethren.

This explains the differences between the two *aravah*-related
mitzvot of Sukkot. The *aravah* of the four kinds has entered and
has been affected by the world of plurality, as evidenced by the
"numberness" of its *halachic* requirements (two twigs, three leaves
on each). Not so the *aravah* of Hoshana Rabbah, whose unadulterated singularity finds expression in its *halachic* criterion of "one
twig and one leaf."

The *aravah* of the four kinds has entered and has been affected by a world of diverse times and conditions. So there are days on which it is taken, and certain calendar configurations on which it is set aside. The *aravah* of Hoshana Rabbah, however, must be kept aloof of the changes and vacillations of this world. If the cycles of time threaten its consistency, we must divert these cycles, manipulating the calendar if necessary, to ensure that the simplicity of the *aravah* should always assert itself on the seventh day of Sukkot.

CHAPTER ELEVEN

Shemini Atzeret and Simchat Torah
Culmination and Integration

Tishrei 22 & 23

Each week of the year, another of the Torah's 54 *parashiot* (sections) is studied, publicly read in the synagogue, and its lessons applied to daily living. Thus the Jew lives with the Torah: The Five Books of Moses are our calendar, their chapters and verses marking, defining, molding, and inspiring the weeks and days of our year.

Simchat Torah ("The Rejoicing of the Torah") is the day on which we conclude the annual Torah-reading cycle. On this day, we read the Torah section of *Vezot Haberachah,* (Deuteronomy 33–34), and immediately begin a new Torah-reading cycle with the reading of the first chapter of Genesis.

The moment marks the climax of the festival-rich month of *Tishrei*. The awe of Rosh Hashanah, the sacredness of Yom Kippur, the unity and joy of Sukkot, all reach their highest expression on Simchat Torah, when we rejoice in the Torah and the Torah rejoices in us (as per the duel meanings of the name "The Rejoicing of the Torah").

On the evening and morning of Simchat Torah, we conduct *hakafot* ("encirclings"): All the Torah scrolls are taken out of the ark and are carried in a procession around the reading table in the center of the synagogue on which they have been read throughout the year. The procession soon dissolves into dancing and singing; embracing the Torah scrolls in our arms, we become the dancing feet of the Torah, as the Torah, too, gives vent to its joy at the conclusion and beginning of another year as the substance of our bond with our Father in Heaven.

In the Land of Israel, Simchat Torah is celebrated on the 22nd of *Tishrei*, coinciding with the one-day festival of Shemini Atzeret. Outside of the Holy Land, where the festival of Shemini Atzeret is observed for two days (*Tishrei* 22 and 23), we conclude and begin the Torah-reading cycle on its second day, and it is this day that we celebrate as "Simchat Torah." Yet the celebration of our joy in the Torah permeates both days of Shemini Atzeret, and, in certain communities, it is the custom to hold *hakafot* on the first night of this festival as well.

"Shemini Atzeret" is a name not easily given to translation. *Shemini* means "eighth"—a reference to the fact that this festival immediately follows the seven days of Sukkot; the word *atzeret* has many meanings, including "assembly," "ingathering," "withholding," "retention," and "absorption." The first essay in this chapter, *Essence*, explains the meaning and function of Shemini Atzeret and its relationship with the festival of Sukkot.

Why do we celebrate our joy with the Torah on the "eighth day" of Sukkot rather than on Shavuot, the day on which we received the Torah at Mount Sinai? This is the question addressed in *Daughters Near and Far*, which explores the parallels and differences between the two "*atzerets*" of the Jewish calendar, Shemini Atzeret and Shavuot.

The two concluding essays of our chapter examine two curiosities of Simchat Torah. *Scrolled* wonders at the fact that we celebrate the gift of the divine wisdom by dancing with, rather than learning and studying, the Torah. *Intuition* notes that the *hakafot* observance of Simchat Torah, which marks the pinnacle of the Jew's service of G-d throughout the month of *Tishrei*, is neither a *mitzvah* nor a rabbinical ordinance, but merely a *minhag* (custom)—prompting an examination of the significance of the "custom" in Jewish life.

For additional essays on the essence and function of Torah, see our chapter on "Shavuot" in volume 3 of this series, pp. 151–206. For more on the Torah-reading cycle, see *The Hard Life* in vol. 1, pp. 225–233.

ESSENCE

G-d spoke to Moses, saying: "...On the fifteenth day of this seventh month shall be the festival of Sukkot for seven days...

On the eighth day shall be a calling of holiness to you... it is an atzeret..."

Leviticus 23:33–36

Once, on the festival of Shemini Atzeret ("The Eighth Day of *Atzeret*" that follows the seven-day festival of Sukkot), chassidic master Rabbi Schneur Zalman of Liadi delivered a discourse on the significance of the day. It was a profound and lengthy discourse, which explored the concept of *atzeret*—a word whose various meanings include "retention," "absorption," "ingathering," and "assembly."

Following the address, one of the chassidim approached Rabbi Schneur Zalman. "Rebbe!" he cried, "I didn't understand a single word. Perhaps you can repeat what you said in simple words, so that a simple mind such as mine could also understand what Shemini Atzeret is?"

Rabbi Schneur Zalman thought for a moment, ran his hand over his forehead, and said: "Shemini Atzeret is the tea essence."

Later, when other chassidim asked the man if he had any idea what the Rebbe might have meant, he said: "Why, exactly what he said—Shemini Atzeret is the tea essence. To make tea essence, you boil a large quantity of tea leaves for a long time, until you get a highly concentrated brew. Then, every time you want a cup of tea, you mix a small amount of the tea essence with hot water—and you have your cup of tea.

"We trembled before the majesty of G-d on Rosh Hashanah, we did *teshuvah* on Yom Kippur, we rejoiced on Sukkot. Now, on Shemini Atzeret, we distill it all into a strong tea essence to supply us throughout the year—until next Rosh Hashanah!"

ONE MORE DAY

Rashi, in his commentary on Torah, explains the significance of Shemini Atzeret with the following parable:

> *There was once a king who invited his children for a banquet of several days. When it came time for them to go, he said to them: "My children, please, stay with me one more day—your parting is difficult for me..."*[1]

Sukkot is a week-long reunion banquet that the supernal King throws for His children, the souls of Israel. For seven days we rejoice in our kinship with G-d and with each other. But then, when it comes time for us to take leave of the festival and return to our everyday pursuits, G-d retains us with the request, "Stay one more day..." Shemini Atzeret, "the eighth day of retention," is one more day of joy and fellowship in the divine palace before returning to the hinterland of material life.

But let us examine this parable more closely. At first glance, the king's request seems little more than an indulgence of sentiment. If his children's return to their lives apart from his is inevitable, what is gained by staying one more day? Other than delaying the pain of parting for several hours, is there anything of enduring significance in an "eighth day of retention"?

---

[1]   Rashi on Leviticus 23:36; cf. *Midrash Rabbah, Song of Songs* 7:4, quoted in the next essay.

SHEMINI ATZERET AND SIMCHAT TORAH (1)   131

THE FESTIVAL OF UNITY

In the parable, the king does not say, "our parting is difficult for
me," but "your parting is difficult for me." Indeed, G-d, of whom it
is said that "no place is void of Him,"[2] never parts from us. It is we
who might "part" from G-d, moving on to a state of diminished
awareness of our relationship with Him.

"Your parting" also has another meaning: our parting from
each other, which, in G-d's eyes, is synonymous to our parting
from Him. When we are one with G-d, we are also one with each
other, united as children of our royal father. The same applies in
reverse: When we are one with each other, united in our common
identity as G-d's children, we are one with G-d.[3]

Sukkot, more than any other festival, emphasizes the unity we
achieve among ourselves through our relationship with G-d. All
mitzvot have this uniting effect, underscoring our common endeavor to fulfill the will of our Father in Heaven; but the *mitzvah*
of *sukkah* is unique in the depth and scope of the unity it awakens
among us.

When two individuals study a chapter of Torah, they deepen
their relationship with G-d and with each other by integrating
the wisdom of G-d into their minds and lives. But their study also
underscores the differences between them, as each understands
and appreciates the divine wisdom in accordance with his or her
distinct intellectual prowess and spiritual sensitivity. When two
individuals fulfill the divine command to give charity, the deed differentiates even as it unites, as each gives in accordance with his or
her generosity and financial capacity. The same is true of virtually

---

2   *Tikkunei Zohar* 57; cf. *Midrash Rabbah, Bamidbar* 12:4.
3   Thus, before we approach G-d in prayer, we pledge: "I hereby accept
    upon myself the commandment, 'Love your fellow as yourself.'"

every other *mitzvah*: While a *mitzvah* unites diverse individuals in the common pursuit of serving the divine will, it also accentuates the diversity of talent, experience, and commitment that each individual brings to the deed.

The *sukkah*, however, is the ultimate equalizer. This *mitzvah* is observed by dwelling in a bough-covered hut for seven days—eating, sleeping, and socializing in it, and otherwise regarding it as one's home, for the duration of the festival. In other words, the *mitzvah* of *sukkah* is not about what you do and how you do it, but *where* you do whatever it is that you do. Two people thinking the same thought are nevertheless thinking differently; the same is true of two people experiencing the same feeling or doing the same deed. But two people inhabiting a particular place are utterly synonymous in the fact of their presence; neither can be more or less or differently *there* (in the empirical, physical sense) than the other. So the *sukkah* relates to all its inhabitants equally: It is the scholar's home no more and no less than it is the simple laborer's; the mystic and the businessman, the scientist and the artist, are housed by its walls without regard to the nature and content of their lives. In the words of the Talmud, "It is fitting that all of Israel should dwell in a single *sukkah*."[4]

THE DAY EIGHTH OF RETENTION

But dwelling in the *sukkah* is a once-a-year experience. After the seven-day unity fest is over, we move from the *sukkah* back to our homes. We move back to a life in which our place of habitat is no longer a *mitzvah*, no longer a primary element in our relationship

---

4 Talmud, *Sukkah* 27b. See *The Easy Mitzvah*, pp. 81–85 above, and *Unity in Three Dimensions*, pp. 106–113 above.

SHEMINI ATZERET AND SIMCHAT TORAH (1)   133

with G-d; and back to a life in which our unity is expressed via the more "individualistic" *mitzvot* of thought, word, and deed.

Yet our parting is distressful to G-d. So He retains us one day longer, for an "eighth day of retention."

He retains us for an "eighth day" of Sukkot—a day on which dwelling in the *sukkah* is no longer a *mitzvah* but on which the unity of Sukkot suffuses us nonetheless. A day on which we are utterly and unequivocally one without the "apparatus" of oneness, without the need for an actual edifice to contextualize our unity.[5]

---

5   Outside of the Land of Israel, Shemini Atzeret is actually observed for two days. This is in commemoration of the time when the Jewish calendar was set on a monthly basis by the *sanhedrin* (highest court of Torah law) in Jerusalem, and all Diaspora communities, who received word of the exact date of the festival days or weeks later, observed an additional day of each festival out of doubt. Thus, the seven-day festival of Passover was observed for eight days, the one-day festival of Shavuot for two days, etc.

On Sukkot, the matter was more complicated. The Torah ordains a seven-day festival, followed by the single day of Shemini Atzeret. Thus, the Diaspora observed a total of nine days—seven days of Sukkot; an eighth day which might have been the last day of Sukkot or, alternatively, the festival of Shemini Atzeret; and a ninth day, in the possibility that this is the "real" Shemini Atzeret.

Today, we follow a fixed calendar, so we are no longer in doubt of the festivals' true dates. Nevertheless, having gained extra days of holiness in our calendar, we are loath to give them up, and so we follow the custom of our ancestors. Following the seven days of Sukkot, we observe two days of Shemini Atzeret, the second of which is called Simchat Torah ("Rejoicing of the Torah"), this being the day on which we conclude, and begin anew, the annual Torah-reading cycle.

On the question of whether one should dwell in the *sukkah* on the first day of Shemini Atzeret, which was initially observed as a day that was possibly the seventh day of Sukkot, the Talmud rules: "One dwells in the *sukkah*, but one does not recite the blessing" on the *sukkah* recited on the first seven days. The omission of the blessing is to emphasize that the *mitzvah* of *sukkah*, as commanded by the Torah, extends only

He retains us for a day of "retention," "absorption," and "ingathering"—a day on which it is not we who are in the *sukkah*, but on which the *sukkah* is within us. A day on which we are empowered to internalize the unity of *Sukkot*, to distill it into a "tea essence" and store it in the pith of our souls so that we may draw on it in the *sukkah*-less months to come.

---

for seven days (Talmud, *Sukkah* 46b–47a; see *Shulchan Aruch* and commentaries, *Orach Chaim* 668:1).

The result of all this is that we have a nine-day festival period of which the first seven are days of full-fledged dwelling in the *sukkah*, followed by one day (the first day of Shemini Atzeret) on which we dwell in the *sukkah* but emphasize that this is not a *mitzvah*, followed, in turn, by a day (the second day of Shemini Atzeret) on which we do not dwell in the *sukkah* at all.

The deeper significance of this is that the unity achieved by the *sukkah* also has these three phases:

a) The seven days of Sukkot, when the *mitzvah* of *sukkah* unites us.

b) The first day of Shemini Atzeret, on which dwelling in the *sukkah* is no longer a *mitzvah*, yet we "retain" and "absorb" the essence of *sukkah* and express this with our custom of dwelling in the *sukkah* one more day.

c) The second day of Shemini Atzeret, on which we have internalized the unity of *sukkah* to such an extent that there is no need even for any "symbolic" expression of it—indeed, no symbol or act can possibly embody its depth and scope, for it transcends any and all representation.

DAUGHTERS NEAR AND FAR

Said Rabbi Joshua ben Levi: The atzeret of the festival of Sukkot ought to have been fifty days later, like the atzeret of Passover. But because the atzeret of Sukkot leads from summer into winter, these are not the days in which to go and come.

Midrash Rabbah, Song of Songs 7:4

The Torah is the stuff of our lives as Jews: our link to our Creator, our national mandate, the purpose of our existence, the blueprint for the perfection for which we yearn. But the Jew is no less crucial for the Torah than the Torah is for the Jew: It is the Jew who devotes his or her life to its study, teaching, and practice; the Jew who carries its wisdom and ethos to all peoples of the earth; the Jew who translates its precepts and ideals into concrete reality. Little wonder, then, that the most joyous festival on the Jewish calendar, both for the Torah and for the Jew, is the festival of Simchat Torah, when the annual Torah-reading cycle is concluded and begun anew.

Simchat Torah means "The Rejoicing of the Torah." For this is both the day when we rejoice in the Torah, lifting its holy scrolls into our arms and filling the synagogue with song and dance; as well as the day on which the Torah rejoices in us. The Torah, too, wishes to dance, but lacking the physical apparatus to do so, it employs the body of the Jew. On Simchat Torah, the Jew becomes the dancing feet of the Torah.

WHY NOT ON SHAVUOT?

Simchat Torah immediately follows the festival of Sukkot. Indeed, the biblical name for Simchat Torah is *Shemini Atzeret*, which means "the eighth day of retention"; for the function of this festival is for us to retain and absorb the attainments of the seven days of Sukkot.[1]

(Outside the Land of Israel, where the festival of Shemini Atzeret/Simchat Torah is observed for two days, the name "Shemini Atzeret" is usually applied to the first day and "Simchat Torah" to the second—the day on which the actual conclusion and beginning of the Torah takes place. In essence, however, the two days constitute a single festival, and the name "Shemini Atzeret" applies to both its days.)

But why celebrate Simchat Torah on Shemini Atzeret, the 22nd (and 23rd) day of the month of *Tishrei*? As a rule, the festivals are located at points on the calendar that mark the historical sources of their significance: Passover is observed on the 15th of *Nissan*, the anniversary of our Exodus from Egypt; Rosh Hashanah occurs on the first of *Tishrei*, the date of the creation of man; and so on. Accordingly, would it not have been more appropriate to rejoice over the Torah on the sixth of *Sivan*, the day in which G-d revealed Himself to us at Mount Sinai and granted us the Torah as our eternal heritage? Indeed, we mark that date with the festival of Shavuot—a festival devoted to reexperiencing the revelation at Sinai and reiterating our covenant with G-d forged by the Torah.

---

[1] See previous essay, *Essence*, pp. 129–134.

SHEMINI ATZERET AND SIMCHAT TORAH (2) 137

Yet our *joy* in the Torah is reserved for the festival of Shemini Atzeret—a date with no apparent historical connection to our relationship with the Torah.

One might explain that our living with the Torah through the annual reading cycle, studying it and implementing it in our daily lives, is of greater significance than our original receiving of it at Sinai. But this itself requires explanation: Why do we conclude and begin the Torah on Shemini Atzeret? Why did Moses, who established the Torah-reading cycle, not schedule it to end and recommence on the festival of Shavuot?

CALENDAR TWINS

Actually, a closer look at Shemini Atzeret and Shavuot reveals a striking resemblance between the two festivals. Shavuot, too, carries the name *atzeret*,[2] for it, too, serves as a vehicle of "retention" and "absorption" for the festival that precedes it. The resemblance is further emphasized by the fact that, like Shemini Atzeret, Shavuot is also an "eighth day of retention"—a one-day festival which culminates a cycle of seven. Shemini Atzeret immediately follows the seven days of Sukkot, while Shavuot closes the seven-week *sefirah* count begun on Passover.

The two *atzeret*s mirror each other across the yearly cycle. The Jewish year is like a circle with two poles: Two key months, *Nissan* and *Tishrei*, are both considered, each in its own realm, to be the "first" and "head" of the entire year.[3] *Nissan* 15 is the date of the Exodus, and begins the seven-day festival of Passover. Exactly six

---

2 "*Atzeret*" is a synonym for Shavuot throughout the Mishnah, Talmud, and the writings of our sages.

3 See *Our Other Head* in vol. 3, pp. 4–12 of this series.

months later, on the 15th of *Tishrei*, begins the other seven-day festival of the Jewish year, Sukkot. And both of these seven-day festivals are capped by a one-day "*atzeret*." The only break in the symmetry is the fact that the *atzeret* of Sukkot is a literal, contiguous eighth to its seven days, while Passover's *atzeret* is a more distant "eighth," following a count of 49 (seven times seven) days that begins on the second day of Passover.

This leads the talmudic sage Rabbi Joshua ben Levi to say: "The *atzeret* of the festival of Sukkot ought to have been fifty days later, like the *atzeret* of Passover."

Why, indeed, does Shemini Atzeret immediately follow Sukkot? Rabbi Joshua offers the following parable in explanation:

> *A king had many daughters. Some of them were married off nearby, and some of them were married off in faraway places. One day, they all came to visit with their father the king. Said the king: Those who are married off nearby have the time to go and come; but those who are married off afar do not have the time to go and come. Since they are all here with me, I will make one festival for them all and I shall rejoice with them.*
>
> *Thus, with the* atzeret *of Passover, when we are coming from winter into summer, G-d says: "They have the time to go and come." But with the* atzeret *of Sukkot, since we are coming from summer into winter, and the dust of the roads is difficult, and the byroads are difficult… G-d says: "They do not have the time to go and come; since they are all here, I will make one festival for them all and I shall rejoice with them."*

SHEMINI ATZERET AND SIMCHAT TORAH (2)   139

What is an "Atzeret"?

To better understand the significance of Rabbi Joshua's question and the answer provided by his parable, we must first examine the concept of "*atzeret*." Why does a festival require an *atzeret*? And what is the difference between an *atzeret* that immediately follows a festival and one that comes several weeks later?

Kabbalistic and chassidic teaching explain that an *atzeret* is the absorption and internalization of what was earlier realized and expressed on a more external level. *Atzeret* is what metabolizing is to eating, what assimilation is to study, what conception is to marital union.

Our receiving of the Torah on Shavuot is the *atzeret* of our liberation from slavery seven weeks earlier. On Passover we became a free people — free of the taskmaster's whip, free of subjugation to the cruelest and most debased society on earth. But what is freedom? How is it to be digested, internalized, and integrated into our day-to-day existence? Is it freedom from responsibility, from the burden of moral choices, from purpose and definition to life? If such is freedom, then the most liberated creature on earth is... the slave! Indeed, this was the freedom some Jews yearned for when they complained to Moses several months later, "We remember the fish which we ate in Egypt, for free."[4]

When G-d revealed Himself to Moses in the burning bush and charged him with the mission of taking the children of Israel out of Egypt, He expressed to him the nature of the freedom to be bestowed upon the newborn nation. "This is your sign that I have sent you," said G-d. "When you take this nation out of Egypt, you shall serve G-d at this mountain."[5]

---

4   Numbers 11:5; see Rashi's commentary.
5   Exodus 3:12.

The purpose of the Exodus was that it should lead to Sinai. The freedom that G-d promised to Israel was not merely freedom from the geographical borders of Egypt, but freedom from all constraints and limitations[6]—physical or psychological, external or internal. Freedom from doubt; freedom from hazard and inconsistency; freedom from servitude to one's own nature, drives, and desires. Freedom which enables the soul to realize her full potential, to experience her intrinsic bond with her essence and source, to actualize her mission and purpose in life. In other words, the freedom to be fully and uninhibitedly oneself. Such freedom is possible only through the Torah, the divinely authored "blueprint for creation" which guides and directs us toward the understanding and actualization of who and what we truly are.

So every year, after receiving the gift of freedom on the 15th of *Nissan*, we embark on a 49-day process of absorbing and internalizing it—a process which culminates in the *atzeret* of Shavuot. For seven weeks we labor to assimilate the true, inner significance of the Exodus into the 49 traits and sub-traits of our souls,[7] to mature a circumstantial liberty into a state of inherent freedom.

Thus we graduate (as Rabbi Joshua expresses it) from winter to summer. From the chill of aimlessness to the warmth of passionate purpose; from the hardship of struggle to the delight of

---

6   The Hebrew word for Egypt, *mitzrayim*, means "constraints" and "limitations."

7   There are seven basic impulses in the heart of man: *chesed* (love, benevolence); *gevurah* (restraint, awe, fear); *tiferet* (compassion, harmony); *netzach* (victoriousness, ambition); *hod* (splendor, devotion); *yesod* (foundation, connectedness); and *malchut* (sovereignty, receptiveness). Each of these traits includes nuances of all seven (e.g., *chesed* of *chesed*, *gevurah* of *chesed*, *tiferet* of *chesed*, etc.) making a total of 49 elements to the human character. See *The Journey* in vol. 3 of this series, pp. 98–108.

SHEMINI ATZERET AND SIMCHAT TORAH (2)   141

achievement; from the gloom of ignorance to the clear summer light of wisdom and understanding.

THE SECOND TABLETS

Then, six months later, come the festivals of *Tishrei*.

For life is not the unbroken progression of development and growth that we plan it to be. Instead, there are blunders, failings, and regressions. Our life as a nation was no different: A few short weeks after we stood at Sinai, beheld our Creator, and attained the pinnacle of freedom and perfection, the Golden Calf was being worshipped in the Jewish camp.

But every fall also provides the momentum for a subsequent rise. The debacle of the Golden Calf gave us Yom Kippur—the holiest day of the year, and the source of an even deeper connection to Torah than the revelation at Sinai on Shavuot had achieved.

Following the revelation at Sinai, G-d gave Moses the "two Tablets of the Covenant" on which He had inscribed the Ten Commandments which encapsulate the entirety of Torah. Upon beholding Israel's violation of everything the Tablets stood for, Moses "threw the tablets from his hands, and broke them at the foot of the mountain."[8] But out of the shattered tablets and covenant was born a second set of tablets—a set of tablets containing the Torah on a level that the earlier set did not, and could not, include. On the 10th of *Tishrei*, observed ever since as Yom Kippur, G-d gave us the "second tablets," conveying to us a dimension of Torah that only the regenerative power of *teshuvah* (repentance, lit. "return") can evoke.

---

8   Exodus 32:19.

On the most basic level, the Torah is a set of divinely-ordained precepts, a list of dos and don'ts which outline the manner in which the Creator of life desired that it be lived; to act accordingly is to achieve connection to G-d by becoming the instrument of His will. This was the dimension of Torah that G-d inscribed on the first tablets. But the Torah is much more than that, as evidenced by the fact that the Torah itself provides the formula for *teshuvah*.

To rebuild a shattered relationship, one must access that part of the relationship that was never damaged in the first place. The possibility of *teshuvah* means that even when a person violates the divine will, G-d forbid, the essence of his or her connection with G-d is not affected. The fact that the Torah itself includes the precept of *teshuvah* means that Torah is the vehicle not only for the connection between ourselves and G-d which is expressed and actualized by our observance of its commandments, but also for the inviolable bond that remains forever unaffected by our deeds. So also one who has shattered the "first tablets" dimension of one's relationship with G-d, can reach deeper into Torah to the very heart of the relationship tapped by the hunger, the longing, the recoil of *teshuvah*, and rebuild it anew.

As long as we did not stray from the path of life ordained by the Torah, there was no need, and no opportunity, to employ the power of *teshuvah*. This is why the first tablets contained only the "conventional" aspect of Torah—the connection with G-d achieved through the fulfillment of His will—while the deeper function of Torah remained locked in sublime potential. It was the second tablets, the product of our repentant response to our first (and prototypic[9]) fall as a people, upon which G-d inscribed the essence of

---

9   "There is no calamity which befalls the world which does not contain something of the Golden Calf in it" (Talmud, *Sanhedrin* 102a).

SHEMINI ATZERET AND SIMCHAT TORAH (2)   143

Torah—the bond between Him and us that transcends the Torah's
own laws and commandments.[10]

HIDDEN AND REVEALED

And Sukkot is the celebration of Yom Kippur.

Teshuvah, by its very nature, is an introverted act. A soul se-
cludes herself with her G-d, anguishes over the distance she has
created between them, and in the depth of her anguish finds the
redeeming element of her iniquities and the power to repair and
sublimate her defective past.

The private nature of *teshuvah* is demonstrated by a marked difference between the manner in which we received the first and
second tablets. On Shavuot, the entire Jewish nation gathered
around Mount Sinai amidst a tremendous display of divine power;
there was thunder and lightning, clouds of fire and smoke, and the
triumphant blast of the *shofar* as the Almighty communicated the
Ten Commandments to all of Israel and summoned Moses to the
top of the mountain to receive the Tablets of the Covenant.[11] But
when Moses received the second set of tablets on Yom Kippur, no
one was there; G-d instructed that it be a silent and private affair,
befitting the still, deep waters of *teshuvah*.[12]

So Yom Kippur is hardly the environment for manifest joy
and celebration. And yet, what greater joy can there be than our
joy in the Torah of the second tablets, in the essence of our eternal, all-enduring bond with our Creator? And the nature of joy is

---

10 See *The 120-Day Version of the Human Story*," pp. 37–43 above, and the
    other essays in our chapter on "Yom Kippur and the Ten Days of Te-
    shuvah" (pp. 33–75)

11 Exodus 19:16ff.

12 Ibid., 34:3.

that it refuses to confine itself to the inner sanctum of the heart. It bursts its seams, floods the body, pours out from the throat in song, and sets the feet dancing. Hence the festival of Sukkot, "the time of our joy,"[13] five days later on the 15th of *Tishrei*. Sukkot is the joy of Yom Kippur come to light—the joy that the solemnity and inwardness of the day had kept concealed.[14]

For seven days the joy mounts. But as with the freedom gained on Passover, the joy of *teshuvah* must be absorbed and internalized. Instead of remaining a once-a-year experience, it must be integrated into our nature and daily existence. So the seven-day festival of Sukkot is followed by an *atzeret*—a day in which our joy with the essence of Torah reaches its peak, and is immediately married to the cycle of our year-round lives.

SUMMER AND WINTER

Thus, the Passover-Shavuot orbit on the one hand, and the Yom Kippur-Sukkot-Shemini Atzeret constellation on the other, represent two dimensions of the Torah and its role as the facilitator of the bond between us and G-d.

The journey from Passover to Shavuot represents the straight and true path outlined by the Torah: the careful climb from the ignorance and selfishness of infancy to spiritual and moral maturity; the step-by-step progress of the righteous individual (*tzaddik*)

---

13 From the festival prayers; see p. 108 above.

14 Sukkot, occurring on the "full moon" of *Tishrei*, reveals what was implicit during Rosh Hashanah, the ten days of *teshuvah*, and Yom Kippur, whose "hidden" nature is reflected in the complete or partial concealment of the moon in the first days of *Tishrei* (see pp. 99–102 above and references noted there).

who labors for a lifetime to develop the inherent goodness and perfection of his or her soul while safeguarding it from the pitfalls of a corporeal and corrupting world.

On the other hand, the "second tablets" of Yom Kippur, and their celebration and internalization on Sukkot and Shemini Atzeret, represent the triumph of the *baal teshuvah* ("master of return") — the one who, having succumbed to the trials of earthly life, has exploited the negativity of his or her condition to touch the very core of his or her soul and stimulate its most quintessential powers.

This is reflected in the alignment of these two festival-systems with the seasons of the year. The springtime festivals of Passover and Shavuot, marking the passage from winter to summer, embody the *tzaddik*'s measured progression from bud to bloom, from darkness and cold to light and warmth, from spiritual infancy to maturity. The autumn festivals of *Tishrei* represent the *baal teshuvah*'s return to the cold and gloom of winter to uncover the positive potentials hidden therein.

THE PARABLE

Now we can understand Rabbi Joshua's parable and how it explains the difference between the *atzeret* of Passover and the *atzeret* of Sukkot.

The Supernal King has many "married daughters" — many souls who have embarked on the mission and challenge of physical life. The soul comes down to earth and is joined to a body in order that their union should yield a progeny of good deeds — deeds which sanctify the material world and fulfill G-d's purpose in creation by developing it as a dwelling for His presence.[15] Hence, the depiction of the soul's earthly sojourn as a "marriage."

Some of the King's daughters are "married off in a near place." These are the souls of the righteous, who, though they descend into physical life, never lose sight of their holy origins. They deal with the material, developing and refining their own physical natures and the world about them; but without falling prey to its adverse influences. They have left their father's home, but never wander too far off.

But the King also has daughters whose marriages have led them to "faraway places": souls whose involvement with the material reality has taken them far from the royal palace; souls who have become deeply enmeshed in the mundanity they came to redeem.

There are *tzaddikim* and there are *baalei teshuvah*, and there is also the *tzaddik* and the *baal teshuvah* within each and every one of us. We each have our moments and areas of perfect righteousness—moments and areas of our lives that remain forever unsullied by the negativity we contend with. And virtually every person has had the experience—to a greater or lesser extent—of grappling with that negativity, being tainted by it, and being challenged to surmount the fall—only to be driven by it to even greater heights than the "perfect" self could ever attain.

Passover is the festival of the *tzaddik,* and of the *tzaddik* within us. On Passover we taste the pure, untarnished freedom of a new-born people. So the *atzeret* of Passover comes fifty days later. For it is springtime; the roads are clear, and we "have the time to go and come." We are free to methodically make our way through the 49 steps from the revelation of Passover to the internalization of

---

15   See *Midrash Tanchuma, Nasso* 16; *Tanya*, ch. 36.

SHEMINI ATZERET AND SIMCHAT TORAH (2)

Shavuot. It is a gradual, step-by-step journey, characteristic of the gradual, step-by-step trajectory of the *tzaddik's* path through life.

But on Sukkot we celebrate our capacity for *teshuvah*, our bond with G-d embodied by the "second tablets." At this reunion of "the daughters that are married afar" with their Father and King, they "have not the time to go and come." For "we are coming from summer into winter, and the dust of the roads is difficult, and the byroads are difficult." We are journeyers along the volatile path of *teshuvah*, where opportunities must be grasped as they come, and lives are unmade and remade in a single, explosive moment.[16]

So we plunge directly from Sukkot into the *atzeret* of Simchat Torah—directly into the immediate internalization of the second tablets edition of Torah and its retention through the winters and summers to come.

---

16   See *Moment*, pp. 57–58 above.

SCROLLED

It is the custom in these lands on the night and day of Simchat Torah to take all the Torah scrolls out of the ark. Psalms and prayers are recited, in each community according to its custom. It is also customary to circle the reading table in the synagogue with the Torah scrolls... all this to increase the joy.

Shulchan Aruch, Orach Chaim 669:1

On Simchat Torah we rejoice with the Torah. We celebrate the joy of being a Jew — the joy of a life defined by and permeated with the divine wisdom and will communicated to us at Sinai.

But where is the Torah?

Where is the all-embracing wisdom of the Five Books of Moses, the inspiration of the Prophets, the music of the Psalms? Where is the brilliance of the Talmud, the guidance of the *Shulchan Aruch*, the mystique of the kabbalistic writings?

Where are the laws, the ethics, and the philosophy that have molded our lives and served as a beacon of light to all of humanity for 33 centuries?

It's all rolled up.

It's all rolled up in a scroll of parchment, girdled with a sash, clothed in an embroidered mantle. This is the Torah we grasp in our arms as we dance away the night and day of Simchat Torah in synagogues across the globe.

Is this how we should celebrate our relationship with the Torah? By embracing a velvet-draped scroll and expending calories

SHEMINI ATZERET AND SIMCHAT TORAH (3)   149

and shoe leather on synagogue floors? Surely the People of the Book could have devised a more appropriate way to rejoice with the essence of all wisdom. Would not the festival be more appropriately observed by immersing oneself in a biblical narrative, page of Talmud, or a work of Torah philosophy?

THE SECOND TIME AROUND

Actually, there are two annual festivals which celebrate our receiving of the Torah: Shavuot and Simchat Torah.

Shavuot is the day on which the entire Jewish nation experienced the divine revelation at Mount Sinai, where G-d communicated the Torah to us and summoned Moses to the top of the mountain to receive the Tablets of the Covenant. These tablets, however, were broken as a result of the violation of their contents by the Jewish people with the sin of the Golden Calf. It is the second tablets, granted us on Yom Kippur, over which we rejoice on Simchat Torah.[1]

In other words, the "first tablets" of Shavuot represent the "conventional" aspect of Torah—Torah as the study of G-d's wisdom and the fulfillment of His will. On this level, a person's relationship with the Torah is determined by his individual talents and behavior. The more one studies, the more one knows; the greater one's mind, the deeper one's comprehension. And if one acts contrary to the Torah's commandments, one is no longer worthy of it—worshipping an idol of gold leads to a shattered tablets and covenant.

But there is also a deeper dimension to Torah, which transcends the externalities of conduct and understanding. This is the

---

[1]   See previous essay, *Daughters Near and Far* (pp. 135–147).

essence of Torah, the quintessential bond between G-d and Jew which is actualized by, but not dependent upon, the Jew's study and observance of the divine wisdom and will. No sin or regression can weaken this bond; on the contrary, it was the breaking of the first tablets that uncovered its power and invincibility. This is the Torah of the second tablets, the Torah we celebrate on Simchat Torah.

On Shavuot we spend the entire night studying. We read selections from the Five Books of Moses, the Prophets, and the Scriptures; we study the first and last paragraphs of each of the Talmud's 60 tractates, selections from the esoteric works *Sefer Yetzirah* and *Zohar*, and Maimonides' list of the 613 *mitzvot*. We are celebrating the manner in which the Torah is realized in our lives—by study and implementation.

But on Simchat Torah we celebrate our bond with the quintessence of Torah. So the Torah remains scrolled and covered—we are grasping *it* rather than its words and precepts. We dance with the Torah rather than study it, because we are relating to that dimension of Torah which embraces each and every Jew equally, regardless of knowledge and spiritual state. And in dancing, we all relate equally to the Torah: The sweat of the scholar is no more profound than that of his illiterate brother, and the feet of the saint move no more piously than those of the boor.

On Simchat Torah we are all equal: equal in our inability to fathom the essence of Torah, and equal in our intrinsic and inviolable connection with it.

INTUITION

To do Your will, my G-d, is my desire; Your
Torah is in my innermost parts.

Psalms 40:9

$\mathcal{T}$ he hallmark of a loving marriage is each partner's readiness
to do the will of the other. If one partner expresses a desire
for something, the other will do everything in his or her power to
bring about its fulfillment.

A greater love is demonstrated when each partner also strives
to fulfill the *implied* will of the other. To the truly devoted spouse,
it makes no difference if a desire has been explicitly expressed or
merely hinted at—he or she will carry it out with the same devotion and commitment to the loved one's gratification.

Finally, there are those very special marriages in which there
is no need for even the merest of allusions. So deep is the bond
between husband and wife that each intuitively knows what the
other wants of him or her. Indeed, when two people love each other to such a degree, there is no greater joy than that experienced
when one has succeeded, all on one's own, in sensing the other's
desire and satisfying it.

THREE DEGREES OF COMMANDMENT

The month of *Tishrei* is a month replete with *mitzvot*—with opportunities for carrying out the divine will. For thirty days, practically our every thought and moment is filled with praying, repenting, fasting, feasting, dancing, building a *sukkah*, acquiring

a set of "four kinds," and dozens of other *mitzvot*, customs, and observances.

The observances of *Tishrei* fall under three general categories. There are "biblical precepts"—commandments that are explicitly stated in the Torah. These include *mitzvot* such as sounding the *shofar*, fasting on Yom Kippur, or eating in the *sukkah*. There are also a number of "rabbinical *mitzvot*"—observances instituted by the prophets and the sages by the authority vested in them by the Torah. For example, the five prayer services held on Yom Kippur and the taking of the four kinds on all but the first day of Sukkot are rabbinical institutions.

Finally, the month of *Tishrei* has many *minhagim* or "customs" such as eating an apple dipped in honey on the first night of Rosh Hashanah or conducting the *kaparot* in the wee hours of the morning on the day before Yom Kippur. The *minhagim* are not mandated by biblical or rabbinical law, but by force of custom: These are things that we ourselves have initiated as ways to enhance our service to our Creator.

Most amazingly, the climax of the month of *Tishrei*, the point at which our celebration of G-d's festivals attains the very pinnacle of joy, is during the *hakafot* of Simchat Torah, when we grasp hold of the Torah scrolls and dance with them around the reading table in the synagogue—a practice that is neither a biblical nor a rabbinical precept, but "merely" a custom.

For it is with our observance of the customs that we express the depth of our love for G-d. The biblical commandments might be compared to the explicitly expressed desires between two people bound in marriage. The rabbinical *mitzvot*, on which G-d did not directly instruct us but which nevertheless constitute expressions

SHEMINI ATZERET AND SIMCHAT TORAH (4)   153

of the divine will,[1] resemble the implied requests between spouses. But the *minhagim* represent those areas in which we intuitively sense how we might cause G-d pleasure—and in this lies our greatest joy.

---

[1] Before performing a rabbinical *mitzvah*, we recite a blessing that begins with the words, "Blessed are You G-d...who has sanctified us with His commandments and commanded us to..." For since G-d commanded us to fulfill the *mitzvot* instituted by the sages, these are divine commandments; the difference between the biblical and rabbinical *mitzvot* is only in that the former are more explicitly the expressed will of G-d. Thus, fulfilling a rabbinical precept is a greater show of commitment, for we thereby exhibit our equal devotion to those divine desires which G-d has not directly related to us.

CHAPTER TWELVE

Cheshvan

The Ordinary Life

The months of the Jewish calendar each have their own distinct quality and "mood": *Nissan* is the month of freedom, *Adar* of joy, *Elul* of introspection, and so on. The festivals and commemorative dates that each month contains, and the *mitzvot* and observances associated with it, impart their auras and essences to the respective places in time that they occupy.

It would appear, however, that the month of *Cheshvan* is an exception to this rule: Coming on the heels of *Tishrei*, the most festival-rich of all months, *Cheshvan* is the only month without a single special date in the Jewish calendar. In truth, however, it is the very ordinariness and regularity of *Cheshvan* that constitutes its distinctive quality: a quality that is no less—indeed, far more—fundamental to our mission and identity than the other eleven qualities that comprise the calendar of Jewish life.

Actually, there does exist one date of particular significance in the month of *Cheshvan*: The seventh day of *Cheshvan* is when we begin to pray for rain in the Land of Israel (in other lands, the request for rain is included in our prayers beginning on the 60th day after the autumnal equinox). But as *The Last Jew*, the single essay to comprise our chapter on *Cheshvan*, shall explain, the "distinction" of this date only further underscores the preeminence of the ordinary in the life of the Jew.

CHESHVAN (1)   157

THE
LAST
JEW

On the seventh day of Cheshvan, *fifteen days
after the conclusion of the festival [of Sukkot],
one begins to pray for rain. This is to allow
the very last Jew to reach the Euphrates River.*

> Talmud, Taanit 10a.

*In many chassidic communities, it was the
custom that the conclusion of the* Tishrei *festival season would be marked by proclaiming
the verse (Genesis 32:2), "And Jacob went on
his way!"*

> The Lubavitcher Rebbe

When the Holy Temple stood in Jerusalem, the festival of
Sukkot (*Tishrei* 15–21) was a time of pilgrimage for all
Jews, when all came to "see and be seen" at the Temple,[1] the seat of
G-d's manifest presence in the physical world. The month of
Cheshvan marked their return to a state of "each under his grapevine, each under his fig tree."[2] The caravans would stream from the
holy city and make the long (physically for some, spiritually for
all) trek back to plow and pruning hook, back to field, vineyard,
and orchard.

---

[1]   Exodus 23:17, as per Talmud, *Sanhedrin* 4b.
[2]   I Kings 5:5.

Today, too, *Cheshvan* marks the end of a period of spiritual focus and experience, and a return to the demands of material life. During the month of *Elul* and the "days of awe" that open the month of *Tishrei*, we occupied ourselves with "repentance, prayer, and charity," striving to improve our relationships with our Creator and with our fellows. Immediately following came Sukkot, the festival of unity and joy; and Simchat Torah, when we celebrated our unique bond with the Almighty by rejoicing with the Torah. *Cheshvan* is the "back-to-normal" month—the month in which we return to our pedestrian involvements after many weeks in which the spiritual was at the forefront of our lives. Indeed, the only "distinguishing feature" of this month is the fact that it is the only month on the Jewish calendar that does not have a single festival or special day.

In truth, however, the month of *Cheshvan*, by virtue of its ordinariness, embodies the very purpose of life on earth. The Jew does not live only for the spiritual experiences of the festivals, merely "tolerating" the stretches of ordinary days and weeks in between. On the contrary: The holy days which dot our year exist for the sake of the so-called "mundane" days of our lives.

THE DWELLING

"G-d desired a dwelling place in the lower realms." With these words our sages describe the divine purpose in creation.[3]

What are the "lower realms"? It is common to refer to the spiritual as "higher" than the material, and to the physical universe as the "lowest" of G-d's creations. But are these designations truly justified? After all, G-d not only created all spiritual and physical

---

3   *Midrash Tanchuma*, *Nasso* 16; *Tanya*, chapter 36.

entities but also the very concepts of "spirituality" and "physicality." He transcends both realms equally and, at the same time, is equally present in both, for His all-embracing truth knows no limit or categorization. So why should the spiritual be deemed loftier than the physical?

To understand why the physical is indeed "lower" than the spiritual, we must first examine the meaning of the term *olam*, the Hebrew word for "world." *Olam* means "concealment." A world is a framework or context within which things exist; and in order for anything to exist, a concealment must first take place.

The reason for this is that the basic (and only) law of existence is that "there is none else beside Him"[4]—that G-d is the only true existence and that nothing exists outside of His all-pervading reality. In order for anything else to possess even the slightest semblance of selfhood or "somethingness," this truth must be veiled and obscured. Hence G-d's creation of "worlds"—concealments within which things may exist distinct and apart (at least in their own conception) from the all-nullifying reality of G-d.

G-d created both "higher" spiritual creations and "lower" physical ones. The difference between them lies not in their essential closeness to or separateness from G-d, but in the degree of the concealment their worlds provide. A lesser concealment may allow for things to "exist," but these existences will be conscious of their Creator and utterly subservient to Him, acknowledging their total dependence upon Him. In this there are many gradations and degrees—the greater the concealment in any given world, the more of a "self" the creations of that world will possess.

In this sense, the physical world is the lowest world of all. So great is the physical world's concealment of G-dliness, that the

---

4   Deuteronomy 4:35.

selfhood of its inhabitants is all but absolute: By nature, the physical object or creature strives only for its own preservation and advancement, regarding its own existence as the axis around which all else revolves. The world of the physical not only dims its divine source but obscures it entirely, even allowing for creations that deny their own origin and essence.

Yet it is this lowest of worlds that is the focus of G-d's creation. G-d wished to create an environment in which His reality is almost entirely concealed; an environment so distant from its source that it can even contain "evil"—elements which resist and deny the all-pervading truth of G-d, despite the fact that they are utterly dependent upon Him for their vitality and existence. And in this lowly realm G-d desired that we construct for Him a "dwelling": a place in which He is at home, an environment in which He is openly and uninhibitedly Himself.

G-d therefore designed us as material creatures whose needs demand a great deal of interaction with the physical reality. And He gave us the ability to direct our material lives to serve a G-dly ideal. Every time we use the yield of our field or business investments to help the needy, every time we utilize our workday involvements as the means by which to carry out the Creator's will, we are vanquishing the self-centeredness which so dominates the nature of the material world. We are vanquishing the "I am" of the physical, thereby transforming its very essence. Instead of being the world that most obscures the reality of G-d, it now becomes a "home" for Him—an environment that expresses and reveals how truly all-pervading His reality is.

Thus, the physical aspects of our existence are the *primary* vehicle for the fulfillment of our life's purpose. The spiritual in ourselves and in creation was created only in order to assist us in the realization of this goal—to inspire and direct us in our interactions

CHESHVAN (1)   161

with the physical.⁵ So one who shuns involvement with the material world and pursues only spiritual and transcendent endeavors, is
abandoning his primary mission in life.

The same applies to the spiritual and material areas of time. The
festivals of *Tishrei* — as all special dates and events of the Jewish
calendar — are for the sake of the "*Cheshvan*" days in our lives. The
spiritual days exist in order to supply us with fortitude and direction so that we may make proper and optimal use of the ordinary
days of the year — the days in which we interact with the physical
reality, each in his or her own occupation and field of endeavor.

THE TREK TO THE EUPHRATES

There does seem, however, to be one breach in the ordinariness of
Cheshvan. The Talmud makes mention of one date of particular
significance in that month:

> *On the seventh day of* Cheshvan, *fifteen days after the*
> *conclusion of the festival [of Sukkot], one begins to pray*

---

5   In the words of Rabbi Schneur Zalman of Liadi: "Clearly, the pur-
     pose of the chain of the worlds and their descent, degree by de-
     gree, is not for the sake of the higher spiritual worlds, for they
     constitute a *descent* from the light of His manifest presence. The ul-
     timate purpose of creation is this lowest world, precisely because of
     its lowliness. For such was G-d's desire: that the negative be sub-
     dued and the darkness transformed into light" (*Tanya*, ch. 36).
     In other words, if G-d's objective in creation were to have been a reality
     which constitutes a lesser concealment of the divine truth, then G-d
     would not have created any world at all, since even the most spiritual
     and loftiest of worlds is already a concealment of His oneness and ex-
     clusivity of being. Obviously, then, the objective *is* concealment, and
     the chain of consecutively coarsened worlds points to its lowest link as
     the environment in which G-d's purpose of creation is to be acted out.

for rain. This is to allow the very last Jew to reach the Euphrates River.[6]

(To this day, Jews living in the Land of Israel add the prayer for rain to their daily prayers beginning on the 7th of *Cheshvan*.)

But upon closer examination, the "distinctiveness" of this day only further underscores the preeminence of the ordinary in the life of the Jew.

For the duration of the festival of Sukkot, the Jew left his field and field-related concerns behind and came to the Holy Temple in Jerusalem, where the miraculous was the norm and the divine presence was openly perceived. But then began the journey back home — home to one's homestead, home to one's mission and purpose. For some it was a journey of several hours, for others of several days, and for the "last Jew" farming his land on the most distant frontier of Jewish settlement in the Land of Israel, it was a fifteen-day journey to the Euphrates. On the 7th of *Cheshvan*, when every last Jew was home on his own land, the entire community of Israel began to pray for rain, beseeching G-d to bless their efforts to work the earth and the earthiness of the world into an abode for His presence.

On a deeper level, the "last Jew" is the most distant Jew in the spiritual sense — the one whose occupation is the most material and earthy of all. Yet all Jews, including those whose missions in life have placed them but a stone's throw from Jerusalem, cannot pray for rain until the last Jew has reached home. For without this last Jew, their work is incomplete; it is this "last Jew," more than any other, who represents the purpose of all their lives.

---

6   Talmud, *Taanit* 10a.

CHAPTER THIRTEEN

Chanukah

Light, Purity, and Spirituality

Kislev 25 to Tevet 3

Chanukah—the eight-day festival of light that begins on the eve of *Kislev* 25—celebrates the triumph of light over darkness, of purity over adulteration, of spirituality over materiality.

More than twenty-one centuries ago, the Holy Land was ruled by the Seleucids (Syrian-Greeks), who sought to forcefully Hellenize the people of Israel. Against all odds, a small band of faithful Jews defeated one of the mightiest armies on earth, drove the Greeks from the land, reclaimed the Holy Temple in Jerusalem, and rededicated it to the service of G-d. When they sought to light the Temple's *menorah*, they found only a single cruse of olive oil that had escaped contamination by the Greeks; miraculously, the one-day supply burned for eight days, until new oil could be prepared under conditions of ritual purity.

To commemorate these miracles, the sages instituted the festival of Chanukah. At the heart of the festival is the nightly *menorah* lighting—a single flame on the first night, two on the second night, and so on till the eighth night of Chanukah, when all eight lights are illuminated. On Chanukah we also recite *hallel* and the *al hanissim* prayer to offer praise and thanksgiving to G-d for "delivering the strong into the hands of the weak, the many into the hands of the few... the wicked into the hands of the righteous." Customs include the eating of foods fried in oil—*latkes* (potato pancakes) and *sufganiot* (doughnuts); playing with the *dreidel* (a spinning top on which are inscribed the Hebrew letters *nun, gimmel, hei, and shin*, an acronym for "a great miracle happened there"); and the giving of Chanukah *gelt*, gifts of money, to children.

Our section on Chanukah consists of eight essays—one for each of the eight flames of Chanukah—which explore the various themes of the festival, the miracles it commemorates, and the laws governing its observance.

The Transparent Body examines the concept of spirituality. Why is Chanukah the most spiritual of the festivals? What lesson is there in this to the great majority of us, whose lives are of a decidedly material nature?

Nightlight focuses on the significance of the Chanukah *menorah* as a generator of light, and its similarities to and differences from its predecessor, the *menorah* in the Holy Temple. *The Lamp* discusses the uniqueness of the lamp as a metaphor for the human soul, which the Torah describes as "a lamp of G-d."

Who were the Greeks, and what was the nature of the challenge they posed to the purity of Israel? That is the question addressed in *The Mudswamps of Hella*. The following essay, *The Miracle*, probes the nature of heroism and self-sacrifice, while *Compromise* discusses another of Chanukah's themes—education—and includes the surprising revelation that the primary miracle of Chanukah was completely unnecessary. *The Towering Servant* offers an insight into the character of the *shamash*, the "service candle" that ignites the Chanukah lamps and stands watch over their light.

Our eighth and concluding essay, *Accumulating Lights*, discusses the specialness of *Zot Chanukah*—the eighth day of Chanukah and the only day of the festival distinguished by a name of its own. We learn of the unique perspective on Chanukah offered by the sages of Hillel, and the challenge of making the most spiritual festival in the Jewish calendar a real and actual force in our lives.

See also the essay *Oil and Wine* on pp. 233–234.

THE TRANSPARENT BODY

Whom have I in heaven but You? And I desire nothing upon earth beside You.
                                        Psalms 73:25

"What is Chanukah?" asks the Talmud, and it then encapsulates the essence of the festival in the following lines:

> When the Greeks entered the Sanctuary, they contaminated all of its oil. When the royal Hasmonean family overpowered and was victorious over them, they searched and found only a single cruse of pure oil that was sealed with the seal of the kohen gadol *(high priest)*—enough to light the menorah *for a single day. A miracle occurred, and they lit the* menorah *with this oil for eight days. The following year, they established these [eight days] as days of festivity and praise and thanksgiving to G-d.* [1]

What is striking about the Talmud's description is that there is only the merest passing reference to the miraculous military victories that preceded and enabled the Hasmoneans' liberation of the Holy Temple. While mentioning that "the royal Hasmonean family overpowered and was victorious over [the Greeks]," the Talmud says nothing of the fact that this was a battle in which a small band of Jews defeated one of the mightiest armies on earth. The focus is

---

[1] Talmud, *Shabbat* 21b.

wholly on the miracle of the oil, as if this were the only significant event commemorated by the festival of Chanukah.

Contrast this with the *al hanissim* prayer, recited on Chanukah to recount "the miracles... that You did for our ancestors in those days, at this time":

> *In the days of Matityahu... the Hasmonean and his sons, when the wicked Hellenic government rose up against Your people Israel to make them forget your Torah and to make them violate the decrees of Your will; You, in Your abounding mercies, stood by them in the time of their distress... You delivered the mighty into the hands of the weak, the many into the hands of the few... the wicked into the hands of the righteous... and you effected a great deliverance and redemption for Your people Israel... Then Your children entered the house of Your dwelling, cleansed Your Temple, purified Your sanctuary, kindled lights in Your holy courtyards, and instituted these eight days of Chanukah to give thanks and praise to Your great name.*

Here, it is the miracle of the oil that is ignored. While the *al hanissim* speaks of "lights" kindled in "Your holy courtyards," this is most probably not a reference to the lights of the *menorah*—whose appointed place was not in the courtyard of the Holy Temple but inside the Sanctuary—but to lights kindled in celebration throughout the Temple compound and the city of Jerusalem (which explains why *al hanissim* speaks of "courtyards," in the plural). In any case, even if the lights in question are those of the *menorah*, there is no mention of the miracles associated with its lighting.

In other words, there seems to be a complete separation between the "physical" and "spiritual" miracles of Chanukah, to the

CHANUKAH (1) 169

extent that the mention of one precludes any mention of the other. When the physical salvation of Israel is remembered and we thank G-d for delivering the "mighty into the hands of the weak, and the many into the hands of the few," we make no reference to the miracle of the oil; and when we relate to the spiritual significance of Chanukah—the triumph of light over darkness—it is free of any association with the physical victories that accompanied it.

THE SPIRITUAL FESTIVAL

The struggles and triumphs chronicled by the Jewish calendar are always more than the struggle for physical survival. The Exodus, commemorated and reexperienced each Passover, was more than a people's liberation from slavery to freedom; it was their extraction from a pagan Egypt to receive the Torah at Sinai and enter into a covenant with G-d as "a nation of priests and a holy people."[2] On Purim we remember that Haman wished to annihilate the Jews because "they are a singular people... whose laws are different from those of all other nations"[3]; Purim thus celebrates not only the salvation of the physical existence of the Jew, but of the Jew's identity and way of life.

Yet the battle waged by the Hasmoneans against the Greeks was the most spiritual battle in Jewish history. The Greeks did not endeavor to physically destroy the Jewish people, or even to deprive them of their religion and way of life; they merely wished to Hellenize them—to "enlighten" their lives with the culture and philosophy of Greece. Keep your books of wisdom, they said to the Jew, keep your laws and customs, but enrich them with our

---

2   Exodus 3:12; 19:6.
3   Esther 3:8.

wisdom, adorn them with our art, blend them into our lifestyle. Worship your G-d in your temple, but then worship the human body in the adjoining sports stadium we will build for you. Study your Torah, but integrate it with the principles of our philosophy and the aesthetics of our literature.

The Hasmoneans fought for independence from Hellenic rule because the Greeks sought to "make them forget Your Torah and make them violate the decrees of Your will." They did not fight for the Torah *per se*, but for "*Your* Torah"—for the principle that the Torah is G-d's law rather than a deposit of human wisdom which might be commingled with other deposits of human wisdom. They did not fight for the *mitzvot* as the Jewish way of life, but for the *mitzvot* as "the decrees of Your will"—as the suprarational will of G-d, which cannot be rationalized or tampered with. They fought not for any material or political end, not for the preservation of their identity and lifestyle, not even for the right to study the Torah and fulfill its commandments, but for the very soul of Judaism, for the purity of Torah as the divine word and its *mitzvot* as the divine will.

The spirituality of Chanukah is emphasized by the festival's principal *mitzvah*, the kindling of the Chanukah lights. We are physical beings, enjoined to anchor our every experience to a physical deed. On Passover, we celebrate our freedom with matzah and four cups of wine; on Purim, we read the *megillah*, give money to the poor, send gifts of food to our friends, and feast and drink. Chanukah, too, has its "ritualistic" element, in which a physical act and object embody the festival's significance. But here the vehicle is the most spiritual of physical phenomena—light. On Chanukah, the overriding emphasis is on the spiritual essence of our struggle, so that even its physical embodiment is an ethereal flame dancing in the night.

CHANUKAH (1)   171

SEPARATION OF MIRACLES

So when the Talmud replies to the question, "What is Chanukah?",
it defines the festival solely in terms of its spiritual miracles—the
discovery of the pure, undefiled cruse of oil, and the rekindling
of the divine light which emanated from the Holy Temple. Since
this is the festival which commemorates our most spiritual battle,
its spiritual content predominates to the extent that it completely
eclipses its physical aspect. Although the military miracles preceded and made possible the lighting of the *menorah* in the Holy
Temple, they are deemphasized when we speak of the miracle that
defines the essence of Chanukah.

This is also the reason that the prayer instituted by our sages
to give thanks to G-d for the military victories omits all mention
of the miracle of the oil. For only when they are regarded on their
own can the military miracles be emphasized and appreciated.
Were they to be discussed in relation to the miracle of the oil, they
would fade to insignificance. Within the supra-spiritual context
of Chanukah's central miracle, they are reduced to a minor detail
scarcely worthy of mention.

THE LESSON

Man is comprised of a soul and a body: a spiritual essence that is
"veritably a part of G-d above,"[1] and the physical vehicle via which
it experiences and impacts the physical world.

The body was designed to serve the soul in its mission to develop the world in accordance with the divine will. Of course, man
has been granted freedom of choice. The body might therefore

---

1   *Tanya*, chapter 2, after Job 31:2.

rebel against the dominion of the soul; it might even subject its master to its own desires, making the pursuit of material things the focus of life and exploiting the soul's spiritual prowess to this end. But in its natural, uncorrupted state, the body is the servant of the soul, channeling its energies and implementing its will.

There are, however, many levels to this submission, many degrees in the servitude of matter to spirit. The body might recognize that the purpose of life on earth lies with the soul's aspirations, yet also entertain an "agenda" of its own alongside the greater, spiritual agenda. Or it might selflessly serve the soul, acknowledging the spiritual as the only goal worthy of pursuit, yet its own needs remain a most visible and pronounced part of the person's life, if only out of natural necessity.

Chanukah teaches us that there is a level of supremacy of soul over body that is so absolute that the body is virtually invisible. It continues to attend to its own needs, because a soul can only operate within a functioning body; but these are completely eclipsed by the spiritual essence of life. One sees not a material creature foraging for food, shelter, and comfort, but a spiritual being whose spiritual endeavors consume his or her entire being.

For all but the most spiritual *tzaddik*, it is not possible, nor desirable, to perpetually maintain this state. Indeed, it is Chanukah for only eight days of the year. But each and every one of us is capable of experiencing moments of such consummate spirituality: moments in which we so completely "lose ourselves" in our commitment to our spiritual purpose that our material cares become utterly insignificant.

NIGHTLIGHT

The mitzvah *of kindling the Chanukah lights begins at sunset... They are to be placed in the outer doorway of one's home; if one lives on the second floor, one should place them in a window which looks out to the street.*

Talmud, Shabbat 21b

$\mathcal{E}$ vening comes early in winter, filling the streets with darkness and cold. One by one the lights come on. Amid the electrical glare, a warmer, purer glow asserts itself. It is the last week of *Kislev*, and from the doorways and windows of Jewish homes, Chanukah lights illuminate the night.

"For a *mitzvah* is a lamp, and Torah, light."[1] The essence of our mission in life is to shed light. Every time we fulfill a *mitzvah* we are lighting a lamp, illuminating a world darkened by ignorance and strife with the wisdom and harmony of its Creator.

Every *mitzvah* is a lamp, but there are two *mitzvot* whose actual form mirrors their quintessential function. These are the two *mitzvot* whose fulfillment involves the generation of physical light: the lamps of the *menorah*, which the Torah instructs to be lit each afternoon in the Holy Temple in Jerusalem; and the Chanukah lights, kindled at nightfall each evening of the eight-day festival of Chanukah.[2]

---

1   Proverbs 6:23.

2   Another *mitzvah* that assumes the form of physical light is the *mitzvah* of kindling the Shabbat lights, with which the Jewish woman ushers the sanctity of Shabbat into the home (see footnote 11 below).

Indeed, the Chanukah lamps are the descendants of those of the *menorah*. The *mitzvah* of lighting the Chanukah lights was instituted by our sages to commemorate the miraculous rebirth of light in the Holy Temple after its suppression, in the 2nd century BCE, by the Hellenist rulers of the Holy Land.

The Temple's *menorah* was a five-foot-high, seven-branched candelabra made of gold and topped with seven oil-burning lamps. Its seven flames, fueled by premium olive oil prepared under special conditions of spiritual purity, were the physical expression of the spiritual light which emanated from the Holy Temple. For the Holy Temple in Jerusalem was the epicenter of G-d's manifest presence in the life of man, the point "from which light went out to the entire world."[3] In their endeavor to supplant the spirituality of Israel with the paganism of Hellas, the Greeks invaded the Temple, defiled it with their decadent images and rites, and contaminated the oil designated for the kindling of the *menorah*.

But one family refused to yield to the darkness. Matityahu the Hasmonean and his sons[4] rallied a small but determined group of fighters and drove the Greeks from the land. After liberating the Holy Temple and rededicating it to the service of G-d, they searched for ritually pure oil with which to light the *menorah*. They found a single cruse of oil that had survived defilement by the Greeks. Miraculously, the one-day supply burned for eight days, until new pure oil could be prepared.

Every winter of the more than 2,100 winters since, we remember and reenact the triumph of light over darkness with the eight flames of the Chanukah *menorah*.

---

3   Jerusalem Talmud, *Berachot* 4:5.

4   Also known as the "Maccabees." After their overthrow of the Greeks, the Hasmonean family ruled an independent Judea for more than 70 years.

CHANUKAH (2)   175

A Different Menorah

There are, however, several marked differences between the Chanukah *menorah* and the *menorah* in the Holy Temple:

a) The Temple *menorah* was lit during the day (no later than
one and one-quarter hours before sunset) and burned through the
night.[5] The Chanukah lights are kindled at night.[6]

b) The original *menorah* stood well indoors, in the inner sanctum of the Holy Temple (called the *heichal*). The Chanukah *menorah* is placed at the perimeter of the home, "on the outer doorway
of one's home" or, "if one lives on the second floor... in a window
overlooking the street."[7]

c) Seven flames burned in the Temple *menorah*. The Chanukah

---

5   According to Talmud, *Pesachim* 59b, the lighting of the Temple *meno-
    rah* immediately followed the afternoon burning of the *ketoret*, which
    was concluded one and one-quarter hours before sunset (see *Lechem
    Mishneh* commentary on *Mishneh Torah, Laws of Prayer* 3:2). Also see
    Mishneh Torah, Laws of Tmidin and Musafin, 3:11.

6   Immediately after sunset according to the custom of some communi-
    ties, or after three stars come out, according to the custom of others.

7   Talmud, *Shabbat* 21b. The two possibilities for the *menorah*'s place-
    ment cited by the Talmud represent two types of spiritual personali-
    ty, and how each fulfills the task of illuminating the street. There are
    those whose lives have "a doorway out to the street"—whose character
    and temperament provide them with ready access to those still outside
    the sphere of the Torah's light. These individuals place their *menorahs*
    "in the outside doorway of their home," incorporating it into the pas-
    sageway by which they venture out to their night-traveling brethren.
    Then there are also those who live in a "loft" (the Talmud's word for
    "second floor," *aliyah*, literally means "loft")—whose nature and ap-
    titudes consign them to a life of spirituality and seclusion. But even
    the most elevated saint must have a window out to the street in which
    to place his *menorah*. If a person's life calling precludes stepping out-
    doors, he or she must still endeavor to shed light, opening portals in
    the walls of their "loft" so that their life might illuminate the world
    outside.

menorah holds eight lamps, all of which are kindled on the eighth and culminating night of the festival.[8]

Why these dissimilarities? Why, in instituting the practice of kindling the Chanukah lights, did our sages so differentiate between them and the lights they come to commemorate?[9]

STANDARD OPERATING PROCEDURE

In the first chapter of Genesis we read:

> *G-d saw the light that it is good, and He separated between the light and the darkness. And G-d called the light "day" and the darkness He called "night"; and it was evening and it was morning, one day.*[10]

In the beginning, darkness and light were one—a single, seamless expression of the goodness and perfection of their Creator. But G-d wanted contrast and challenge in His world. So He separated between light and darkness, between revealed good and concealed good, challenging us to cultivate the day and sublimate the night.

On the most fundamental level, our task is to harness the light of day so that it extends to illuminate the night. We strive to preserve and develop all that is good and G-dly in our world, and to direct these positive forces to overcome and transform the negativity of the "dark side" of creation. This process was exemplified by the *menorah* in the Holy Temple. Kindled in the light of day, its rays reached deep into the night. Kindled in an inner sanctum

---

8   One light is kindled on the first evening of Chanukah, two on the second, three on the third, etc.

9   Especially in light of the dictum that "All rabbinical institutions are modeled after their biblical prototypes" (Talmud, *Pesachim* 30b).

10   Genesis 1:4–5.

CHANUKAH (2)   177

brimming with divine light, it radiated its glow to the mundane
world without.

But there are times when this "standard operating procedure"
is no longer operative. Times when darkness invades the divine
lighthouse, extinguishing the *menorah* and defiling its oil. Times
when we can no longer draw from the day to illuminate the night.

At such times, we must turn to the night itself as a source of
light. We must search for the hidden "single cruse of pure oil," for
the undefiled and indefilable essence of creation. We must delve
below the surface realities of "day" and "night" to unearth the primordial singularity of light and darkness.

Therein lies the significance of Chanukah, when the *menorah*
moves from within the Holy Temple out into the street, and from
the daytime to the evening. Chanukah transforms the *menorah*
from a tool that disseminates the light of day into a tool that extracts the luminous essence of darkness itself.[11]

---

11 More specifically, the lighting of the Temple and Chanukah *menorah*s,
    together with the third light-generating *mitzvah*, the lighting of the
    Shabbat lights, chart a three-phased progression of light through place
    and time.

    The Temple *menorah* stood in the holiest place on earth, in the ed-
    ifice that was the seat of G-d's manifest presence in the physical world.
    The Shabbat lights find a source of light in a less sacred environment
    —in the home, a place that embraces both our holy endeavors (Torah
    study, prayer, acts of charity, etc.) as well as our more mundane ac-
    tivities. Yet the home is our private sanctum; here we are in control,
    making the task of achieving harmony between the spiritual and ma-
    terial components of home life, if not always easy, then within rea-
    sonable reach. The Chanukah lights, however, test the very limits of
    our light-generating capacities. Placed in the doorway or in a window,
    they straddle the private and public areas of our lives, the boundary
    between the home and the street.

    In terms of their placement in time, the Temple's *menorah* was kin-
    dled in early afternoon, the Shabbat candles are lit eighteen minutes

178   INSIDE TIME: VOL. II

CYCLE AND CIRCUMFERENCE

This is also the significance of the difference between the number of lamps in the Temple and Chanukah *menorahs*.

Seven is the number of creation. G-d created the world in seven days, employing the seven divine attributes (*sefirot*) which He emanated from Himself to serve as the seven spiritual building blocks of the created reality. Seven is thus the dominant number in all natural cycles and processes. Hence, the "standard operating procedure" to bring light to the darker corners of creation is associated with the seven-branched *menorah* of the Holy Temple.

If seven is the cycle of nature, the number eight represents the encompassing element (*shomer hahekef*) that defines and contains it, the pre-creation reality that both transcends and pervades the created reality. If the seven lamps of the Temple *menorah* embody the normative process of overriding darkness with light, the eight lamps of the Chanukah *menorah* represent the endeavor to access

---

before sunset, and the Chanukah lights are kindled at or after nightfall. This also corresponds to the sequence of their appearance on the macro-historical level. The Temple *menorah* came first, in the luminous years when G-d still communicated openly with man; commanded by G-d at Sinai, the *mitzvah* to kindle the Temple *menorah* was written into the Torah (Exodus 27:20–21). The Shabbat lights came in later, spiritually darker times, a rabbinical institution designed to foster harmony in the home on the holy day. (Jewish women, beginning with Sarah and Rebecca, kindled the Shabbat lights from the very beginning of Jewish history—see *Midrash Rabbah* on Genesis 24:67; and *Likutei Sichot*, vol. 15, 168–173—but as a *halachic* obligation they date from the time they were instituted as a rabbinical ordinance.) Most recent in linear time are the Chanukah lights, instituted 21 centuries ago in commemoration of the miracle of Chanukah.

So goes the journey of light through time and space to ever duskier vistas, to increasingly alien environments: a journey from midday in Jerusalem to the darkest reaches of a world awaiting redemption.

CHANUKAH (2)   179

a higher reality—a reality in which darkness is but another ray of
divine truth.[12]

---

12 See *The Seventh Element* (in vol. 1 of this series, pp. 77–88), and *The
    Eighth Dimension* (vol. 1, pp. 127–138).

THE
LAMP

The soul of man is a lamp of G-d.
Proverbs 20:27

For a mitzvah *is a lamp, and Torah, light.*
Ibid. 6:23

$\mathcal{F}$ ew sights are as warming to the soul as the sight of a burning flame. Though a physical phenomenon, the flame—luminous, pure, ethereal—is everything the physical is not; hence its appeal to man, a spiritual being entrapped in a material world.

But the flame is more than a symbol of spirituality. The flame is our own mirror, in which are reflected the strivings of our deepest self. In the words of the book of Proverbs: "The soul of man is a lamp of G-d."

The flame surges upward, as if to tear free from the wick and lose itself in the great expanses of energy that gird the heavens. But even as it strains heavenward, the flame is already pulling back, tightening its grip on the wick and drinking thirstily of the oil in the lamp—oil that sustains its continued existence as an individual flame. And it is this tension of conflicting energies, this vacillation from being to dissolution and back again, that produces light.

We, too, yearn for transcendence, yearn to tear free of the entanglements of material life and achieve a self-nullifying reunion with our Creator and Source. At the same time, however, we are also driven by a will to be, a will to live a physical life and make our mark upon a physical world. In the lamp of G-d that is man, these

CHANUKAH (3)   181

polar drives converge in a flame that illuminates its surroundings
with a G-dly light.

THE INGREDIENTS

A lamp consists of oil, a wick, and a vessel containing them so that
the oil is fed through the wick to a burning flame.

Oil and wick are both combustible substances, but neither
could produce light on its own with the efficiency and stability of
the lamp. The wick, if ignited, would flare briefly and die, utterly
consumed. As for the oil, one would find it difficult to ignite at
all. But when wick and oil are brought together in the lamp, they
produce a controlled and steady light.

The soul of man is a lamp of G-d whose purpose in life is to
illuminate the world with divine light. G-d provided us with the
"fuel" that generates His light—the Torah and its commandments
(*mitzvot*), which embody the divine wisdom and will and convey
its luminous truth.

The divine oil requires a "wick" to channel its substance and
convert it into an illuminating flame. The Torah is the divine wisdom; but for divine wisdom to be manifest in our world, there
must be physical minds that study it and comprehend it, physical
mouths that debate it and teach it, and physical media that publish
it and disseminate it. The *mitzvot* are the divine will; but for the
divine will to be manifest in our world, there must be a physical
body that actualizes it, and physical materials (animal hide for *tefilin*, wool for *tzitzit*, money for charity) with which it is actualized.[1]

---

[1]   See *Torah Ohr, Mikeitz* 33c; *Shaarei Orah, Shaar HaChanukah*, s.v. *Ki
      Atah Neri*; *Igrot Kodesh*, vol. IV, p. 228.

And just as the divine oil cannot produce light without a material wick, neither can a wick without oil. A life without Torah and *mitzvot*, however aflame with the desire to come close to G-d, is incapable of sustaining its flame. It might generate flashes of ecstatic spiritual experience, but lacking oil of genuine divine substance, these quickly die out and fail to introduce any enduring light into the world.

To realize its role as a "lamp of G-d," a human life must be a lamp that combines a physical existence (the "wick") with the divine ideas and deeds of Torah (the "oil"). When the wick is saturated with oil and feeds its spiritual yearnings with a steady supply of the same, the resultant flame is both luminous and sustainable, preserving the existence and productivity of the wick and illuminating the corner of the world in which it has been placed.

THE PENDULUM OF LIFE

The "wick" is both prison and liberator for the flame, both tether and lifeline. It holds the soul in its distinctiveness from the divine whole, in its apartness from its Creator. And yet, it is this distinctiveness and apartness, this incarnation in a physical life, which allows the soul to connect to G-d in the deepest and most meaningful way—by fulfilling His will.

So when divine command, physical body, and human life come together as oil, wick, and lamp, the result is a flame: a relationship with G-d that is characterized by two conflicting drives, by a yearning to come close coupled with a commitment to draw back. The materiality of life evokes in the soul a desire to tear free of it and fuse with the Divine. But the closer the soul is drawn to G-d, all the more does it recognize that it can fulfill G-d's will only as a distinct and physical being. So while the corporeality of the wick

CHANUKAH (3)

triggers the flame's upward surge, the divine will implicit in the oil sustains its commitment to existence and life.

ACTUAL LAMPS

Every *mitzvah* is oil for the soul. With every act that constitutes a fulfillment of the divine will, our lives are rendered into burning lamps, alight with flames that vacillate from heaven to earth and back again, illuminating the world in the process.

Every *mitzvah* generates light — whether it involves giving a coin to charity, binding *tefilin* on one's arm and head, or eating matzah on Passover. But certain *mitzvot* not only transform us into metaphorical lamps, but also assume the actual form of a lamp. A real, physical lamp, with physical oil, a physical wick, and a physical flame that produces physical, tactual light.

Thus we have the *mitzvah* to kindle the *menorah* in the Holy Temple and produce a literal representation of the divine light that emanated from there to the entire world. Every Friday evening, the Jewish woman invites the light of Shabbat into her home by kindling the Shabbat candles — another *mitzvah* whose function is reflected in its form.

And once a year comes Chanukah, the festival of lights. For eight days, a nightly growing number of flames are kindled in the doorways and windows of our homes, so that the light generated by our lives as "lamps of G-d" should spill outdoors and illuminate the street.

THE MUDSWAMPS OF HELLA

He raised me from a tumultuous pit, from the Yavanite mire.   Psalms 40:3

"Yavan" means mud.   Rashi, ibid.

*C*hanukah celebrates the victory of Judea over Greece, of a small band of Jews over those who sought to subvert their faith and profane the sanctity of their lives.

In the course of the four millennia of Jewish history, many ideologies and cultures have sought to compromise our allegiance to G-d and His Torah. But there is something unique about the challenge posed by the Hellenists 21 centuries ago—something that marks Chanukah as the ultimate triumph of spirit over matter and of light over darkness.

SOIL AND WATER

In general, the factors that might undermine the integrity of a Jew's faith and his commitment to G-d fall into two categories.

Most blatant are the challenges of a material sort. The Jew living in Middle-Ages Europe had a choice: Cleave to your faith and suffer humiliation, poverty, frequent expulsion, and outright slaughter; or submit to the faith of your "hosts." Twentieth-century America offered the same choice, albeit in more humane terms, beckoning to the Jew to shed Shabbat, *tefilin*, and *kashrut*

CHANUKAH (4)   185

for smoother distillation in the melting pot and enhanced access
to the American dream. On the individual level, we are daily challenged by the choice of devoting our lives to serving our Creator
and fulfilling the purpose of our creation, or to the pursuit of
physical gratification and material gain.

More subtle are the ideological challenges: doctrines and
philosophies that lay claim to virtue and truth, and might even
espouse altruistic behavior and transcendent aims, but are utterly
alien to the Jewish soul. A Jew disconnected from his roots and
ignorant or unappreciative of his heritage is ready prey for the foreign waters that offer to quench his or her spiritual thirst.

But most noxious of all is a third category: doctrines that blend
the soil of materialism and the fountains of reason into a lethal
muck.

A person buried in corporeality can claw and dig his way out to
sunlight. A person sinking in a sea of spurious reason can struggle
to the surface and swim to shore. But he who adds water to his
soil—who saturates his materialism with intellectual fluid—creates a morass from which it is far more difficult to extricate himself.
When his soul is moved to reach beyond the mundanity of the
material, a host of rationalizations rise to still its yen; and when his
mind begins to wake to the fallacy of the alien creed, the grasp of
earth pulls him down. The person is thus steadily sucked down, as
his efforts of mind and will to rise above his mired state are coun-
teracted by the bog of idealized hedonism.

Such was the challenge that faced our forefathers during the
Greek domination of the Holy Land. *Yavan*, the Hebrew word for
the Hellenic culture, means "mud"[1]: The Hellenists did more than

---

[1]   See Psalms 40:3, and the Rashi and *Metzudat Zion* commentaries on
       this verse.

entice and coerce the people of Israel to embrace the body-worship of Greece; they also sought to indoctrinate them with a philosophy that exalted the physical and made its worship a virtue and an ideal. The Greek was not merely pagan; his was a paganism aestheticized by art, glorified by poetry, and hallowed by reason. The Greek was no mere materialist, but one who kneaded his earthiest wants with the subliminal waters of his intellect to form a mucilage that fastened on the soul and drew it, inch by inch and limb by limb, into the quagmire of *yavan*.[2]

HOLY MUD

Mud can be made with the putrid water of sophism. But even water from the most pristine well turns to mud when mixed with soil.

Thus, our sages have said: "If the student of Torah is meritorious, the Torah becomes an elixir of life for him; if he does not merit, it becomes a death-potion for him."[3] The Hebrew word *zechut* ("merit") also means "refinement"; so the above statement can also

---

2   The deadliness of the mudswamp is further illustrated by the very form of the Hebrew word *Yavan* (יון), whose three letters are three lines, each descending an increment lower than its predecessor. Unlike water, in which one might sink swiftly to the bottom but can also, equally swiftly, pull himself out, the mud of *yavan* works slowly, drawing the person down bit by bit, step by step. At first, it only demands a slight, barely discernible departure from one's convictions and morals. But its downward pull is steady and all but irreversible—indeed, all efforts to extract oneself by the means of one's conventional faculties are doomed to failure—except by the extremely potent power of faith, as explained in the text.

3   Talmud, *Yoma* 72b. The emphasis is that Torah becomes a potion of death *for him,* for the corrupt student, since "the words of Torah (themselves) are not susceptible to contamination" (ibid., *Berachot* 22a).

be read, "If the student of Torah refines himself, the Torah becomes an elixir of life for him; if he does not refine himself, it becomes a death-potion for him." If a person does not refine his soul, cleansing his character from the soil of its baser instincts, the pure waters of Torah become for him a mudpit of depravity: Instead of buoying and nourishing his soul, his wisdom and knowledge only feed his ego, justify his iniquities, and aid his manipulation and distortion of the truth.

This is the eternal lesson of Chanukah. Intellect might be man's highest faculty, but it can also be the instrument of his degradation to the lowest depths. Chanukah celebrates the cleansing of the Holy Temple from Hellenic corruption, the triumph of the pristine essence of the Jewish soul—represented by the small, pure cruse of oil that burned in the *menorah* for eight days—over the "mud" of Greece.

We each possess such a "small, pure cruse of oil" in the pith of our souls, a reserve of *suprarational* commitment to our Creator, with the power to illuminate our lives with a pure, inviolable ligh that ensures that our search for water does not leave us mired in mud.

THE
MIRACLE

What is Chanukah? …When the royal Hasmonean family overpowered and was victorious over [the Greeks], they searched and found only a single cruse of pure oil… enough to light the menorah *for a single day.*

A miracle occurred, and they lit the menorah *with this oil for eight days.*

On the following year, they established these [eight days] as days of festivity and praise and thanksgiving to G-d.

Talmud, Shabbat 21b

any miracles, great and small, accompanied the liberation of Israel from Hellenic dominance and the reclaiming of the Holy Temple as the lighthouse of G-d. But there is one particular miracle, the Talmud is saying, that is the sum and substance of Chanukah: the miracle of the small cruse of pure oil that burned for eight days.

The challenge faced by the Jewish people at that time was unlike any that had confronted them before. Hellenism, a noxious blend of hedonism and philosophy, could not be resisted by the conventional tools of Jewish learning and tradition.[1] Only the "cruse of pure oil," representing the Jew's *mesirat nefesh* — the suprarational, supra-egotistical essence of the Jewish soul, from which stems the

---

[1]　See previous essay, *The Mudswamps of Hella*, pp. 184–187.

Jew's intrinsic self-sacrificial loyalty to G-d—could illuminate the way out of the mudswamps of Hella. Only by evoking this inner reserve of incontaminable oil were we able to banish the pagan invader from the divine dwelling and rekindle the torch of Israel as a "light unto the nations."

But this was oil sufficient for only a single day. This, too, reflects the nature of the soul's "pure oil" of *mesirat nefesh*. By nature, our highest powers flare brightly and fleetingly, soon receding to the supra-conscious, supra-behavioral place from which they have come. When a person's deepest self is challenged, the essential oil of his soul is stimulated, and no force on earth can still its flame. But then the moment passes, the cataclysmic levels off into the routine, and the person is left with his ordinary, mortal self.[2]

The miracle of Chanukah was that "they lit the *menorah* with this oil for eight days"—that the flame of selfless sacrifice blazed beyond a moment of truth, beyond a day of reckoning; that the "small pure cruse of oil" burned beyond its one-day lifespan for an additional week, illuminating the seven chambers of the soul. This was no mere flash of light in a sea of darkness, but a flame destined to shed purity and light for all generations, under all conditions.

The Talmud therefore tells us that it was only on "the following year" that these eight days were established as the festival of Chanukah. A year is a microcosm of time, embodying all of time's seasons and transmutations.[3] So it was only on the following year, after it had weathered all fluctuations of the annual cycle, that the victory of Chanukah could be installed as a permanent fixture in our lives.

---

2   See *Tanya*, chapters 18–19.
3   See *A Seasoned Life* in vol. 1, pp. 181–183 of this series.

COMPROMISE

*With the measure that a person metes out, so
is meted out to him.* Talmud, Sotah 1:7

A close examination of the story of Chanukah reveals that its primary miracle—the miracle of the oil—was completely unnecessary.

Every Jewish schoolchild knows the story: The Greeks had defiled the Holy Temple's store of olive oil, so that when the Maccabees liberated the Temple, they could not find ritually pure oil with which to kindle the *menorah*. Then, a single cruse of uncontaminated oil was found, enough to keep the *menorah* lit for a single day. Miraculously, the oil burned for eight days, until new oil could be prepared.

Strictly speaking, none of this was necessary. The law which forbids the use of ritually impure oil in the Temple would not have applied under the circumstances which then prevailed. According to Torah law, "The prohibition of impurity, if affecting the entire community, is waived"—if the entire community, or all the *kohanim* (priests), or all the Temple's vessels, are ritually impure, it is permissible to enter the Temple and conduct the Temple services under conditions of impurity.[1] Nevertheless, because G-d wished to show His love for His people, He suspended the laws of nature in order to enable them to rededicate the Temple without any compromise on its standards of purity—even a perfectly legal and permissible compromise.

---

1 Talmud, *Pesachim* 79a; *Mishneh Torah, Laws of Entering the Temple*, 4:12.

CHANUKAH (6)   191

Going Overboard

Every Chanukah, we reciprocate in kind. How many lights must
be kindled on the Chanukah *menorah*? Most would reply: one on
the first night, two on the second, and so on. The law, however, is
otherwise. According to the Talmud,

> *The mitzvah of Chanukah is [fulfilled with] a single light
> for each household. Those who do more than is obligatory,
> kindle a single light for each individual. Those who do
> more than those who do more than is obligatory... kindle
> one light on the first day and add an additional light on
> each succeeding day.*[2]

There are those who buy the least costly *tefilin* on the market, who
give the absolute minimum that the laws of charity mandate, who
employ every *halachic* exemption and loophole they can find. But
when was the last time you saw a single light in the window of a
Jewish home on the sixth night of Chanukah? On Chanukah, we
all "do more than those who do more than is obligatory"—after all,
G-d did the same for us.

Fanatical Educator

The name "Chanukah" comes from the word *chinuch*, which
means "inauguration." Chanukah celebrates the renewal of the
service in the Holy Temple after it was liberated from the Greek

---

2 Talmud, *Shabbat* 21a. The ascending lights of Chanukah carry the lesson that one must always "ascend in holiness": that what is complete
   and perfect today, is not sufficient for tomorrow. Yesterday the "lamp
   of G-d" that is your soul may have been illuminated to its full capacity;
   today its light must be increased.

defiler, purified, and rededicated as the seat of the divine presence in our world.

Chanukah thus serves as a model for all inaugurations, including the most significant inauguration of all—education, a child's inauguration into life (indeed, *chinuch* is also the Hebrew word for "education"). The uncompromising insistence on purity and perfection which Chanukah represents holds an important lesson regarding the essence of the educator's task.

Compromise is anathema to education. To a mature tree, a gash here or a torn limb there is of little or no consequence. But the smallest scratch in the seed, the slightest nick in the sapling, results in an irrevocable deformity, in a flaw which the years to come will deepen rather than erase.

Virtually every life is faced with demands for compromises—some tolerable, others not. The educator who wishes to impart a set of values and priorities that will weather them all, must deliver, by teaching and by example, a message of impeccable purity, free of even the slightest and most "acceptable" compromise.

THE TOWERING SERVANT

If I am only for myself, what am I?
Ethics of the Fathers 1:14

t's the first night of Chanukah, and a single flame is glowing the night away at the right-hand end of the *menorah*.

One flame? Aren't there two?

Two? Oh, you mean the *shamash*. He doesn't count.

Night after night, the *shamash* ("service candle") dutifully goes about his task of lighting lights. Each evening, he welcomes the newcomer and settles him into his rightful place in the growing row: two flames, three flames, four flames... The *shamash* coaxes them to life and then stands watch over them, lest one falter and require a fresh boost of light.

Still the *shamash* doesn't count. An imparter of light to others, he never attains the station of a Chanukah light in his own right.

Despite—indeed because—of this, the *shamash* towers above all the other lights of the *menorah*. To forgo one's own luminary potential in order to awaken a flame in others—there is no greater virtue.

ACCUMULATING LIGHTS

The School of Shammai says: On the first day, one lights eight lights; from here on, one progressively decreases.

The School of Hillel says: On the first day, one lights a single light; from here on, one progressively increases.

Talmud, Shabbat 21b

*O*isit, or simply pass by, a Jewish home on any of the eight evenings of Chanukah, and there will be the lights burning in the doorway or window proclaiming the celebration of the Chanukah miracle to the street and to the world at large. They will also be proclaiming which night of Chanukah it is. On each of the eight nights of Chanukah, a different number of flames is kindled, expressing that night's particular place in the festival. On the first night of Chanukah, there will be one flame illuminating the street; on the second night, two flames; and so on.

Actually, the Talmud records two opinions on how each Chanukah night should identify itself and radiate its unique light into the world. This was one of the *halachic* issues debated by the two great academies of Torah law, the School of Shammai and the School of Hillel. The sages of Hillel held that the Chanukah lights should increase in number each night, in the familiar ascending order. The sages of Shammai, however, were of the opinion that eight flames should be lit on the first night, seven on the second,

CHANUKAH (8)

and so on in descending number, until the eighth night of Chanukah, when a single flame should be lit.[1]

The Talmud explains that the sages of Shammai saw the Chanukah lights as representing the "upcoming days" of the festival —the number of days still awaiting realization. Thus, the number of lights decrease with each passing night, as another of Chanukah's days is "expended." On the first night, we have eight full days of Chanukah ahead of us; in the second night, seven days remain, and so on. The sages of Hillel, on the other hand, see the lights as representing Chanukah's "outgoing days," so that the ascending number of flames reflect the accumulation of actualized milestones in our eight-day quest for light.

In practice, we follow the opinion of the Hillel school, and an ascending number of lights chronicle the progress of the festival. This is even alluded to in the very name of the festival: the Hebrew word "Chanukah" forms an acronym of the sentence *chet neirot vehalachah k'veit Hillel*—"Eight lights, and the law follows the School of Hillel."[2]

Our acceptance of Hillel's perspective on Chanukah is also expressed by the name traditionally given to the eighth day of Chanukah—the only day of the festival to be distinguished by a name of its own—"Zot Chanukah."

The name "Zot Chanukah" is based on a phrase from that day's Torah reading, and literally means "This is Chanukah." This is in keeping with the Hillelian vision of Chanukah, in which the final day of Chanukah—the day on which all eight days of light have been actualized—marks the climax of the festival. Only on the eighth day can we say, "This is Chanukah. Now we 'have' the

---

[1]   Talmud, *Shabbat* 21b.

[2]   Avudraham, *Seder Hadlakat Ner Chanukah.*

entire Chanukah." (From the Shammaian perspective, the *first* day of Chanukah would be Zot Chanukah.)

What is the basis for these two visions of Chanukah? And why is the view of the School of Hillel so decisively embraced, to the extent that it is implicit in the very name "Chanukah," and in the name given to its culminating day?

THE DEBATE

There are two primary ways in which one might view something: a) in light of its potential, or b) by its actual, manifest state. We might say of a certain person: "He has tremendous potential, but his actual performance is poor." The same can be said of a business venture, a relationship, an experience, or anything else. Or we might say: "There's potential for disaster here, but it can be contained and prevented from actualizing."

Some of us are potential-oriented, which means that we would admire the person, invest in the venture, stick it out with the relationship, and treasure the experience—depending upon its potential. Some of us are more actual-oriented, viewing things in terms of their actual, tactual impact upon our reality.

This is a recurring theme in many of the disputes between the schools of Shammai and Hillel. For example, the sages of Shammai consider the moment of the Exodus to have been the eve of *Nissan* 15, when the people of Israel were free to leave Egypt, while the sages of Hillel place the moment at midday of the following day, when the Jews actually exited Egypt's physical borders.[3] In another debate, the sages of Shammai consider a fish susceptible

---

3   The question of the precise moment of the Exodus has certain *halach-ic* repercussions, such as the procedure for reciting *hallel* on the *seder*

CHANUKAH (8)   197

to ritual impurity from the moment the fisherman pulls his catch
out of the water, since at this point the fish has been removed
from the environment in which it might possibly live; the sages
of Hillel disagree, contending that as long as the fish is actually
alive (though its potential for continued life has been destroyed),
it is immune to contamination, as are all other living plants and
animals.[4]

This is also the basis of their differing perspectives on Chanukah. The School of Shammai, which views things in terms of their
potential, sees the first day of Chanukah, with its potential for
eight days of light, as the point in which all eight days are "there."
After one day has "gone by" and passed from potential into actuality, there are left only seven days in their most meaningful form—
the potential form. The sages of Hillel, on the other hand, see
the actual state as the more significant. To them, the eighth day
of Chanukah, when all eight dimensions of the festival have been
actualized, is when the festival is at its fullest and most "real."

G-D'S REALITY

We are creatures of the actual. We cannot live on potential nourishment, or be emotionally satisfied by potential relationships. On
the whole, we judge people by their actual conduct, as opposed
to their potential to behave a certain way. Reality, to us, is what is,
not what might be.

---

right. See Talmud, *Pesachim* 116b; Jerusalem Talmud, *Pesachim* 10:5;
Rashi on Deuteronomy 16:1.

4   Talmud, *Uktzin* 3:8; Bartenura's commentary, ad loc. For more examples of Shammai-Hillel debates that hinge on the question of potential
vs. actual, see *Beit HaOtzar* 1:27 and 2:2; *L'Or HaHalachah, LeShitot
Beit Shammai U'Veit Hillel*; *Sefer HaSichot* 5748, vol. II, pp. 645–668.

This is largely due to the fact that we are physical beings. It is a most telling idiosyncrasy of our language that "immaterial" means "insignificant": if we cannot touch it or see it, it's not real to us. Also, because of our finite and limited nature, we possess potentials that we will never actualize because we haven't enough energy, resources, or willpower to carry them out, or simply because we won't live long enough to do so. So the existence of a potential or possibility for something is not enough, for how do we know that it will amount to anything? Indeed, we often judge a thing's potential by the actual: If this much has been actualized, this "proves" that there is potential worthy of regard.

Envision, however, a being who is neither physical nor finite; a being not limited by space, time, or any other framework. In such a being, potential does not lack actualization, as everything is "as good as done." On the contrary: Potential is the purest and most perfect form of every reality—the essence of the thing, as it transcends the limitations and imperfections imposed upon it when it is translated into physical actuality.

For G-d, then, the potential is a higher form of being than the actual. This is why we say that, for G-d, the creation of the world did not constitute an "achievement" or even a "change" in His reality. The potential for creation existed in Him all along, and nothing was "added" by its translation into actuality. It is only we, the created, who gained anything from the actual creation of the world.

So when the sages of Shammai and Hillel debate the question of which is more significant from the perspective of Torah law, the actual or the potential, they are addressing the more basic question: Whose Torah is it—ours or G-d's? When Torah law enjoins us to commemorate the Exodus, when it legislates the laws of ritual impurity, or when it commands us to kindle the Chanukah lights, does it regard these phenomena from the perspective of its divine author, in whom the potential is the ideal state, or from the perspective of its human constituency, who equate real with actual?

THE TORAH

Whose Torah is it, ours or G-d's? Both Shammai and Hillel would agree that it is both.

The Torah is the wisdom and will of G-d. But as we proclaim in the blessing recited each morning over the Torah, G-d has *given* us His Torah, for He has delegated to mortal man the authority to interpret it and apply it. Thus, G-d did not communicate His will to us in the form of a detailed manifesto and a codified list of instructions. Instead, He communicated a relatively short (79,976-word) "Written Torah" (the Five Books of Moses), together with the "Oral Torah"—a set of guidelines by which the Written Torah is to be interpreted, decoded, extrapolated, and applied to the myriads of possibilities conjured up by the human experience.

So while the entire body of legal, homiletic, philosophical, and mystical teaching we know as "Torah" is implicit within the Written Torah, G-d designated the human mind and life as the tools that unlock the many layers of meaning and instruction contained within its every word.

The Torah is thus a partnership of the human and the divine, where a kernel of divine wisdom germinates in the human mind, gaining depth, breadth, and definition, and is actualized in the physicality of human life. In this partnership, our human finiteness and subjectivity become instruments of the divine truth, joining with it to create the ultimate expression of divine immanence in our world—the Torah.

Which is the more dominant element of Torah, divine revelation or human cognition? Which defines its essence? What *is* Torah — G-d's vision of reality, or man's endeavor to make his world a home for G-d? At times the Torah indicates the one; at times, the other. We have the rule that "The words of Torah are not susceptible to contamination."[5] A person who is in a state of ritual impurity (*tum'ah*) is forbidden to enter the Holy Temple; but there is no prohibition for him to study Torah. Why is he forbidden to enter a holy place but permitted to think and speak holy words? Because the Torah is not only "holy" (i.e., an object subservient to G-d and receptive to His presence) — it is divine. It is G-d's word, and the divine cannot be compromised by any impurity.

On the other hand, another law states that "A teacher of Torah who wishes to forgive an insult to his honor, can forgive it." This is in contrast to a king, who if insulted, has no right to forgive the insult, and no recourse but to punish the one who insulted him. For a king's honor is not his personal possession, but something that derives from his role as the sovereign of his people; one who insults the king insults the nation, and this is an insult that not even the king has the authority to forgive. Yet does not one who insults a Torah scholar insult the Torah? How does the scholar have the right to forgive the Torah's insult? The explanation given is that "the Torah is his." He who studies Torah acquires it as his own; G-d's wisdom becomes his wisdom.[6]

Whose Torah is it — ours or G-d's? Both descriptions are valid; both are part of the Torah's own self-perception. In certain laws and circumstances, we find the divinity of Torah emphasized; in others, its human proprietorship.

---

5   Talmud, *Berachot* 22a.
6   Ibid., *Kidushin* 32a.

CHANUKAH (8)   201

Thus, in a number of laws, the schools of Shammai and Hillel debate which definition of Torah is the predominant one. The sages of Shammai believe that in these particular applications of Torah law, the divinity of the Torah predominates. The Torah's perspective is synonymous with G-d's perspective, meaning that the potential of a thing is its primary truth. The sages of Hillel see these laws as belonging to the "human" aspect of Torah, so that the Torah's vision of reality is the human, actual-based perspective.

THE HUMAN FESTIVAL

In the great majority of disputes between the sages of Shammai and Hillel, the final *halachic* ruling follows the opinion of the School of Hillel. *Halachah* is the application of Torah to day-to-day life. In this area of Torah, it is the human element which predominates; here, reality is defined in terms of the actual and tactual, rather than the potential.

But nowhere is the supremacy of the Hillelian view more emphasized than in the debate on Chanukah, where the very name of the festival, and the name given to its final day, proclaim that "the law follows the School of Hillel." For Chanukah is the festival that, more than any other, underscores the human dynamic in Torah.

As noted above, the Torah consists of two parts: a) the divinely dictated words of the Written Torah; b) the Oral Torah, also communicated by G-d, but delegated to man. In the Oral Torah, G-d provides the guidelines and principles, while human beings follow these guidelines and apply these principles to derive and express the divine will.

The Oral Torah has two basic functions: to interpret the Written Torah, and to legislate the necessary laws, ordinances, and customs required to preserve the Torah and Jewish life through the generations.

Most of the festivals are explicitly ordained in the Written Torah. This is not to say that there is no "human element" involved in the biblically ordained festivals: the Oral Torah is still required to clarify each festival's laws and observances. For example, the Written Torah commands us to dwell in a *sukkah* and take the "four kinds" on Sukkot, but the Oral Torah is needed to interpret the oblique biblical allusions that tell us how a *sukkah* is to be constructed and which plant species are to be taken. Still, the festivals themselves were instituted by direct divine revelation.

There are two festivals, however, that are rabbinical institutions: Purim and Chanukah. These belong to the second function of the Oral Torah — to institute laws and observances that derive not from a verse in the Written Torah, but which arise out of the historical experience of the people of Israel.

These, too, are Torah, for they were enacted in accordance with the principles revealed at Sinai. Before reading the *megillah* on Purim, or kindling the Chanukah lights, we say: "Blessed are You, G‑d... Who has sanctified us with His commandments, and commanded us to read the *megillah*," or: "...to kindle the Chanukah lamp." *G‑d* is commanding us to observe these *mitzvot*, for it is He who granted the leaders of each generation the mandate to institute laws, ordinances, and festivals. Yet in these festivals, it is the human aspect of the Torah which predominates, while the divine aspect is more subdued.

Of the two rabbinical festivals, Chanukah is even more "human" than Purim. Purim was instituted during the era of prophecy, when G‑d still communed directly with the greatest individuals of the generation. The story of Purim was written down and incorporated within the Holy Scriptures that are appended to the Written

Torah. Thus, while Purim is technically an "Oral Torah" festival, it is closely related to the Written Torah.

Chanukah, however, occurred several hundred years later, when prophecy had ceased and the canon of the twenty-four books of the *Tanach* (Bible) had been closed. It thus belongs wholly to the Oral Torah—to the predominantly human aspect of the partnership. So Chanukah is the environment in which the Hillelian perspective on Torah—Torah as it relates to our tactual experience of the world in which we live—reigns supreme.

CHAPTER FOURTEEN

Tevet
Winter

The tenth day of the month of *Tevet* is the first of four annual fast days that commemorate a series of events that culminated in the destruction of the Holy Temple in Jerusalem and the onset of the *galut* (exile and spiritual displacement) of the Jewish people. The significance of these fast days, and of the Temple's destruction, will be examined in the essays in our chapter on "The Three Weeks and Tishah B'Av" (vol. 3, pp. 207–271 of this series); in this chapter, we will confine ourselves to the significance of the 10th of *Tevet* in the context of the month in which it occurs.

Tevet, whose 29 days fall in the months of December and January, is the coldest month of the year. But as the Talmud notes, conditions of external cold deepen our delight in our bodies' own, internal warmth. The essay *Spirit and Substance* applies this physiological truism to the cosmic relationship between us and G-d: During times of spiritual winter, when the frigid night of *galut* dulls the mind and freezes the heart, it is left to our physical self to discover its inherent warmth and its quintessential bond with its Creator.

SPIRIT
AND
SUBSTANCE

We are Your mate, and You are our lover.

High Holiday liturgy

hroughout the Torah, our relationship with G-d is compared to the marriage bond between husband and wife. The prophet Jeremiah speaks of how G-d recalls the Exodus as "the kindness of your youth, your bridal love, your following Me into the desert, into an unsown land."[1] King Solomon refers to the covenant at Mount Sinai as "the day of His betrothal."[2] When the people of Israel violated that covenant by transgressing the commandments of the Torah, the prophets admonished them as a wayward wife who has betrayed her husband.[3] And an entire book of the Torah, "Song of Songs," employs the language and imagery of marital love to describe the love between the bride Israel and her supernal Groom.

A deeper dimension of this metaphor is revealed in the talmudic passage which describes the month of *Tevet* as "the month in which a body derives pleasure from a body" because of the extreme cold that prevails in that time of the year.[4] The Talmud is referring to the verse in the book of Esther that relates how "Esther was

---

1 Jeremiah 2:2.
2 Song of Songs 3:11, as per Talmud, *Taanit* 26b.
3 Jeremiah 3:8; et al.
4 Talmud, *Megillah* 13a, as explained by Rashi.

taken to King Achashveirosh, into his royal house, in the tenth month, the month of *Tevet*."[5] The month is significant, says the Talmud, in that divine providence contrived that Esther should be brought to Achashveirosh at a time of year that would heighten his desire for her, thereby ensuring that he would choose her as his queen. As everything in Torah, this observation has many layers of meaning; in the words of the sages, "The Torah speaks about the physical world and alludes to the supernal worlds."[6] So in the supernal version of this detail of the Purim story, it relates to the relationship between "The King to Whom the End and Beginning are His" (*acharit vereishit shelo*—an acronym of "Achashveirosh") and His bride Israel ("Esther").[7]

The marriage of man and woman has both a spiritual and physical dimension. There is the spiritual bonding of minds and hearts —the fulfillment each derives from the other's intellect, emotions, and character. But the "pleasure" in the relationship, in the most potent and palpable sense of the word, lies in its physical aspect, in the contact and union of their bodies.

The same is true of the supernal prototype from which all male-female relationships derive and which they all mirror—the bond between G-d and His bride Israel. Here, too, there is both a "spiritual" and a "bodily" aspect. And here, too, the most powerful aspect of the relationship is the one in which, in the words of the Talmud, "a body derives pleasure from a body."

---

5   Esther 2:16.
6   See Nachmanides' introduction to his commentary on Torah; Shaloh 14a; et al.
7   See *Me'orei Ohr,* s.v. "Achashveirosh."

Our Two Selves

The body is often regarded as but a container and tool of the soul. In truth, however, the body is also the soul's counterpart and counterpole. While the soul is the seat of our spiritual identity —our sense of mission and purpose, our sense of connectedness to a higher truth—the body is the source of our material self, of our sense of distinctiveness and apartness of being. The soul is ever conscious of its insignificance in the face of its divine source; the body, on the other hand, has been imbued with a concreteness and substantiality which, in effect, smother all awareness of its Creator. It is the body that creates the "I am" feeling that underlies the egocentrism of physical life and which constitutes the greatest challenge to the truth that "There is none else besides Him."[8]

Comprised of both body and soul, we enlist them both in our relationship with G-d. We serve G-d with our spiritual self, imbuing our mind with His wisdom through the study of His Torah, and stimulating a love and awe of Him in our hearts through prayer. In these and other ways, we strive to exercise the mastery of mind over matter, the supremacy of spirit over substance. We strive to subordinate the body's selfish drives and express our soul's self-nullifying attachment to its Creator.

But this is only one aspect of the relationship. The body, too, serves G-d, not only as an instrument of the soul, but also with its own resources and with the material identity it generates.

The purpose of creation, say our sages, is that "G-d desired a dwelling in the lower realms."[9] The "lower realms" is our physical world—lowly because of its spiritual distance from its source, its

---

8   Deuteronomy 4:35.
9   *Midrash Tanchuma, Nasso* 16; *Tanya,* ch. 36. See *The Last Jew,* on pp. 157–162 above.

illusion of self-sufficiency, its virtual blackout of anything transcendent and divine. But it is here that G-d wished to make His home, desiring that this "lower realm" be made to house and express His quintessential self.[10]

Thus, we serve G-d primarily with physical deeds and objects: with the physical acts of binding the *tefilin* on one's arm and head, eating matzah on Passover, sounding a ram's horn on Rosh Hashanah, and with all the other *mitzvot* which govern our business dealings, family life, diet, and dress. Even the spiritual act of prayer has a physical vehicle in the form of audible sounds formed by moving lips. Indeed, virtually every material resource on earth, and every organ and limb of the human body, has its prescribed *mitzvah*—G-d's way of establishing how it can become an instrument of His will.

Furthermore, the making of "a dwelling in the lower realms" is not only about using physical actions and materials to fulfill G-d's commandments. It also incorporates the very essence of physicality, the very features which deem it lowly. Ego, individuality, pride —the antitheses of the soul's affirmation of the divine truth—these, too, are forces that can be harnessed and directed to drive our efforts to build the world which G-d desires.

This is the physical aspect of our relationship with the Almighty. We may not be experiencing G-d the way we do in its spiritual dimension, but with our physical drives and deeds we relate

---

10 Man constructs many edifices to serve his needs: shops, warehouses, office buildings, schools, houses of worship, recreational facilities, etc. Each of these serve a specific area of our lives, and each one will find us projecting a different self and personality. A home, however, is what we build to house our "essence"—to serve as the place where we can be uninhibitedly ourself. Thus, the metaphor of "dwelling" is used to express the purpose for which G-d created the physical world: that it serve and express His very essence.

TEVET (1)   211

to Him in a way that is no less significant—by fulfilling His desire in creation.

THE DIVINE ESSENCE

So much for the body and soul of the "bride." What about the supernal Groom?

G-d, of course, does not possess a "body" or a "soul" or any other component parts. But precisely because G-d is not divisible or definable in any way, *we* must distinguish between two things whenever we think about, discuss, or "experience" the divine: G-d Himself (the divine "body"), and our perception of His reality (the divine "soul").

Because of the finite and definitive nature of everything human, any understanding we may have of His truth, any articulable perception we may have of His reality, belongs to the second category. G-d desired that we relate to Him and experience Him, so He projected various humanly perceivable manifestations of Himself (His "wisdom" in the Torah, His "artistry" in nature, His "providence" in history) into our world. None of this is actually *Him*, any more than the sun's rays are the sun. They are reflections of His being, not His substance.

When we serve G-d with our spiritual selves, we are actually relating to manifestations of G-dliness rather than to G-d Himself. These divine manifestations will always be "spiritual" (i.e., intangible), since our perception of G-d is of a being of absolute abstraction, infinity, omnipresence, and omnipotence; of a being before which everything submits and nullifies itself, before which any vestige of selfhood is in variance with the truth that "there is nothing else besides Him." Indeed, to perceive Him in any other way would be a gross definition of His undefinable being. But is this G-d Himself? Obviously not, if we are perceiving it or experiencing it.

But when we serve G-d with our physical selves, we are relating to more than a spiritual manifestation of His truth. These physical actions by our physical self may be devoid of any perception or experience of their divine significance; but with them we are in touch with the very essence and "substance" of G-d—with the "body" of His reality rather than its soul. Because from where do we derive our self, our sense of individuality and distinctiveness? From where does the physical existence derive its brute immanence, its unyielding substantiality? Ultimately, G-d is the supreme source of all. The blatant "I am" exuded by the physical is but a reflection of the unequivocalness of G-d's being. In this regard, the world of the body stems from a far deeper place in the divine essence than the world of spirit.

So when we serve G-d with our body and bodily identity, we are accessing what our physicality and ego are really all about: the unexperienceable essence of G-d.

And it is in this "blind" coming together of bodies that the most profound pleasure of the relationship lies. G-d's "mind" may be in the Torah, His "heart" may be in the yearnful notes of prayer, but His "desire" is in the dwelling that we make for Him out of our physical self and world.

The Frigid Nights of Tevet

The history of our relationship with G-d has known spiritually sunny times, in which G-d's involvement in our lives was openly perceivable. Times when the Holy Temple stood in Jerusalem, a beacon of His manifest presence in our midst. The divine "sun" shone brightly, and we basked in the warmth of its rays.

TEVET (1)

213

But on the 10th of *Tevet* in the year 3336 from Creation (426 BCE) began our plunge into a winter from which we have yet to emerge. On that day, Babylon's armies laid siege to Jerusalem; two and a half years later they breached the city's walls, torched the Temple, and exiled the Jewish people. *Galut*, the physical and spiritual displacement of Israel, commenced.[11]

The sun came out for another four centuries in the time of the Second Temple, but this was a more reserved revelation of G-dliness: Some of the Temple's most overt signs of divine immanence were lacking.[12] In addition, prophecy had ceased — the Divine Groom was no longer directly communicating to His bride. Then the Second Temple, too, was taken from us.

Ever since, we have been out in the cold. But if the spiritual winter of *galut* all but eclipses the perceptive and experiential side of our relationship with G-d, it is a time of heightened pleasure in its physical aspect — the frigid nights of Tevet only intensify our bodies' delight in each other. If a cold and dark world mutes the light of G-d and dulls our minds and hearts, it only accentuates the most basic and essential element of our relationship: the bond between the physical self of man and the quintessential being of G-d.

---

11 *Tevet* is also the month whose weekly Torah readings describe our descent into our first (and prototypic) *galut* — our exile and enslavement in Egypt.

12 Talmud, *Yoma* 21b: "Five things distinguished the First Temple from the Second Temple: the holy ark (containing the tablets engraved with the Ten Commandments) with its cover and *cherubim*, the divine fire (which descended upon the altar), the *Shechinah* (divine presence), the holy spirit, and the *urim vetumim* (G-d's communication and guidance via the gems of the High Priest's breastplate)."

CHAPTER FIFTEEN

Tu BiShevat

The New Year for Trees

The 15th of Shevat

Tu BiShevat, the 15th day of the month of *Shevat*, marks the beginning of a "New Year for Trees." This is the season in which the earliest-blooming trees in the Land of Israel emerge from their winter sleep and begin a new fruit-bearing cycle.

Legally, the new year for trees relates to the various tithes that must be separated from produce grown in the Holy Land. These tithes differ from year to year in the seven-year *shemittah* cycle; *Shevat* 15 is the point at which a budding fruit is considered to belong to the next year of the cycle.

We mark the day by eating fruit, particularly the "seven fruits" that are singled out by the Torah in its praise of the bounty of the Holy Land: wheat, barley, grapes, figs, pomegranates, olives, and dates. On this day we remember that "man is a tree of the field" (Deuteronomy 20:19) and reflect on the lessons we can derive from our botanical analogue.

A sampling of these lessons is presented in the two essays that comprise this chapter. *Of Trees and Men* looks at the various parts of the tree (roots, trunk, branches, leaves, fruit, seeds, etc.) and their corresponding elements within the human being. *Fruit for Thought* defines the seven areas of our lives represented by the "seven fruits."

Also see *Agricultural Man* in vol. 1 of this series, pp. 190–192.

TU BISHEVAT (1)

OF TREES
AND MEN

And G-d said: Let the earth sprout forth greenery... fruit trees that produce fruit after its kind whose seed is in itself...

Genesis 1:11

For man is a tree of the field.

Deuteronomy 20:19

"Man is a tree of the field," and the Jewish calendar reserves one day each year—the "New Year for Trees" on the 15th of Shevat—for us to contemplate our affinity with our botanical analogue and what it can teach us about our own lives.

The tree's primary components are: the roots, which anchor it to the ground and supply it with water and other nutrients; the trunk, branches, and leaves which comprise the body of the tree; and the fruit, which contains the seeds by which the tree reproduces itself.

The spiritual life of man also includes roots, a body, and fruit. The roots represent faith, our source of nurture and perseverance. The trunk, branches, and leaves are the "body" of our spiritual lives—our intellectual, emotional, and practical achievements. The fruit is our power of spiritual procreation—the ability to influence others, to plant a seed in a fellow human being and see it sprout, grow, and bear fruit.

Roots and Body

The roots are the least glamorous of the tree's parts, and the most crucial. Buried underground, virtually invisible, they possess neither the majesty of the tree's body, the colorfulness of its leaves, nor the tastiness of its fruit. But without roots, a tree cannot survive.

Furthermore, the roots must keep pace with the body: If the trunk and leaves of a tree grow and spread without a proportional increase in its roots, the tree will collapse under its own weight. On the other hand, a profusion of roots makes for a healthier, stronger tree, even if it has a meager trunk and few branches, leaves, and fruit. And if the roots are sound, the tree will rejuvenate itself if its body is damaged or its branches are cut off.

Faith is the least glamorous of our spiritual faculties. Characterized by a "simple" conviction and commitment to one's Source, it lacks the sophistication of the intellect, the vivid color of the emotions, or the sense of satisfaction that comes from deed. And faith is buried underground, its true extent concealed from others and even from ourselves.

Yet our faith, our suprarational commitment to G-d, is the foundation of our entire "tree." From it stems the trunk of our understanding, from which branch out our feelings, motivations, and deeds. And while the body of the tree also provides some of its spiritual nurture, the bulk of our spiritual sustenance derives from its roots, from our faith in and commitment to our Creator.

A soul might grow a majestic trunk, numerous and wide-spreading branches, beautiful leaves, and lush fruit. But these must be equaled, indeed surpassed, by its "roots." Above the surface, there might be much wisdom, profundity of feeling, abundant experience, copious achievement, and many disciples; but if these are not grounded and vitalized by an even greater faith and commitment, it is a tree without foundation, a tree doomed to collapse under its own weight.

On the other hand, a life might be blessed with only sparse knowledge, meager feeling and experience, scant achievement, and little "fruit." But if its roots are extensive and deep, it is a healthy tree: a tree fully in possession of what it does have; a tree with the capacity to recover from the setbacks of life; a tree with the potential to eventually grow and develop into a loftier, more beautiful, and fruitful tree.

FRUIT AND SEED

The tree desires to reproduce, to spread its seeds far and wide so that they take root in diverse and distant places. But the tree's reach is limited to the extent of its own branches. It must therefore seek out other, more mobile couriers to transport its seeds.

So the tree produces fruit, in which its seeds are enveloped by colorful, fragrant, and tasty fibers and juices. The seeds themselves would not rouse the interest of animals and men; but with their attractive packaging, they have no shortage of "customers" who, after consuming the external fruit, deposit the seeds in those diverse and distant places where the tree wants to plant its seeds.

When we communicate with others, we employ many devices to make our message attractive. We buttress it with intellectual sophistication, steep it in emotional sauce, dress it in colorful words and images. But we should bear in mind that this is only the packaging—the fruit that contains the seed. The seed itself is essentially tasteless—the only way that we can truly impact others is by conveying our own simple faith in what we are telling them, our own simple commitment to what we are espousing.

If the seed is there, our message will take root in their minds and hearts, and our own vision will be grafted into theirs. But if there is no seed, there will be no progeny to our effort, however tasty our fruit might be.

FRUIT
FOR
THOUGHT

For the L-rd your G-d is bringing you to a good land: ...A land of wheat, barley, grapes, figs, and pomegranates; a land of oil-yielding olive and [date] honey.

Deuteronomy 8:8

Our sages tell us that, originally, all trees bore fruit, as will also be the case in the era of Moshiach.[1] A fruitless tree is a symptom of an imperfect world, as the ultimate function of a tree is to produce fruit.

If "man is a tree of the field"[2] and fruit is the tree's highest achievement, there are seven fruits that crown the human and botanical harvest. These are the seven fruits and grains singled out by the Torah as exemplars of the Holy Land's fertility: wheat, barley, grapes, figs, pomegranates, olives, and dates.

The 15th day of the month of *Shevat* is the day designated by the Jewish calendar as the "New Year for Trees." On this day, we celebrate the trees of G-d's world, and the tree within us, by partaking of these seven "fruits," which typify the various components and modes of human life.

---

1   Nachmanides on Genesis 1:11.

2   Deuteronomy 20:19.

FOOD AND FODDER

The kabbalistic masters tell us that each and every one of us possesses not one, but two souls: an "animal soul," which embodies our natural, self-oriented instincts; and a "G-dly soul" embodying our transcendent drives—our desire to escape the "I" and relate to that which is greater than ourselves.[3]

As its name implies, the animal soul constitutes that part of ourselves that is common to all living creatures: the instinct for self-preservation and self-perpetuation. But man is more than a sophisticated animal. There are qualities that are unique to us as human beings—the qualities deriving from our "G-dly soul." The point at which we graduate beyond the self and its needs ("How do I survive?" "How do I obtain food, shelter, money, power, knowledge, satisfaction?") to a supra-self-perspective ("Why am I here?" "What purpose do I serve?") is the point at which we cease to be just another animal in G-d's world and begin to realize our uniqueness as human beings.

This is not to say that the animal self is to be rejected in favor of the divine/human self. These are our two souls, both of which are indispensable to a life of fulfillment and purpose. Even as we stimulate the divine in us to rise above the merely animal, we must also develop and refine our animal selves, learning to cultivate the constructive aspects of selfhood (e.g., self-confidence, courage, perseverance) while weeding out the selfish and the profane aspects.

"Wheat," a staple of the human diet,[4] represents the endeavor to nourish what is distinctly human in us, to feed the divine aspirations that are the essence of our humanity. Barley, a typical

---

3   Rabbi Chaim Vital, *Shaar HaKedushah* 1:1–2; *Tanya*, chapter 1 ff.

4   "Bread satiates the heart of man"—Psalms 104:15.

animal food,[5] represents the endeavor to nourish and develop our animal soul—a task no less crucial to our mission in life than the cultivation of our G-dly soul.[6]

EXCITEMENT

Wheat and barley, the two grains among the "seven fruits," represent the "staples" of our inner makeup. Following these come five fruits—"appetizers" and "desserts" on our spiritual menu—which add flavor and zest to our basic endeavor of developing our animal and G-dly souls.

The first of these is the grape, whose defining characteristic is joy. As the grapevine describes its product in Jotham's Parable, "my wine, which makes joyous G-d and men."[7]

Joy is revelation. A person ignited by joy has the same basic traits he or she possesses in a non-joyous state—the same knowledge and intelligence, the same loves, hates, wants, and desires. But in a state of joy, everything is more pronounced: The mind is keener, the loves deeper, the hates more vivid, the desires more aggressive. Emotions that ordinarily show only a faint intimation of their true extent now come out into the open. In the words of the Talmud, "When wine enters, the concealed emerges."[8]

A joyless life might be complete in every way, yet it is a shallow life; everything is there, but only the barest surface is showing.

---

5   "The barley and the straw for the horses and the mules"—I Kings, 5:8. See also Talmud, *Sotah* 14a.

6   Indeed, according to Torah law, a person is obligated to first feed his animals before he feeds himself (Talmud, *Berachot* 40a; *Mishneh Torah, Laws of Slaves* 9:8).

7   Judges 9:13.

8   Talmud, *Eruvin* 65a.

Both the G-dly and the animal souls contain vast reservoirs of insight and feeling that never see the light of day because there is nothing to stimulate them. The "grape" represents the element of joy in our lives—the joy that unleashes these potentials and adds depth, color, and intensity to everything we do.

INVOLVEMENT

We might be doing something fully and completely; we might even be doing it joyously. But are we there? Are we involved?

Involvement means more than doing something right, more than giving it our all. It means that we care, that we are invested in the task. It means that we are affected by what we are doing, for the better or for the worse.

The fig, the fourth of the "seven fruits," is also the fruit of the "Tree of Knowledge of Good and Evil"—the fruit of which Adam and Eve tasted, thereby committing the first sin of history.[9] As chassidic teaching explains, "knowledge" (*daat*) implies an intimate involvement with the thing known (as in the verse, "And Adam knew his wife"[10]). The sin of Adam and Eve derived from their refusal to reconcile themselves with the notion that there are certain things from which they must distance themselves; they desired to intimately know every corner of G-d's world, to become involved with every one of G-d's creations. Even evil, even that which G-d had declared out of bounds to them.

Adam and Eve's fig was one of the most destructive forces in history. In its equally powerful constructive guise, the fig represents our capacity for a deep and intimate involvement in our

---

9   Genesis 3:7; Rashi, ad loc.
10   Genesis 4:1.

TU BISHEVAT (2)   225

every positive endeavor — an involvement which signifies that we
are one with what we are doing.

DEED

"Your lips are like a thread of scarlet," extols King Solomon in Song
of Songs, his celebration of the love between the Divine Groom
and His bride Israel. "Your mouth is comely; your temple is like
a piece of pomegranate within your locks."[11] As interpreted by
the Talmud, the allegory of the pomegranate expresses the truth
that, "Even the empty ones amongst you are full of good deeds as
a pomegranate (is full of seeds)."[12]

The pomegranate is not just a model for something that contains many particulars. It also addresses the paradox of how an individual may be "empty" and, at the same time, be "full of good
deeds as a pomegranate."

The pomegranate is a highly compartmentalized fruit: each of
its hundreds of seeds is wrapped in its own sac of pulp and is separated from its fellows by a tough membrane. In the same way, it
is possible for a person to do good deeds — many good deeds — yet
they remain isolated acts, with little or no effect on his nature and
character. He may possess many virtues, but they do not become
him; he may be full of good deeds, yet he remains morally and
spiritually hollow.

If the fig represents our capacity for total involvement and
identification with what we are doing, the pomegranate is the fig's

---

11 Song of Songs 4:3.
12 Talmud, *Berachot* 57a. *Raka*, the Hebrew word used by the verse for
    "temple," is related to the word *reik*, "empty." Thus, "your temple is like
    a .. pomegranate" is homiletically rendered "the empty ones amongst
    you are like a pomegranate.")

antithesis, representing our capacity to overreach ourselves and act in a way that surpasses our internal spiritual state. It is our capacity to do and achieve things that are utterly incompatible with who and what we are at the present moment.

The pomegranate is "hypocrisy" in its noblest form: the refusal to reconcile oneself to one's spiritual and moral station as defined by the present state of one's character; the insistence on acting better and more G-dly than we are.

STRUGGLE

For most of us, life is synonymous with struggle. We struggle to forge an identity under the heavy shadow of parental and peer influence; we struggle to find a partner in life, and then we struggle to preserve our marriage; we struggle to raise our children, and then struggle in our relationship with them as adults; we struggle to earn a living, and then struggle with our guilt over our good fortune; and underlying it all is the perpetual struggle between our animal and G-dly selves, between our self-oriented instincts and our aspiration to transcend the self and touch the divine.

The "olive" in us is that part of ourselves that thrives on struggle, that revels in it, that would no more escape it than escape life itself. "Just like an olive," say our sages, "which yields its oil only when pressed," so, too, do we yield what is best in us only when pressed between the millstones of life and the counterforces of a divided self.[13]

---

13 *Midrash Rabbah, Shemot* 36:1.

PERFECTION

As the "fig" is countered by the "pomegranate," so, too, is the "olive" in us contrasted by our seventh fruit, the "date," which represents our capacity for peace, tranquility, and perfection. While it is true that we're best when we're pressed, it is equally true that there are potentials in our soul that well forth only when we are completely at peace with ourselves, when we have achieved a balance and harmony among the diverse components of our souls.

Thus the Psalmist sings: "The *tzaddik* (perfectly righteous person) shall bloom as the date palm." The *Zohar* explains that there is a certain species of date palm that bears fruit only after seventy years.[14] The human character is comprised of seven basic attributes, each consisting of ten subcategories; thus, the *tzaddik*'s blooming "after seventy years" is the fruit of absolute tranquility, the product of a soul whose every aspect and nuance of character has been refined and brought into harmony with oneself, one's fellow, and one's G-d.

While the "olive" and "date" describe two very different spiritual personalities, they both exist within every individual. For even in the midst of our most ardent struggles, we can always find comfort and fortitude in the tranquil perfection that resides at the core of our souls. And even in our most tranquil moments, we can always find the challenge that will provoke us to yet greater achievement.

---

14   Psalms 92:13; *Zohar* 3:16a.

CHAPTER SIXTEEN

Purim

Nature, Physicality, Choice

Adar 14 & 15

Purim celebrates the salvation of the Jewish people, in the year 356 BCE, from Haman's plot "to destroy, kill, and annihilate all the Jews, young and old, infants and women, in a single day." Endorsed by King Achashveirosh, whose dominion extended from India to Ethiopia, Haman's decree boded the physical destruction of every Jew on the face of the earth.

While the sage Mordechai rallied the Jews to prayer and repentance, his cousin, Queen Esther, engineered Haman's downfall at a private wine-party to which she invited the king and the minister. She prevailed upon Achashveirosh to hang Haman and to issue a second decree, empowering the Jews to defend themselves against those who sought to destroy them.

On the 13th of *Adar*—the day selected by Haman's *pur* (lottery)—numerous battles were fought throughout the empire between the Jews and those who attempted to carry out Haman's decree (which was never actually revoked). The following day, *Adar* 14, became a day of feasting and rejoicing in celebration of the Jews' victory over their enemies. In the ancient walled capital, Shushan, where the battle went on for two days, the victory celebration was held on *Adar* 15.

Mordechai and Esther instituted that these two days be observed for posterity as the festival of Purim —*Adar* 15 in walled cities, and *Adar* 14 in unwalled towns—by public readings of the story of the miracle as recorded in the "Scroll of Esther"; sending food portions to friends; giving gifts of money to the poor; and enjoying a festive meal accompanied with inebriating drink (recalling the fateful wine-party at which Esther turned Achashveirosh against Haman).

A time-honored Purim custom is for children to dress up and disguise themselves—an allusion to the fact that the miracle of Purim was disguised in natural garments. This is also the significance behind a traditional Purim food, the *hamantash*—a pastry whose filling is hidden within a three-cornered crust. The day before Purim is the "Fast of Esther," in commemoration of the fasts of Esther and her people as they prayed for G-d's salvation from Haman's decree.

Our chapter on Purim includes eight essays on the various themes and aspects of Purim, and the significance of its observances and customs.

<u>Oil and Wine</u> contrasts Purim with its alter ego, Chanukah. While Chanukah commemorates a series of supernatural miracles, Purim focuses on the natural and commonplace events that clothe the divine hand in the affairs of man. If Chanukah is about the purity of the Jewish soul, Purim is about the Jew's physical existence.

This theme is further developed in *Esther's Story*, which probes the nature and essence of our physicality.

The next essay, *A Roll of Dice*, examines the significance of the lottery cast by Haman to set the date for his proposed annihilation of the Jews—a lottery which gives the festival of Purim its name.

A central theme of Purim is choice. What do we really want? As explained in *The Thousand-Year Difference*, Purim marked the first time in our history that we confronted this question free of all outside influences and compulsions. Purim is thus the final frontier in the forging of our identity as G-d's chosen people, culminating a process begun a thousand years earlier with the Exodus and the revelation at Sinai.

A Feast and a Fast explores the various faces and uses of nature in the story of Purim. *A Singular People* raises the question of whether there is anything truly unique about the Jew amidst the profusion of religions and philosophies, symbols and ceremonies, heroes and martyrs that distinguish the national identities of other peoples—and finds the answer in Purim's celebration of the specialness of Israel. *The Purim Drunk* enjoys the spectacle of the Purimly-drunken Jew.

Our concluding essay, *The Beginning and the End*, is about *Purim Katan*, the "minor Purim" which occurs seven times in 19 years and which illustrates how joy is the signature emotion of the Jew and the grand finale of his or her life cycle.

PURIM (1)   233

OIL
AND
WINE

Oil permeates the entire substance of a thing.

Shulchan Aruch, Yoreh De'ah 105:5

When wine enters, secret emerges.

Talmud, Eruvin 65a

O il is in. Oil shuns superficiality—you won't find it riding a fad or angling for a photo opportunity. When oil comes in contact with something, it saturates it to the core, permeating it in its entirety.

When set aglow, oil is the master of understatement. Soundlessly it burns—not for the oil lamp the vulgar cackling of firewood or even the faint sizzle of candlewax. Its light does not burst through the door and bulldoze the darkness away; instead, it gently coaxes the gloom to shimmer with a spiritual luminescence.

Wine is a tabloid reporter. Wine barges past the security guard of the mind to loosen the lips, spill the guts, and turn the heart inside out. Wine smears the most intimate secrets across the front pages of life.

Chanukah is oil, Purim is wine.

Chanukah is the triumph of the Jewish soul. The Greeks had no designs on the Jew's body; it was the soul of Israel they coveted, seeking to indoctrinate her mind with their philosophy and tint her spirit with their culture. We fought not for the freedom of our material self, but to liberate our spiritual identity from Hellenist domination.

Haman and company did not bother with such subtleties. They had one simple goal: the physical destruction of every Jew on the face of the earth. Purim remembers the salvation of the Jew's bodily existence.

Chanukah is commemorated with oil. Chanukah celebrates the innerness of the Jewish soul, the essence which permeates and sanctifies every nook and cranny of the Jew's life. Chanukah celebrates the secret glow of the spirit, which, rather than confronting the darkness, infiltrates it and transforms it from within.

On Purim we pour out the wine. Purim is a noisy party, a showy parade, a costumed extravaganza. Purim celebrates the fact that the Jew is not just a soul, but a body as well. Purim celebrates the fact that our Jewishness is not only an internal spirituality but also a palpable reality; that it not only permeates our beings from within, but also spills out into the externalities of our material lives.

ESTHER'S STORY

The decree of Esther was fulfilled regarding the words of this Purim, and they were written in a book.

Esther 9:32

*E*ach year, on the fourteenth day of the month of *Adar*, we observe the festival of Purim, fulfilling the observances of the day as they have been practiced for more than 2,300 years. We read the *megillah*, the "scroll of Esther"; we send gifts of food to our friends; we increase in charity to the poor; and we partake of a festive meal, replete with food, drink, and unbridled joy.

Originally, however, there were two different conceptions of how the miracle of Purim should be commemorated, propagated by the two heroes and founders of Purim, Mordechai and Esther.

The observances of *mishloach manot* (sending of food-portions), *matanot l'evyonim* (gifts to the poor), and *mishteh v'simchah* (feasting and rejoicing) were jointly proposed by Mordechai and Esther. However, the concept of the *megillah* came solely from Esther: It was she, not Mordechai, who advocated that the story of Purim should be written in a scroll and included among the 24 books of the *Tanach* (Bible), and that this written account should be publicly read each Purim.[1]

---

1 Thus, in Esther 9:32 we read that "The decree of *Esther* was fulfilled regarding the words of this Purim, and they were written in a scroll," while the aforementioned institutions of "festivity and joy, sending food-portions to one's friends and gifts to the poor" (Ibid., v. 22) are described as "what has been established for [the Jewish people] by

Another difference between the two leaders was that it was Mordechai, rather than Esther, who wished to make Purim a full-fledged *yom tov*—a day of sabbatical rest like the first and last days of Passover and Sukkot.[2]

The different Purims envisioned by Mordechai and Esther reflect their respective roles in the events of the time. It was Mordechai who personified the faith of his people with his refusal to bow to Haman; it was he who identified the spiritual source of Israel's vulnerability to Haman's decree, who called upon the people to repent and return to G-d, who led them in three days of fasting and prayer, who gathered thousands of Jewish children and studied Torah with them in order to arouse the mercy of Heaven. Esther, on the other hand, was the one who risked her life by approaching King Achashveirosh on the matter, who provoked the king's wrath against Haman, and who prevailed upon him to empower the Jewish people to defend themselves against their enemies.

In other words, Mordechai was the soul of Purim—the one who rectified the spiritual state of his people and summoned forth the divine salvation. Esther was Purim's body, the one who manipulated the physical events through which the salvation came about.

So Mordechai envisioned Purim as a *yom tov*, a day on which the Jew eschews all creative involvement with the material world, while Esther saw it as a day that is very much part of the physical reality. And it was Esther who insisted that the story of Purim be written down, and read aloud each Purim, while Mordechai

---

Mordechai the Jew and Queen Esther" (v. 31). See also Talmud, *Megillah* 7a: "Esther wrote to the sages: "Establish me (i.e., the reading of my story—Rashi) for all generations... Write me down (as a book in Torah —Rashi) for all generations..."

2   Talmud, *Megillah* 5b; *Torah Ohr*, Esther 100a.

PURIM (2)   237

felt that it was enough that it be "remembered and observed"[3]
when the events of the day are commemorated by a series of observances, as is the case with the other festivals. For Mordechai,
it was enough that future generations be *reminded* of the miracle
when they observe the rituals of Purim, whereas Esther felt that
the events should be perpetuated not only as thoughts in the consciousness of Israel but also in the physical form of written and
verbalized words.[4]

THE RESOLUTION

When the observances of Purim were institutionalized by the
sanhedrin[5] on the first anniversary of the miracle, it was Esther's
vision that prevailed: The Purim we observe today is Esther's physical Purim rather than Mordechai's spiritual model. Indeed, the
section of the Torah devoted to the story of Purim is called "The
Book of Esther"—not "The Book of Mordechai" or "The Book of
Mordechai and Esther," or even "The Book of Esther and Mordechai." Purim has been decisively established as Esther's story, Esther's miracle, Esther's festival.

For Purim is the festival of the Jewish body. Mordechai, too,
recognized this when, together with Esther, he instituted a series
of decidedly physical observances for Purim: gifts of food and
money, and the joy achieved through feasting and drinking.

---

3   Esther 9:28.
4   According to kabbalistic and chassidic teaching, the spiritual is the
    "male" element of creation, while the physical is its "female" aspect.
    Thus Mordechai related to the spiritual or "masculine" constitu-
    ent of Purim, while Esther identified with its physical or "feminine"
    dimension.
5   Council of 71 sages that was the supreme legal and judicial authority.

On the most basic level, this is because

> *The decree was to destroy and kill the bodies of the Jewish people... not their souls (as, for example, was the endeavor of the Greeks at the time of Chanukah)... hence, the salvation is commemorated by physical means.*[6]

Also, the physicality of Purim reflects the "natural" form of the miracle it commemorates. No seas split on Purim, no oil yielded eight times its natural kindling capacity, no divine voice issued from a flaming mountain. To the perfunctory observer, the events of Purim do not appear miraculous at all, but a series of fortunate coincidences. Indeed, the name of G-d is not once mentioned in the Book of Esther (!)—an absence fully consistent with its story line of a palace intrigue involving an evil minister, a beautiful queen, and a fickle king. While other festivals celebrate G-d's supranatural interventions in history for the sake of His people, Purim extols the hand of G-d concealed within the natural world, the divine providence implicit within even the most mundane workings of the physical reality.

A MATTER OF BEING

On a deeper level, the physical nature of Purim is at the heart of its unique contribution to the relationship between G-d and Israel.

Common wisdom has it that spirit is superior to matter. The physical is finite and temporal, while the spiritual is not bounded by time and space; the physical is inert, the spiritual vibrant and transcending. Yet the physical body relates to the divine truth in a way that is beyond the scope of the loftiest spiritual reality.

---

6   *Levush, Orach Chaim* 670:2.

PURIM (2)   239

The soul of man was forged in the "image of G-d."[7] Its qualities
and virtues—its intelligence, its compassion, its sense of beauty
and harmony—are divine qualities, divine attributes reflected in
the human spirit. But these are merely divine *qualities*, rather than
true expressions of G-d's essence. To say that G-d is wise, compassionate, or harmonious is to refer to a superficial aspect of His
being, one that is wholly extraneous to the divine essence.

There is, however, one element of G-d's creation that reflects
His quintessential being: the physical reality. The physical object
is—unequivocally and definitively. "I am," it proclaims, "and my
being is wholly defined by my own existence." Ostensibly, this
makes the physical the greatest concealment of the divine truth,
the most blatant denial of the axiom, "There is none else besides
Him."[8] But it is precisely for this reason that, in all of creation, the
physical object is also the most fundamental expression of the divine being. For in the physical object we have a model for absolute
existence.[9]

Our calendar is replete with spiritual avenues of relationship
with G-d: the experience of freedom on Passover, the reliving of
the revelation at Sinai on Shavuot, the imperial awe of Rosh Hashanah, the *teshuvah* of Yom Kippur, the sublime joy of Sukkot and
Simchat Torah, the subtle light of Chanukah. But once a year we
access a dimension of our relationship with G-d that no spiritual
experience can capture. On Purim, it is our physicality that affirms
our commitment to G-d, expressing the truth that the definitive
being of our bodies is but a reflection of the absolute being of G-d.

---

7   Genesis 1:27.

8   Deuteronomy 4:35.

9   Indeed, it is only as an analogue of its Creator's being that the physical
    object can possess this quality, which, in essence, is the exclusive pre-
    rogative of the Divine. See *Spirit and Substance* on pp. 207–213 above.

A ROLL OF DICE

For Haman the son of Hamdata the Agag-
ite, the enemy of all the Jews, had schemed
against the Jews to destroy them, and had
cast a pur *— that is, the lot — to consume*
them, and to destroy them...

  Therefore they called these days "Purim"
after the pur...
Esther 9:24–26

*M*any developments contributed to the salvation of the Jewish people from Haman's decree: Esther's replacement of Vashti as queen; Mordechai's rousing the Jews of Shushan to repentance and prayer; Achashveirosh's sleepless night, in which he is reminded that Mordechai had saved his life and commands Haman to lead Mordechai in a hero's parade through the streets of Shushan; Esther's petition to the king and her confrontation with Haman; the hanging of Haman; the great war between the Jews and their enemies on the 13th of *Adar*.

Each of these events played a major role in the miracle of Purim. And yet, the name of the festival—the one word chosen to express its significance—refers to a seemingly minor detail: the fact that Haman selected the date of his proposed annihilation of the Jews by casting lots (*pur* is Persian for "lot"). Obviously, the significance of the lot lies at the very heart of what Purim is all about.

Why, indeed, did Haman cast lots? Why didn't he simply choose the first convenient day or days on which to carry out his evil decree?

PURIM (3)   241

The Angel and the Drunk

There is another day on the Jewish calendar associated with the casting of lots: Yom Kippur. In one of the most dramatic moments of the Yom Kippur service in the Holy Temple, the *kohen gadol* (high priest) stood between two goats and cast lots to determine which should be offered to G-d and which should carry off the sins of Israel to the desert.[1]

It would seem that one could hardly find two more dissimilar days in the Jewish calendar. Yom Kippur is the most solemn day of the year. It is a day of soul-searching and repentance; a day on which we connect with the inviolable core of purity within us — with the self that remains forever unsullied by our failings and transgressions — to draw from it atonement for the past and resolve for the future.[2] So it is only natural that Yom Kippur should be a day of unfettered spirituality, a day on which we transcend our very physicality in order to commune with our spiritual essence. The Torah commands us to "afflict ourselves" on Yom Kippur[3] — to deprive the body of food and drink and all physical pleasures. Yom Kippur is the day on which terrestrial man most resembles the celestial angel.

Purim, on the other hand, is the most physical day of the year. It is a day of feasting and drinking — the Talmud goes so far as to state that "a person is obligated to drink on Purim until he does not know the difference between 'cursed be Haman' and 'blessed be Mordechai.'"[4] As our sages explain, Purim celebrates the salvation of the body of the Jew. There are festivals (such as Chanukah)

---

1   Leviticus 16:7–10.
2   See our chapter on "Yom Kippur and the Ten Days of *Teshuvah*" pp. 33–75 above.
3   Leviticus 16:31, et al.
4   Talmud, *Megillah* 7b.

242   INSIDE TIME: VOL. II

that remember a time when the Jewish soul was threatened, when
our enemies strove to uproot our faith and profane the sanctity of
our lives; these are accordingly marked with "spiritual" observances (e.g., lighting the *menorah*, reciting *hallel*). On Purim, on the
other hand, it was the Jewish body that was saved—Haman did
not plot to assimilate or paganize the Jews, but to physically destroy every Jewish man, woman, and child on the face of the earth.
Purim is thus celebrated by reading the *megillah*,[5] lavishing money
on the poor, sending gifts of food to friends, eating a sumptuous
meal, and drinking oneself to oblivion.

On Yom Kippur we fast and pray; on Purim we party. Yet the
Zohar sees the two days as intrinsically similar, going so far as to
interpret the name *Yom HaKippurim* (as the Torah calls Yom Kippur) to mean that it is "a day like Purim" (*yom k'purim*)![6]

REASON AND LOTS

The casting of lots expresses the idea that one has passed beyond
the realm of motive and reason. A lottery is resorted to when there
is no reason or impetus to choose one option over the other, so
that the choice must be surrendered to forces that are beyond
one's control and comprehension.

---

5   All the festivals are "testimonials"—days that commemorate a pivotal
     event in our history. Purim is unique in that its laws mandate that the
     events of the day be inscribed in a scroll (*megillah*) from which they are
     read aloud publicly, underscoring the physical nature of the festival:
     Its story is not confined to the realm of thought (i.e., evoked by the ob-
     servances of the day), or even speech (as in *kiddush* on Shabbat or the
     discussion of the Exodus on Passover), but must assume the physical
     form of parchment and ink (see the previous essay, *Esther's Story*).
6   *Tikkunei Zohar*, 57b.

PURIM (3)   243

Therein lies the significance of the lots cast by the *kohen gadol* on Yom Kippur. After all is said and done, implied the lots, no man is worthy in the eyes of G-d. We all stand before G-d with our faults and iniquities, and by all rational criteria, should be found lacking in face of the divine judgment. So we impel ourselves beyond the realm of nature and reason, beyond the realm of merit and fault. We disavow all the accoutrements of physical identity — food and drink, earthly pleasures, and our very sense of reason and priority. We cast our lot with G-d, confident that G-d will respond in kind and relate to us in terms of the quintessential bond between us rather than by the ontological scales of pro and con.

Haman's lot-casting was his attempt to exploit the supra-reality of the divine to an opposite end. The Jewish people, said Haman to himself, might be the pursuers of G-d's wisdom on earth and the implementers of His will, thus meriting His favor and protection. But surely G-d, in essence, is above it all—above our earthly reason and its notions of "virtue" and "deservedness," beyond such concepts as "good" or "evil." Ultimately, the divine will is as arbitrary as a roll of dice. Why not give it a shot? I might just catch a supernal caprice running in my direction.

As the Talmud relates, "When the lot [cast by Haman] fell on the month of *Adar*, he greatly rejoiced, saying: 'The lot has fallen for me upon the month of Moses' death.'"[7] This is what I've been saying all along, exulted Haman. Moses might have given Israel the Torah, the document that so endears them to G-d; but Moses, too, is mortal. Moses, too, is part of the physical, rational reality— a reality transcended by the "lot" reality I have accessed. My lots indicate that I have superseded Moses—superseded Israel's merit in the eyes of G-d.

---

7   Talmud, *Megillah* 13b.

What Haman failed to realize, adds the Talmud, was that while *Adar* was the month of Moses' passing, it was also the month of Moses' birth. In the final analysis, the import of Haman's lots was the very opposite of what he had understood. On the physical-existential plane, the lots were saying, there might be variations and fluctuations in G-d's relationship with His people. At times, they might be more deserving of His protection and blessing; at times, less so.[8] On this level of reality, Moses might even "die." But G-d's relationship with His people transcends the fluctuations of the terrestrial reality. Also on the level on which "darkness is as light,"[9] and "good" and "evil" are equally insignificant before Him, G-d chooses—for no reason save that such is His choice—the nation of Israel.

In the words of the prophet, "So says G-d: Is not Esau a brother to Jacob? But I love Jacob."[10] Also when reality seems as "arbitrary" as a throw of dice—for the righteous Jacob is no more worthy (for "worthiness" is a moot point) than the wicked Esau—the divine lot invariably falls with G-d's chosen people.

Thus, the festival of Purim derives its name from the lots cast by Haman. For this is not some incidental detail in the story of Purim, but the single event that most expresses what Purim represents.

DOES MATTER MATTER?

Yom Kippur is indeed "a day like Purim." Both are points in physical time that transcend the very laws of physical existence, points

---

8   Indeed, the reason that Haman was given license to threaten the Jewish people in the first place was that they had bowed to Nebuchadnezzar's image and had participated in the banquet given by Achashveirosh to celebrate the destruction of the Holy Temple (Ibid., 12a).

9   Psalms 139:12; cf. Job 35:6.

10   Malachi 1:2.

at which we rise above the rational structure of reality and affirm our suprarational bond with G-d: a bond not touched by the limitations of mortal life, a bond as free of cause and motive as the free-falling lot.

But there is also a significant difference between these two days. On Yom Kippur, our transcendence is expressed by our disavowal of all trappings of physical life. But the very fact that these would interfere with the supra-existential nature of the day indicates that we are not utterly free of them. Thus Yom Kippur is only "a day *like* Purim" (*k'purim*), for it achieves only a semblance of the essence of Purim.

The ultimate mark of transcendence is that the transcended state is not vanquished or suppressed, but that it itself serves the transcendent end. The miracle of Purim was G-d's assertion of His supra-existential choice of Israel, yet it was a miracle wholly garbed in nature. Everything happened quite naturally: Esther's beauty pleased Achashveirosh, and he made her his queen; Mordechai happened to overhear a plot to kill Achashveirosh, and years later the event was remembered by the king on a sleepless night; Esther contrived Haman's fall from grace in the royal court, had him hanged, and maneuvered Mordechai into his vacated position; and so on. But it is for this very reason that Purim is the greatest of miracles—a miracle in which the natural order is not merely circumvented or superseded, but in which nature itself becomes the instrument of the miraculous.

The same is true on the individual level. The ultimate transcendence of materiality is achieved not by depriving the body and suppressing the physical self, but by transforming the physical into an instrument of the divine will. So Purim is the day on which we are our most physical, and at the same time exhibit a self-abnegation to G-d that transcends all dictates and parameters of the physical-rational state—transcending even the axioms "cursed be Haman" and "blessed be Mordechai."

Yom Kippur is the day that empowers the Jew to rise above the constraints of physicality and rationality. Purim is the day that empowers the Jew to live a physical life that is the vehicle for a supra-physical, suprarational commitment to G-d.

PURIM (4)   247

THE THOUSAND-YEAR DIFFERENCE

The Jews fulfilled and accepted upon them-
selves... to observe these days of Purim...

Esther 9:27

"Fulfilled and accepted"— they fulfilled (on
Purim) that which they had already accepted
back then (at Mount Sinai).

Talmud, Shabbat 88a

aman's decree "to destroy, kill, and annihilate all the Jews, young and old, infants and women"[1] was neither the first nor the last such attempt by our enemies to destroy us. But this was the only time in our history that the threat to our physical existence was so immediate and all-inclusive. A single day—the 13th of *Adar*—was set aside for the total extinction of the people of Israel. The Persian Empire included 127 provinces, from India to Ethiopia; every Jew on the face of the earth lived in this domain and was subject to Haman's decree.

The comprehensive nature of Purim extends also to its inner significance. Underlying the physical events recounted in the Book of Esther was a spiritual drama involving each and every Jew and profoundly affecting the very essence of our nationhood and

---

1   Esther 3:13.

our relationship with G-d. Paradoxically, Purim represented both a nadir in terms of the divine presence in our lives as well as a "moment of truth" which galvanized our covenant with G-d and set it upon its eternal foundations.

A Jarring Experience

On the sixth day of *Sivan* in the year 2448 from creation (1313 BCE), the entire nation of Israel assembled at the foot of Mount Sinai. There, G-d chose us as His people and we committed ourselves to observe the laws of life as outlined in His Torah.

The Talmud points out, however, that nearly one thousand years were to pass before our covenant with G-d was sealed. As formulated at Sinai, the contract between G-d and Israel contained certain vulnerabilities; in fact, its very validity was contestable. It was only nine and a half centuries later, with the events of Purim, that our acceptance of the Torah was established upon an unshakable foundation.

The Torah tells us that prior to the revelation at Sinai, the people of Israel "stood beneath the mountain."[2] How does one stand "beneath" a mountain? The Talmud interprets this to mean that "G-d held the mountain over them like a jar and said to them: 'If you accept the Torah, fine; if not, here shall be your grave.'" But a most basic rule of Torah law is that a contract entered into under duress is not binding. Hence, concludes the Talmud, there was a standing contest to the legality of our commitment to observe the Torah.

---

2   Exodus 19:17. "Beneath the mountain" is the literal translation of the Hebrew words *betachtit hehar*. Common translations render it "at the foot of the mountain" and the like (see Rashi, ad loc.).

But during the events of Purim, the Jewish people reaffirmed their acceptance of the Torah without any hint of coercion from Above. In the words of the Book of Esther, "they fulfilled and accepted"— they established as valid and incontestable that which they had accepted a millennium earlier at Sinai.

THE DARK AGES

At Sinai, G-d revealed His very essence to man. As the Torah describes it, "G-d descended upon Mount Sinai" and we "saw the G-d of Israel." On that day, we "were shown to know that G-d is the Supreme Being—there is none else besides Him"; "Face to face G-d spoke to [us], on the mountain, from within the fire."[3]

In terms of any open signs of the divine presence in our lives, the events of Purim were the diametric opposite of the revelation at Sinai. G-d's home on earth, the Holy Temple in Jerusalem, lay in ruins, its rebuilding, ordered fourteen years earlier by the emperor Cyrus, halted by Achashveirosh's decree. The era of prophecy—G-d's direct communication to man—was coming to a close. We were in exile, at the mercy of our enemies, and G-d seemed oblivious to the fate of His chosen people. Even the miracle of Purim was so completely clothed in natural events that G-d's guiding hand in all that occurred was shrouded by the illusion of fortunate coincidence. This is most powerfully demonstrated by the fact that in the entire Book of Esther, there is not a single mention of G-d's name! This is also alluded to by the fact that "Esther," the name of the heroine of Purim and the name of the biblical book that recounts its story, is from the Hebrew *hester*, "concealment."

---

3   Exodus 19:20; ibid., 24:10; Deuteronomy 4:35; ibid., 5:4.

How did this spiritual blackout affect our commitment to G-d? It spurred us to what can be described as the greatest demonstration of our loyalty to G-d in our history. For eleven months, a decree of annihilation hung over the entire community of Israel. As the Book of Esther relates, even after Haman had fallen out of favor with the king and was hanged, the decree he initiated remained in effect; the only thing that Esther was able to achieve was to prevail upon Achashveirosh to issue a second decree, in which the Jews were given the right to resist those who came to kill them. The first decree, calling upon all citizens of the realm to annihilate the Jewish minority in their midst on the 13th of *Adar*, remained in force until that date, when the Jews were victorious in their war against their enemies, killing 75,000 of their attackers.[4]

For that entire year, when being a Jew meant that one's life was free for the taking by imperial decree, not a single Jew broke ranks from his or her people to seek safety by assimilating into the pagan populace. In fact, the Book of Esther records that that period saw many conversions to Judaism! So strongly did the Jews radiate their faith in G-d and their confidence in G-d's salvation, that many of their neighbors were motivated to join a people with such a powerful and immutable relationship with G-d.

Therein lies the deeper significance of the "coercion" to accept the Torah at Sinai, and of the validation of our covenant with G-d achieved on Purim.

At Sinai, we had no choice. Faced with such an awesome revelation of the divine truth, one could hardly doubt or dissent. In effect, we were "forced" to accept the Torah: Overwhelmed and completely enveloped by the divine reality ("the mountain held

---

4   Esther, chapters 8–9.

over them like a jar"), we could not but commit ourselves to our divinely ordained mission and role.

But a thousand years later, we reaffirmed this commitment under entirely different conditions. The divine presence did not envelop us, compelling us to recognize its truth. On the contrary: the divine face was hidden. We were on our own, our commitment to G-d stemming wholly from within, from an inner choice to cleave to G-d regardless of how invisible He remained to us.

THE PROOF

This is not to say that on Purim a new, valid contract replaced the original, "contestable" one. If that were the case, what was the point of the revelation at Sinai? Certainly, the Torah was a binding commitment between ourselves and G-d for the 950 years from Moses to Esther. Rather, as the Talmud interprets the Book of Esther, "They fulfilled what they had already accepted." Purim was the fulfillment and corroboration of a truth that had already been established at Mount Sinai.

That truth is that our relationship with G-d is not bounded by reason. It is not dependent upon our understanding of it, or even upon our conscious awareness of its existence. It transcends our conscious self, residing in the very core of our souls.

This was why we were "compelled" to receive the Torah at Mount Sinai. Not because we would not have freely chosen to do so on our own, but because a consciously chosen commitment could not begin to express the true extent of our acceptance of the Torah. Our covenant with G-d extends beyond the finite realm of our conscious desires, embracing the infinite expanses of our supra-conscious self—the supra-conscious self that always "sees" G-d and is unequivocally aware of His truth. At Sinai, this supra-conscious self was revealed. Our conscious self, comprising but a minute corner of our soul, was completely overwhelmed and its "choice-making" mechanisms were completely silenced.

This was the true significance of what occurred when we "stood beneath the mountain." But for many centuries, the events at Sinai were open to misinterpretation. In our own minds, we remembered the event as a time when we were overwhelmed by the divine truth and compelled to accept it. Did this come from within, from a place in our souls not accessible by the conscious self? Or perhaps it came from without, from an external force which coerced us, against our own true will, into our covenant with G-d?

Then came Purim, with its total eclipse of all perceivable G-dliness. To remain a Jew, to remain loyal to our covenant with G-d, was a choice uninfluenced by any supra-conscious revelations. By choosing to accept the Torah under such circumstances, we affirmed that this is our true will. We affirmed that our "coercion" at Sinai was not against our will, but completely consistent with what we truly desire.

THE WILLFUL MITZVAH

Thus Purim revealed a new dimension to our observance of Torah, establishing it as a freely elected way of life, as opposed to a set of compelling duties. And this thousand-year difference is reflected in several of the *mitzvot* of Purim.

The festival observances are usually specially ordained *mitzvot* unique to their festival, such as sounding the *shofar* on Rosh Hashanah, or eating matzah on Passover. But there are two Purim observances about which there appears to be nothing "original," as they seem to be only extensions of general, year-round precepts of the Torah.

PURIM (4) 253

On Purim we send gifts of food, called *mishloach manot*, to friends and neighbors in order to promote fellowship and love between us. Another Purim *mitzvah*, *matanot l'evyonim*, is to seek out a minimum of two paupers and give them gifts of money. But to "love your fellow as yourself" and to give charity are year-round duties for the Jew.[5] What makes these distinctly Purim observances?

But the Torah does not obligate us to initiate gestures of friendship, or to seek out the needy. The commandment "Love your fellow as yourself" only mandates that when you do come in contact with your fellow, you treat him with love and respect. The laws of charity mandate that when a needy person asks for your help, you are obligated to render assistance. What is unique about the way we fulfill these *mitzvot* on Purim is that we actively seek out opportunities to do so.

For Purim emphasizes our *desire* to fulfill the commandments of the Torah. One who does something only out of a sense of duty may also do the deed properly and wholeheartedly. Conceivably, two individuals may be doing the same thing, one of them out of a deep-felt desire to do so and the other because he feels obligated, and we may not be able to tell the difference between the two. But what if no obligating circumstances exist? Does one pursue the deed and seek to obligate oneself? Here is where the difference is revealed—this is what distinguishes the willing, desirous actor from the merely obedient one.

The Purim *mitzvot* of *mishloach manot* and *matanot l'evyonim* highlight the "choice" element in our relationship with G-d: that this is a relationship not only bound by ties of duty but also cemented with the bond of will.

---

5   Leviticus 19:18; Deuteronomy 15:7–11.

A FEAST
AND
A FAST

*In the third year of his reign... the king made
a seven-day feast for all the people, from great
to small, who were to be found in Shushan
the capital...*   Esther 1:3–5

*Go and gather all the Jews who are to be
found in Shushan, and fast for my sake, do
not eat and do not drink for three days, night
and day; also I and my maidens will so fast...*
                                                   Esther 4:16

"Why was annihilation decreed on the Jews of that generation?" asks the Talmud, wondering at the ease with
which Haman obtained license to murder every Jew alive before
his plans were foiled by the events of Purim. One of the reasons
given is "Because they enjoyed the feast of the wicked [King
Achashveirosh]."[1]

The Jewish people had many compelling reasons to attend the
week-long banquet thrown by King Achashveirosh to celebrate
the consolidation of his rule over the 127 provinces of the Persian
Empire. All residents of the capital were invited, and to turn down
the royal invitation would have been a grievous insult—something

---

1   Talmud, *Megillah* 12a.

PURIM (5)

that a small minority, scattered throughout the empire and threatened by many enemies, could ill afford to do.

It is true that the Jews are not like the other nations of the world, whose fortune rises and falls with the political tide. In the words of the Talmud, "The people of Israel are not subject to 'fate,'"[2] as they are under the singular province of G-d. Indeed, our millennia of survival as a "lone sheep surrounded by seventy wolves"[3] belies every law of history. Yet it is also true that we are commanded to construct a natural "vessel" through which the divine protection and blessing might flow.[4] Surely the Jews of the Persian Empire recalled the words spoken by the prophet Jeremiah seventy years earlier, when they were first exiled from their homeland: "Seek the peace of the city to which I have exiled you, and pray for it... for in its peace shall you have peace." [5]

Even if participating in the feast of Achashveirosh was neither desirable nor necessary, was it forbidden by the laws of the Torah? The Book of Esther implies that it was not. We are told that Achashveirosh had instructed that no man be pressured to partake of any food or drink that did not agree with his constitution or his religious beliefs. He had even arranged for kosher food for his

---

2   Talmud, *Shabbat* 156a; et al.

3   *Midrash Rabbah*, Esther 10:11; et al.

4   Cf. Deuteronomy 15:18: "G-d will bless you in *all that you will do.*" See discourses on this verse by Rabbi Schneur Zalman of Liadi (*Sefer HaMaamarim* 5565, vol. II, p. 648; 5568, vol. I, p. 165), Rabbi DovBer of Lubavitch (introduction to *Derech HaChaim*), Rabbi Menachem Mendel of Lubavitch (*Derech Mitzvotecha, Mitzvat Tiglachat Metzora*, ch. 2), and Rabbi Shalom DovBer of Lubavitch (*Kuntres U'Maayan*, *Maamar* 17). Also see *Bread from Heaven* in vol. 1 of this series, pp. 106–118.

5   Jeremiah 29:7.

Jewish subjects, in full conformity with the exacting standards of none other than Mordechai himself![6]

In any case, even if there were something amiss in the Jews' attendance at the feast of Achashveirosh, was this a transgression so terrible that it warranted Haman being given license to "annihilate, slaughter, and destroy every Jew, young and old, women and children, in a single day"?

JEWS IN POLITICS

But the problem was not that the Jews participated in Achashveirosh's feast; it was, as the above-quoted talmudic passage emphasizes, that "they enjoyed the feast" of the Persian emperor.

As a people in exile we are indeed enjoined to employ the tools that, by natural criteria, aid our survival under foreign rule. But we must always remember that this is no more than a vessel or channel for G-d's protection. Politics, business, natural law—these are no more than a front, an elaborate facade which G-d desires that we construct to encase and disguise His supranatural providence of our lives. They are not something to be revered, much less to get excited about.

Yet the Jews experienced joy at having been invited to Achashveirosh's feast. As they took their places among the Persians, Medians, Babylonians, Chaldeans and the other nationalities of the realm, they felt content and secure. After seventy years of exile, they had "made it"; they were now a member of equal standing in the family of nations at Achashveirosh's table, with *glatt* kosher dinners issuing from the royal kitchens.

With their joy over their invitation to Achashveirosh's feast,

---

6   Esther 1:8; *Targum* ad loc.; Talmud, *Megillah* 12a.

the Jewish people disavowed their uniqueness as a nation under the special protection of G-d. Their feelings demonstrated that they now perceived the niche they had carved for themselves in the good graces of an earthly emperor as the basis for their survival. But the world they so gleefully embraced is a capricious one. One day a Jew, Mordechai, is a high-ranking minister in Achashveirosh's court, and another Jew, Esther, is the emperor's favorite queen; a day later, Haman becomes Prime Minister and prevails upon Achashveirosh to sign a decree of annihilation against the Jewish people.

THE REVERSAL

When Mordechai informed Esther of Haman's plans and urged her to use her influence with the king to annul the decree, Esther instructed him to "gather all the Jews who are to be found in Shushan, and fast for my sake, do not eat or drink for three days, night and day; also I and my maidens will so fast. Thus I shall go to the king, against the law..."[7]

It was forbidden, on pain of death, for anyone to go to the king unsummoned. Esther's only chance was to charm the king into not killing her and to turn him against his favorite minister in favor of her people. The last thing for her to do under such circumstances was to approach the king looking like a woman who had not eaten for three days!

So would dictate the norms of human nature and palace politics. But Esther recognized that the key to saving her people was to reestablish the relationship between G-d and Israel on its original, supranatural terms. The Jews must repent their regression to

---

7   Esther 4:16.

a political people; they must draw on their only true resource—G-d's love for them and His commitment to their survival. They must storm the gates of heaven with their fasting and prayer, and rouse G-d's compassion for His people.

Certainly, she must go to Achashveirosh and do everything in her power to make him change his mind. But this is merely a formality. She must go through the motions of doing things the "normal" way, because that is what G-d wants her to do—because this is the garment in which He chooses to cloak His salvation. But she will not appeal less fervently to G-d because she fears it will make her less attractive to Achashveirosh—that would be like a soldier discarding his rifle because it creases his uniform.

In this way, Esther rectified the error of those who enjoyed Achashveirosh's feast. They had exalted the facade, abandoning the essence of Jewish survival for the sake of the superficial vessel. Esther's approach to dealing with the threat of Haman's decree reiterated the true priority of the Jew, and evoked G-d's reassertion of His singular providence over the fate of Israel.

PURIM (6)   259

A
SINGULAR
PEOPLE

To the Jews was light, happiness, joy, and
prestige.   Esther 8:16

"Light," is Torah, "happiness" are the festivals,
"joy" is circumcision, and "prestige" are the
tefilin.   Talmud, Megillah 16b

$\mathcal{P}$ urim is about being different.

Haman complained to King Achashveirosh that
"There exists a singular people, scattered and divided among the
peoples in all the provinces of your kingdom, whose laws are different from those of all peoples..." A "singular people," Achashveirosh
agreed, different and unique despite their dispersion, cannot be
tolerated; he concurred with Haman that "it is not worthy that
the king let them be... it must be decreed that they be destroyed."[1]

The Jewish response to Haman's decree was to intensify their
singularity. Instead of continuing the assimilationist trends that
began with their exile from the Holy Land three generations earlier,[2] they rallied under the leadership of Mordechai with a renewed commitment to their uniqueness as G-d's people.

---

1   Esther 3:8–9
2   Indeed, the deterioration of their identity and commitment to G-d is
    what made them vulnerable to Haman's plot in the first place—see
    Talmud, *Megillah* 12a.

After relating the story of Haman's downfall and Israel's victory, the Book of Esther sums up the miracle of Purim in one sentence: "To the Jews was light, happiness, joy, and prestige." The Talmud interprets these words as a reference to the four primary distinguishing features of the Jewish people: the Torah, the festivals, circumcision, and *tefilin*. There are, of course, 613 *mitzvot* (divine commandments) and numerous principles, laws, and customs that comprise the Jewish way of life; but these four are singled out as the matrices of Jewish singularity.

Distinguishing Similarities

On the face of it, it would seem that the very opposite is the case— that these four precepts actually reflect Israel's *similarity* to other nations.

Scholarship is not unique to the Jews. Virtually every community and culture has its creed and philosophy, a canon of writings on which they are based, and an army of scholars and jurists to study, interpret, and apply it. Furthermore, even the Torah *qua* Torah is not confined to the people of Israel; several faiths are based on it, including two that embrace more than half the human race. Even some of the specifically Jewish expositions on Torah (such as the Talmud, the writings of Maimonides, or the teachings of kabbalah) are universally known and studied.

Festivals are also a common feature of all societies. It is true that only Jews eat matzah on Passover and sound the *shofar* on Rosh Hashanah; but the concept of a festival, of a date designated for commemoration and observance, is universal. Every nation, culture, and religion has its calendar of dates that mark the historical events that forged them, and commemorates these dates with appropriate rituals and customs.

PURIM (6)   261

The same is true of *tefilin*. Only the Jew binds these leather boxes
and straps on his arm and head as the symbol of his commitment
to G-d, but again the concept is a universal one. The married woman's ring, the soldier's uniform, the tribal chief's headdress—all
these are signs worn as a demonstrations of one's allegiance to a
certain group or cause. As for circumcision, it is a fairly common
procedure, practiced by many for health and other reasons.

And yet, the Torah, the festivals, circumcision, and *tefilin*—or,
as the Book of Esther refers to them, "light," "happiness," "joy," and
"prestige"—are the cornerstones of Jewish distinction. True, other
nations and societies have similar, or virtually identical, elements
in their doctrine and lifestyle; but the Jewish experience of these
selfsame elements is different from—even antithetical to—their
universal counterparts.

Indeed, this is the ultimate mark of distinction: how one differs from his fellows not in those areas in which he is obviously
different, but in those areas in which he is externally similar but
internally worlds apart.

FEMALE WISDOM

How does the Jew's Torah differ from the universal concept of
learning and scholarship? The key lies in the Book of Esther's
choice of the Hebrew word *orah*—which is the feminine form of
ohr, "light"—as a reference to Torah.

All wisdom, whose function is to illuminate and enlighten, is
light; but there is masculine light and feminine light. Masculine
light is self-generated, original, and aggressive; feminine light is
receptive. Masculine intellect is the mind exploring the unknown,
originating new ideas, debunking old misconceptions. Feminine
intellect is the mind opening itself to receive from a higher source,

ingesting a seed of revealed wisdom and developing the myriad of details and applications inherent within it.

Torah study employs both the masculine and feminine functions of the mind, but the greater, defining emphasis is on the feminine. Indeed, for all its talmudic hair-splitting, the Torah is not about intellect at all; the intellect is but a "garment," a medium by which to convey the suprarational essence it enclothes. To study Torah is, first and foremost, to surrender to a revelation of divine truth, to make one's mind a receptacle for the wisdom and will of G-d. The mind of the Torah sage is not a generator of ideas but a womb that receives the divine truth and then develops it as a rationally structured principle or law.

THE PRESENT PAST

The universal function of the festival or holiday is to celebrate and commemorate the past. The function of the Jewish festival is to reexperience the past — or rather, to unearth the timeless essence of a past event that makes it real to one's present existence.

The Jew does not merely remember the Exodus on Passover. Through his observance of Passover's divinely ordained *mitzvot*, he accesses the divine gift of freedom that the Exodus is, thereby achieving a personal "exodus" — a liberation from the constraints that enslave his own life. The same is true of the giving of the Torah on Shavuot, the attaining of forgiveness on Yom Kippur, and so on: The Jewish festival is a timeless window in time, making "past" events accessible and realizable.[3]

A festival is a "happy" occasion. But, again, the happiness experienced by the Jew, while superficially similar to the happiness of

---

3   See *Appointments in Time* in vol. 1 of this series, pp. 38–45.

PURIM (6)   263

the non-Jewish celebrant, is radically different. To the non-Jewish celebrant, a festival is an escape: immersing himself in a joyous and rosy past, he can temporarily disregard the trouble-and responsibility-burdened present. Little wonder that holidays often induce lavish spending, moral laxity, and barroom brawls.

The Jew also transcends the present on his festivals, and for him, too, this is a source of joy. But this is not an escapist joy. On the contrary, it is the joy of penetrating to the essence of one's present-day self to discover the timeless self within. So the Jew's festival joy is a disciplined joy, a joy that shatters external barriers while amplifying internal focus. A joy that makes the celebrant more responsible, more caring, more committed.[4]

The holiday on which the distinction of Jewish festival celebration most vividly comes to light is Purim. On Purim the Jew is commanded to "drink until one cannot distinguish between 'cursed be Haman' and 'blessed be Mordechai.'"[5] Drinking, especially drinking to the point of irrationality, is generally anathema to the Jew; it is on Purim that we are accorded the rare sight of a drunk Jew. And the Purim drunk is a sight worthy of beholding: emotionally uninhibited yet morally controlled; rationally incoherent yet spiritually true.[6]

THE JOY OF SACRIFICE

Circumcision is a fairly common practice. Many undergo it for reasons of health, others for religious reasons. In either case, the decision to circumcise is a question of weighing the pain against

---

4   See citation from Maimonides on p. 109 above.
5   Talmud, *Megillah* 7b; *Shulchan Aruch, Orach Chaim* 695:2.
6   See the following essay, *The Purim Drunk*.

the gain. The procedure is painful, there is an element of risk involved (as with all surgical procedures), and it is said to lessen sexual pleasure. The American who decides to circumcise his or her son might say: "Certainly, there are disadvantages, but the health benefits make it worthwhile." The Moslem boy might say: "Sure it hurts, but it gains me entry into heaven."

What is unique about the Jew is that the circumcision itself is perceived as something positive and desirable. Anyone who has ever attended a *brit milah* understands why the Book of Esther refers to it as a "joy"—one does not get the impression that we are "paying a price" for some future reward.[7] It is the giving of self for G-d that the Jew joyfully desires, not the results or rewards of the sacrifice.

Indeed, circumcision can be said to be representative of all "sacrifice"—it is a giving of oneself in the most physically literal sense. The concept of sacrifice is, of course, a universal one —people constantly make sacrifices for the sake of their future, their loved ones, their country, their convictions. But sacrifice is always either for the sake of some future return (in one's lifetime or in the hereafter) or an inescapable duty. For the Jew, sacrifice at G-d's behest is a joy.

Hence the amazing, rationally inexplicable phenomenon: Virtually *all* Jews, regardless of religious commitment,

---

7   In fact, what is commonly perceived as the greatest disadvantage of circumcision is, to the Jew, one of its benefits. Almost 800 years ago, Maimonides wrote (in his *Guide for the Perplexed*, part 3, chs. 35 & 49) that circumcision enhances a person's spiritual sensitivity through its tempering of his corporeal drives. (This is not to say that this is the reason *why* the Jew circumcises himself. Yet as with all *mitzvot*, which are essentially suprarational divine decrees, we also identify the spiritual and material benefits which naturally result from a life lived in conformity with the design of its Creator—as we might speak of the spiritually healthy kosher diet or the enhancement of the marriage relationship through the laws of *niddah*.)

PURIM (6)   265

practice circumcision. Jews who define themselves as "atheists" and "non-practicing" circumcise their sons. Jews who emerged from seven decades of Soviet rule bereft of any knowledge or appreciation of Judaism immediately arranged circumcisions for themselves, their children, and their grandchildren. Circumcision, to the Jew, is about what he is, not about what it does for him.

BLACK BOXES

The fourth definer of Jewish uniqueness are the *tefilin* — black leather boxes, containing scrolls inscribed with selected passages from the Torah, that are bound on the arm and head as the symbol of our relationship with G-d.

Every community and culture has garments and adornments that are worn as symbols of its identity. Because of what they represent, these naturally reflect their wearers' conceptions of beauty and prestige: the shimmering gold of the bride's ring, the impeccable tailoring of the general's uniform, the rainbow of colors in a people's national dress, all embody a person's or group's pride in who they are.

The *tefilin* stand out in their austere simplicity. Two austere boxes, which Torah law mandates to be unadorned and painted black. For the *tefilin* convey not pride, but our subjugation of our mind, heart, and deeds to the Almighty.

Yes, *tefilin* are the prestige of the Jew, but the Jew's prestige does not lend itself to aesthetic depiction. Jewish prestige lies in our servitude to G-d, in the binding of our intellect, emotions, and talents to the supernal will.

Purim celebrates the salvation of a singular people: a people whose learning, festivities, sacrifices, and badge of honor are so similar, yet so unique, in the family of man.

THE PURIM
DRUNK

Rava said: A person is obligated to drink on Purim until he does not know the difference between "cursed be Haman" and "blessed be Mordechai."
Talmud, Megillah 7b

oy is a perpetual presence in the life of the Jew. "Serve G-d with joy,"[1] exhorts the Psalmist, and the Jew is constantly serving G-d, whether through the actual performance of a *mitzvah* (divine command), by doing "all your deeds for the sake of Heaven," or by "knowing Him in all your ways."[2]

On this level, however, joy is not an activity in its own right, but an accessory to another endeavor. The endeavor is to serve G-d; in order to serve G-d in the most optimal manner, one's deeds must be saturated with joy. (For example: Giving charity begrudgingly aids the recipient materially, but demoralizes him; giving cheerfully nurtures the pauper's body and refreshes his soul).

---

[1] Psalms 100:2.

[2] "All your deeds shall be for the sake of Heaven" (*Ethics of the Fathers* 2:12), means that everything one does is a means to that end: one eats in order to have the energy to pray, one earns money in order to give to charity, etc. "Know Him in all your ways" (Proverbs 3:6) expresses the ideal that our "mundane" activities are not only a means to a G-dly end, but are themselves ways of experiencing G-d. For example, one's business activities are not only a means toward earning money which will in turn be used to do a *mitzvah*, but an opportunity to observe the hand of G-d in the dozens of "lucky coincidences" that add up to a single business deal and gain a deeper appreciation of His providence.

PURIM (7)   267

A second, higher joy is that connected with the festivals, our "seasons for rejoicing."[3] Here, our joy is not an accompaniment to some other activity, but the substance of the endeavor itself. On the festivals, it is a *mitzvah* to be joyful.

Nevertheless, this is still not joy for its own sake. The objective remains the fulfillment of the will of G-d, who commanded that the festivals be celebrated joyously.

A third, yet higher type of joy is the joy associated with the month of *Adar*. "When *Adar* commences, one increases in joy"[4] not because it is a *mitzvah*, but as a natural response to the joyous nature of the month. The joy of *Adar* is not joy with an objective, but simply a state of being.

Finally, the epitome of joy is achieved on Purim, when "A person is obligated to drink on Purim until he does not know..." Not only is this joy not qualified by any objective, it is free even of the objective to be joyous. On Purim, we are so consumed with joy that we are oblivious to all, including the fact that we are rejoicing.

A Drunken Jew?

But can a Jew actually drink, as the talmudic sage Rava enjoins, "until he does not know the difference between 'cursed be Haman' and 'blessed be Mordechai'"? Our grandparents knew that *shikker is ah goy*—Jews don't get drunk. How, indeed, do we reconcile the *halachah* (Torah law) to get drunk on Purim[5] with our under-

---

3   *Kiddush* for the festivals; cf. Deuteronomy 16:14–15.
4   Talmud, *Taanit* 29a.
5   The question of whether and how Rava's injunction to drink on Purim —to the point that "one does not know..."—should be implemented in practice is a matter of disagreement between various *halachic* authorities. The question, however, is not what Rava means, but whether or

standing of the kind of life that the Torah commands us to lead? Can we allow ourselves to relinquish control over our behavior one day a year, or even once in a lifetime? Can we abnegate our awareness of the difference between good and evil for even a single moment?

The drunk that most people know (from TV, the neighborhood bar, or, unfortunately, in their own homes) is a vulgar and often violent creature. Is this because drinking generates vulgarity and violence? Obviously not. What excessive drink does is cloud the intellect and incapacitate cognition, freeing the passions of the heart from their internal jurist and regulator. The drunk who starts a fight at the slightest provocation is also inclined to do so when sober; it is only that when sober, his mind is capable of recognizing the folly of the deed and of controlling his behavior. The drunk who shouts obscenities in the street is only expressing

---

not the Talmud contains another opinion, contrary to Rava's (see Ran and *HaMaor* on Talmud, *Megillah* 7b; *Bach* and *Beit Yosef* on *Tur, Orach Chaim*, 695). Many of the greatest *halachists* follow Rava's ruling. Maimonides writes: "What is the obligation of the [Purim] feast? That one should eat meat...and drink wine until one is drunk and falls asleep from drunkenness" (*Mishneh Torah, Laws of Megillah*, 2:15). Rif, Rosh, *Tur,* and *Shulchan Aruch* all cite Rava's dictum without any qualification. Rema, on the other hand, comments that "There are others who say that one need not become that drunk, but rather that one should drink more than is one's custom." Rema concludes: "Whether one drinks more or drinks less, the main thing is that his intention is for the sake of Heaven."

To summarize: All *halachic* authorities are unanimous in ruling that it is a *mitzvah* to drink, and drink to excess, on Purim, though there are differences of opinion as to whether the obligation is to get as drunk as Rava enjoins, or to a lesser degree. In any case, the concept of becoming intoxicated on Purim to the point that one's reason is totally incapacitated is a legitimate *halachic* position, which requires understanding regardless of whether or not it is accepted in practice.

thoughts and urges he harbors all the time, but which he usually has sense enough to keep to himself.

But if the intellect stems what is worst in us, it also stymies what is best in us. We all know the feeling of being unable to "find the words" to adequately convey our thoughts, which are so much more subtle than the words and idioms available to us in the languages in which we speak and write. But reason itself is a "language" which captures but an infinitesimal fraction of what is sensed and felt by our deepest selves. To live a rational life is to filter our essentially suprarational self through the constricting lens of reason. To confine our relationship with G-d, our people, and our family to the realm of the intelligible is to repress all but a finite facet of their infinite depth and scope.

For 364 days a year, we have no other choice. Our mind must exercise control over our emotions and behavior, lest the animal in us rage rampant and trample to death all that is good in ourselves and our world. Furthermore, we need the mind not only as guardian and regulator, but also as facilitator of our highest potentials. It is the mind that navigates the workings of nature, enabling us to sustain and improve our lives in the service of our Creator; it is the mind that recognizes the goodness and desirability in certain things and the evil and danger in others, thereby guiding, developing, and deepening our loves and aversions, our joys and fears; it is with our minds that we imbibe the wisdom of the Torah, allowing us an apprehension of the divine truth.

If the mind does all these things within the finite parameters of reason, concealing galaxies of knowledge with every ray of light it reveals and suppressing oceans of feeling with every drop it distills, it nevertheless remains the most effective tool we have with which to access the truths that lie buried in the core of our souls and reside in the subliminal heavens above.

But there is one day in the year in which we enjoy direct, immediate access to these truths. That day is Purim. The Jew who rejoices on Purim—who rejoices in his or her bond with G-d without equivocation—has no need for reason. For then the Jew is in touch with his or her truest self—a self before which our animalistic drives are neutralized, a self which requires no medium by which to express itself and no intermediaries by which to relate to our source in G-d.

On Purim we no longer require the mind to tell us the difference between "cursed be Haman" and "blessed be Mordechai"; we are above it all, relating to the divine truth that transcends the bifurcation of good and evil. On Purim, the mind is utterly superfluous, something which only encumbers the outpouring of our soul, something which only quantifies and qualifies that which is infinite and all-pervading. So we put the mind to sleep for a few hours, in order to allow our true self to emerge.

The Marriage Broker

A time-honored institution in many Jewish communities is the *shadchan*, or marriage broker. The *shadchan* is more than a "dating service"; he or she is a middleman who accompanies the deal from its inception all the way to its conclusion. The *shadchan* meets with the respective families; notes their desires, demands, and expectations; and presents them with a proposal. The *shadchan* then presides over the negotiations, convincing each side to make the concessions required so that the deal can be closed. Then the boy meets the girl, and the *shadchan*'s work begins in earnest. The boy wanted someone more beautiful, the girl wanted someone with better prospects. The *shadchan* explains, cajoles, clarifies, and exaggerates; he or she gives long speeches on love and what is important in life. The *shadchan* succeeds in arranging a second meeting and then a third. More meetings follow, and the engagement is formalized. In the critical period between the engagement and the wedding, the *shadchan* advises, encourages, assuages doubts, and heads off crises.

Then comes the wedding. The bride and groom stand under the canopy, and the *shadchan* is the proudest person in attendance. At this point, the *shadchan* is discreetly taken aside and told: "Thank you very much for what you did. Without you, this union could never have been achieved. Now take your commission and get out of our lives. We don't want to see you ever again."

In the cosmic marriage between G-d and Israel, the intellect is the *shadchan*. Without it, the relationship could not have been realized. But there comes a point at which the *shadchan*'s brokering is no longer needed, for something much deeper and truer has taken over. At this point, the *shadchan*'s continued presence is undesirable, indeed intolerable.

Purim is a wedding at which the *shadchan* has been shown the door, a feast celebrating the quintessential bond between G-d and Israel. There are "drunks" at this feast who have achieved a state of cognitive oblivion; but in no other way do they resemble the stereotypical drunk.

You will not see them hurling fists, insults, or obscenities at each other, or slobbering over their domestic troubles. What you will see is outpourings of love to G-d and to man. You will see pure, unbridled joy.

You will see people who are disciplined and aware: not with a discipline imposed by the watchdog of reason, not with an awareness brokered by the mind, but with a discipline and awareness which derive from the uninhibited expression of the spark of divine truth that is the essence of the human soul.

THE BEGINNING
AND THE END

I set G-d before me always.

Psalms 16:8

One who is of good heart is festive always.

Proverbs 15:15

"The beginning is embedded in the end," say the kabbalists, "and the end in the beginning."[1]

Everything has a beginning and an end. The beginning precedes all other stages and particulars, and the end follows them all. But the beginning, if it is a true beginning, contains the seeds of all that is to follow; and the end, if it is a true end, is the culmination and fulfillment of everything that preceded it.

So the beginning and the end each embody the entire process, each in its own way. Each is the mirror image of the other: A true understanding of the beginning reveals the end, while a true understanding of the end uncovers the essence of the beginning.

Orach Chaim ("the way of life") is the first of the four sections of the *Shulchan Aruch*, the codification of Torah law that has been universally accepted as the most basic guide to Jewish life. As its name indicates, *Orach Chaim* is the section that deals with the day-to-day life of the Jew: the daily prayers, the laws of *tzitzit* and *tefilin*, the observance of Shabbat and the festivals, and so on.[2]

---

1 *Sefer Yetzirah* 1:7.

2 The other three sections of the *Shulchan Aruch* deal with subjects that

PURIM (8)   273

Like every book, *Orach Chaim* has a beginning and an end. And
here, too, "The beginning is embedded in the end, and the end in
the beginning."

THE COULD'VE-BEEN PURIM

In the opening lines of *Orach Chaim,* the *Shulchan Aruch* quotes
Psalms 16:8: "I set G-d before me always." "This is a great principle
in Torah," it goes on to say. "When a person sets in his heart that
the great king, the Holy One, blessed be He, whose presence fills
the entire world, stands over him and sees his deeds... he will immediately achieve a fear of G-d and submission to Him..."[3]

Orach Chaim closes with another verse—from Proverbs 15:15:
"He who is of good heart is festive always." The subject under discussion is *Purim Katan,* the "minor" Purim. The "major" Purim—
the fourteenth of the month of *Adar*—is the day established by
Mordechai and Esther as a day of "feasting and rejoicing"[4] in commemoration of the Purim miracle. But approximately once every
three years, the Jewish calendar produces a "leap year" containing not one but two months called *Adar*—*Adar* I and *Adar* II.[5]
Which is the "real" *Adar* and which is the addition? When should
Purim be celebrated—in *Adar* I or *Adar* II? The Talmud rules that

---

   are generally the province of rabbis and judges: *kashrut,* marriage and
   divorce, civil law, and the like.

3 *Shulchan Aruch, Orach Chaim* 1:1. The *Shulchan Aruch* consists of a
   code compiled by Rabbi Joseph Caro (1488–1575), and the annotations
   and glosses appended to it by the Rema (Rabbi Moshe Isserles, approx.
   1525–1572). The "beginning" and "end" cited in this essay are from the
   Rema's glosses on the first and last *halachot* of *Orach Chaim.*

4 Esther 9:22.

5 See *Jewish Time* in vol. 1 of this series, pp. 195–202.

Purim is to be celebrated in *Adar* II.[6] Nevertheless, the fourteenth day of *Adar* I is also a special day. It is "the minor Purim"—the day that would have been Purim had the year not been a leap year.

What do we do on *Purim Katan*? We don't read the *megillah*, nor is there any special *mitzvah* to send food-portions to friends or give gifts to the poor, as is the case on Purim proper. The *Shulchan Aruch* cites an opinion that one should increase in festivity and joy, but rules that there is no *halachic* obligation to do so. "Nevertheless," the *Shulchan Aruch* continues, "a person should increase somewhat in festivity, in order to fulfill his duty according to the opinion that it is obligatory." By way of explanation, it concludes with the quote from Proverbs: "One who is of good heart is festive always." Joy and festivity are always desirable, so if an opportunity presents itself in the form of a day that might have been Purim— the most joyous day of the year—one should certainly rejoice and celebrate.[7]

The Two Constants

The beginning is embedded in the end, and the end is embedded in the beginning.

I set G-d before me always. One who is of good heart is festive always. Always, always. Always fearful, always joyous.

The foundation of all is fear of G-d. Unless we perceive ourselves as constantly in the presence of G-d, unless we tremble before the immensity of the import G-d places on our every act, there can be no *Shulchan Aruch*, no divine law for life.

---

6   Talmud, *Megillah* 6b.
7   *Shulchan Aruch, Orach Chaim* 697:1.

PURIM (8)   275

The culmination of all is joy. When we conclude the *Orach Chaim* section of *Shulchan Aruch*—when the "the way of life" becomes *our* way of life from morning to night and from Passover to Purim[8]— our every moment becomes a link in a chain of perpetual joy. We are realizing our purpose in life, actualizing our deepest potentials; and there is no greater joy.

But fear is not only the beginning, nor is joy only the end. As the foundation of all, the fear of G-d pervades our every hour and deed, from the most solemn moments of Yom Kippur to the ine- briating joy of Purim. As the culmination of all, joy, too, pervades every nook and cranny of Jewish life: Also in the "days of awe" of Rosh Hashanah and Yom Kippur, we are enjoined to "tremulously rejoice."[9]

Fear and joy are as diverse as any two emotions to reside in the human heart. But the *Shulchan Aruch* synergizes them as a perpet- ual state of joyous trembling and tremulous joy. For the beginning is embedded in the end, and the end is embedded in the beginning.

---

8 Though the Jewish year begins on Rosh Hashanah, the calendar of the festivals is reckoned by the Torah as running from Passover to Purim (Talmud, *Rosh Hashanah* 2a), and this is the format followed by the *Shulchan Aruch*. See *Our Other Head* in vol. 3 of this series, pp. 4–12.
9 Psalms 2:11; *see Likutei Torah, Devarim* 47a; et al.

INSIDE TIME

*A Chassidic Perspective on
the Jewish Calendar*

VOLUME THREE

PASSOVER TO ELUL

Inside Time
Volume Three: Passover to Elul

First Edition — 2015

Published by
Meaningful Life Center
ISBN 978-1-886587-52-6

© Meaningful Life Center 2015

INSIDE TIME

*A Chassidic Perspective on
the Jewish Calendar*

VOLUME THREE

PASSOVER TO ELUL

Based on the works of the Lubavitcher Rebbe
Adapted by Yanki Tauber

Publication of this book
was made possible
through the generosity
of
Kevin Bermeister and family

Lovingly dedicated
in memory of
Avraham Chaim ben Ze'ev — Allan Bermeister

Niftar 18 Elul 5774

CONTENTS*

VOLUME III: PASSOVER TO ELUL

CHAPTER XVII: NISSAN I
The Miraculous Month

> *Essay 1*: **Our Other Head**................................4
> The month of *Nissan* as the year's other "Rosh Hashanah."

> *Essay 2*: **The Coiled Spring**...........................13
> The spiritual significance of the season of spring, and its connection with the Exodus.

> *Essay 3*: **The Great Shabbat**...........................15
> The significance of the miracle of *Shabbat HaGadol*, and why its date of commemoration is set according to the day of the week rather than the day of the month.

CHAPTER XVIII: PASSOVER 23
Freedom, Faith, and Nationhood

> *Essay 1*: **Endless Lives**..................................28
> If the goal of the Exodus was the covenant at Sinai with its multitude of restrictions on human life, why is Passover the festival of freedom?

> *Essay 2*: **Midnight**...34
> Why the Exodus took place at midnight. The two *mitzvot* by which the people of Israel "deserved" their redemption—the Passover offering and circumcision.

---

* A full Table of Contents of the chapters and essays for all three volumes of *Inside Time* is provided at the beginning of Volume I.

CONTENTS   III

Essay 3: **The Festival of the Child** 42

The child as the personification of freedom. The "Four Sons" of the *Haggadah*, and the elusive fifth child of our day.

Essay 4: **Hillel's Paradox** 47

To be or to belong? The role of the Passover offering in our birth as a people, and the ever-present dichotomy between individual and communal identity.

Essay 5: **Bread of Faith** 53

The three matzot and the four cups of wine of the *seder*. Simple faith vs. understanding and appreciation.

Essay 6: **A Speck of Flour** 62

The all-out prohibition against leaven on Passover. The progression from the "barley offering" of the second day of Passover to the "two loaves" offering of Shavuot. The custom to eat matzah *sheruyah* ("wetted matzah") on the eighth day of Passover.

Essay 7: **The Vegetarian Era** 71

The significance of the "great wealth" the people of Israel took out of Egypt. The three staples of the *seder*—the Passover offering, matzah, and *maror*—in the Jew's approach to materiality.

Essay 8: **The Muddy Path** 80

The deeper significance of the "Splitting of the Sea" on the seventh day of Passover. Two paths through the "sea" of our internal hidden worlds.

Essay 9: **Miriam's Song** 86

The womanly strain in the "Song at the Sea," and the woman's role in the redemption from Egypt and the future redemption

Essay 10: **Passovering Time** 91

Remembrance and anticipation; the eighth day of Passover and its connection with the messianic redemption

IV INSIDE TIME

CHAPTER XIX: THE COUNTING OF THE OMER 95
Growth and Self-Refinement

> *Essay 1*: **The Journey** 98
> The history and significance of the *omer* count. The "days" and "weeks" in the journey from Exodus to Sinai as a collusion between the sublimity of the goal and the mortality of the journeyer.

> *Essay 2*: **Accumulative Time** 109
> What happens to time when we count it? Instead of "running out," it accumulates.

> *Essay 3*: **A Month of Mitzvot** 111
> The specialness of the month of *Iyar* in that each of its 29 days has its own *mitzvah*.

CHAPTER XX: PESACH SHEINI 113
Second Chance

> *Essay 1*: **The Distant Road** 115
> The differences between the first and second Passovers as the difference between the orderly and compartmentalized life of the righteous person, and the frenzied and inclusive life of the "returnee."

> *Essay 2*: **The Missing Complaint** 126
> The cry and demand, "Why shall we be deprived?"; our right and duty to protest G-d's imposition of the state of *galut* (exile) and His diminishing of His presence in our lives.

CHAPTER XXI: LAG BAOMER 129
The Mystic Dimension

> *Essay 1*: **24,000 Plus One** 132
> Rabbi Akiva's disciples and Rabbi Shimon bar Yochai; reconciling love with truth.

CONTENTS V

Essay 2: **Long-Range Missile** 138
The custom of playing with bow-and-arrow on Lag BaOmer; the mystical "inner soul" of Torah—reaching inward to fly outward.

Essay 3: **The Many and the Few** 144
Rabbi Shimon bar Yochai's approach of "Torah is one's sole occupation" and its relevance to otherwise occupied lives.

CHAPTER XXII: SHAVUOT 151
Law, Truth, and Peace

Essay 1: **Doing Nothing** 155
The first six days of *Sivan* and the series of preparations for receiving the Torah. Torah as the divine wisdom and will, requiring an absolute *bittul* (self-abnegation) on the part of its student.

Essay 2: **Truth** 162
Relative and absolute truth. The deeper significance of Rav Yosef's statement, "Were it not for this day (Shavuot), how many Yosefs are there in the marketplace!"

Essay 3: **Peace** 166
Torah as the harmonizing force in a diverse and fragmented world. The connection of Torah with the number "3."

Essay 4: **Law** 170
The "limitations" imposed by Torah on human behavior as the ultimate liberators of human potential.

Essay 5: **The Breakthrough** 171
The giving of the Torah at Sinai as the revocation of the "decree" that had separated the supernal and the earthly. The concept of a *cheftza shel kedushah*, a physical object made holy through its actualization of a divine desire and command.

VI   INSIDE TIME

Essay 6: **Real Estate**...177
The legal battle between Moses and the angels when Moses came to
bring the Torah "down from heaven." The transformation of Torah
from a spiritual manifesto into the instrument of our development of
the physical world into a "dwelling" for G-d.

Essay 7: **The Mathematics of Marriage**........................187
Torah as the vehicle of relationship between G-d and man; as a collaboration of divine revelation and human intellect.

Essay 8: **The Three Names of Shavuot**........................193
The three names of Shavuot—"The Time of the Giving of Our Torah," "The Festival of Weeks," and "The Day of the First Fruits"—as
they describe the Torah's influence upon our behavior, character, and
environment.

Essay 9: **The Phantom Days of Shavuot**.......................201
The "substitute days" of Shavuot (*Sivan* 7–12). Why Shavuot has no
special *mitzvah*. The concept of a "chosen people."

CHAPTER XXIII:
THE THREE WEEKS AND TISHAH B'AV 207
Exile and Redemption

Essay 1: **The Pinch**..212
The deeper reason why the three weeks from *Tammuz* 17 to *Av* 9 are
referred to as *bein ha'metzarim,* "between the strictures."

Essay 2: **Good Grief**..214
The difference between *merirut*, constructive grief, and *atzvut*, destructive grief.

Essay 3: **Postponed**...215
The essence of the fast day as "a day of goodwill before G-d."

Essay 4: **Difficult Days**...220
The making and worship of the Golden Calf on *Tammuz* 16 and 17. The
two related events of the Torah's translation into Greek, and the temporary triumph of Shammai's stringent approach to Torah law.

CONTENTS VII

Essay 5: **Shabbat of Vision** 234

Rabbi Levi Yitzchak of Berdichev's metaphor for the "Shabbat of Vision" that precedes the Fast of *Av* 9.

Essay 6: **The Subterranean Temple** 239

Our 3,000-year journey, along the "hidden, convoluted tunnels" built by King Solomon in the Holy Temple.

Essay 7: **The Legalities of Destruction** 244

Was G-d's destruction of the Holy Temple a violation of Torah law? The Ninth of *Av* as the birthday of Moshiach. The practice of "calculating deadlines" for Moshiach's arrival.

Essay 8: **The Intimate Estrangement** 253

The "three weeks of rebuke" and the "seven weeks of consolation" as the mind and heart of our relationship with G-d. The meaning of an enigmatic passage in the Talmud describing the destruction of the Holy Temple as a most intimate moment in the marriage of G-d and Israel.

Essay 9: **Regret** 262

The meaning of the talmudic statement that G-d "regrets" the creation of *galut* (exile). The "split personality" of the Jew in exile.

Essay 10: **Cholent** 268

With all the benefits of *galut*, we still cry: Enough already!

CHAPTER XIV: THE 15TH OF AV 273
Love and Rebirth

Essay 1: **The Day of the Breaking of the Ax** 275

The mystery of *Av* 15: What is the significance of five relatively minor historical events that occurred on this day, and why do they signify it as our "greatest festival"?

Essay 2: **The Dancing Maidens of Jerusalem** 285

The three types of prospective brides who danced in the vineyards on *Av* 15—the "beautiful," those of "good lineage," and the "ugly"—and their counterparts in the Jew's love of G-d.

Essay 3: **No and Yes**...291

The Sinaitic and messianic phases of our marriage to G-d. The correlation between Torah's positive and negative laws and the positive/negative architecture of our binary world.

CHAPTER XXV: ELUL 295

Compassion and Introspection

Essay 1: **A Haven in Time**.................................298

The month of *Elul* as a "city of refuge." The spiritual meaning of "unintentional murder."

Essay 2: **Month of the Bride**.............................301

Elul's astral sign of "virgin" and how it relates to the dynamics of the cosmic marriage of G-d and Israel.

Essay 3: **The King in the Field**..........................304

The month of *Elul* as a time when "the King is in the field." The relationship between the 39 forbidden labors of Shabbat and the 39 constructive acts of the building of the *mishkan* ("sanctuary"), and why these are categorized primarily as "the order of bread-making." *Elul* as a month of "spiritual workdays."

ADDENDA 315

The Jewish Calendar (Infographic)......................316

Sources...318

Glossary..324

Index...360

CHAPTER SEVENTEEN

Nissan
The Miraculous Month

The Jewish year is a cycle with two beginnings, a body with two heads. The first two days of the month of *Tishrei* are Rosh Hashanah, the "head of the year." But six months later is the month of *Nissan*, designated by the Torah as the "head of months" and the "first of the months of the year."

For while *Tishrei* marks the creation of the natural world and the onset of human history, *Nissan* marks the beginning of Jewish time. On the first of *Nissan* in the year 2448 from creation, G-d spoke to Moses and Aaron in the land of Egypt and instructed them to establish a calendar based on the monthly birth of the new moon. Two weeks later, on *Nissan* 15, the people of Israel exited the land of Egypt to begin their march through history as "a nation of priests and a holy people." *Nissan* is also the month when, one year after the Exodus, the Sanctuary (forerunner of the Holy Temple in Jerusalem) was erected in the Sinai desert to serve as the abode of the divine presence and the focus of the Jew's endeavor to serve G-d.

Nissan's thirty days are all but consumed with our commemoration of these signature events in our history. The first thirteen days of the month are distinguished by daily readings of the "*nassi*," which describe the inauguration of the Sanctuary. *Shabbat HaGadol* ("the great Shabbat") commemorates the mutiny of the Egyptian firstborn on the Shabbat before Passover, and culminates a month-long study of the laws and customs of Passover with the traditional pre-Passover sermon delivered in the synagogue. *Nissan* 14 is "the eve of Passover," followed by Passover itself and its eight-day celebration of freedom on *Nissan* 15–22.

"Since the majority of the month has passed in holiness," concludes the *Shulchan Aruch* (code of Jewish law), "the entire month is observed as a holy and festive time" throughout which we omit the recitation of *tachanun* (the confession for sins) from our daily prayers and refrain from scheduling unjoyous occasions such as eulogies or fast days.

Three essays comprise our chapter on *Nissan*. The first, <u>Our Other Head</u>, examines *Nissan*'s role as the "head of months," and the parallels and differences between the *Nissan*-to-*Adar* year and the *Tishrei*-to-*Elul* year. The second essay, <u>The Coiled Spring</u> looks at the spiritual significance of spring and its connection with the month of the Exodus.

On the face of it, the events of the Shabbat before Passover are but one of many miracles that paved our way to redemption. But as <u>The Great Shabbat</u> demonstrates, this was a miracle unique among the miracles of Jewish history, resulting in an "appointment in time" that is unique among the special dates on the Jewish calendar.

OUR OTHER HEAD

G-d spoke to Moses and Aaron in the land of Egypt, saying: "This month shall be to you the head of months — the first of the months of your year."   Exodus 121:–2

Rabbi Eliezer says: The world was created in Tishrei... *Rabbi Joshua says: The world was created in* Nissan.   Talmud, Rosh Hashanah 10b–11a

The Talmud relates an exchange between the wise men of Athens and Rabbi Joshua. The Greek philosophers challenged the talmudic sage to identify the exact center of the world. Rabbi Joshua pointed to a field atop a nearby hill, and said: "In the middle of that field is a well. That well is the center of the world. You can take ropes and measure it, if you wish."[1]

As every schoolchild knows today, the earth is a sphere, meaning that its every point can be considered its center. If a certain point is regarded as the "top" or "bottom" of the globe, or a certain half designated as its "eastern" or "western" hemisphere, these are expressions of a particular historical or conceptual view of our world. In purely geometrical terms, the surface of a sphere has no

---

[1]   Talmud, *Bechorot* 8b.

NISSAN (1)   5

definitive top, bottom, or center, just as a circle is a line with no
definitive beginning or end.

The time we inhabit is also circular in form. As we travel through
time, we come in contact with the various qualities imbued in it by
its Creator: freedom on Passover, awe on Rosh Hashanah, joy on
Sukkot, and so on. But each year we return, like a traveler circling
the globe, to the same point in the annual cycle at which we stood
a year earlier. Theoretically, any point in this cycle can be regarded
as its "beginning."

This explains a curiosity of the Jewish calendar. We know that
the Jewish year begins on the first of *Tishrei*—a day we observe
as Rosh Hashanah, "the head of the year"—and ends twelve (or
thirteen)[2] months later, on the 29th of *Elul*. But if the "head of the
year" is on the first of *Tishrei*, why does the Torah (in Leviticus 23)
refer to *Tishrei* as the *seventh* month of the year? And why is the
month of *Nissan*, occurring midway through the *Tishrei*-headed
year, designated (in Exodus 12) as the "head of months, the first of
the months of your year"?

But like a sphere with two poles, the Jewish year has two
"heads," each of which is equally its beginning. Our annual journey
through time is actually two journeys—a *Tishrei*-to-*Elul* journey,
and a *Nissan*-to-*Adar* journey. Each day on the Jewish calendar
can be experienced on two different levels, for it simultaneously
exists within these two contexts.[3]

---

2   A 13th month is added seven times in 19 years to keep our lunar-based
    calendar in sync with the solar seasons. See *Jewish Time* in vol. 1 of this
    series, pp. 195–202.

3   *Tishrei* 1 and *Nissan* 1 are the two primary "heads" of the year. In addi-
    tion, the year has other "heads" as well, such as the "Rosh Hashanah for
    trees" on *Shevat* 15 and the "Rosh Hashanah for animal tithes" on *Elul*
    1 (Talmud, *Rosh Hashanah* 2a). Rabbi Shalom DovBer of Lubavitch
    declared Kislev 19 to be the "Rosh Hashanah for Chassidism." Also, a

For example: In the *Tishrei*-to-*Elul* year, Yom Kippur is the climax of the "ten days of repentance" that begin on Rosh Hashanah;[4] whereas on the *Nissan*-to-*Adar* calendar, Yom Kippur is the second "giving of the Torah," culminating a 120-day process that begins on Shavuot.[5] In the *Tishrei*-to-*Elul* year, the seventh day of Passover is the cosmic "birth of the souls," following their "conception" on Shemini Atzeret, the "eighth day" of Sukkot;[6] whereas in the *Nissan*-to-*Adar* year, Passover is the first festival,[7] commencing a cycle that culminates in Purim, the "last miracle" and final frontier in our quest for connection with G-d.[8]

A MIRACULOUS PEOPLE

As already noted, both these beginnings for the Jewish year are referred to in the Torah as "heads." The first of *Tishrei* is Rosh Hashanah, "the head of the year," while the month of *Nissan* is designated as "the head of months."

---

person's birthday is his personal Rosh Hashanah, marking the beginning and culmination of each complete year of life.

4 See *Day One* in vol. 2, pp. 65–71 of this series.

5 See *The 120-Day Version of the Human Story* in vol. 2, pp. 37–43 of this series.

6 *Pri Etz Chaim, Shaar HaLulav*, end of chapter 8; *Tanya, Igeret HaKodesh* 20 (p. 130b); *Likutei Torah, Tzav* 16c.

7 Talmud, *Rosh Hashanah* 2a.

8 Ibid., *Yoma* 29a. See vol. 2 of this series, *The Thousand-Year Difference* (pp. 247–253) and *Esther's Story* (pp. 235–239). In fact, the order of the festivals basically follows the *Nissan*-to-*Adar* year, *Nissan* 1 being "the head of the year in regard to festivals" (Talmud, *Rosh Hashanah* 2a), while the placement of the festivals in the context of the *Tishrei*-to-*Elul* year is the exception rather than the rule. This is consistent with the fact that the festivals are set by the day of the month, and *Nissan* is the "head of months" (see footnote 11 below).

NISSAN (1)   7

The head is the highest part of the body, both in the literal, spatial sense, as well as in the sense that it is the seat of its loftiest and most sophisticated faculties. More significantly, it serves as the body's nerve and command center, providing the consciousness and direction that guides the body's diverse components toward a unified goal.[9]

And the Jewish year has not one but two heads. For Jewish life embraces two different—indeed, contrasting—modes of existence, each with its own nerve-center and "headquarters."

The "head of the year" with which we are all familiar—the one on which we sound the *shofar* and pray for a healthy and prosperous year—occurs on the first of *Tishrei*. The first of *Tishrei* is the anniversary of G-d's creation of the world, particularly His creation of man.[10] On this day we reaffirm our commitment to G-d as our creator and king, and ask that G-d inscribe us in the book of life.

But if the first of *Tishrei* is the first day of human history, the month of *Nissan* marks the birth of Jewish time. On the first of *Nissan*, 2,448 years after the creation of Adam, G-d commanded His first *mitzvah* to the fledgling nation of Israel—to establish a calendar based on the monthly lunar cycle.[11] On the fifteenth of that month, the Jewish people exited the land of Egypt and embarked on their seven-week journey to Mount Sinai.

---

9   See *The Neurology of Time* in vol. 2 of this series, pp. 5–7.

10   See *The Man in Man* in vol. 2 of this series, pp. 8–16.

11   Hence, the Jewish month was born on the first of *Nissan*. In contrast, the seven-day week is a product of G-d's creation of the world in the seven days that culminated in the month of *Tishrei*. Thus, the *Nissan*-headed and *Tishrei*-headed years reflect another duality in our experience of time: the fact that every day in our life simultaneously exists within the seven-day weekly cycle, the matrix of "natural time," and within the monthly-lunar cycle, the vector of "miraculous time." See *The Great Shabbat* on pp. 15–21 below.

The Jew is a citizen of G-d's world—a status he or she shares with all other peoples and all other creations. As such, our "head of the year" is the first of *Tishrei*, the birthday of mankind and the Rosh Hashanah of the natural world. But we also inhabits another reality—a reality born of the supernatural events of the Exodus, the splitting of the Red Sea, and the divine revelation at Sinai. This dimension of our lives has its own "head"—the miraculous month of *Nissan*.

For the first twenty-five centuries of human history, the basic, "natural" relationship between Creator and creation held sway. The Torah records miracles and supernatural events prior to the Exodus, but these are exceptions, temporary departures on the part of G-d from His normal manner of running the world in accordance with the predefined formula we call "the laws of nature." The Exodus, on the other hand, produced the people of Israel, whose very existence is a perpetual miracle. The Jew makes "redemption" a constant, living a life in which the miraculous is the norm. In the words of the Midrash,

> *When G-d chose His world, He established heads of months and years; and when He chose Jacob and his children, He established the head of the month of redemption.* [12]

G-d of the Exodus

This is why when G-d revealed Himself to us at Mount Sinai, He proclaimed: "I am G-d your G-d, who has taken you out from the land of Egypt, from the house of slavery." [13] Would it not have been

---

12   *Midrash Rabbah, Shemot* 15:11.

13   The first of the Ten Commandments, Exodus 20:2.

more appropriate, ask the commentaries, for G-d to introduce Himself as the creator of the heavens and the earth? Is not the fact that we owe our very existence to G-d more significant than the fact that G-d took us out of Egypt?[14]

But G-d as the creator of the heavens and the earth, G-d as the author of nature, is the G-d that Israel shares with the rest of creation. At Sinai, however, G-d did not speak to us as the G-d of creation, but as the G-d of the Exodus. At Sinai, a new chapter was opened in divine-human relations, as G-d and the people of Israel committed themselves to a *miraculous* relationship—a relationship that does not recognize the dictates of convention and normalcy.

It is for this reason that our sages question the very inclusion of the first 25 centuries of history in the Torah. "Why does the Torah begin, 'In the beginning [G-d created the heavens and the earth]'?" asks the Midrash. "It should have begun, 'This month shall be to you [the head of months],' which is the first *mitzvah* commanded to Israel."[15] If the Torah is the document that outlines our mandate as a people not constricted by the laws of nature and history, of what relevance are the events of the pre-Exodus era? And even if they are of historical and educational value, should the Torah *begin* with these stories?

CROSS-REFERENCES

And yet, the Torah does not begin with that first *mitzvah*, commanded on the first of *Nissan*, but with the creation of the world on the first of *Tishrei*. Our covenant with G-d, though a product

---

14   Cf. Ibn Ezra on Exodus 20:1.
15   Cited in Rashi on Genesis 1:1.

of the Exodus and of a *Nissan*/miraculous character, has its roots in the natural soil of *Tishrei*.

In fact, the Exodus itself also has its beginnings in the month of *Tishrei*. The process of our liberation from Egypt began on the first of *Tishrei*, when the hard labor imposed upon our forefathers by the Egyptians ceased six months before they actually left Egypt.[16]

The reverse is also true: the creation of the natural world on *Tishrei* has its origins in the month of *Nissan*. Our sages tell us that while the physical world was created in the six days that culminate in the first of *Tishrei*, the "thought" or idea of creation was created six months earlier (conceptual "months," that is, since physical time is itself part of the physical creation), on the first of *Nissan*.[17]

In other words, the natural and the miraculous time-systems are mutually interconnected, each serving as the basis for the other.

As Jews, we follow both cycles, simultaneously inhabiting both worlds. On the one hand, even the most "natural" aspects of our lives are predicated upon the miraculous, and are permeated with a norm-transcending vision. On the other hand, our most miraculous achievements are grounded in the natural reality.

---

16   Talmud, *Rosh Hashanah* 11a.

17   The Talmud (Ibid., 10b–11a) cites a debate between two sages: "Rabbi Eliezer says: The world was created in *Tishrei*... Rabbi Joshua says: The world was created in *Nissan*." The kabbalists explain that Rabbi Eliezer and Rabbi Joshua are not debating the date of G-d's actual creation of the universe. Rather, both sages agree that the physical world was created in *Tishrei*, and that the "idea" of creation was created in the month of *Nissan*. Where the two sages differ is on the question of priority and emphasis: Is the day that the physical universe was completed to be regarded as the primary anniversary of creation, or is the world's true date of birth the day that it was conceived in the divine mind?

NISSAN (1)   11

For our mission in life can be achieved only by being a part of the
natural world and, at the same time, rising above it to transcend its
strictures and limitations.

The Paradox

Our mission in life is to transform the very nature of reality; in
the words of the Midrash, to build "A dwelling for G-d in the lower realms."[18] "This," writes Rabbi Schneur Zalman of Liadi in his
Tanya, "is what man is all about; this is the purpose of his creation
and the creation of all the worlds"—that we transform the "lower
realms" (i.e., the natural, material world which, by its nature, conceals the face of its Creator) into an environment receptive to the
divine truth; into a place where the goodness and perfection of
G-d is "at home" and is the dominant reality.[19]

But here comes the paradox: Are we ourselves part of these
"lower realms" we are to transform, or are we a step above them?
If we are part and parcel of the material world, how can we truly
change it and uplift it? As the talmudic axiom goes, "A prisoner
cannot release himself from prison"[20]—if he himself is bound by
its parameters, from where might derive his ability to supersede
them? On the other hand, if we are, in essence, transcendent beings, existing beyond the confines of the natural reality, then whatever effect we have upon the world cannot truly be considered "a
dwelling for G-d in the lower realms." For the world *per se* has not
been transformed—it has only been overwhelmed by a superior

---

18 *Midrash Tanchuma, Nasso* 16.
19 *Tanya*, chapter 36. See *Real Estate* on pp. 177–186 below, and sources
    cited there.
20 Talmud, *Berachot* 5b.

force. The true meaning of a "dwelling in the lower realms" is that the "lowly realms" themselves change, from within.

So to achieve His aim in creation for "a dwelling in the lower realms," G-d created the Jew, a hybrid of the *Tishrei* and *Nissan* realities. For only in incorporating both these time-cycles in our lives, combining a norm-defying approach with a natural-pragmatic *modus operandi*, can we achieve the redemption of ourselves and our world. Only by drawing from above to change from within can we make our world a home for G-d.[21]

---

21 Another way of viewing the *Nissan-Tishrei* duality is in terms of the difference between the *tzaddik* (perfectly righteous person), and the *baal teshuvah* (penitent, or "master of return"). See *Daughters Near and Far* in vol. 2, pp. 135–147 of this series. Also see footnote 16 on p. 94 of that volume.

THE COILED SPRING

And Moses said to the people: "Remember this day on which you went out from the land of Egypt, from the house of slavery... Today you are going out, in the month of spring."

Exodus 13:3–4

"Keep the month of spring," instructs the Torah, "and make a Passover-festival for G-d your G-d; for in the month of spring G-d took you out of Egypt."[1] Indeed, the imperative to preserve *Nissan*, the month of the Exodus and Passover, as "the month of spring" has far-reaching implications for the arrangement of the Jewish calendar, necessitating the insertion of an additional month before *Nissan* seven times in a 19-year cycle.[2]

Keep the month of spring...

Observing the bare branches and the frozen earth of winter, one sees not a sign of life and growth; the juices of nature appear to have run dry. But come spring, the pent-up energies break the surface. Suddenly, practically before our eyes, a seemingly dead world becomes bedecked in green and vitality.

Obviously, the lifeless gray of winter was a deceptive front. Behind a veneer of inertia, the sap of life had coursed along, garnering its energies, rejuvenating its potency. Winter turns out to

---

[1]   Deuteronomy 16:1
[2]   See *Jewish Time* in vol. 1 of this series, pp. 195–202.

have been a retreat for the sake of a forward thrust, a recoil only to spring forth life and renewal.

...for in the month of spring G-d took you out of Egypt.

For more than two centuries, the people of Israel languished under the yoke of Pharaoh and sank deeper and deeper in the morass of Egyptian paganism and depravity. The seedling planted by Abraham, Isaac, and Jacob appeared to have atrophied. Generations of slavery had deadened their hearts, numbed their minds, and stifled all outward signs of spiritual life.

Then came the Exodus. In a flash, a clan of slaves blossomed into a free and holy people. In just forty-nine days, 210 years of repression were undone, and a nation of ex-idolaters stood at Mount Sinai ready and worthy to be elected as G-d's chosen people and to serve as a guiding light for all of humanity.

The spiritual winter of Egypt was now shown to have harbored and nurtured the Jewish soul below its frozen surface, forging it in the smelting pit of exile and endowing it with the fortitude to fuel Israel's birth and growth as a nation.

Keep the month of spring...

In every individual's life there are patches of barrenness and fruitlessness. Yet to turn one's back on these seemingly "dead" periods is to forgo the most precious resources that life can yield. Buried beneath these fallow surfaces lie the germinating seeds of renewal, awaiting discovery and utilization as the springboard for the attainment of otherwise unimaginable heights.

THE GREAT SHABBAT

The Shabbat before Passover is called "The Great Shabbat" (Shabbat HaGadol), *because a great miracle occurred on that day...*

Why was [the commemoration of the miracle] not instituted on the tenth of Nissan, regardless of whether it falls on Shabbat or on a weekday, as all other commemorative dates were instituted?

Shulchan Aruch HaRav, Orach Chaim 430:1

 cursory look at our calendar indicates that we measure time in an awkward and inconvenient manner.

To distinguish a certain day, we refer to two different time-cycles: the seven-day weekly cycle, and the 29.5 day lunar cycle, which give us an alternating 29- and 30-day month. These two time-systems are asynchronous—a day's place in the month has no bearing on its place in the week.[1] So if the 10th of *Nissan* falls on Shabbat

---

1   There *are* certain dates on the Jewish calendar that are confined to certain days of the week: for example, the first day of Passover (*Nissan* 15) cannot fall on a Monday, Wednesday, or Friday. But this is only because our calendar today follows a preset system, and is configured so as to avoid certain undesirable confluences of the two cycles (for example, if the seventh day of Sukkot would fall on Shabbat, we would not be able to fulfill the *mitzvah* of *aravah*). In essence, however, if our months were guided solely by the phases of the moon, any monthly date could fall on any day of the week.

one year (as it did in the year of the Exodus), it may fall on a Monday the next year; and if the Shabbat before Passover is *Nissan* 10 one year, it might be *Nissan* 14 the next. Would it not have been much simpler to employ a single cycle in which a fixed number of "weeks" make up the "month," so that any given day may be placed in a single, unvarying context?

But life itself is not a singular state of being, or even a series of compatible states. Life is a multifaceted phenomenon, with certain facets diverging from, or even clashing with, the others. The absence of synchrony between the week and the month is due to the fact that these two time-cycles reflect two very different areas of our lives.

The Miraculous Month

G-d created the universe in seven days: six days of creative involvement, followed by a seventh day of rest and withdrawal. As a result, a seven-day cycle of work and rest has been ingrained in creation as nature's inner clock.[2] This is the significance of the *mitzvah* of Shabbat: that we attune our lives to G-d's creation, alternating a six-day exercise of our own creative powers with a day of withdrawal from material creativity.

But G-d wanted more: more than our development of His world in harmony with its built-in cycle of creation, more than our realization of our inborn potentials. He wanted us to be miracle-workers: to be forever reinventing and recreating ourselves, forever challenging the status quo imposed by nature and habit, forever transcending the strictures of normalcy and convention. To this end, G-d introduced lunar time into our lives, instructing

---

2   See *The Seventh Element* in vol. 1, pp. 77–88, of this series.

NISSAN (3)   17

us, in the first *mitzvah* commanded us as a people, to establish a
calendar based on the phases of the moon.

In contrast with the regular, monotonous week, the lunar
month is forever changing and regenerating itself. As the moon
wanes and waxes in the nighttime sky, the lunar month follows
suit, growing with the expanding moon in the first half of the
month, reaching its climax with the "full moon" on the 15th, dwindling to nothingness with the shrinking moon of the second half
of the month, and being reborn on the night of the "new moon."
Indeed, the Hebrew word for "month," *chodesh*, means "renewal."
For while the week represents the natural potential of man, the lunar month stands for what is innovative, original, and miraculous
in our achievements.[3]

This explains why all the festivals on the Jewish calendar are
set in accordance with the day of the month, rather than the day
of the week.[4] The festivals represent a transcendence of the natural order—the Exodus on Passover, the miracles of Chanukah and

---

3   The difference between the week and the month can also be seen in the
     history of the two time-cycles: The week was established with the cre-
     ation of nature, while the Jewish lunar month came into being 2,448
     years later with the miraculous month of *Nissan*, the month of the Ex-
     odus and the splitting of the Red Sea. See *Our Other Head* on pp. 4–12
     above.

4   There is one festival—the festival of Shavuot—that is not designated
     by the Torah as a certain day of a certain month. Instead, the Torah in-
     structs us to count seven weeks (i.e., 49 days), beginning on the second
     day of Passover, and observe Shavuot on the 50th day; indeed, the very
     name "Shavuot" means "weeks." However, these are not natural weeks,
     but "weeks" created by counting days in groups of seven. Shavuot is not
     consigned to a certain day of the natural week—it is the 50th day after
     the first day of Passover; and since the first day of Passover has a lunar
     date—*Nissan* 15—Shavuot is ultimately a product of the monthly cycle
     (see *The Journey* on pp. 98–108 below).

Purim, and so on. These days are landmarks of the miraculous in the terrain of time, signposts indicating stores of norm-surpassing potential. Every year, as we arrive at these junctures in our journey through time, we are afforded the opportunity to tap these reservoirs of the supernatural and translate them into personal miracles.

THE MUTINY OF THE FIRSTBORN

There is, however, one exception to this rule—one case in which the date of a miraculous event in our history is identified for posterity by its place in the weekly cycle. This exception is *Shabbat HaGadol*, "the great Shabbat," which commemorates a "great miracle" that transpired shortly before our Exodus from Egypt.

That miracle occurred on Shabbat, the 10th of *Nissan*, 2448 (1313 BCE), five days before the Exodus on *Nissan* 15 of that year.[5] But instead of commemorating the miracle on the lunar date of its original occurrence, as is done with all other festivals and commemorative dates of the Jewish calendar, the event is remembered each year on the Shabbat before Passover.

Various reasons are given for this departure from the standard practice.[6] But the name given to this day, "the great Shabbat,"

---

5   The Exodus occurred on a Thursday (see Talmud, *Shabbat* 87a, and *Tosafot*, ad loc.), meaning that, in that year, *Nissan* 10 was the Shabbat before Passover.

6   One reason is that 40 years after the Exodus, Moses' sister, the prophetess Miriam, died on *Nissan* 10, and a fast day was instituted on that date to mourn her passing; so the celebration of the miracle was relegated to the weekly cycle (*Magen Avraham, Orach Chaim* 430; *Shulchan Aruch HaRav*, ad loc.). Another reason is that since another miracle, the splitting of the Jordan River, is commemorated on *Nissan* 10, the miracle of the firstborn was relegated to the Shabbat before Passover (*Taz*, ad loc.).

NISSAN (3)

suggests a deeper reason as well—a reason connected with the very significance of Shabbat and the weekly cycle.

What happened on that "great Shabbat," five days before the Exodus?

On the eve of their departure from Egypt, the Jewish people were commanded to bring a "Passover offering" (*korban pesach*) to G-d:

> *On the tenth of this month, every man shall take a lamb for his family, one lamb for each household... It should be held in safekeeping until the fourteenth of this month; the entire community of Israel shall then slaughter their sacrifices in the afternoon. They shall take the blood and place it on the two doorposts and on the lintel... They shall eat the meat that night, roasted over fire, with matzot and bitter herbs...*
>
> *I will pass through Egypt on that night, and I will smite every firstborn in Egypt, man and beast... The blood will be a sign for you on the houses where you are staying; I will see the blood and pass over you—there will not be any deadly plague among you when I strike the land of Egypt.*[7]

The Talmud relates what happened when thousands of Jews began rounding up their lambs on the 10th of *Nissan*. The lamb was worshipped as a deity in ancient Egypt, so this caused quite a commotion. The firstborn of Egypt, who held the key social and religious positions in Egyptian society, confronted the Jews, and were told: We are preparing an offering to G-d. In four days hence, at the stroke of midnight, G-d will pass through Egypt in order to

---

7   Exodus 12:3-13.

execute the tenth and final plague. All firstborn will die, and the Jewish nation will be freed.

The firstborn of Egypt, who had already witnessed the first nine plagues occurring exactly as Moses had warned, were understandably alarmed. They approached Pharaoh and his generals and demanded that the Jews be freed immediately. When Pharaoh refused, the firstborn took up arms against Pharaoh's troops, killing many of them. This event is alluded to by the Psalmist, who sings: "[Offer thanks to G-d,] who smote the Egyptians with their firstborn."[8]

WHERE'S THE MIRACLE?

What was so "great" about this miracle? Indeed, what *was* the miracle? That the firstborn took up the cause of the Israelites was a natural and understandable development. After all, all of Egypt had nine times witnessed the fulfillment, with deadly accuracy, of the previously forecasted plagues. (What is amazing is the extent of Pharaoh's self-destructive stubbornness, possible only because G-d had "hardened his heart".)[9] Furthermore, the firstborns' mutiny was not successful. Though they inflicted heavy casualties on Pharaoh's forces, they failed in their attempt to force the freedom of the Jewish people. Our conditions in Egypt were unchanged by the events of "the great Shabbat."

This explains why this event belongs to the "weekly" or natural of our life's time-cycles, rather than to its "monthly" or miraculous orbit. The "great miracle" was in fact a perfectly natural

---

8 Psalms 136:10; Talmud, *Pesachim* 87a; *Shulchan Aruch HaRav, Orach Chaim* 430:1.

9 Exodus 10:1.

occurrence, both in the predictability of its development, and in that it did not in any way change the essential nature of the prevailing circumstances.

Yet we mark the event as a miracle, indeed as a uniquely "great miracle." For true greatness lies not in overturning the circumstances of one's existence, but in working within these circumstances to "miraculize" them.

In the miraculous trajectory of our lives, we transcend the natural and the normal. But a greater feat, a more miraculous miracle, is to elevate and perfect the natural and the normal; to create, within their confines and parameters, a higher and more transcendent reality.

This is what we achieved in Egypt on the "great Shabbat." We were slaves to the Egyptians; yet we refused to be intimidated by a society that deified the material and proclaimed a lamb a god, and we proceeded to slaughter the idol of our masters. Without hesitation we explained our actions to the leading citizens of the superpower that ruled us.

On that "great Shabbat," a transformation took place. Not a transformation that overturned the natural parameters of our reality, but a transformation in which that very reality was converted to our cause. By acting courageously in our fulfillment of the divine will, we caused the most prestigious segment of Egyptian society to press for our redemption.

Whether or not their effort was successful is far less relevant than the fact that the natural and normal became instruments of the miraculous. Indeed, the fact that it was *not* successful places the greater emphasis on the true significance of what happened on that "great Shabbat"—the Shabbat that most powerfully exemplifies the "natural time" dimension of our lives.

CHAPTER EIGHTEEN

Passover

Freedom, Faith, and Nationhood

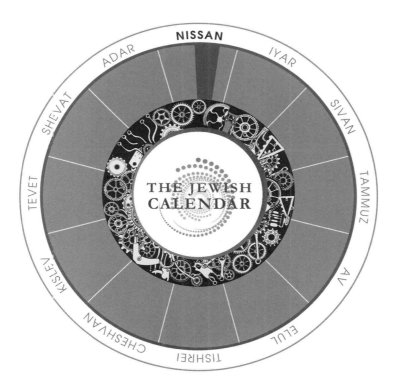

Nissan 15 to 22

"Has such a great thing ever been," proclaimed Moses forty years later, "or has the like of it ever been heard? Has G-d ever endeavored to come and take for Himself a nation from the womb of a nation, amidst trials, signs, wonders and battles... as G-d has done for you in Egypt before your eyes?"

A nation from the womb of a nation. On the 15th of *Nissan* in the year 2448 from creation (1313 BCE), a new entity, the people of Israel, was born, delivered by G-d "from slavery into freedom, from darkness into a great light, from bondage into redemption." Seven days later, our rescue from Egypt was complete when the sea split to allow us passage and drowned Pharaoh's armies in its waters.

The eight-day festival of Passover (seven days in the Land of Israel), which straddles these two events, is our annual "appointment in time" to access the freedom of the Exodus. But first, all leaven—which represents the self-bloating egotism that is the greatest obstacle to true freedom—must be eradicated from our homes and hearts. In the weeks before Passover, the Jewish home is the scene of all-out war against every last breadcrumb seeking refuge between the floorboards. On the eve of *Nissan* 14, we conduct a solemn search for any survivors; on the following morning, we burn the proceeds of that search and renounce all ownership of any leaven which might have escaped our notice.

When the Holy Temple stood in Jerusalem, the Passover offering was brought there on the afternoon of *Nissan* 14; today, it is commemorated with the "shankbone" placed on the *seder* plate, and with the *afikoman*— a portion of matzah eaten in its stead at the end of the *seder* meal. Nissan 14 is also the "fast of the firstborn," who remember that G-d "passed over" them when He killed all firstborn Egyptians in the last of ten plagues visited upon Egypt.

On the eve of *Nissan* 15 we conduct the *seder*— the "order" of observances which recall and relive the events of the Exodus. We tell the story of enslavement and liberation in response to the "Four Questions" asked by the child. We eat the matzah, the unleavened "bread of faith" in which we taste the poverty of servitude, the freedom of redemption, and the self-effacing commitment of a people taken by G-d as His own. We eat *maror* (bitter herbs) dipped in *charoset* (a paste of apples, nuts, and wine) to recall the bitterness of slavery and the "mortar and bricks" of our labor in Egypt. We drink the four cups of wine representing the "four expressions of redemption" in G-d's vow to make us a free people, and pour a fifth cup for Elijah the Prophet, herald of the future redemption.

On second night of Passover, begins the 49-day "*omer* count" to the festival of Shavuot, linking the Exodus to its objective and *raison d'être*, the giving of the

Torah at Mount Sinai. On the eighth day of Passover we read Isaiah's prophecy on the coming of Moshiach and partake of "Moshiach's feast"; for on this day we are granted a foretaste of the day that will eternalize the freedom gained at the Exodus, institutionalized at Sinai, and pursued for 33 centuries by the nation that G-d took from the womb of a nation amidst great trials, signs, and wonders.

What is "freedom"? Is the person who accepts constraints on his behavior and internal life more free or less free than his uninhibited fellow? *Endless Lives* finds the answer in its examination of the nature of our enslavement in Egypt, and of the ultimate purpose of the Exodus.

Midnight examines the significance of that point in time as the exact moment of the Exodus. *The Festival of the Child* explains the special connection of the child to our annual experience of freedom, discusses the "four children" of the Passover *seder*, and identifies a "fifth child" unique to our day. *Hillel's Paradox* addresses the dichotomy between our individual and communal identities, as reflected in the laws governing the bringing of the Passover offering.

Passover is the "festival of matzot" and a time of utter intolerance for the tendency of flour and water to ferment and swell when mixed. *Bread of Faith* delves into the significance of the *seder*'s three matzot and four cups of wine. *A Speck of Flour* explains the war on leaven and the unexpected appearance of "wet matzah" on the eighth day of Passover. *The Vegetarian Era* defines the three staples of the *seder*—matzah, bitter herbs, and the meat of the Passover offering—as three approaches to the "great wealth" we carried out of Egypt at the time of the Exodus.

Our chapter's last three essays discuss themes associated with the closing days of Passover. The deeper significance of the "splitting of the sea" is explored in *The Muddy Path*, and the woman's role in redemption in *Miriam's Song*. Memory and prophecy make their two-pronged onslaught on the tyranny of time in *Passovering Time*, lending insight into the connection of Passover's eighth day with the age of Moshiach.

ENDLESS LIVES

Go to Pharaoh... and say to him: G-d, the G-d of the Hebrews, has sent me to you, saying: "Let My people go, that they may serve Me."
Exodus 7:15–16

(O)ur sages call the festival of Passover *zeman cheiruteinu*, "the time of our freedom."[1] For the Exodus from Egypt was more than one of the many salvations of Jewish history; it was the first and ultimate bestowal of freedom upon man. Before the Exodus, there was no true freedom; and having experienced the Exodus, the Jew is forever and invariably free, and no force on earth can enslave him.[2]

What is "freedom"? A most basic definition would be that freedom is a state in which a person is not subject to any constraints upon his behavior and self-expression. But if that were all there was to freedom, Passover would hardly qualify as "the time of our freedom." For while the Exodus freed us from Pharaoh and his taskmasters, it also committed us to a greater, more embracing servitude.

"When you take this nation out of Egypt," G-d said to Moses from the burning bush at the foot of Mount Sinai, where He first revealed Himself to him and commissioned him to redeem the people of Israel, "you shall serve G-d at this mountain." Standing

---

1 From the prayers of the day, authored by the "Great Assembly" in the 4th century BCE.
2 Maharal, *Gevurot Hashem*, chapter 61.

PASSOVER (1)

before Pharaoh, Moses did not merely demand in the name of G-d, "Let My people go," but, "Let My people go, that they may serve Me." The purpose of the Exodus was to bring the children of Israel to Mount Sinai to be bound in a covenant with G-d as His "nation of priests and holy people"—a covenant delineated by the 613 commandments of the Torah.[3]

INTERNAL SLAVERY

To understand the freedom achieved by the Exodus, we must first examine the deeper significance of Israel's enslavement in Egypt.

Our sages state that "all exiles are called by the name of Egypt."[4] The name *Mitzrayim* (Hebrew for "Egypt") means "boundaries" and "constraints." Every time we are limited—by a foreign power, by a hostile or merely alien environment, by the corporeality of our bodies, the deficiencies of our character, or by the subjectivity of our minds—we are in *mitzrayim*. If freedom means the absence of constraint, *mitzrayim* is the limitation of man on all levels— physically, emotionally, intellectually, morally, or spiritually.

The person who has all externally-imposed constraints neutralized but remains a prisoner of his or her own habits, compulsions, biases, and ego, is hardly free. In fact, he or she is even more a slave than the literal slave. For this person's *mitzrayim* is internal. He or

---

3   Exodus 3:12, 7:16, and 19:6. Thus the festival of Shavuot, which marks the day on which we received the Torah at Sinai, is the only festival that has no calendar date: The Torah designates Shavuot not as a certain day of a certain month—as it does all other festivals—but as the 50th day after Passover. This is to emphasize that Shavuot is an extension and fulfillment of Passover, as the purpose of the Exodus was realized only on the day we stood at Sinai.

4   *Midrash Rabbah, Bereishit* 16:7.

she carries it wherever they go, the keys to their prison clenched tight in their own fists.

The only way to achieve freedom from this internal enslavement is by tapping a power that transcends all that is petty and narrow in oneself, and at the same time is the source and empowerer of all that is lofty and true within oneself. The Torah, G-d's blueprint for creation and G-d's script for a soul's ultimate self-expression, is that higher power. In the words of the Talmud, "There can be no free person, other than one who occupies himself with Torah."[5] The physical freedom attained by the children of Israel at the time of the Exodus was but the prelude for the ultimate freedom they achieved when they stood at Mount Sinai and committed themselves to a life defined and guided by Torah.

THE PILFERING OF INFINITY

But there is yet a deeper dimension to our enslavement in Egypt, and to the freedom we attained with the Exodus and with our acceptance of the Torah.

The first chapter of the book of Exodus describes the enslavement of the children of Israel by the Egyptians as follows:

> They embittered their lives with hard labor, with mortar and bricks and in all manner of work in the field; all the work to which they subjected them was crushing labor.[6]

The phrase "crushing labor" (*avodat perech*) appears repeatedly in the Torah's account of the Egyptian exile, in the text of the

---

5   Ethics of the Fathers 6:2.
6   Exodus 1:14.

PASSOVER (1)   31

Passover *Haggadah*, and in the symbolism of the *seder* observances.[7] What is "crushing labor"? Maimonides defines it as "work that
has no limit and no purpose."[8] Work—even the most difficult
work—that has a defined end-point and a defined objective is not
as demoralizing as endless, futile work. The Egyptians, whose aim
in enslaving the Jewish people was to break their spirit, refused to
impart any schedule, logic, efficiency, or utility to their work. They
worked them at the most irrational hours, gave to each of them the
task most ill-suited to his or her abilities, and repeatedly destroyed
what they had built only to order them to rebuild it again and
again.[9]

Pharaoh had whip-wielding taskmasters to enforce his work-
edict. Today, our world has "progressed" to the point that millions
voluntarily subject themselves to "work that has no limit and no
purpose": work that spills over from its official work-hours to
invade every moment and thought of the day; work that is dictated not by the capabilities and resources of the worker but by
status and vogue; work that is not a means to an end but a "career"—a self-perpetuating enterprise that becomes its own aim
and objective.[10]

---

7   *Karpas*, the vegetable dipped in salt-water at the beginning of the *sed-
    er*, isd an acronym for *samech perech*—"sixty myriads (600,000) en-
    slaved by crushing labor."
8   *Mishneh Torah, Laws of Servitude* 1:6; see *Hagahot Maimoniot*, ad loc.
9   See *Midrash Tanchuma, Vayeitzei* 9; *Midrash Rabbah, Shemot* 1:14–15.
10 Therein lies the deeper significance of Pharaoh's decree, "Every son
    that is born you shall cast into the Nile" (Exodus 1:22). The Nile, which
    irrigated the fields of rain-parched Egypt, was the mainstay of its econ-
    omy and therefore its most venerated god. "Throwing one's child into
    the Nile," in the spiritual sense, means to immerse him in a culture
    which deifies the "career"—which worships the earthly vehicles of ma-
    terial sustenance as an end in itself.

By nature, the physical self is finite and pragmatic. What drives it to, and sustains it in, such infinite labor? What can be the source of its infinite perseverance in pursuit of the ever-receding goal of material "success"? Such boundless commitment and energy can only have one source: the "spark of G-dliness" that is the essence of the human soul. Only the soul, which draws upon the infinity of its divine source, can exhibit such vigor; only the soul, whose commitment to its Creator is not contingent upon envisionable goals and calculable objectives, can be the driving force behind "work that has no limit and no purpose."

Thus, the soul that finds itself imprisoned within a materialistic life is subjected to a double exile. Not only is it prevented from expressing its true self, but it is forced to express itself in ways that are *contrary* to its true desires. Not only is it constrained by a material self and world—it also suffers the usurpation of its quintessential powers to drive the material self's mundane labors. Not only is the soul's capacity for infinite and objectiveless commitment inhibited and repressed—it is distorted into an endless quest for material gain.

The Discipline of Freedom

The road out of Egypt passes through Sinai.

The Torah regulates our involvement with the material world. It instructs that we may—and should—work, create, and do business six days a week; but that on the seventh day, not only must all work cease, but we should assume a state of mind in which "all your work is done."[11] On a daily basis, it tells us to set aside inviolable islands in time devoted to Torah study and prayer. And at

---

11 Exodus 20:9, according to Rashi, ad loc.

PASSOVER (1)   33

all times, a multitude of Torah laws define the permissible and the forbidden in business and pleasure.

The Torah also enjoins us to "eat of the toil of your hands"[12] — to invest only our marginal faculties in the business of earning a living, leaving our choicest talents free to pursue more spiritual goals. And it insists that all material pursuits should be but a means to an end—but a vessel to receive G-d's blessings, and a tool to aid us in our life's work of bringing sanctity and G-dliness into our world.[13]

In so restricting our physical lives, the Torah liberates our souls. By limiting the extent and the nature of our material involvements, Torah extricates our capacity for infinite commitment from its material exile, freeing it to follow its natural course: to serve G-d in a manner of "no limit and no purpose" in the positive sense—in a manner that transcends the parameters of self, self-gain, and our very concept of "achievement."

---

12   Psalms 128:2.
13   See *Bread from Heaven* in vol. 1, pp. 106-118 of this series. Also see *The Many and the Few* on pp. 144-149 below.

MIDNIGHT

So said G-d: "At midnight, I shall go out into
the midst of Egypt."   Exodus 11:4

t midnight of *Nissan* 15, 2448 (1313 BCE), G-d broke the last manacle of Egyptian bondage by killing all of the Egyptian firstborn, and the nation of Israel was born as a free people.[1] The time is significant: Twice the Torah emphasizes that the event occurred exactly at midnight, and to this day, "midnight" is a factor in our annual reexperience of the Exodus at the *seder* held each year on the eve of the 15th of *Nissan*.[2]

But can an event actually take place at midnight? It would seem not. If midnight is the line that divides the night in two, then it is not a time period of any duration. No matter how minute a time-particle we might envision as occupying the center of the night, this particle can itself be halved; its first half would belong to the first half of the night and its second half to the post-midnight half of the night. Indeed, a more literal translation of the Hebrew words *kachatzot halailah*, rendered above as "at midnight,"

---

1   The Jews physically left Egypt twelve hours later, at midday of *Nissan* 15. But from the moment the firstborn were killed, the last vestige of Egyptian resistance to their release crumbled and they were a free people.

2   Exodus 11:4 (see Rashi) and 12:29. Midnight is the deadline for the eating of the matzah and the bitter herbs, and, when the Holy Temple stood in Jerusalem, for the eating of the meat of the Passover offering (today it is the deadline for eating the *afikoman*, which represents the Passover offering at our *seder*). See *Tosafot, Megillah* 21a; *Shulchan Aruch, Orach Chaim* 477a; Rema and *Dagul Mirvavah*, ad loc.

PASSOVER (2)   35

would read, "as the night divides."[3] How, then, can anything be said to occur at the time that "the night divides"?

The Midrash cites two opinions as to the nature of the night's division that first Passover eve. According to Rabbi Yishmael, "The night's Creator halved it"; according to Rabbi Judah ben Beteira, "He who knows His times and moments halved it."[4]

Radbaz[5] explains the reasoning behind these two opinions. Rabbi Yishmael is saying that G-d, who created night, day, and time itself, can obviously manipulate them at will. G-d literally split the night in two, opening an expanse of timelessness between its halves. In this "time-vacuum," G-d smote the Egyptian firstborn and freed the Children of Israel. Rabbi Judah, however, is of the opinion that G-d effected the Exodus within physical time, not in some time-transcendent reality. What G-d did was to coordinate His action with the exact midpoint of the night, so that the initial state ended with the night's first half, and the state effected by His action began with the onset of its second half. This He was able to do because "He knows His times and moments" absolutely.[6]

(In other words, every action is the effecting of a change from state A to state B. So in truth, no time duration is required in which to effect a change, only a point in time[7] to mark the end of

---

3   As per Rashi's first interpretation, which he considers the "straightforward meaning, which best explains the verse in its context." But also according to the second interpretation cited by Rashi, which translates *kachatzot* as "about midnight," the plague of the firstborn took place exactly at midnight—see there.

4   *Mechilta*, Exodus 12:29.

5   16th-century sage Rabbi David ibn Zimra.

6   *Radbaz Responsa*, vol. I, ch. 814.

7   In geometry, a point occupies no area, representing not a quantity of space but a position relative to which area is defined. It is in this context that we use the term "point" to connote the same in regard to time.

state A and the beginning of state B. But since no physical instrument, human or artificial, can measure time with absolute accuracy, man, in timing his deeds, can, at best, define a stretch of time — perhaps, even, a very small stretch of time — within which the change will take place. G-d, however, who has absolute knowledge of "His times and moments," can position His deed — in this case, the taking of the lives of the Egyptian firstborn and Israel's transformation from slavery to freedom — exactly on the duration-less line that halves the night, effecting a change at the very point that lies between the night's former and latter parts.)

What is the point in all this? Why did the plague of the firstborn have to transpire precisely at midnight? And what is the significance of the differing scenarios of Rabbi Yishmael and Rabbi Judah?

THE TENTH PLAGUE

The plague of the firstborn was the tenth of a series of plagues visited upon the Egyptians. But there was a basic difference between this plague and the first nine — a difference that touches on the nature and function of the plagues themselves.

The primary objective of the first nine plagues was to prove a point — to instill an awareness among the Egyptians. In Moses' words to Pharaoh: "So said G-d: 'With this you shall know that I am G-d. Behold, I will strike... the waters of the Nile, and they shall turn to blood"; "If you do not let My people go, I will send swarms of wild beasts at you... in order that you know that I am G-d"; "Once again, I am sending all My plagues... In order that

---

See the section titled "The Geometry of Time," in the essay, *The Seventh Element*, on pp. 82–85 of vol. 1 of this series.

PASSOVER (2)   37

you know that there is none like Me in the land."[8] The tenth plague,
however, was more than a demonstration of divine power. It came
to punish and to break Egypt, and free Israel from its midst.[9]

This explains a puzzling difference between the first nine
plagues and the plague of the firstborn. The first nine plagues
threatened only the Egyptians; the children of Israel were immune
to them.[10] The Midrash tells us that during the plague of blood, if
an Egyptian and a Jew drank from the same cup, the Jew drank
water while the Egyptian drank blood; that during the plague of
darkness, a Jew could enter an Egyptian's home in broad daylight
while to the Egyptian the world was shrouded in darkness.[11] But in
the case of the plague of the firstborn, the Jews were as vulnerable
to the plague as their Egyptian neighbors, and a series of protec-
tive measures had to be taken so that the Jewish firstborn would
not also die.

The Jews were commanded to make a "Passover offering" (korban pesach) to G-d—slaughter a lamb or goat, sprinkle its blood
on the two doorposts and the lintel of their homes, and eat its
meat that night with matzah and bitter herbs. That night, the Jewish people also circumcised themselves. It was only in the merit
of these two *mitzvot* that the Jewish firstborn were spared. In fact,
in the words of the prophet Ezekiel, "I passed over you, and I saw
you weltering in your blood [i.e., the blood of circumcision and

---

8   Exodus 7:17, 8:17–18 and 9:14.

9   In ancient Egypt, the firstborn held all the key religious and govern-
     mental positions (Pharaoh himself was a firstborn, and was spared
     only so that he should witness the liberation of Israel and the destruc-
     tion of his army). The death of all firstborn spelled the demise of Egyp-
     tian power and prestige.

10   Exodus 8:18–19, 9:6, 9:26, and 10:23.

11   *Midrash Rabbah, Shemot* 9:9 and 14:3.

the blood of the *korban pesach*] and I said to you: By your blood you shall live!"[12]

The Jews in Egypt were a people meritorious in faith but deficient in behavior. On the one hand, we are told that their faith in G-d and His promise of redemption never wavered, even in the darkest moments of their ordeal;[13] on the other hand, they had assumed the pagan practices of their enslavers.[14] Thus, the first nine plagues, whose function was "in order that you know that I am G-d," had no cause to afflict the Jewish people, whose awareness of the divine truth was beyond reproach. But when the tenth plague came to punish and destroy the Egyptians for their sins and to "take out a nation from the womb of a nation"—to extract the Jew from the society of which he was a part and forge him into a holy people—here, G-d's "attribute of justice" had cause to argue: "How are these any different from these? These are idol-worshippers, and these are idol-worshippers!"[15]

Thus, on the night of *Nissan* 15, it was necessary to differentiate between Egyptian and Jew. G-d had to *pass over* the homes of the Jews when the Egyptian firstborn were killed—indeed, it is this divine discrimination that gives "Passover" (*Pesach*, in the Hebrew) its name. To this end, G-d clothed a nation "bare and naked of virtues"[16] with *mitzvot*, in order to distinguish them from their neighbors.[17]

---

12   Ezekiel 16:6.

13   See Exodus 4:31; *Mechilta, Shemot* 14: 31.

14   See *Zohar Chadash*, beginning of *Yitro*; *Yalkut Reuveni, Shemot* 14:27; *Zohar* 3:170b.

15   *Yalkut Reuveni* and *Zohar* in previous footnote.

16   Ezekiel 16:7; Rashi on verse.

17   To this day, all Jewish firstborn are obligated to fast on the day before Passover in acknowledgment that they, too, deserved to die in the plague of the firstborn.

Two Visions of Midnight

However, there is still much that requires clarification. If we were no less deserving of punishment than our enslavers, and no more deserving of redemption — if the divine sense of justice dictated that "these are no different than these" — what moved G-d to grant us the *mitzvot* to distinguish us from the Egyptians? And if, on the other hand, G-d wished to redeem us despite all, why the need for these special *mitzvot* to protect us from the plague of the firstborn?

Indeed, G-d chose to redeem us not because we were any "better" than the Egyptians, but because of His intrinsic love for us. In the words of the prophet Malachi: "Is not Esau a brother to Jacob?... But I love Jacob."[18] Even when there is no cause to distinguish between Jacob and Esau, G-d chooses Jacob. At the very onset of Moses' mission to free the Jewish people, G-d told him to communicate to Pharaoh that "Israel is My child, My firstborn."[19] I love him with a father's unconditional love, G-d is saying: a love that transcends considerations of virtue and deservedness.

This, explain the Kabbalistic masters, is the reason why the Exodus took place at midnight. The first half of the night embodies the divine attribute of justice (*din* or *gevurah*), and its second half, the divine attribute of benevolence (*chesed*). Midnight is the juncture that fuses and supersedes them both, since the power to join two opposites can only come from a point that transcends their differences.[20] "Midnight" is thus an expression of a divine involvement in creation that transcends all standard criteria for punishment or reward.

---

18   Malachi 1:2.
19   Exodus 4:22.
20   See *Twilight* in vol. 1, pp. 139–147 of this series.

"At midnight," said G-d to Moses, "I shall go out into the midst of Egypt." As the sages interpret this verse: "'I'—and not an angel; 'I'—and not a messenger."[21] At midnight I shall disregard all the "attributes," norms, and processes I have established to define My governance of the world, and relate to you as I am and as I choose.[22]

At the same time, G-d provided us with *mitzvot* with which to *deserve* our redemption. For a most basic feature of the covenant which G-d desired to forge with us is that the deepest aspects of our relationship with Him should be manifested in our daily lives via the *mitzvot* of the Torah—that the most sublime spiritual truths be actualized by the means of physical deeds. So although G-d superseded all standards of deservedness and undeservedness to redeem us, He granted us the means by which to deserve our redemption—the *mitzvot* of *korban pesach* and circumcision.[23]

---

21 Exodus 12:2; *Sifri* on Deuteronomy 26:8; *Passover Haggadah.*

22 Nevertheless, at the Exodus G-d did insist on one condition in His choice of us—that we desire to be chosen. Those who did not wish to be taken out of Egypt to become G-d's people were not redeemed. It was only at Sinai that G-d's truly unconditional choice of Israel took place, and we entered a covenant with G-d that supersedes even the desire to be chosen. See the following essay, *The Festival of the Child* (pp. 42–46 below). Also see *The Phantom Days of Shavuot* on pp. 201–206 of this volume, and *The Thousand-Year Difference* in vol. 2, pp. 247–253.

23 Both these *mitzvot* embody, on a human scale, the divine response they were designed to elicit. The offering of the *korban pesach* was an act that defied all conventions of logic and feasibility. The Jews were commanded to take a lamb—one of the deities of Egypt—and keep it bound in their homes for four days, slaughter it, sprinkle its blood on their doorposts, and eat its flesh. Reason argued: "Can we slaughter the idol of Egypt before their eyes, and they won't stone us?" (Exodus 8:22) But reason was set aside to do the will of G-d. G-d responded in kind, setting aside the divine norms of "justice" and "benevolence."

Circumcision, the bodily sign of our covenant with G-d, also emphasizes its suprarational basis. The Jewish child is circumcised at the age of eight days, when he cannot possibly appreciate the significance

PASSOVER (2)   41

HALVING THE NIGHT

Hence the alternate interpretations offered by Rabbi Yishmael and Rabbi Judah as to the nature of the midnight of the Exodus.

Rabbi Yishmael sees the Exodus as a supranatural, suprarational event. To him, midnight of *Nissan* 15 is no temporal landmark in time. To take the Jews out of Egypt, G-d stopped the clocks of creation, splitting night, time, and natural order apart to reveal the quintessential divine will that underlies and transcends all.

Rabbi Judah, on the other hand, focuses on the natural dimension to the Exodus. True, to pass over the homes of the Israelites while their Egyptian peers were destroyed, to extract a nation from a nation it all but resembled morally and spiritually, there had to be a divine choice that superseded the rules and standards that G-d built into creation. But is it not also true that this choice had to be accessed and actualized from within the terms of these rules and standards themselves? Is not the entire point of the Exodus, and of the revelation at Sinai to which it led, that man make himself a worthy vessel to the divine, and that our finite, physical world be developed as a receptacle to the infinite goodness and perfection of its Creator?

To Rabbi Judah, midnight of *Nissan* 15 is a point in time—a point of entry for the all-transcending truth of G-d, but an integral part of our conventional existence all the same.

---

of the deed or even be aware of it. Why don't we wait until the age of intellectual maturity (as we do, for example, with the *mitzvah* of *tefilin*)? Because this is a *mitzvah* given to us by the Almighty to access the reason- and rule-transcending essence of our relationship.

THE FESTIVAL OF THE CHILD

And you shall tell your son on that day: "This is done because of what G-d did for me, when I came out of Egypt.   Exodus 13:8

 W hen did you last experience freedom? For many of us, burdened by our jobs, our familial and social responsibilities, and the other entanglements of the human conditions, freedom seems as rare as it is essential, as elusive as it desirable. We want it, we need it, yet how do we achieve it?

But look at the child. Observe him at play, immersed in a book, asleep and smiling at his dreams. Assured that father and mother will feed her, protect her and worry about all that needs worrying about, the child is free. Free to revel in his or her inner self, free to grow and develop, open to the joys and possibilities of life.

This is why Passover, the festival of freedom, is so much the festival of the child. For it is the child who evokes in us the realization that we, too, are children of G-d, and are thus inherently and eternally free. It is the child who opens our eyes to the ultimate significance of Passover: that in taking us out of Egypt to make us His chosen people, G-d has liberated us of all enslavement and subjugation for all time.

The child is thus the most important participant at the Passover *seder*. Many of the *seder* customs are specifically designed to mystify the child, to stimulate her curiosity, to compel him to ask:

PASSOVER (3)   43

Mah nishtanah halailah hazeh... "Why is this night different from all other nights?" For the entire *Haggadah*—the "telling" of the story of our redemption from Egypt at the *seder*—is built around the concept of "When your child shall ask you... You shall tell your child."[1] On Passover, we want to enter the child's mind, to view reality from his perspective. For how else might we taste freedom?

FOUR CHILDREN

But children, as every parent will attest, come in many shapes and forms. An examination of the Torah's discussion of the *seder* dialogue reveals several versions of the child's questions and the parent's response. The *Haggadah* explains that, "The Torah is addressing itself to four children: the wise, the wicked, the simple, and the one who does not know how to ask." Depending on how (and if) the child articulates his question, the Torah offers four different approaches to explaining the message of the festival and the significance of our freedom.

The "wise child" asks intelligent, detailed, and well-structured questions that reflect the thoroughness of his observations and his desire to know, appreciate, and participate.[2] The proud father responds with a detailed explanation of the *seder* observances from beginning to end, all the way to the law that "one should not serve up any dessert after the meat of the Passover offering" so that its taste should linger in our mouths long after the *seder*.[3]

The "wicked child," observing the labor and expense that go into the making of the *seder*, asks: "Whatever for is this work of

---

1   Exodus 13:8 and 14.
2   Deuteronomy, 6:20.
3   *Haggadah*. Today, the same law applies to the *afikoman*, the matzah eaten at the end of the meal in commemoration of the Passover offering.

yours?"[4] "This work of *yours*," notes the *Haggadah*—this is something he wants no part of himself. "This is because of what G-d did for me," replies the father in kind, "when I left Egypt."[5] "For *me*... when *I* left Egypt" implying, explains the *Haggadah*, since "had he (the wicked child) been there, he would not have been redeemed."

To the "simple child," who can manage only a lame "What is this?", the father responds with an appropriately elementary explanation of the night's significance.[6] And to the father of "the son who does not know how to ask," the Torah instructs: "You shall tell your child."[7] You initiate the discussion; you prod him into conversation and participation.

There and Here

Of the above responses, our answer to the "wicked child" begs clarification. Why do we tell him that he would have been left behind in Egypt at the time of the Exodus?

Factually, this was indeed the case. Our sages tell us that only one out of five Jews departed Egypt for Sinai on the first Passover.[8] The other four-fifths refused to leave, preferring slavery to Pharaoh over commitment to G-d. These Jews were not redeemed. For though G-d accepted the Jews in Egypt as they were, despite their lowly spiritual station after two centuries of enslavement to the most debased society on earth, there was one condition: One had to desire freedom in order to deserve it.

---

4   Exodus 12:26.
5   Ibid. 13:8.
6   Ibid., verse 14.
7   Ibid., verse 8.
8   Rashi on Exodus 13:18.

PASSOVER (3) 45

Still, what is to be gained by telling the wicked son that "had he been there, he would not have been redeemed"? Do we wish to further alienate an already alienated child?

In truth, however, our response to the wicked son is not a message of banishment and rejection, but one of acceptance and promise. The emphasis is on the word "there" in our reply. Had he been *there*, we tell him, he would not have been redeemed. The Exodus from Egypt was before the giving of the Torah at Mount Sinai, before G-d's ultimate choice of Israel. There, in Egypt, redemption was contingent upon the Jew's choice and consent. Had the "wicked child" been there, he would still be there. But he was not there—he is here.

"Here" is after Sinai. Here, free is what we are rather than something that we might elect or decline to be. True, we are currently in exile, but "on that day," prophesies Isaiah, "you will be gathered up one by one, O children of Israel."[9] When G-d shall again come to redeem us, not a single Jew will be left behind.

THE FIFTH CHILD

As different as they may be, the "four children" of the *Haggadah* have one thing in common: whether involved, challenging, inept, or indifferent, they are all present at the *seder* table. They are all relating, albeit in vastly differing ways, to our annual reliving of the Exodus and our birth as a nation. The line of communication is open; the potential "wise child" that resides within every Jewish child is approachable.

Today, however, in our era of spiritual displacement, there also exists a fifth child: the Jew who is absent from the *seder* table. He

---

9   Isaiah 27:12.

or she asks no questions, poses no challenges, displays no interest. For she knows nothing of the *seder*, nothing of the significance of the Exodus, nothing of the revelation at Sinai at which we assumed our mission and role as Jews.

To these children of G-d we must devote ourselves long before the first night of Passover. We must not forget a single Jewish child; we must invest all our energies and resources to bringing every last "fifth child" to the *seder* table of Jewish life.

HILLEL'S PARADOX

G-d said to Moses and Aaron in the land of Egypt, saying:

"...Speak to the entire congregation of Israel... and they shall take for themselves, every man, a lamb for each family, a lamb for each house... And you shall hold it in safekeeping until the fourteenth day of this month; and the entire community of the congregation of Israel shall slaughter it toward evening... And they shall eat the meat that night, roasted by fire, with matzot and bitter herbs..."

Exodus 12:1–8

Man is a lonely creature. No other inhabitant of G-d's world harbors a sense of individuality as pronounced and as determined as that cultivated by the human being. No other creature perceives itself as apart and distinct of its fellows.

Yet we are also the most social of creatures, weaving intricate webs of familial and communal relations in our quest for validation and acceptance by others. Never content to merely be ourselves, we group by profession, class, nationality, and other providers of a self-definition that transcends the personal.

If we are aware of a contradiction between our individual and communal identities, this does not lessen our need and striving for both. For while we are convinced that we are what we make of ourselves, we also know that alone, we are less than what we are and can be. In the words of the great sage Hillel, "If I am not for myself, who is for me? And if I am only for myself, what am I?"[1]

The Passover Offering

Hillel's paradox confronts us in countless guises every day of our lives. In Hillel's own life, it took the form of a question of Torah law that was instrumental in his ascension (in the year 32 BCE) to the leadership of his people: Should the Passover offering be brought when the 14th of *Nissan* falls on Shabbat?

When the Holy Temple stood in Jerusalem, the primary vehicle of man's service of his Creator were the *korbanot* (animal and meal offerings) offered on its altar to G‑d. The *korbanot* fall under two general categories:

a) "Individual offerings" (*korbanot yachid*) brought by private citizens, such as the "generosity offering" brought as a donation, the "thanksgiving offering" brought to express one's gratitude to G‑d for a personal salvation, or the "sin offering" brought to atone for a transgression.

b) "Communal offerings" (*korbanot tzibbur*), such as the daily morning and afternoon offerings brought by the people of Israel as a whole from a fund to which every Jew contributed an annual half-*shekel*.

While most offerings belong completely to one class or the other, the Passover offering straddles both categories. On the one hand, it possesses certain features (such as the fact that it is purchased with private funds and eaten by those who brought it) which would define it as an individual offering. On the other hand, there are things about it that are characteristic of the communal

---

[1]   *Ethics of the Fathers* 1:14.

PASSOVER (4)   49

offering (such as the fact that it is brought en masse by "the entire community of the congregation of Israel").[2]

When the 14th of *Nissan*—the day on which the Passover offering is brought—falls on a Shabbat, the question of its categorization becomes crucial. Torah law forbids the bringing of individual offerings on Shabbat, but permits and obligates the bringing of communal offerings.[3] Should the Passover offering be regarded as an "individual offering" which cannot be brought on Shabbat, or as a "communal offering" whose obligation supersedes the prohibition of work on the day of rest?

The Talmud relates that one year when *Nissan* 14 fell on Shabbat, the leaders of the *sanhedrin* (highest court of Torah law) were unable to resolve the question of whether the Passover offering should be brought. Hillel, a scholar newly arrived in the Holy Land from Babylonia, demonstrated that the communal aspect of the Passover offering is its more dominant element, meaning that it should be offered also when its appointed time coincides with Shabbat. In recognition of his superior scholarship, the leaders of the *sanhedrin* stepped down and appointed Hillel as their head.[4]

---

2   Exodus 12:6. Indeed, we find the Passover offering alternately described as an individual and a communal offering—cf. Jerusalem Talmud, *Pesachim* 6:1; *Tosafot, Pesachim* 70b, s.v. *Ha vadai*; Maimonides' *Commentary on the Mishnah,* introduction to *Seder Kodashim*; *Mishneh Torah, Laws of the Preparation of the Offerings* 1:3; and sources cited in *Likutei Sichot,* vol. 18, p. 105, notes 15 and 19.

3   Talmud, *Temurah* 14a; see *Likutei Sichot,* vol. 18, p. 105. (text and notes).

4   Jerusalem Talmud, *Pesachim* 6:1. A communal offering can be brought on Shabbat only if it must be brought on that very day—e.g., the *tamid* offering, commanded by the Torah to be brought every morning and evening, or the *musaf* offerings specifically designated to be brought on certain dates. A communal offering that has no designated time (e.g., the *par he'elem davar shel tzibbur* brought in atonement for a transgression erroneously committed by the entire people) may not be

Isaiah and Jeremiah

Echoing Moses' description of the Exodus as a time when G-d "took a nation from the womb of a nation," the prophet Ezekiel describes the event as the "birth" of the Jewish people.[5] Before the Exodus, the children of Israel shared a common ancestry, culture, and heritage,[6] but they did not constitute a nation; on that first Passover, the entity "Israel" was born.

Passover can thus be seen as representing the ascendancy of the communal over the individual—the point at which numerous distinct personalities surrendered to a common mission and identity. Indeed, as Hillel showed, in the Passover offering it is the communal element which dominates, and determines the *halachic* status of the *korban*.

So why isn't the Passover offering a full-fledged communal offering like the others? Why is it a hybrid of the individual and the communal, in which both elements find expression and vie for

---

brought on Shabbat (see sources cited in previous note). The Passover offering, which the Torah instructs to be brought on *Nissan* 14, would therefore meet the criteria for a Shabbat offering if it were regarded as a "communal offering."

Hillel alludes to this factor as well in his above-quoted saying. The full saying, as it appears in *Ethics of the Fathers*, reads: "If I am not for myself, who is for me? And if I am only for myself, what am I? And if not now, when?" Here are all the issues in the *halachic* question which raised Hillel to the presidency of the *sanhedrin*: a) the individualistic aspect of the Passover offering—"If I am not for myself, who is for me?"; b) its communal element—"And if I am only for myself, what am I?"; c) the fact that it must be brought at a specific time—"And if not now, when?"

5   Deuteronomy 4:34; Ezekiel 16.

6   "The Jews in Egypt... did not abandon their distinctive names, language... and dress" (*Midrash Rabbah, Vayikra* 32:5; *Lekach Tov, Shemot* 6:6).

PASSOVER (4)   51

supremacy? Because G-d's purpose in forging many individuals
into a single people was not the obliteration of their individuality, but the incorporation of each member's distinct personality
within the communal whole. The community of Israel is not just
a vehicle for the transcendence of the limitations of individuality
and the attainment of goals unachievable by ego-encumbered individuals; it is also the framework within which each individual
might optimally develop and realize his or her personal best.

Our relationship with G-d includes "individual offerings,"
which represent the devotion of our individual resources to G-d,
as well as "communal offerings," which express the surrender of our
individuality to our communal mission. But the Passover offering,
which played a formative role in our birth as a people, must belong
to *both* categories.[7]

---

7 More specifically, the first Passover offering, which was brought by the
   Jewish people while they were still in Egypt, was predominantly an "individual offering," while the later Passover offerings belong more to
   the "communal" category. In Egypt, each family slaughtered its offering, and performed all the rituals associated with it, in its own home;
   thus the blood of the offering was sprinkled on "the two side-posts
   and the upper doorpost of the homes in which it will be eaten" (Exodus 12:7). Beginning with the second Passover, observed a year later
   in the Sinai Desert, all Jews brought their Passover offerings to the
   Sanctuary to be slaughtered there and have its blood sprinkled upon
   the Sanctuary's altar. Indeed, the first Passover offering was brought
   on a weekday (as per the Talmud, *Shabbat* 87b, the Exodus occurred
   on a Thursday, meaning that the Passover offering was slaughtered on
   Wednesday afternoon), while the second Passover offering was actually brought on Shabbat (that year, the 1st of *Nissan* was a Sunday (Ibid.),
   meaning that *Nissan* 14 was Shabbat).

   But even the first Passover offering had certain communal characteristics—the Midrash (*Shemot Rabbah* 19:5) describes how all Jews ate
   from Moses' Passover offering, and the above-quoted verse describing
   it as an offering brought by "the entire community of the congregation of Israel" speaks of that first Passover offering brought in Egypt.

As the *mitzvah* that marks the birth of the nation of Israel, the Passover offering must express our commonality as G-d's people; this is indeed its dominant theme. But it must also express the truth that even as we set aside our differences to devote ourselves to a common goal, our individual strengths and challenges continue to define us as distinct and unique entities. It must express the truth that the paradox of individuality and community is at the heart of who and what we are, and that the tension between these two strivings is a necessary and desirable component of our relationship with G-d.

Even at the very end of days, when the whole of human history culminates in the divinely perfect and harmonious age of Moshiach, this duality will continue to define our identity and nationhood. The ultimate redemption will be a communal redemption, when, as the prophet Jeremiah proclaims, "A great community shall return here"; but it will also be the realization of Isaiah's vision of a time when "You shall be collected, one by one, O children of Israel."[8]

On the other hand, even after it became a predominantly "communal offering" in the year after the Exodus, the Passover offering retained many of its "individualistic" elements, such as the fact that it is eaten by each family or family group at their own family *seder*.

8   Jeremiah 31:7; Isaiah 27:12.

BREAD OF FAITH

And they baked unleavened cakes of the dough which they brought out of Egypt, for it did not [have time to] leaven; for they were driven out of Egypt and could not tarry...

Exodus 12:39

For seven days, you shall eat... matzah, the bread of poverty... Thus you shall remember the day of your exodus from Egypt, all the days of your life.

Deuteronomy 16:3

atzah, the unleavened bread, is the most prominent item at the Passover *seder*. It is the "bread of poverty" that symbolizes our hardship under Egyptian slavery. It is also the "hasty bread" that did not have time to rise, reminiscent of the nature of our redemption — the sudden, drastic, overwhelming change that the Almighty wrought in our lives. At the stroke of midnight on Passover eve, G-d instantaneously transformed a materially and morally impoverished clan of slaves into a free people — into the nation chosen to be a "light unto the nations" and to play the central role in the divine purpose of creation.[1]

Virtually the entire *seder* centers on the three matzot on the *seder* plate, from the recitation of the *Haggadah* over the smaller

---

1   Isaiah 49:6; Rashi on Genesis 1:1.

half of the middle matzah, to the eating of the "after matzah" (*afikoman*) at the meal's end. Indeed, the biblical name for Passover is *chag hamatzot* ("the festival of matzot"), for it is the matzah that embodies the essence of the Exodus.

So why aren't there *four* matzot?

The number four is a recurring theme at the *seder*. We drink four cups of wine, ask the "four questions," speak of the "four children" — to name but a few of the fours associated with the festival of freedom. Our sages explain this recurrence of the theme of "four" on Passover as deriving from the "four expressions of redemption" in G-d's promise to Moses (Exodus 6:6–7):

> *I will bring you out from under the hardship of Egypt, and I will save you from their bondage; I will redeem you with an outstretched arm and with great judgments. I will take you to Myself as a nation, and I will your G-d.*

As the commentaries explain,[2] the "four expressions of redemption" relate to the four aspects of our liberation from Egypt: 1) "I will bring out"—our physical removal from the geographical boundaries of Egypt. 2) "I will save"—our delivery from Egyptian hegemony.[3] 3) "I will redeem"—the elimination of any future possibility of enslavement by the "great judgments" inflicted upon the Egyptians.[4] 4) "I will take you to Myself as a nation, and I will be

---

2 Nachmanides, Sforno, et al.

3 Egypt was a superpower that enslaved and oppressed many nations and peoples outside its borders.

4 Had the Egyptians' power not been broken by the ten plagues and the drowning of its army in the sea, they would have posed a future threat to the freedom of Israel (indeed, no sooner had the people of Israel left Egypt than Pharaoh chased after them to try to force their return). Freedom that exists under the threat of slavery is not true freedom.

PASSOVER (5)

your G-d"—our election as G-d's chosen people at Mount Sinai, the purpose of the Exodus.

So why aren't the "four expressions of redemption" represented in the most basic symbol of the Exodus, the matzah? Why are there only three matzot arranged on the *seder* plate?[5]

FLASH OF FAITH

The matzah, as we said, expresses both our poverty at the time of the Exodus and the haste with which the redemption came about. The two are interrelated: It was because we were impoverished—spiritually as well as materially—that our redemption had to be such a hasty affair. Our sages explain that we had become so entrenched in the paganism and depravity of Egypt that the Exodus came at the very last possible moment. Had we remained slaves in Egypt a moment longer, there would have been no "people of Israel" to redeem.[6]

---

5   The practical reason for the three matzot is that "bread of poverty" is best represented by a *piece* of matzah, rather than a whole matzah; on the other hand, we honor every Shabbat and festival meal with *lechem mishneh*—two whole loaves of bread. We therefore place three matzot on the *seder* plate. At the beginning of the *seder*, we break the middle matzah in two; the larger half is set aside for the *afikoman*, and the smaller half serves as the "bread of poverty" upon which the *Haggadah* (the "telling" of the story of the Exodus) is recited. To observe the *mitzvah* of eating matzah, we eat both from the broken matzah as well as from the top whole matzah. The third matzah is used for *koreich*, the matzah-and-*maror* sandwich.

But everything is Jewish life is significant, especially on the *seder* night, when everything we do is replete with symbolism and meaning. So in addition to any "technical" reason, there must be a deeper import as well to the matzah's departure from the foursomeness that pervades the *seder*.

6   In the *Haggadah* we say: "If G-d had not taken our forefathers out of

Thus, we could not afford the luxury of an orderly, methodical redemption. We simply did not have the time to divest ourselves of our slave mentality and pagan ways, to comprehend the significance of the role for which we were being chosen, or to develop the proper emotional response to this unprecedented event in human history.[7] All we had was our faith in G-d—a faith that had persevered throughout our long and harrowing exile.[8] On Passover eve, G-d ignited this faith with a tremendous revelation of His might and truth, wrenching our souls free of the chains that had imprisoned them in an internal slavery more nefarious than any physical bondage. It was this faith, and this faith alone, that took us out of Egypt and set us on the road to Sinai. The prophet Jeremiah describes the moment when he says: "So says G-d: I remember your youthful love, your bridal devotion, following Me out to the desert, to an unsown land."[9]

But faith alone was not enough. Faith can move mountains, but it cannot remake the essence of man. For faith is a transcendent force, and therein lies both its power and its limitations: It can lift us to unprecedented heights, but these remain "otherworldly" experiences, extraneous to our inner self.

Faith got us out of Egypt, but it could not get Egypt out of us. To become truly, inherently free we had to change from within, by means of a gradual process of internal growth and development.

Egypt, we, our children, and our children's children, would still be enslaved to Pharaoh in Egypt..." If the redemption had not come when it did, it could not have come at all (see sources cited in the Rebbe's *Haggadah Im Likutei Taamim Minhagim u'Biurim*, p. 30).

7   In contrast, of the future redemption it is said, "For you shall not go out in haste, nor go in flight" (Isaiah 52:12).

8   *Yalkut Shimoni*, Hosea 519; cf. *Midrash Rabbah*, *Shemot* 3:15. See *Midnight* on pp. 34–41 above.

9   Jeremiah 2:2.

PASSOVER (5)   57

So following the instant exodus of Passover, G-d embarked us on a
systematic regimen of self-refinement and transformation. Only at
the end of a forty-nine-step process (which we reexperience each
year with the 49-day *omer* count) did we enter into our covenant
with G-d at Mount Sinai.[10]

Thus, while the "I will bring out," "I will save," and "I will redeem" elements of the Exodus were realized on Passover itself, the
fourth element came to fruition seven weeks later, with the giving
of the Torah at Mount Sinai (marked each year with the festival of
Shavuot). At Sinai, G-d's promise that "I will take you to Myself
as a nation" was realized, after we had internalized the faith of the
Exodus, attaining an understanding and appreciation of our mission as G-d's "treasured people among the nations... a kingdom of
priests and a holy nation."[11]

FLAT CAKE AND SENSUAL DRINK

These two stages in our redemption are personified by two staples
of the *seder*: matzah and wine.

Matzah, the "bread of poverty" and the "bread of haste," is the
"bread of faith"[12] which represents the state of the Jewish people at
the moment of the Exodus. The matzah dough must be kneaded
hastily, and placed immediately in the oven; allowing it to rise and

---

10 The human character consists of seven basic attributes, each of which
    contains elements of each of the others, making a total of 49 traits and
    nuances of personality. Hence the 49-step program of self-refinement.
    See next essay, *A Speck of Flour.*

11 Exodus 19:5–6.

12 *Zohar* 2:41a (see the Rebbe's notes on page 116 of *Sefer HaMaamarim
    5708*).

assume the richness of full-bodied bread renders it *chametz* (leaven), forbidden for consumption (or even possession) on Passover. Also, in order to be valid for use at the *seder,* the matzah must consist of flour and water only: Any innovative attempt at a gourmet matzah (e.g., mixing in eggs or fruit juice) disqualifies it for the *mitzvah* of eating matzah on Passover eve.[13] Matzah thus reflects the intellectual and emotional poverty of one who, roused by a flash of divine truth, follows G-d into the desert with nothing but his faith and commitment: one who understands nothing, feels nothing, "tastes" nothing save his awe before the majesty of his Creator and his firm resolve to serve Him.[14]

Wine, on the other hand, is the epitome of sense and experience. Wine, the palatable beverage that "gladdens G-d and man,"[15] represents the spiritual richness of the people who stood at the foot of Mount Sinai—a people who had undergone the process of internalizing the divine truth so that it excited and invigorated their minds and hearts.

Thus we have three matzot and four cups of wine at the Passover *seder.* With the three matzot, we reexperience the event of the Exodus itself: the flash of faith that "brought out," "saved," and "redeemed" us from Egypt, but which fell short of the fourth expression of redemption that enables us to taste and experience the substance of our freedom. With the four cups of wine, we savor also the fourth dimension of the Exodus—the flavor and fragrance of the spiritual maturity attained at Sinai.

---

13 *Shulchan Aruch, Orach Chaim,* 462:2; see also *Magen Avraham,* ad loc., 461, subsection 7.

14 Cf. Talmud, *Nedarim* 41a: "There is no true poverty save the poverty of mind."

15 Judges 9:13.

PASSOVER (5)

THE SENSITIVE SERVANT

And yet, matzah is not the "tasteless" food that many an undiscerning palate would judge it to be. Indeed, the taste of matzah is mandated by Torah law.

Actually, we find two seemingly conflicting rulings in *halachah* (Torah law) regarding the taste of matzah. On the one hand, there is the law which states that even if a person does not taste the matzah he is eating, he has nevertheless fulfilled the *mitzvah* of eating matzah on Passover eve. For example, if a person grinds the matzah into a powder and swallows it, he has observed the *mitzvah*. Another law, however, stipulates that the matzah must retain its distinctive taste; if, for whatever reason, the taste of matzah is suppressed or altered (e.g., it is cooked or mixed with other foods) it is not valid for the *mitzvah*. Rabbi Schneur Zalman of Liadi explains: "Although one need not taste the matzah in his mouth, the matzah itself must possess the taste of matzah." Matzah need not be tasted, but it must be tasteable.[16]

For matzah does have a taste: the taste of faith, the taste of commitment, the taste of self-abnegation. Matzah is not wine—it has not the keen tang of intellectual inquiry or the intoxicating high of emotional passion. But the sensitive servant of G-d will savor its simple yet subtle flavor, its austere yet deeply satisfying consistency.

One who does not taste the matzah he is eating—one who does not appreciate the flavor of faith and the delectability of commitment—nevertheless fulfills the *mitzvah* of eating matzah on the *seder* night. For also our forefathers, beholding the truth of truths for the first time that night, were not in a position to "taste"

---

16   *Shulchan Aruch, Orach Chaim*, 475:3 and 461:4; *Shulchan Aruch Ha-Rav* 461:12.

their faith and experience its sublime delights. The overwhelming revelation of G-dliness which they experienced was just that: overwhelming and unreal to their still unperfected selves.

But the matzah must have its distinct flavor, even if the one ingesting it is incapable, as of yet, of relishing it. Faith, true faith, always carries the potential for a deep and satisfying relationship with G-d—no less satisfying than the most luscious vintage of the mind and heart.

MATZAH, WINE, AND MATZAH

So it is matzah, not wine, that is the symbol of the Exodus. The sensory austerity of matzah is not merely an initial phase to be overcome and surpassed on the road to Sinai; if this were the case, the robust cup of wine, rather than the flat matzah cake, would be upheld as the symbol of our freedom. But it is the matzah which embodies the ultimate goal of the redemption, the matzah that we are to refer to, "all the days of your life,"[17] for the ultimate significance of our freedom and nationhood.

Certainly, we should strive to stimulate our senses with an appreciation of our purpose in life and our relationship with our Creator. But the purpose of it all is a return to the genesis of our journey, a return to the unequivocal commitment that transcends reason and experience.

This is not a return to the "tasteless" faith of childhood, to a faith whose simplicity stems from the limitations of the not-yet-matured mind. It is not a return to a sense-poor Exodus that was dictated by the circumstances of the Egyptian *galut*. Rather, it is a reaffirmation of faith and commitment that comes *after* we have

---

17 Deuteronomy 16:3, quoted at the beginning of this essay.

comprehended all that is in our power to comprehend and we have experienced all that we are capable of experiencing. It is the acknowledgment that no matter how high our sensory self might reach, there is always something higher, a truth to which we can relate only with the simple acceptance of faith. Having supplemented our matzah with wine, we must now graduate to a higher order of matzah, to a matzah that is not bereft of thought and feeling but which surmounts them and supersedes them.

Matzah hurriedly chewed on an empty stomach is virtually tasteless; but at the meal's end, especially after a glass or two of wine, it is a feast for the senses.

A SPECK OF FLOUR

On the first day, you shall annihilate leaven from your houses... For seven days, no leaven shall be found... and no leaven shall be seen...
Exodus 12:15, 19; 13:7

$\mathcal{I}$ t is rare to find a substance so utterly proscribed by the Torah. There are other foods whose consumption is forbidden; but this the Torah forbids us to eat, benefit from in any way, or even keep in our possession. Usually, a forbidden substance becomes "nullified" if it mixes with a much greater quantity of permissible substances;[1] of this, the Torah forbids the slightest trace — even if it blends with something a million times its volume, the entire lot becomes unfit for consumption.

We are speaking, of course, of *chametz*, or leaven, on Passover. In the weeks before the festival, the Jewish home is the scene of an all-out war of extermination. Floorboards are scraped, furniture dismantled, countertops boiled. On the night before the festival we conduct a solemn search for any survivors and consign them

---

[1] E.g., while the Torah forbids the mixing of milk and meat, if a drop of milk accidentally falls into a pot of meat-stew, the stew is only forbidden for consumption if the milk was more than one-sixtieth of the stew. Certain forbidden substances are nullified if they constitute a minority of the mixture; others if they are less than one-sixtieth, less than one part in one hundred, or less than one part in two hundred. It should be noted that it is forbidden to intentionally nullify a prohibited substance.

PASSOVER (6)   63

to the flames on the next morning. The enemy: the most minute breadcrumb, beer stain, or pasta residue—anything in which grain and water have come together and fermented, rendering the product *chametz* and utterly intolerable for eight days a year.

On the spiritual level, leaven, whose primary feature is that it rises and inflates itself, embodies pride. This explains our uncompromising rejection of *chametz*. Other negative traits might be tolerable, or even useful, in small, greatly diluted doses. Depression, for example, has been declared "a grave sin,"[2] for man is commanded to "serve G-d with joy";[3] but a small dash of melancholy, counterbalanced by a hundredfold helping of joy, may serve a positive function, reflecting a necessary concern over one's shortcomings and the commitment to rectify them.[4] The same applies to anger, stubbornness, brazenness, and a host of other negative character traits: As a rule, they are undesirable, yet in the proper context and in the right proportions, each has its positive applications. Arrogance and pride, however, are of such spiritual toxicity—the Talmud states that G-d says of the arrogant one, "I and he cannot dwell in the same world"[5]—that we must forgo any attempt to exploit them, and must totally eradicate them from every crevice of our hearts.[6]

THE 49-DAY DIFFERENCE

And yet, despite the severity of the prohibition of *chametz*, it is only forbidden for eight days and several hours a year, while other,

---

2   Addendum to *Keter Shem Tov*, section 205.
3   Psalms 100:2.
4   *Tanya*, chapter 26. Also see *Good Grief* on pp. 214 below.
5   Talmud, *Erchin* 15b.
6   Cf. Maimonides' commentary to *Ethics of the Fathers* 4:4.

less "toxic" elements are forbidden year-round.[7] In other words, there is a state of being, which Passover represents, in which arrogance and pride are objectionable in any context and quantity. After "Passover," however, *chametz* becomes permissible and even desirable.

This duality is also expressed in the laws governing the offerings brought to G-d in the Holy Temple in Jerusalem. In the Holy Temple, it was "Passover" all year round: all grain offerings had to be unleavened, in keeping with the divine command that, "No leaven... may be brought as a fire-offering to G-d."[8] This, too, reflects G-d's utter abhorrence of arrogance and pride. Nevertheless, on the festival of Shavuot, two loaves of bread, specifically commanded to be "baked leavened,"[9] were offered in the Holy Temple.

Thus, Passover and Shavuot represent two extremes in the desirability of pride. On Passover *chametz* is wholly and utterly forbidden, while on Shavuot it is not only permitted but is a *mitzvah*, commanded and desired by G-d.

Passover marks our birth as a people, when G-d extracted a clan of slaves from the "forty-nine gates of depravity" of Egypt and set them on the journey toward Sinai, where G-d took Israel as His eternal bride on Shavuot.[10] Connecting Passover and Shavuot is the 49-day "counting of the *omer*": The Torah commands that beginning on the eve of the second day of Passover, we should con-

---

7   *Chametz* is forbidden for consumtion from midmorning of the day before Passover, until nightfall of the eighth day (seventh day in the Land of Israel). However, the most stringent aspects of the prohibition of *chametz* (such as the law that "the slightest trace is forbidden") apply only from nightfall on Passover eve (see note 13 below).

8   Leviticus 2:11.

9   Ibid., 23:17.

10   See *Zohar Chadash*, beginning of *Parashat Yitro*; Shaloh, *Masechet Pesachim*, s.v. *Mah Nishtanah*; *Megalleh Amukot, Emor*; et al.

PASSOVER (6)   65

duct a daily count of the days that have passed from the day after the Exodus.

The teachings of kabbalah explain that the human personality consists of seven basic attributes (love, awe, harmony, ambition, devotion, connection, and receptiveness),[11] reflecting the seven divine attributes (*sefirot*) which G-d invested in creation. Each *sefirah* contains elements of all seven, making for a total of forty-nine divine channels of relation to our reality, and forty-nine corresponding traits in the human heart.[12] Thus, the Kabbalists speak of the utterly corrupt society of Egypt as a moral nadir of "forty-nine gates of depravity." These are paralleled by "forty-nine gates of understanding"—the ladder and process by which one achieves the refinement and perfection of all elements in one's character.

Therein lies the significance of the forty-nine-day count and climb from Passover to Shavuot. On the first day of Passover, we were physically removed from the land of Egypt. But we still had to remove the "Egypt" from within us, to cleanse our hearts and minds of the residue of two centuries of pagan environment and practice. So on the second day of Passover begins a forty-nine-day count, chronicling a daily internal exodus from another of Egypt's "gates of depravity," and a daily entry into another of the "gates of understanding." After forty-nine days, we attain the internal purity required to receive the divine election and communication of Shavuot.

Hence the difference between Passover and Shavuot regarding *chametz*. One who is still burdened with negative drives and emotions (though he or she has already "come out of Egypt" in

---

11   See *The Journey* on pp. 98–108 below.

12   E.g., *chesed* of *chesed*, (loving love), *gevurah* of *chesed* (awed love), etc.

the most literal sense by abandoning the negative behavior they engender) lacks the ability to sublimate the most potent and corruptible of the heart's traits—pride. So immediately following the Exodus, *chametz* is banned.[13] It is only upon attaining the full refinement of all forty-nine compartments of the heart on Shavuot that the offering of leaven to G-d becomes a *mitzvah*, appropriate and desirable.

On this level, pride is no longer the self-inflating *chametz* of the "Passover" personality, but the selfless pride of one who has cleansed one's heart of every last vestige of self-interest and has dedicated it exclusively to the service of one's Creator. This is a pride not in what a person is or has achieved, but an expression of the majesty of the Higher Being that the person serves and whose reality the person conveys in his or her every thought, word, and deed.[14]

WET MATZAH

This also explains an interesting law regarding *Acharon Shel Pesach*, the eighth and final day of Passover.

One example of the extremes to which we go to avoid the slightest trace and chance of *chametz* on Passover is the practice, in many communities, of refraining from eating matzah *sheruyah* ("soaked matzah") on the festival.

---

13   On the other hand, for one who is still "in Egypt"—still imprisoned by his negative habits—the evocation of pride might be the only means by which he can overcome them, notwithstanding its negative effect on his internal self.

14   As in II Chronicles 17:6: "And his heart was lifted up in the ways of G-d."

PASSOVER (6)   67

Matzah is made of water and flour that have been quickly and thoroughly blended and speedily baked, to avoid any chance of leavening. Once baked, the flour in the matzah will not leaven; matzah (or "matzah meal" made by grinding matzah to a fine "flour") may now conceivably be mixed with water and other liquids in the preparation of food for the festival. However, there remains an extremely slight chance that some of the flour might have failed to mix completely with the water at the time of the matzah's original baking, leaving a few particles of raw flour at risk of leavening should they come in contact with water. For this reason, many *halachic* authorities, including Rabbi Schneur Zalman of Liadi, rule that it is best to avoid the use of matzah *sheruyah* on Passover.[15] This ruling has been accepted by many communities, to the extent that there are those who are careful not to even place matzah on the table during mealtimes unless it is securely covered, lest a single drop of liquid alight on a piece of matzah. This is one of the many examples of the unparalleled lengths to which we go in the avoidance of *chametz* on Passover.

On the other hand, Rabbi Schneur Zalman permits the use of matzah *sheruyah* on the eighth day of Passover. Furthermore, his successors, the rebbes of Chabad-Lubavitch, made a point of wetting matzah at every course of the meals of *Acharon Shel Pesach*.

There are those who are wont to explain this leniency by the fact that the eighth day of Passover is a rabbinical institution, as opposed to the first seven days, which are biblically ordained.[16] But the observance of the rabbinical "added days" to the festivals

---

15   Responsa 6, printed at the end of *Shulchan Aruch HaRav*.

16   Outside of the Land of Israel, a rabbinically-instituted "additional festival day of the Diaspora" is added to each festival. See the section, "The Dividend of Doubt," in the essay *Three Times Three* in vol. 1, p. 214–217 of this series.

68   INSIDE TIME: VOL. III

are just as binding for the Jew as their biblical sisters. In fact, Torah
law is even more stringent regarding certain aspects of their observance, for the very reason of forewarning any inclination to treat
them lightly.[17] Indeed, with the exception of the eating of "soaked
matzah," we are no less diligent in our rejection of leaven on Passover's final day. Why, then, this exception?

A Taste of Future

As we have discussed, the forty-nine-day count from Passover to
Shavuot represents the process of refining the seven basic traits
(*sefirot*) of the heart, as each comprises elements of all seven, making for a total of forty-nine traits. This is why the Torah speaks of
the count as consisting of weeks ("Seven weeks you shall count for
yourselves...").[18] In our daily count, we, too, emphasize its weeks:
On the twenty-fifth day, for example, we say, "Today is twenty-five
days, which are three weeks and four days to the *omer* [count]."
Indeed, *Shavuot*—the name of the festival that culminates the
counting of the *omer*—means "weeks." For our internal "count"
also consists of seven "weeks," being the refinement of seven attributes of the heart that are each a unit of seven.

Thus, each week of the count is a microcosmic *omer* count of
its own, involving seven "days" or sub-traits as they are reflected in
the various nuances of that week's *sefirah*.

The eighth day of Passover is the seventh day of the count and
the final day of its first week. It therefore represents the point at
which elements of each of the seven attributes (as they are present within the attribute of "love") have been refined and elevated.

---

17   See *Tur, Shulchan Aruch,* and commentaries, *Orach Chaim*, section 491.
18   Deuteronomy 16:9; see also Leviticus 23:15.

PASSOVER (6)   69

The eighth day of Passover is thus a mini-Shavuot, and shares its leaven-tolerant quality. While outright *chametz* is still strictly forbidden, we mark this milestone on the road to perfection with the positive use of a *chametz*-vulnerable element, employing wetted matzah to enhance our festival meal.

This corresponds to another feature of the eighth day of Passover—its identification with the era of Moshiach. The *haftarah* (reading from the Prophets) for this day, Isaiah 10:32–12:6, describes the coming of Moshiach and the harmonious perfection of a time when "the world shall be filled with the knowledge of G-d as the waters cover the sea." Rabbi Israel Baal Shem Tov instituted a special festive meal, "the meal of Moshiach," to be held on the afternoon of the eighth day of Passover, this being a time that is profoundly suited to "taste" and experience the divinely perfect world we are creating with our positive efforts—a world in which "the spirit of impurity shall cease from the earth"[19] and everything, including the pride so abhorrent to G-d today, shall be sublimated as a wholly positive and altruistic force.[20]

---

19 Zechariah 13:2.

20 The "feast of Moshiach" offers another, even more extreme example of *Acharon Shel Pesach*'s "tolerance" for *chametz*. On Passover (as on all other festivals) a special section—*Yaaleh veyavo*—is added to the *Grace after Meals* recited at the conclusion of each meal; this section includes the passage, "Remember us for good, on this day of Passover." The law is that if a person begins his meal on the last day of a festival and continues it after nightfall, he is to recite the *Yaaleh veyavo* at the conclusion of this meal, even though, for everyone else, the festival has ended many hours ago. Nevertheless, it is permissible to eat *chametz* immediately after nightfall of the last day of Passover, even in the middle of a meal that began before nightfall. Thus we have the paradox of a *Passover meal*, at whose conclusion we still consider ourselves "on this day of Passover," during which it is permissible to eat *chametz*! (*Shulchan Aruch HaRav, Orach Chaim,* 491:3. See also *Mishnah Berurah,* ibid.; *Likutei Sichot,* vol. 22, p. 36, notes 62–64).

Therein lies the lesson of the eighth day of Passover: Even if perfection seems a far-off goal, you possess the ability to create a "taste" of perfection in the here and now. Start with a single trait of your personality, or with a small corner of your community. If you wholly devote yourself to it, you will find in it elements of your entire self, indeed of the entire universe. Your creation of this small model of perfection will serve as the catalyst for its realization on a holistic, and ultimately universal, level.

PASSOVER (7)

THE
VEGETARIAN
ERA

*Rabban Gamliel would say: Whoever did
not speak of the following three things at the
Passover [seder], has not fulfilled his obligation [to relate the story of the Exodus]. These
are: the Passover offering, matzah, and maror.*

The Passover Haggadah

wo centuries before Jacob and his seventy children and
grandchildren settled in the land of Egypt, the Egyptian
exile and Exodus were foretold by G-d to Abraham at the "covenant between the parts." As described in the book of Genesis,

*As the sun began to set, a deep slumber fell upon Abram;
and, behold, a dread, a great darkness, descended upon
him. And [G-d] said to Abram: "Know that your children
shall be strangers in a land not theirs, and they will enslave them and afflict them... and afterward they will go
out with great wealth."*[1]

The "great wealth" referred to here is a recurrent theme in the
Torah's account of the Exodus — to the extent that one gets the
impression that this was the very purpose of our exile and enslavement in Egypt. In G-d's very first communication to Moses, when
G-d revealed Himself to Moses in a burning bush and charged

---

1   Genesis 15:12–14.

Moses with the mission of taking the Jewish people out of Egypt, G-d makes sure to include the vow that "when you go, you will not go empty-handed. Every woman will ask from her neighbor, and from the one who dwells in her house, vessels of gold and vessels of silver and garments... and you shall salvage Egypt."[2]

During the plague of darkness, when the land of Egypt was plunged into a darkness so thick that the Egyptians could not budge from their places, the Jewish people—whom the plague did not affect—were able to move about freely inside the Egyptians' homes. This, says the Midrash, was in order that the Jews should be able to take an "inventory" of the wealth of Egypt, so that the Egyptians could not deny the existence of any valuable objects the Jews asked for when they left Egypt.[3]

And just prior to the Exodus, G-d again says to Moses: "Please, speak into the ears of the people, that each man ask his [Egyptian] fellow, and each woman her fellow, for vessels of silver and gold."[4] G-d is virtually *begging* the children of Israel to take the wealth of Egypt! The Talmud explains that the Jewish people were disinclined to hold up their departure from Egypt in order to gather its wealth:

> *To what is this comparable? To a man who is locked up in prison and is told: "Tomorrow you shall be freed from prison and be given a lot of money." Says he: "I beg of you, free me today, and I ask for nothing more" ... [Thus, G-d had to beseech them:] "Please! Ask the Egyptians for gold and silver vessels, so that the righteous one (Abraham) should not say: He fulfilled 'they will enslave them and*

---

2   Exodus 3:21-22.
3   *Midrash Rabbah, Shemot* 14:3.
4   Exodus 11:2.

afflict them,' but He did not fulfill 'and afterward they will go out with great wealth.'"[5]

But would not Abraham, too, have been prepared to forgo the promise of "great wealth," if this were to hasten his children's liberation? Obviously, the gold and silver we carried out of Egypt were more than our compensation for generations of wageless labor in service of the Egyptians,[6] but an indispensable component of our redemption.

SCATTERED SPARKS

The great kabbalist Rabbi Isaac Luria taught that every object, force, and phenomenon in existence has a "spark of holiness" at its core. Every time that we utilize something to serve the Creator, we reveal its divine essence, thereby realizing its function within G-d's overall purpose for creation.

Each soul has its own "sparks" scattered about in the world, which actually form an integral part of the soul itself: No soul is complete until it has redeemed those sparks that belong to its mission in life. Thus we move through life, impelled from place to place and from occupation to occupation by seemingly random forces; but everything is by divine providence, which guides each of us to those possessions and opportunities whose "spark" is intimately connected with our soul.[7]

---

5 Talmud, *Berachot* 9b.
6 See Talmud, *Sanhedrin* 91a.
7 These consist of two general types, alluded to in the verse, "Every woman shall ask from her neighbor, and from the one who dwells in her house, vessels of gold and vessels of silver." Every soul has permanent "dwellers in her house"—routine involvements, dictated by its natural

Thus we find that Jacob risked his life to retrieve some "small jugs" he had left behind after crossing the Yabbok River.[8] "The righteous," remarks the Talmud, "value their possessions more than their bodies."[9] For they recognize the divine potential in every bit of matter, and see in each of their possessions a component of their own spiritual integrity.

Therein lies the deeper significance of the "great wealth" we carried out of Egypt: the sparks of holiness contained within these "gold and silver vessels and garments" constituted the spiritual harvest of our Egyptian Exile.

A MIXED APPROACH

One might surmise from the above that it is our sacred duty to partake of the material world to the greatest possible extent, so that we may achieve the sublimation of the "sparks of holiness" that dwell therein. In fact, however, the Torah's instructions on the matter are mixed, following a middle, and seemingly not always consistent, path between indulgence and self-denial.

On the one hand, the Torah admonishes the *nazir* (one who vows to abstain from wine), "Is what the Torah has forbidden not

---

talents and inclinations. It also has "neighbors" or casual acquaintances—the chance encounters of life, in which it comes in fleeting contact with something, unintentionally, or even unwillingly. Both of these, however, must be exploited as a source of "gold" and "silver." The very fact that a certain resource or opportunity has presented itself to a person indicates that it constitutes part of his or her mission in life; that it is the purpose of his or her *galut* (subjugation) to that particular corner of the material world; that this person, and this person alone, can redeem the spark it contains by utilizing it toward a G-dly end.

8   Genesis 32:25; Rashi, ad loc.
9   Talmud, *Chulin* 91a.

PASSOVER (7)

enough, that you assume further prohibitions upon yourself?" and calls him a "sinner" for having deprived himself of one of G-d's blessings.[10] "A person," says the Talmud, "is obligated to say: 'The entire world was created for my sake, and I was created to serve my Creator.'"[11] In other words, not only the necessities of life, but the entirety of creation—including those elements whose sole human utility is to make life more pleasurable—can, and should, serve a life devoted to the service of its Creator. Our sages go so far as to say that "A person will have to answer for everything that his eye beheld and he did not consume."[12]

On the other hand, we find expressions in Torah of a decidedly ascetic approach to life. In addition to the numerous prohibitions and restrictions pertaining to diet, sexual relations, and other areas of life commanded in the Torah, the Talmud interprets the injunction, "Be holy," as a commandment to "abstain also from that which is permissible to you" and a warning against being "a hedonist with the Torah's permission" who indulges in every permissible pleasure.[13] The *Ethics of the Fathers* declares: "This is the way of Torah: Eat bread with salt, drink water in small measure, sleep on the ground, and live a life of hardship."[14] These biblical and talmudic injunctions are at the root of the chassidic doctrine of *iskafia* ("self-conquest") in all that pertains to the body's physical needs and desires. It is told that the very first thing that students coming to study under the tutelage of Rabbi Schneur Zalman of

---

10 Talmud, *Sanhedrin* 37a.
11 Ibid., *Kidushin* 82a.
12 Ibid., *Nedarim* 10a; Jerusalem Talmud, *Nedarim* 9:1; Talmud, *Kidushin* 82b; Jerusalem Talmud, *Kidushin* 4:12.
13 Leviticus 19:2; Talmud, *Yevamot* 20a; Nachmanides on Leviticus 19:2.
14 *Ethics of the Fathers* 6:4.

Liadi were taught was: "What is forbidden, one must not; what is permitted, one need not."[15]

How, then, are we to regard the physical self? Is it a mere tool, to be exploited but never indulged? Should it be provided only with the bare minimum it needs to hold the soul and support the soul's spiritual pursuits, or is there value or even virtue in the experience of physical pleasure and the enhancement of physical life with objects of luxury and beauty?

Bread, Vegetable, and Meat

One approach to the resolution to this contradiction can be found in the three primary symbols of the Exodus: the Passover offering, matzah, and *maror* (the "bitter herb").

All three are foods and, eating being the most physical of human activities, can be seen as representative of the various areas of physical life. Matzah, the humble "bread of poverty,"[16] represents the bare necessities of life. The Passover offering—a yearling lamb or kid slaughtered in the Holy Temple, roasted whole, and eaten at the *seder*—represents luxuries whose function is solely to give pleasure. *Maror*, a vegetable, represents a middle ground between these two extremes: more than the minimalist bread, less than the sumptuous meat.[17]

A further examination of these three *seder* observances yields

---

15 *HaYom Yom, Adar* II 25.

16 Deuteronomy 16:3; see *Bread of Faith*, pp. 53–61 above.

17 Cf. Talmud, *Chulin* 84a: "The Torah (Leviticus 17:13 and Deuteronomy 12:20) is teaching proper behavior, to eat meat only on occasion... only as a delicacy... Thus Rabbi Elazar ben Azariah said: 'One who possesses a *maneh* (a certain sum of money) should purchase vegetables for his pot... [if he has] fifty *maneh*, he should purchase meat...'"

PASSOVER (7)   77

another distinction between these three foods: they each differ
from the others in the extent to which their observance has been
affected by the destruction of the Holy Temple in Jerusalem — an
event which rendered many of the *mitzvot* of the Torah impossible
to fulfill, or observable only in a diminished, or merely commemorative, form.

Ever since the Holy Temple was destroyed, we have been unable to bring the Passover offering. Today, it is present at the *seder*
table only in the form of the uneaten, purely commemorative, *zeroa* ("shankbone") placed on the *seder* plate.[18]

As for the "bitter herb," we do eat *maror* today, but doing so is
not the full-fledged *mitzvah* it was at the time that the Holy Temple stood in Jerusalem. According to Torah law, the bitter herb is
to be eaten as an accompaniment to the meat of the Passover offering; when there is no Passover offering, there is no biblical obligation to eat *maror*. Nevertheless, our sages instituted that *maror*
should be eaten on the night of Passover in commemoration of the
"real" *maror* commanded by the Torah.

On the other hand, eating matzah on the night of Passover is
a *mitzvah* in its own right. Thus, matzah remains the only one of
the three Passover foods that has the full status of a "biblical commandment" (*mitzvah mide'oreita*) today.[19]

"From the day that the Holy Temple was destroyed," say our sages, "it was decreed that the homes of the righteous should be in ruins... The servant need not be better off than the master."[20] As long

---

18   Furthermore, it is the custom to remove almost all the meat from the
     zeroah bones, to avoid any suggestion that we actually have a Passover
     offering today. The Passover offering is also represented in the *seder* in
     our eating of the *afikoman* — which is a piece of matzah!
19   Talmud, *Pesachim* 120a; *Shulchan Aruch HaRav, Orach Chaim*, 475:15.
20   Talmud, *Berachot* 58b.

as G-d remains homeless, expelled from His manifest presence in the physical realm, the Jew, too, is a stranger in the material world. Ultimately, physical matter is no less a creation of G-d, and no less capable of serving and expressing His truth, than spirit; but in times of dimmed divine presence, the substantiality of the physical all too readily obscures, rather than reveals, its G-dly essence. In such times, we must limit our involvement with the material, lest our immersion in it dull our spiritual senses and blur the divine objectives of our lives.

Thus, no Passover offering is possible in our present-day world: dealing with the bare bones of physicality is challenge enough without the meat of opulence clogging our lives. Indeed, as seen from the most basic vantage point on life (the "biblical" perspective), only the austere matzah is needed. Anything beyond that is a foray into hostile territory whose risks rival its potential rewards.

Nevertheless, our sages have opened a tract of this territory to exploration and development, empowering us to make positive and G-dly use of much of physical life. While steering clear of the overtly superfluous "meat," they broadened our physical fare to include "vegetables"—physical goods and experiences that, while not of the strictest necessity, are more of a need than a luxury. "Meat," however—pleasure for the sake of pleasure—remains out of bounds, constituting a degree of involvement with materiality that cannot be dealt with in our era of spiritual darkness.

(Indeed, a clear distinction must also be drawn between the "bread" and "vegetable" realms: *maror* is a *bitter* vegetable, emphasizing the fact that whenever our material involvements extend beyond life's strictest necessities, they constitute a most difficult and trying challenge, demanding a greater degree of vigilance not to allow the means to obscure the end.)

Life on the Road

None of this means that we are to regard the physical as evil or irredeemable. On the contrary—we know that "meat" was, and will again be, a basic component of the *seder*. We know that in the proper spiritual environment, the most physical of experiences can be as pure an expression of the G-dly essence of existence as the most sublime prayer. And it is this knowledge that enables us to keep the proper perspective on whatever aspect of physical life we are capable of engaging with under our present circumstances.

The story is told of the visitor who, stopping by the home of Rabbi Dov Ber of Mezheritch,[21] was outraged by the poverty he encountered there. Rabbi Dov Ber's home was bare of all furnishing, save for an assortment of rough wooden planks and blocks that served as benches for his students during the day and as beds for his family at night. "How can you live like this?" demanded the visitor. "I myself am far from wealthy, but at least in my home you will find, thank G-d, the basic necessities: some chairs, a table, beds..."

"Indeed?" said Rabbi Dov Ber. "But I don't see any of your furnishings. How do you manage without them?"

"What do you mean? Do you think that I carry all my possessions with me wherever I go? When I travel, I make do with what's available. But at home—a person's home is a different matter altogether!"

"Ah, yes," said Rabbi Dov Ber. "At home, it is a different matter altogether..."

---

21   Second leader of the chassidic movement; d. 1772.

THE MUDDY PATH

All that exists on land, exists in the sea

Talmud, Chulin 127a

On the seventh day of Passover, we commemorate the miracle of the "splitting of the sea." As related in 13th and 14th chapters of the book of Exodus, Pharaoh and his army chased after the children of Israel in order to force their return to Egypt. Miraculously, the sea split to allow the children of Israel to pass, and closed in over the pursuing Egyptians.

On a mystical level, this event was more than a divine intervention to save the Israelites from the Egyptians. The Midrash relates that when "Moses stretched out his hand over the sea... and the waters split,"

> *All the waters in the world split... the waters in the cisterns, in the ditches... in the pitchers and in the cups... the supernal waters and the earthly waters...*[1]

We each inhabit two worlds. One world is the "revealed" portion of our existence: our professional, social, and family lives; our conscious thoughts and feelings. Simultaneously, we inhabit a "hidden" world—a world of subconscious drives and desires, of innately known truths and deeply-held convictions that rarely, if ever, see the light of day.

---

[1] Exodus 14:21; *Mechilta,* ad loc.

PASSOVER (8)   81

The teachings of kabbalah and chassidism refer to these two worlds as our "land" reality and our "sea" reality. On land, things are out in the open—so much so, that they often seem disconnected from their environment and source of life. (Looking at a throng of suited businesspersons striding down a busy city sidewalk, it is hardly apparent that they derive their nourishment from the earth.) In the sea, on the other hand, everything is submerged and hidden. At most, we might catch a shadowy glimpse of what transpires close to its surface; of what lurks in its depths we see nothing at all.

What is the case on the individual level is also true of creation as a whole. There are the "revealed worlds," which include the material and physical realities, as well as those spiritual realities that are fathomable and accessible to us. But beyond this "land" lies the mysterious sea, the supranatural and suprarational strata of creation.

Much of the pain and frustration in our lives stems from the rift between our land and sea personalities. If only we could reconcile our revealed life with our subconscious self! If only we could recognize our true will and understand our deepest yearnings; if only the countless choices we make each day in our "terrestrial" existence would reflect who we truly are and what we truly desire. On the cosmic level, too, the strife and discord that grips the "known" universe is the result of its disconnection from its mystic dimension.

This, explain the chassidic masters, is the spiritual significance of the "splitting of the sea" on the seventh day of Passover. When G-d split the Red Sea for the children of Israel, He also split "all the waters in the world"—from the physical seas on earth, to the individual sea of every soul, to the cosmic sea that suffuses the deepest secrets of creation. In the words of the Psalmist, G-d "transformed the sea into dry land; they traversed the river on foot."[2] What is ordinarily submerged and inaccessible became manifest and tactual, and traversing the depths of one's soul was like walking on firm terrain.

After "the children of Israel passed through the midst of the sea on dry land," the waters reassumed their natural course.[3] Once again the sea reality was obscured; once again the subconscious became a mystic and secret place. But a precedent had been established, a potential implanted in our souls. Never again was the sea to be impregnable; never again were the revealed and hidden in man to constitute two hermetic worlds. By splitting all seas of creation, G-d empowered us to penetrate our individual seas, to blaze pathways of dry land on the ocean floors of our souls.

HOW DRY?

In the *dayeinu* hymn, sung at the Passover *seder*, we enumerate fifteen things that G-d did for us when He liberated us from Egypt and took us to be His chosen people. We thank G-d for each of these things individually, recognizing each as a distinct and unique gift. Thus we say: "If He had taken us out of Egypt, but had not punished [the Egyptians] — it would have sufficed for us... If He had fed us the manna, but had not given us the Shabbat — it would have sufficed for us..." and so on.

In the stanza that relates to the splitting of the sea, we sing:

> *If He had split the sea for us, but did not take us across it on dry land — it would have sufficed for us.*

---

2   Psalms 66:6.

3   Exodus 14:27–28.

PASSOVER (8)   83

A number of the commentaries on the *Haggadah* are puzzled by
the meaning of these lines: What does it mean that it would have
sufficed for us if G-d had "split the sea for us" but did not "take us
across it on dry land"? Of what use would the splitting of the sea
have been to us, had it not enabled us to cross to the other side and
escape Pharaoh's pursuing armies?

Avudraham[4] explains that the emphasis is on the fact that we
crossed the sea *on dry land*. In order to save us from the Egyptians, it would have been enough that the sea split and we trudged
through the mud and silt that naturally covers the sea bottom. To
show His love for His people, G-d performed an additional miracle, making our path as dry and firm as land that has never been
covered by water.

But the fifteen things enumerated by the author of *dayeinu* are
not simply a list of miracles performed by G-d in the course of
the Exodus (of which there were many others). These are all major
developments in Jewish history: the Exodus itself, the splitting of
the sea, the manna, the giving of the Torah, the entry into the Holy
Land, the building of the Holy Temple—events that profoundly
impacted our lives as Jews to this very day. What, then, is the lasting significance of the fact that not only did the sea split for us, but
that it also revealed to us a wholly dry passage through its depths?

THE INTERMEDIATE MAN

In his *Tanya*, Rabbi Schneur Zalman of Liadi describes three spiritual personalities: the *rasha* (sinner), the *tzaddik* (perfectly righteous person), and the *beinoni* (the "intermediate").

---

4   Classic commentary on the *Siddur* by Rabbi David Avudraham
    (14th-century Spain).

The *rasha* is one whose "revealed" life—his deeds, speech, and conscious thoughts—is at odds with his hidden essence. His soul is "veritably a part of G-d above,"[5] but his daily life includes acts that are a transgression of the divine will. His quintessential desire is to be faithful to his Source, but he consciously desires things that impede his relationship with G-d.

In the *tzaddik*, there is perfect harmony between the hidden and revealed portions of his self. The *tzaddik*'s intrinsic love of G-d spills over into his "revealed" life, so that he desires only that which enhances his bond with the Almighty and is repelled by anything that threatens it. The *tzaddik* is a person who has transformed his "sea" into "dry land"—whose quintessential self and manifest self are one and the same.

Between the *rasha* and the *tzaddik* is the *beinoni*, the "intermediate." Like the *rasha*, the *beinoni* desires evil; but he never allows his negative impulses to find expression in action, speech, or willful thought. In other words, the *beinoni* is a behavioral *tzaddik* and a psychological *rasha*. On the behavioral level, the *beinoni*'s life is in complete conformity with his inner identity as a spark of the divine torch. Psychologically, the dissonance between his essence and his conscious self remains.

The *beinoni* is one who has split his sea, but who still struggles along its muddy bottom. He has penetrated his hidden self enough to "get across to the other side." He gets the same "results" as the *tzaddik*: his daily life is a perfect reflection of his innermost self. But his sea has not been transformed into dry land. Life, for the *beinoni*, is a constant struggle with the contradiction between sea and land.

---

5   *Tanya*, ch. 2, after Job 31:2.

A Twofold Split

After describing the inner life of these three spiritual prototypes, the *Tanya* goes on to declare that every individual has the capacity to be a *beinoni*—to gain complete mastery over his behavior and not allow a single evil impulse to find expression in actual deed. But few can attain the status of the *tzaddik*, and it is not expected, or even desirable, that all but a select few should achieve this state. For there is something about the *beinoni*, something about his perpetual battle with evil, that makes his life richer and more G-dly than the perfect existence of the *tzaddik*. G-d desires both *beinonim* and *tzaddikim* in His world, for each realizes a dimension of the divine purpose in creation that the other cannot fulfill.

On a more subtle level, our lives include both states. We each have our *beinoni* periods of struggle and our *tzaddik* moments of harmony—both of which are integral to a complete self.

In the final analysis, then, we each experience two splittings-of-the-sea in our lives, paralleling the two "versions" of the miracle itemized in the *dayeinu* song. There is a "splitting of the sea" in which the path through our oceanic self struggles through the mud, and a "splitting of the sea" in which we tread resolutely and tranquilly cross on dry land.

On the seventh day following the Exodus, G-d granted us the capacity for both these modes of life: for challenge as well as for perfection, for divine struggle as well as for harmonious wholeness. G-d split the sea for us, empowering us to manifest our hidden self in our daily lives. And G-d transformed the sea into dry land, enabling us to aspire to a complete synthesis of our mystic essence and our terrestrial personality.

MIRIAM'S SONG

Miriam the prophetess... took the tambourine in her hand; and all the women followed her with tambourines and dances.

And Miriam called to them: "Sing to G-d..." Exodus 15:20–21

e don't sing when we are frightened, despairing, sleepy, or after a heavy meal. We sing when we are pining after a loved one, when we are yearning for better times, when we are celebrating an achievement, or anticipating a revelation.

We don't sing when we are complacent. We sing when we are striving for something, or when we have tasted joy and are climbing it to the heavens.

Song is prayer, the endeavor to rise above the petty cares of life and cleave to one's source.[1] Song is the quest for redemption.

The Midrash[2] enumerates ten preeminent songs in the history of Israel—ten occasions on which our experience of redemption

---

[1] Throughout the Torah, song is used as a synonym of prayer (e.g., Jeremiah 7:16 and 11:14, II Chronicles 6:19 and 20:22, Psalms 17:1 and 61:2). The offering of the *korbanot* in the Holy Temple—the forerunner of our daily prayers—was accompanied by the vocal and instrumental music of the Levites.

Aside from the traditional intonations of the reader who leads the prayer service, Jews have always recited their prayers in a full, melodious voice. This is especially the custom amongst chassidim; indeed, many great chassidic melodies are, in fact, spontaneous compositions which emerged from personal prayer.

[2] *Midrash Tanchuma, Beshalach* 10.

PASSOVER (9)   87

found expression in melody and verse. The first nine were: the song sung on the night of the Exodus in Egypt,[3] the "song at the sea,"[4] the "song at the well,"[5] Moses' song upon his completion of writing the Torah,[6] the song with which Joshua stopped the sun,[7] Deborah's song,[8] King David's song,[9] the song at the dedication of the Holy Temple,[10] and King Solomon's song extolling the love between the Divine Groom and His bride Israel.[11]

The tenth song, says the Midrash, will be the *shir chadash*, the "new song" of the ultimate redemption—a redemption that is global and absolute; a redemption that will annihilate all suffering, ignorance, jealousy, and hate from the face of the earth. A redemption of such proportions that the yearning it evokes, and the joy it brings, require a new song—a completely new musical vocabulary—to capture the voice of creation's ultimate striving.

ENCORE

The most well-known of the ten songs of redemption is *shirat hayam*, the "song at the sea" sung by Moses and the children of Israel upon their crossing of the Sea of Reeds. We recite this song every day in our morning prayers, and publicly read it in the synagogue twice a year: on the seventh day of Passover (the anniversary of the splitting of the sea and the song's composition), and on a

---

3   Isaiah 30:29.
4   Exodus 15:1–21.
5   Numbers 21:17–20.
6   Deuteronomy 31–32.
7   Joshua 10:12–13.
8   Judges 5.
9   II Samuel 22.
10   Psalms 30.
11   The biblical book of "Song of Songs."

midwinter Shabbat in the course of the annual Torah-reading cycle—a Shabbat which is therefore distinguished with the name *Shabbat Shirah*, "Shabbat of Song."

The song at the sea praises G-d for His miraculous redemption of Israel when He split the sea for them and drowned the pursuing Egyptians in it, and expresses Israel's desire that G-d lead them to their homeland and rest His presence amongst them in the Holy Temple. It concludes with a reference to the ultimate redemption, when "G-d will reign for all eternity."

Actually, there are two versions of the song at the sea—a male version and a female version. After Moses and the children of Israel sang their song,

> *Miriam the prophetess, the sister of Aaron, took the tambourine in her hand; and all the women followed her with tambourines and dances. And Miriam called to them: "Sing to G-d, for He is most exalted; horse and rider He cast in the sea…"*[12]

The men sang, and then the women. The men sang, and then the women sang, danced, and tambourined. The men sang—sang their joy over their deliverance, sang their yearning for a more perfect redemption. But something was lacking—something that only a woman's song could complete.

FEELING AND FAITH

Miriam, the elder sister of Moses and Aaron, presided over the female encore to the song at the sea. Miriam, named "Bitterness"

---

12   Exodus 15:20–21.

PASSOVER (9)   89

because at the time of her birth the people of Israel entered the harshest phase of the Egyptian exile.[13] Miriam, who when the infant Moses was placed in a basket at the banks of the Nile, "stood watch from afar, to see what would become of him."[14]

For it was Miriam, with her deep well of feminine feeling, who truly experienced the bitterness of *galut* (exile and persecution). And it was Miriam, with her woman's capacity for endurance, perseverance, and hope, who stood lonely watch over the fledging life in a basket at the edge of a mammoth river; whose vigilance over "what would become of him" and his mission to bring redemption to her people never faltered.

The image of the young woman standing watch in the thicket of rushes at the edge of the Nile, the hope of redemption persevering against the bitterness of *galut* in her heart, evokes the image of another watching matriarch—Rachel. As the prophet Jeremiah describes, it is Rachel who, in her lonely grave on the road from Bethlehem to Jerusalem, weeps over her children's suffering in *galut*. It is she, more than the male patriarchs or leaders of Israel, who feels the depth of our pain; so it is her intervention before G-d, after theirs has failed, which brings the redemption.[15]

Miriam and her chorus brought to the song at the sea the intensity of feeling and depth of faith unique to womankind. Their experience of the bitterness of *galut* had been far more intense than that of their menfolk, yet their faith had been stronger and more enduring. So their yearning for redemption had been that much more potent, as was their joy over its realization and their striving toward its greater fulfillment.

---

13 *Midrash Rabbah, Shemot* 26:1; Ibid., *Shir HaShirim* 2:11.
14 Exodus 2:4.
15 Jeremiah 31:14–15; *Pesikta Rabbati* 3.

TODAY

The great kabbalist Rabbi Isaac Luria writes that the last generation before the coming of Moshiach is the reincarnation of the generation of the Exodus.

Today, as we stand at the threshold of the ultimate redemption, it is once again the woman whose song is the most poignant, whose tambourine is the most hopeful, whose dance is the most joyous. Today, as then, the redemption will be realized "in the merit of righteous women."[16] Today, as then, the woman's yearning for Moshiach—a yearning which runs deeper than that of the man, and inspires and uplifts it—forms the dominant strain in the melody of redemption.

---

16   Talmud, *Sotah* 11b; *Yalkut Shimoni*, Ruth 606.

PASSOVERING
TIME

In order that you should remember the day
you went out of Egypt, all the days of your
life.   Deuteronomy 16:3

"In each and every generation," our sages enjoin in a key passage of the Passover *Haggadah*, "a person is obligated to see himself as if he himself has come out of Egypt."

True freedom is freedom from limitation—whether external or internal, whether physical, psychological, or spiritual. *Mitzrayim*, the Hebrew word for "Egypt," means "boundaries" and "constrictions"; *yetziat mitzrayim*, "going out of Egypt" (the Torah's term for the Exodus) is the endeavor to transcend limitation, to rise above all that inhibits the soul of man.

One of the most constricting elements of the human condition is the phenomenon of time. Time carries off the past and holds off the future, confining our lives to a temporal sliver of "present." But on the first night of Passover, we break the bonds of time, having received a mandate to experience the Exodus "as if he himself has come out of Egypt." We recall the Exodus in our minds, verbalize it in the telling of the *Haggadah*, digest it in the form of matzah and *maror*. As we passover the centuries, memory—those faded visages of past that generally constitute our only answer to the tyranny of time—becomes experience, and history is made current and real.

LEAP TO THE FUTURE

Passover is an eight-day festival, with two opening and two closing days of heightened observance and commemoration.[1] While the theme of freedom runs as a current throughout the festival, the first days of Passover focus primarily on the "first redemption"— our liberation from Egypt thirty-three centuries ago—while the last days highlight the "final redemption": the future era of divine goodness and perfection heralded by Moshiach.

On the first two nights of Passover, we conduct the *seder*, replete with the rituals and discussion which recall the Exodus. On the seventh day of Passover, we read the "song at the sea," which contains an important allusion to the messianic era.[2] On the eighth day, the *haftarah* (reading from the Prophets) consists of one of the most vivid descriptions of the future redemption (Isaiah 10–12) to be found in the Torah. The founder of chassidism, Rabbi Israel Baal Shem Tov, instituted the custom of partaking in a special festive meal toward the evening of the last day of Passover, which he named "Moshiach's meal," explaining that on the last day of Passover there is a revelation of the light of the future redemption.

Thus our transcendence of time enters a new, heightened phase in Passover's closing days. It is one thing to elevate a memory of the past to the point of actual reexperience, but quite another to "remember forward"—to experience an event that lies in the future, especially an event that has no precedent or parallel in human history. Yet in the closing hours of Passover, we enter into the world

---

[1] Called *yom tov*. These include the "additional festival-days of the Diaspora" added outside of the Land of Israel. In Israel, Passover is observed for seven days, with one opening day and one closing day of *yom tov*.

[2] Talmud, *Sanhedrin* 91b; see previous essay, *Miriam's Song*, pp. 86–90.

of Moshiach. Having vaulted over millennia of the past on the *seder* night, we now surmount the blank wall of future, to taste the matzah and wine of the ultimate redemption.

CHAPTER NINETEEN

The Counting of the Omer
Growth and Self-Refinement

Nissan 16 to Sivan 5

"When you take this people out of Egypt," said G-d to Moses when He revealed Himself to him in a burning bush at the foot of Mount Sinai, "you shall serve G-d on this mountain."

It took seven weeks to reach the mountain. The children of Israel departed Egypt on the 15th of *Nissan*; on the 6th of *Sivan*, celebrated ever since as the festival of Shavuot, they assembled at the foot of Mount Sinai and received the Torah from G-d.

The teachings of kabbalah explain that the 49 days that connect Passover with Shavuot correspond to the 49 traits and drives of the human heart. Each day saw the refinement of one of these "*sefirot*," bringing the people of Israel one step closer to their election as G-d's chosen people and their receiving of G-d's communication to humanity.

Every year, we retrace this inner journey with our "counting of the *omer*." Beginning on the second night of Passover, we count the days and weeks: "Today is one day to the *omer*"; "Today is two days to the *omer*"; "Today is seven days, which are one week to the *omer*"; "Today is eight days, which are one week and one day to the *omer*"; and so on, until "Today is forty-nine days, which are seven weeks to the *omer*." Shavuot, the "festival of weeks" is the product of this count, driven by the miracles and revelations of the Exodus but achieved by a methodical, 49-step process of self-refinement within the human soul.

(In addition to the nightly *mitzvah* of "counting the *omer*," there are certain customs that are associated with other events that occurred in the period between Passover and Shavuot; we will discuss these in our chapter on "Lag BaOmer")

Three essays comprise our chapter in the *omer* count. *The Journey* explores the history, purpose, and dynamics of the count. *Accumulative Time* looks at the manner in which our experience of time is altered by our counting it; and *A Month of Mitzvot* dwells on the different ways in which we relate to the "routine" and "special" moments of our lives.

THE JOURNEY

You shall count for yourselves from the morrow of the Shabbat, from the day on which you bring the omer *offering, seven complete weeks they shall be; until the morrow of the seventh week, you shall count fifty days... And you shall proclaim that very day a holy festival...* Leviticus 23:15–21

There was once a people who lived in a deep valley ringed by high mountains. A perpetual mist, trapped by the mountain walls, hung over the valley, allowing only a dim light to penetrate. Generation after generation were born, lived, and died in this gray world.

The old men of the valley told stories of a brighter, warmer world beyond the mountains, a world made joyous and beautiful by a thing called "the sun." At times, a listener of these stories would be inspired to set out for this sunlit world. But the mountains were steep, the trails treacherous, the maps uncertain, and the goal but a fanciful idea. They all came back empty-handed.

One day, a strong wind forced a breach in the cloud-cover; for a fleeting minute, the valley was flooded with light and warmth. For the first time in their lives, the people of the valley beheld the face of the sun. Then the wind receded, the breach was closed, and once again they were in their familiar, sunless world.

THE COUNTING OF THE OMER (1) 99

"So this is the sun!" exclaimed the people of the valley. "This is sunlight! This is what it is like to live a life of light, beauty, and joy! We must leave this dark, cold place. We must set out for the sun-blessed world beyond the mountains."

So the people began climbing out of the valley. The mountains were as steep as ever, the trails as fraught with hardship and uncertainty. But whenever they faltered in their climb, whenever they began to doubt the attainability of their goal, they would remember that moment of sunlight, and it would drive them to press on. Inspired and prodded by that vision, they climbed out of the clouds to the world of the sun.

THE CLIMB TO SINAI

For 210 years, our ancestors lived in darkness. Enslaved by the Egyptians, the most debased society on earth, the children of Israel inhabited a spiritual fog which shut off every vestige of manifest G-dliness.

Their elders spoke of an age-old promise, made by the G-d of their fathers, that they would one day leave this sunless world. They spoke of a mountain top upon which G-d would show Himself to them, take them as His chosen people, and grant them His Torah, the revelation of His wisdom and will. They spoke of a land, basking in the light of divine providence, in which they would fulfill their destiny as "a light unto the nations."

But this was little more than a fantasy. The darkness of their world seemed impregnable. They had no idea what this place in the sun was like, much less how to get there.

Then, at the stroke of midnight on *Nissan* 15, 2448 (1313 BCE), a breach opened up in the clouds of their exile and they beheld the face of their Creator. On that night, "the Holy One, Blessed be He, revealed His very self to them and redeemed them."[1]

G-d, of course, could have simply lifted them out of Egypt and brought them to Mount Sinai that very night. But G-d wanted it to be their journey, their achievement. So after that momentary vision, the face of G-d receded.

Then began the arduous climb to Sinai. The Jews were out of Egypt, but Egypt was still deeply embedded within the Jews. For seven weeks they struggled to refine the seven traits of their souls, to cleanse it of the profanity of Egypt and make themselves worthy candidates for the divine choice.

This was something that they had to achieve on their own, in the darkness of their deficiencies and the coldness of their alienation. But it was that initial vision of the divine light that inspired, encouraged, and drove them in their journey.

Every year, on the first night of Passover, we commemorate the events of the night of the Exodus. Through the *seder* observances, we reexperience the liberating vision which drives our annual emergence from our personal "Egypt" and our internal liberation "from slavery to freedom, from darkness to a great light."[2]

But the revelation of the Exodus is but a brief, momentary flash. On the following day we begin our 49-day trek to Sinai, reenacted each year with the "counting of the *omer*."[3] Beginning with the second night of Passover, we count the days traversed from the

---

[1]   Passover *Haggadah*.

[2]   Ibid.

[3]   On the second day of Passover, the day on which the count begins, an *omer* (approx. 43 oz.) of barley was offered at the Holy Temple in Jerusalem, representing the refinement of the "animal soul" of man (barley being the representative animal food—see I Kings 5:8, and Talmud, *Sotah* 14a) which is the objective of the count (see *The Three Names of Shavuot* on pp. 193–200, below).

THE COUNTING OF THE OMER (1)   101

Exodus, chronicling the milestones and stations of our journey of self-refinement.

The 50th day is the festival of Shavuot, our annual reexperience of the giving of the Torah, when we once again stand at Sinai to receive G-d's communication of His wisdom and will and be chosen as G-d's very own "kingdom of priests and a holy nation."[4]

DAYS AND WEEKS

In commanding us to count the days from Passover to Shavuot, the Torah instructs:

> You shall count for yourselves from the morrow of the Shabbat, from the day on which you bring the omer offering, seven complete weeks they shall be; until the morrow of the seventh week, you shall count fifty days... And you shall proclaim that very day a holy festival...

In other words, not only the days, but also the *weeks* are to be counted. Thus, on the seventh day of the count we say, "Today is seven days, which are one week, to the *omer*"; on the 25th day we say, "Today is twenty-five days, which are two weeks and three days, to the *omer*"; and so on to the last night of the count, when we say, "Today is forty-nine days, which are seven weeks, to the *omer*." Indeed, the very name of the festival that culminates the count, *Shavuot*, means "weeks," emphasizing that it is the product of the seven-week count from the second day of Passover.[5]

---

4   Exodus 19:6.
5   As a result, Shavuot is the only festival that does not have a fixed calendar date, but is defined as the 50th day of the *omer* count.

    (Today we follow a fixed calendar in which the month of *Nissan* always has 30 days and the month of *Iyar*, 29 days. Thus, the 50th day

Kabbalistic teaching explains that there are seven basic drives in the human character: *chesed* (love and benevolence), *gevurah* (awe and restraint), *tiferet* (harmony and compassion), *netzach* (victory and ambition), *hod* (humility and devotion), *yesod* (bonding) and *malchut* (sovereignty and receptiveness).[6] Each of these traits

---

of the count, which begins on *Nissan* 16 [the second night of Passover], always coincides with the 6th of *Sivan*. However, this is only because today we do not have a functioning *sanhedrin* [supreme court of Torah law]. In essence, the Jewish calendar is supposed to be fixed by eyewitness sightings of the new moon, based on which the *sanhedrin* proclaims the new month. By this process, which will recommence with the coming of Moshiach and the reestablishment of the *sanhedrin*, any month may consist of either 29 or 30 days; Shavuot might thus occur on the 5th, 6th, or 7th of *Sivan*.

But the fact that the true "date" of Shavuot is the 50th day of the *omer* rather than the 6th of *Sivan* can, in certain circumstance, be pertinent today as well. For example, there exists a *halachic* dilemma in the case of a traveler who crosses the international date line during the period between Passover and Shavuot, thereby "gaining" or "losing" a day. Regarding all other festivals, whose dates are determined by the calendar, an individual's loss or gain of a day is irrelevant. But since Shavuot is defined solely as the 50th day from the second day of Passover, the question arises: Is this traveler to observe Shavuot on *his* 50th day, or is he to defer to the 50th day as counted by the community with whom he is observing the festival?)

6   There are, in fact, ten *sefirot*, and ten corresponding attributes of the human soul. The first three (*chochmah*, *binah*, and *daat*) are "intellectual" or perceptual faculties and beyond the scope of the *sefirah* count, which involves the refinement of the human character and emotions.

Each of these attributes are multifaceted and multinuanced, and there are no English words that can be said to capture its essence; thus, each has several translations in contemporary English literature on kabbalah and chassidism, depending on the context and the author's preference. For a comprehensive discussion of these seven attributes as they exist in the human character, and for examples of the seven aspects within each attribute, see *A Spiritual Guide to the Counting of the Omer* by Simon Jacobson (Meaningful Life Center 1996) and *Ten Keys*

THE COUNTING OF THE OMER (1)   103

includes nuances of all seven (e.g., *chesed* of *chesed*, *gevurah* of *chesed*, *tiferet* of *chesed*, etc.) making a total of 49 aspects to the human character.[7]

Thus, the basic journey is one of seven weeks, each devoted to perfecting another of our seven primary attributes. The days are details and aspects of the weeks—a count within a count, a journey within a journey.[8]

For Understanding Human Nature by Mattis Kantor (Zichron Press, NY, 1994).

7 *Gevurah* of *chesed*, for example, is the capacity for restraint in love—of maintaining a degree of distance and respect for the loved one's individuality in one's loving. For additional examples, see the works referred to in the previous note.

8 Therein lies the significance of a difference in *halachic* status between the counting of the "weeks" and the counting of the "days" in the *omer* count.

According to most *halachic* authorities, the count has true significance only when it follows the offering of the *omer* in the Holy Temple (see footnote 3 above); hence, our counting today is not a full-fledged biblical commandment (*mitzvah mide'oreita*), but a rabbinical ordinance that merely commemorates the *mitzvah* fulfilled in the times of the Temple (See Talmud, *Menachot* 66a; *Tosafot*, ad loc.; *Shulchan Aruch HaRav, Orach Chaim* 489:2, 17; et al.). Maimonides, however, is of the opinion that even today, counting the *omer* is a biblical precept (*Mishneh Torah, Laws of Regular and Additional Offerings*, 7:22). A third opinion is a combination of the first two: according to Rabbeinu Yerucham, it is a biblical *mitzvah* to count the days also when the Holy Temple is not extant, but the *mitzvah* to count the weeks applies only when the *omer* is offered, and is thus today only a rabbinical precept (*Toledot Adam VeChavah, Sefer Adam*, path 5, section 4).

In terms of our internal "counting of the *omer*," this means that while we are able today to refine specific elements of our character—perhaps even all 49 of them—we lack the capacity to piece these together into a perfect self. In other words, the *quest* for perfection proceeds at all times and under all conditions, even in the darkest hours of *galut*; advances are made in this quest, pinpoints of perfection achieved within an imperfect self and world; but actual perfection—including

THE CONTRADICTION

The Torah's emphasis on the *weeks* of the *omer* count gives rise to a seeming contradiction in its instructions as to how the count is to be conducted. The Talmud devotes a lengthy discussion to resolve this inconsistency and arrive at a decisive interpretation of the Torah's words.

The Torah not only instructs us to count seven weeks from the second day of Passover—it says that these should be "seven *complete* weeks." This seems to imply that the count should include seven full calendar weeks, each running from Sunday to Shabbat. This would mean that the festival of Shavuot will always fall on a Sunday—the day after the seventh "complete" week has been concluded.[9]

The Talmud, however, rejects this hypothesis. For the Torah explicitly instructs, "You shall count fifty days." Obviously, then, the "complete weeks" of the *omer* count are not the Sunday-to-Shabbat weeks that populate our calendar, but "man-made" weeks—

---

the actual perfection of a complete portion of the soul—can only be attained when the divine home is restored in our midst.

Today, we might hold all the pieces of the puzzle in our hands, yet the complete picture eludes us. Only upon our emergence from *galut* will the 49 days of our soul amount to seven complete weeks.

In this context, see *The Eighth Dimension* in vol. 1, pp. 127–138 in this series.

9 Indeed, the *Baitusim* (a breakaway Jewish sect who rejected the "Oral Torah"—the traditional interpretation of Torah handed down through the generations) contended that this is how the count is to be conducted. The *Baitusim* based their interpretation on the Torah's instruction to begin the count "on the morrow of the Shabbat," which they understood as a reference to the weekly Shabbat. The traditional interpretation, however, is that the "Shabbat" to which the Torah is referring is the first day of Passover. (A festival day is also referred to in the Torah as *Shabbat*, for on these days we cease from our workday labors.)

THE COUNTING OF THE OMER (1)   105

seven-day units created by our count. Otherwise, the count would,
in most years, total more than fifty days. (For example, if the first
day of Passover occurs on a Tuesday, and we were to insist on seven
"complete" Sunday-to-Shabbat weeks, Shavuot will occur on the
54th day of the count.)

But there are certain years, concludes the Talmud, in which the
configuration of the calendar is such that there is no inconsistency,
and the Torah's words can be implemented in their most literal
sense. When the first day of Passover falls on a Shabbat, the seven
weeks of the *omer* are "complete" in every sense. They are fully personal weeks, each containing seven days of our individual count;
and they are also complete calendar weeks, corresponding to the
seven-day cycle which G-d instituted at the very beginning of creation, and which continues to define our experience of time.[10]

THE MAN-MADE WEEK

But why are the Torah's instructions expressed so ambiguously,
fraught with inconsistency and open to misinterpretation? And
why is the counting of the *omer* structured in such a way that in
certain years the count is more "complete" than in others?

As explained above, the entire point of the *omer* count is that
our journey to Sinai be a personal one, the product of our own
efforts. Obviously, no human achievement can equal the loftiness
and perfection of a divine gift; but that which is granted us from
Above, however lofty and perfect, is never as deeply appreciated

---

10   Talmud, *Menachot* 65b; Rashi, ad loc.; *Midrash Rabbah, Kohelet* 1:3;
     Matanot Kehunah on *Midrash Rabbah, Kohelet* 1:3. In these years, the
     verse instructing us to begin the count "on the morrow of the Shabbat"
     (see previous note) is likewise fulfilled in its most literal sense.

or as intensely identified with as that which we attain with our own finite capabilities. In the words of the Talmud, "A person would rather have a *kav* of his own [grain] than nine *kavim* of his fellow's."[11]

The only truly "complete weeks" are G-d's weeks—the weeks that are the product of G-d's original work of creation. Man-made weeks are forever bound by the limitations and deficiencies of their mortal creator. Yet man-made weeks are what connect Passover and the Exodus with Shavuot and Sinai. "You shall count *for yourselves*," instructs the Torah. This is your climb, your journey.

Hence the contradiction—an inconsistency built in to the very nature of the *omer* count. On the one hand, we are striving toward Sinai, toward our election as G-d's chosen people. The goal is perfection: the refinement of all seven dimensions of the heart and all their 49 sub-aspects. On the other hand, it is *we* who are conducting the count, we who are struggling up the steep slopes of our valley, we who compose and define the weeks of the *omer*.

The inherent paradox in these two objectives is reflected in the contrary implications in the Torah's instructions. On the one hand, the Torah insists on seven "complete"—apparently G-d-made—weeks. On the other hand, it emphasizes that these are to be personal weeks, the product of our count rather than of divine creation.

In truth, however, the *omer* count is a place where the finite and the infinite converge, where divine revelation and human effort combine to move a people toward their encounter with G-d. For although the actual count begins "on the morrow of the Shabbat"—on the day *after* the first of Passover—it is driven by the revelation of the Exodus. Although the actual count is conducted

---

11 Talmud, *Bava Metzia* 38a.

in the valley of human subjectivity, it is that original, momentary flash of light that penetrates the darkness of our valley, impels us on our journey, and empowers us to forge upward and attain the summit.

WHEN PASSOVER FALLS ON SHABBAT

So there are two elements in our every journey: that which we receive and that which we achieve. As we traverse the quests and climbs of life, at times one of these elements dominates while the other recedes to the background, and at times the reverse occurs.

At times, the divine influence in our lives dominates. We sense a higher power carrying us along, granting us the understanding and vision with which to meet life's challenges, and the courage and fortitude to surmount them. At such times, we appreciate that we are part of something greater than ourselves; that our achievements are the outgrowth of a perfection that transcends the human, reflecting the divine source of all our gifts.

At other times, our selfhood and individuality dominate. The divine influence recedes, heightening our sense of our own strengths and weaknesses, of our own responsibility for our failures and successes. We experience difficulty and disappointment, alienation and despair; but also fulfillment, pride, and true identification with our achievements.

Finally, there are those moments, rare and exquisite, when the received and the achieved coalesce in our journey; when our vision of the summit is fully integrated into our struggle up the mountainside. Times when we sense the enormity of what has been revealed and granted to us, and at the same time, fully identify with it. Times when we are not only aware of what is divine and infinite in our lives, but when our experience of these gifts is an intensely personal experience, for we have incorporated them into our self and personality.

The seven weeks of the *omer* count are *always* "complete weeks"—complete in that they represent the optimum of our personal efforts at self-perfection, and complete in that they are driven by a vision that has the perfection of the divine. Usually, however, these two aspects of "completeness" are in conflict with each other, as an overt emphasis on the divinely granted vision will detract from our sense of fulfillment and identification with our achievements. So the divine input into our lives retreats to the realm of "memory," "intuition," and "spiritual experience," so as to allow for our construction of wholly man-made weeks to join Passover and Shavuot.

But there are certain years in which these man-made weeks coincide with the divinely-ordained weeks of creation. When the first day of Passover falls on Shabbat, each of "our" weeks is also a Sunday-to-Shabbat week, alluding to a special window of opportunity. In these years we are particularly empowered to integrate our divine endowments with our personal achievements.

In these years, our journey from Exodus to Sinai is comprised of "seven complete weeks" in every sense: weeks that combine the perfection of the divinely granted with the depth of the personally achieved.

ACCUMULATIVE TIME

Today are two days to the omer.

Siddur, text of counting of the *omer* for Nissan 17

We are accustomed to thinking of time as a fixed yardstick against which our lives are measured. We "pass through" time (or time passes us by) at an unalterable pace. Time deeply affects everything about us and everything we do, but we have no effect on it.

Physical science has since refuted this cursory perception of time, demonstrating how time, as any other physical phenomenon, is in fact malleable. It can be concentrated, stretched, speeded up, slowed down, or stopped altogether. This, of course, is achieved mostly on paper or by computer simulation. In practice, time's dictatorial rule of our lives seems absolute. The irrevocability of the past, the uncompromising temporality of the present, the impregnable fog of the future—the human being still seems very much a creature subject to time, rather than the other way around.

The Torah, however, insists that we can master time, transcend it, and redefine it. One example of our triumph over time is *teshuvah* ("return")—the power to reach back in time and recreate the nature of one's past deeds.[1] And time itself, according to Torah, is a resource to be molded and developed, as we are charged to mold and develop all resources of G-d's creation. Time can be

---

[1]   Talmud, *Yoma* 86b; *Tanya*, Chapter 7. See *The Distant Road*, pp. 115–125 below, and the essays *Sin in Four Dimensions* and *Ketoret* in vol. 2 of this series, pp. 44–56 and 59–64.

sanctified—made more porous and absorbent of the all-pervading reality of its Creator—as it is when it is utilized toward good and G-dly ends. Time can be imbued with joy, freedom, love, awe, wisdom, and a host of other spiritual characteristics—as we do when we set the calendar and thereby determine the dates of the festivals. And time can be accumulated.

From Passover to Shavuot, we conduct a daily count of the days and weeks in reenactment of the 49-day process of self-refinement that led from the Exodus on the first day of Passover to the revelation at Sinai on Shavuot.[2] "Today is one day of the *omer*," we pronounce on the second evening of Passover; "Today are two days...," we say on the following evening. Seven weeks later, we conclude the count and climb to Sinai with the statement, "Today are forty-nine days, which are seven weeks of the *omer*."

Two questions come to mind concerning the text of the count. If we are counting the days to Sinai, why don't we state how many remain until Shavuot, instead of the number that have passed since Passover? Also, "Today are two days" seems awkward if not inaccurate; would it not be more correct to say, "Today is the second day," etc.?

But we do not merely pass through the days between Passover and Shavuot—we accumulate them. Each of these 49 days embodies another spiritual achievement—the refinement of another aspect of our personality and character. Each of these days becomes a component of our reborn selves, as we internalize the freedom obtained at the Exodus. On the second day of the count, we *possess* two days of the *omer* process; by its final day, we shall have amassed forty-nine units of time, and the specific qualities they embody, with which to approach this year's experience of Sinai.

---

2   See previous essay, *The Journey*, pp. 98–108.

A MONTH OF MITZVOT

Each and every day, the Torah should be as desirable to you as if you received it this very day at Mount Sinai.

Midrash Tanchuma, Ki Tavo 1

The *mitzvot* of the Torah are the means by which we sanctify our world: an object, a feeling, an occasion, becomes the vehicle of connection to one's Creator.

Mitzvot not only afford us the opportunity to fulfill G-d's will (for which a Torah comprised of a single divine commandment would have sufficed) but also enable us to involve every aspect of our existence in the endeavor. There are *mitzvot* which involve actions, and *mitzvot* which are fulfilled by refraining from action; *mitzvot* involving the mind, and *mitzvot* involving the heart; *mitzvot* pertaining to one's home, diet, dress, family life, and business affairs. No nook or cranny of the human experience is without the potential to become something more, to serve a higher purpose.

The *mitzvot* are also distinguished by the various ways in which they intersect with our experience of time. There are perpetual *mitzvot* (e.g., awareness of G-d, love your fellow), daily *mitzvot* (prayer, *tefilin*), seasonal *mitzvot* (sounding the *shofar* on Rosh Hashanah, eating matzah on Passover), and once-in-a-lifetime *mitzvot* (circumcision). Each of these affect us in different ways. The more frequently occurring *mitzvot* become a fixture of our daily life and an integral part of our consciousness. The rarer *mitzvot* inspire a sense of specialness and uniqueness in their performance.

BEST OF BOTH WORLDS

The Jewish month of *Iyar*, whose 29 days fall sometime in the months of April and May, is unique in that it combines both distinctiveness and consistency in a single *mitzvah*. The *mitzvah* is the commandment to "count the *omer*," by which we annually re-experience our forefathers' 49-day spiritual journey from the Exodus to Sinai. Every evening, from the second night of Passover to the eve of Shavuot, we verbalize the day's number in the count, after first reciting the blessing, "Blessed are You, G-d... Who has sanctified us with His commandments, and commanded us concerning the counting of the *omer*."

As a *mitzvah* associated with a particular time of the year, the counting of the *omer* is accompanied by the anticipation and sense of occasion that is the hallmark of the seasonal *mitzvah*. At the same time, for a period spanning the latter 15 days of *Nissan*, all of *Iyar's* 29 days, and the first five days of *Sivan*, this yearly event becomes a fixed part of our daily schedules.

So while the other months of the year serve as the background for their special days, the month of *Iyar*, whose each and every day is the date for a "seasonal" *mitzvah*, *is* its special days. While in other months these occasions are spiritual peaks surrounded by a plain of ordinariness, in Iyar, the unique becomes routine.

CHAPTER TWENTY

Pesach Sheini
Second Chance

The 14th of Iyar

"There's no such thing as a lost case," is how the sixth Lubavitcher Rebbe, Rabbi Yosef Yitzchak Schneersohn, defined the eternal significance of *Pesach Sheini*, the "Second Passover" occurring on the 14th of *Iyar*, one month after the first, "regular" Passover.

When the Holy Temple stood in Jerusalem, this day served as a "second chance" for those who were unable to bring the Passover offering on its appointed day because they were in a state of ritual impurity or "on a distant road." Today, we commemorate the day by eating matzah and dwelling on its significance as an opportunity to correct the failings and missed opportunities of the past.

We have already had the occasion (in our chapter on "Yom Kippur and the Ten Days of *Teshuvah*") to dwell at length on G-d's unique gift to us of *teshuvah*—the power to return in time to rectify, and even redefine, the past. In this chapter, <u>The Distant Road</u> reexamines the concept of *teshuvah* in light of the specific lessons and insights provided by the laws of the "Second Passover."

Our second essay, <u>The Missing Complaint</u>, dwells on another lesson of the Second Passover: that we need not, and must not, ever accept that G-d has chosen to limit His involvement in our lives.

PESACH SHEINI (1)   115

THE
DISTANT
ROAD

On the Second Passover, leaven and matzah
are with him in the house.

Talmud, Pesachim 95a

he fourteenth day of the month of *Iyar* is *Pesach Sheini*,
the "Second Passover." When the Holy Temple stood in
Jerusalem, this day served as a second chance for those who were
unable to bring the Passover offering on its appointed day one
month earlier, on the 14th of *Nissan*.

In the ninth chapter of the book of Numbers, the Torah re-
lates the circumstances which led to the institution of the Second
Passover. On the 1st of *Nissan* in the year 2449 from creation (1312
BCE), two weeks before the first anniversary of the Exodus,

> *G-d spoke to Moses in the Sinai desert... saying: "The*
> *children of Israel should prepare the Passover [offering]*
> *at its appointed time. On the fourteenth of this month, in*
> *the afternoon... in accordance with all its decrees and*
> *laws..."*
>
> *There were persons who had become ritually impure*
> *through contact with a dead body and could not prepare*
> *the Passover offering on that day. They approached Moses*
> *and Aaron... and they said: "...Why should we be de-*
> *prived, and not be able to offer G-d's offering in its time,*
> *amongst the children of Israel?"*

And Moses said to them: "Wait here, and I will hear what G-d will command concerning you."

And G-d spoke to Moses, saying: "Speak to the children of Israel, saying: Any person who is contaminated by death, or is on a distant road, whether among you now or in future generations, shall prepare a Passover offering to G-d. They shall prepare it on the afternoon of the fourteenth day of the second month, and they shall eat it with matzot and bitter herbs..."[1]

THE POWER OF RETURN

The eternal significance of the Second Passover, says the sixth Lubavitcher Rebbe, Rabbi Yosef Yitzchak Schneersohn, is that it is never too late to rectify a past failing. Even if a person has failed to fulfill a certain aspect of his or her mission in life because they have been "contaminated by death" (i.e., in a state of disconnection from the divine source of life)[2] or "on a distant road" from their people and G-d, there is always a "Second Passover" in which they can make good on what they have missed.

The Second Passover thus represents the power of *teshuvah* — the power of "return." *Teshuvah* is more than "repentance," more than turning over a new leaf and achieving forgiveness for past sins. It is the power to go back in time and redefine the past.

---

1 Numbers 9:1–12.
2 "Life," in the true and ultimate sense of the word, is attachment to G-d, the creator and provider of life. In the words of the Torah, "Love G-d your G-d... for He is your life" (Deuteronomy 30:20); "You, who cleave to G-d your G-d, are all alive today" (Ibid., 4:4). Thus our sages have said: "The righteous, even in death, are regarded as alive; the wicked, even in their lifetimes, are regarded as dead" (Talmud, *Berachot* 18a–b).

PESACH SHEINI (1)   117

Teshuvah is achieved when a negative deed or experience is applied in a way that completely transforms its significance. When
our contact with death evokes in us a striving for life we would
never have mustered without that experience, when our wanderings on distant roads awaken in us a yearning for home we would
never have otherwise felt, these hitherto negative experiences are
literally transformed. Contact with death is converted into a more
intense involvement with life; distance into a greater closeness.[3]

BEYOND TORAH

This explains the unique circumstances under which the institution of the Second Passover became part of Torah.

Virtually all of the *mitzvot* of the Torah, including those governing rare and unforeseeable circumstances, were unilaterally
commanded by G-d to Moses. The law of the Second Passover, instituted in response to the outcry of those who protested, "Why
shall we be deprived?", is one of the few instances in which a *mitzvah* was elicited from G-d by a petition from mortal men.[4]

Why wasn't the provision for a "Second Passover" included in
the Torah's initial legislation of the laws of Passover? Because the

---

3   This is why the principle that "There is no earlier or later in Torah" is
     derived from the verses describing the institution of the Second Pass-
     over (see next essay, *The Missing Complaint*, pp. 126–128). The simple
     meaning of this rule is that the events recounted by the Torah do not
     necessarily follow in chronological order of their occurrence, as the
     Torah will often disregard the time-context of an event for the sake of
     an insight or lesson that can be derived from its appearance in proxim-
     ity to earlier or later events. On a deeper level, this law alludes to the
     power of *teshuvah* to go against the conventional direction of the flow
     of time and transform the nature and significance of a past event.
4   Another example is the law of inheritance by female heirs, elicited by
     the petition of Tzelafchad's daughters (Numbers 27).

gift of *teshuvah* could not have been granted through the regular channels of Torah law.

Torah is the articulation of the divine will via a body of 613 commandments and prohibitions. In other words, the very definition of "Torah" is that there are certain things that G-d desires that we do, and certain things which He desires that we not do. So if Torah defines a certain deed or situation as contrary to the divine will, it cannot subsequently regard it as positive and desirable. In the words of the Midrash:

> They asked Wisdom, "What is the punishment for the sinner?" Wisdom replied: "Evil pursues sinners."
>
> They asked Prophecy... and Prophecy replied: "The soul who sins shall die."
>
> They asked the Torah... and the Torah replied: "He shall bring a guilt-offering and he shall be forgiven."
>
> They asked G-d... and G-d replied: "He shall do te-shuvah *and he shall be forgiven.*"[5]

Torah can provide a formula for repentance; but it can see no way of escaping the fact that the person has transgressed the divine will. At most, it can forgive the deed and reconnect the person to their source of life. But it cannot change the negativity of sin—the fact that, at a certain point in time, the person had been in a state of disconnection from G-d. *Teshuvah*, in its ultimate sense of "return" (i.e., to redefine and transform the negativity of a past deed or state) can only come from G-d Himself—from a place in G-d that supersedes the articulation of the divine will via the commandments of the Torah.

---

5   *Yalkut Shimoni*, Tehillim 702. For a detailed discussion of these four perspectives on sin, see the essay *Sin in Four Dimensions,* in vol. 2 of this series, pp. 44–56.

PESACH SHEINI (1)   119

So the Second Passover, with its premise that nothing is beyond rectification, could not have entered our lives through the conventional process of Torah. It took a small group of Jews, contaminated by death and languishing on a distant road, to elicit the gift of *teshuvah* from G-d.

Their cry of "Why shall we be deprived?", expressing a depth of yearning for attachment to G-d that only their currently distant state could have evoked, prompted G-d to supersede the formulation of His will as articulated in the Torah and grant them a mandate to redefine the past with a "Second Passover."

AN INSTANT LIFE

A central principle in chassidic teaching is that the entirety of the divine wisdom, from the most technical deliberations of *halachah* (Torah law) to the most esoteric kabbalistic passage, form "one Torah." The Torah may possess a "body" and a "soul," but these together constitute a single, wholly integrated organism: The soul, or the spiritual significance, of a law is reflected in its body, and every "limb" and "organ" of its body has its corresponding significance in its soul.

The same is true of the laws governing the first and second Passovers. An entire tractate in the Talmud (*Pesachim*) details the many laws that apply to the Passover offering. Most of these apply equally to both Passovers; but there are several significant differences. In the words of the Talmud:

> *What is the difference between the first Passover and the second? The first Passover is observed for seven days; the second, for a single day...*
> *On the first Passover, leaven is forbidden "to be seen*

and to be found"; on the second, leaven and matzah are with him in the house...[6]

These "technical" differences reflect the deeper conceptual import of the two Passovers: the original Passover observed by the "straight and true," and the Second Passover established for the *baal teshuvah*, the "returnee."

One difference between the two Passovers is that the Passover offering brought on the afternoon of *Nissan* 14 is followed by a seven-day festival,[7] while the Second Passover is but a single day.

The number "seven" signifies a process, a routine, a natural course of action. G-d created the world in seven days and thereby stamped a seven-day work/rest cycle into the very fabric of the natural reality. The heart of man possesses seven major traits (love, awe, harmony, ambition, devotion, connection, and sovereignty), reflecting the seven divine attributes (*sefirot*) that G-d invested in His seven-day creation.[8] So when we speak of a seven-day Passover, we speak of the graduated, step-by-step accomplishments of the *tzaddik* — the righteous individual who builds his relationship with G-d and fulfills his mission in life in accordance with the formula set forth in the Torah.

Not so the *baal teshuvah*, the one who strays from the natural course of his or her soul and then rebounds with a thirst for life that only those who have wandered in a deathly wasteland can experience. The Talmud tells the story of Elazar ben Durdaia, a man who transgressed virtually every sin in the book. One day, a harlot

---

6   Talmud, *Pesachim* 95a; *Tosefta*, ad loc. 8:3

7   Outside the Land of Israel, we observe an "additional festival day of the Diaspora," making a total of eight days. The original, biblically ordained festival is for seven days only.

8   See *The Journey*, pp. 98–108 above, and *The Seventh Element* in vol. 1, pp. 77–88 of this series.

PESACH SHEINI (1)   121

said to him, "Elazar ben Durdaia could never repent." The recognition of how far he had gone shook him to the very core of his soul;
"he placed his head between his knees, and wailed and sobbed until
his soul departed from his body." Upon hearing the story of this
man, Rabbi Judah HaNassi wept and said: "There are those who
acquire their world through many years' toil, and there are those
who acquire their world in a single moment."[9]

The essence of *teshuvah* is a single wrench of self, a single flash
of regret and resolve. "There are those who acquire their world in
many years," said the greatest *tzaddik* of his day, building it step by
step with the conventional tools of achievement; "and there are
those who acquire their world in a single moment"—in a single
instant that molds their future and redefines their past.

Not every *baal teshuvah* achieves the instantaneous transformation of Elazar ben Durdaia. But the one-day duration of the
Second Passover expresses the nature of *teshuvah*: not the conventional, progressional life of the *tzaddik*, but the *baal teshuvah*'s
drastic leap from extreme to extreme.[10]

Conquering Inflation

Another *halachic* difference between the two Passovers concerns
the prohibition against leavened foods.

The first Passover wages an all-out war on all leavened substances; not only is the eating of any form of leaven severely forbidden,
but every last speck and crumb must be banished from our premises. Not so on the Second Passover. Although the Passover offering

---

9   Talmud, *Avodah Zarah* 17a.
10 See the essays, *Moment* (vol. 2 of this series, pp. 57–58) and *Daughters
    Near and Far* (vol. 2, pp. 135–147).

is then, too, eaten with the unleavened matzah, there is no need to rid ourselves of leaven. In the words of the Talmud, "leaven and matzah are with him in the house."

Chassidic teaching explains the spiritual significance of the prohibition of leaven on Passover. Leaven, dough that has risen and inflated, represents the tendency of the human ego to rise and swell. Leaven must be completely eradicated from our premises, since a risen ego is the source of all evil. The entire Torah is based on the premise that "There is none else besides Him"[11] — that G-d is the only true reality, since every created thing is completely dependent on G-d continually suppling it with life and existence. One who perceives himself as an existence in his own right, ultimately rejects the entire Torah. Our sages go so far as to declare: "G-d says of the egotistical person: 'I and he cannot dwell in the same world.'"[12]

The *tzaddik's* reality consists of two distinct spheres: the permissible and the forbidden; that which he develops and that which he disavows. The 248 positive commandments of the Torah relate to those elements of his environment and his own being which he utilizes in his service of G-d; the Torah's 365 prohibitions define what is not within his power to redeem and sublimate, and is therefore off limits to him. Leaven and everything that it represents has no place in his life.

The *baal teshuvah*, however, is one who, having already wandered off into the forbidden realm, now exploits these negative elements and experiences to fuel his quest for a divine life. In his home, leaven and matzah both reside. What is beyond the ken of

---

11   Deuteronomy 4:35.
12   Talmud, *Erchin* 15b.

the *tzaddik* and his "first Passover," forms an integral part of the *baal teshuvah*'s service of G-d.

Indeed, the story behind the Second Passover is a classic example of how the "me" instinct, generally a most destructive force to man's relationship with his Creator, was transformed into an impetus for greater commitment to G-d. A group of Jews approached Moses with the prototypically selfish complaint, "Why should we be deprived?" But in their case, these words did not express a need to have and be, but a desire to give and serve. In their petition, the ferment and "leavening" of their selves was not the antithesis of humble and self-effacing matzah, but rather its complement. Leaven and matzah coexisted in their souls, as ego and self-abnegation jointly gave rise to a desire to serve one's Creator.

On the "Second Passover," the festival that came into being out of their "egotistical" cry, there is no need to banish leaven from our homes. For when the self asserts itself in such a manner, it is a welcome participant in our celebration of the freedom we achieved at the Exodus—the freedom to actualize our quintessential identity as "servants of G-d."[13]

THE REPENTANT RIGHTEOUS

The Talmud cites a dispute between the sages regarding the status of the Second Passover:

> *Rabbi Chananiah ben Akavia is of the opinion that the Second Passover is a fulfillment of the first... Rabbi [Judah HaNassi] is of the opinion that it is a festival in its own right.*[14]

---

13   See *Endless Lives* on pp. 28–33 above.

14   Talmud, *Pesachim* 93a.

There are several practical ramifications to this issue. For example, if one reaches the age of legal maturity (*bar mitzvah*) during the month between the two Passovers, or if a non-Jew converts to Judaism during this period, should they bring a Passover offering on the Second Passover? If the Second Passover is defined as a "fulfillment of the first"—i.e., solely as a second chance for a failed opportunity—then it would apply only to those who were obligated to observe the first and failed to do so. The new adult or the new Jew has no deficiency to fulfill. On the other hand, if it is "a festival in its own right," then anyone who has not brought a Passover offering on the First Passover can do so on the Second Passover.

These two definitions of the Second Passover apply to its "soul" as well as to its "body." In fact, it is only in the soul of the law that both opinions can be fully applied. Regarding the "body" of Torah law, we can only follow one opinion: Though we regard both as legitimate Torah views (in the words of the Talmud, "these and these are both the word of the living G-d"[15]), in practice, we follow the majority opinion.[16] But when it comes to the soul of Torah— to the conceptual-spiritual significance of the law—all opinions are equally applicable.

On the most basic level, *teshuvah* is the result of a sin in the literal sense, making the terms *baal teshuvah* and *tzaddik* mutually exclusive: One who hasn't actually transgressed the divine will cannot experience *teshuvah* and the powerful attraction to G-d only it can bring. This is the equivalent of seeing the Second Passover exclusively as a "fulfillment of the first"—a phenomenon that comes only as the result of actual failing.

Yet there is also another, more universal *teshuvah*. The essence of *teshuvah* is the drive to return to one's former, unblemished

---

15   Ibid., *Eruvin* 13b.
16   See Exodus 23:2; Talmud, *Berachot* 9a.

state—a drive that is fueled by the presently deficient state itself. Ordinarily, we consider the sin-free soul of a *tzaddik* to be perfect in its relationship with G-d, and thus devoid of the possibility for *teshuvah*. Yet in truth, the very placement of the soul into a physical body, and its subsequent enmeshment in material needs and concerns, is itself a compromising of the soul's original, uninhibited bond with G-d. The very birth of the human being means that the physical faculties of the body are now the medium through which the soul must perceive, experience, and relate to its Creator, greatly limiting the quality and scope of its spiritual life.

But as with the standard *teshuvah* for "real" sins, the distant road of physical life holds the potential for an even more intense, more meaningful bond with G-d than before. In this sense, the Second Passover is "a festival in its own right," offering an opportunity for a *teshuvah* that is not limited to the literal sinner—an opportunity to exploit the distance and spiritual lifelessness of the material world as an impetus to greater and deeper connection with one's source.

THE
MISSING
COMPLAINT

There were persons who had become ritually impure... and could not prepare the Passover offering on that day. They approached Moses and Aaron... and they said: "...Why should we be deprived, and not be able to offer G-d's offering in its time, amongst the children of Israel?"
Numbers 9:6–7

𝔗 he Talmud points out that the above verses appear in the Torah out of chronological context. The events leading to the establishment of the Second Passover took place in the month of *Nissan* in the year 2449 from creation (1312 BCE); chronologically, this would place these events in the very first chapter of the book of Numbers. Instead, Numbers begins with an account of the census taken of the Jewish people a month later, in *Iyar* of that year. From this, the Talmud derives the rule that "There is no earlier and later in Torah."[1]

Why, indeed, aren't these events transcribed in the order in which they occurred? Our sages explain that the Torah does not wish to begin the book of Numbers with the account of the Second Passover because,

> *This is a disgrace for Israel. For in the forty years that*

---

1   Talmud, *Pesachim* 6b; Rashi on Numbers 9:1.

PESACH SHEINI (2)   127

the people of Israel were in the desert, this was the only
Passover offering they brought.[2]

But why should this be regarded as a "disgrace"? The reason that
our ancestors brought no other Passover offering until they entered the Land of Israel was that G-d did not allow them to. G-d
had instructed that the annual Passover offering should be observed only "when you come into the land that G-d shall give to
you."[3] The first two Passovers—the one observed in Egypt, and the
one observed in the desert on the following year—were exceptions
to this rule, specifically commanded by G-d. So of what deficiency
in Israel's behavior are our sages speaking?

The answer lies in the story of the "Second Passover" itself. A
group of people had found themselves in a state which, by divine
decree, absolved them from the duty to bring the Passover offering.
Yet they refused to reconcile themselves to this. They refused to
accept that this avenue of relationship with G-d should be closed
to them. And their impassioned plea and demand, "Why should
we be deprived?", swayed G-d to establish a new institution, the
"Second Passover," to enable them, and all who will find themselves
in a similar situation in future generations, "to offer G-d's offering
in its time, amongst the children of Israel."

Therein lies the "disgrace" in those thirty-eight Passover-less
years in the Sinai Desert. Why did the people of Israel reconcile
themselves with the divine decree? Why did they accept this void
in their relationship with G-d? Why did they not clamor for the
opportunity to serve G-d in the full and optimum manner that
the *mitzvot* of the Torah describe?

---

2   *Sifri* on Numbers 1; Rashi on Numbers 1.
3   Exodus 12:25; see Rashi on verse.

THE LESSON

For more than nineteen-hundred years now, our Passovers have been incomplete. We eat the matzah and the bitter herbs, we drink the four cups of wine, and we ask and answer the four questions, but the heart and essence of Passover, the Passover offering, is absent from our *seder* table. For G-d has hidden His face from us, and has removed the Holy Temple, the seat of His manifest presence on physical earth, from our midst.

The lesson of the "displaced" ninth chapter of the book of Numbers is clear: G-d desires and expects of us that we refuse to reconcile ourselves with the decree of *galut* and its diminution of His manifest involvement in our lives. He desires and expects of us that we storm the gates of heaven with the plea and demand: "Why shall we be deprived?!"

CHAPTER TWENTY-ONE

Lag BaOmer
The Mystic Dimension

The 18th of Iyar

The weeks between Passover and Shavuot are a time of anticipation and preparation, as we retrace our ancestors' journey from the Exodus to Mount Sinai with our nightly "counting of the *omer*." They are also a time of sadness: No marriages are conducted during this period; like mourners, we don't cut our hair or enjoy the sound of music. For it was in this period that Rabbi Akiva's 24,000 disciples died in a plague because "they did not conduct themselves with respect for each other."

One day stands out as an isle of joy in these despondent weeks. On Lag BaOmer, the 33rd day of the *omer* count, the laws proscribing joy during the *omer* period are suspended, children are taken out on outings and play games with bows and arrows, and the day is marked as a festive and joyous occasion.

There are two reasons for this joy. One is that the plague that raged among Rabbi Akiva's disciples ceased on this day. A second reason is that it is the anniversary of the passing of Rabbi Shimon bar Yochai, whose teachings heralded a new epoch in the revelation and dissemination of the mystical dimension of the Torah known as the "kabbalah." Lag BaOmer, the day on which Rabbi Shimon's life's work achieved its culminating perfection, is thus celebrated as the festival of the esoteric soul of Torah.

Our three essays on Lag BaOmer explore the inner significance of the customs of the day, and the lessons to be derived from the deeds and teachings of Rabbi Akiva and Rabbi Shimon bar Yochai.

Can a person fulfill the precept "love your fellow as yourself" without compromising the integrity of his own principles and convictions? *24,000 Plus One* addresses the paradox of love and truth as played out in the lives of the two heroes of Lag BaOmer.

Long-Range Missile delves into the nature of the mystical teachings revealed by Rabbi Shimon bar Yochai, and the significance of the Lag BaOmer custom to play with bows and arrows.

Rabbi Shimon's example of "One whose Torah is his sole occupation" is beyond the ken of all but a select few; nevertheless, *The Many and the Few* shows how his approach might also be applied by that vast majority of us whose lives are often otherwise occupied.

24,000 PLUS ONE

Love your fellow as yourself.

Leviticus 19:18

T here was once a man who had twenty-four thousand disciples. He taught them to love, but their love was too absolute, too true, to be loving. They died, and their death spawned a period of mourning that darkens our calendar to this very day.

This man had one disciple who devoted his entire life—literally his every minute—to the pursuit of truth. Yet his truth was true enough to love. He, too, passed from this world, and the anniversary of his passing is celebrated as a day of joy and festivity to this very day.

This, in a word, is the story of Lag BaOmer—the story of Rabbi Akiva and his greatest disciple, Rabbi Shimon bar Yochai.

A Celebrated Death

The 18th of *Iyar* is "Lag BaOmer," the 33rd day of the *omer* count which spans the seven weeks from Passover to Shavuot. Two joyous occasions are associated with this day. During the *omer* period we mourn the deaths of 24,000 students of Rabbi Akiva who died in a plague because "they did not conduct themselves with respect for each other"; Lag BaOmer is the day on which the plague ended

LAG BAOMER (1)   133

and the dying ceased.[1] Lag BaOmer is also the anniversary of the passing of Rabbi Akiva's greatest disciple, Rabbi Shimon bar Yochai. Before his death (many years later, without connection to the plague), Rabbi Shimon referred to the day of his passing as "the day of my happiness" and instructed his disciples that it be observed each year as a day of joyous celebration.[2]

Why is the passing of Rabbi Akiva's other disciples mourned as a national tragedy, while the passing of Rabbi Shimon bar Yochai is remembered with celebration and joy? Indeed, the very same day that celebrates the end of the dying of Rabbi Akiva's disciples, celebrates the death of his greatest disciple! To unravel the paradox of Lag BaOmer, we must first examine the root of the "disrespect" that caused the plague amongst Rabbi Akiva's disciples.

Rabbi Akiva taught that "Love your fellow as yourself" is a "cardinal principle in Torah";[3] indeed, this is the most famous of his teachings. One would therefore expect that Rabbi Akiva's disciples would be the foremost exemplars of this principle. How was it that they, of all people, were deficient in this area?

But their very diligence in fulfilling the precept, "Love your fellow as yourself," was their undoing. Our sages have said that "Just as each person's face differs from the faces of his fellows, so, too, each person's mind differs from the minds of his fellows."[4] When the twenty-four thousand disciples of Rabbi Akiva studied their master's teachings, the result was twenty-four thousand nuances of understanding, as the same concepts were assimilated by twenty-four thousand minds—each unique and distinct from its

---

1   Talmud, *Yevamot* 62b; Me'iri on Talmud, ad loc.; *Tur* and *Shulchan Aruch, Orach Chaim,* 493:1-2.
2   *Zohar* 3:296b; *Pri Etz Chaim, Shaar Sefirat HaOmer* 7.
3   Leviticus 19:18; *Torat Kohanim* ad loc.
4   *Midrash Tanchuma, Pinchas* 10.

23,999 fellows. Had Rabbi Akiva's students loved each other less, this would have been a matter of minor concern; but because each disciple loved his fellows as he loved himself, he felt compelled to correct their "erroneous" thinking and behavior, and to enlighten them as to the true meaning of their master's words. For the same reason, they found themselves incapable of expressing a hypocritical "respect" for each other's views when they sincerely believed that the other's understanding was lacking, even in the slightest degree.

The greater a person is, the higher are the standards by which he is judged; in the words of our sages, "With the righteous, G-d is exacting to a hairsbreadth."[5] Thus what would be considered a minor failing for people of our caliber, had such a devastating effect upon the disciples of Rabbi Akiva.

The Thirteenth Year

But there was one disciple of Rabbi Akiva's who learned to overcome the pitfalls of uncompromising love and uncompromising truth, as exemplified by the following incident in the life of Rabbi Shimon bar Yochai:

The Talmud relates that when the Roman rulers of the Holy Land placed a price on the heads of Rabbi Shimon and his son Rabbi Elazar, they hid in a cave for twelve years. During this time, they spent every minute of their day studying Torah. When they emerged from the cave, they were shocked to discover people plowing and sowing: How could people set aside the eternal life that is Torah and occupy their days with the transitory life of the material? So intense was their wrath at such folly that whatever

---

5   Talmud, *Yevamot* 121a.

LAG BAOMER (1)   135

met with their burning glance went up in flames. Proclaimed a voice from heaven: "Have you come out to destroy My world? Return to your cave!" Rabbi Shimon's thirteenth year of study, while increasing his knowledge and appreciation of the truth of Torah, also taught him the value of endeavors other than his own. Now, wherever he went, his look would heal rather than destroy.[6]

The 4,000-year history of Jewish learning has known many great and diligent students of Torah; yet none epitomized the absolute devotion to the pursuit of the divine truth to the extent exemplified by Rabbi Shimon bar Yochai. Throughout the writings of our sages, his example is cited as the ultimate case of *torato um'nato*, "one whose study of Torah is his sole vocation."[7]

Certainly, Rabbi Shimon's commitment to truth was no less absolute than that of Rabbi Akiva's other disciples. Yet his truth was true enough to love. In his thirteenth year in the cave, he attained a dimension of the divine truth that tolerates, indeed embraces, the many and diverse avenues of connection to G-d which the Creator has provided to a humanity whose minds, characters, and temperaments are as diverse as their number. In his thirteenth year in the cave, Rabbi Shimon attained a level of truth in which he could utterly devote himself to the "eternal life" that is Torah, and advocate such devotion for everyone else,[8] while at the same time appreciating and respecting the path of those who serve G-d via the "temporal life" of material endeavors.

So the very same day that celebrates the end of the plague amongst Rabbi Akiva's disciples also celebrates the passing of Rabbi Shimon bar Yochai. The chassidic masters explain that the passing of a righteous person marks the point at which "all his deeds,

---

6   Ibid., *Shabbat* 33b.

7   Ibid., 11a.

8   See Talmud, *Shabbat* 35b, cited on pp. 144–145 below.

teachings, and works" attain the pinnacle of fulfillment and realization, and the point of their most powerful influence upon our lives.[9] And the "deeds, teachings, and works" of Rabbi Shimon bar Yochai are the ultimate rectification of Rabbi Akiva's disciples' tragic failure to achieve the proper synthesis of love and truth that would make their love true and their truth loving.

As Yourself

As noted above, it is only among men of the caliber of Rabbi Akiva's disciples that such a failing could bode such devastating results. But our sages chose to record their story for posterity, and to fix it in our lives with a series of laws that govern our behavior in the weeks between Passover and Shavuot each year.[10] Obviously, we, too, have something to learn from what happened to Rabbi Akiva's disciples.

The lesson is twofold: We must learn from their virtues as well as from their mistakes. We must learn to care enough for our fellows not to indulge their errors and accommodate their failings. This might be the easiest and most socially comfortable way to behave, but, rather than "tolerance," it bespeaks an indifference toward their welfare. On the other hand, we must never allow our commitment to our fellow's betterment to lessen in the slightest our respect and esteem toward him or her, no matter how misguided and unresponsive he or she might be.

---

9   *Tanya, Igeret HaKodesh* 27. Thus, while every death is a negative and sorrowful event, which the Torah instructs to honor with the appropriate mourning practices, the *yahrtzeit* (anniversary of the passing) of a righteous person is traditionally celebrated as a joyous occasion (see footnote 4 on p. 139 below).

10   See *Shulchan Aruch, Orach Chaim,* 493.

LAG BAOMER (1) 137

If this seems paradoxical, it is. But the ability to embrace this paradox is at the very heart of the Torah's commandment to "Love your fellow as yourself." In regard to ourselves, this is a paradox with which we are quite comfortable: We love ourselves unconditionally and, at the same time, incessantly strive to improve ourselves. This paradox we must also cultivate in our relationship with others: On the one hand, we must never compromise our efforts to improve our fellow; on the other hand, we must never allow these efforts to compromise our love and respect for him or her.

For to succumb to either compromise is to fail to love our fellow as we love ourselves—a principle which Rabbi Akiva considered fundamental to G-d's blueprint for life and of which Hillel said: "This is the entire Torah; the rest is commentary."[11]

---

[11] Talmud, *Shabbat* 31a.

LONG-RANGE MISSILE

Jonathan said to David: "…On the third day… you shall go to the place where you hid yourself on that day, and remain by the Ezel Stone. And I will shoot three arrows… and I will send the lad, saying, 'Go, find the arrows.'

"If I say to the lad, 'Behold, the arrows are here, to this side of you, take them' — then you can come, for peace is to you… But if I say to the youth, 'Behold, the arrows are there, further away from you' — go, for G-d has sent you."   I Samuel 20:18–22

*L*ag BaOmer, the 33rd day of the *omer* count, is the anniversary of the passing of the great Torah sage, Rabbi Shimon bar Yochai (c. 165 CE).

Although Rabbi Shimon was one of the most prolific expounders of the "revealed" part of Torah — the vast body of Torah law that legislates the civil, marital, and ritual laws of Jewish life[1] — he is most deeply identified with its "hidden" or mystical element. He is the author of the *Zohar*, the most basic kabbalistic work, and

---

[1] Indeed, almost every one of the Talmud's 523 chapters contains at least one law cited in the name of Rabbi Shimon (see *Likutei Sichot*, vol. 12, p. 194).

LAG BAOMER (2) 139

the initiator of a new era in the history of Torah's transmission through the generations.

Up until Rabbi Shimon's time, the "soul" of Torah—which charts the sublime expanses of the divine reality, the processes of creation, G-d's relationship to our existence, and the inner recesses of the human soul—was transmitted only in the form of terse, cryptic maxims, and only in private to a very few individuals in each generation. Rabbi Shimon was the first to expound upon these most intimate secrets of the divine wisdom, and he set in motion the process by which, in the generations that followed, these secrets gained a widening audience and an increasingly detailed and explicit elucidation. This process was accelerated by the 16th-century kabbalist Rabbi Isaac Luria, who proclaimed that "in these times, we are allowed and duty-bound to reveal this wisdom," and more recently, by Rabbi Israel Baal Shem Tov and his disciples.

The chassidic masters have explained that the growing popularity and accessibility of the inner dimensions of Torah reflect history's progression toward the day when, with the advent of the messianic era, "The earth will be filled with the knowledge of G-d, as the waters cover the sea."[2] The *Zohar* itself expresses this truth when it declares, "With this book shall Israel be mercifully redeemed."[3]

Before his passing, Rabbi Shimon instructed his disciples to observe his *yahrtzeit* as a day of joy and festivity, as it marks the culminating point of all he achieved in the course of his physical life.[4] Thus we celebrate Lag BaOmer as Rabbi Shimon's personal

---

2   Isaiah 11:9.

3   *Zohar* 3:124b.

4   In the words of King Solomon, "Greater is... the day of death than the day of birth" (Ecclesiastes 7:1). As chassidic teaching explains, the coming together of many particulars often creates a whole that is

festival, as well as the day that made accessible to each and every one of us the mystical soul of Torah.

On Lag BaOmer it is customary to take the children to parks and fields to play with bows and arrows. One of the explanations given for this custom is that it is told of Rabbi Shimon that no rainbow appeared in the sky in the course of his lifetime. The rainbow is a sign of human failing: As related in the ninth chapter of Genesis, G-d promised that whenever mankind shall be as undeserving as it was in the generation of the Flood, the rainbow will remind G-d of His vow to never again destroy His world. But for as long as Rabbi Shimon was alive, his merit alone was enough to ensure that G-d would not regret His creation. Hence the connection of the bow (*keshet*) to Lag BaOmer.[5]

According to this, however, the bow is a negative symbol, reflecting the decrease in merit that the world experienced upon Rabbi Shimon's passing. There is, however, a positive aspect to the phenomenon of the bow as well, since the bow also serves as an indicator and catalyst for the ultimate redemption. In the words of the *Zohar*: "Do not anticipate the coming of Moshiach until you see the shining colors of the rainbow."[6]

What does the bow symbolize, and what is its connection with the messianic era and with the life and accomplishments of Rabbi Shimon bar Yochai?

---

greater than the sum of its parts. The moment of a person's passing, which is the product of everything he or she experienced and achieved in the course of his or her lifetime, encapsulates the whole of a life—a whole that is infinitely greater than the sum of its parts.

5 Jerusalem Talmud, *Berachot* 9:2; *Benei Issaschar, Maamarei Chodesh Iyar* 3:4.

6 *Zohar* 3:72b; *Tikkunei Zohar, Tikkun* 18.

The Sword and the Bow

The first weapons devised by man were designed for hand-to-hand combat. But a person's enemy or prey is not always an arm's length away, or even within sight. Soon the warrior and hunter were inventing an array of weapons capable of reaching targets which are a great distance away, or which lie invisible and protected behind barriers of every sort.

Chief among these weapons was the bow and arrow. The inventor of this device conceived how the tension in an arched bough of wood can be exploited to propel a missile for great distances. To do so, he first had to grasp the paradox that the deadly arrow must be pulled back toward one's own heart in order to strike the heart of the enemy; and that the more it is drawn toward oneself, the more distant a foe it can reach. Indeed, virtually all long-range weapons operate on this principle: they cause an action by the means of an opposite action; they impel up and away by means of a force that is exerted down and back toward the launch-point.

Therein lies the deeper significance of the bow and its connection to Lag BaOmer.

The "revealed" part of Torah is like the close-range weapon, in that it aids us in meeting the obvious challenges of life. It teaches us to distinguish between good and evil, and between the holy and the profane. Do not kill or steal, it tells us; feed the hungry, hallow your relationship and family life with the sanctity of marriage, remember the Shabbat day, eat only kosher foods—for thus you will preserve the order that G-d instituted in His world and develop it in accordance with the purpose for which He created it.

But not everything is as upfront as the explicit dos-and-don'ts of the Torah. What about the ambiguities of intent and motive, love and awe, ego and commitment? What about the subtleties of comprehending the divine essence of reality and vanquishing the cosmic heterogeneity that is the subtle source of evil? How are we to approach these challenges, so distant from our sensory reach and so elusive of our mind's perception?

This is where the mystical dimension of Torah comes in. Delve into yourself, it explains, retreat to your own essence, to the very core of your soul. There you will uncover the selfless heart of the self, the "spark of G-dliness" within you that is one with its Creator and with creation. There you will gain the insight and foresight to deal with the most distant and obscure adversary; from there you will catapult your redeeming influence to the most forsaken corner of G-d's world.

On Lag BaOmer, Rabbi Shimon bar Yochai gave us the bow.

DAVID AND JONATHAN

In the 20th chapter of the first book of Samuel, we read of the drama of David's escape from King Saul—a drama in which a bow and arrows plays a crucial part.

David had been anointed by the prophet Samuel to be the next king of Israel, much to King Saul's chagrin, for Saul desires that his son, Jonathan, should succeed him. David, who until then had been a welcome guest at the royal table, has reason to fear that Saul intends him harm. Jonathan, whose love for David transcends all self-interest and filial loyalty, promises to inform him of any threat to his life. They devise a code: David will hide in a field, concealed behind a large stone. Jonathan will come to that field, ostensibly for shooting practice, accompanied by a servant. He will shoot three arrows and send his lad to fetch them. If he cries to the youth, "The arrows are here, to this side of you," all is well, and David can safely come to the palace. If, however, he calls, "The arrows are there, further away," David must flee.

Our sages tell us that had Saul been faithful to his mission as king of Israel, he would have merited to build the Holy Temple in Jerusalem and would have achieved the ultimate peace for Israel and for the entire world. In other words, the first king in Jewish history would also have been its culminating leader, Moshiach, who brings about the final redemption. This is what David had to know: Has Saul risen to the task, or has he failed? Have we shot the final arrow of history, in which case eternal peace and perfection will reign? Or do we still lag behind in the cosmic battle, in which case David must embark on his struggle to attain the throne?

On the appointed day, David heard Jonathan utter the fateful words: "The arrows are there, further away from you." The struggle must go on. Many bows must still be stretched, many lives pulled back to their deepest limits to impel themselves toward far and hidden challenges, before the harmonious world envisioned by G-d at creation shall be realized. "Go on," was Jonathan's message to David, "for G-d has sent you."

THE MANY
AND
THE FEW

All the days that I have been bound in this world, in one bond have I been bound with Him, with G-d. My soul is united with Him, burns in Him, cleaves to Him.

Rabbi Shimon bar Yochai

"Many did like Rabbi Yishmael, and succeeded," said the talmudic sage Abayei. "Many did like Rabbi Shimon, and did not succeed."[1]

Abayei is referring to a debate, recorded in the Talmud,[2] between Rabbi Shimon bar Yochai, the hero of Lag BaOmer, and his contemporary, the great sage and High Priest, Rabbi Yishmael. Citing the verse, "You shall harvest your grain, your wine, and your oil,"[3] Rabbi Yishmael asks:

> *What does this come to teach us? But since it says, "This book of Torah shall not cease from your mouth [and you shall study it day and night],"[4] I would have thought that one should take these words literally. Comes the verse to teach us: "You shall harvest your grain"—conduct yourself also in the ways of the world.*

---

1   Talmud, *Shabbat* 35b.
2   Ibid.
3   Deuteronomy 11:14.
4   Joshua 1:8.

LAG BACMER (3)   145

Rabbi Shimon bar Yochai disagrees:

> If a person plows in the plowing season, sows in the sowing
> season, reaps in the reaping season, threshes in the thresh-
> ing season, and winnows when there is wind, what shall
> become of the Torah? But when Israel does the will of the
> Almighty, their work is done by others, as it is written,[5]
> "Strangers will stand and graze your sheep..."

Rabbi Shimon bar Yochai was the ultimate example of "one whose
Torah is his sole occupation"—one who is loath to expend a single
moment of life on any activity other than the actual study of Torah. Indeed, he was profoundly shocked when witnessing the fact
that there are people who actually work for a living, "setting aside
eternal life to preoccupy themselves with transitory life."[6] For the
Torah is the wisdom and will of G-d, and the mind that studies it
and integrates it into itself thereby unites with the eternity and
infinity of its Author. In the words of Rabbi Schneur Zalman of
Liadi:

> When a person knows and grasps in his mind a Torah
> law... he thereby grasps and holds and encompasses with
> his mind the divine wisdom and will... while his mind
> is simultaneously enveloped within them. This makes for
> a wonderful union, like which there is none other, and
> which has no parallel anywhere in the material world,
> whereby complete oneness and unity, from every side and
> angle, is attained.[7]

---

5   Isaiah 61:5.
6   Talmud, *Shabbat* 33b.
7   *Tanya*, chapter 5. Cf. *Zohar* 3:73a: "There are three connections that
     are bound to each other: G-d, the Torah, and Israel. The people of Is-
     rael bind themselves to the Torah, and the Torah is bound with G-d."

How, then, wondered Rabbi Shimon, can a person set aside the eternal life of Torah to preoccupy himself with the transitory life of the material? "I am my Beloved's, and His desire is to me," said Rabbi Shimon to his disciples on the day of his passing, "All the days that I have been bound in this world, in one bond have I been bound with Him. My soul is united with Him, burns in Him, cleaves to Him."[8]

Five generations later, Abayei reported that many succeeded in following Rabbi Yishmael's counsel of pursuing a path through life in which one's spiritual endeavors are supported by the conventional ways of earning a livelihood; but that only a few succeeded in following Rabbi Shimon's example of leading a life in which the Torah is one's "sole occupation." Indeed, Rabbi Yishmael's approach has been universally accepted as the proper way of life for all but a select few. "Beautiful is the study of Torah together with the ways of the world," says Rabban Gamliel in *Ethics of the Fathers*. The talmudic sage Rava issued the following decree to his students: "Do not show yourselves to me during the days of *Nissan* and *Tishrei*"—two important months for work in the fields—"so that you should not be worried by your material sustenance all year."[9]

A MINOR THING

The word *torah* means "instruction"—if the Torah tells us of something, it is applicable, in some way, to each and every one of us. If we have been told the story of Rabbi Shimon bar Yochai, there is something in his approach to life for us to emulate.

---

8   *Zohar* 3:288a and 3:292a.
9   *Ethics of the Fathers* 2:2; Talmud, *Shabbat* 35b.

LAG BAOMER (3)   147

This "pretentious" approach to the examples of the greatest and
loftiest of our leaders was established by none other than Moses
himself. In his speech to the people of Israel before his passing,
Moses proclaims: "And now, Israel, what does the L-rd your G-d
ask of you, but to fear G-d?"[10] Asks the Talmud: "Is the fear of
G-d a minor thing?" Answers the Talmud: "Yes, for Moses it is a
minor thing."[11]

But who's talking about Moses? The verse distinctly says "What
does G-d ask of *you*"—of the entire community of Israel!

Every Jewish soul, explains Rabbi Schneur Zalman of Liadi in
his *Tanya*, contains a spark of the soul of Moses. So, "although
who is the man who dares presume in his heart to approach and
attain even a thousandth part of the level of the faithful shepherd,
nevertheless, an infinitesimal fringe and minute particle of his
great goodness and light illuminates every Jew in each and every
generation."[12]

The same is true regarding Rabbi Shimon bar Yochai, who was
the "Moses of his generation."[13] There is a spark of his soul in each
and every one of us, which means that, on a certain level, we can
each make our bond with G-d the "sole occupation" of our lives.

MEANS OR END

How are we to apply Rabbi Shimon's utter and perpetual attachment to G-d to our lives? Even if we establish our relationship
with G-d as the basis and axis of our existence, a great part of our

---

10   Deuteronomy 10:12.
11   Talmud, *Berachot* 33b.
12   *Tanya*, chapter 42.
13   *Emek HaMelech, Dikna Kadisha*, chapter 10.

time and energies will, by necessity, be devoted to supplying our physical existence with its wants and needs. In what way can we make the Torah our "sole occupation"?

On the most basic level, we can ensure that in the daily hours or minutes which we do set aside for Torah study, this should be our "sole occupation." We can create islands in time in which our material cares are not merely "on hold," but utterly nonexistent; in which our attachment to G-d is no less real and all-consuming than if we were to lead a wholly spiritual existence twenty-four hours a day.

On a deeper level, we have it within our power to be "bound with Him in one bond" at all times, even while engaged in the "ways of the world." For our material involvements can be made an integral part of the "Torah" aspect of our lives.

Chassidic teaching explains that there are two ways in which we might regard our "worldly" activities: a) as auxiliary, supportive elements to our relationship with G-d; b) as component parts of the relationship itself. The first approach is expressed by Rabbi Yossei in the second chapter of the *Ethics of the Fathers* when he says, "All your doings should be for the sake of Heaven."[14] The second approach is expressed by King Solomon in the book of Proverbs—"Know Him in all your ways."[15]

"All your doings should be for the sake of Heaven" means that everything one does ultimately *serves* a Heavenly purpose. In this approach to life, when we eat, or work to earn the means to eat, or train ourselves in a profession so that we will be able to work and earn the means to eat—we do so for the purpose of utilizing the energy derived from our food to study G-d's Torah and implement

---

14 *Ethics of the Fathers* 2:14.
15 Proverbs 3:6.

LAG BAOMER (3)   149

G-d's will by fulfilling the *mitzvot* He commanded. So even if only a relatively small quantity of our time and prowess are devoted to achieving attachment to G-d, this is the focus and objective of everything we do.

On the other hand, "Knowing Him in all your ways" is an approach to life in which everything is not only "for the sake of" Heaven, but a way of knowing G-d. To eat is not only to eat for a G-dly purpose, but to experience G-d—to sense the divine essence of our food, the "spark of G-dliness" within it that imbues it with its life-nurturing quality.[16] To engage in business or a profession is not only to do so as a means toward a G-dly end, but to experience G-d—to discern the divine providence in every development in the marketplace or our chosen endeavor. To acquire "worldly" knowledge is not only to do so toward a G-dly purpose, but to experience G-d—to appreciate His all-transcendent, all-pervading truth as expressed by every science and field of study.

"Making Torah one's sole occupation," as applied to a life which includes "conducting oneself in the ways of the world," means that everything we do is not only a means to a holy end, but an act of relating to and unifying ourselves with the Creator.

---

16 See *The Vegetarian Era* on pp. 71–79 above.

CHAPTER TWENTY-TWO

Shavuot

Law, Truth, and Peace

Sivan 6 & 7

They call us the "people of the book" because of our legendary devotion to it. By law, we are required to pursue it every spare moment of our day and night. When a child is born, we wish its parents, "May you merit to raise him to Torah." For 4,000 years, the study of Torah has been the life's occupation of the Jewish people and our highest mark of achievement.

To the Jew, the Torah is nothing less than the basis and objective of all existence. In the words of the Midrash, "G-d made a condition with the work of creation: If the people of Israel accept the Torah, you will exist; if not, you will revert to chaos and nothingness."

The festival of Shavuot is a surprisingly simple commemoration for so momentous an event as the giving of the Torah at Mount Sinai. Passover and Sukkot are week-long festivals; Shavuot is observed for a single day (two outside the Holy Land). Passover has its matzah, Sukkot its *sukkah* and "four kinds," Rosh Hashanah its *shofar*; Shavuot has no special *mitzvah* to lend it grandeur and occasion. Indeed, what ritual could possibly convey Shavuot's essence? What deed or experience could possibly capture the revelation at Sinai, where we literally "saw the G-d of Israel" and apprehended the truth of all truths?

There are, however, a number of observances associated with the festival. On Shavuot we assemble in the synagogue to hear the reading of the Torah's account of G-d's descent upon Mount Sinai and His proclamation of the Ten Commandments. It is customary to eat dairy foods, because the Torah is compared to nurturing milk, and because on that first Shavuot, the Jewish people did not eat meat until they could begin implementing their newly-received kosher dietary laws.

In the days of the Holy Temple, an offering of "two loaves" made with wheat flour was brought on Shavuot, closing the "counting of the *omer*" begun fifty days earlier with the barley offering brought on Passover. This progress from animal food to the staple of the human diet symbolized the refinement of our animal self and the actualization of our uniquely human qualities. Shavuot also marked the time when the Israelite farmer brought a gift of "first fruits" (*bikurim*) to the Holy Temple, representing our dedication of the first and finest of our resources to G-dly ends.

In this chapter, nine essays explore the nature and functions of the Torah, the significance of the revelation at Sinai, the history of Shavuot, and the meaning of its laws and observances.

Doing Nothing retraces the events of the week from *Sivan* 1 to *Sivan* 6, analyzing the ways in which our ancestors prepared for the giving of the Torah.

"The world is sustained by three things," proclaims the Talmud. "Law, truth, and peace." The next three essays examine these three guises and functions of Torah: _Truth_, in both its relative and absolute forms, is the subject of the essay by that name. _Peace_ defines Torah as the harmonizing factor in the diversity of creation. _Law_ looks at the "limitations" which a code of behavior seems to impose upon the bond-resistant spirit of man.

Noting that the Torah was studied and practiced for many generations before Sinai, _The Breakthrough_ address the question of what exactly was "given" to us at the giving of the Torah. _Real Estate_ describes a legal battle waged in heaven over the relocation of Torah to material earth. _The Mathematics of Marriage_ delves into the Torah's role as the vehicle of relationship between G-d and man.

"The time of the giving of our Torah," "The festival of weeks," and "The day of the first fruits" are _The Three Names of Shavuot_—delineating Torah's influence upon our behavior, personality, and environment. Lastly, _The Phantom Days of Shavuot_ explains how the "diminished" form of this festival—its single day and its lack of a distinguishing _mitzvah_—in fact reflects the enormity of what transpired at Sinai.

See also the following essays: *The 120-Day Version of the Human Story* (vol. 2 of this series, pp. 37–43); *Daughters Near and Far* (vol. 2, pp. 135–147); and *The Thousand-Year Difference* (vol. 2, pp. 247–253).

SHAVUOT (1)   155

DOING
NOTHING

[On the 1st of Sivan,*] Moses did not say any-*
thing at all to the people, because they were
weary from the journey.
                                        Talmud, Shabbat 86b

O n the first day of the month of *Sivan* in the year 2448
from creation (1313 BCE), six weeks after the Exodus, the
people of Israel arrived at Mount Sinai. Six days later, the entire
nation stood at the foot of the mountain as G-d revealed Himself
to them and gave them the Torah. Ever since, we celebrate the festival of Shavuot (*Sivan* 6–7) as "the time of the giving of our
Torah."

The 19th chapter of the book of Exodus describes this final
week of preparation for the revelation at Sinai. Analyzing the Torah's account, the Talmud[1] pieces together the following chronicle
of events for these six days, the 1st through the 6th of *Sivan*:

Sivan 1: "Moses did not say anything at all to the people, because they were weary from the journey."

Sivan 2: At dawn, Moses ascends Mount Sinai. He brings back
the following message from G-d: "You have seen what I have
done to Egypt, and how I bore you upon the wings of eagles and
brought you to Myself. Now, if you will obey My voice and keep
My covenant, you shall be My chosen treasure from among all the
nations, for all the earth is Mine. You shall be to Me a kingdom

---

1   Talmud, *Shabbat* 86b; see also Rashi's commentary on Exodus 19.

156   INSIDE TIME: VOL. III

of priests and a holy nation."[2] With these words, G-d expressed
His desire that we become His "chosen people." The day is accordingly marked in our calendar as *yom ha'meyuchas*, "the day of
designation."

Sivan 3: G-d commands Moses to fence-in Mount Sinai, marking the boundaries where everyone is to stand when G-d reveals
Himself upon the mountain and gives them the Torah. The *kohanim* (priests) may approach closer than the rest of the people,
Aaron may approach closer than the *kohanim*, while Moses alone
will be summoned by G-d to ascend to the top of the mountain.[3]

Sivan 4: The people are instructed to purify and sanctify themselves in preparation for the giving of the Torah by suspending
marital relations and immersing in a *mikveh*.[4]

Sivan 5: Moses builds an altar at the foot of the mountain and
seals the covenant between G-d and Israel. The entire people proclaim, "All that G-d commands, we will do and we will hear."[5]

Sivan 6: The giving of the Torah. "When morning came, there
was thunder and lightning, and a thick cloud upon the mountain...
The voice of the *shofar* sounded, growing stronger and stronger...
G-d descended upon Mount Sinai... and spoke the following
words, saying: 'I am G-d your G-d, who has taken you out of the
land of Egypt...'"[6]

A MYSTERIOUS BLANK

The revelation at Sinai was the culmination and fulfillment of
the Exodus. Many months earlier, also at Sinai, when G-d first

---

2   Exodus 19:4–6.
3   Ibid., v. 12 (see Rashi on v. 24).
4   Ibid., v. 14–15.
5   Ibid. 24:4–8.
6   Ibid. 19:16–20:2.

SHAVUOT (1) 157

appeared to Moses in a burning bush and commanded him to lead
the people of Israel out of Egypt, He had said: "This is your sign
that I have sent you: When you take this nation out of Egypt, you
will serve G-d on this mountain."[7]

From the moment that Moses brought them word of the promised redemption, the people of Israel eagerly awaited the revelation at Sinai. For Moses had promised them more than an escape
from Egypt and their "hard labor in mortar and bricks"[8]; he had
promised them the ultimate freedom—freedom from their own
mortality, freedom from the finiteness and mundanity of a mate-
rial-bound existence. He had promised them a vision of the divine
reality, and a mandate to incorporate its boundlessness and eternity into their lives. So from the day they left Egypt, the people
literally counted the days to the morning on which they would
gather to "serve G-d on this mountain" and be granted the liberating truth of truths. (To this very day, we reenact their 49-day
count with our own "counting of the *omer*."[9])

In light of this, the event—or rather, the non-event—of the
first of *Sivan* is most difficult to understand. This was the day on
which "Moses did not say anything at all to the people, because
they were weary from the journey." But human nature is such that
the closer one comes to an anticipated point in time, the stronger
one's yearning and desire becomes. After six weeks of anticipation
and preparation for the great day, would everything come to a halt
merely because the people were "weary from the journey"? Is it
possible that on the very day on which they arrived at Mount Sinai
they did not do *anything at all* in preparation for their receiving
of the Torah?

---

7 Ibid., 3:12.
8 Ibid., 1:14.
9 See *The Journey*, pp. 98–108 above, and *The Three Names of Shavuot*, pp.
193–200 below.

The Silencing of the Jewish Mind

Let us take a closer look at what the Torah tells us about the doings of the people of Israel on the 1st of *Sivan*:

> *In the third month of the exodus of the children of Israel from the land of Egypt, on that day, they arrived in the Sinai desert. They journeyed from Rephidim and came to the Sinai desert, and camped in the desert; and Israel camped there, before the mountain.*[10]

In his commentary on these verses, Rashi notes the grammatically unconventional use of the singular *vayichan* ("and he camped," rather than *vayachanu*, "and they camped") in speaking of the entire people of Israel. Rashi explains that the Torah wishes to inform us that "They camped as a single person, with a single heart, unlike all other encampments, which were accompanied by dissent and dispute."

Indeed, we find many instances of quarreling and even rebellion in the course of the Israelites' journeys in the desert. Still, was it really as bad as that? Were "all other encampments" (there were 42 of them altogether, as enumerated in the 33rd chapter of Numbers) ridden with strife, and Sinai the only peaceful exception?

But the "dissent and dispute" which characterized the Israelite camp need not be understood only in the negative sense. Our sages tell us that G-d created the human being in such a way that "Just as no two are alike in their features, no two are alike in mind and character."[11] Each individual's distinct mindset and temperament leads him or her to apply the same truths in their own unique way. So differences of opinion do not necessarily stem from selfishness

---

10 Exodus 19:1–2.
11 Talmud, *Berachot* 58a.

SHAVUO⁻ (1)   159

and animosity; they can also arise out of a sincere search for the truth and the desire to fully realize one's potential as an individual. In fact, when not corrupted by self-interest, dissent and differences of opinion can prove positive and constructive.

Nevertheless, what was acceptable, even desirable, in the other forty-one encampments, was intolerable at the encampment at Sinai. For an important part of our preparations to receive the Torah was—and remains—the eradication of all differences in outlook and understanding.

The reason for this is best understood by examining the difference between pre- and post-Sinaitic study of Torah. Also before Sinai, the Torah was studied and observed by our ancestors. Shem, the son of Noah, headed an academy for Torah study together with his great-grandson, Eber.[12] Abraham, Isaac, and Jacob established "*yeshivot*" for Torah study.[13] All through the Egyptian exile, the tribe of Levi (who were not enslaved) occupied themselves with the study of Torah.[14] At Sinai we were not granted a code of law or body of wisdom which had not been previously known; what did happen was that we were the recipients of a revelation which completely transformed the nature of our relationship with the Torah.

Prior to Sinai, the human intellect was the tool with which to access the Torah. The divine wisdom had been put into words and ideas comprehensible to the human mind, and the human mind labored to grasp and digest them—to the extent that it was capable. Since every mind is unique in both its strengths and its weaknesses, the scope and depth of each student's understanding differed. Obviously, *no* mind was capable of apprehending the entirety of

---

12   Rashi on Genesis 26:5.
13   Talmud, *Yoma* 28b.
14   Rashi on Genesis 46:28; *Chizkuni* on Exodus 5:4.

Torah, as the infinite wisdom of G-d could never be contained by the finite human mind.

But at Sinai, G-d *gave* us His Torah. All of it. He chose to impart the whole of His wisdom to us, regardless of the limits of our intellect. At this moment, Moses and the most simple Jew were equal: equal in their inability to grasp the essence of G-d's wisdom with their own intellect, and equal in that G-d had granted them this understanding as a gift—that He "inserted" the infinity of His wisdom into the simplest of Torah's verses in the mouth of the simplest of Jews.[15]

To prepare for the divine *giving* of the Torah at Sinai, the people had to abnegate their individual intellects. They had to make the transition from active apprehension of Torah to passive reception of a gift from Above.

Thus, the 1st of Sivan, the day on which the Jews arrived at Sinai, was far from an uneventful day. On the contrary, it was a day of intense preparation, involving an unprecedented activity: to establish a camp that was "as a single person with a single heart." To not only reach a consensus on a unified course of action ("as a single person"), but that each should also surrender his or her individual approach, outlook, and intuition to a singular egoless receptiveness ("a single heart").[16]

---

15 Hence the law is that one who reads a single verse of Torah, even if he merely mouths the words without understanding their meaning, recites the obligatory blessing on Torah study—"Blessed are You, G-d... Who gives the Torah" (Rabbi Schneur Zalman of Liadi's *Hilchot Talmud Torah* 2:12–13, and sources cited there).

16 Hence the importance of reciting a blessing over the Torah before approaching to study it (see previous note), thereby acknowledging that it is, first and foremost, something that is *given* to us from G-d. The sages go so far as to say, "The Land of Israel was destroyed only because they did not first make a blessing on the Torah" (Talmud, *Nedarim* 81a).

SHAVUOT (1)   161

This was a most "wearying journey." It was not the physical journey from Rephidim that so drained them,[17] but the psychological transition from a six-week active preparation to utter passivity.
On this day, "Moses did not say anything at all" to them, and his
non-verbalization of the order of the day was its strongest articulation: to transcend one's individual comprehension of Torah and
make oneself an "empty vessel" to receive what G-d would bestow.

RETURN TO SELF

Following the great "non-event" of Sivan 1 came five days of active
preparation for Sinai.

Initially, the definitiveness and individuality of the mind is an
impediment to receiving the infinite, intangible essence of the divine wisdom. But after we open ourselves to receive G-d's Torah,
we must reactivate our individual faculties in order to absorb and
assimilate what we have received.

Once again, differences will emerge. Moses, Aaron, the priests,
and the common folk—each will have his boundaries clearly
marked. For each must now take the very essence of Torah, which
they all received equally, and apply it to his own life with the tools
of his own cognition and experience.

---

17   In fact, the day that the people of Israel arrived at Sinai was either a
     Sunday or a Monday (see Talmud, *Shabbat* 86b), shortly after the 24-
     hour rest of Shabbat.

TRUTH

On Shavuot, Rav Yosef would say: "Prepare me a third-born calf... Were it not for this day, how many Yosefs are there in the marketplace!"
Talmud, Pesachim 68b

"here are many paths to the truth. Every man must seek G-d in his own heart, in his own way."

"Truth, by definition, is absolute and unequivocal. To speak of 'different truths' is a contradiction in terms."

"If something is true, it exists under all circumstances and on all levels of reality. There might be one ultimate truth, but it has many faces and manifestations."

"'Faces' and 'manifestations' are expressions of a truth, not the truth itself. If one desires the truth itself, one must surrender all personal conceptions and inclinations and relate to the truth solely on its, the truth's, terms."

Which of the above statements are true? All of them, of course. They just describe two different perspectives: the view from the "bottom up," and the view from the "top down."

Imagine a group of people contemplating a piano. They have never seen or heard of a piano in their lives, nor, for that matter, any other musical instrument—they live in a world in which the very concept of music is unknown.

"It's a piece of wood," says one.

"It's an exquisitely fashioned piece of furniture," says another, a cabinetmaker by profession.

"It's obviously some sort of machine," says the engineer in the group.

A musician from another galaxy enters the room. "It's a piano," he tells them, "a musical instrument." He seats himself at the keyboard and plays them a concerto. He teaches them how to read, play, and compose music.

These people were each seeking the truth in their own way, drawing on their own knowledge and experience to decipher the significance of the object before them. The conclusions they reached were true—a piano *is* a piece of wood, a piece of furniture, a machine. But they grasped only an outermost edge of the truth. This was not because their reasoning was faulty, or because it was based on faulty data; it was because the piano belongs to a world—the world of music—which lay beyond the parameters of their reality. So they perceived not the piano for what it is, but the piano as it exists in their respective worlds—the world of physical objects, the world of cabinetmaking, the world of engineering. They were looking at it from the bottom up. Then an ambassador from the world of music came and introduced a new perceptive: a perceptive from the "top down"—a vision of the piano from its, the piano's, world.

The Marketplace

The Talmud relates that Rav Yosef would celebrate Shavuot with a particular enthusiasm and joy, calling for a "third-born calf" (a special delicacy) to be prepared in honor of the festival. "Were it not for this day," he explained, "how many Yosefs are there in the marketplace!"

Simply understood, Rav Yosef's words express his joy over having been privileged to devote his life to the study and practice of

Torah. Shavuot marks the day on which we received the Torah from G-d at Mount Sinai. Were it not for the day of Shavuot, Rav Yosef is saying, what would distinguish him from the many "Yosefs" out there, involved with the mundane pursuits of the marketplace?

There is, however, a deeper significance to Rav Yosef's words, in which the "marketplace" of which he speaks is a spiritual marketplace, populated by seekers and propagators of G-dliness and truth. How many "Yosefs" are there in this marketplace? Indeed, many. Every individual is unique, with his or her own particular mindset, character, and spiritual persona. It follows, therefore, that there would be many approaches in humanity's striving for meaning to life.

The fact that there are many Yosefs in the marketplace does not mean that they are all on the wrong track. G-d is the ultimate singularity, but He is also the ultimate and exclusive source of our diverse and multifarious world. Every reality is an expression of His being, every perspective a path to His truth. But these are all quests "from the bottom up"—quests generated, driven, and defined by the human condition. Everything human is finite, and the finite and the infinite are two different worlds—as different from each other (to grossly understate the fact) as cabinetmaking and music. So the most sublime human discoveries only touch upon the outermost "edge" of the divine truth—on the finite expressions of an infinite reality.

But on the sixth day of Sivan, "G-d descended upon Mount Sinai,"[1] allowing man a glimpse, "from the top down," of the divine essence.[2] G-d gave us the Torah, in which He revealed to us

---

[1] Exodus 19:20.

[2] Thus, Rav Yosef says, "were it not for *this day*..." (not "were it not for the Torah," etc.). The Torah was studied and practiced prior to the revelation at Sinai, but until then it was comprehensible and implementable

SHAVUOT (2)   165

His truth from *His* perspective, and provided us with the tools to comprehend, relate to and realize His reality on *His* terms. On Shavuot, the many Yosefs of the marketplace graduated to the singular Yosef—the student and practitioner of Torah.

---

only as part of the human quest for truth, not as a revelation of the divine essence. On Shavuot, G-d dissolved the dichotomy, inherent in His creation, between the human and the divine, imparting to man the divine perspective on reality and enabling man to relate to Him on *His* terms. See previous essay, *Doing Nothing* (pp. 155–161), and *The Breakthrough* (pp. 171–176 below).

PEACE

An architect who builds a palace does not do so on his own — he has scrolls and notebooks which he consults how to place the rooms, where to set the doors. So it was with G-d: He looked into the Torah and created the world.

Midrash Rabbah, Bereishit 1:2

𝔗 he number "three" figures prominently in everything connected with the giving of the Torah. The Torah was given in Sivan, the third month of the Jewish year, on the third of a three-day period of preparation. It was given through Moses, the third child of Amram and Jocheved, to the people of Israel, who comprise three classes (*Kohanim*, Levites and Israelites). The Torah itself consists of three parts: Torah (the "Five Books of Moses"), Prophets, and Scriptures. In the teachings of kabbalah, the Torah is identified with *tiferet* ("harmony"), the third of the seven supernal *sefirot* (divine attributes), and was therefore given in the third millennium of history. The Talmud expressed it thus:

> *Blessed be the Merciful One, who gave a threefold Torah to a threefold people through a third-born on a third day in the third month.*[1]

Chassidic teaching explains that Torah embodies the number three because "the Torah was given to make peace in the world,"[2] and three is the number of peace.

---

1   Talmud, *Shabbat* 88a.
2   *Mishneh Torah, Laws of Chanukah* 4:14; cf. Proverbs 3:17.

The number "one" implies a monopolizing individuality. Where "one" dominates, there cannot be peace, for "one" insists on the absoluteness and exclusivity of its being. Where "one" dominates, everything else (if there is anything else) must surrender its identity before its all-nullifying singularity. True, there is no conflict, for there is only one; but neither is there peace, which is the harmonious integration of two (or more) distinctive elements.

"Two" represents diversity. As the number implies, we are dealing with two parallel entities. One may be greater than the other, yet they are equal if only in that each is a distinct existence. Twoness is often the cause of conflict, but even when it is not, it still precludes true peace. As long as each entity retains its separateness, the most they can achieve is a noncombative coexistence. Dichotomized by their respective individualities, they cannot merge into a synthesized whole.

So what is peace? If it is neither "one" nor "two," neither the affirmation of difference nor its surrender, what is it? Indeed, peace is a paradox—a paradox expressed by the number "three."

Peace is when two distinct entities find common ground in a third reality which transcends the differences between them: a third element which embraces them both to orient them towards a higher goal; a third element within whose broader context their unique and even opposite features complement and fulfill the other; a third element which preserves their differences—and exploits them as the very ingredients of harmony.

A PERSONAL EXAMPLE

We can see a model for the dynamics of peace in our own diversified selves. The mind and the heart, for example, are two very different systems, with differing and conflicting approaches and priorities. The mind is cold, aloof, and objective; the heart is heated, involved, and gloriously *subj*ective. Yet they both inhabit the same individual and serve as active forces in his or her life.

In a person who leads an uncompromisingly singular existence—let us call him a "one" personality—either the mind or the heart will become the exclusive arbitrator in all areas of his or her life. Either the heart will yield to the mind and become a passionless void, or the mind will surrender its discriminating judgment to the heart's biased affections.

In the case of a "two" personality, both mind and heart will each hold their ground, and the person will go through life torn between two perspectives on every issue that he or she confronts.

But then there is the individual in whom the mind remains a mind and the heart remains a heart, yet each is an integral part of a third and inclusive entity—the human being. Humanness does not negate intellect or feeling—it includes them both, and includes them in a way that combines the two (and numerous other faculties) into a cohesive approach to life.

In other words, when each of the two elements sees itself and its inclinations as a self-contained entity, there will never be true peace. But when each sees itself as part—a distinctive part, but a part nonetheless—of a greater whole, the result is the paradox of peace: the paradox of diversity and disparity as the harbingers of unity.

The Blueprint

"The Torah was given to make peace in the world."

The world: a chaos of diversity and seeming randomness. Here and there we may observe patches of cohesiveness, communities and systems driven by a unanimity of purpose. But on the whole,

SHAVUOT (3)   169

the world seems a jumble of elements, forces, species, nations, and individuals, each with its own nature and agenda. We know that there must be something that holds it all together; we know that underneath it all, they're all headed toward a common goal. But on the surface, the world seems doomed to conflict, as each pursues its individual aspirations.

If only we could somehow get ahold of the master plan, of the grand blueprint for existence! If only we could read the Creator's mind, to discern His intended use for each creature's particular traits and tendencies! If only we had a vision of the "third element" of creation, a vision that incorporates all created things as the component parts of a single organism!

If we had that blueprint, we would no longer have to struggle to force some sort of balance between individual wants, to keep the world from tearing itself apart. If we had that blueprint, there would be no need to compromise differences for the sake of peace, since the properly guided pursuit of each entity's differences would result in the realization of the quintessential harmony which underlies all.

Torah, given in a flurry of threes, is that blueprint. Torah lays down the dos-and-don'ts of life, not as a curb on individual freedom but as the description of every individual's deepest and truest strivings. It outlines the manner in which every element of creation is to be developed and utilized, not as a program to change them but to bring to light their innate essence and function.

The Torah was given to make peace in the world.[3]

---

3   For another interpretation of the threesome-ness of Torah, see *The Mathematics of Marriage*, pp. 187–192 below.

LAW

According to the dictum of the Torah which they shall teach you... you shall do. You shall not turn away from what they shall instruct you to the right or to the left.

Deuteronomy 17:11

Among the great technological achievements of the 20th century is the development of the laser beam. The nature of light is such that it scatters as it moves away from its source, thereby lessening its intensity and effect. The laser overcomes this limitation by concentrating its energy in a straight line, so that it retains its potency even at a great distance from its point of origin; with the result that its utility (as light, heat, or other use) can be exploited in ways previously unimaginable.

We often hear the argument that a life that is faithful to the precepts of the Torah is greatly "constricted" and "confined." Why limit myself in any way? Why not give free reign to my thoughts, feelings, and inclinations, and let them lead me where they may? Why automatically exclude certain pursuits and experiences from the possible paths my life might take?

On the face of it, any code of behavior is limiting—something that detracts from the great variety of possibilities that life has to offer. In truth, however, the very opposite is the case. A life without parameters is a life that quickly dissipates in the cosmic heterogeneity in which we exist, draining it of all power and impact. As the example of the laser beam demonstrates, it is precisely the "limitations" imposed on a force that extend and amplify its potential and enable its optimal realization.

SHAVUOT (5)   171

THE BREAKTHROUGH

*And it came to pass on the third day, when
morning came, that there were thunders and
lightnings, and a thick cloud upon the mountain, and the sound of the* shofar *exceedingly
loud; and the entire people within the camp
trembled. And Moses brought the people out
of the camp to meet with G-d, and they stood
at the foot of the mountain...*

*G-d came down upon Mount Sinai, on the
top of the mountain. And G-d called Moses to
the top of the mountain, and Moses ascended.*

Exodus 19:16–20

𝔍 he most momentous event in history took place on Shabbat, the sixth day of the month of *Sivan*, in the year 2448
from creation (1313 BCE). On that day, the entire people of Israel—
more than two million men, women, and children,[1] as well as the
souls of all future generations of Jews—gathered at the foot of
Mount Sinai to receive the Torah from G-d. Ever since, the event
has been marked on our calendar as the festival of Shavuot—"the
time of the giving of our Torah."

But the Torah we received at Sinai had already been in our
possession for many generations. Our ancestors had studied and
"fulfilled the entire Torah even before it was given."[2] No new

---

1   A census taken eleven months later counted 603,550 males between
    the ages of 20 and 60.
2   Talmud, *Yoma* 28b; see *Doing Nothing*, pp. 155–161 above and sources

document was unveiled at Sinai, and no hitherto unknown code of behavior was commanded there. What, then, was given to us at "the giving of our Torah"?

The Midrash[3] explains the significance of the event with the following parable:

> *Once there was a king who decreed: "The people of Rome are forbidden to go down to Syria, and the people of Syria are forbidden to go up to Rome." Likewise, when G-d created the world He decreed and said: "The heavens are G-d's, and the earth is given to man."[4] But when G-d wished to give the Torah to Israel, He rescinded His original decree, and declared: "The lower realms may ascend to the higher realms, and the higher realms may descend to the lower realms. And I, Myself, will begin"—as it is written, "G-d descended on Mount Sinai," and then it says, "And to Moses He said: Go up to G-d."[5]*

For the first twenty-five centuries of history, there existed a *gezeirah*—a "decree" and "schism"—which split reality into two hermetic worlds: the spiritual and the physical. The spiritual could not be truly brought down to earth—its very nature defied actualization. Nor could the physical be made transcendent and divine— its very nature kept it imprisoned within the finiteness and mortality of the "lower realms." So Torah, the divine wisdom and will, could have no real effect upon the physical world. It was a wholly spiritual manifesto, pertaining to the soul of man and to the

---

cited there.

3   *Midrash Tanchuma, Va'eira* 15; *Midrash Rabbah, Shemot* 12:4.

4   Psalms 115:16.

5   Exodus 19:20 and 24:19.

SHAVUOT (5)   173

spiritual reality of the "heavens."[6] While its concepts could, and
were, applied to physical life, physical life could not be elevated.
The physical could be improved and perfected to the limits of its
potential, but it could not transcend its inherent coarseness and
subjectivity.

At Sinai, G-d revoked the decree which had confined matter
and spirit to two distinct realms. G-d came down on Mount Sinai,
bringing the spirituality of the heavens down to earth. He summoned Moses to the top of the mountain, empowering physical
man to raise his physical self and world to a higher state of existence. The Torah could now sanctify physical life.

The encounter between G-d and man at Sinai introduced a new
phenomenon—the *cheftza shel kedushah* or "holy object." After Sinai, when we take a physical coin, earned by our physical toil and
talents, and gives it to charity; or when we bake flour and water
as unleavened bread (matzah) and eat it on the first night of Passover; or when we form a piece of leather to a specified shape and
dimensions, insert into it parchment scrolls inscribed with specified words, and bind them to our head and arm as *tefilin*—the
object with which we have performed our *mitzvah* (divine commandment) is transformed. A finite, physical thing becomes "holy,"
as its substance and form come to embody the realization of a divine desire and command.

The *mitzvot* could be, and were, performed before the revelation at Sinai. But because they had not yet been *commanded* by
G-d, they lacked the power to bridge the great divide between matter and spirit. Only as a command of G-d, creator and delineator
of both the spiritual and the physical, could the *mitzvah* supersede

---

6   See next essay, *Real Estate*. pp, 177–186.

174   INSIDE TIME: VOL. III

the natural definitions of these two realms. Only after Sinai could
the *mitzvah* actualize the spiritual and sanctify the material.

Thus we find that when Abraham required his servant Eliezer
to take an oath, he told him to "place your hand under my thigh."[7]
An oath is taken while holding a sacred object such as a Torah
scroll or *tefilin*; here Abraham is telling Eliezer to swear on the
part of his own body sanctified by the *mitzvah* of circumcision.
But since "Abraham observed the entire Torah even before it was
given"—i.e., he studied Torah, put on *tefilin*, affixed a *mezuzah* on
his doorpost—it would seem that he had no shortage of "sacred
objects" available to him. Why, then, did he have Eliezer place his
hand "under his thigh," contrary to all common standards of mod-
esty and propriety? But as we said, the import of Abraham's pre-Si-
nai *mitzvot* were of a wholly spiritual nature. Since G-d had not
commanded him to do them, they remained subject to the cosmic
law that separated the supernal from the material. While Abraham's *mitzvot* had a profound effect on his own soul, the souls of
his descendants, and the spiritual essence of creation, they had no
impact on the material substance of the universe. The single exception was the *mitzvah* of circumcision, which G-d *did* command
to Abraham (as related in Genesis 17), imparting to this *mitzvah*
something of the nature of the post-Sinaitic *mitzvot*.[8] Hence, this
was the only "sacred object" available to Abraham.

---

7   Genesis 24:2; cf. Jacob's similar administration of an oath to Joseph,
    Genesis 47:29.

8   Nevertheless, Abraham's *mitzvah* of circumcision was only a *precedent*
    for the divine commandments issued at Sinai, and not a full revocation
    of the decree dissevering heaven from earth. It was the closest thing he
    had to an "object of holiness," but not a complete sanctification of the
    physical, which is possible only after Sinai. Thus Maimonides writes:
    "Pay close attention to the major principle expressed by [the words] 'It
    was said at Sinai'... For everything from which we refrain or which we
    do today, we do only because of G-d's command to Moses at Sinai, not

SHAVUOT (5)   175

An Absorbent World

Therein lies the significance of a curious detail related by our sages regarding the revelation at Sinai.

The Torah tells us that G-d spoke the Ten Commandments in "a great voice, which did not cease."[9] The Midrash offers a number of interpretations for this description of the divine voice. One interpretation is that the divine did not confine itself to the holy tongue but reverberated in the seventy languages of mankind. A second meaning is that the voice did not cease on that particular Shabbat morning thirty-three centuries ago: Throughout the generations, all prophets and sages who taught and expounded upon the wisdom of the Torah are the extension of that very voice, for they added nothing that was not already inherent in the Ten Commandments. Finally, the Midrash offers a third explanation of the voice's "unceasing" nature: The divine voice at Sinai was unique in that it had no echo.[10]

The first two interpretations obviously point to the universality and timelessness of Torah. But what is "great and unceasing" about a voice that has no echo? Why should the divine voice at Sinai have been distinguished in this manner from all other sounds?

In truth, however, the echoless nature of the divine communication conveys the very essence of what transpired at Sinai. An

---

because of any communication by G-d to earlier prophets. For example, the fact that we do not eat a limb from a live animal is not because G-d forbade this to Noah, but because Moses forbade it to us by commanding at Sinai that the prohibition of eating a limb from a live animal should remain in force. Similarly, we do not circumcise ourselves because our father Abraham circumcised himself and the members of his household, but because G-d commanded us through Moses that we should circumcise ourselves as did Abraham" (Maimonides' *Commentary on the Mishnah, Chulin* 7:6).

9   Deuteronomy 5:19.
10   *Midrash Rabbah, Shemot* 28:4.

echo is created when a sound meets with a substance which resists it: instead of absorbing its waves, the substance repels them, bouncing them back to the void. Prior to Sinai, the voice of Torah had an "echo." Belonging to the spirituality of the heavens, it could not truly penetrate the physicality of the earth. The world might "hear" of Torah and be affected by it; but there remained a certain degree of resistance, as the Torah and the physical world each remained bound in their respective "higher" and "lower" realms. At Sinai, however, G-d rescinded the decree which had severed the heavens from the earth. The world could now fully absorb the divine voice; a physical object could now become one with its mission and role.

THE EMPOWERING PRECEDENT

Therein lies an important lesson to us as we pursue our mission in life to implement the ethos and ideals of Torah in our world.

At Sinai we were charged to serve as a "light unto the nations"— to actualize in our own lives, and to teach all of humanity, that no matter what the conditions of a particular time, place, or society may be, there is an all-transcendent, unequivocal, divinely ordained truth and moral code of behavior to adhere to.

At times, we might be confronted with a seemingly unresponsive and even resisting world. It may appear that one or another of Torah's precepts does not "fit in" with the prevalent reality. So the Torah tells us that the voice which sounded G-d's message to humanity had no echo.

The voice of the Ten Commandments permeated every object in the universe. So any "resistance" we may meet in implementing them is superficial and temporary. For at Sinai, the essence of every created being was made consistent with, and wholly receptive to, the goodness and perfection which G-d desires of it.

REAL ESTATE

G-d desired a dwelling in the physical world.

Midrash Tanchuma, Nasso 16

*A*ccording to Torah law, your neighbor is not just the fellow on the other side of the fence, but someone toward whom you have certain responsibilities and obligations. One of these is spelled out in the law of *bar mitzra* (literally, "the one on the boundary"), which states that when a person wishes to sell his field, his neighbors (i.e., those who own land bordering the land being sold) must be given first priority to purchase it. This law is enforced by the court, to the extent that if the property is sold to an outside buyer without first being offered to a neighbor, the neighbor has the right to pay the purchase price to the buyer and evict him from the land.[1]

Halachah (Torah law) is more than a code of behavior for life on earth: it also describes G-d's own "code of behavior," the manner

---

1   Talmud, *Bava Metzia* 108a; *Mishneh Torah, Laws Regarding Neighbors*, chs. 12–14; *Shulchan Aruch, Choshen Mishpat* 175:5–63. The Talmud cites this law as a classic case of "one profits, while the other suffers no loss." The buyer profits in that he can cultivate both properties as a single contiguous field, saving him the added expense of cultivating two fields in two separate places; the seller suffers no real loss, since he gets his price; nor does the prospective non-neighboring buyer, who can purchase a field of equal quality and value somewhere else. Thus, the court enforces the precept, "You shall do what is just and good" (Deuteronomy 6:18)—i.e., it is forbidden to act maliciously, even if it is within your "legal" rights.

in which G-d chooses to relate to His creation. Thus, we find G-d observing Shabbat, donning *tefilin*, and otherwise fulfilling the requirements of Torah law. In the words of the Midrash, "G-d's way is not like the way of flesh and blood. The way of flesh and blood is that he instructs others to do, but does not do so himself; G-d, however, what He Himself does, that is what He tells Israel to do and observe."[2] So if G-d commanded us the law of *bar mitzra*, He conforms to it Himself.

Thus, the Talmud tells us that when Moses "ascended to heaven" to receive the Torah from G-d,

> The angels protested to G-d: "What is a human being doing amongst us?" Said He to them: "He has come to receive the Torah."
>
> Said they to Him: "This esoteric treasure, which was hidden with You for nine hundred and seventy-four generations before the world was created, You wish to give to flesh and blood? ...Place Your glory upon the heavens!"
>
> Said G-d to Moses: "Answer them."
>
> Said [Moses]: "Master of the Universe! This Torah that You are giving to me, what is written in it? 'I am G-d your G-d, who has taken you out from the land of Egypt.'"
>
> "Have you descended to Egypt?" asked Moses of the angels. "Have you been enslaved to Pharaoh? So why should the Torah be yours?
>
> "What else does it say? 'You shall have no alien gods.' Do you dwell amongst idol-worshipping nations?
>
> "What else does it say? 'Remember the Shabbat day.' Do you work?... What else does it say? 'Do not swear falsely.'

---

2   *Midrash Rabbah, Bereishit* 11:5; Talmud, *Berachot* 6a; *Midrash Rabbah, Shemot* 30:4.

SHAVUOᵀ (6)   179

Do you do business? What else does it say? 'Honor your
father and your mother.' Do you have parents? What else
does it say? 'Do not kill,' 'Do not commit adultery,' 'Do
not steal.' Is there jealousy among you? Do you have an
evil inclination?"[3]

As the commentaries[4] explain, the angels had a *legal* claim on the
Torah — the neighbor's prerogative stipulated by the law of *bar
mitzra*. For the Torah is G-d's "esoteric treasure": before it was giv-
en to us at Sinai it was a wholly spiritual manifesto, "written of
yore before Him in black fire upon white fire,"[5] relating exclusively
to the spiritual infrastructure of creation. Thus we are told that at
Sinai G-d spoke to us "from the heavens," and that Moses "ascended to heaven," entering into a spiritual state of being in order to
receive the Torah.[6] We, argued the angels, are the Torah's natural
neighbors; it should be offered to us before it is translated into a
doctrine for physical life for some distant earthly customer.[7]

---

3   Talmud, *Shabbat* 89a.
4   *Shetei Yadot, Terumah*; *She'eirit Yaakov, Bamidbar*; Chida (*Penei Dovid
    and Rosh Dovid, Yitro*; *Chasdei Avot*, 3:14); *Be'er Yitzchak, Yitro* (2);
    Maarchei Lev, Mattan Torah (12); *Berit Avot, Yitro*; *Sefat Emet, Yitro*;
    Nachal Yitzchak, Pesach, Shaar I and II; et al.
5   Rashi, Deuteronomy 33:2.
6   Exodus 20:19 and Deuteronomy 4:31; Talmud, *Shabbat* 89a, and in nu-
    merous other places; see Exodus 34:28: "And [Moses] was there (atop
    Mount Sinai) with G-d for forty days and forty nights; bread he did
    not eat, and water he did not drink."
7   This also explains why Moses could not simply reply to the angels:
    "Open up the Torah and have a look: Virtually every section is pref-
    aced with the words, 'Command the children of Israel,' 'Speak to the
    children of Israel,' and the like." For the law of *bar mitzra* gives the
    neighbor the right to purchase the field even *after* it has been sold to
    the non-bordering buyer.

FIVE ANSWERS

G-d acknowledged that the angels had a basis for their claim in Torah law, telling Moses to "answer them" before he could receive the Torah and take it down to earth.[8] How, indeed, might Moses defend the legality of the contract between G-d and Israel? The commentaries offer the following *halachic* solutions:

1) The law of *bar mitzra* applies only to a sale, not to a gift — the owner is obviously free to make a gift of his field to whomever he desires.[9] Since G-d *granted* us the Torah, the angels' claim has no basis.

2) The law of *bar mitzra* applies only to real estate, not to transportable objects.[10] The Torah, which is a portable entity (as evidenced by the fact that it was "transported" to earth), is thus exempt from this law.

3) If a person wishes to sell his field to a family member, he is permitted to do so without first offering it to his neighbor.[11] The people of Israel are G-d's children[12] and His "close relatives."[13]

---

8   According to Rashi on Talmud, *Bava Metzia* 108a, the law of *bar mitzra* pertains primarily to the prospective purchaser, forbidding him to purchase a field desired by its neighbor and obligating him to resell it to the neighbor should he actually purchase it (see *Likutei Sichot*, vol. 19, pp. 55–57). This explains why G-d directed the angels' claim to Moses, who, as the "purchaser," was the alleged violator of the *bar mitzra* law.

9   Talmud, *Bava Metzia* 108b; *Mishneh Torah, Laws Regarding Neighbors* 13:1; *Shulchan Aruch, Choshen Mishpat* 175:54.

10   *Mishneh Torah, Laws Regarding Neighbors* 13:4; *Shulchan Aruch, Choshen Mishpat* 175:53.

11   Rif, cited in *Shitah Mekubetzet* on Talmud, *Bava Metzia* 108b; *Bahag*, cited by *Beit Yosef* on *Tur, Choshen Mishpat* 175; *Shach* on *Shulchan Aruch, Choshen Mishpat* 175:30.

12   Deuteronomy 14:1

13   *Kerovim*, in the Hebrew; ibid. 4:7.

SHAVUOT (6)   181

Thus, the law of *bar mitzra* is not applicable to Israel's purchase of
the Torah.

4) A sale to a partner is likewise exempt from the *bar mitzra*
requirement.[14] The Talmud states that "Any judge who judges law
with an utter exactitude of truth becomes a partner with G-d in
creation."[15] Moses, being such a juror of Torah law,[16] is thus considered G-d's partner, and may purchase property from Him over the
objections of the property's supernal neighbors. (Keeping Shabbat
also renders one "a partner with G-d in creation."[17] Since the Jewish people had been given the *mitzvah* of Shabbat several weeks
before Sinai,[18] they, too, are G-d's "partners," and thus free to "purchase" the Torah).

5) The Torah refers to Moses as a "man of G-d"—half mortal,
half supernal.[19] So he was no less a "neighbor" to the spiritual Torah than his celestial competitors. (Again, the same could be said
regarding the people of Israel, whose souls are "carved from beneath the supernal throne" of G-d.[20])

However, each of these defenses has its difficulties. Regarding
the first defense, while it is true that the Torah is called a "gift"
from Above (as in Numbers 21:18, and in the text of the blessing
recited on the Torah), it is also called an "inheritance" (Deuteronomy 33:4), and a "purchase" (Proverbs 4:2; *Midrash Rabbah*,

---

14 *Mishneh Torah, Laws Regarding Neighbors* 12:5; *Shulchan Aruch, Chosh-
    en Mishpat* 175:49.
15 Talmud, *Shabbat* 10a, as per Exodus 18:13.
16 Indeed, the verse from which the Talmud derives this is speaking
    about Moses.
17 Talmud, *Shabbat* 119b.
18 During their encampment in Marah, as per Talmud, *Sanhedrin* 56b.
    See also Exodus 16:29–30.
19 Deuteronomy 33:1; Psalms 90:1; *Midrash Rabbah, Devarim* 11:4.
20 *Zohar* 3:29b.

Shemot 33:1). These three metaphors describe three distinct elements in Torah and the manner of its "possession" by the people of Israel. Thus, the angels' claim to the Torah stands, at least in regard to the "purchase" aspect of Torah.

As for the second defense, the reason the law of *bar mitzra* does not apply to a portable object is because a portable object has no defined place, and thus no true neighbors: anyone can acquire it anywhere and transport it to his property. In our case, however, the Torah's defining "place" is the very issue at hand. The angels were insisting that it should remain "in heaven" and spiritual in essence, while Moses' purchase would mean its removal to earth and the redefinition of its primary function from a spiritual manifesto to a doctrine for physical life. Indeed, after we received it at Sinai, the Torah is expressly "not in heaven," and completely under terrestrial jurisdiction.[21] The "sale" of Torah to Israel meant that the angels would no longer have access to the Torah—at least not as something of their own environment (in the same way that the Torah's remaining "in heaven" would have meant that we could relate to it only on the esoteric level, not as a sanctifier of physical life).[22] It follows, then, that as regards the law of *bar mitzra,* the Torah is indeed supernal "real estate," and ought to be subject to the neighbor's prerogative claimed by the angels.

---

21 Deuteronomy 30:12. See Talmud, *Bava Metzia* 59b, quoted on p. 192 below.

22 As it was prior to the giving of the torah—see previous essay, *The Breakthrough,* pp. 171–176.

The law of *bar mitzra* applies only when comparable fields are available at other locations, and the issue is only who should be subjected to the trouble of purchasing elsewhere (see note 1 above). This is consistent with the debate between Moses and the angels as to whether the Torah might be "sold" to earth: In either case, both the angels and the people of Israel would still be able to study the Torah, but only one of them would enjoy the Torah as something that is of their own element.

SHAVUOT (6)   183

Finally, all five explanations beg the question: Where is there mention of any of this in Moses' response? If the basis of the angels'
argument to G-d, "Place Your glory upon the heavens!" is the law
of *bar mitzra*, then Moses must explain why this clause is not applicable in this case. Yet nowhere in Moses' words do we find a
sign of any of the five defenses enumerated above. Indeed, as far
as the third, fourth, and fifth defenses are concerned, Moses seems
to be saying the very opposite. The gist of Moses' response is that,
unlike the angels, the Jewish people are physical beings inhabiting
a profane and even heretical world—a world marked by jealousy,
dishonesty, and idolatry—and thus they have need of and right
to the Torah. Instead of refuting the angels' claim by speaking of
Israel's innate spirituality (defense #5) or their relationship or partnership with G-d (defenses #3 and #4), Moses seems to be *confirm-
ing* their claim by emphasizing Israel's distance from their divine
origins and the spirituality of the heavens.

THE HOME

Our sages teach that "The purpose of the creation of all worlds, supernal and ephemeral," is that "G-d desired a dwelling in the lowly
realms."[23] G-d desired to create a "lowly realm"—a world that is
virtually devoid of all manifest expression of His truth—and that
this lowly realm should be made into a home for Him, a "dwelling"
that serves and facilitates His presence.

Thus, the world was created "for the sake of the Torah and for
the sake of Israel"[24]—the people of Israel are the builders of this
home for G-d, and the Torah is the instrument of its construction.

---

23   *Midrash Tanchuma, Nasso* 16; *Tanya*, chapter 36.
24   Rashi, Genesis 1:1.

The people of Israel inhabit the physical universe — the "lowly realm" where G-d desires to dwell. The Torah instructs us how to transform material things such as animal hides and palm fronds into holy and G-dly things such as *tefilin* and a *lulav*. With the Torah as our blueprint and empowerer, we transform a mundane world into an environment that is receptive and subservient to the divine reality.

Why is the sanctification of the physical world referred to as the making of a "dwelling" for G-d? Because the home is the human model which most expresses the significance of what we achieve through our fulfillment of the Torah's blueprint for life.

There are many environments and structures that "house" a person and serve his needs. A person might spend many toilsome hours in a field, tilling its soil to derive sustenance from the earth; others mark time in offices, factories, and laboratories to earn a livelihood. Man also constructs buildings to serve his educational, medical, legal, and recreational needs. But what all these containers of man have in common is that they each house a specific aspect of the person, as opposed to the person himself. They shelter and facilitate the farmer, the businessman, the student, the patient, the art critic, and the vacationer in the person, rather than the person himself. All these are places where a person fulfills a certain role or fills a certain need; only at home is he himself. Echoing the talmudic adage, "A man without a homestead is not a man,"[25] Chassidic teaching defines the dwelling as "a place that houses a person's very essence."[26]

This is what is meant when we say that "G-d desired a dwelling in the lowly realms." G-d has many venues for the expression of

---

25 *Yevamot* 63a, as per *Tosafot*.
26 *Ohr HaTorah, Balak* 997; *Yom Tov Shel Rosh Hashanah 5666*, p. 3; et al.

SHAVUOT (6)   185

His reality—He created many spiritual worlds or "realms," each of
which conveys another face of G-d's infinitely faceted truth. But
only the physical world can be G-d's home, the environment that
houses His essence.

For the wisdom of the sage is not revealed in his scholarly discourse with his colleagues, but in his ability to explain the
loftiest of concepts to the simplest of minds. The benevolence of
the philanthropist is seen not in his generosity to his family and
friends, but in his kindness toward the most undeserving of recipients. The power of the torch is expressed not by the light it
sheds upon its immediate surroundings, but by its illumination
of the most distant point its light can reach. By the same token,
the infinity and all-pervasiveness of the divine is expressed not in
the spirituality of the heavens, but in the sanctification of material
earth. When the physical world—"whose workings are harsh and
evil and the wicked prevail there," for it is dominated by forces that
seem indifferent and even opposed to the divine will[27]—is made
to express the divine truth, it becomes a "dwelling" for G-d. When
the lowliest and most profane of G-d's creations is made to serve
Him, a true home has been constructed for Him, an edifice that
houses His very essence.

Therein lies the ultimate refutation of the angels' claim on the
Torah. The law of *bar mitzra* states that "If the distant buyer wishes to build homes on the land, and the neighbor wishes to seed it,
the distant buyer retains the land, since the habitation of the land
takes precedence, and the law of *bar mitzra* is not applied in this
case."[28]

---

27 *Tanya*, chapters 6 and 36.
28 *Mishneh Torah, Laws Regarding Neighbors* 14:1; Talmud, *Bava Metzia*
    108b; *Shulchan Aruch, Choshen Mishpat* 175:26.

Thus Moses said to the angels: Do you have an evil inclination? Do you deal with the mundanities of the marketplace? Do you dwell in a pagan world? So to what end should you be given the Torah? To cultivate another lush garden of spiritual delights? But we will build a *home* with the Torah—as only we can. Only we, who daily grapple with the deceit, the strife, and the profanity that mark the lowliest stratum of G-d's creation, can construct with the Torah a dwelling for Him, a place to house His quintessential self.

SHAVUOT (7)

THE MATHEMATICS OF MARRIAGE

When a person knows and grasps in his mind a Torah law... he thereby grasps and holds and encompasses with his mind the divine wisdom and will... while his mind is simultaneously enveloped within them. This makes for a wonderful union, like which there is none other and which has no parallel anywhere in the material world, whereby complete oneness and unity, from every side and angle, is attained.

Tanya, chapter 5

*M*arriage comes in three varieties: the singular marriage, the twosome marriage, and the three-dimensional marriage.

In a singular marriage, one partner is completely consumed by the dominant other. Two have joined to become one, yet theirs is not so much a union as a singularization. One partner either abnegates their own understanding, feelings, and very self to the other's; or else his or her ego swallows up the other's mind, heart, and very being.

In the twosome marriage, each partner preserves his or her distinction as an individual. They share thoughts, feelings, and resources, and deeply affect and are affected by each other; but each does so on his or her own terms, assimilating the marital bond as part of his or her own experience and identity. So what we have here is not a union, only a "relationship" between individuals.

Then there is marriage in its true and ultimate sense: a marriage in which two individuals collaborate in the creation of a third reality which embraces and suffuses them both, while preserving their differences as the very dynamics of their union. A true marriage houses not a single, all negating being, nor two distinct beings, but a threesome that is the essence of unity: the individual selves of the marriage partners, and the marriage itself—the "third element" within whose context their two beings unite into a harmonious whole.

CHANNELS

As human beings, we inhabit a finite and corporeal reality—a reality which, by nature and definition, precludes all contact with anything truly infinite, transcendent, and absolute. Nevertheless, the Creator has established channels of awareness and experience which extend beyond the boundaries of our existence and allow us to relate to His all-transcendent truth.

These outlets to a higher reality assume many forms, but may be divided into three general categories, akin to the three types of "marriages" described above.

On the "unilateral" level of relationship, there are occasions when the Almighty chooses to overwhelm us with a supranatural, suprarational dose of His reality. For example, we may witness a miracle which shatters the very foundations of how we understand ourselves and our world—an experience which we cannot assimilate in any humanly sensible way except to be overcome with awe and humility. Another example of the unilateral relationship is

SHAVUOT (7)   189

when a person, confronted with a challenge to his deepest convictions, will choose to sacrifice his or her very existence for the sake of a higher truth.

In both these cases, the wall which encloses our self-bound existence has been breached. Yet the result is not so much a union of the human with the divine, but the negation of the human, the exposure of its insubstantiality in the face of the divine.

Then there are the "twosome" type relationships between Heaven and earth—natural, humanly digestible points of contact between our world and the divine reality. Every sunrise, every beat of the human heart, and every flutter of an insect's wings, is G-d acting upon our reality. While these divine deeds are no less miraculous than the splitting of the Sea of Reeds, nature is G-d's way of affecting our world through a veil of constraint, routine, and predictability—a veil which filters His input into our lives in a way that is readily absorbable by our finite senses and minds. On our part, the whole of human science is man's attempt to gain insight into what lies behind and beyond the mere facts of our existence.

Through these natural channels of connection we relate to the divine truth "on our own terms," without annihilating the norms of human existence and experience. On the other hand, however, they cannot be said to truly *unite* the earthly and the divine—only to establish a connection between them as two distinct and irreconcilable realms.

MEETING OF MINDS

But on the sixth day of *Sivan* in the year 2448 from creation (1313 BCE), G-d descended on Mount Sinai and "gave a threefold Torah to a threefold people through a third-born on a third day in the third month."[1] Torah is the "third element" of our relationship with G-d—the element which makes our relationship a true marriage.

In the words of the Midrash, at Sinai, "The higher realms descended to the lower realms" with G-d's descent upon Mount Sinai, while "the lower realms ascended to the higher realms" with Moses' ascent to the top of the mountain.[2] Had there only been a descent from Above to below, the divine reality would have totally overwhelmed the earthly reality, resulting in a one-sided marriage —a relationship that is wholly defined by the nature and character of only one of its partners. If there had been only an ascent from below to Above, our encounter with the divine would have been characterized by the finiteness of our physical existence, resulting in a "twosome" marriage in which each side relates to the other from behind the defining walls of self. But at Sinai there occurred a descent from above by G-d as well as a rising upward of man. In other words, this was an encounter in which each partner not only relates to and connects with the other, but also participates in defining the nature of the relationship between them, so that the relationship affirms his individual identity even as it expands it to include the very different identity of the other partner.[3]

---

1   Talmud, *Shabbat* 88a; see the essay *Peace* on pp. 166–169 above.

2   *Midrash Tanchuma, Va'eira* 15; *Midrash Rabbah, Shemot* 12:4; see *The Breakthrough* on pp. 171–176 above.

3   Thus there were three stages to the union of heaven and earth: 1) the descent of the "higher realms" to the lower; 2) the ascent of the "lower realms" to the higher; and 3) the collusion or merger of these two movements in a single "marriage" and union.

On the historical level, the first millennium of history, which was characterized by an abundant flow of life and nurture from Above, was a time in which the relationship between heaven and earth was defined exclusively by the "higher realms." The second millennium, which saw the refinement and self-elevation of earth, was a time of upward

SHAVUOT (7)   191

For at Sinai was introduced the "third element" of Torah, where the finiteness of man unites with the infinity of G-d in a union that is both finite and infinite, both human and divine.

Torah is the wisdom and will of G-d. But G-d did not communicate His wisdom and will as a detailed manifesto and a codified list of instructions. Instead, G-d gave us a relatively short (79,976-word) "Written Torah" (the Five Books of Moses), together with the "Oral Torah"—a set of guidelines by which the Written Torah is to be interpreted and expounded, and applied to the myriads of possibilities conjured up by the human experience. So while the Written Torah encapsulates the immense sea of legal, homiletic, philosophical, and mystical teaching we know as "Torah,"[4] it is the human mind and life which G-d designated as the tools

---

striving on the part of the "lower realms." And the third millennium, which commenced the "age of Torah," saw the union of the supernal and the earthly in the convergence of the two.

In the immediate events leading to the revelation at Sinai, these three stages were actualized in: 1) the Exodus, which was a unilateral, divinely initiated revelation and redemption from Above; 2) the seven-week period of preparation and self-refinement between the Exodus and the revelation at Sinai (reenacted each year with our "counting of the *omer*"); and 3) the giving of the Torah, in which G-d came down on Mount Sinai and Moses ascended the mountain (see *The Journey* on pp. 98–108 above).

On another level, the revelation at Sinai, though it included elements of the "lower realms ascending," was primarily a revelation from Above. This is followed by many centuries of self-refinement and self-perfection on our part, to be followed by the era of Moshiach and its ultimate union of heaven and earth (see *No and Yes* on pp. 291–294).

4   In the words of the Talmud: "Scripture, Mishnah, Talmud, and *aggadah*, and even everything that a qualified student is destined to innovate—all was already said to Moses at Sinai" (Jerusalem Talmud, *Pe'ah* 2:4).

with which to unlock the many layers of meaning and instruction implicit in its every word.

This is most powerfully demonstrated by the Talmud's account of a *halachic* dispute between Rabbi Eliezer and his colleagues:

> *Rabbi Eliezer brought them all sorts of proofs, but they were rejected... Finally, he said to them: "If the law is as I say, may it be proven from heaven!" There then issued a heavenly voice which proclaimed: "What do you want of Rabbi Eliezer—the law is as he says..."*
>
> *Rabbi Joshua stood on his feet and said: "The Torah is not in heaven!"[5]... We take no notice of heavenly voices, since You, G-d, have already, at Sinai, written in the Torah to follow the majority.[6]*
>
> *Rabbi Nathan subsequently met Elijah the Prophet and asked him: "What did G-d do at that moment?" [Elijah] replied: "He smiled and said: 'My children have triumphed over Me, My children have triumphed over Me.'"[7]*

Torah is where the human and the divine fuse to one: where a kernel of divine wisdom germinates in the human mind, gaining depth, breadth, and definition, and is then made tangible in the physicality of human life.

In this marriage, our humanity is not obliterated within the infinite expanse of the divine; but neither does it remain distinct from it. In this marriage, our human finiteness and subjectivity themselves become instruments of the divine truth, joining with it to create the ultimate expression of divine immanence in our world: the Torah.

---

5   Deuteronomy 30:12.

6   Exodus 23:2.

7   Talmud, *Bava Metzia* 59b.

THE THREE
NAMES
OF SHAVUOT

*You have granted to us with love, L-rd our G-d
... this festival day of Shavuot... the Time of
the Giving of Our Torah...*

Siddur, from the festival prayers

*Seven weeks shall you count; from the time
that you begin to put the sickle to the corn,
you shall commence to count seven weeks.
And you shall make a Festival of Weeks to the
L-rd your G-d.* Deuteronomy 16:9–10

*And the Day of First Fruits, when you bring a
new meal-offering to G-d on your Festival of
Weeks, shall be for you a calling of holiness.*

Numbers 28:26

A t first, our entire focus is on figuring out how this thing
works, as if life was a giant machine and we just had to
learn to push the right buttons. We discover that crying elicits nurture and attention; we perceive that certain of our actions are met
with approval and others with censure; we figure out which skills
and resources are required to preserve and perpetuate our
existence.

At a certain point, however, we realize that there's more to life
than mastering a set of behaviors. We discover an inner self of ideas,

drives, feelings—a personality. No longer content with just doing things the right way, we strive to better ourselves—to expand our mind, hone our feelings, refine our character.

Finally, there comes a time when this goal, too, pales in significance before a far more ambitious endeavor. Why content ourselves with the perfection of the self, when we can transform the world? Why relegate our quest for peace to the search for inner harmony, when a conflict-ridden race of seven billion cries out for our aid? Why limit our capacity for growth and discovery to the interior of our souls, when an entire universe awaits exploration and development?

THE MANDATE AT SINAI

On the sixth day of *Sivan* in the year 2448 from creation (1313 BCE), the people of Israel stood at the foot of Mount Sinai. There G-d revealed Himself to us and gave us the Torah, His "blueprint for creation" and our charter as "a holy people" and "a light unto the nations."[1] Ever since, the day has been celebrated as the festival of Shavuot.

The Torah functions on many levels. On the most basic level, it is a guide to life in the most elementary and technical sense. Its 613 commandments (*mitzvot*) instruct us in the dos-and-don'ts of life, delineating the permissible and the forbidden, the sacred and the profane, the beneficial and the injurious to our bodies and souls.

But the Torah is more than a regulator of behavior. It "was given to refine the person,"[2] to weed out the bad and cultivate the good in our hearts; to develop our minds as vectors of the divine

---

1   *Midrash Rabbah, Bereishit* 1:2; Exodus 19:6; Isaiah 42:6.
2   *Midrash Rabbah, Bereishit* 44:1.

truth; to bring to light the "divine image"[3] in which our souls have been molded.

Finally, the Torah is the vehicle for the most enterprising of our potentials: to "make the physical world a home for G-d"[4]—a place that houses, expresses, and serves the perfection of the divine.

THREE NAMES

The festival on which we commemorate and reexperience the revelation at Sinai has three names, corresponding to these three areas of the day's influence in our lives.

In the Shavuot prayers, we refer to the day as *Zeman Mattan Torateinu*, the "Time of the Giving of Our Torah."

In the Torah, it is called *Chag Shavuot*, "Festival of Weeks."[5] This, because the festival follows, and is the product of, a seven-week count that begins on the second day of Passover.[6]

A third name for the festival, also of biblical origin, is *Yom Ha-Bikurim*, "The Day of the First Fruits."[7] On this day, the *bikurim*, the first-ripened fruits of the Israelite farmer's orchard, were presented to the *kohen* (priest) in the Holy Temple, as commanded by the Torah in the 26th chapter of Deuteronomy.

Torah means "law" and "instruction." The most basic significance of Shavuot is that it is the "time of the giving of our Torah"—the day on which the 600,000 souls gathered at Sinai were

---

3   Genesis 1:26.

4   *Midrash Tanchuma, Nasso* 16; *Tanya*, chapter 36.

5   Exodus 34:22; Deuteronomy 16:10 and 16:16.

6   See our chapter on "The Counting of the Omer," pp. 95–112 above.

7   Numbers 28:26.

instructed on "the path along which they should walk and the deeds which they should do."[8]

But Shavuot is not only the time of the giving of our Torah—it is also the "Festival of Weeks," the culmination of a seven-week journey of self-discovery and self-refinement. In the 23rd chapter of Leviticus, the Torah instructs:

> *You shall count for yourselves, from the morrow of the Shabbat, from the day on which you bring the raised* omer— *seven complete weeks shall there be. Until the morrow of the seventh week, you shall count fifty days; and you shall offer a new meal-offering to G-d. From your habitations you shall bring two breads for raising... made of fine flour... And you shall proclaim that very day a holy festival...*

On the second day of Passover ("the morrow of the Shabbat") a measure—*omer*[9]—of barley was "raised up" and offered in the Holy Temple in Jerusalem. This marked the beginning of a seven-week count—the "counting of the *omer*"—which culminated in the "raising up" of the *shtei halechem*, an offering of two loaves of bread, on the festival of Shavuot.

Chassidic teaching explains that the progress from animal fodder (barley)[10] to human food (the "two loaves," prepared from finely ground wheat flour) signified the refinement of our "animal soul"—our base and materialistic instincts—and its elevation to

---

8   Exodus 18:20.

9   The *omer* is a biblical measure, equivalent to approximately 43 ounces by volume.

10   "The barley and the straw for the horses and the mules"—I Kings 5:8. Cf. Talmud, *Sotah* 14a: "Since her deeds were the deeds of an animal, her offering is [of barley,] the food of animals."

SHAVUOT (8)

the human level of a soul forged in the image of the divine. The seven weeks of the intervening count correspond to the seven basic drives of the human personality, each of which includes aspects of all seven. Each week of the count is devoted to the task of refining one of these drives, and each day of the week's seven days to another of its seven aspects. On the 50th day we attain Shavuot, the Festival of Weeks—the perfection of all seven "weeks" of the human character.[11]

The festival's third name, "Day of the First Fruits," speaks of the endeavor to go beyond the perfection of self to develop and elevate the material resources of our world.

In Deuteronomy 26 we read:

> *When you enter the land which G-d your G-d is giving you as a heritage, and you inherit it and settle it, you shall take from the first fruits of the land... and place them in a basket. And you shall go to the place which G-d will choose to dwell His name...*

Every year, the Israelite farmer repeated the process, selecting from the first and finest of his orchard to bring to the Holy Temple in Jerusalem on the festival of Shavuot. By doing so, he proclaimed: My days are consumed with working the land, my nights with thoughts of seed, soil, and weather; but the purpose of it all is not development of the material for material ends, but to make this world a home for G-d. See—the first and best of my produce I have brought here, to the place chosen by G-d to house His presence.

---

11 See *The Journey*, pp. 98–108 above.

Diminished Weeks

The history of a nation—like the story of an individual life—knows periods of greater and lesser spiritual sophistication. Just as in our own lives we experience times of profound personal and social achievement as well as periods in which merely "functioning" is a struggle, so, too, it is in the progress of Israel through the generations.

If we contemplate the three names of Shavuot, we note that they vary in the degree of their realization from era to era and from generation to generation.

The first and most basic definition of the festival is also the least subject to the flux of time. Each morning we thank G-d for His gift of truth with the words, "Blessed are You G-d, who gives the Torah"—*gives*, in the present tense, since "every day the words of Torah should be as new in your eyes, as if you received them from Sinai today."[12] The divine instruction of daily life is unaffected by the rises and slumps of spiritual awareness and achievement: Shavuot is equally the "time of the giving of our Torah" to every generation.

This has not been the case, however, regarding its designation as the "festival of weeks." The *omer* offering can only be brought in the Holy Temple in Jerusalem. Since the Torah defines the seven-week count from Passover to Shavuot as beginning on "the day on which you bring the raised *omer*," it is the opinion of most *halachic* authorities that there is no biblical obligation to conduct the counting of the *omer* when the Temple is not extant.[13] Today, we

---

12 *Lekach Tov*, Deuteronomy 6:6.

13 Actually, there are three opinions cited in *halachic* literature on the status of the *omer* count in times when there is no *omer* offering. According to most *halachic* authorities, the counting of the *omer* today is wholly a rabbinical *mitzvah*. Others, however, are of the opinion that

SHAVUOT (8)

still conduct a nightly count of the days and weeks between Passover and Shavuot, but this is a rabbinical institution, established by the sages in order to commemorate the "real" count which was conducted when the divine presence was a manifest reality in our lives. In our present-day circumstances, until such time as the Temple will be rebuilt with the coming of Moshiach, Shavuot is the "festival of weeks" in a lesser form, as there is no full-fledged status to the *omer* count and its results.

If only a diminished version of the "festival of weeks" can be actualized in this spiritually infirm age, the "day of the first fruits" is completely absent from our observance of the festival today. The *bikurim*, too, require the presence of the nation of Israel on their land and of the divine home in Jerusalem. Nor is there, in this case, any "rabbinical" version of this *mitzvah*. Our present-day experience of Shavuot does not include any actual observance connected with this aspect of the festival.

A Task, a Struggle and a Dream

One thing has not changed in all of history's winding path through the light and shadow of spiritual time: At all times, and under all circumstances, we have our G-d-given guide to daily living. No

---

even today, it remains a biblical precept. A third opinion, expressed by 14th-century sage Rabbeinu Yerucham, is that it remains a biblical *mitzvah* to count the *days*, but the commandment to count the *weeks* applies only when the *omer* is offered, and is thus today only a rabbinical commandment. In terms of the internal "count" that the counting of the *omer* represents, the third mediating opinion implies that while we are able to perfect specific elements of our character—perhaps even all 49 of them—also in our present spiritual state, we lack the capacity to piece these together into "weeks" of fully perfected traits.

matter how trying the struggles in the interior of our souls, no matter how elusive the goal of a harmonious and righteous world, we can always do the right thing. We can always access the Torah that G-d has given us, learn what He desires us to do in any given circumstance, and make our behavior conform with the divine will.

In the quest for self-perfection, the picture is less definitive, our abilities more circumscribed. We can still count the *omer*; we can still climb the 49-step mountain to the seven-week wholeness of heart. But our present-day "festival of weeks" is but an echo of what is attainable in more spiritually luminous times.

As for the dream of a world united in the service of its G-d, of a physical reality which reveals rather than obscures the harmonious truth of its Creator, we have only the memory of a time when Shavuot was the "day of the first fruits." All we can do is recall the Israelite farmer's dedication of the choicest of his field to G-d, strive to do the same in our respective fields of endeavor, and pray for the day when we can again experience the divine in our lives and truly make our world a home for G-d.[14]

---

14 The difference between the three aspects of Shavuot is also reflected in the order in which they became part of the festival. Shavuot was "the time of the giving of the Torah" beginning with the revelation at Sinai less than three months after the Exodus; but it was not "the festival of weeks" (i.e., the 50th day of the *omer* count) until the following year. (As explained in *Shulchan Aruch HaRav, Orach Chaim* 494:1, the children of Israel left Egypt on a Thursday, and the Torah was given on a Shabbat; thus, that year, the 6th of *Sivan* occurred 51 days after the Exodus, not 50 as in our calendar today.) And it did not become the "day of the first fruits" until the Jewish people's conquest and cultivation of the Holy Land a generation later.

This reflects the sequence in which we actualize the spiritual aspect of the three names of Shavuot in our own lives. We begin with the correction of our behavior, then go on to the refinement of our character, and thence to the sanctification of our environment (as described in the opening paragraphs of this essay).

THE PHANTOM DAYS OF SHAVUOT

You have chosen us from all the nations; You loved us and desired us; You raised us above all the tongues, and You sanctified us with Your commandments.

Siddur, the festival prayers

O ur sages relate that when the people of Israel stood at Sinai and G-d spoke the Ten Commandments, so overwhelming was the experience that, "with each and every utterance, their souls flew from their bodies."[1]

We can perhaps envision "being blown" away by an utterance such as "I am G-d your G-d." But what of pedestrian commandments such as "Honor your father and your mother," and "Do not steal"? Other than the fact that they were spoken by G-d, there seems nothing divine or transcendent about these statements. Indeed, need G-d descend upon a mountaintop for us to appreciate the necessity of these laws?

CHOICE

The day we stood at Sinai (on the 6th day of *Sivan*, marked each year by the festival of Shavuot) is more than the day we received

---

[1]   Talmud, *Shabbat* 88b.

the Torah from G-d. This was also the occasion on which the Almighty chose us as His people.[2]

What was the significance of this choice? While we were still in Egypt, G-d already referred to us as "My firstborn child, Israel."[3] More than 400 years earlier, G-d had "found [Abraham's] heart faithful before [Him], and entered with him into the covenant" that deeded the Holy Land to Abraham's descendants and established them as the bearers of G-d's word to humanity.[4] What new degree of chosenness did we gain at Sinai?

"Choice" exists on many levels. A person might choose something because of its positive qualities—because it is the most tasty dish on the menu, the most attractive suit of clothes on the rack, or the most lucrative job offer. But these are "compelled" choices— the positive qualities of these things have dictated that they be chosen. A true choice is a *free* choice—a choice that is not influenced by anything, a choice that is a pure expression of the chooser's quintessential desire.

When G-d chose Abraham because "He found his heart faithful before Him," this was not a choice in the ultimate sense of the word. Here was a man who, alone in a pagan world, had discovered the One G-d, and had devoted his life to bringing a monotheistic faith and ethos to mankind. Whom else would G-d choose when selecting a man to father a nation that will serve as the harbingers of His truth to the world?

In Egypt, too, we were chosen for our qualities. True, two centuries of subjugation to the most debased society on earth had taken their toll—we had sunken into the "forty-nine gates of impurity,"

---

2 Exodus 19:5–6; see *Magen Avraham* commentary on *Shulchan Aruch, Orach Chaim* 60:2.

3 Exodus 4:22.

4 Nehemiah 9:8; cf. Genesis 18:18–19.

SHAVUOT (9)   203

assuming the pagan mores of our enslavers. But throughout it all, we had clung to our identity as Jews and to our faith in G-d.[5] Most importantly, we never forgot our promised destiny as G-d's people, and yearned for redemption with every fiber of our being. Indeed, those who did not wish to be redeemed were not included in the divine choice: The Midrash tells us that only one in five of the Jewish people were taken out of Egypt; the rest, who preferred slavery in a hedonist land to a covenant with G-d in the desert, perished in the three days of darkness prior to the Exodus.[6]

But at Sinai we were truly chosen, in a choice free of all reasons and conditions. At Sinai was established that "A Jew, although he has sinned, is a Jew,"[7] simply because he is the object of G-d's quintessential choice.

RESPONDING IN KIND

"As water mirrors the face it is shown, so does the heart of one man to another,"[8] and so does the soul of man respond to her Creator. When G-d chose us for our positive qualities, we responded in kind, choosing Him for *His* "positive qualities." We appreciated His greatness and majesty as Creator. We understood that a life devoted to serving G-d is a life most beneficial to ourselves, both materially and spiritually. We recognized that only our relationship with G-d would imbue our existence with purpose and significance.

---

5   *Midrash Rabbah, Vayikra* 32:5; *Yalkut Shimoni*, Hosea 519.
6   *Midrash Rabbah, Shemot* 14:3; see *The Festival of the Child* on pp. 42–46 above.
7   Talmud, *Sanhedrin* 44a.
8   Proverbs 27:19.

When G-d chose us at Sinai, we again responded in kind. When there He chose with a choice free of motive or reason, we, too, chose Him thus. After Sinai, our bond to Him no longer depends on His love for us, or on the benefits of being His people. Our commitment to His laws has nothing to do with the wisdom and righteousness they display. We choose Him as He chose us: because our very self—the quintessential "I" that transcends all reason and calculation—so desired.

So when we heard the divine voice at Sinai proclaim "Do not steal," we accepted it not merely as a sane and rational law of civilized life, but as the will of G-d. When we heard "Honor your father and your mother," we embraced it as far more than a dictum of decency and gratitude—we embraced it as the will of G-d. We committed ourselves to G-d's commands not for their beneficial qualities, but as a response to G-d's unequivocal, unreasoned choice of us as His people.

BEYOND RITUAL

This explains two curious things about the festival of Shavuot, our annual reexperience of our chosenness and our choice at Sinai.

All other festivals are equipped with a series of observances, or *mitzvot*, which evoke the special quality of the day. Matzah and the eradication of leaven on Passover, the *sukkah* and the "four kinds" on Sukkot, sounding of the *shofar* on Rosh Hashanah, kindling of lights on Chanukah, and so on. The single exception is Shavuot, which has no specific *mitzvah* to capture and actualize the nature of the festival.

For each of the festivals embodies a certain quality of our relationship with G-d: freedom on Passover, unity and joy on Sukkot, the divine sovereignty on Rosh Hashanah, light and spirituality on

SHAVUOT (9)   205

Chanukah, and so on. Shavuot, however, is our experience of the essence of this relationship, of our mutual choosing of each other with a choice that transcends reason and qualification. There is no ritual or symbol that can capture or express this essence. On Shavuot, our Jewishness is what we are, not what we do or feel.

BEYOND HOLINESS

This also explains the second curiosity of Shavuot—the fact that more than 85 percent of the festival is not a festival at all.

The Torah decrees three "pilgrimage" festivals: Passover, Shavuot, and Sukkot. On these three festivals, every Jew was obligated to journey to Jerusalem and offer *korbanot* at the Holy Temple. These offerings could be brought at any time during the seven days of the festival. But while Passover and Sukkot are both seven-day festivals, the Torah designates but a single day as the festival of Shavuot.[9] Nevertheless, Shavuot, too, has a seven-day period for its *korbanot*, which may be brought up to, and including, the 12th of *Sivan*.[10]

In other words, Passover and Sukkot each have seven days that are defined by the Torah as "callings of holiness"—days on which we "call forth" and actualize a divine quality and sanctity by marking the distinctiveness of the day and observing its *mitzvot*.[11] Shavuot, however, has only one such "holy" day; the six days that

---

9   Outside the Land of Israel, where we observe an "additional festival-day of the Diaspora," Passover is observed for eight days, Sukkot/Shemini Atzeret for nine days (instead of eight), and Shavuot for two days.

10 Talmud, *Chagigah* 17a.

11 Leviticus 23:4. See *Appointments in Time* in vol. 1, pp. 38–45 of this series.

follow are ordinary days, no holier than any other day in the mundane stretches of calendar between the festivals. And yet, these days are an integral part of Shavuot, as attested by the fact that the festival offerings may then be offered. (In fact, the Talmud cites the opinion of the sages of Shammai, who rule that these offerings cannot be brought on Shavuot itself, but *only* on the following day.[12])

The six "phantom days" of Shavuot express the quintessential nature of the festival. As the time when the "choice" element of our relationship with G-d is realized, Shavuot is a festival that goes beyond the qualified sanctity of all other festivals, beyond, even, sacredness itself.

---

12 Talmud, *Beitzah* 19a. *Shulchan Aruch HaRav, Orach Chaim* 494:19: "In this matter, the sages of Hillel also conducted themselves thus, and many of Israel did likewise."

CHAPTER TWENTY-THREE

The Three Weeks and Tishah B'Av

Exile and Redemption

Tammuz 17 to Av 9

For 830 years there stood an edifice upon a Jerusalem hilltop which served as the point of contact between heaven and earth. So central was this edifice to our relationship with G-d that nearly two-thirds of the *mitzvot* are contingent upon its existence. Its destruction is regarded as the greatest tragedy of our history, and its rebuilding will mark the ultimate redemption—the restoration of harmony within G-d's creation and between G-d and His creation.

A full three weeks of our year—the three weeks "between the strictures" of *Tammuz* 17 and *Av* 9—are designated as a time of mourning over the destruction of the Holy Temple and the resultant *galut*—physical exile and spiritual displacement—in which we still find ourselves.

On *Tammuz* 17 of the year 3829 from creation (69 CE), the walls of Jerusalem were breached by the armies of Rome; three weeks later, on the 9th of *Av*, the Holy Temple was set aflame. *Av* 9 is also the date of the First Temple's destruction by the Babylonians in 3339 (423 BCE), after the Temple service was disrupted on Tammuz 17. (The breaching of Jerusalem's walls at the time of the first destruction was on *Tammuz* 9.) These dates had already been the scene of tragic events in the very first generation of our nationhood. *Tammuz* 17 was the day Moses smashed the Tablets of the Covenant upon beholding Israel's worship of the Golden Calf;

Av 9 was the day that G-d decreed that the generation of the Exodus would die out in the desert, after they refused to proceed to the Holy Land in the wake of the demoralizing report by the spies sent by Moses to scout the Land. In these events lay the seeds of a breakdown in the relationship between G-d and Israel — a breakdown which reached its nadir in the destruction of the Temple.

Tammuz 17 is a fast day, on which we refrain from eating and drinking from dawn to nightfall. *Av* 9 (Tishah B'Av) is a more stringent fast: It commences at sunset of the previous evening, and additional pleasures (washing, anointing, wearing leather shoes, and marital relations) are also proscribed. On Tishah B'Av we gather in the synagogue to read the book of Lamentations composed by Jeremiah, and *kinot* (elegies) on the Destruction and exile.

Beginning on the Shabbat before *Tammuz* 17, we read the "three of rebuke" — three weekly readings from the Prophets which prophesy the Destruction, describe the sins which caused it, and admonish us to repent our ways. During the "three weeks", no weddings or other joyous events are held; like mourners, we do not cut our hair or purchase new clothes. Additional mourning practices are assumed during the "Nine Days" beginning on *Av* 1, such as refraining from eating meat, drinking wine, and enjoying music.

But there is more to the "three weeks" than fasting and lamentation. The prophet describes the fasts as "days of goodwill before G-d"—days of opportunity to exploit the failings of the past as the impetus for a renewed and even deeper bond with G-d. A sense of purification accompanies the fasting, a promise of redemption pervades the mourning, and a current of joy underlies the sadness. The Ninth of Av, say our sages, is not only the day of the Temple's destruction—it is also the birthday of Moshiach. The "three of rebuke" are thus followed by "seven of consolation"—seven weekly readings describing the future redemption and the rebuilding of the marriage of G-d and Israel.

Three short introductory essays open our chapter. *The Pinch* explains the prophet's reference to the "three weeks" as "between the strictures." *Good Grief* defines the difference between destructive and constructive sadness. *Postponed* uncovers the essence of the fast day as a "day of goodwill" and a future festival.

Difficult Days explores the significance of *Tammuz* 17 in light of three historical events—the making of the Golden Calf, the Torah's translation into Greek, and a momentary triumph of the sages of Shammai over their colleagues of the Hillelian school—all three of which introduced a dangerous, yet potentially fruitful, "otherness" into Jewish life.

210

The next four essays focus on the Holy Temple and its role as the "marital home" of our relationship with G-d. *Shabbat of Vision* speaks of an annual window of opportunity on the Shabbat before Tishah B'Av. *The Subterranean Temple* describes a 3000-year journey through the "hidden, convoluted tunnels" built into the Temple by King Solomon. *The Legalities of Destruction* questions the legality of G-d's actions on *Av 9* even as it shows them to have been the salvation of Israel. *The Intimate Estrangement* defines the Destruction as the most intimate moment in the marriage of G-d and Israel, and explores the mystical significance of the "three of rebuke" and the "seven of consolation."

The deeper significance and purpose of *galut* is the subject of the last two essays of our chapter. *Regret* describes it as an existence whose essential quality is that it does not, in truth, exist. *Cholent* expresses our profound yearning to escape *galut* even as we acknowledge it as the most fruitful epoch of our history.

See also the essays *The Hard Life* in vol. 1 of this series, pp. 225–233; and *Spirit and Substance* in vol. 2, pp. 207–213.

THE
PINCH

From the straits I call G-d; He answers me
with the expanse of the Divine.　　Psalms 118:5[1]

"Between the strictures" is the prophet Jeremiah's description of the period between the 17th of *Tammuz*, the day the walls of Jerusalem were breached, and the 9th of *Av*, when the Holy Temple was destroyed and the exile of Israel commenced.[2] To date, these two days are observed as days of fasting, and the three-week "strait" between them as a period of mourning and repentance.

The narrow strait, however, is not a roadblock; on the contrary, it is a mechanism for increased productivity. Hydraulic power plants, rockets, and garden hoses employ it to squeeze a greater degree of power and velocity from the element they constrain. The *shofar*, sounded to awaken man to repentance, is also such a device, its narrow mouth-end pinching the stream of air expelled from the blower's lungs into the piercing note that emerges from its wide, upward-sweeping end.

The same is true of the strictures of *Tammuz* 17 and *Av* 9 and the two thousand years of physical exile and spiritual darkness they mourn. Twenty centuries of suppression have wrenched the Jewish soul through the funnel of *galut*, revealing its deepest convictions and provoking its highest potentials. From these terrible

---

[1] Recited before the sounding of the *shofar* on Rosh Hashanah.
[2] Lamentations 1:3; see *Midrash Rabbah* on verse.

THE THREE WEEKS AND TISHAH B'AV (1) 213

straits we have never ceased to seek G-d, and it is this seeking that will yield the "divine expanse" of ultimate redemption and the perfect world of the messianic age.

"On that day," proclaims the prophet, "the great *shofar* will be sounded. And they will come, those lost in the land of Assyria and those forsaken in the land of Egypt,[3] and bow before G-d on the holy mountain, Jerusalem."[4] On that day, the goodness and perfection of G-d's creation will burst through the straits of concealment and blossom into unconstrained realization.

---

3   The Hebrew *eretz mitzrayin* (land of Egypt) literally translates as "the land of the strictures."

4   Isaiah 27:13.

GOOD GRIEF

There nothing as whole as a broken heart.

Chassidic saying

Depression is not a sin; but the damage that depression does, no sin can do.

Chassidic saying

*I*s sad bad? Chassidic teaching differentiates between two types of sorrow: *merirut*, a constructive grief, and *atzvut*, a destructive grief.

Merirut is the distress of one who not only recognizes his failings but also cares about them. One who agonizes over the wrongs he has committed, over his missed opportunities, over his unrealized potential; one who refuses to become indifferent to what is deficient in himself and his world. *Atzvut* is the distress of one who has despaired of himself and his fellow man, whose melancholy has drained him of hope and initiative. *Merirut* is a springboard for self-improvement; *atzvut* is a bottomless pit.

How does one distinguish between the two? The first is active, the second, passive. The first one weeps, the second's eyes are dry and blank. The first one's mind and heart are in turmoil, the second's are still with apathy and heavy as lead. And what happens when it passes, when they emerge from their respective bouts of grief? The first one springs to action: resolving, planning, taking his first faltering steps to undo the causes of his sorrow. The second one goes to sleep.

THE THREE WEEKS AND TISHAH B'AV (3)   215

POSTPONED

Can this be called a fast day, a day of good-
will before G-d?   Isaiah 58:5

The fast of the fourth month, the fast of the
fifth, the fast of the seventh, and the fast of
the tenth[1] shall be transformed into gladness,
joy, and festival days for the House of Judah.
       Zechariah 8:19

"Since it has been postponed, let it be postponed altogether."[2] Such was the opinion of Rabbi Judah HaNassi regarding a time when the fast day of Tishah B'Av (the 9th of *Av*) fell on Shabbat.

There are four fast days in the Jewish calendar that were instituted by the prophets and sages to commemorate the destruction of the two Holy Temples in Jerusalem:

1) The 10th of *Tevet*, on which Nebuchadnezzar's armies laid siege to Jerusalem, in the time of the first Holy Temple.

2) The 17th of *Tammuz*, the day on which the Temple service was disrupted in the time of the first Temple, and on which the walls of Jerusalem were breached by the Romans in the time of the second Temple.[3]

3) The 9th of *Av*, on which both Temples were destroyed—the

---

1   I.e., the fasts of *Tammuz* 17, *Av* 9, *Tishrei* 3 and *Tevet* 10, occurring in the 4th, 5th, 7th and 10th months (counting from *Nissan*—see p. 5 above).

2   Talmud, *Megillah* 5b.

3   The 17th of *Tammuz* is also the date of other tragic events in our

first Temple by the Babylonians in the year 3338 from creation (423 BCE) and the second Temple by the Romans in 3829 (69 CE).[4]

4) The 3rd of *Tishrei*, which commemorates the assassination of Gedaliah ben Achikam, the governor of Judea. The murder of Gedaliah spelled the end of the small Jewish community that remained in the Holy Land after the destruction of the first Temple.

On these days we deprive our bodies of food and drink, stirring ourselves to repent the sins and failings which twice caused the destruction of G-d's home and our banishment into *galut* (exile). The strictest of these fast days is the 9th of *Av*, on which the fast begins at sunset of the previous evening (whereas the other three fasts begin at dawn of that day), and on which additional physical pleasures are also forbidden.[5]

On Shabbat, however, it is a *mitzvah* to pleasure ourselves with food and drink—a *mitzvah* which supersedes the injunction to fast. So when a fast day falls on Shabbat, the fast is postponed to the following day, while on Shabbat itself—even if it is the 9th of *Av*—"One should eat meat and drink wine... and set his table even like the feast of Solomon during his kingship."[6]

---

history, including Moses' breaking of the Tablets of the Covenant as a result of Israel's worship of the Golden Calf (Talmud, *Taanit* 26a-b; see following essay, *Difficult Days*, pp. 220–233; and *The 120-Day Version of the Human Story*, in vol. 2 of this series, pp. 37–43).

4 The 9th of *Av* is also the date of numerous other tragic events in Jewish history, beginning with the decree that the generation that left Egypt would die in the desert, as a result of the sin of the Spies (Talmud, *Taanit* 26b).

5 Washing, anointing, wearing (leather) shoes, and marital relations.

6 *Shulchan Aruch, Orach Chaim* 552:10. This applies only to the rabbinical fast days, not to the biblically instituted fast day of Yom Kippur. There is also an opinion that if *Tevet* 10 were to fall on Shabbat, we would nevertheless fast; but this is not possible in the current configuration of our calendar.

THE THREE WEEKS AND TISHAH B'AV (3)   217

In this context, the Talmud cites Rabbi Judah HaNassi's opinion
that "since it has been postponed, let it be postponed altogether."
According to Rabbi Judah, when the 9th of *Av* falls on Shabbat,
the fast ought to be canceled completely.

CORE AND HUSK

The prophet Isaiah refers to the fast day as "a day of goodwill before G-d."[7] In other words, the negative aspects of the fast day—
the mourning, the recollection of our failings, the deprivation of
the body—are not what define its essence. At its core, the fast day
is a wholly positive phenomenon: a day of opportunity for us to
bring ourselves closer to our Creator.[8]

Why, then, the need to deny ourselves food and drink on such
a day? Only because the material trappings of life tend to erect
barriers between ourselves and G-d. We must therefore lessen our
involvement with the material—to the extent of forswearing some
of our body's most basic needs—thereby freeing our soul to take
advantage of the "day of goodwill before G-d" without hindrance
and obstruction from our physical selves.

This explains why in the era of Moshiach the fast days will
be "transformed into days of gladness and joy... festival days."[9] In
the perfect world of Moshiach, the physical creation will no longer obscure the face of its Creator; on the contrary, the physical
will equal, and even surpass, the spiritual as an expression of the
all-pervasiveness of the divine truth.[10] So there will be no need to

---

7   Isaiah 58:5.
8   See the two following essays in this chapter, *The Legalities of Destruc-
    tion*, pp. 244–252, and *The Intimate Estrangement*, pp. 253–261.
9   Zechariah 8:19; *Mishneh Torah, Laws of Fasts* 5:19.
10 See *Reverse Biology* in vol. 2 of this series, pp. 72–75.

suppress the physical self in order to actualize the positive essence of the fast days. Rather, these will be festivals, on which the body's joy and pleasure will contribute to the deepening of the bond between us and G-d.

A Taste of Future

Shabbat is a weekly foretaste of "the day that is wholly Shabbat and tranquility, for life everlasting."[11] Thus, when a fast day falls on Shabbat, there occurs a process similar to that which will transpire in the time of Moshiach, when the fast days will be stripped of their negative husk and their wholly positive core will be exposed.

In other words, a fast day occurring on Shabbat is not a clash between two opposing elements in which the stronger element (Shabbat) overpowers the weaker (the fast day) and pushes it off to another time. Rather, the essence of Shabbat and the essence of the fast day are fully compatible; Shabbat only repels certain external aspects of the fast day. So it's not that the fast day is not being observed on Shabbat; it is being observed in a different manner —a manner that is actually *more* consistent with its true function. The fast day is being observed in the manner in which it will be observed in the perfect world of Moshiach.

This explains Rabbi Judah's view that when a fast day falls on Shabbat, the fasting should be "postponed altogether." For on such a year, the futuristic essence of Shabbat has enabled us to actualize the function of the fast day as a "day of goodwill before G-d" without the negative externalities it requires when it occurs on an ordinary weekday. There is no further need, maintains Rabbi Judah, for a day of fasting.

---

11   Talmud, *Tamid* 33b; Shabbat addendum to *Grace after Meals*.

THE THREE WEEKS AND TISHAH B'AV (3)   219

ON THE THRESHOLD

In actual practice, we do not follow Rabbi Judah's view. When a fast day falls on Shabbat, we observe the day in its joyous, messianic form on that day; but on the next day, we observe it again, this time with the negative trappings that accompany a fast day in our still unperfected world.

For Shabbat is only a "taste" of a future perfection. We still inhabit a world in which our material involvements tend to obscure, rather than enhance, our spiritual sensitivities; a world in which the needs of physical life tend to interfere with, rather than facilitate, our relationship with G-d. Even on Shabbat, we experience only a semblance of the absolute harmony between Creator and creation that Moshiach will bring. So after sampling a messianic Tishah B'Av on Shabbat, we must observe another, "ordinary" Tishah B'Av on Sunday in order to fully exploit the day of goodwill granted us by G-d.

Nevertheless, Shabbat leaves its mark: The laws of a "postponed" Sunday fast are more lenient than a non-postponed fast day.[12] And ever present in our awareness is the vision of Rabbi Judah HaNassi—a vision even more pertinent today as we stand on the threshold of the era of Moshiach and the elimination of all negative elements that still cling to the periphery of our lives.

---

12   See *Shulchan Aruch* and commentaries, *Orach Chaim* 559:9.

DIFFICULT DAYS

[Aaron] took [the gold] from them and formed it in a mold, casting it into a calf... And Aaron announced: "Tomorrow is a festival unto G-d."

Exodus 32:4–5

Seventy sages translated the Torah into Greek for King Ptolemy. That day was as difficult for the people of Israel as the day on which the [Golden] Calf was made; for the Torah could not be fully translated.

Talmud, Sefer Torah 1:8

A count was conducted, and it was found that the sages of Shammai were more numerous than the sages of Hillel. Eighteen ordinances were enacted on that day... and that day was as difficult for the people of Israel as the day on which the [Golden] Calf was made.

Ibid., Shabbat 13b; 17a

𝔗he translation of the Torah into a foreign language is not, in itself, undesirable. A thousand years before King Ptolemy ordered the translation of the Torah into Greek, Moses had, by divine command, translated the Torah into the seventy languages of the world.[1] Nor can it be said that the Greek language is partic-

---

[1]   Deuteronomy 1:5 (according to *Midrash Tanchuma* and Rashi on

THE THREE WEEKS AND TISHAH B'AV (4)   221

ularly problematic for the Torah's translation, as Greek is one of
the seventy basic languages[2] into which the Torah was translated
by Moses. In fact, the Talmud states that, of all languages, Greek is
the *most* suited for the translation of Torah.[3]

So what is it about the translation ordered by Ptolemy that was
so "difficult for the people of Israel"? And why does the Talmud
compare it to one of the greatest tragedies of Jewish history—"the
day on which the Golden Calf was made"?

The making of the Golden Calf is also cited as a model for another "difficult day" in Jewish history: the day on which the disciples of Shammai outnumbered the disciples of Hillel. The Torah
decrees that, in cases of disagreement between the sages on matters of Torah law, one should "follow the majority."[4] The disciples
of Hillel were more numerous than the disciples of Shammai, so
that the final ruling on the disputations between these two schools
of Torah scholarship almost always follows the more lenient approach of Hillel. On one occasion, however, the disciples of Shammai constituted the majority of sages in the study hall, and eighteen laws were enacted following their stricter interpretation of
Torah law. "That day," says the Talmud, "was as difficult for the
people of Israel as the day on which the Golden Calf was made."

Again, the comparison with the Golden Calf seems extreme, if
not inappropriate. The enactment of these laws might have "burdened" us with additional and stricter prohibitions, but even the
365 basic prohibitions of the Torah can be said to be "difficult" until
one appreciates their value as divine guidelines for a constructive

---

   verse); Ibid., 27:8 (according to *Talmud*, Sotah 32a). The seventy languages are enumerated in the 10th chapter of Genesis.
2 See Genesis 10:2.
3 Jerusalem Talmud, *Megillah* 1:9.
4 Exodus 23:2.

and meaningful life.[5] The eighteen Shammaian laws were enacted in full accordance with the authority vested by the Torah in the sages. From the moment they were endorsed by a majority of the sages, they became part of Torah law, as binding and crucial to the Jew as the most basic of the Torah's precepts. So why does the Talmud consider the event to be "as difficult for the people of Israel as the day on which the Golden Calf was made"?

THE MAKING OF THE CALF

The Golden Calf was made by Moses' brother, Aaron, on the 16th day of the month of *Tammuz*, in the year 2448 from creation (1313 BCE).

Forty days earlier, Moses had ascended Mount Sinai to receive the Torah from G-d. Due to a miscalculation, the children of Israel expected him to return on the morning of the 16th of *Tammuz* (after 40 days on the mountain, counting the day of the ascent), instead of the morning of the 17th (after 40 days, *not* counting the day of the ascent). When Moses failed to appear when expected, "They massed upon Aaron, and said to him: Arise! Make us a god that shall walk before us. For the man Moses, who brought us up out of the land of Egypt—we do not know what has become of him."[6]

When Aaron saw that the people could not be dissuaded from their plan, he took charge of the operation himself in the hope of postponing the actual worship of the idol. He collected their gold and smelted it into the form of a calf. He then announced: "Tomorrow is a festival unto G-d!"[7] "Tomorrow," of course, was the 17th of *Tammuz*, the date of Moses' return from Mount Sinai.

---

5   See *Law*, pp. 170 above.

6   Exodus 32:1.

7   Ibid. v. 5; see Rashi there.

THE THREE WEEKS AND TISHAH B'AV (4)   223

Were it not for the people's all-consuming enthusiasm for their new idol, which roused them from their beds at the crack of dawn the next morning, the 17th of *Tammuz* would indeed have been "a festival unto G-d" in the sense that Aaron had intended—the day on which Moses prevented Israel's error and rededicated them to the true service of G-d. But when Moses descended from the mountain, the deed was already done. The people of Israel had violated their newly-made covenant with G-d, transgressing the commandment, "You shall have no other gods before Me."[8]

It is significant that the Talmud compares the day of the Torah's translation into Greek, and the day of Shammai's triumph over Hillel, to "the day on which the Calf was *made*," as opposed to the day on which it was actually worshipped. The day on which the Golden Calf was worshipped was the most tragic day in Jewish history—the day that spawned all subsequent regressions and calamities experienced by our people.[9] But on *Tammuz* 16, the day on which the Golden Calf was *made*, this was still a calamity in potential, with an equal potential for its prevention, and even its transformation into a positive occurrence.

The Quest for Divinity

What led the people of Israel to worship an icon of gold? If they were seeking a replacement for Moses, why did they not appoint another leader in his place? What is the connection between the perceived "disappearance" of Moses and their desire for a material representation of divinity?

---

8   Exodus 20:3—the second of the two commandments which the people of Israel heard directly from G-d at Sinai.

9   In the words of the Talmud (*Sanhedrin* 102a, based on Exodus 32:34), "There is no calamity that comes upon the world that does not contain a fraction of the punishment of the original calf."

Chassidic teaching explains that Moses was more than a leader to the people of Israel; he was a living model of the divine immanence. As the Torah attests, Moses was an *ish elokim* ("man of G-d")[10]—a human being who so completely conformed to the divine will, who so completely negated his self to G-d, that his mind, his personality, his very being, were pure, unadulterated expressions of the divine truth. In Moses, the people of Israel perceived how "there is none else besides Him"[11]—how a creature as individualistic and self-centered as man can manifest the truth that, in essence, he is but a ray of the divine light.

With Moses' "disappearance," the people of Israel felt the need for a visual, tangible exemplar of all-pervasiveness of G-d. But this time they wanted a physical object as their prototype, in the belief that this would constitute an even greater testimony to the truth that "there is none else besides Him." If we take an icon of gold, they reasoned, the epitome of materiality, and hallow it as a representation of the divine immanence, this will truly demonstrate how even the most mundane being is not separate from the divine reality.

Indeed, several months later, the people of Israel were instructed to do just that: to construct a "sanctuary" for G-d out of fifteen physical materials, the most dominant of which was gold. At the heart of the Sanctuary was to stand the gold-plated ark, topped by two *keruvim* (cherubs) hammered out of a block of solid gold. The golden *keruvim* symbolized the relationship between G-d and Israel and marked the seat of G-d's manifest presence within the physical universe. Furthermore, Israel's construction of this Sanctuary was to serve as their atonement for the sin of the Golden Calf!

---

10 Deuteronomy 33:1, as per *Midrash Rabbah*, Devarim 11:4.

11 Deuteronomy 4:35.

THE THREE WEEKS AND TISHAH B'AV (4)   225

Why was the Golden Calf the gravest of sins and the most per-
fidious of betrayals, while the golden *keruvim* were the epitome
of holiness? Often, an extremely fine line distinguishes between
the purest truth and the most distortive falsehood. Though ostensibly similar, the *keruvim* were the very antithesis of the Golden
Calf. When *G-d* commands to construct a material receptacle for
His presence, it becomes a holy, G-dly object; when *man* chooses
a material representation of the divine presence, this is idolatry—
a detraction from, rather than an affirmation of, the truth that
"there is none else besides Him." For it is not the sanctified object that expresses the all-pervasiveness of G-d, but the fact that it
is serving as an instrument of man's fulfillment of the divine will.
Where there is a divine commandment to make a certain physical
object or do a certain physical deed, the fulfillment of this commandment attests that the divine will has permeated the whole of
creation, down to and including the object or deed that realizes it.
Where there is no such commandment, only the human choice of
a certain object or ritual to embody man's relationship with G-d,
this is idolatry—the attribution of divine qualities to something
other than G-d Himself.[12]

THE THIRTEEN IMPRECISIONS

Therein lies the parallel between the making of the Golden Calf
and the translation of the Torah into Greek.

---

12 Indeed, the essence of idolatry is not the denial of G-d's existence and
    supreme power, but the veneration of "other gods before Me"—the at-
    tribution of divine significance to anything other than G-d. If man, by
    his own initiative, chooses a certain object or force as a representation
    of the divine or as a vehicle of relationship with G-d, this is idolatry
    (see *Mishneh Torah, Laws Regarding Idol Worship* 1:1-2).

When G-d commanded Moses to translate the Torah into the languages of the world, this achieved the introduction of the word of G-d into all strata of human existence. Words and idioms, distilled from the most foreign of cultures and lifestyles, became a "sanctuary" housing the divine wisdom. This was a divine endeavor, achieved via Moses—the same medium through which G-d first "translated" His supra-literary truth into the words of the Holy Tongue.

But when the seventy sages translated the Torah at Ptolemy's behest, this was a human endeavor, initiated by a mortal ruler. As such, it boded the possibility of becoming a Golden Calf—a humanly-defined vessel for the divine truth. There existed the danger that instead of faithfully conforming to their sacred content, the foreign garments in which the Torah was being dressed would allow the distortion of its original sense.

Therefore, the day that the Torah was translated into Greek was "as difficult as the day on which the Golden Calf was made." The Golden Calf was not an idol until it was worshipped the following morning; but the potential for idolatry was there—the potential for the pagan feast that Moses found upon his descent from the mountain as opposed to the "festival for G-d" that Aaron had hoped for. By the same token, the Torah's translation into Greek constituted the introduction of a dangerous otherness to Torah, with the potential for subsequent distortion of the divine truth.

This time, however, the negative possibilities of the endeavor were averted, or at least greatly minimized. The Talmud relates that Ptolemy isolated the seventy sages in seventy different houses to prevent their collaboration on an imprecise translation: The Hellenic king wanted a literal rendering of the Torah, so that he and his scholars would be free to interpret it according to their own understanding and not be dictated by the Mosaic tradition

THE THREE WEEKS AND TISHAH B'AV (4) 227

of the Jews. Nevertheless, the seventy translators departed from the literal meaning of the Torah's words in thirteen places where such a translation would be open to misinterpretation, each independently recognizing the problematic places and substituting an identical word or phrase which, while not a precise translation from the Hebrew into the Greek, was a faithful rendition of the Torah's intent.

This is the deeper meaning of the Talmud's words that the "difficulty" lay in that "the Torah could not be fully translated." Had the seventy sages fully — that is, precisely and exactly — translated the Torah into Greek, it would have been exposed to misinterpretation and distortion. It was only because they succeeded in presenting Ptolemy with a less than literal translation that this tragedy was averted. Indeed, their translation yielded the positive result of bringing G-d's word to the Greek world, and showing the way for the subsequent translators of Torah who would spread the light of Torah to all peoples and cultures of the earth.[13]

THE WORLD ACCORDING TO HILLEL

The parallel between the Golden Calf and the Torah's translation into Greek is an extremely subtle one. The first was outright

---

13 According to tractate *Sofrim* 1:7–8, there were two attempts at the translation of Torah, by two King Ptolemys (there were several rulers of the Greek-Egyptian empire who went by that name): the first by five sages, which is compared to "the day of the making of the Golden Calf," and the second by 72 sages, who made the thirteen "changes" in the translation, as described above (see *Kissei Rachamim* and Yaavetz's glosses on *Sofrim*, ad loc.; *Meor Einayim, Imrei Binah*, ch. 8). According to this version of events surrounding the Torah's translation into Greek, the first translation was indeed vulnerable to distortion, and this state of affairs was rectified by the second, amended translation.

idolatry, the gravest of sins proscribed by the Torah; the second was a permissible, and, in many ways, beneficial, endeavor to expand the influence of the Torah in the world. Nevertheless, the potential danger of the translation is, in essence, the very same danger posed by idolatry: the introduction of a foreign element into our relationship with G-d, an "otherness" that belies the divine exclusivity expressed by the axiom of our faith, "there is none other besides Him."

Even more subtle is the parallel between the making of the Golden Calf and the triumph of Shammai over Hillel in eighteen disputations of Torah law. For here we speak of a legitimate development of Torah law, sanctioned and mandated by G-d's instructions as to how His will should be applied to our lives. Shammai's disciples' understanding of the Torah, even when rejected by the final ruling, is a valid expression of the divine will; when endorsed by the majority of Torah sages, it becomes the *only* valid way in which to implement the divine will in practice. Nevertheless, the triumph of the Shammaian approach to Torah carries the potential for the very same "otherness"—albeit in the subtlest of forms—represented by the Golden Calf.

As mentioned above, the school of Hillel tended to a more lenient application of Torah law, while the expositions of the school of Shammai were characterized by strictness and severity. This was not a matter of a benevolent group of sages on the one hand and a group of harsh, uncompromising jurists on the other, but the product of two different perspectives on the very function of Torah.

Living as a Jew means daily grappling with a basic dissonance in our perception of reality. On the one hand, we affirm that "there is none else besides Him." On the other hand, we are daily

THE THREE WEEKS AND TISHAH B'AV (4)   229

confronted with a world that blatantly exhibits its else-ness and
besides-ness.

To address this dissonance, G-d gave us the Torah, which is a
set of guidelines on how to impose the divine will upon the world.
By implementing Torah in our lives, we create a world that is not
separate from G-d but subservient to Him; a world that does not
contradict the exclusivity of the divine reality, but is the instrument of its realization.

The 613 *mitzvot* (divine commandments) of the Torah consist
of 365 prohibitions (e.g., not to work on Shabbat, not to eat meat
with milk) and 248 positive commandments (to give charity, to
put on *tefilin*). In other words, the Torah has a two-pronged approach to resolving the seeming contradiction between the divine
unity and the world's perceived separateness: a) abnegation; b)
cultivation.

In the "abnegation" mode, the negation of a part of the physical
universe vanquishes its otherness. For example: the human appe-
tite might desire a nonkosher food; the Torah commands not to
eat it; by suppressing our craving for the sake of our commitment
to the divine will, we demonstrate that our physical desire, and the
desired physical object, are devoid of value and significance. They
might exist, but they are "nothing" to us. The only "something" is
G-d, for He is the only being of any significance.

In the "cultivation" mode of Torah, a part of the world is developed into an instrument of the divine. A piece of leather exists,
bearing no manifest relationship with G-d; the piece of leather is
fashioned into a pair of *tefilin*, an object whose obvious function is
to fulfill a divine command. A physical object has transcended its
otherness to exhibit its subservience to G-d. It has not been made
into nothing; indeed, its "somethingness" has been cultivated and
developed. But its somethingness is no longer separate from (and

thus opposed to) the divine being, but is now its extension and expression.

Which of these two modes of Torah's interaction with the world is more primary to its overall function? This is the underlying difference between the two most basic schools of Torah law, the House of Shammai and the House of Hillel. From the Shammaian perspective, the Torah is basically "negative," its primary function being to expose the nothingness of the physical reality. True, the Torah also includes cultivative elements, but these, too, are a function of its abnegative effect on the world. When the Torah commands to develop a piece of leather into a pair of *tefilin*, this is just another way of abnegating the physical reality—by demonstrating how even the spiritually "useful" elements of the physical world possess no significance of their own, save for their capacity to serve G-d.

Thus, when Torah allows for both a prohibitive and a permissive interpretation of a certain law, the school of Shammai naturally embraces the option that is consistent with its understanding of Torah's overall function: to proscribe and prohibit, thus negating the "somethingness" of the physical reality.

Hillel and his disciples had a different perspective on Torah. In their view, the Torah comes not to negate the physical reality, but to reveal how its "somethingness" is of a piece with the "somethingness" of G-d. So it is the Torah's cultivating *mitzvot* that express its ultimate function. The Torah, of course, also includes many prohibitions, but these are only the necessary ground rules that allow for the proper cultivation of the world as a vehicle of G-dliness. For the physical world includes certain elements whose divine potential is beyond our capacity to reveal; unless these are "abnegated," they will interfere with our cultivation of those elements which we *are* equipped to deal with. But when faced with two possible interpretation of a law in Torah, the Hillelian school will opt for the permissive rather than the prohibitive, for it is inclined to include as much of the world as possible in the Torah's "cultivative" domain.

Both the Shammaian and Hillelian approach are legitimate perceptions of Torah; both affirm the truth that "there is none else besides Him." But in a very subtle way, the approach of Shammai recognizes an "otherness" to the world that is completely absent from the Hillelian view. In effect, the perspective of Shammai says: The world exists; therefore it must be abnegated. The world challenges the singularity of G-d; therefore it must be disavowed.

From the perspective of Hillel, however, the "existence" of the world is not an adversary to be vanquished, but an enigma to be revealed; not a rebellion against the divine sovereignty to be put down, but a potential to be realized. The world according to Hillel possesses no "otherness" in the first place. What we perceive as its independence and separateness of being is but the expression of the divine being that pervades it.

A Mitigating Victory

As long as the Shammaian approach to Torah was subservient to the Hillelian, it posed no threat to the integrity of Israel's relationship with G-d. On the contrary, it complemented it as a parallel vision of the divine blueprint for life. For our service of G-d includes both the cultivation of our self and world as a receptacle for G-dliness, as well as the abnegation of self and world before the all-transcending truth of G-d. There are times in a person's life that the first element must take precedence, and times when the second element should be accentuated; times when he must view the world as a Hillelian sage, and times when he must look at it with a Shammaian eye.

But the day that the sages of Shammai outnumbered the sages of Hillel and their vision of Torah became the basis of its actual practice, was "as difficult for the people of Israel as the day on which the Golden Calf was made." When the abnegating approach of Shammai supplanted the cultivating approach of Hillel in the actual, day-to-day practice of Torah, the danger existed that we might eventually be led to view our world as something "other" than G-d, something alien to the truth of its Creator. In this sense, it was a day rife with a potential threat akin to that posed by the making of the Golden Calf.

But unlike the day on which the Golden Calf was made, which led to the day on which it was actually worshipped, the danger implicit in the brief reign of Shammai had no adverse results. The numerical superiority of the school of Shammai was short-lived; on the following day, the majority reverted to Hillel and his disciples. With the exception of the eighteen laws voted on that day, the actual practice of Torah law follows the Hillelian approach.

In fact, the momentary victory of Shammai's disciples had a mitigating effect on their severity. For even as their view triumphed over that of the school of Hillel, it was influenced by the very process of debate and defense against the other opinion. In a number of cases, we actually find the disciples of Shammai propagating a more lenient view than Hillel's disciples.[14] This was the result of the day on which eighteen laws were decided according to the opinion of Shammai, but not without being influenced by the defeated opinion of Hillel.

Because of this day, even when we must, by necessity, adapt a "Shammaian" approach, it is mitigated by the vision of Hillel. Even

---

14 Cf. Talmud, *Eiduyot* chapter 4

THE THREE WEEKS AND TISHAH B'AV (4)   233

when the circumstances necessitate the abnegation of the materiality of our existence, this is accompanied by the recognition that, ultimately, there are no alien or "other" elements in G-d's world, where everything is one with its Creator and Source.

Tomorrow

Our sages tell us that the words of a *tzaddik* (perfectly righteous person) are never without result. Even if they are not realized immediately, they ultimately achieve fulfillment.

The same applies, says the great kabbalist Rabbi Isaac Luria, to Aaron's proclamation, "Tomorrow is a festival unto G-d!" On that first "tomorrow," Aaron's hope was not realized. The 17th of *Tammuz* became the day on which the Golden Calf was worshipped, the Tablets of the Covenant constituting the "marriage contract" between G-d and Israel were broken, and the very day fated to become the scene of many tragedies in Jewish history—including the breaching of Jerusalem's walls, which led to the destruction of the Holy Temple three weeks later on the 9th of *Av*, and to the exile of Israel from their land.

But as the prophet promises,[15] G-d will transform the 17th of *Tammuz* into a festival and a day of joy, when the tribulations and sufferings of *galut* will yield the divine harmony and perfection of the messianic era. Then, the positive resolution of the making of the Golden Calf anticipated by Aaron will be realized, as the error and regression of Israel's sin will be transformed into a heightened appreciation of the all-pervading reality of G-d.

---

15   Zechariah 8:19.

SHABBAT OF VISION

And I, Daniel, alone saw the vision, and the people with me did not see it; but a great terror befell them, and they fled into hiding.

Daniel 10:7

If they did not see the vision, why were they terrified? Because although they themselves did not see, their souls saw.

Talmud, Megillah 3a

On the ninth day of the month of *Av* ("Tishah B'Av") we fast and mourn the destruction of the Holy Temple in Jerusalem. Both the first Temple (833–423 BCE) and the second Temple (353 BCE–69 CE) were destroyed on this date. The Shabbat preceding the fast day is called the "Shabbat of Vision," for on this Shabbat we read a chapter from the Prophets entitled "The Vision of Isaiah."[1]

But there is also a deeper significance to the name "Shabbat of vision," expressed by chassidic master Rabbi Levi Yitzchak of Berdichev with the following metaphor:

A father once prepared a beautiful suit of clothes for his son. But the child neglected his father's gift and soon the

---

[1] Isaiah 1:1–27. This reading is the third of a series of readings, called the "three of rebuke," that are read on the three *Shabbatot* preceding the 9th of *Av*.

suit was in tatters. The father gave the child a second suit of clothes, but this one, too, was ruined by the child's carelessness. So the father made a third suit. This time, however, he withheld it from his child.

Every once in a while, in special and opportune times, the father shows the suit to the child, explaining that when the child learns to appreciate and properly care for the suit, it will be given to him. This induces the child to improve his behavior, until it gradually becomes second nature to him, and he will be worthy of his father's gift.

On the "Shabbat of Vision," says Rabbi Levi Yitzchak, each and every one of us is granted a vision of the third and final Temple—a vision that, to paraphrase the Talmud, "though we do not see ourselves, our souls see." This vision evokes a profound response in us, even if we are not consciously aware of the cause of our sudden inspiration.

The Divine Dwelling

The Holy Temple in Jerusalem was the seat of G-d's manifest presence in the physical world.

A basic tenet of our faith is that "The entire earth is filled with His presence" and "There is no place void of Him."[2] But G-d's presence and His involvement in His creation are masked by the seemingly independent and arbitrary workings of nature and history. The Holy Temple was a breach in this mask, a window through which G-d radiated His light into the world. Here G-d's involvement in our world was openly displayed by an edifice in

---

2   Isaiah 6:3; *Tikkunei Zohar, Tikkun* 57.

which miracles were a "natural" part of its daily operation,[3] and whose very space expressed the infinity and all-pervasiveness of the Creator.[4] Here G-d showed Himself to us, and we presented ourselves to G-d.[5]

Twice we were given the gift of a divine dwelling in our midst. Twice we failed to prove worthy of this gift and banished the divine presence from our lives.

So G-d built us a third Temple. Unlike its two predecessors, which were of human construction and therefore subject to debasement by man's misdeeds, the third, divinely made Temple is eternal and invincible. But G-d has withheld this "third suit of clothes" from us, confining its reality to a higher, heavenly sphere, beyond the sight and experience of our earthly selves.

Each year, on the "Shabbat of vision," G-d shows us the third Temple. Our souls behold a vision of a world at peace with itself and its Creator, a world suffused with the knowledge and awareness of G-d, a world that has realized its divine potential for goodness and perfection. It is a vision of the third Temple in heaven— in its spiritual and elusive state—like the third set of clothes in the analogy, which the child sees but cannot have. But it is also a vision with a promise: a vision of a divine home poised to descend

---

3 See *Ethics of the Fathers* 5:5.

4 The Talmud (*Yoma* 21a) relates that the Temple and its furnishings defied the most fundamental characteristic of physical objects—that they take up space—in that "the space of the ark was not part of the measurement." The Holy of Holies measured 20 cubits (approx. 30 feet) by 20 cubits; the ark which stood in its center measured 2.5 by 1.5 cubits; yet the distance from each of the outside walls of the ark to the walls of the chamber was a full 10 cubits. In other words, the ark, though itself a physical object with spatial dimensions, did not take up any of the space in the room.

5 Exodus 23:17, as per Talmud, *Sanhedrin* 4b.

THE THREE WEEKS AND TISHAH B'AV (5)

to earth, inspiring us to correct our behavior and hasten the day when the spiritual Temple becomes a tangible reality.

Through these repeated visions, living in the divine presence becomes more and more "second nature" to us (as Rabbi Levi Yitzchak says in his analogy), progressively elevating us to the state of worthiness to experience the divine in our daily lives.

THE WEARABLE HOUSE

The metaphors of our sages continue to speak to us long after the gist of their message has been assimilated. Beneath the surface of the metaphor's most obvious import lie layer upon layer of meaning, in which each and every detail of the narrative is significant.

The same applies to Rabbi Levi Yitzchak's analogy. Its basic meaning is clear, but many subtle insights are enfolded within its details. For example: Why, we might ask, are the three Temples portrayed as three suits of clothes? Would not the example of a building or house have been more appropriate?

The house and the garment both "house" and contain the person. But the garment does so in a much more personal and individualized manner. While it is true that the dimensions and style of a home reflect the nature of its occupant, they do so in a more generalized way—not as specifically and as intimately as a garment suits its wearer.

On the other hand, the individual nature of the garment limits its function to one's personal use. A home can house many; a garment can clothe only one. I can invite you into my home, but I cannot share my garment with you. Even if I give it to you, it will not clothe you as it clothes me, for it "fits" only myself.

G-d chose to reveal His presence in our world in a "dwelling"— a communal structure that goes beyond the personal to embrace an entire people and the entire community of man.[6] Yet the Holy Temple in Jerusalem also had certain garment-like features. It is these features that Rabbi Levi Yitzchak wishes to emphasize by portraying the Holy Temple as a suit of clothes.

For the Holy Temple was also a highly compartmentalized structure. There was a "women's court" and a courtyard reserved for men; an area restricted to the *kohanim* (priests); a "sanctuary" (*heichal*) imbued with a greater sanctity than the "courtyards;" and the "Holy of Holies"—a chamber into which only the High Priest could enter, and only on Yom Kippur, the holiest day of the year. The Talmud enumerates eight domains of varying sanctity within the Temple complex, each with its distinct function and purpose.[7]

In other words, although the Temple expressed a single truth—the all-pervasive presence of G-d in our world—it did so to each individual in a personalized manner. Although it was a "house" in the sense that it served many individuals—indeed the entire world—as their meeting point with the infinite, each individual found it a tailor-made "garment" for his or her specific spiritual needs, according him or her a personal and intimate relationship with G-d.

Each year, on the Shabbat before Tishah B'Av, we are shown a vision of our world as a divine home—a place where all G-d's creatures will experience His presence. But this is also a vision of a G-dly "garment"—the distinctly personal relationship with G-d, particularly suited to our individual character and individual aspirations, that we will each enjoy when the third Temple descends to earth.

---

6   For more on the significance of the "dwelling" analogy as it relates to the divine presence in our lives, see *Real Estate* on pp. 177–186 above.

7   Talmud, *Keilim* 1:6.

THE SUBTERRANEAN TEMPLE

I am asleep, but my heart is awake.

Song of Songs 5:2

Our sages tell us that "when King Solomon built the Holy Temple, knowing that it was destined to be destroyed, he built a place in which to hide the ark, [at the end of] hidden, deep, winding passageways." It was there that King Josiah placed the ark twenty-two years before the Temple's destruction, as related in the book of Chronicles.[1]

The Holy Temple in Jerusalem was built by King Solomon in the year 2928 from creation (833 BCE), and was destroyed 410 years later, on the 9th day of the month of *Av*, by the armies of the Babylonian emperor Nebuchadnezzar. Seventy years later it was rebuilt; the second Temple stood for 420 years, until its destruction by the Romans, also on the 9th of *Av*, in 3829 (69 CE). Ever since, the *Av* 9 has been a day of fasting and repentance—a day on which we mourn the Destruction and pray for the coming of Moshiach, when the third and final Temple will be restored to its place as the divine epicenter of the world.

The Holy Temple was G-d's home, the place in which G-d chose to manifest His all-pervading truth. How, then, could it have been destroyed by human hands? Only because the very structure of the

---

[1] *Mishneh Torah, Laws of the Holy Temple,* 4:1; Talmud, *Yoma* 53b; II Chronicles 35:3.

Temple allowed for this possibility. This is the deeper significance of the fact that King Solomon built the Holy Temple "knowing that it was destined to be destroyed" and incorporated into it a hiding place for the ark for that eventuality. Had the Temple not been initially constructed with the knowledge of, and the provision for, what was to happen on the 9th of *Av*, no mortal could have moved a single stone from its place.

THE PLACES OF THE ARK

The fact that the ark's hiding place was built into the Holy Temple from the very beginning also carries another implication: It means that the first, second, and third Temples are not three different structures, but the continuum parts of a single edifice.

The ark contains the two stone tablets, inscribed with the Ten Commandments by the hand of G-d, which Moses brought down from Mount Sinai. It was the holiest object in the Temple, and the sole object in the Temple's innermost chamber, the "Holy of Holies." Indeed, our sages define the primary function of the Holy Temple as the housing of the ark, for the ark constitutes "the resting place of the *Shechinah* (divine presence)."[2]

Thus, the underground chamber built by Solomon is much more than another "part" of the Holy Temple. The fact that it was constructed for the express purpose of containing the ark means that it is of a piece with the "Holy of Holies"—the very heart of the Temple and its *raison d'être*.[3]

---

2   Nachmanides' commentary on the Torah, introduction to Exodus 25. See *Likutei Sichot*, vol. 4, p. 1346, note 24.

3   Thus the Talmud says that "The ark was concealed in *its place*" (*Yoma*, 53b).

THE THREE WEEKS AND TISHAH B'AV (6)

This is further underscored by the fact that the ark has remained in this chamber from the time that it was placed there by Josiah, twenty-two years before the destruction of the first Temple, to this very day. This means that for the 420 years of the second Temple, the ark was not in the above-ground Holy of Holies, but in its underground chamber. But if the most fundamental function of the Temple is to house the ark, how can there be a Holy Temple without an ark? Also, at the time that Josiah hid the ark, there was not yet any threat to the Holy Temple or to the Jewish sovereignty over Jerusalem, only the prophetic knowledge that the Temple was destined to be destroyed. If the essence of the Holy Temple would have been negated by the removal of the ark below ground, this would certainly not have been done until there was actual danger that the ark might fall into enemy hands. Obviously, then, the underground hiding place of the ark is no less part of the Holy Temple, and no less valid a place for the ark, than the (above-ground) Holy of Holies.

In other words, the Holy Temple was initially designed and built to exist in two states: a revealed state and a concealed state. Accordingly, there were two designated places for the ark in the Holy Temple — the above-ground portion of the Holy of Holies, and the chamber hidden at the end of "deep, winding passageways." In its revealed state, the Holy Temple was a beacon of divine light, a place where humanity openly perceived and experienced the divine presence.[4] In its concealed state, the divine revelation in the Holy Temple is muted, or almost completely obscured. But as long as the Temple houses the ark, it continues to serve as the dwelling of G-d.

---

4   See Exodus 23:17 (as interpreted by the Talmud, *Chagigah* 2a), 25:8 and 40:34–35; I Kings, chapter 8; *Ethics of the Fathers*, 5:5; et al.

In the thirty centuries since it was first built, the Holy Temple has never ceased to fulfill its fundamental function as the seat of the divine presence in the world. There were times in which the entire structure stood in all its glory atop the Temple Mount in Jerusalem, times in which it existed in a diminished form (as in the Second Temple Era), and times in which it was almost entirely destroyed. But a certain part of the Holy Temple has never been disturbed, and there its heart has never ceased to beat. When the third Temple will be built, speedily in our days, and the ark restored to its above-ground chamber, it will not be a new edifice, or even a "rebuilding," but a revelation and reasserting of what has been present all along.

Deep and Winding

"Because we have sinned before You... our city was destroyed, our Sanctuary laid waste; our grandeur was banished, and the glory departed from our House of Life; no longer are we able to fulfill our duties in Your chosen home, in the great and holy house upon which Your name is proclaimed..."[5]

As these lines express, the Temple's susceptibility to destruction is, on the most basic level, a negative thing. Because G-d knew that we might prove unworthy of His manifest presence in our lives, He instructed that the Holy Temple be built in such a way as to allow for periods of diminution and concealment.

But our vulnerability to sin is but G-d's "awesome plot on the sons of man."[6] G-d created us with the capacity to do wrong

---

5   From the *musaf* prayer for Shabbat *Rosh Chodesh*.

6   Psalms 66:5; see *The 120-Day Version of the Human Story* in vol. 2 of this series, pp. 37–43.

THE THREE WEEKS AND TISHAH B'AV (6) 243

only to enable us to uncover "the greater light that comes from darkness"[7]—to enable us to exploit the momentum of our lowest descents to drive our highest achievements. There is much to be achieved through the virtuous development of our positive potential; but nothing compares with the fervor of the repentant sinner, with the passion of one who has confronted his darkest self to recoil in search of light. No man can pursue life with the intensity of one who is fleeing death.

For centuries the Holy Temple has lain desolate, its essence contracted in a subterranean chamber deep beneath its ruined glory. But this terrible descent is, in truth, but the impetus for even higher ascent, even greater good, even more universal perfection, than what shone forth from the Temple in its first and second incarnations.

The paths to this chamber are hidden, deep, and winding. This is not the straight and true path of the righteous, but the furtive, convoluted path of the "returnee" (*baal teshuvah*)—a path that plunges to the depths of his soul to unleash the most potent forces buried therein.

---

7 Ecclesiastes 2:13, as per *Zohar* 3:47b and *Tanya*, chapter 26.

THE LEGALITIES OF DESTRUCTION

One who breaks a single stone of the altar or the temple or the temple courtyard in a destructive manner [violates a biblical prohibition] as it is written, "You shall smash their altars... You shall not do the same to the L-rd your G-d."

Mishneh Torah, Laws of the Holy Temple 1:17

"G-d's way is not like the way of flesh and blood," the Midrash assures us. "The way of flesh and blood is that he instructs others to do, but does not do so himself; G-d, however, what He Himself does, that is what He tells Israel to do and observe."[1] The laws which He decreed to govern our lives also delineate His own conduct in relating to His creation.

But each year, on the 9th day of the month of *Av*, we mourn an act of G-d that was not only tragic but seemingly illegal as well—a divine act which, at first glance, seems to violate laws He set down in His Torah.

On that day, in the year 3338 from creation (423 BCE), the Holy Temple in Jerusalem was destroyed.[2] The actual burning of the Temple was done by the armies of Babylonian emperor Nebuchadnezzar, but G-d takes full responsibility for the deed. In the

---

[1] *Midrash Rabbah, Shemot* 30:6.

[2] The second Temple was destroyed by the Romans on the very same date 490 years later.

THE THREE WEEKS AND TISHAH B'AV (7) 245

years before the destruction, the Almighty had warned: "Behold, I shall dispatch the nations of the north... and Nebuchadnezzar, king of Babylonia, My servant, and I shall bring them upon this land and its inhabitants..." "I shall deliver this city into the hands of the king of Babylonia..." "I shall do to the House upon which My name is called... what I have done to Shiloh."[3]

G-d's destruction of the Holy Temple seems a violation of two Torah prohibitions. The first is *lo tashchit*, the prohibition to destroy anything of value. The source of this law is Deuteronomy 20:19, where the Torah prohibits the cutting down of a fruit tree in the course of war; Torah law (*halachah*) interprets this as a prohibition against all wanton destruction:

> *One who breaks vessels, tears clothes, demolishes a building, stops a spring, or disposes of food in a ruinous manner, transgresses the prohibition of* lo tashchit.[4]

Regarding the Holy Temple, there is an additional law that would seem to proscribe G-d's devastation of His home. In Deuteronomy 12:3–4 we read:

> *Destroy all the places in which the nations [of Canaan] served their gods... Tear down their altars, break their monuments, burn their* asheirah *trees, and smash their idols... You shall not do the same to G-d your G-d.*

From these verses, the *halachic* codifiers derive that it is a biblical prohibition to "break a single stone of the altar or the temple

---

3   Jeremiah 25:9, 32:3, and 7:14. (The sanctuary at Shiloh, which served as the central house of worship prior to the Temple's construction, was also destroyed in punishment for Israel's sins.)

4   *Mishneh Torah, Laws of Kings* 6:10; *Shulchan Aruch HaRav, Laws of Bal Tashchit* 14; see *Talmudic Encyclopedia* under *Bal Tashchit.*

or the temple courtyard in a destructive manner... as it is written,
'...You shall not do the same to G-d your G-d.'"

How, then, could G-d destroy the Holy Temple, without transgressing laws which He has commanded and to which He has committed Himself?

Constructive Mayhem

The legality of G-d's action, at least in regard to the *lo tashchit* law, can be explained on the basis of another law, this from the laws of Shabbat.

There are thirty-nine categories of "work" forbidden on Shabbat. A basic legal requisite for an action to be considered "work" is that it be constructive. Thus, while the list of 39 forbidden labors includes categories such as "demolishing" and "tearing," these are strictly of the constructive sort, such as breaking down a wall in order to renovate a building, or tearing a seam in order to make alterations to a garment; one who *destructively* rips or demolishes has not violated the prohibition to do work on Shabbat. Nevertheless, the law is that "one who tears something apart out of rage, or [grief] over the death [of a loved one], violates the Shabbat, for he is soothed by this and his temper is relaxed. Since his rage is abated by this action, it is considered a constructive deed."[5]

The same could be said of G-d's destruction of the Holy Temple. Noting that Psalm 79—which describes how "alien nations have entered Your estate, they have defiled Your Holy Temple, they have laid Jerusalem in ruins"—carries the caption "A song to Asaf," the Midrash asks:

---

5   *Mishneh Torah, Laws of Shabbat*, 1:17 and 10:10.

THE THREE WEEKS AND TISHAH B'AV (7)

> *Should not the verse have said "A weeping to Asaf," "A wail to Asaf," "A lament to Asaf"? Why does it say "A song to Asaf"?*
>
> *But this is analogous to a king who built a nuptial home for his son, and had it beautifully plastered, inlaid, and decorated. Then this son strayed off to an evil life. So the king came to the nuptial canopy, tore down the tapestries, and broke the rails. Upon which the prince's tutor took a flute and began to play. Those who saw him, asked: "The king is overturning the nuptial canopy of his son, and you sit and sing?" Said he to them: "I am singing because the king overturned his son's nuptial canopy, and did not vent his wrath upon his son."*
>
> *So, too, was asked of Asaf: "G-d destroyed the Temple and Sanctuary, and you sit and sing?" Replied he: "I am singing because G-d vented His wrath upon wood and stone, and did not vent his wrath upon Israel."*[6]

The destruction of the Temple, then, was a constructive deed. Our sins had threatened our relationship with the Almighty; by "venting His wrath" upon the wood and stone of the Temple, G-d deflected the damage to the physical "nuptial home" of the relationship, preserving the integrity of the relationship itself.

This, however, still does not explains why G-d's destruction of the Temple did not violate the specific prohibition to destroy "even a single stone" of the Holy Temple. The fact that the Temple's destruction is a means toward a worthy end would not mitigate

---

6   *Midrash Rabbah* on Lamentations 4:11, where Jeremiah proclaims: "G-d has spent His wrath, He poured out His fury; He set fire to Zion and consumed its foundations."

this prohibition, which specifically forbids inflicting damage on the Temple, even if one has a constructive purpose in mind.

Unless the destruction of the Temple were to somehow be constructive to the Temple itself. As quoted above from Maimonides' *Mishneh Torah*, the prohibition is to demolish any part of the Temple "in a destructive manner." "To demolish in order to improve," explain the commentaries, "is obviously permitted."[7] Indeed, the Talmud relates how the sages advised and encouraged Herod to demolish the Holy Temple in order to rebuild it in greater splendor.[8] In other words, while it is forbidden to demolish any part of the Holy Temple even for a constructive purpose, it is permitted to do so for the *Temple's* betterment.

This distinction can also be seen in the manner in which this law is applied to the "minor sanctuary" of today, the synagogue, which has assumed the Temple's role of housing the Jew's service of his Creator. It is forbidden to demolish a synagogue, or any part thereof, even for a most positive and G-dly purpose—unless the purpose is to rebuild or improve the synagogue itself, in which case "the demolition is itself an act of building."[9]

And so it was with G-d's destruction of the Temple—the demolition was itself an act of building. The first two Temples were edifices built by human hands, and thus subject to the mortality of everything human.[10] G-d came to dwell in the work of man; but the work of man can be corrupted by the deeds of man, driving the divine presence from its earthly abode.

---

7   *Kesef Mishneh* on *Mishneh Torah, Laws of the Holy Temple* 1:17.

8   Talmud, *Bava Batra* 4a.

9   Mordechai on Talmud, *Megillah*, section 826; *Shulchan Aruch* and *Rema*, *Orach Chaim* 152; *Tzemach Tzedek Responsa*, *Orach Chaim*, Responsa 20; *Torat Chesed* Responsa, *Orach Chaim*, Responsa 4.

10   *Zohar* 3:221a.

THE THREE WEEKS AND TISHAH B'AV (7) 249

The two mortal Temples were destroyed in order that the eternal third Temple may be built.[11] Indeed, the Temple was originally designated to be a divinely-constructed edifice — Moses described it as "The base for Your dwelling that You, G-d, have made; the Sanctuary, O L-rd, that Your hands have established."[12] If this was preceded by the Temples built by Solomon and Ezra, these were but stages in the construction of the third Temple, the divine edifice which shall descend from heaven with the advent of Moshiach, speedily in our day.

SIGHTING THE END

The law that allows tearing down a house of worship in order to rebuild it is most stringent. The new building must be superior (in size, beauty, etc.) to the one being torn down.[13] If the circum-

---

[11] In the words of the Midrash, "The lion came, under the constellation of lion, and destroyed the Lion of G-d, *in order that* the Lion shall come, under the constellation of lion, and build the Lion of G-d." Meaning: "'The lion came'—this is Nebuchadnezzar, of whom it is written 'The lion came up from his thicket' (Jeremiah 4:7); 'Under the constellation of lion'—[as it says] 'Until the exile of Jerusalem in the fifth month' (Jeremiah 1:3; i.e., the month of *Av*, which falls under the constellation Leo); 'And destroyed the Lion of G-d ("Ariel")'—[as it says] 'Woe, Ariel, Ariel, city of David's camp' (Isaiah 29:1); 'In order that the Lion shall come'—this is the Holy One Blessed Be He, of whom it is written 'The Lion has roared, who fears not?' (Amos 3:8); 'Under the constellation of lion'—[as it says] 'I shall transform their mourning day to joy' (Jeremiah 31:12; i.e., the redemption shall come at the time when we are mourning the Destruction); 'And build the Lion of G-d'—[as it says] 'G-d builds Jerusalem, the forsaken of Israel He gathers' (Psalms 147:2)." (*Yalkut Shimoni*, Jeremiah 259).

[12] Exodus 15:17.

[13] As per the precedent of Herod's tearing down of the Temple. *Masaat*

stances are such that the old building must be demolished before the new one is built, the new building's construction must begin immediately and must be pursued "day and night, lest difficulties arise that will cause it to remain desolate—even for a time."[14] The Talmud relates that when the deteriorating synagogue in Matta Mechasia had to be torn down, Rav Ashi moved his bed into the construction site and did not leave the site "until the gutter-pipes were affixed."[15]

In keeping with this law, G-d began His reconstruction of the Temple immediately upon its destruction. As the Talmud relates:

> *On the day that the Holy Temple was destroyed, a Jew was plowing his field when his cow suddenly called out. An Arab was passing by and heard the low of the cow. Said the Arab to the Jew: "Son of Judah! Unyoke your cow, free the stake of your plow, for your Holy Temple has now been destroyed."*
>
> *The cow then lowed a second time. Said the Arab to the Jew: "Son of Judah! Yoke your cow, reset the stake of your plow, for the redeemer has now been born..."*
>
> *Said Rabbi Bon: "Do we need to learn this from an Arab? The Torah itself says so. The verse predicts, "The Cedar of Lebanon[16] shall be felled by the mighty one."[17] And what is written in the very next verse? "There shall come forth a shoot out of the stem of Yishai."[18]*

Binyomin Responsa, cited in the *Tzemach Tzedek Responsa* referred to above.

14   *Shulchan Aruch* and *Taz* commentary, *Orach Chaim* 152.
15   Talmud, *Bava Batra* 3b.
16   A reference to the Holy Temple; cf. Deuteronomy 3:25.
17   Isaiah 10:34.
18   Jerusalem Talmud, *Berachot* 2:4.

THE THREE WEEKS AND TISHAH B'AV (7)   251

As the Temple ruins lay smoldering, the process of rebuilding was already underway. Moshiach, the divine emissary empowered to bring redemption to the world and the eternal Sanctuary to Jerusalem, was born on the 9th of *Av*.[19]

This explains a curious phenomenon in the history of our exile. Many of our sages—including such prodigious figures as Rabbi Shimon bar Yochai, Rabbi Saadiah Gaon, Maimonides, Nachmanides, Rabbeinu Bechayei, and Rabbi Schneur Zalman of Liadi—predicted various dates for the revelation of Moshiach and the rebuilding of the Holy Temple, despite the Talmud's admonishment of those who "calculate deadlines" for the Redemption.[20]

For these great visionaries had a view of history that penetrated beyond the surface mayhem of the Destruction. They understood that G-d could not have destroyed the Temple if the very moment of the destruction was not also the moment which commenced its reconstruction in its greater, eternal form. They understood that *galut* is not a void or hiatus in G-d's presence in our world, but an

---

19   "In every generation is born a descendent of Judah who is worthy to become Israel's Moshiach" (Bartinoro on Ruth). "When the time will come, G-d will reveal Himself to him and send him, and then the spirit of Moshiach, which is hidden and secreted on high, will be revealed in him" (*Chatam Sofer*).

20   Talmud, *Sanhedrin* 97b, cited by Maimonides (who himself calculates the date of Moshiach's coming in his famed *Yemen Letter*) as a *halachic* prohibition in his *Mishneh Torah, Laws of Kings* 12:2.

The obvious difference between what the Talmud warns against and what these sages did, is that a "deadline" implies that "If the time of the deadline comes and [Moshiach] has not arrived, then he won't come at all" (Talmud, *Sanhedrin* 97b); while these leaders of Israel pointed out those junctures of history at which the opportunity for redemption—an opportunity which, as mentioned above, has existed from the moment of the Temple's destruction—was most palpably within reach.

integral part of the process of redemption. To them, the 9th of *Av* was, above all, the birthday of Moshiach.

They saw, beneath the veneer of *galut*, the eternal abode of G-d rising from the rubble. They saw the opportunity, which has existed from the day of the Temple's destruction, growing more realizable with each passing generation. Seize the moment, they urged us, the climax of history is in ready reach.

THE THREE WEEKS AND TISHAH B'AV (8)

THE
INTIMATE
ESTRANGEMENT

When the pagans entered the Holy Temple,
they saw the keruvim *cleaving to each other.*
They took them out to the streets and said:
"These Jews… is this what they occupy them-
selves with?!" With this, they debased [the
Jewish people], as it is written (Lamentations
1:8): "All who had honored her have despised
her, for they have seen her nakedness."

Talmud, Yoma 54b

𝔍 he prophets compare the bond between G-d and Israel to
the marriage relationship between husband and wife. The
prophet Jeremiah describes G-d recalling the Exodus as "the kindness of your youth, your bridal love, your following Me into the
desert, into a land that was not sown."[1] King Solomon refers to
the covenant at Mount Sinai as "the day of His betrothal," for the
Torah, which outlines our duties as G-d's people and His eternal
commitment to us, is the marriage contract (*ketubah*) between
ourselves and G-d.[2]

Thus, when we violated the commandments of the Torah, the
prophets admonished us as a wayward wife who has betrayed her
husband. They described the resultant *galut*—the destruction of

---

1 Jeremiah 2:2.
2 Song of Songs 3:11; see Talmud, *Taanit* 26b; Rashi to Exodus 34:1.

the Holy Temple in Jerusalem and our banishment into exile—as a period of estrangement and "separation" in the marriage. The messianic redemption is accordingly presented as the promise of a restoration of the relationship to its original state and the forging of a renewed, even deeper bond of love between the bride Israel and her Supernal Groom.

In the innermost chamber of the Holy Temple, the "Holy of Holies," stood a golden ark, containing the two stone tablets on which G-d had inscribed the Ten Commandments, and the original Torah scroll written by Moses. Topping the ark were the *keruvim*, two winged figures, one male and one female, hammered out of a block of pure gold. The *keruvim* represented the relationship between G-d and His people. The Talmud tells us that when the people of Israel rebelled against the will of the Almighty, the *keruvim* would turn away from each other. When Israel was faithful to her G-d, they would face each other. Times in which the love and goodwill between G-d and His bride were at their peak were reflected in the *keruvim's* embrace "as a man cleaves to his wife."[3]

The Talmud relates that when the enemies of Israel invaded the Temple, they entered into the Holy of Holies—a place so sacred that entry into it was permitted only to a single individual, the High Priest, and only on Yom Kippur, the holiest day of the year. There they saw the *keruvim* embracing each other. They dragged them out of the Temple and into the streets, perverting and vulgarizing their sacred significance.[4]

---

3 Talmud, *Bava Batra* 99a and *Yoma* 54a.

4 Ibid.; Rashi, ad loc. (The Ark of Testimony, with the *keruvim* atop its cover, were hidden in an underground chamber in the Holy Temple twenty-two years before the destruction of the first Temple, where they remain to this day [see *The Subterranean Temple*, pp. 239–243 above]. So neither the Babylonians nor the Romans would have found the ark

THE THREE WEEKS AND TISHAH B'AV (8)

THE PARADOX

In our prayers we remind ourselves that "Because of our sins, we were exiled from our land... and we are no longer able to ascend and show ourselves and bow before You... in Your chosen home, in the great and holy house upon which Your Name is called."[5]

For 830 years,[6] G-d dwelled in a physical edifice on a Jerusalem mountaintop, granting us a tangible experience of His presence in our lives. But we proved unworthy of such closeness and intimacy with the divine presence. The Holy Temple was taken from us, and we were cast into *galut*—a state of existence in which the divine face is hidden and G-d's love and concern for us is concealed—so that the void in our lives should impel us to repent our ways and repair the damage to our marriage inflicted by our misdeeds.

But if *galut* is a time of estrangement between G-d and Israel, why were the *keruvim* embracing each other at the time of the Temple's destruction? Wouldn't the destruction of the Holy Temple mark a nadir in our relationship with the Almighty? What greater paradox can there be: the Divine Groom is destroying His marital home, allowing His nuptial chamber to be violated and His bride to be carried off by strangers, while the barometer of their marriage indicates the ultimate in intimacy and union!

---

in the Holy of Holies. The Talmud explains that the *keruvim* that were dragged out into the streets were not the *keruvim* from on top of the ark, but reliefs which decorated the walls of the Holy of Holies and which likewise acted as a "barometer" of the state of marriage between G-d and Israel.)

5   *Musaf* prayer for the festivals.
6   The first Temple stood 410 years, the second, 420.

THREE AND SEVEN

Every Shabbat, following the reading of the weekly Torah portion, a weekly selection from the Prophets, called the *haftarah,* is read in the synagogue. Usually, the content of the *haftarah* corresponds to the week's Torah reading. However, there are weeks when the *haftarah* instead reflects events connected with the time of the year. Such is the case during the last ten weeks of the year, when ten special *haftarot*—called the "three of rebuke" and the "seven of consolation"—are read.

The "three of rebuke" are read in conjunction with the three weeks from *Tammuz* 17 to *Av* 9, during which we remember and mourn the destruction of the Temple and the onset of our *galut.*

On the 17th of *Tammuz* in the year 3829 from creation (69 CE), the walls of Jerusalem were breached by the besieging armies of Rome. After three weeks of fighting, during which the Romans advanced with great difficulty through the city, they succeeded in breaking into the Temple; on *Av* 9 they set it aflame.[7] These two days are observed as fast days, and the three weeks between them as a time of mourning. In this period, the *haftarah* readings consist of selections from the Prophets in which the prophet rebukes Israel for her crimes and iniquities and her betrayal of her covenant with G-d.[8]

The "three of rebuke" are followed by "seven of consolation." For seven weeks, beginning with the Shabbat after the 9th of *Av,* the *haftarah* readings consist of prophecies describing G-d's consolation of His people and the rehabilitation of their relationship.[9]

---

7 The 9th of *Av* is also the date of the first Temple's destruction, by the Babylonians, in the year 3339 (423 BCE).

8 The "three of rebuke" are: Jeremiah 1:2–2:3; ibid. 2:4–2:28 and 3:4; and Isaiah 1:1–27.

9 The "seven of consolation" are: Isaiah 40:1–26; 49:14–51:3; 54:11–55:5;

THE THREE WEEKS AND TISHAH B'AV (8)   257

Thus we reexperience each year the process of rebuke and condo-
lence, destruction and rebuilding, estrangement and reunion.

But why, specifically, a ten-week process? And what is the significance of its division into three phases of withdrawal and seven
degrees of reconciliation? Chassidic sage Rabbi Hillel of Paritch
explains that the "three of rebuke" and the "seven of consolation"
correspond to the ten attributes of the soul, which are likewise
divided into sets of three and seven. The soul of man possesses
three basic intellectual faculties (conceptualization, comprehension, and application), and seven basic emotional drives (love, awe,
harmony, ambition, devotion, bonding, and sovereignty).[10] For it
is the interrelation between mind and heart that enables us to understand the true nature of the "estrangement" of *galut*.

MIND AND HEART

The mind, by nature and necessity, is aloof and detached. To apprehend a concept it must assume an objective distance, divesting itself of all involvement with or affinity for its subject and adopting
a reserved, even callous attitude toward the studied entity. Only
then can its analysis and comprehension be exact and complete.

The heart, on the other hand, is involved, attached, gloriously
*subj*ective. The heart *relates* to the object of its affections, bridging
distances, surmounting the barriers between self and other.

Yet true and enduring attachments are born only out of understanding. Feelings that are based on nothing more than impulse
or instantaneous attraction are ultimately as shallow as they are

---

51:12–52:12; 54:1–10; 60:1–22; and 61:10–63:9.

10 See *A Speck of Flour* (pp. 62–70 above) and *The Journey* (pp. 98–108)
and references cited there.

impassioned, as transient as they are intense. It is those emotions that are conceived in the womb of the mind which possess depth and continuity. It is the love that is founded upon an understanding and appreciation of the beloved that can transcend the fluctuations of feeling, the letdowns, the lethargy, and the many other pitfalls of time and change.

So the seemingly cold and distant mind is, in truth, the source and essence of any meaningful relationship. The detachment associated with rational examination actually lies at the heart of our emotive capacity to bond with others.

G-D'S "MIND"

"From my own flesh, I perceive G-d."[11] The human is a metaphor of the divine; by examining our own physiological and psychological makeup, we learn much about the divine reality and the manner in which G-d chooses to relate to His creations.

The mind-heart paradox—the manner in which mental detachment is the essence and foundation of true emotional attachment—provides us with a model for the paradox of *galut*.

G-d's relationship with us also includes both "intellectual" and "emotional" elements. At times, we sense what appear to be signs of detachment and disinvolvement on His part. G-d seems to have shifted the focus of His attention from our lives, abandoning us to the whims of chance and fate. Our existence seems bereft of all direction and purpose. G-d is distancing Himself from us, our lives apparently no longer worthy of His concern.

In truth, however, this divine "objectivity" carries the seeds of greater connection. It is a disengagement for the sake of a more

---

11   Job 19:26; cf. Genesis 1:27: "And G-d created man in His image."

THE THREE WEEKS AND TISHAH B'AV (8)   259

enduring relationship, a withdrawal to create an even more meaningful closeness. Ostensibly, *galut* is a breakdown, a diminution of
the bond between ourselves and G-d; in truth, it is the essence of a
deeper identification with and commitment to each other.

G-d's hiding His face from us in *galut* is an act of love. Despite
our painful incomprehension, it serves to deepen our attachment
to Him. In the "three of rebuke," we experience abandonment,
alienation, and distance; but these give birth to the "seven of consolation." Bereft of the outward expressions of our relationship
with G-d, we are impelled to uncover its essence, the quintessential bond which transcends all physical and spiritual distance.
Thus, it is only through the experience of *galut* that the deepest dimensions of our marriage are realized. Externally, the "three weeks"
are a period of detachment and estrangement; in essence, they are
the height of attachment and connection.[12]

---

12   Chassidic teaching also offers another analogy for the paradox of *ga-
     lut*, this one from within the world of intellect itself:
          A teacher is in the midst of communicating a concept to his disci-
     ple. Suddenly, he has a flash of inspiration: a new, infinitely deeper and
     more profound concept has erupted in his mind—a concept which he
     immediately senses to be of great value for his disciple. Practically in
     mid-sentence, he falls silent; his eyes, which have been focused upon
     the attentive disciple, close; the disciple's questions and remarks are
     repelled with a brusque motion of his hand. The teacher's every iota of
     mental power is now concentrated on the task of absorbing and retain-
     ing the still nebulous concept hovering at the periphery of his mind.
          The disciple is devastated. Why has his beloved master turned
     from him? Why has he shut him out so abruptly? Things go from bad
     to worse. At first he was brushed aside—now he is being completely ig-
     nored. At first his master closed his eyes—now he has turned his back
     on him entirely.
          The teacher senses the anguish of his pupil. If he cared less for
     him, he would reassure him with a word or two. But he knows that the
     slightest diversion at this critical time would impair his efforts to fully

Hence the pagan armies entering the Holy of Holies found the *keruvim* in intimate embrace. Without, Israel was being

---

capture his newly conceived idea before the flash of enlightenment recedes. He is loath to relinquish even a single nuance of the concept which will so enrich his disciple. So despite the manner in which it is received by the pupil, the teacher's act of "rejection" is, in truth, an act of love—an act which is not only fully in keeping with the nature of their relationship but which serves to deepen and enhance it. On the surface, they are cut off one from the other; in essence, they have never been closer to each other.

This analogy also explains why *galut* increases in severity the closer we move toward our rapprochement with G-d. If the function of *galut* were only to serve as a punishment for sin, then its intensity ought to lessen as time goes by and we atone for our transgressions. Historically, the very opposite is true—the nearer we reach Redemption, the darker the concealment of *galut* grows. A case in point is our first *galut*, our 210-year sojourn in Egypt. For their first generation in Egypt, our forefathers flourished; for the next century or so their situation deteriorated; but the outright slavery and cruel tortures associated with this *galut* came only in its final 86 years, and the most difficult and trying period came in the final year of the Egyptian exile, *after* Moses had already prophesied its end. The same is true of our present exile: The spiritual state of our lives—the most basic factor of *galut*—has known a steady decline from the day of the Temple's destruction more than 1,900 years ago. In its earlier generations, an era populated by the great sages of the Talmud, our relationship with the Almighty, though obscured by the concealment of *galut*, was still a deeply felt reality in many people's lives. As the generations progress, we find an increasing coarsening and materialization of life, leading to the almost total blackout of spirituality and sensitivity to the divine which characterizes our present-day existence. This, despite the fact that each successive generation has brought us closer to the ultimate redemption.

But this pattern reflects the process of the metaphorical teacher's "abandonment" of his disciple. The deeper the teacher delves into the concept, the more he must retreat into himself, distancing himself even further from the distraught pupil. Yet each successive retreat represents a greater regard for his disciple and a greater commitment to his role as teacher.

vanquished and exiled, and the Holy Temple set ablaze. Externally the marriage was crumbling, the husband alienated, and the wayward wife banished to a foreign land. But within the Holy of Holies—within the chamber which housed the essence of their marriage—the bond between G-d and His people was at the height of closeness and unity.

REGRET

There are four things whose creation G-d regrets every day. The first is galut.

Talmud, Sukkah 52b[1]

To say that G-d "regrets" something is obviously at odds with our understanding of His omniscience and omnipotence. Regret implies that one now knows something that one did not know before; that one's earlier decision or deed was flawed or ill informed; that one has now matured to the point that he can look back and reject a deficient past. None of this, of course, can be related to G-d. In the words of the verse, "G-d is not a man that He should lie; nor a son of Adam that He should regret."[2]

Attributing regret to G-d represents a further problem: If G-d regrets the creation of something, how could that thing continue to exist? As the sages and mystics explain,[3] creation is a perpetual act on the part of G-d. When the Torah tells us that "G-d said, 'There shall be light,' and there was light," it isn't describing a one-time event which took place on the first day of creation; it is telling us that what we experience as "light" is the embodiment of G-d's continued articulation of His desire that there be light. In every fraction of every moment of time, G-d "says" the words "There shall be light," and it is this divine utterance that constitutes

---

1   The words "every day" in this quote are from the version cited in *Dikdukei Sofrim*.

2   Numbers 23:19.

3   See *The Now* in vol. 1 of this series, pp. 31–37, and sources cited there.

THE THREE WEEKS AND TISHAH B'AV (9)   263

the essence of physical light. For no being or phenomenon can possibly exist independently of G-d's constant involvement in its creation.

[The story is told of a young man who left his hometown for several years to study under the tutelage of chassidic master Rabbi Dov Ber of Mezheritch. When he returned, one of his friends asked him: "Why did you have to leave your family and community to go study in some distant town? What did you learn in Mezheritch that you couldn't have learned in our own study halls from our own rabbis?"

"Tell me," said the young chassid, "do you believe in G-d?"

"Certainly I believe in G-d."

"If G-d no longer wanted this table to exist, what would happen?"

"What kind of question is that? G-d can do everything! If He no longer wanted this table to exist, He could destroy it immediately."

"What might He do?"

"What might He do? Whatever He wants! He could send forth a fire and incinerate it on the spot."

"But if G-d incinerates the table, there would still remain the ashes."

"G-d can create such a mighty fire that nothing whatsoever would remain."

"If such is your conception of G-d," said Rabbi Dov Ber's new student, "you might as well throw yourself, together with this god of yours, into that fire. What is this table, if not the embodiment of G-d's desire that it be? The moment G-d no longer desires its existence, it has no existence!"]

So if G-d regrets the creation of *galut* every day, why are we still in exile? How could *galut* exist, even as a concept, without G-d's continued desire that it be?

THE ART OF METAPHOR

Then again, nothing we say about G-d can imply quite the same thing it does when applied to a mortal being. For example, when we say that G-d "hears" our prayers, do we mean that sound waves generated by our vocal chords vibrate a divine eardrum and stimulate a divine brain in order for G-d to "hear" our request? Do we even mean that our prayers inform G-d what it is we lack—G-d who knows our every desire before we are ourselves aware of it, indeed, before we were born? Obviously not. When we say that G-d hears our prayers, we mean "hear" in a purely conceptual sense— hear as in "take notice of" and "pay attention to" and, hopefully, "respond to."

In discussing G-d, we inevitably use terms whose meaning is colored by the dynamics of our experience—an experience bounded by time, space, and our human limitations. Our only other option would be not to speak of G-d at all.[4] So in using these terms, we must always take care to strip them of their mortal and temporal trappings and apply only their pure, noncorporeal essence to our understanding of G-d's relationship to our existence.

Thus, when the Torah tells us that G-d regrets something, it expects us to strip the term "regret" down to its bare conceptual

---

4   Which is not an option, since G-d has command us to not only believe in His existence, but also to know and comprehend it to the extent to which we are capable. As Moses says to the children of Israel, "You have been shown to know... Know today and bring it unto your heart, that G-d is the G-d... there is none else" (Deuteronomy 4:35–39). In the words of King David, "Know the G-d of your fathers and serve Him with a whole heart" (I Chronicles 28:9). See Tzemach Tzedek's *Derech Mitzvotecha*, pp. 88ff. (*Mitzvat HaAmanat HaElokut*) and sources cited there.

bones; to divest it of all connotations of failing, past ignorance — indeed, of time itself — before applying it to G-d.

Regret, to us, means that something is both desired and not desired — desired in the past, but not desired in the present. Applied to a timeless G-d, "regret" implies both these states simultaneously: something that is both desired and not desired, with the desire belonging to the more distant dimension of the thing (its "past"), and the non-desire belonging to its more apparent and immediate dimension (its "present").

This is G-d's attitude to *galut* "every day" — including the very day on which He destroyed the Holy Temple and banished us from the Holy Land.

G-d desires *galut* and does not desire it at the same time. He desires its positive functions — the fortitude it reveals in us, the depths of faith to which it challenges us, its globalization of our mission as His "light unto the nations." But He abhors its manifest reality — the physical suffering and spiritual displacement to which *galut* subjects us. Upon our ultimate deliverance from exile, the positive essence of *galut* will come to light — but then, of course, we shall no longer be in a state of *galut*. *Galut*, by definition, is a state in which the externalities of life obscure its inner content. Thus, the state of *galut* is a state of "regret": a state whose not desirable element is manifest and "present," while its desirable aspect is "in the past" — distant and obscured.

And since a thing's existence is the expression of a divine desire that it be, the state of *galut* exists only in a very limited sense — only inasmuch as G-d desires it. Only its "desired" element possesses true existence; its "not-desired" element, despite its ostensibly greater, more "present" reality, is a nonentity, nothing more than the illusionary shadow of its truly real, though presently obscured, positive function.

Two Lessons

Today, *galut* is no longer what it used to be. Although we still suffer the spiritual rootlessness of *galut*, its more blatant expressions are fading away. Today, a Jew can live practically anywhere in the world in freedom and prosperity.

But to feel comfortable in *galut* is the greatest *galut* there can be, the ultimate symptom of alienation from one's essence and source. To feel comfortable in *galut*—to perceive it as a viable, even desirable, state of affairs—is to live in contradiction to G-d's daily regret of *galut*. The Jew who lives in harmony with G-d will always regard the *galut* state as abhorrent and undesirable.[5]

At the same time, we know that *galut*, devoid of all but the faintest echo of divine desire, possesses no true reality, no matter how formidable a face it may represent to us. We understand that it stands ever poised on the brink of dissolution; that at any moment, its desirable essence can manifest itself and banish the *galut* "reality" to the regretted past that it is.[6]

---

5 Thus the *Haggadah* tells us that Jacob descended to Egypt to begin the first (and archetypal) *galut* of Israel "forced by the divine command." On the face of it, this seems inconsistent with our sages' depiction of Jacob as a *merkavah* ("chariot" or "vehicle") of the divine will, whose "every limb was totally removed from physical concerns and served only as a vehicle to carry out G-d's will every moment of his life" (*Midrash Rabbah*, *Bereishit* 82:6; *Tanya*, chapter 23). Would a *merkavah* feel "forced" to fulfill a divine command?

   In truth, however, it was *because* Jacob was so absolutely attuned to the divine will that he felt "forced" into his exile in Egypt. Because he experienced *galut* as G-d relates to it—as a "regretted" thing, as something whose "present" is undesirable—his attitude toward *galut* was one of antipathy and aversion, even as he readily entered it to harvest its positive, yet hidden, potentials.

6 The non-reality of *galut* is a theme which pervades the Rebbe's writings and talks. This was much more than an "idea" to him—in the Rebbe, one saw a person who lived and experienced the reality described in

THE THREE WEEKS AND TISHAH B'AV (9)

the last paragraph of this essay. Here, for example, is a freely-translated transcript of his words at a gathering on *Shabbat Parashat Pinchas*, 5744 (the Shabbat on which the Torah section of *Pinchas* is read in the Jewish year 5744—i.e., July 14, 1984):

"...In regard to what has been discussed above—the redemption and the era of Moshiach—there are those who wonder (though, for obvious reasons, they do not openly express their amazement): How can a person appear in public, week after week, and repeatedly speak of one subject—the coming of Moshiach? Furthermore, this person always stresses that he is not merely speaking of the concept, but of the actual coming of Moshiach, here on physical earth, and immediately, on this very day—*Shabbat Parashat Pinchas*, 5744! He then instructs, on each occasion, to sing 'May the Holy Temple be rebuilt speedily in our days,' emphasizing that 'speedily in our days' should not be understood as 'speedily, tomorrow,' but as 'speedily, today'!

"Certainly, every Jew believes that Moshiach can come at any moment—after all, 'I await his coming every day' is one of the fundamental principles of the Jewish faith. Still—they wonder—to sense that Moshiach will come at *this very moment* is hardly consistent with the reality of our lives. So why does this man speak incessantly about this, on every occasion, and with such single-minded intensity, as if to forcefully ram the idea into the minds of his listeners?

"Their conclusion is that all this is a nice dream (and, as we say in our prayers, 'May all my dreams be positively fulfilled for me and for all of Israel')—nice, but not very realistic. So what's the point of speaking, in such length and frequency, about one's dreams?

"The truth, however, is the very opposite.

"In a discourse based on the verse 'When G-d returns the exiles of Israel, we shall be as those who have dreamed' (Psalms 126:1), the Alter Rebbe (Rabbi Schneur Zalman of Liadi) explains that our current state of *galut* is comparable to a dream, in which a person's sense of perception can tolerate the most contradictory and irrational things.

"In other words, our current 'reality' is a dream, while the world of Moshiach is the true reality. In a single moment, we can all wake from the dream of *galut* and open our eyes to the true reality of our existence—the perfect world of Moshiach. It is in the power of each and every one present in this room to immediately wake himself from his dream, so that today, *Shabbat Parashat Pinchas*, 5744, before we even have a chance to recite the *minchah* prayer, indeed this very moment, we all open our eyes and see Moshiach, in the flesh, with us, here in this room!"

CHOLENT

G-d, how long?!   Psalms 90:13

The story is told of a simple, unlettered Jew who kept a tavern on a distant crossroads many weeks' journey from the nearest Jewish community. One year he decided to make the trip to the Jewish town for Rosh Hashanah.

When he entered the *shul* on Rosh Hashanah morning, it was already packed with worshippers and the service was well underway. Scarcely knowing which way to hold the prayer book, he draped his *tallit* over his head and took an inconspicuous place against the back wall.

Hours passed. Hunger was beginning to gnaw at his insides, but impassioned sounds of prayer around him showed no signs of abating. Visions of the sumptuous holiday meal awaiting him at his lodgings made his eyes water in pain. What was taking so long? Haven't we prayed enough? Still the service stretched on.

Suddenly, as the cantor reached a particularly stirring passage, the entire congregation burst into tears. "Why is everyone weeping?" wondered the tavern-keeper. Then it dawned on him. Of course! They, too, are hungry. They, too, are thinking of the elusive meal and endless service. With a new surge of self-pity he gave vent to his anguish; a new wail joined the others as he, too, bawled his heart out.

But after a while the weeping let up, finally quieting to a sprinkling of exceptionally pious worshippers. Our hungry tavern-keeper's hopes soared, but the prayers went on. And on. Why have they stopped crying? he wondered. Are they no longer hungry?

THE THREE WEEKS AND TISHAH B'AV (10)   269

Then he remembered the *cholent*. What a *cholent* he had waiting for him! Everything else his wife had prepared for the holiday meal paled in comparison to that *cholent*. He distinctly remembered the juicy cut of meat she had put into the *cholent* when she set it on the fire the previous afternoon. And our tavern-keeper knew one thing about *cholent*: The longer it cooks, the more sumptuous your *cholent*. He'd glanced under the lid on his way to the synagogue this morning, when the *cholent* had already been going for some eighteen hours. Good, he'd sniffed approvingly, but give it another few hours, and Ahhhh... A few hours of aching feet and a hollow stomach are a small price to pay, considering what was developing under that lid with each passing minute.

Obviously, that's what his fellow worshippers are thinking, as well. They, too, have a *cholent* simmering on their stovetop. No wonder they've stopped crying. Let the service go on, he consoled himself, the longer the better.

And on the service went. His stomach felt like raw leather, his knees grew weak with hunger, his head throbbed in pain, his throat burned with suppressed tears. But whenever he felt that he simply could not hold out a moment longer, he thought of his *cholent*, envisioning what was happening to that piece of meat at that very moment: the steady crisping on the outside, the softening on the inside, the blending of flavors with the potatoes, beans, *kishkeh*, and spices in the pot. Every minute longer, he kept telling himself, is another minute on the fire for my *cholent*.

An hour later, the cantor launched into another exceptionally moving piece. As his tremulous voice painted the awesome scene of divine judgment unfolding in the heavens, the entire congregation broke down weeping once again. At this point, the dam burst in this simple Jew's heart, for he well understood what was on his fellow worshippers' minds. "Enough is enough!" he sobbed.

"Never mind the *cholent*! It's been cooking long enough! I'm hungry! I want to go home...!"

SCATTERED SPARKS

Jewish history is a *cholent*.

The Talmud states that "The people of Israel were exiled amongst the nations only so that converts may be added to them."[1] On the most basic level, this is a reference to the literal converts to Judaism who, in the centuries of our dispersion, have come in contact with the Jewish people and decided to join their covenant with G-d. Chassidic teaching, however, explains that the Talmud is also referring to the many other "souls" which we have transformed and elevated in the course of our exile—the "sparks of holiness" contained within the physical creation.

Every created entity has a spark of G-dliness within it, a pinpoint of divinity that constitutes its "soul"—its spiritual function and design. And when we utilize something to serve the Creator, we penetrates its shell of mundanity, revealing and realizing its divine essence.

It is to this end that we have been scattered across the six continents—so that we may come in contact with the "sparks of holiness" that await redemption in every corner of the globe. So that a printing press in Boston should print a work of Torah learning on paper manufactured by a Pennsylvania mill from a tree which grew in Oregon. So that a forest clearing in Poland should serve as the site for a wandering Jew's prayers, and that a scientific theory developed in a British university should aid a mystic in his appreciation of the divine wisdom inherent in the natural world.

---

1   Talmud, *Pesachim* 87b.

THE THREE WEEKS AND TISHAH B'AV (10)   271

And the holier the spark, the deeper it lies buried. The kabbalists employ the analogy of a collapsed wall—the highest stones are the ones which fall the farthest. By the same token, when G-d invested His will in His creation, He caused its loftiest elements to descend to the most distant and spiritually desolate corners of the earth. Hence our *galut*—our exile from the Holy Land, our subjugation to alien governments and cultures, the cessation of G-d's open and direct involvement in our lives, and our seeming abandonment to chance and fate. All this is "a descent for the sake of ascent," a mission to the most forsaken points of earth—spiritually as well as geographically—to extract the exceptionally lofty "sparks" they contain.[2]

Thus, the more painful the *galut*, the more challenging its trials, the lowlier the elements it confronts us with—the greater its rewards. Every additional minute of *galut* represents more sparks of holiness redeemed, and its every further descent brings a deeper dimension of the divine purpose to fruition.

But there comes a point at which every Jew must cry out from the very depths of his being: "Enough already! The *cholent* has been cooking long enough! We want to come home!"

---

2   Therein lies the deeper significance of the "great wealth" that was the harvest of our exile in Egypt—see *The Vegetarian Era*, pp. 71–79 above.

CHAPTER TWENTY-FOUR

The Fifteenth of Av
Love and Rebirth

The 15th of *Av* is undoubtedly the most mysterious day of the Jewish calendar. A search of the *Shulchan Aruch* (code of Jewish law) reveals no observances or customs for this date, except for the instruction to increase one's study of Torah, since at this time of the year the nights begin to grow longer and "the night was created for study." And the Talmud tells us that many years ago the "daughters of Jerusalem would go dance in the vineyards" on the 15th of *Av*, and "whoever did not have a wife would go there" to find himself a bride.

And this is the day which the Talmud considers the greatest festival of the year, with Yom Kippur a close second!

Indeed, the 15th of *Av* cannot but be a mystery. As the "full moon" of the tragic month of *Av*, it is the festival of the future redemption, a day whose essence is unknowable to our unredeemed selves.

Yet also the unknowable is ours to seek and explore, as we shall do in the three essays of this chapter. *The Day of the Breaking of the Ax* approaches the mystery of *Av* 15 by examining a number of events which occurred on this day. *The Dancing Maidens of Jerusalem* sees in the Talmud's account of their match-seeking dance a model for the various dimensions of our relationship with G-d. *No and Yes* charts the progress of our marriage with G-d from its Sinaitic beginnings to its messianic maturity.

THE DAY
OF THE
BREAKING
OF THE AX

The descent of the soul is for the sake of ascent.

Rabbi Schneur Zalman of Liadi

"𝔍 here were no greater festivals for the people of Israel," declared the talmudic sage Rabban Shimon ben Gamliel, "than the 15th of *Av* and Yom Kippur."[1]

The Talmud goes on to list several joyous events which occurred on the 15th day of the month of *Av*:

a) *The dying of the generation of the Exodus ceased.* Several months after the people of Israel were freed from Egyptian slavery, the incident of "the spies"[2] demonstrated their unpreparedness for the task of conquering the land of Canaan and developing it as the "Holy Land." G-d decreed that that entire generation would die out in the desert, and that their children would enter the land in their stead. After 40 years of wandering through the wilderness, the dying finally ended, and a new generation stood ready to enter the Holy Land. It was the 15th of *Av* of the year 2487 from creation (1274 BCE).

b) *The tribes of Israel were permitted to intermarry.* In order to ensure the orderly division of the Holy Land between the twelve

---

[1]   Talmud, *Taanit* 26b and 30b-31a.

[2]   Numbers chapters 13-14.

tribes of Israel, restrictions had been placed on marriages between members of two different tribes. A woman who had inherited tribal lands from her father was forbidden to marry out of her tribe, lest her children—members of their father's tribe—cause the transfer of land from one tribe to another by inheriting her estate.[3] This ordinance was binding on the generation that conquered and settled the Holy Land. When the restriction was lifted, on the 15th of *Av*, the event was considered a cause for celebration and festivity.

c) *The tribe of Benjamin was permitted to enter the community.* *Av* 15 was also the day on which the tribe of Benjamin, which had been excommunicated for its behavior in the incident of the "concubine at Gibeah,"[4] was readmitted into the community of Israel.

d) *Joshua ben Eilah opened the roads to Jerusalem.* Upon the division of the Holy Land into two kingdoms following the death of King Solomon, Jeroboam ben Nebat, ruler of the breakaway northern Kingdom of Israel, set up roadblocks to prevent his citizens from making the thrice-yearly pilgrimage to the Holy Temple in Jerusalem, capital of the southern Kingdom of Judea. These were finally removed more than 200 years later by Joshua ben Eilah, the last king of the northern kingdom, on *Av* 15, 3187 (574 BCE).

e) *The dead of Betar were allowed to be buried.* The fortress of Betar was the last holdout of the Bar Kochba rebellion against the Romans. When Betar fell on the 9th of *Av*, 3893 (133 CE), Bar Kochba and many thousands of Jews were killed. The Romans massacred the survivors of the battle with great cruelty, and would not even allow the Jews to bury their dead. When the dead of Betar were finally brought to burial on *Av* 15, 3908 (148 CE), an

---

3   Ibid., chapter 36.

4   Judges chapters 19–21.

THE FIFTEENTH OF AV (1)   277

additional blessing (*hatov veha'meitiv*) was added to the *Grace after Meals* in commemoration.

f) *"The day of the breaking of the ax."* When the Holy Temple
stood in Jerusalem, the annual cutting of firewood for the altar
was concluded on the 15th of *Av*. The event was celebrated with
feasting and rejoicing, as is the custom upon the conclusion of a
holy endeavor,[5] and included a ceremonial breaking of the axes
which gave the day its name.

These events may all be worthy of commemoration and celebration; but how do they explain Rabban Shimon's amazing statement that "There were no greater festivals for Israel"? In what way
is the 15th of *Av* greater than Passover, the day of our Exodus from
Egypt, or Shavuot, the day we received the Torah? Rabban Shimon even places it before his other "great festival," Yom Kippur!

LUNAR TIME

To understand the significance of *Av* 15, we must first examine the
workings of the Jewish calendar.

The most basic feature of our calendar is that it is primarily a
lunar calendar—a calendar whose months are set in accordance
with the phases of the moon.[6] The *Zohar* explains that the people
of Israel mark time with the moon because we are the moon of
the world. Like the moon, we know times of growth and diminution, our moments of luminous fullness alternating with moments
of obscurity and darkness. And like the moon, our every regres-

---

5   Cf. the *siyum*, a festive meal held upon the conclusion of the study of
    an entire tractate of the Talmud.
6   Exodus 12:2; *Mechilta* on verse.

sion and defeat is but a prelude to yet another rebirth, yet another renewal.[7]

At a certain point in its 29.5 day circuit of the earth (the point at which it is closest to the sun) the moon "disappears" from the nighttime sky. The night on which the moon is first visible to the earthly observer after its concealment marks the beginning of a new month on the Jewish calendar. For the next two weeks, the Jewish month grows with the moon, reaching its apex on its 15th night—the night of the full moon. There then follow two weeks of decreasing moonlight, until the night when the moon falls completely dark and the month dwindles to a close. The rebirth of the moon, 29 or 30 nights after its previous birth, ushers in the next month: a new climb to fullness, followed by another descent to oblivion, followed by yet another rebirth.

Accordingly, the 15th of the Jewish month marks the high point of that month's particular contribution to Jewish life. For example: *Nissan* is the month of redemption, and it was on the first day of *Nissan* that the process of our liberation from Egypt began; but the results of this process were fully manifest only on the 15th of *Nissan*, with our actual exodus from Egypt. So it is on the 15th of *Nissan* that we celebrate the festival of Passover and experience the divine gift of freedom through the observances of the *seder*.

Another example is the month of *Tishrei*. On the 1st of *Tishrei* (Rosh Hashanah) we crown G-d as king of the universe, re-dedicating the entirety of creation to the purpose for which it was created and evoking in G-d the desire to continue to create and sustain it. But the celebration of the divine coronation is eclipsed by the days of solemnity and awe which occupy the first part of

---

7   *Zohar* 1:236b. See our chapter on "The Month" in vol. 1 of this series, pp. 149–178.

THE FIFTEENTH OF AV (1)   279

Tishrei, and comes out in the open in the joyous festival of Sukkot, which commences on the 15th of the month. (This is the deeper significance of the verse, "Sound the *shofar* on the moon's renewal, which is concealed until the day of our festival."[8] The *shofar*, whose trumpet-like blast signifies our "coronation" of the Almighty, is sounded on the 1st of *Tishrei*, the day of the moon's renewal; but like the moon itself, the experience remains "concealed" and largely unexpressed until "the day of our festival"—Sukkot, on the 15th of *Tishrei*.)

The same is true of each of the twelve months of the Jewish year. Each month possesses a character and quality uniquely its own, which undergoes a cycle of diminution and growth, concealment and expression, reaching its climax on the 15th of the month.

THE REBOUND

Therein lies the specialness of the 15th of *Av*.

The greater the momentum of an object's plunge down a mountainside, the greater the impetus that carries it up the next mountain; the further an arrow is pulled back on the bow, the greater the force that will carry it forward when it is let fly. This basic law of physical nature also governs the flow of lunar time and the spiritual qualities it enfolds: the lower the descent, the loftier the ascent to follow.

Hence, the month of *Av* must indeed possess the greatest 15th of them all. For what darker eclipse is there than the one preceding the full moon of *Av*?

The latter half of *Tammuz* and the first days of *Av* mark a breakdown in the very heart of the universe and the onset of a spiritual

---

8   Psalms 81:4, as per Talmud, *Rosh Hashanah* 8a.

winter from which we have yet to emerge. On the 17th of *Tammuz* in the year 3829 from creation (69 CE), the lunar orbit of Jewish life swung into the steepest decline of its 4,000-year history. On that day the walls of Jerusalem were breached by the Roman armies; for the next three weeks, from *Tammuz* 17 to *Av* 9 (observed to this day as three weeks of mourning), the enemy steadily advanced through Jerusalem, invaded the Holy Temple, and, on the 9th of *Av*, set it aflame.[9]

The destruction of the Temple was but the physical counterpart of a deeper, spiritual loss. The Holy Temple in Jerusalem was the seat of G-d's manifest presence in our world—the source of everything spiritual and G-dly in our lives and the focus of our efforts to implement the divine purpose in creation of "making a dwelling for G-d in the physical world." Its destruction marked the withdrawal of the direct and open relationship between G-d and His creation, and the onset of a state of *galut*—a hiding of the divine face, a shrouding of the true, underlying reality of creation behind the mask of the corporeal and fragmented world we experience today.

And yet, the greater the descent, the greater the ascent which springs from it. The great darkness of the latter days of *Tammuz* and the first days of *Av* carries the seeds for an equally great "full moon" on the 15th of *Av*—a full moon that represents the perfect and harmonious world of Moshiach which is the product and outgrowth of our long and bitter *galut*.

---

9   Av 9 is also the date of the destruction of the First Temple in the year 3338 (423 BCE) and numerous other calamities in Jewish history (see below in text).

The Events

Therein lies the significance of the various joyful events recounted by the Talmud as having occurred on the 15th of *Av*: They each mark a step in the climb out of the descent of *Av* 9.

The destruction of the Temple on *Av* 9 was preceded by another tragic event on the very same date many centuries earlier. It was on the eve of *Av* 9 that the twelve spies sent by Moses returned from their reconnaissance of the Holy Land and dissuaded the people of Israel from settling the land, causing G-d to decree that the generation of the Exodus would die out in the desert.

Indeed, the two events are deeply interrelated. Our sages tell us that if Moses' generation would have merited to enter the Land of Israel and to build the Holy Temple in Jerusalem, it would have been an eternal edifice, inviolable and indestructible. The goal of a "dwelling place for G-d in the physical world" would have been fully and perfectly realized, avoiding the need for any subsequent regressions or descents.[10] Thus, the events of that *Av* 9 in the desert were the source and harbinger of the destruction and *galut* which the day eventually wrought.

So when the dying of the generation of the Exodus ceased on *Av* 15,[11] this also marked the beginnings of the "ascent" of *Av*. A

---

10 See Talmud, *Sotah* 9a; *Megalleh Amukot, Ofan* 185; *Ohr HaChaim* on Deuteronomy 1:37 and 3:25; *Ohr HaTorah, Va'etchanan*, pp. 65, 93 and 2201.

11 According to the Jerusalem Talmud (*Taanit* 4), the deaths actually ceased on *Av* 9, but the people of Israel were not aware of this until the 15th, which is why the 15th was made a day of celebration. This is consistent with the significance of the 15th as the apex of the month. The moon, of course, is always full; the "full moon" is the point in its cycle at which its fullness is *visible* to us and we maximally enjoy its light. By the same token, the descents and ascents of Jewish history are descents and ascents only *in our perception and our experience* of our closeness to G-d. In essence, however, there are no descents, for even on the 9th of

new generation stood poised to enter the land and lay the foundations for renewal and reconstruction.

And when the barriers between the tribes were removed, allowing their members to unite in marriage with one another, another element of the "descent" was being rectified. Our sages tell us that the primary cause for the destruction of the Temple was divisiveness within the community of Israel. Accordingly, the key to the ascent of redemption is the fostering of unity and harmony amongst us. Such is also the significance of another two of the special events associated with *Av* 15: The reacceptance of the errant tribe of Benjamin into the community, and the removal of the roadblocks which had rent the people of Israel into two nations and had prevented the Holy Temple from serving as the unifying force between brothers torn apart by political strife.

The fall of Betar on *Av* 9, which spelled the end of the last significant effort to free the Land of Israel from Roman rule, was the culmination of the tragedy of the destruction of the Holy Temple and the exile of Israel on that same date a generation earlier. The first respite from this crushing blow to the Jewish people — the bringing to burial of the dead of Betar on the 15th of *Av* — is another example of how *Av* 15 achieves the redemption and rectification of the 9th of *Av*.

SHATTERED IRONS

The manner in which the conclusion of the wood-cutting for the Temple service was celebrated on *Av* 15 is yet another manifestation

---

Av, at the very moment of the destruction, our relationship with G-d was not diminished in the slightest (see *The Intimate Estrangement*, pp. 253–261 above, and *The Sixteenth Increment*, in vol. I, pp. 151–159 of this series).

THE FIFTEENTH OF AV (1) 283

of the significance of the day. The breaking of axes expresses the ultimate purpose of the Holy Temple, whose destruction we mourn on the 9th of *Av* and whose rebuilding will herald the harmonious world of Moshiach.

Why break the axes? Why not store them for next year's cutting? Because the ax represents the very antithesis of what the altar, and the Temple as a whole, stood for.

Regarding the making of the altar, G-d had instructed: "When you build a stone altar for Me, do not build it of cut stone; for if your sword has been lifted upon it, you have profaned it"; "Do not lift iron upon it... The altar of G-d shall be built of whole stones."[12] If any metal implement as much as touched a stone, that stone was rendered unfit for use in the making of the Altar.

Our sages explain: "Iron was created to shorten the life of man, and the altar was created to lengthen the life of man; so it is not fitting that that which shortens should be lifted upon that which lengthens."[13] Iron, the instrument of war and destruction, has no place in the making of the instrument whose function is to bring eternal peace and harmony to the world.

AWAITING THE LIGHT

Of course, these events were only first glimmers of the full moon of Moshiach—a full moon which has yet to emerge from the darkness that envelops it. So today, Av 15 is a relatively minor event in our experience of the yearly cycle. We mark the day, but without the grandeur of Passover, the joy of Sukkot, or the exultation of Purim. For unlike these festivals, whose "full moon" we have already

---

12 Exodus 20:22; Deuteronomy 27:5–6.
13 Talmud, *Middot* 3:4.

experienced, the luminance of *Av* 15 has yet to shine forth. We are still in *galut*, still in the dark stretch of this cycle, still climbing out of the descent in which we have been plunged by the events of *Tammuz* 17–*Av* 9.

But the date is already fixed in our calendar as the greatest "15th" of them all. And with the imminent coming of Moshiach, the true import of the "day of the breaking of the ax" will come to glorious light, and the 15th of *Av* will be truly revealed as our greatest festival.

THE DANCING
MAIDENS
OF JERUSALEM

Your G-d shall rejoice with you as a groom
rejoices with his bride.   Lecha Dodi hymn

The closing pages of the talmudic tractate *Taanit* contain a description of how matchmaking was conducted in the Land of Israel many centuries ago:

> There were no greater festivals for Israel than the 15th of Av and Yom Kippur. On these days the daughters of Jerusalem would go out… and dance in the vineyards. What would they say? "Young man, raise your eyes and see which you select for yourself…"
>
> What would the beautiful ones among them say? "Look for beauty, for a woman is for beauty."
>
> What would those of prestigious lineage say? "Look for family, for a woman is for children."
>
> What would the ugly ones say? "Make your acquisition for the sake of Heaven, as long as you decorate us with jewels."[1]

As the Talmud and its accompanying commentaries go on to explain, the choice of these two dates as a time to seek and find a marriage partner is significant: Yom Kippur and the 15th of *Av* are the respective betrothal and marriage days of G-d and Israel. Yom

---

1   Talmud, *Taanit* 26b and 31a.

Kippur—the day on which the Second Tablets were given to Moses, marking the fulfillment of the covenant at Mount Sinai[2]—is the day of Israel's betrothal to G-d. *Av* 15—the day that represents the rebirth which follows the great fall of the Holy Temple's destruction on the 9th of *Av*[3]—celebrates the ultimate consummation of our marriage with the final redemption of Moshiach.[4]

This also explain the deeper significance of the three different types of maidens the above talmudic passage describes, and the manner in which they called out to their prospective grooms. For the marriage of G-d and Israel also includes these three categories of brides. The souls of Israel include "beautiful" souls, souls "of prestigious lineage," and "ugly" souls, each of whom contribute their own unique dimension to our relationship with G-d.

Two Types of Love

"You shall love G-d"[5] is a crucial component of our relationship with the Almighty. Aside from the fact that loving G-d is one of the 613 *mitzvot* (divine commandments) of the Torah, it is also a prerequisite for the proper observance of all the other commandments. *Mitzvot* which are not motivated by a love of G-d are

---

2   See the essays *The 120-Day Version of the Human Story* (vol. 2 of this series, pp. 37–43), and *Daughters Near and Far* (vol. 2, pp. 135–147).

3   See the previous essay, *The Day of the Breaking of the Ax* (pp. 275–284).

4   According to Torah law, the marital union between husband and wife consists of two stages: *kidushin* ("consecration" or "betrothal") and *nissu'in* ("marriage"). As will be explained in the next essay (*No and Yes*, pp. 291–294), the giving of the Torah at Mount Sinai constituted the "betrothal" in the marriage of G-d and Israel, while the ultimate consummation of our union awaits the rebuilding of our eternal home in the age of Moshiach.

5   Deuteronomy 6:5.

THE FIFTEENTH OF AV (2)   287

performed mechanically and erratically; only one who loves G-d serves Him in a manner that is both integral and enduring.[6]

The chassidic classic *Tanya* explains that there are two types of love, and thus two ways that the *mitzvah* to love G-d can be fulfilled. There is a love that is generated by the person's own mind and heart, when a person meditates upon the beloved's greatness and desirability and thereby develops feelings of love and attraction. By contemplating the greatness of G-d's works, and studying what G-d has revealed about Himself to us in His Torah and meditating upon these truths, one develops a feeling of love toward G-d— a desire to approach G-d's great and magnificent being, to unite and become one with it. Indeed, this is one of the primary functions of prayer, "the service of the heart"[7]: to generate a feeling of love for the Creator by meditating on His greatness and majesty.

But also the person who does not succeed in creating a "self-generated" love by these means, can still attain a love of G-d. For there also exists another type of love: a love that we have not created ourselves, but which resides in our heart from birth as a natural bond and attraction implanted in us by virtue of who and what we are. We each possess such an inborn love for G-d as "an inheritance from our forefathers."[8] Abraham, the first Jew, was the very embodiment of divine love,[9] and G-d rewarded him with the gift of "fatherhood"—with the ability to bequeath this love to his

---

6   *Tanya*, chapter 4.

7   Deuteronomy 11:13, as per Talmud, *Taanit* 2a. One of the meanings of the Hebrew word for prayer, *tefilah*, is "attachment."

8   *Tanya*, chapter 18.

9   In G-d's words to Isaiah, "Abraham, who loves Me" (Isaiah 41:8). *Sefer HaBahir* states: "The attribute of *chesed* (divine benevolence and love) said to G-d: 'Master of the Universe! From the day that Abraham is in the world, there is no need for me to do my work, as Abraham fills my role'" (quoted in *Pardes*, portal 22, chapter 4).

descendants. So each and every one of us has Abraham's love of G-d encoded in his or her spiritual genes. As with all inborn characteristics, this love may be buried in the subconscious, stifled by the dross of material life; but it can always be wakened and called upon to stimulate and vitalize our observance of the *mitzvot*.

The advantages of the second type of love are obvious. Every one of us possesses it—and the ability to realize it—regardless of the extent of our cognitive and meditative skills or the degree of our spiritual sensitivity. Furthermore, a self-generated love will always be limited by the finite capacities of the mind and heart which have created it, and will fluctuate in accordance with the person's mental and emotional state at any given moment; our inborn love, being divinely granted, is infinite and unequivocal.

But there are advantages to self-generated love as well. Though lesser in essence and scope, it is more keenly felt, more exuberantly experienced. For such is our nature: What we create is more precious to us than the most valuable endowment; what we conceive of ourselves is more relevant and real to us than what is learned from the greatest teacher. So although the stimulation of our inherited love for G-d would suffice to drive our observance of the *mitzvot*, we should nevertheless strive to enhance our relationship with Him with the ecstasy and passion that only a love created by our own faculties can bring. In the words of our sages, "Although a fire came down [on the Altar] from the heavens, it is imperative to also kindle a man-made fire."[10]

---

10   Talmud, *Eruvin* 63a.

Three Brides

Therein lies the deeper significance of the Talmud's description of how "the beautiful ones," "those of prestigious lineage," and "the ugly ones" among the daughters of Jerusalem conducted their courtship dance in the vineyards on *Av* 15.

The dancing maidens of Jerusalem calling out their virtues to their prospective bridegrooms echo the call of the souls of Israel to their Divine Groom. Among these are the beautiful souls, those who have achieved a best-of-both-worlds perfection in their love of the Almighty: a passionate, self-generated love set upon the immutable foundation of inherited love. "A woman is for beauty," call these souls to G-d. Take us as your bride, and You will be rewarded by the pleasure You derive when Your creations realize the potential for perfection You have invested in them.

Then there are the souls of "prestigious lineage." We cannot offer you the flawless beauty of our perfect sisters, they call to G-d, but we have unearthed the hereditary love You have implanted in us. "A woman is for children": Our relationship might not, as of yet, yield beauty, but it will bear fruit—the *mitzvot* generated by our natural love for You. For is not Your ultimate purpose in creation that Your creations fulfill your will? Our love for you might not excite our senses and illuminate our lives, but we offer You the rewards of family—the good deeds that are the tangible, enduring offspring of Israel's commitment to her Creator.[11]

And the ugly ones? Those who have neither roused their minds and hearts to desire their Creator, nor wakened their hereditary loyalty to Him? Those who never generated a self-created love, and whose inborn love lies dormant under a squalid veneer of apathy

---

11   In the words of the sages, "The offspring of the righteous are good deeds" (*Tanchuma*, Rashi, and *Lekach Tov* to Genesis 6:9).

and iniquity? They cry: "Make Your acquisition for the sake of Heaven!"

"Do for *Your* sake, if not for ours,"[12] call the "ugly" souls of Israel. Take us as Your own, despite our appearance, because only You know what lies behind our appearance, and only You know the truth of what You can inspire in us. For You know that, in truth, "The daughters of Israel are beautiful, it is only that poverty obscures their beauty."[13] You know that our "ugliness" is not our true essence, but imposed upon us by the spiritual poverty of *galut*.

If we have failed to realize our potential for beauty and fruitfulness, then it is left to You to "decorate us with jewels"—to shower us with the gifts that will awaken our quintessential bond to You and bring to light our innate perfection.[14]

---

12   From the *selichot* prayers.

13   Talmud, *Nedarim* 66a.

14   The three categories described here correspond to the *tzaddik*, *beinoni*, and *rasha* as classified in the first eighteen chapters of *Tanya*.

THE FIFTEENTH OF AV (3)   291

NO
AND
YES

In this world, it was a betrothal — as it is
written, "I shall betroth you to Me forever"...[1]
But in the days of Moshiach there shall be the
marriage — as it is written, "Your husband,
your maker."[2]

Midrash Rabbah, Shemot 15:30

e inhabit a reality defined by two basic states: being and
naught. A thing either is or is not, is either manifest or
repressed, in motion or at rest, positive or negative. Even the most
complex phenomena are the sum of so many gradations of presence and absence: After all is said and done, everything boils down
to the sum of so many times "yes" and so many times "no." The
"nos" delineate the parameters of a thing, establishing what it is
not, while the "yesses" fill the space within these parameters with
the essence of what the thing is.

The binary nature of creation is a reflection of the fact that the
Torah, the "blueprint" into which "G-d looked and created the
world,"[3] is divided into positive and negative realms. "I am G-d
your G-d"— the most fundamental of the positive commandments (*mitzvot assei*)— is complemented by "You shall have no
other gods before Me"— the essence of all divine prohibitions

---

[1]   Hosea 2:21.
[2]   Isaiah 54:5.
[3]   *Midrash Rabbah, Bereishit* 1:2

(*mitzvot lo taasseh*).[4] "Love your fellow as yourself" is the positive counterpart to "You shall not hate your brother in your heart."[5] The Torah commands to create life and forbids destroying it; it commands to aid the needy and forbids pressing them for their debts; it instructs to eat unleavened bread on Passover, and forbids all leavened foods for the duration of the festival; and so on.[6]

The institution of marriage, as defined and legislated by the Torah, also includes both an "affirmative" and a "negative" component. According to Torah law, a marriage consists of two distinct steps.

The first step is the *kidushin* ("consecration," also called *eirusin*,[7] "betrothal"). The groom gives the bride something of value (by common practice, a ring), in return for which the bride consecrates herself to him, with the effect that "she becomes forbidden to the rest of the world."[8] From this point on, for another man to have relations with her constitutes adultery, and to dissolve the *kidushin* requires a *get* (writ of divorce), as for a full-fledged marriage.

Of course, the purpose of marriage is not merely to preclude "the rest of the world," but to effect a union between two people. This is the function of the second step, the *nissu'in* ("marriage")—

---

4   The first two of the Ten Commandments, Exodus 20:2-3; see *Tanya* chapter 20 ff.

5   Leviticus 19:17-18.

6   Genesis 1:28; Exodus 20:13; Deuteronomy 15:8; Exodus 22:24, 12:18, and 13:3.

7   The term *eirusin* is often erroneously applied to an "engagement," which is merely the pledging of the two parties to marry at some future date. On one occasion, the Rebbe urged that this error—which can also be *halachically* problematic—be corrected, and that engagements should be referred to only by their correct Hebrew term, *shidduchin*.

8   Talmud, *Kidushin* 2b.

THE FIFTEENTH OF AV (3)   293

achieved by the *chupah* (wedding canopy), *yichud* (private seclusion), and *sheva berachot* (seven marriage benedictions)—which unites them as husband and wife.

In other words, the *kidushin* defines the parameters of the relationship, clearing a "space" within which it might exist, while the *nissu'in* fills this space with the essence of the relationship itself.

MANNING THE BORDERS

As we said, *kidushin* and *nissu'in* are two distinct phases in the marriage process. Indeed, originally, the *kidushin* would be held at an earlier date, after which the bride continued to live with her parents as the couple prepared for the *nissu'in*, which was usually held one year later. (It was only in recent centuries, when the tribulations of exile undermined the stability of Jewish life and often caused the sudden dispersion of communities, that it was deemed unwise to create a marriage-bond between a man and woman who would not actually be living together. Hence the present-day practice of conducting the *nissu'in* immediately following the *kidushin*, passing through both stages of marriage in a single ceremony.)

Our sages tell us that at Mount Sinai, where G-d revealed Himself to us and gave us the Torah, we consecrated ourselves to Him as His bride. This, however, was only the *kidushin* stage of our marriage. Our bond with Him will be complete only in the era of Moshiach, at which time G-d and Israel will unite in *nissu'in*.

This is not to say that our relationship with G-d today is an exclusively "negative" one—as noted above, our commitment to G-d includes "positive commandments" as well as "prohibitions." But today we are only capable of establishing the parameters of the relationship, not of realizing its essential content. Today, our relationship with G-d is defined by our commitment to Him and by our striving to unite with Him, but without the tangible experience of the union itself. We yearn for G-d as a bride yearns for her betrothed, but whose most rapturous feelings are but a faint intimation of post-marriage love.

For thirty-three centuries, we have been creating the "space" of our marriage with G-d and zealously defending its borders. We have remained faithful to Him in the face of all the cultures and "isms" that have sought to seduce us. We have established our identity as His people, consecrated to Him alone. Now we are ready for the real thing—for an actual experience of the divine as the most intimate truth of our lives.

CHAPTER TWENTY-FIVE

Elul

Compassion and Introspection

"Though summer still lingered and the day was bright and sunny, there was a change in the air. One already smelled the *Elul*-scent; a *teshuvah*-wind was blowing. Everyone grew more serious, more thoughtful... All awaited the call of the *shofar*, the first blast that would announce the opening of the gates of the month of compassion."

So describes the sixth Lubavitcher Rebbe, Rabbi Yosef Yitzchak Schneersohn, the onset of the month of *Elul* in the town of Lubavitch. A month of trepidation on account of the approaching "days of awe" of Rosh Hashanah and Yom Kippur; but also a gentle month, softened by the reconciliatory prophesies of the "seven of consolation" and the vibes of divine compassion that linger from the time that Moses spent the whole of *Elul* on the summit of Mount Sinai procuring G-d's wholehearted forgiveness for Israel's first sin.

As the last month of the year, *Elul* is a time for review and stocktaking for the closing year, as well as a time of preparation for the coming year. Throughout the month, at the close of the weekday morning prayers, the *shofar* sounds its call to *teshuvah* (repentance), urging us to ready ourselves for the divine coronation and universal day of judgment on Rosh Hashanah. In our letters to family and friends we include the wishes, "May you be inscribed and sealed for a good year." And in the last week of Elul, we rise at an early hour to recite the solemn *selichot* prayers. *Teshuvah* is in the air.

In our chapter on *Elul*, <u>A Haven in Time</u> discusses the month's role as a "city of refuge" for the spiritual refugees of life. In <u>Month of the Bride</u>, we examine *Elul*'s astral sign of "virgin" (*betulah*), and how it relates to the dynamics of the marriage of G-d and Israel.

The closing essay of our series redefines the "appointments in time" that have been the topic of all our previous chapters. For eleven months of the year, touching base with a day's spiritual content means distancing oneself, to a greater or lesser degree, from its material surface. Not so the month of *Elul*. Analyzing Rabbi Schneur Zalman of Liadi's famous analogy, <u>The King in the Field</u> introduces the "spiritual workday"—a phenomenon unique to the closing month of the year.

See also the following essays: *Shammai's Shabbat* (vol. 1 of this series, pp. 219-224) and *The 120-Day Version of the Human Story* (vol. 2, pp. 37-43)

A
HAVEN IN
TIME

Three cities you shall set aside within the
land... and they shall be for all murderers to
escape there. This is the case of the murderer
who shall flee there and live: One who strikes
his fellow unintentionally...
Deuteronomy 19:2–4

$\mathcal{T}$he unintentional murderer is not innocent. He is guilty of criminal negligence — negligence which has resulted in the destruction of a life. But for his sake, G-d commanded that "cities of refuge" should be established in the Holy Land. Cities to serve him both as a haven and as a place of punitive exile; cities to which he is banished to atone for his deed as well as to rebuild his life anew.

There are cities of refuge in space, and there is a city of refuge in time. And while the spatial cities of refuge await the coming of Moshiach and the restoration of Torah law in the Holy Land to be reinstated, the haven in time that G-d has established for us in the calendar is there for us at all times, under all conditions.

This haven in time is the month of *Elul*—the last month of the Jewish year and the month which leads to the "days of awe" that commence the new year. This is alluded to in one of the verses which discuss the law of the "cities of refuge." The central words in the verse, "And for one who did not lie in wait [to kill premeditatedly], but G-d has caused it to happen to him, I shall establish

ELUL (1)   299

for you a place to which he can flee"[1] are *inah le'yado vesamti lach*; master kabbalist Rabbi Isaac Luria points out that the first letters of these words (*alef, lamed, vav, lamed*) spell the word "*Elul*."[2]

THE HISTORY OF ELUL

On the morning of *Elul* 1, 2448 (1313 BCE) Moses ascended Mount Sinai, for the third time in as many months. Moses' first ascent was on the 7th of *Sivan*, a day after the revelation at Sinai, to receive the Torah from G-d; but when he descended the mountain 40 days later, on the 17th of *Tammuz*, he found the people of Israel worshipping a calf of molten gold. Upon witnessing Israel's betrayal of her marriage with G-d, Moses destroyed the "marriage contract," smashing the Tablets of the Covenant upon which G-d had inscribed the Ten Commandments.

After destroying the Golden Calf, punishing the idolaters, and rebuking the errant nation, Moses returned to the summit of Sinai for a second 40 days—from the 19th of *Tammuz* to the 29th of *Av*—to plead on behalf of his people for G-d's forgiveness. On the 29th of *Av*, G-d said to Moses:

> *Hew for yourself two tablets of stone like the first; and I will inscribe upon these tablets the words which were on the first tablets, which you broke.*
>
> *Be ready for morning. In the morning, you shall ascend Mount Sinai, and present yourself to Me there, on the top of the mountain.*[3]

---

1   Exodus 21:13
2   *Shaar HaPesukim, Parashat Mishpatim.*
3   Exodus 34:1-2.

Moses' third 40 days on Mount Sinai included the whole of the month of *Elul* and the first ten days of *Tishrei*. In this period, G-d revealed to Moses the greatest secret of creation: the "thirteen attributes of divine mercy" which are the source of the power of *teshuvah*—the power to rectify past wrongs and failings and even exploit them as a force for previously unimaginable achievements.

Ever since, the month of *Elul* has been the city of refuge for all "inadvertent murderers" who seek the protection of its walls. For every transgression against the will of G-d is, by definition, an act of "inadvertent murder": murder, because one has violated the essence and *raison d'être* of one's own life;[4] inadvertent, because man is inherently and intrinsically good, and all evil deeds result only from a lapse of awareness of one's own true will. In the words of our sages, "A person does not sin unless a spirit of insanity has entered into him."[5]

The twenty-nine days of *Elul* offer an isle in time, a sanctum for introspection and self-assessment, for atonement and rehabilitation. It is a place to which we might flee from our subjugation to the struggles and entanglements of material life to audit our spiritual accounts and restore the sovereignty of our true will over our lives. It is a month in which to resolve that, henceforth, no accidental iniquity will mar the quintessential goodness of our soul.

---

4   Cf. Deuteronomy 4:4: "And you who cleave to G-d are all alive today"; ibid. 30:20: "Love the L-rd your G-d... for He is your life..."; and Talmud *Berachot* 18a-b: "The wicked, even in their lifetimes, are considered dead... The righteous, even in death, are considered alive."

5   Talmud, *Sotah* 3a. See citation from Maimonides in vol. 2 of this series, on p. 47.

ELUL (2)   301

MONTH
OF THE
BRIDE

I am to my beloved, and my beloved is to me.

Song of Songs 6:3

§ n every relationship, there are times when the "male" or giving partner takes the initiative, and times when the "female" or receiving partner is the first to express her feelings and thereby stimulate the feelings of her partner.

The question of who takes the initiative has a profound effect on the nature of the relationship. For though the end result is that both of them express their love for each other, the initiating partner determines the nature of the other's response. When initiated by the giving partner, the response stimulated in the recipient will likewise be a "masculine" response; when initiated by the recipient, the giver's response will also be of a "feminine" nature, for it will be influenced and shaped by the source of its arousal.

In Song of Songs, which explores the relationship between G-d and Israel through the metaphor of the love between a bride and her groom, we find expressions of both male-initiated and female-initiated love. In one verse, the narratress proclaims, "My beloved is to me, and I am to him." In another, she says, "I am to my beloved, and my beloved is to me."[1]

There are times when the Almighty showers us with love and kindness, arousing in us a response in kind ("My beloved is to me,

---

1   Song of Songs 2:16 and 6:3.

and I am to him"). But there are also times in which we take the initiative, expressing our love and devotion to G-d despite His apparent distance from us, thereby awakening His love for us ("I am to my beloved, and my beloved is to me").

It may be argued that the divinely-initiated love produces a higher and loftier love than the love which is initiated by ourselves. When the initial arousal comes from G-d, it is a show of love that is as infinite and sublime as its source, arousing in us feelings that we could never have produced ourselves. Nevertheless, such a love cannot be said to be truly our own. We have been overwhelmed by something that is infinitely greater than ourselves, and our own response is likewise "larger than life," bearing little relation to who and what we are in our natural state.

On the other hand, the love we generate ourselves may be less magnificent and glorious, but it is a deeper and truer love. It is an integral love—a love that comes from within and expresses our deepest yearnings. And when we awaken such a love in ourselves, G-d responds in kind, showing us an integral, intimate love—a love that embraces us as we are, rather than transporting us to sublime yet alien peaks of spirituality and transcendence.

THE ACRONYM

The month of *Elul* is a time of special closeness between the Divine Groom and His bride Israel. This is alluded to by the fact that, in Hebrew, the first letters of the verse "I am to my beloved and my beloved is to me" (*ani ledodi v'dodi li*) spell the word *Elul*.

It is significant that the acronym for *Elul* comes from the verse that describes a love that is initiated by the bride, rather than the verse in which the initial show of love comes from the groom. For despite its designation as a time for special closeness with G-d,

ELUL (2)

Elul is a most "ordinary" month, conspicuously devoid of festivals and holy days. In other words, *Elul* is not a time in which we are lifted up from our daily routine to the more spiritual state of a festival day. Rather, it is a time in which we remain in our natural environment as material beings inhabiting a material life.[2]

For the month of *Elul*, whose astral sign is the sign of *betulah* ("virgin"), is the month of the bride. *Elul* is a time when the initiative comes from our side of the relationship, and the divine response to our love is one that relates to us as finite, material beings and embraces our natural self and personality.

---

2   See next essay, *The King in the Field*, pp. 304–313.

THE KING IN THE FIELD

There is a profit in the land over all else, for the king is sustained by the field.

Ecclesiastes 5:8[1]

 lul, the last month of the Jewish year, is a time of paradox— a time of what might be termed, "spiritual workdays."

The Jewish calendar distinguishes between two general qualities of time: "mundane" (*chol*) and "holy" (*kodesh*). Ordinary workdays are "mundane" portions of time; Shabbat and the festivals are examples of "holy" time. On "holy" days, we disengage ourselves from the material involvements of life to devote ourselves to the spiritual pursuits of study and prayer. These are also days enriched with special spiritual resources (rest on Shabbat, freedom on Passover, awe on Rosh Hashanah, etc.), each providing its unique quality to the journeyer through calendar and life.[2]

In the latter respect, the month of *Elul* resembles the "holy" portions of the calendar. *Elul* is a haven in time, a "city of refuge" from the ravages of material life;[3] a time to audit one's spiritual accounts and assess the year gone by; a time to prepare for the "days of awe" of Rosh Hashanah and Yom Kippur by repenting the failings of the past and resolving for the future; a time to increase

---

[1] As per ibn Ezra on verse.
[2] See *Appointments in Time* in vol. 1 of this series, pp. 38–45.
[3] See *A Haven in Time*, pp. 298–300 above.

ELUL (3) 305

in Torah study, prayer, and charitable activities.[4] *Elul* is the opportune time for all this because it is a month in which G-d relates to us in a more open and compassionate manner than He does in the other months of the year. In the terminology of kabbalah, it is a time when G-d's "thirteen attributes of mercy" illuminate His relationship with us.[5]

Yet unlike Shabbat and the festivals, the days of *Elul* are workdays. On Shabbat, the Torah commands us to cease all physically constructive work (*melachah*). The festivals, too, are days on which *melachah* is forbidden.[6] Regarding the month of *Elul*, however, there are no such restrictions. The transcendent activities of *Elul* are conducted amidst our workday lives in the field, shop, or office.[7]

---

4   The Talmud's *Ethics of the Fathers* defines these as the three "pillars" of life: "The world stands on three things: Torah, divine service [i.e., prayer], and deeds of kindness." In Hebrew, the word *Elul* forms the acronym for each of three biblical phrases, alluding to these three activities: "I am to my beloved, and my beloved is to me" (*ani ledodi v'dodi li*—Song of Songs 6:3) refers to the bonding of the soul to G-d through prayer. "A man to his fellow and gifts to the poor" (*ish lerei'eihu umatanot la'evyonim*—Esther 9:22) is a reference to charity. And Elul's role as a "city of refuge," alluded to in the verse, "...has caused it to happen to him, I shall establish for you..." (*inah le'yado vesamti lach*—Exodus 21:13) is a reference to Torah Study, which likewise serves as a "city of refuge" (Talmud, *Makot* 10a). *Elul* also is an acronym of "[And G-d shall circumcise] your heart and the heart [of your children]" (*et levavcha ve'et levav*—Deuteronomy 30:6), a reference to the atmosphere of *teshuvah* (repentance) which pervades the month.

5   As established by Moses' third 40-day period on the mountain—*A Haven in Time,* above, and the essay *The 120-Day Version of the Human Story* in vol. 2 of this series, pp. 37–43.

6   The laws prohibiting work on Shabbat apply, with several exceptions, to the festivals as well.

7   The Jewish calendar contains other spiritually enriched days on which work is not forbidden to the extent that it is on Shabbat and the festivals, such as *Rosh Chodesh* (the opening day or days of the month), the

Rabbi Schneur Zalman of Liadi explains the paradox of Elul with the following analogy: The king's usual place is in the capital city, in the royal palace. Anyone wishing to approach the king must go through the appropriate channels in the palace bureaucracy and gain the approval of a succession of secretaries and ministers. He must journey to the capital and pass through the many gates, corridors, and antechambers that lead to the throne room. His presentation must be meticulously prepared, and he must adhere to an exacting code of dress, speech, and mannerism upon entering into the royal presence.

However, there are times when the king comes out to the fields outside the city. At such times, anyone can approach him, and the king receives them all with a smiling face and a radiant countenance. The peasant behind his plow has access to the king in a manner unavailable to the highest ranking minister in the royal court when the king is in the palace.

The month of *Elul*, says Rabbi Schneur Zalman of Liadi, is when the king is in the field.[8]

THE FIELD

Bread is the "staff of life" that "sustains the heart of man."[9] There was a time when most everyone plowed, sowed, and harvested the

---

intermediate *Chol HaMoed* days of Passover and Sukkot, the rabbinical festivals of Chanukah and Purim, etc. But each of these carry some restriction of *melachah*. On the other hand, the 29 days of *Elul* (with the exception of the four *Shabbatot* the month contains) are full-fledged workdays, carrying no *halachic* restriction on the extent of one's creative involvement with the physical world.

8 *Likutei Torah*, *Re'eh* 32b.
9 Leviticus 26:26; Psalms 104:15.

grain that sustained themselves and their families. But also today, when only a small percentage of us farm the land, we all labor for bread. Everyone works in the field—be it the wheatfield or cornfield, or the field of banking, steelmaking, medicine, or advertising.

Indeed, the field is the prototype employed by Torah law to define the "work" that distinguishes between the holy and mundane days of the calendar. The talmudic passage which lists the types of work forbidden on Shabbat reads:

> *The father-categories of work are forty minus one:*[10] *sowing, plowing, reaping, making sheaves, threshing, winnowing, picking the chaff from the grain, milling, sifting, kneading, baking...*[11]

Each of these activities is a "father-category" which includes many different types of work. For example, leveling the ground to make a tennis court is tantamount to "plowing"; mixing cement is a form of "kneading"; sorting laundry would fall under the category of "picking the chaff from the grain." But the prototypes that head and dominate the list of activities to be refrained from on Shabbat are labors of the field. In the words of the Talmud, "The author of the Mishnah follows the process of bread-making."[12]

For eleven months of the year, our lives alternate between the field and the palace, between the "process of bread-making" of material life and the sublime moments when we leave the field to enter into the royal presence. During the ordinary workdays we are in the field; on Shabbat and the festivals, we enter the palace. In the month of *Elul*, however, the king comes to the field.

---

10 I.e., thirty-nine.

11 Talmud, *Shabbat* 73a.

12 Ibid , 74b.

What happens when the king comes to the field? The field is not transformed into a palace, yet neither is the king any less a king when he greets the farmer in his soiled overalls. Back in the throne room, however, in the aura of sanctity that surrounds the king, the sweat and mundane toil of the field seem a million miles away. How do these two worlds meet and what happens when they do?

To understand the essence of *Elul*, we must first examine the relationship between the palace and the field—between Shabbat and the workweek, between the very concepts of "holy" and "mundane." Are they really as distant from each other as their very different faces suggest?

THE SANCTUARY

A glance at the calendar reveals that the mundane days of the year far exceed the holy. Of course, it would be extremely difficult to earn a living if the week consisted of a single workday followed by six days of Shabbat. This, however, is an outgrowth of how G-d created us, encumbering us with a host of material needs and placing us in a world that requires a great deal of plowing, sowing, and reaping (or crafting or selling) to satisfy these needs. Why did G-d so order our lives as to necessitate the investment of the bulk of our time and energy in material endeavors? How is this consistent with the mission with which He charged us at Mount Sinai—to be His "kingdom of priests and holy people"?

The answer lies in G-d's instruction to the people of Israel, following the revelation at Sinai, to construct a physical edifice to serve as a "sanctuary" for Him.[13] Fifteen materials (including gold, silver, copper, wood, flax, wool, and animal skins) are to be

---

13   Exodus 25 ff.

ELUL (3) 309

fashioned into a "dwelling for G-d in the physical world."[14] The construction of the Sanctuary represents the purpose of our soul's placement within a physical body and world: to imbue our material involvements with a sanctity of purpose, so that our workday life becomes a "home" for G-d, an abode for His goodness and perfection. Indeed, the Talmud tells us that when a soul ascends to heaven upon the completion of its earthly life, the very first question it is asked—before any questions about the fervor of its prayer or the depth of its Torah study—is, "Have you dealt faithfully in business?" In no other area of life is our purpose in this world fulfilled more than in our day-to-day material dealings.[15]

This explains the rather roundabout way by which the Torah defines the types of work from which we must desist on Shabbat. In both the 31st and the 35th chapters of Exodus, the commandment to keep Shabbat and G-d's instructions concerning the construction of the Sanctuary immediately follow each other. The Talmud explains that the juxtaposition of these two seemingly unrelated laws is to teach us that the thirty-nine creative acts which the construction of the Sanctuary necessitated are the same thirty-nine categories of work that are forbidden to us on Shabbat:

> A person is guilty of violating the Shabbat only if the work he does has a counterpart in the work of making the Sanctuary. They sowed [the herbs from which to make dyes for the tapestries—Rashi]; you, too, shall not sow [on Shabbat]. They harvested the herbs; you, too, shall not harvest. They loaded the boards from the ground onto the wagons;

---

14 *Midrash Tanchuma, Nasso* 16.

15 Talmud, *Shabbat* 31a.

you, too, shall not bring an object from a public domain into a private domain...[16]

In other words, the work forbidden on Shabbat and the festivals—the work that defines the difference between the "holy" and "mundane" days of our lives—is not mundane work at all. It is holy work—the work of forming the physical world into a home for G-d. Why, then, are the days on which this work is done regarded as the "mundane" days of our lives? And why are the days on which we are commanded to *cease* this work for the favor of purely spiritual endeavors, "holier" than the days on which this work is done?

The Lookout Tower

Indeed, the difference between the "holy" and "mundane" times of our lives is not a difference in essence, only a difference in perspective. Yet the reality of physical life is that to achieve this change of perspective, one must change the place and position from which one looks.

Beyond its mundane surface, the material world possesses a deeper truth: its potential to house the goodness and perfection of its Creator. The purpose of our workday lives is to reveal this potential—to develop the material world as a home for G-d. But on the workdays of our life, this potential is all but invisible to us, obscured by the very process that serves to bring it to light. Our very involvement with the material prevents us from experiencing its spiritual essence. To do so, we must rise above it.

A "holy" day is an elevation in the terrain of time, a lookout tower that rises above the surface of our workday lives to behold

---

16 Ibid., 49b.

ELUL (3)   311

the true essence of our world—the essence we are laboring to actualize.[17] Rising to these lookout points means interrupting our life's
work; but without these periodic glimpses from a higher, more
detached vantage point, our involvement in the material may well
become an enmeshment. Instead of sanctifying the mundane, we
may find ourselves being profaned by it.

So one day a week, and on special occasions throughout the
year, we cease our work in "the field" to gain a more transcendent
view of our workday labors. Then, when we reenter the so-called
"mundane" days of our lives, the Shabbat or festival experience lin-
gers on. Enriched with insight into the true nature of our labors,
fortified by the vision of what our involvement with the material
will ultimately achieve, our workday lives become more focused
on their goal, and less susceptible to the diversions and entanglements of the mundane.

This explains the curious manner in which the Talmud refers
to the number of categories of work forbidden on Shabbat—"The
categories of work are forty minus one." Why not simply say, "The
categories of work are thirty-nine"? The talmudic commentaries
explain that, in truth, there are forty categories of work, alluded to
by the fact that the word *melachah* ("work") appears forty times
in the Torah. Yet when we count the categories of work involved
in the construction of the Sanctuary, we find only thirty-nine.
The missing endeavor is the spiritual work in which we engage on
Shabbat—"the work of Heaven." In other words, there are actually forty elements to our work-life: our thirty-nine creative labors
within the material world, and a fortieth, spiritual element that
must pervade this work, and whose source is the spiritual "work"
of Shabbat.

---

17   In the words of our sages, "Shabbat is a taste of the World to Come"
     (Talmud, *Berachot* 57b; et al).

The King and his Bread

For eleven months of the year, our lives alternate between the holy and the mundane — between the material labor of life and the spiritual vision of that labor's objective. For eleven months of the year, we must, at regular intervals, cease our involvement with the material and rise above it in order to glimpse its soul and purpose.

The exception to this rule is the month of *Elul*. For during the month of *Elul*, the king comes to the field.

The king is the heart and soul of the nation, the embodiment of its goals and aspirations. The king, though sequestered behind the palace walls and bureaucracy, though glimpsed, if at all, through a veil of opulence and majesty, is a very real part of the farmer's field. The king is the why of the farmer's plowing, the reason for his sowing, the objective of his harvest. No farmer labors for the sake of labor. He labors to transcend the dust of which he and his field are formed, to make more of what is. He labors for his dreams. He labors for his king.

So is the king in the field an apparition out of its element? Hardly. We may not be used to seeing him here, but is not the royal heart, too, sustained by bread? His bread may be baked in the palace, its raw ingredients discreetly delivered to a back entrance; the golden tray on which it is served may in no way evoke the loamy bed from which it grew; but it is the yield of the field all the same.

The king in the field is making contact with the source of his sustenance, with the underpinnings of his sovereignty. And the field is being visited by its *raison d'être*, by its ultimate function and essence.

Shabbat is when the farmer is invited to the palace. On Shabbat, his overalls are replaced with the regulation livery, his vocabulary and manners are polished, his soul and fingernails are scrubbed of the residue of material life. On Shabbat, the farmer is whisked from the hinterland to the capital and ushered into the throne room to glimpse and experience the ultimate purpose of his daily toil.

But Elul is when the king comes to the field.

When the farmer sees the king in his field, does he keep on plowing? Does he behave as if this were just another day in the fields? Of course not. Elul is not a month of ordinary workdays. It is a time of increased Torah study, more fervent prayer, more generosity and charity. The very air is charged with holiness. We might still be in the field, but the field has become a holier place.

On the other hand, when the farmer sees the king in his field, does he run home to wash and change? Does he rush to the capital to school himself in palace protocol? But the king has come to the field, to commune with the processors of his bread in their environment, and on their terms.

In the month of Elul, the essence and objective of life become that much more accessible. No longer do the material trappings of life conceal and distort its purpose, for the king has emerged from the concealment of his palace and is here, in the field. But unlike the holy days of the year, when we are lifted out of our workday lives, the encounter of Elul is hosted by our physical selves, within our material environment, on our workingman's terms.

ADDENDA

The Jewish Calendar (Infographic)............................316

Sources...318

Glossary..324

Index...360

| 1 ROSH HASHANAH | 2 ROSH HASHANAH | 3 | 4 | 5 | 6 | 7 | 8 | 9 | 10 YOM KIPPUR | 11 | 12 | 13 | 14 | 15 SUKKOT |

TISHREI (APPROX. SEPTEMBER–OCTOBER)

| 1 | 2 | 3 | 4 | 5 | 6 | 7 | 8 | 9 | 10 | 11 | 12 | 13 | 14 | 15 |

CHESHVAN (APPROX. OCTOBER–NOVEMBER)

| 1 | 2 | 3 | 4 | 5 | 6 | 7 | 8 | 9 | 10 | 11 | 12 | 13 | 14 | 15 |

KISLEV (APPROX. NOVEMBER–DECEMBER)

| 1 CHANUKAH | 2 CHANUKAH | 3 CHANUKAH | 4 | 5 | 6 | 7 | 8 | 9 | 10 | 11 | 12 | 13 | 14 | 15 |

TEVET (APPROX. DECEMBER–JANUARY)

| 1 | 2 | 3 | 4 | 5 | 6 | 7 | 8 | 9 | 10 | 11 | 12 | 13 | 14 | 15 TU B'SHEVAT |

SHEVAT (APPROX. JANUARY–FEBRUARY)

| 1 | 2 | 3 | 4 | 5 | 6 | 7 | 8 | 9 | 10 | 11 | 12 | 13 | 14 "MINOR PURIM" | 15 "MINOR SHUSHAN PURIM" |

ADAR I (APPROX. FEBRUARY–MARCH)

| 1 | 2 | 3 | 4 | 5 | 6 | 7 | 8 | 9 | 10 | 11 | 12 | 13 | 14 PURIM | 15 SHUSHAN PURIM |

ADAR (OR ADAR II) (APPROX. MARCH–APRIL)

| 1 | 2 | 3 | 4 | 5 | 6 | 7 | 8 | 9 | 10 | 11 | 12 | 13 | 14 | 15 PASSOVER |

NISSAN (APPROX. MARCH–APRIL)

| 1 | 2 | 3 | 4 | 5 | 6 | 7 | 8 | 9 | 10 | 11 | 12 | 13 | 14 PESACH SHEINI | 15 |

IYAR (APPROX. APRIL–MAY)

| 1 | 2 | 3 | 4 | 5 | 6 SHAVUOT | 7 SHAVUOT | 8 | 9 | 10 | 11 | 12 | 13 | 14 | 15 |

SIVAN (APPROX. MAY–JUNE)

| 1 | 2 | 3 | 4 | 5 | 6 | 7 | 8 | 9 | 10 | 11 | 12 | 13 | 14 | 15 |

TAMMUZ (APPROX. JUNE–JULY)

| 1 | 2 | 3 | 4 | 5 | 6 | 7 | 8 | 9 TISHAH B'AV | 10 | 11 | 12 | 13 | 14 | 15 |

AV (APPROX. JULY–AUGUST)

| 1 | 2 | 3 | 4 | 5 | 6 | 7 | 8 | 9 | 10 | 11 | 12 | 13 | 14 | 15 |

ELUL (APPROX. AUGUST–SEPTEMBER)

The Jewish Calendar – Key & Notes

 Festival and special days. The festivals are shown here as observed outside of the Land of Israel. In Israel, the festivals of Shemini Atzeret/Simchat Torah, Passover, and Shavuot are one day shorter.

 Rosh Chodesh, the "head of the month." When a month has 30 days, the 30th day of the month also serves as the first of two *Rosh Chodesh* days for the next month.

Fast days.

THE JEWISH CALENDAR

16	17	18	19	20	21	22	23	24	25	26	27	28	29	30
SUKKOT	SUKKOT	SUKKOT	SUKKOT	SUKKOT	SUKKOT HOSHANAH RABBA	SHEMINI ATZERET	SIMCHAT TORAH							

TISHREI

16	17	18	19	20	21	22	23	24	25	26	27	28	29	30

CHESHVAN

16	17	18	19	20	21	22	23	24	25	26	27	28	29	30
									CHANUKAH	CHANUKAH	CHANUKAH	CHANUKAH	CHANUKAH	CHANUKAH

KISLEV

16	17	18	19	20	21	22	23	24	25	26	27	28	29	

TEVET

16	17	18	19	20	21	22	23	24	25	26	27	28	29	30

SHEVAT

16	17	18	19	20	21	22	23	24	25	26	27	28	29	30

ADAR I

16	17	18	19	20	21	22	23	24	25	26	27	28	29	

ADAR (OR ADAR II)

16	17	18	19	20	21	22	23	24	25	26	27	28	29	30
PASSOVER	PASSOVER	PASSOVER	PASSOVER	PASSOVER	PASSOVER	PASSOVER								

NISSAN

16	17	18	19	20	21	22	23	24	25	26	27	28	29	
		LAG BAOMER												

IYAR

16	17	18	19	20	21	22	23	24	25	26	27	28	29	30

SIVAN

16	17	18	19	20	21	22	23	24	25	26	27	28	29	

TAMMUZ

16	17	18	19	20	21	22	23	24	25	26	27	28	29	30

AV

16	17	18	19	20	21	22	23	24	25	26	27	28	29	

ELUL

KEY & NOTES *(continued)*

These months or days occur only on certain years but not on others:

(A) The month of *Adar* I. Every two or three years (i.e., in the 3rd, 6th, 8th, 11th, 14th, 17th, and 19th years of a 19-year cycle), an additional month is added between the months of *Shevat* and *Adar*, in order to bring the Jewish year in sync with the solar seasons. The additional month is called "*Adar* I" (with the regular *Adar* named "*Adar* II").

(B) *Cheshvan* 30 and *Kislev* 30: While all other months are set at either 29 or 30 days, these two months vary from year to year. In certain years, both *Cheshvan* and *Kislev* have only 29 days. In certain years, *Cheshvan* has 29 days and *Kislev* 30 days. And in certain years, both months have 30 days. The eight-day festival of Chanukah, which begins on *Kislev* 25, may therefore end on *Tevet* 2 or on *Tevet* 3.

Thus, while a "regular" year on the Jewish calendar (i.e., no leap year, with *Cheshvan* having 29 days and *Kislev* 30 days) has 354 days, the Jewish year can also have 353, 355, 383, 384, or 385 days, depending on the number of days that *Cheshvan* and *Kislev* have, and on whether the 30-day "*Adar* I" is added or not.

SOURCES

NOTE: The 113 essays included in the three volumes of *Inside Time* are adaptations, rather than direct translations, of the teachings of the Lubavitcher Rebbe, Rabbi Menachem M. Schneerson, and of his predecessors, the rebbes of Chabad-Lubavitch. The listing below provides the primary sources which served as the basis and the inspiration for each essay. All works listed are from the Rebbe, unless otherwise attributed.

VOLUME ONE

CHAPTER ONE: ON THE ESSENCE OF TIME

(1) **The Evolution of Time** • Likutei Sichot, vol. 26, pp. 359–365. Also see discussion in Likutei Sichot, vol. 10, pp. 176–177, and sources cited there.

(2) **The First Creation** • Likutei Sichot, vol. 20, pp. 315–322 and 333; Ibid., vol. 21 pp. 64–65; et al.

(3) **The Now** • Likutei Sichot, vol. 1, pp. 1–2 ; Sichot Kodesh 5732, vol. 2, p. 72 ; Torat Menachem Hitvaaduyot 5744, vol. 3, pp. 1674–1675.

(4) **Appointments in Time** • Likutei Sichot, vol. 32, pp. 127–133. Parable by chassidic sage Rabbi Yechezkel Panet (1783–1845), as told by Rabbi Zvi Meir Steinmetz.

(5) **Routine and Occasion** • Likutei Sichot, vol. 28, p. 182–190; Ibid., vol. 26, pp. 16–17; et al.

(6) **Masculine Moment, Feminine Time** • Likutei Sichot, vol. 31, pp. 93–98.

CHAPTER TWO: THE DAY

(1) **Garments for the Soul** • Likutei Sichot, vol. 20, pp. 315–322; Sefer HaSichot 5750, vol. 2, pp. 596–599.

(2) **Evening and Morning** • Torat Menachem Hitvaaduyot 5711, vol. 1, pp. 23–25; Ibid., 5745, vol. 1, pp. 104–106; Sefer HaSichot 5751, vol. 1, pp. 63–65; Igrot Kodesh, vol. 3, p. 480.

(3) **The Threshold** • Inyana Shel Torat HaChassidut, section 9–18; Likutei Sichot, vol. 34, pp. 150–152; Torat Menachem Hitvaaduyot 5752, vol. 2, pp. 368–369.

CHAPTER THREE: THE WEEK AND SHABBAT

(1) **The Seventh Element** • Likutei Sichot, vol. 17, pp. 59–61; Reshimot #3, pp. 46–47; Sefer HaSichot 5752, pp. 502–514.

(2) **The World of Thought** • Sefer HaSichot 5750, vol. 2, p. 397; Rabbi Schneur

SOURCES 319

Zalman of Liadi, Likutei Torah, Shabbat Shuvah 66c-d; Rabbi Yosef Yitzchak of Lubavitch, Sefer HaMaamarim 5703, p. 38.

(3) **A Private World** • Likutei Sichot, vol. 11, pp. 68-72.

(4) **Bread from Heaven** • Likutei Sichot, vol. 16, pp. 173-182; Ibid., vol. 2, p. 535; ibid., vol. 17, pp. 294-299; et al.

(5) **Havdalah** • Sichot Kodesh 5736, vol. 1, pp. 365 ff.; Likutei Sichot, vol. 7, p. 66; Sichot Kodesh 5751, vol. 1, pp. 7 ff.

(6) **The Eighth Dimension** • Likutei Sichot, vol. 7, pp. 170-174; Sefer HaSichot 5751, vol. 1, pp. 437 ff.; et al.

(7) **Twilight** • Torat Menachem Hitvaaduyot 5742, vol. 4, pp. 2240-2243 and 2249-2253; Ibid., 5745, vol. 4, pp. 2068-2069 and 2079-2080; et al.

CHAPTER FOUR: THE MONTH

(1) **The Sixteenth Increment** • Sefer HaSichot 5752, pp. 122-133 and 155-159; et al.

(2) **G-d on the Moon** • Likutei Sichot, vol. 30, pp. 8-15.

(3) **Locating the Moon** • Likutei Sichot, vol. 31, pp. 62-67.

(4) **The Monthly Bridge** • Sichot Kodesh 5735, vol. 2, pp. 201-202; et al.

CHAPTER FIVE: THE YEAR AND THE SEASONS

(1) **A Seasoned life** • Reshimot #3, p. 17; Torat Menachem Hitvaaduyot 5750, vol. 1, pp. 439-440.

(2) **A Rising Mist** • Torat Menachem Hitvaaduyot 5750, vol. 1, pp. 406 and 423; Ibid., p. 419, footnote 71; Reshimot #1, pp. 8-9; Rabbi Levi Yitzchak Schneerson, Likutei Levi Yitzchak, Igrot Kodesh, pp. 205 and 217.

(3) **Agricultural Man** • Sefer HaMaamarim Melukat, vol. 5, pp. 169-176.

CHAPTER SIX: THE LEAP YEAR

(1) **Jewish Time** • Likutei Sichot, vol. 34, pp. 632-637.

(2) **A Complete Year** • Likutei Sichot, vol. 20, pp. 281-291.

CHAPTER SEVEN: CONFLUENCE

(1) **Three Times Three** • Sefer HaSichot 5751, vol. 2, pp. 859-882; Ibid., vol. 1, pp. 3-6.

(2) **Shammai's Shabbat** • Sefer HaSichot 5751, vol. 2, pp. 750-755.

(3) **The Hard Life** • Likutei Sichot, vol. 18, pp. 378 ff; Ibid., vol. 28, pp. 279 ff.; et al.

VOLUME TWO

CHAPTER EIGHT: ROSH HASHANAH

(1) **The Neurology of Time** • Sefer HaMaamarim Melukat, p. 332. See also Rabbi DovBer of Lubavitch, Ateret Rosh, Shaar Rosh Hashanah.

(2) **The Man in Man** • Igrot Kodesh, vol. 12, pp. 377-379; Torat Menachem Hitvaaduyot 5749, vol. 4, pp. 366-69.

(3) **To Will a World** • Sefer HaMaamarim Melukat, vol. 4, pp. 4-5; Ibid., vol. 1, pp. 429-438; et al.

(4) **A Glass of Milk** • Likutei Sichot, vol. 19, pp. 291-297.

CHAPTER NINE:
YOM KIPPUR AND THE TEN DAYS OF TESHUVAH

(1) **The 120-Day Version of the Human Story** • Sefer HaSichot 5752, pp. 423-439.

(2) **Sin in Four Dimensions** • Igrot Kodesh, vol. 5, p. 3; Likutei Sichot vol. 7, pp. 22-23.

(3) **Moment** • Likutei Sichot, vol. 19, pp. 593-596.

(4) **Ketoret** • Likutei Sichot, vol. 14, pp. 129-131; Torat Menachem Hitvaaduyot 5746, vol. 3, pp. 583-584; et al.

(5) **Day One** • Likutei Sichot, vol. 4, pp. 1144-1154.

(6) **Reverse Biology** • Sefer HaSichot 5750, vol. 1, p. 30.

CHAPTER TEN: SUKKOT

(1) **The Easy Mitzvah** • Likutei Sichot, vol. 2, pp. 417-418.

(2) **The Four Mysteries of King Solomon** • Reshimot #62, pp. 16-20.

(3) **The Taste of Water** • Likutei Sichot, vol. 2, pp. 426-432.

(4) **Unity in Three Dimensions** • Likutei Sichot, vol. 19, pp. 348-355; ibid., p. 224, note 35; et al. See also Rabbi Schneur Zalman of Liadi, Siddur Im D'ach, Shaar HaLulav 264d.

(5) **One Twig and One Leaf** • Likutei Sichot, vol. 19, pp. 220-228.

CHAPTER ELEVEN: SHEMINI ATZERET AND SIMCHAT TORAH

(1) **Essence** • Likutei Sichot, vol. 2, pp. 433-434; Ibid., vol. 9, pp. 225-236.

(2) **Daughters Near and Far** • Torat Menachem Hitvaaduyot 5742, vol. 1, pp. 241-246.

(3) **Scrolled** • Torat Menachem Hitvaaduyot 5742, vol. 1, pp. 241 ff.

(4) **Intuition** • Based on a talk given by the Rebbe in the 1940s, as related by Rabbi Zalman Posner. Also see Rabbi Schneur Zalman of Liadi, Likutei Torah, Derushim LeSukkot 80c; Likutei Sichot, vol. 26, p. 216-217; Sichot Kodesh 5717, Leil Simchat Torah; Sichot Kodesh 5731, Shabbat Parashat Re'ei; et al.

SOURCES   321

CHAPTER TWELVE: CHESHVAN

(1) **The Last Jew** • Likutei Sichot, vol. 25, pp. 38–46.

CHAPTER THIRTEEN: CHANUKAH

(1) **The Transparent Body** • Likutei Sichot, vol. 25, pp. 235–242.
(2) **Nightlight** • Maamar Tanu Rabanan Mitzvat Ner Chanukah 5738; Reshimot #1, p. 16.
(3) **The Lamp** • Likutei Sichot, vol. 12, p. 149; Ibid., vol. 5, pp. 445–446; et al.
(4) **The Mudswamps of Hella** • Reshimot #3, pp. 10–24.
(5) **The Miracle** • Reshimot #3, p. 17.
(6) **Compromise** • Likutei Sichot, vol. 1, pp. 81–82.
(7) **The Towering Servant** • Based on an address by the Rebbe (date unkown).
(8) **Accumulating Lights** • Likutei Sichot, vol. 25, pp. 243–251.

CHAPTER FOURTEEN: TEVET

(1) **Spirit and Substance** • Likutei Sichot, vol. 15, pp. 382ff.

CHAPTER FIFTEEN: TU BISHEVAT

(1) **Of Trees and Men** • Igrot Kodesh, vol. 1, pp. 247–250.
(2) **Fruit For Thought** • Sefer HaSichot 5750, vol. 1, pp. 273–282; Sefer HaSichot 5752, vol. 1, pp. 325–328; et al.

CHAPTER SIXTEEN: PURIM

(1) **Oil and Wine** • Likutei Sichot, vol. 2, pp. 482–484.
(2) **Esther's Story** • Likutei Sichot, vol. 16, pp. 352–358.
(3) **A Roll of Dice** • Likutei Sichot, vol. 4, pp. 1278–1279.
(4) **The Thousand-Year Difference** • Likutei Sichot, vol. 16, pp. 365–366; Rabbi Schneur Zalman of Liadi, Torah Ohr, 98d–99a.
(5) **A Feast and a Fast** • Likutei Sichot, vol. 31, pp. 170–176.
(6) **A Singular People** • Likutei Sichot vol. 3, pp. 916–923.
(7) **The Purim Drunk** • The first six paragraphs of this essay are based on Likutei Sichot, vol. 4, p. 1274. The rest of this essay is from the editor's reply to a reader who questioned the legitimacy of reaching a state of inebriation of Purim, published in the Week In Review, vol. VIII, no. 26. While it was written in the spirit of the Rebbe's teachings, it is not based on any particular talk or work of the Rebbe. The "matchmaker" parable is told in the name of the legendary mashgiach (mentor) of the Lakewood Yeshivah, Rabbi Nosson Wachtfogel.
(8) **The Beginning and the End** • Likutei Sichot, vol. 26, pp. 209–218.

Volume Three

CHAPTER SEVENTEEN: NISSAN

(1) **Our Other Head** • Likutei Sichot, vol. 1, pp. 233–236; Rabbi Shalom DovBer of Lubavitch, Yom Tov Shel Rosh Hashanah 5666, p. 156ff.; Rabbi Yosef Yitzchak of Lubavitch, Sefer HaMaamarim Kayitz 5700, pp. 19–30.

(2) **The Coiled Spring** • Igrot Kodesh, vol. 4, pp. 267–268.

(3) **The Great Shabbat** • Likutei Sichot, vol. 27, pp. 44–47.

CHAPTER EIGHTEEN: PASSOVER

(1) **Endless Lives** • Likutei Sichot, vol. 3, pp. 848–852.

(2) **Midnight** • Likutei Sichot, vol. 3, pp. 864–872; Ibid., vol. 21 pp. 55–61; Rabbi Menachem Mendel of Lubavitch (Tzemach Tzedek), Ohr HaTorah, Bereishit, Vol. 1, pp. 149 ff.

(3) **The Festival of the Child** • Likutei Sichot, vol. 11, p. 2; Igrot Kodesh, vol. 15, pp. 33–34.

(4) **Hillel's Paradox** • Likutei Sichot, vol. 18, pp. 104–116.

(5) **Bread of Faith** • Likutei Sichot, vol. 26, pp. 43–48.

(6) **A Speck of Flour** • Likutei Sichot, vol. 22, pp. 30–38.

(7) **The Vegetarian Era** • Likutei Sichot, vol. 3, pp. 823–827; Reshimot #10, pp. 35–38.

(8) **The Muddy Path** • Likutei Sichot, vol. 3, pp. 1016e–1016f.

(9) **Miriam's Song** • Sefer HaSichot 5752, 303–307.

(10) **Passovering Time** • Likutei Sichot, vol. 7, pp. 272–273.

CHAPTER NINETEEN: THE COUNTING OF THE OMER

(1) **The Journey** • Sefer HaSichot 5751, vol. 2, pp. 437–440; Torat Menachem Hitvaaduyot 5711, vol. 2, pp. 65–66.

(2) **Accumulative Time** • Likutei Sichot, vol. 7, p. 284.

(3) **A Month of Mitzvot** • Likutei Sichot, vol. 1, pp. 263–264; et al.

CHAPTER TWENTY: PESACH SHEINI

(1) **The Distant Road** • Likutei Sichot, vol. 18, pp. 117–125; Ibid., p. 62–72; Rebbe's Haggadah (1991 ed.), pp. 880–881; et al.

(2) **The Missing Complaint** • Likutei Sichot, vol. 23, pp. 62–72.

CHAPTER TWENTY-ONE: LAG BAOMER

(1) **24,000 Plus One** • Likutei Sichot, 22, pp. 138–142; Ibid., vol. 32, pp. 149–152; et al.

(2) **Long-Range Missile** • Torat Menachem Hitvaaduyot 5711, vol. 2, pp. 50–58 and 77–81.

(3) **The Many and the Few** • Sefer HaSichot 5748, vol. 2, pp. 440–444.

SOURCES   323

CHAPTER TWENTY-TWO: SHAVUOT

(1) **Doing Nothing** • Likutei Sichot, vol. 28, pp. 7–14.

(2) **Truth** • Sefer HaSichot 5750, vol. 2, pp. 493–503.

(3) **Peace** • Likutei Sichot, vol. 21, pp. 110–114; Sefer HaSichot 5751, vol. 2, pp. 550–553; et al.

(4) **Law** • Based on an address delivered by the Rebbe on Chanukah, 5730 (1970).

(5) **The Breakthrough** • Likutei Sichot, vol. 3, pp. 887–892; Ibid., vol. 4, pp. 1092–1098; Ibid., vol. 8, pp. 105–113; et al.

(6) **Real Estate** • Likutei Sichot, vol. 18, 28–34.

(7) **The Mathematics of Marriage** • Based on the Rebbe's talks on numerous occasions.

(8) **The Three Names of Shavuot** • Reshimot #10, pp. 40–45.

(9) **The Phantom Days of Shavuot** • Likutei Sichot, vol. 28, pp. 76–84.

CHAPTER TWENTY-THREE:
THE THREE WEEKS AND TISHAH B'AV

(1) **The Pinch** • Sefer HaSichot 5749, vol. 2, pp. 581–583; et al.

(2) **Good Grief** • Rabbi Schneur Zalman of Liadi, Tanya, chapter 31; see Biurei Rabbi Shlomo Chaim, p. 39.

(3) **Postponed** • Sefer HaSichot 5751, vol. 2, pp. 683ff. and 721ff.; et al.

(4) **Difficult Days** • Likutei Sichot, vol. 24, pp. 1–11.

(5) **Shabbat of Vision** • Likutei Sichot, vol. 29, pp. 18–25.

(6) **The Subterranean Temple** • Likutei Sichot, vol. 21, pp. 156–163.

(7) **The Legalities of Destruction** • Likutei Sichot, vol. 29, pp. 9–17.

(8) **The Intimate Estrangement** • Likutei Sichot, vol. 2, pp. 359–363; Sefer HaSichot 5749, vol. 2, pp. 609–611; Ibid., p. 614, note 45.

(9) **Regret** • Likutei Sichot, vol. 24, pp. 167–176; et al.

(10) **Cholent** • The second part of this essay is based on numerous talks by the Rebbe, including on Hoshana Rabbah, 5744 (1983).

CHAPTER TWENTY-FOUR: THE 15TH OF AV

(1) **The Day of the Breaking of the Ax** • Likutei Sichot, vol. 24, pp. 47–56, et al.

(2) **The Dancing Maidens of Jerusalem** • Likutei Sichot, vol. 9 pp. 261–263; Rabbi Schneur Zalman of Liadi, Tanya, chapters 3–4 and 13–18.

(3) **No and Yes** • Torat Menachem Hitvaaduyot 5711, vol. 2, p. 142; Likutei Sichot, vol. 19, 215–220; Sefer HaMaamarim Melukat, vol. 4, pp. 237–241; et al.

CHAPTER TWENTY-FIVE: ELUL

(1) **A Haven in Time** • Likutei Sichot, vol. 2, pp. 623–626; et al.

(2) **Month of the Bride** • Sefer HaSichot 5750, vol. 2, pp. 631–633; et al.

(3) **The King in the Field** • Sefer HaSichot 5750, vol. 2, pp. 642–648.

GLOSSARY

Italicized terms are Hebrew unless otherwise indicated. Names (e.g., Rashi), or words that have entered common English usage (e.g., kabbalah), are not italicized.

Terms appearing in the text with a dotted underline are themselves entries in this glossary.

Terms that are translated and/or explained inside the essays in which they appear are not included in this glossary.

A

Aaron Elder brother of Moses. Served as *Kohen Gadol* (high priest) during the Israelites' travels through the desert following the Exodus from Egypt.

Abayei 278–338 CE; Pumbeditha, Babylonia. A prominent talmudic sage, whose debates on matters of Torah law with his colleague Rava are classics of the talmudic dialectic.

Abraham The first Jew, and the first of the three patriarchs (Heb., *avot*) of the Jewish people—Abraham, Isaac, and Jacob. Born into pagan Mesopotamia in the 18th century BCE, Abraham discovered the truth of a one G-d and devoted his life to spreading the teachings and ethos of monotheism. By divine instruction he traveled to the Holy Land, where G-d promised to make his descendants into a great people and bequeath the Land to them as their eternal inheritance.

Acharon Shel Pesach The eighth and last day of the festival of Passover.

Achashveirosh Ruler of the Persian Empire during the events of Purim (4th century BCE).

Adam The first man, created by G-d on the sixth day of creation.

Adar Twelfth month of the Jewish calendar, or the sixth month counting from *Tishrei*. (For the significance of the two different systems for numbering the months of the Jewish year, see entry for *Nissan*.) Approximately February–March. In Jewish leap years, when an extra month is added so that the lunar months keep pace with the solar year, there are two months called *Adar: Adar I* and *Adar II*. The holiday of Purim is celebrated on the 14th of *Adar* (*Adar II* on leap years). Also see infographic "The Jewish Calendar" on pp. 316–317 of this book.

Adon Olam "Master of the world." Opening words of a hymn which summarizes the thirteen principles of the Jewish faith. Recited or sung at the beginning of the morning prayers.

Afikoman An Aramaic term meaning "dessert." In the Passover *seder*, a piece of

GLOSSARY   325

matzah that is hidden and then eaten at the conclusion of the meal to commemorate the Passover offering.

Aggadah Non-legal Torah teachings, including ethics, homilies, narratives, etc. Sometimes contrasted with *halachah* (teachings pertaining to Torah law). The Talmud, for example, is seen as consisting of both *halachic* and *aggadic* portions.

Akeidat Yitzchak A commentary on the Bible by Rabbi Yitzchak Arma (1420–1494, Spain and Italy) comprised of lengthy essays that blend explanations of the text and narrative with philosophical and kabbalistic thought. It greatly influenced many later Torah commentaries. Also referred to as "*Akeidah.*"

Akiva, Rabbi 1st and 2nd century; Benei Berak, Israel. One of the most important personalities in the history of the transmission of Torah through the ages. Rabbi Akiva was a descendant of converts to Judaism and was an illiterate shepherd until the age of 40, when he was "discovered" by his employer's daughter Rachel who promised to marry him on the condition that he devote his life to the study of Torah. Soon after his marriage he left home to study under the leading sages of his day; after twenty-four years of study he returned with thousands of students of his own. His disciples became seminal figures in Torah's chain of tradition, and much of the material in the Mishnah and the Midrashim is based on the teachings they received from him. Toward the end of his life Rabbi Akiva defied a Roman ban on teaching Torah publicly, and was arrested and cruelly executed.

Al hanissim Lit., "for the miracles." Special addenda to the *amidah* prayer and *Grace after Meals* recited on Chanukah and Purim, which recount the miracles commemorated by these festivals.

Amidah Lit., "standing." The central portion of each of the daily prayers, so called because it is recited while standing, as at an audience with a king. It is also known as *shemoneh esreh* ("eighteen"), after the number of blessings in its original composition (a nineteenth blessing was added in the late 1st century under the direction of Rabban Gamliel). The first three blessings of the *amidah* offer praise to G-d; the middle thirteen blessing are requests from G-d for various personal and communal needs (health, sustenance, redemption, etc.); and the three concluding blessings are expressions of thanks to G-d. The versions of the *amidah* for Shabbat and most Jewish holidays contain seven blessings, with the thirteen middle blessings of the weekday version replaced with a single blessing on the theme of the day.

Amram Father of Miriam, Aaron, and Moses.

Annual Torah-reading cycle In keeping with a tradition dating back to the days of Moses to hold public readings of the Torah each Shabbat, the Five Books of Moses are divided into 54 portions or *parashiot* (singular, *parashah*), each of which serves as the weekly reading in an annual cycle beginning on the Shabbat after the holiday of Simchat Torah, and ending on Simchat Torah of the following year.

Due to the varying lengths of the Jewish year, and the coincidence of certain holidays with Shabbat (in which case the regular weekly *parashah* is superseded by a reading relating to the holiday), there are often less than 54 Shabbat readings in the course of the year; in those cases, two *parashiot* are combined into one reading on certain weeks.

Aravah; aravot (pl.) Willow branch. One of the "four kinds" taken on the festival of Sukkot. Also used, on its own, in the observances of Hoshana Rabbah, the seventh day of Sukkot.

Ari Rabbi Isaac Luria (1534–1572) of Safed, Israel. Preeminent master of kabbalah, whose interpretations of the *Zohar* and other kabbalistic texts are widely considered the most authoritative basis of all subsequent study in this area.

Ariel "Lion of G-d." A reference to the Holy Temple and to the city of Jerusalem.

Ark, The | Heb. *aron.* The receptacle containing the "tablets of the covenant" which G-d gave to Moses at Mount Sinai. It stood in the innermost chamber of the *mishkan* and later of the first Holy Temple. The ark was absent in the second Temple, and according to most opinions it was hidden underground in advance of the first Temple's destruction. The structure that houses the Torah scrolls in a synagogue is also referred to as the "ark" or "holy ark."

Asheirah A tree that was the object of idol worship by the biblical Canaanites.

Ashi, Rav Talmudic sage (d. 427) who headed the Torah academy at Matha Mechasya, Babylonia for more than sixty years. Redacted the Babylonian Talmud together with his colleague, Ravina.

Assyria A Mesopotamian kingdom and empire, c. 2500–650 BCE.

Av Fifth month of the Jewish calendar, or the eleventh month counting from *Tishrei.* (For the significance of the two different systems for numbering the months of the Jewish year, see entry for *Nissan.*) Approximately July–August. Also known as *Menachem Av.* The ninth day of Av is *Tishah B'Av*, a day of mourning for the destruction of both Holy Temples and various other calamities in Jewish history; conversely, the fifteenth day of the month is a holiday celebrating various joyful events in Jewish history. Also see infographic "The Jewish Calendar" on pp. 316–317 of this book.

Avodat HaKodesh Seminal kabbalistic work by Rabbi Meir ibn Gabbai, c. 1480–1540, Spain and Turkey.

Avudraham Rabbi David Avudraham, 14th century, Seville, Spain. Author of a classic commentary on the *Siddur* (prayer book).

GLOSSARY   327

B

Baal Shem Tov Rabbi Israel Baal Shem Tov, 1698–1760, Mezhibuzh, Ukraine. Founder of the chassidic movement.

Baal teshuvah; baalei teshuvah (pl.) Lit. "returnee" or "master of return." A person who returns to G-d in *teshuvah* (repentance) after willful or unknowing transgression of the Torah's commandments. The "*baal teshuvah* movement" has been a widespread phenomenon, beginning in the 1960s, in which Jews from secular or not fully observant backgrounds decide to undertake full Torah observance.

Bach Halachic work by Rabbi Joel Sirkis (1561–1640; Belarus, Poland, and Ukraine), written as a commentary on *Tur*.

Bahag Early *halachic* work, commonly attributed to 9th-century Babylonian *gaon* Rabbi Simeon Kayyara.

Balaam Midianite prophet who attempted to curse the children of Israel in the desert, as recounted in Bible (Numbers 22–24).

Bar Kochba Jewish leader of a failed revolt against the Roman rulers of the Holy Land in the 2nd century.

Barley offering See *Omer*.

Bartinoro Rabbi Ovadiah of Bartinoro, late 15th to early 16th centuries, Italy and Jerusalem. Author of a lucid commentary to the Mishnah which became a primary point of reference for the study of that work.

Bechayei Rabbi Bechayei (or Bachya) ben Asher ibn Chalawah, c. 1255–1340, Zaragoza, Spain. Author of an extensive commentary on the Bible.

Be'er Yitzchak A work by Rabbi Isaac ben Elijah Sangi, published in Thessaloniki, Greece in 1735.

Beinoni; beinonim (pl.) lit., "intermediate one." In the Talmud, this term is used for someone who is neither a righteous nor a wicked person. Rabbi Schneur Zalman of Liadi defines a *beinoni* as the ideal "everyman," who has an active evil inclination but successfully combats it to avoid transgressing the divine will in thought, speech, or deed.

Beit HaOtzar Encyclopedia of talmudic concepts authored by Rabbi Joseph Engel, 1858–1919, Bedzin and Krakow, Poland.

Beit Yosef Voluminous talmudic and *halachic* work by Rabbi Joseph Caro, 1488–1575, Turkey, Bulgaria, and Safed, Israel. Composed as a commentary on *Tur*, it served as the basis for Caro's *Shulchan Aruch*.

Benei Issaschar Classic chassidic work by Rabbi Zvi Elimelach Spira of Dinov, 1783–1841, Poland and Ukraine.

328   INSIDE TIME

Benjamin The youngest of Jacob's twelve sons. Also refers to the Israelite tribe descendant from him.

Bereishit Rabbah An early (3rd to 4th century) collection of midrashic expositions on the biblical book of Genesis.

Berit Avot Work by Rabbi Abraham Koriyat, 1800–1845, Mogador, Morocco.

Bet din Court of Torah law.

Bitter herbs Heb., *maror*. A vegetable with a bitter taste (commonly horseradish or romaine lettuce) eaten at the Passover *seder* in commemoration of the hard labor with which the Egyptians "embittered the lives" of the Israelites (Exodus 1:14) during the Egyptian exile.

Brit milah "Covenant of circumcision." As commanded to Abraham in Genesis 17 (and reiterated to Moses in Leviticus 12:3), all Jewish males are circumcised as a sign of the covenant between G-d and the people of Israel. Also referred to simply as *brit* ("covenant").

Broken tablets See Tablets of the Covenant.

C

Chabad; Chabad-Lubavitch Branch of chassidism, founded in 1772 by Rabbi Schneur Zalman of Liadi, emphasizing the role of the mind in assimilating divine truths and developing and guiding a person's emotions and behavior. The name "Chabad" is an acronym for the three intellectual faculties *chochmah, binah,* and *daat*. The movement is also called "Chabad-Lubavitch," or simply "Lubavitch," after the Russian town, Lyubavichi, which served as its headquarters from 1813 to 1915. (The two terms are not completely synonymous, however, since there also existed other branches of Chabad, headquartered in other towns.)

Chafetz Chaim Rabbi Israel Meir Kagan, 1838–1933, Radun, Belarus. Known as "Chafetz Chaim" (Lit., "Desirer of Life"), after his first published work of that name.

Challah; challot (pl.) Lit., "loaf." Commonly refers to the bread (usually braided) baked in honor of Shabbat and Jewish holidays. In Torah law, "*challah*" is a portion of dough given as a gift to a *kohen* (priest), who will eat it under conditions of ritual purity. As today such conditions rarely exist, the piece is generally burned instead.

Chametz Leavened products derived from one of the "five grains" (wheat, barley, oat, spelt, and rye). *Chametz* is forbidden throughout the festival of Passover.

Chanah 10th century BCE, Israel. Mother of the biblical prophet Samuel.

Chanukah An eight-day festival beginning on the 25th of the Jewish month of

GLOSSARY   329

Kislev, celebrating the Hasmoneans' recapture of the Holy Temple from the Syrian-Greeks and its rededication to the service of G-d in the 2nd century BCE. The
holiday is marked by the kindling of lights, in commemoration of a miracle where
the single day's supply of oil available sufficed to keep the Temple *menorah* lit for
eight days.

Chasdei Avot See Chida.

Chassid; chassidim *(pl.)* Adherent of chassidism (see following entry). Also used in
the sense of a follower of a specific chassidic leader or rebbe, as in "Moshe was a
chassid of the Baal Shem Tov."

Chassidism; chassidic Jewish revivalist movement founded in 1726 by Rabbi Israel
Baal Shem Tov, stressing the mystical dimension of Torah, joyfulness in serving
G-d, love of all Jews regardless of material or spiritual station, intellectual and
emotional involvement in prayer, finding G-dliness in every aspect of one's existence, the elevation of the material universe, and the role of the *tzaddik* (righteous
leader) in guiding and facilitating a person's relationship with G-d. Many of the
ideas of chassidism are based on the *Zohar* and the teachings of Ari, and of later
mystics such as Maharal and Shaloh. Its in-depth exploration of the esoteric soul
of Torah attracted many of the great minds of European Jewry, and at the same
time it enfranchised the unlettered masses by teaching that sincere faith and good
deeds are no less precious in the eyes of G-d than the Torah learning of the most
accomplished scholar. By the time of the passing of its second leader, Rabbi Dov
Ber of Mezheritch, in 1772, the movement had spread throughout Eastern Europe, with many of Rabbi Dov Ber's disciples establishing followings in different
towns and regions. Thus were born the various branches or schools within chassidism, each with its own leader or rebbe.

Chatam Sofer Collective name given to the prolific works of Rabbi Moses Schreiber
(1762–1839), a leader of Austro-Hungarian Jewry.

Cheshvan Eighth month of the Jewish calendar, or the second month counting from
Tishrei. (For the significance of the two different systems for numbering the
months of the Jewish year, see entry for *Nissan*.) Approximately October–November. Also known as *Marcheshvan*. There are no Jewish holidays in this month. Also
see infographic "The Jewish Calendar" on pp. 316–317 of this book.

Chida Rabbi Chaim Joseph David Azulai, 1724–1806, Israel and Italy. Author of numerous talmudic and kabbalistic works, including *Chasdei Avot*, *Kissei Rachamim*,
Penei David, and *Rosh David*.

Chizkuni Commentary on the Bible by Rabbi Hezekiah ben Manoah, of mid-13th-
century France.

Cholent Traditional slow-cooking stew, prepared before the start of Shabbat and kept warm or simmering on a low flame overnight, so as to provide hot food for the Shabbat meal while avoiding the prohibition against cooking on Shabbat.

Circumcision See *Brit milah.*

City of refuge Special cities set up in biblical times to serve as a place of exile and refuge for someone who accidentally killed another person.

Concubine at Gibeah The incident which sparked the civil war against the tribe of Benjamin during the period of the Judges (13th–10th centuries BCE), when the Benjaminites refused to give up for punishment the persons responsible for a brutal rape and murder in the town of Gibeah (see Judges 19–21).

Counting of the *omer.* A biblically (Leviticus 23:15–21) mandated forty-nine-day count which commences on the second day of Passover and culminates on the eve of the festival of Shavuot. Also see *Omer.*

Cubit Heb. *amah*, lit. "arm." A measure of length used in the biblical and talmudic eras, and for assorted *halachic* purposes. It is defined as the distance from the average person's elbow to the tip of the middle finger. Various *halachic* authorities put the length of the standard cubit at between approximately 48 and 63 centimeters.

D

Dagul Mirvavah A commentary on *Shulchan Aruch* (Code of Jewish Law) by Rabbi Yechezkel Landau (1713–1793; Poland and Bohemia).

David, King 907–837 BCE; Bethlehem and Jerusalem. First Judean king and composer of the biblical book of Psalms.

Days of awe First ten days of the Jewish year, which include the holidays of Rosh Hashanah and Yom Kippur and the intervening "days of repentance." During this time we crown G-d as sovereign of the world and recommit ourselves as subjects of the divine sovereignty; this is also the time that every person is judged and his or her fate for the coming year is decided in the heavenly court.

Deborah Active 1125–1085 BCE; Mount Ephraim, Israel. One of the "Judges" (and the only woman among them), and one of the seven prophetesses in Jewish tradition. Together with Barak (whom some say was her husband) she led the Israelites in a successful war against the Canaanites, and her song of triumph on their victory is one of the ten classic "songs" of Jewish history.

Derech HaChaim A work by Rabbi DovBer of Lubavitch (1773–1827).

Derech Mitzvotecha A work by Rabbi Menachem Mendel of Lubavitch (1789–1866).

Diaspora, The General term for the "dispersed" Jews living outside of the Jewish homeland, Israel.

GLOSSARY 331

Dikdukei Sofrim Compilation of variances in the talmudic text from numerous manuscripts and editions of the Talmud, compiled by Rabbi Raphael Nathan Rabinovitch (1835–1888).

Dov Ber of Mezheritch, Rabbi Also known as "Maggid of Mezheritch." Successor of the Baal Shem Tov as the leader of the chassidic movement. d, 1772.

DovBer of Lubavitch, Rabbi 1773–1827, Lyubavichi, Russia. Son of Rabbi Schneur Zalman of Liadi, and his successor as leader of the Chabad branch of chassidism. In 1813 he settled in the town of Lubavitch, which became the headquarters of the Chabad-Lubavitch movement for the next 102 years.

E

Eiruv Lit., "combination." A halachic procedure, involving the fashioning of an enclosure around an area and the creation of a common meal area, which "combines" a courtyard, street, or even an entire city into a single "private domain," thereby allowing the transfer of objects from home to home within the *eiruv* area on Shabbat.

Eitz Chaim Kabbalistic work by Rabbi Chaim Vital (1543–1620)

Elazar ben Azariah, Rabbi Late 1st century; Yavneh, Israel. A mishnaic sage, who at the age of 18 was appointed *nassi* (president of the sanhedrin) to replace the deposed Rabban Gamliel, and later shared the position with him.

Eliezer, Rabbi Rabbi Eliezer ben Hyrcanus, 1st century, Lod, Israel. A mishnaic sage, also known as Rabbi Eliezer ha-Gadol (Rabbi Eliezer the Great). Rabbi Eliezer was an illiterate farm worker in his father's fields when he ran away from home to study in the academy of Rabbi Jochanan ben Zakkai, where he developed into a leading Torah scholar; Rabbi Jochanan said of him that he could outweigh all of the other sages in his breadth of knowledge. His disciples included Rabbi Akiva.

Elijah the Prophet The leading prophet of his era in 8th century BCE, Israel. The biblical book of Kings relates that Elijah ascended bodily to heaven on a chariot of fire, and Jewish tradition records his reappearances on earth through the generations to teach great sages, such as Rabbi Joshua ben Levi, Rabbi Anan (compiler of *Tana d'Vei Eliyahu*), and the Baal Shem Tov, and to assist people in distress. The prophet Malachi foretells of Elijah's future appearance as the herald of Moshiach.

Elul Sixth month of the Jewish calendar, approximately August–September. It is also the last month of the Jewish year, when counting from Tishrei. (For the significance of the two different systems for numbering the months of the Jewish year, see entry for Nissan.) The month of *Elul* is traditionally a time devoted to repentance and soul-searching in preparation for the "high holidays" of Rosh

Hashanah and Yom Kippur. Also see infographic "The Jewish Calendar" on pp. 316–317 of this book.

Emek HaMelech 17th-century kabbalistic work by Rabbi Naftali Hertz Bacharach of Frankfurt, Germany.

Esther Mid-4th-century BCE, Shushan (Susa), Persia. Esther was the queen of the Persian empire, and author (together with her cousin Mordechai) of the biblical book of Esther, which tells of how she was taken to the palace of King Achashveirosh and chosen to become his queen, and how she used her position to foil the genocidal plot of the Jew-hating prime minister Haman. The book of Esther (also called *Megillat Esther*, "the scroll of Esther") is read publicly on the holiday of Purim, which celebrates the salvation of the Jewish people from Haman's evil decree.

Ethics of the Fathers Tractate of the Talmud, mostly containing ethical and religious maxims by sages of successive generations, from those of the "Great Assembly" (4th century BCE) to Rabban Gamliel III, son of Rabbi Judah HaNassi (early 3rd century CE).

Etrog Citron fruit. One of the "four kinds" taken on the festival of Sukkot.

Eve The first woman, created by G-d on the sixth day of creation.

Exodus, The The miraculous liberation of the children of Israel from Egyptian slavery under the leadership of Moses, and their exodus from that land for the purpose of receiving the Torah at Mount Sinai and settling the Holy Land in fulfillment of their destiny as G-d's chosen people.

Ezra Active c. 348–315 BCE, Jerusalem, Israel. Spiritual leader of the Jewish community at the beginning of the Second Temple Era, Ezra successfully combated assimilation and intermarriage prevalent in the Jewish community at the time after decades of exile in Babylon, and headed the "Great Assembly." The biblical book "Ezra" describes the events of this period and the preceding decades.

F

First Tablets See Tablets of the Covenant.

First Temple See Holy Temple.

First Temple Era 733 to 423 BCE, the period during which the first Holy Temple stood in Jerusalem.

Five Books of Moses The core text of Judaism, which Moses received from G-d and taught to the people of Israel during their 40 years in the Sinai Desert. Moses completed his transcription of these texts on the last day of his life, in the biblical year 2488 (1273 BCE). The five books are: Genesis, Exodus, Leviticus. Numbers, and Deuteronomy. The Five Books of Moses are also referred to as the *Chumash* (short for *chamishah chumshei Torah*, Hebrew for "the five fifths of the Torah"),

GLOSSARY 333

the *Pentateuch* (Greek for "five books"), as well as simply the Torah ("teaching"). The five books constitute the first of the three sections (Torah, Prophets, and Scriptures) of the Jewish bible. Also see entry for Written Torah.

Four kinds As instructed in Leviticus 23:40, four plant species are taken in hand on the festival of Sukkot: the citron fruit (*etrog*), palm frond (*lulav*), myrtle twigs (*hadasim*), and willow twigs (*aravot*).

Future Redemption See entry for Moshiach.

G

Galut Lit., "exile." The state of physical and spiritual displacement experienced by the Jewish people for much of their history: in Egypt prior to the Exodus, in Babylonia and Persia following the destruction of the first Holy Temple, under the hegemony of Greece during the Second Temple Era, and following the destruction of the second Temple by the Romans.

Gamliel, Rabban Late 1st century, Yavneh, Israel. A mishnaic sage who served as president of the *sanhedrin*.

Gaon; geonim (pl.); geonic Lit., "exalted one." The title given to the heads of the central academies for Torah learning in Babylonia and in the Land of Israel from the late 6th to early 11th centuries. In later times, the title *gaon* came back into use an honorific for exceptional scholars (as in "Gaon of Vilna" or "Rogatchover Gaon").

Gedaliah ben Achikam Governor of Judea following the destruction of the first Holy Temple in the 5th century BCE. His assassination spelled the end of the small Jewish community that remained in the Holy Land after the Destruction.

Giving of the Torah The revelation at Mount Sinai on the 6th of *Sivan* of the biblical year 2448 (1313 BCE), where G-d spoke the Ten Commandments to the assembled children of Israel and summoned Moses to the top of the mountain to receive the Torah, as related in Exodus 19–20 and 24.

Golden Calf The idol made and worshipped by the children of Israel, thus violating their newly-made covenant with G-d only 40 days after the revelation at Mount Sinai (as related in Exodus 32).

Grace after Meals Heb., *birkat hamazon*; also popularly called by the Yiddish term *bentching*. A prayer, consisting of four blessings, recited after eating bread.

Great Assembly c. 371–273 BCE; Babylon and Israel. Also referred to as "Men of the Great Assembly" (Heb., *Anshei Kenesset HaGedolah*). A body of 120 prophets and sages who led the people of Israel during the return from Babylon to the Holy Land at the beginning of the Second Temple Era. Members included Haggai, Zechariah, Malachi, Mordechai, Ezra, Nehemiah, and Shimon HaTzadik. The Great Assembly fixed the biblical canon, standardized the text of the prayers, and enacted numerous other ordinances which became integral features of Jewish life to this day.

Guide for the Perplexed Classic work of Jewish philosophy by Maimonides (Rabbi Moses ben Maimon, c. 1135–1204).

H

Hadas; Hadassim (pl.) Myrtle twig. One of the "four kinds" taken on the festival of Sukkot.

Haftarah; haftarot (pl.) Selected readings from the "Prophets" section of the Bible, which are read following the public Torah reading on Shabbat and the festivals. The *haftarah* is either thematically connected with the Torah reading of the week, or else related to the time of year in which it is read.

Haggadah Lit. "telling." The text used for telling and expounding on the story of the Exodus in the course of the Passover *seder* feast, including the instructions for each step of the procedure.

Hakafot Lit., "encirclings" The custom to carry the Torah scrolls in a procession around the reading table in the synagogue on the festival Simchat Torah, followed by singing and dancing with the Torah scrolls.

Halachah; halachic Torah law; the rulings pertaining to the details of the biblical commandments (*mitzvot*) and the rabbinical ordinances. In particular, those works of Torah literature devoted to weighing the different arguments and opinions appearing in the Talmud and the talmudic commentaries to arrive at a final ruling. Central *halachic* works include the *Mishnah*; the codes authored by Maimonides and *Tur* along with their commentaries; the *Shulchan Aruch* and its commentaries; and the vast body of *halachic* responsa.

Half-shekel The *shekel* (lit. "weight") is a silver coin, equivalent to approximately 10–12 grams of silver, that served as the standard monetary unit in biblical and talmudic times. The half-*shekel* was the mandated annual contribution given by each Jew as their participation in the communal offerings (*korbanot*) brought in the Holy Temple.

Hallel Psalms of praise recited on special occasions, particularly on festivals that commemorate miracles of salvation, such as Passover or Chanukah.

Haman Evil prime minister of King Achashveirosh who plotted to annihilate the Jewish people in the 4th century BCE. See entry for *Purim*.

HaMaor Halachic work by Rabbi Zerachiah ben Isaac HaLevi Gerondi (d. circa 1186, Lunel, France).

Hasmoneans The family of priests—Matityahu and his five sons Judah, Simeon, Elazar, Jochanan, and Jonathan—who led the revolt against the Syrian-Greek rulers

GLOSSARY   335

of the Holy Land in the 2nd century BCE, which culminated in the victory and
miracles of Chanukah. Also referred to as the "Maccabees." Their descendants
ruled the Holy Land for more than a century.

Havdalah Lit. "differentiation." Ritual marking the end of the Shabbat or festival day
and the start of the mundane workdays.

HaYom Yom A calendar which includes a daily chassidic saying culled from the writings and talks of the sixth Lubavitcher Rebbe, Rabbi Yosef Yitzchak Schneersohn
(1880–1950). Compiled in 1943 by Rabbi Yosef Yitzchak's son-in-law and successor, Rabbi Menachem Mendel Schneerson.

Hella The Greek or Hellenist culture.

Herod Ruler of Judea in the 1st century BCE. A slave, Herod murdered the entire
Hasmonean royal family and seized the throne with the aid of the Romans. He
also massacred the Torah sages of the time to cement his rule. He later rebuilt the
Holy Temple (which was in bad repair, having been built more than three centuries earlier by the impoverished community returning from Babylonian exile) as
an atonement for his crimes.

Hilchot Talmud Torah Halachic work, detailing the laws of Torah study, authored by
Rabbi Schneur Zalman of Liadi (1745–1812).

Hillel First century BCE, Babylonia and Israel. A descendant of King David, Hillel served as president of the *sanhedrin* (highest court of Torah law) during the
Second Temple Era, a position filled thereafter almost exclusively by his descendants. Famous for his legendary devotion to Torah study under conditions of extreme poverty in his first years as a student of Torah. He was also famed for his
approachability and patience, and is the author of the maxim: "What is hateful to
you, do not do to your fellow man. This is the entire Torah; the rest is commentary—now go and study it!" In his rulings on Torah law, Hillel tended toward the
lenient position, in contrast with the more stringent approach of his colleague
Shammai. Each of them gathered a following of like-minded disciples, which developed into two schools of Torah thought and law: the "House of Hillel" and the
"House of Shammai."

Hillel of Paritch, Rabbi Rabbi Hillel Malisov, 1795–1864, a senior disciple of the
second and third rebbes of Chabad-Lubavitch.

Holy Ari See *Ari*.

Holy of Holies Heb. *kodesh hakodashim*. The innermost and most sacred room of
the *mishkan* and later the Holy Temple, which housed the ark containing the
"Tablets of the Covenant" inscribed with the Ten Commandments.

Holy Temple Heb. *beit hamikdash* (lit., "house of holiness"). The seat of G-d's manifest presence in the physical world, and the location where *korbanot* (animal and

meal offerings) were to be offered exclusively; located on Mount Moriah (the "Temple Mount") in Jerusalem. The first Holy Temple was built by King Solomon and stood for 410 years (733–423 BCE) until its destruction by the Babylonians. The second Temple was built by the Jews returning from exile under the leadership of the "Great Assembly" and stood for 420 years (353 BCE to 69 CE) until its destruction by the Romans. The third Temple, whose details are described in the biblical book of Ezekiel, is to be built by Moshiach.

Hoshana Rabbah The seventh day of the festival of Sukkot (see Volume II of this series, p. 121).

House of Hillel See *Hillel*.

House of Shammai See *Shammai*.

I

Ibn Ezra Rabbi Abraham ibn Ezra, c. 1089–1164, Spain, Italy, and France. Author of one of the classic commentaries on the Bible.

Igrot Kodesh Lit. "holy letters." Name given to published collections of letters by saintly rabbis and leaders. In this book, it refers to the published letters of the Lubavitcher Rebbe (Rabbi Menachem Mendel Schneerson, 1902–1994).

Isaac 17th and 16th centuries BCE, the Holy Land. Son of Abraham and Sarah, and the second of the three "patriarchs" or founding fathers of the Jewish people.

Isaiah Biblical prophet, active in the 7th and 6th centuries BCE. The biblical book of Isaiah contains his recorded prophesies, which include many references to the future coming of the messiah (Moshiach) and describe the universal peace, goodness, and perfection of the messianic era.

Issachar One of the twelve sons of Jacob. Also refers to the Israelite tribe descendant from him.

Iyar Second month of the Jewish calendar, or the eighth month counting from Tishrei. (For the significance of the two different systems for numbering the months of the Jewish year, see entry for *Nissan*.) Approximately April–May. The holiday of Lag BaOmer, celebrating the lives and works of Rabbi Akiva and Rabbi Shimon bar Yochai, is on the 18th of this month. Also see infographic "The Jewish Calendar" on pp. 316–317 of this book.

J

Jacob Also called "Israel." 16th and 15th centuries BCE, the Holy Land and Egypt. Son of Isaac and Rebecca, and the third of the three "patriarchs" or founding fathers

GLOSSARY   337

of the Jewish people. His twelve sons became the progenitors of the twelve tribes of Israel.

Jeroboam ben Nebat Led the rebellion against King Solomon's son Rehoboam to establish the kingdom of Israel in the north of the Holy Land. Reigned 797–776.

Jerusalem Talmud During the talmudic era (see entry for Talmud), there were two major centers of Torah learning—in the Land of Israel and in Babylonia; consequently there are two recensions of the Talmud: the "Jerusalem Talmud" and the "Babylonian Talmud." The Jerusalem Talmud records 150 years of teachings and discussions in the academies of the Land of Israel, approximately 200–350 CE. The term "Talmud," without further qualification, generally means the Babylonian version, which as the later and more comprehensive recension, is considered the more decisive conclusion in matters of Torah law.

Job One of the books of the Bible, which tells the story of Job, a prosperous, charitable, and G-d-fearing man who undergoes a litany of personal and family tragedies, leading to a series of debates between him and his three friends on the meaning of life and of suffering, and in particular, why bad things happen to righteous people. The Talmud cites an opinion attributing its authorship to Moses.

Jochanan ben Zakkai, Rabbi c. 40 BCE to 80 CE, Israel. A mishnaic sage and disciple of both Hillel and Shammai, who served as vice-president of the *sanhedrin* in the period before and after the destruction of the second Holy Temple and was instrumental in ensuring that Judaism would continue to flourish despite the loss of the Temple.

Jocheved Mother of Miriam, Aaron, and Moses.

Joseph Eleventh son of Jacob. Sold into slavery by his brothers, he rose to the position of viceroy of Egypt and saved his family from famine. The saga of Joseph was instrumental in bringing Jacob and his family to settle in Egypt, and the subsequent exile and enslavement of the Israelites in Egypt.

Joshua 1355–1245 BCE. Joshua was the principal disciple of Moses, whom he succeeded as leader of the people of Israel. Joshua brought the Israelites into the Promised Land, led them in the battles for the land's conquest, and oversaw its apportionment amongst the twelve tribes of Israel. The biblical book of Joshua, which he authored, describes the events during his time of leadership.

Joshua ben Chanania, Rabbi Mid-1st to early 2nd century; Peki'in, Israel. A prominent mishnaic sage and vice-president of the *sanhedrin* under Rabban Gamliel. Rabbi Joshua was exceptionally skilled at refuting hostile and heretical interpretations of the Torah, and is recorded to have bested the Roman emperor Hadrian in several such debates.

Joshua ben Levi, Rabbi Early 3rd century; Lod, Israel. A member of the transitional generation between the sages of the Mishnah and the sages of the Talmud, he taught many of the talmudic sages of the next generation. He is also recorded as having the rare privilege of frequently meeting with Elijah the Prophet.

Joshua, Rabbi See *Joshua ben Chanania, Rabbi.*

Jotham's Parable As related in chapter 9 of the biblical book of Judges, Jotham was the sole survivor of the massacre of the 70 sons of Gideon by their brother Abimelech. He pronounced his parable from the top of Mount Grezzim, rebuking the people of Shechem for supporting the murderous usurper.

Jubilee Heb., *yovel.* Occurring every fifty years, the jubilee year was a time to "proclaim liberty throughout the land and to all inhabitants thereof" in the Land of Israel (Leviticus 25:10). All indentured servants, including those who had sold themselves for lifetime labor, were set free, and all ancestral lands that had been sold reverted to their original owners.

Judah Fourth son of Jacob. Also refers to the Israelite tribe descendant from him. The tribe of Judah was assigned the role of the leadership of Israel: The kings of the royal House of David, as well as the future redeemer Moshiach, are descendants of Judah. The name "Judah" (and its derivatives, "Judean" and "Jew") can also refer to the whole of the Jewish people.

Judah ben Beteira, Rabbi 1st-century mishnaic sage

Judah HaNassi, Rabbi c. 120–190 CE; Tiberias, Bet Shearim, and Sepphoris, Israel. President (*nassi*) of the sanhedrin, and redactor of the Mishnah, the first official transcription of the laws of the Oral Torah. He is also known simply as "Rebbi" ("master" and "teacher" *par excellence*) in recognition of this accomplishment, and of the great number of prominent sages who were his disciples.

Judges A series of national leaders who led the people of Israel in war and peace during the four-century period between the passing of Joshua and the establishment of the Israelite monarchy (13th–10th centuries BCE). Also the name of the biblical book recounting the deeds and achievements of the Judges, and the events of that period, authored by the prophet Samuel.

K

Kabbalah; kabbalistic The mystical dimension of the Torah transmitted by tradition from master to disciple (hence the name *kabbalah*, meaning "that which is received"). The teachings of kabbalah explore the relationship between G-d and creation, the significance of the various names of G-d, the structure of the spiritual cosmos, the nature and purpose of evil, the function of the *mitzvot*, and the mission of the human soul which descends into the world to repair its breaches and unite creation with its Creator. Core texts of kabbalah include *Zohar, Sefer*

GLOSSARY

Yetzirah, Sefer HaBahir and the teachings of the Safed kabbalists Rabbi Moshe Cordovero (1522–1570) and Ari (1534–1572).

Kaparot Lit., "atonements." Atonement ceremony performed before Yom Kippur, traditionally while holding a fowl, fish, or money which is then given to charity.

Kashrut The kosher dietary laws.

Keli Yakar Commentary on the Bible, by Rabbi Ephraim of Luntschitz (Leczyca, Poland), c. 1540–1619.

Keruvim Angels. Also refers to two winged figures, hammered out of a block of solid gold, that were part of the cover of the ark in the Holy Temple.

Kesef Mishneh Commentary on Maimonides' *Mishneh Torah,* by Rabbi Joseph Caro (1488–1575).

Keter Shem Tov Compilation of teachings of Rabbi Israel Baal Shem Tov (1698–1760).

Ketoret The incense offered twice daily in the *mishkan* and later in the Holy Temple, as well as by the high priest in the Holy of Holies on Yom Kippur.

Kiddush Lit., "sanctification." A declaration, consisting of some biblical passages and one or two blessings, recited over a cup of wine, expressing the sanctity of the Shabbat or of a festival.

Kiddush hachodesh "Sanctification of the new month." The process by which the Jewish calendar was set by the *sanhedrin* in the Holy Land until the 4th century. See volume I of this series, pp. 169 ff.

Kislev Ninth month of the Jewish calendar, or the third month counting from *Tishrei.* (For the significance of the two different systems for numbering the months of the Jewish year, see entry for *Nissan.*) Approximately November–December. The holiday of Chanukah begins on the 25th of this month. Also see infographic "The Jewish Calendar" on pp. 316–317 of this book.

Kissei Rachamim See entry for *Chida.*

Kohen; kohanim (pl.) "Priest." A descendant of Aaron in the male line, responsible for the service in the Holy Temple, where they were assisted by the Levites. In the present day the *kohanim* perform the "priestly blessing" in the synagogue, and are honored there with being called first for the Torah reading.

Kohen Gadol The "high priest" elected as leader of the *kohanim.* The *kohen gadol* wore special priestly garments, and performed the Yom Kippur service in the Holy Temple.

Korach A cousin of Moses who led a mutiny against Moses' leadership (as related in Numbers 16).

Korban; korbanot (pl.) Lit., "a bringing near." An offering brought to G-d (as a rule, in the Holy Temple), generally an animal, a bird, or a measure of flour. The

340   INSIDE TIME

various *korbanot* and their laws are enumerated in the biblical books of Leviticus and Numbers, and discussed at length in the Mishnah and Talmud.

Kuntres U'Maayan A series of discourses of chassidic teaching authored by Rabbi Shalom DovBer of Lubavitch (1860–1920).

Kuzari Twelfth-century work discussing the principles of Judaism in the form of a dialogue between a Jewish scholar and a non-Jewish king. The author, poet, and philosopher Rabbi Judah HaLevi (1075–1141, Spain), took as his framework the story of the Khazars, a people living in parts of present-day Ukraine, the Caucasus, and Kazakstan, whose king had converted to Judaism some four centuries earlier following a search for the true religion.

L

Lag BaOmer The 33rd day of the *omer* count (see entry for Counting of the *omer*), equivalent to the 18th of the month of *Iyar*. A festive day celebrating the lives and works of Rabbi Akiva and Rabbi Shimon bar Yochai. See volume III of this series, pp. 129 ff.

Leap Year. On the Jewish calendar, a year in which a 13th month is added in order to realign the Jewish year, which is comprised of lunar months, with the solar seasons. See volume I of this series, pp. 193–206. Also see infographic "The Jewish Calendar" on pp. 316–317 of this book.

Lechem Mishneh A commentary on Maimonides' *Mishneh Torah* by Rabbi Abraham Chiyya de Boton, c. 1560–1605, of Salonica (Thessaloniki), Greece.

Lekach Tov Midrashic anthology and commentary on the Five Books of Moses by Rabbi Toviah ben Eliezer, late 11th century, Kastoria, Greece.

Levi; Levites The third of twelve sons of Jacob. Also refers to the Israelite tribe descendant from him, who served as spiritual leaders, and as *kohanim* (priests) and "Levites" (priestly assistants) in the Holy Temple.

Levi Yitzchak of Berdichev, Rabbi 1740–1809, Belarus and Ukraine. Chassidic leader legendary for his defenses of the Jewish people against their critics both in heaven and on earth. Served as rabbi of Berdychiv, Ukraine, from 1785. One of the foremost disciples of Rabbi Dov Ber of Mezheritch.

Levush Halachic work by Rabbi Mordechai Yaffe, 1530–1612, Bohemia, Italy, and Poland.

Liadi A town in White Russia. Served as the headquarters of Rabbi Schneur Zalman of Liadi and Chabad branch of chassidism, which he founded, from 1801 to 1812.

Likutei Sichot A 39-volume collection of essays adapted from the talks of the Lubavitcher Rebbe (Rabbi Menachem Mendel Schneerson, 1902–1994) and edited by him.

GLOSSARY   341

Likutei Torah A book of discourses of chassidic teaching by Rabbi Schneur Zalman
of Liadi (1745–1812).

L'Or HaHalachah A collection of essays by Rabbi Shlomo Yosef Zevin (1886–1978,
Israel).

Lubavitch The town in White Russia, Lyubavichi, that served as the seat of the rebbes of the Chabad-Lubavitch branch of chassidism for 102 years, from 1813 to
1915. The Chabad-Lubavitch movement is also known by the name "Lubavitch."

Lubavitcher Rebbe, The The seventh rebbe or leader of Chabad-Lubavitch, Rabbi Menachem Mendel Schneerson (1902–1994). Commonly referred to as "The
Rebbe."

Lulav Closed frond of the date palm. One of the "four kinds" taken on the festival
of Sukkot.

Luria, Rabbi Isaac See entry for *Ari*.

M

Maamar; maamarim (pl.) A discourse of chassidic teaching.

Maarchei Lev Work by Rabbi Rephael Yosef Hazan, 1741–1822, Turkey and Israel.

Magen Avraham Halachic work by Rabbi Abraham Abele Gombiner, c. 1635–1682,
Kalisz, Poland.

Maggid Mishneh Commentary on Maimonides' *Mishneh Torah*, by Rabbi Vidal of
Toulouse, France (1283–1360).

Maggid of Mezheritch See entry for *Dov Ber of Mezheritch, Rabbi.*

Maharal Rabbi Judah Loew, c. 1520–1609, Poland and Bohemia. Rabbi in several
communities, most notably Prague. A prolific author on many areas of Torah,
whose works strongly influenced later Jewish thinkers and schools of thought.

Maimonides Rabbi Moses ben Maimon, c. 1135–1204, Spain, Morocco, and Egypt.
Also known by the acronym "Rambam." One of the foremost authorities in Torah
law and in Jewish philosophy.

Manna The miraculous "bread from heaven" that sustained the children of Israel in
their travels through the desert, as related in Exodus 16 and Numbers 11.

Maror See *bitter herbs.*

Masaat Binyomin Halachic responsa by Rabbi Benjamin Aaron Solnik, 1530–1620,
Poland.

Matanot Kehunah Commentary on *Midrash Rabbah*, by Rabbi Issachar Ber Katz,
late 16th century, Poland.

Matityahu the Hasmonean See *Hasmoneans.*

Matzah; matzot (pl.) Unleavened bread (the antonym of _chametz_), eaten during the holiday of Passover. _Matzah_ is made and baked quickly before the dough can leaven and rise, and hence commemorates the haste with which the Jews left Egypt during the Exodus.

Mechilta Midrash on the book of Exodus, first century, Israel.

Mefaane'ach Tzefunot A work by Rabbi Menachem Kasher (1895–1983), deciphering and analyzing the writings of the "Rogachover Gaon," Rabbi Joseph Rosin (1858–1936).

Megalleh Amukot Kabbalistic work by Rabbi Nathan Nata Spira, 1585–1633, Krakow, Poland.

Me'iri Rabbi Menachem HaMeiri, c. 1249–1315, Perpignan, France.

Melachah "Work." In Torah law, a physically constructive action that, if it meets a specific set of criteria, is forbidden on the Shabbat.

Menachem Mendel of Lubavitch, Rabbi 1789–1866, Lyubavichi, Russia. The third rebbe of the Chabad-Lubavitch branch of chassidism. Also known as "Tzemach Tzedek," after the collection of his responsa on Torah law and talmudic commentary published under that title.

Menorah A candelabrum. In the _mishkan_ and later in the Holy Temple, the _menorah_ was made of gold and had seven branches. It was kindled every afternoon and burned through the night, representing the divine light which radiated to the entire world from the "dwelling place" of the divine presence. Also refers to the candelabrum (regardless of its shape) which holds eight lights, used on Chanukah to commemorate the miracle that occurred when the Temple's _menorah_ remained lit for eight days on one day's supply of oil.

Meor Einayim Work by Rabbi Azariah dei Rossi, c. 1513–1578, Mantua, Italy.

Me'orei Ohr Encyclopedia of midrashic and kabbalistic teachings compiled by 17th-century kabbalist Rabbi Meir HaKohen Papirash.

Messiah; messianic See _Moshiach_.

Metzudat Zion One of a pair of biblical commentaries by 18th-century sage Rabbi David Altschuler, who lived in Jaworow, Galicia. His _Metzudat Zion_ explains individuals words, and his _Metzudat David_ elucidates the meaning of the text.

Mezuzah; mezuzot (pl.) Lit., "doorpost." A parchment scroll, containing biblical verses encapsulating fundamental beliefs and practices of Judaism (Deuteronomy 6:4–9 and 11:13–21), affixed to the right post of each doorway in a Jewish home or business.

Midrash; midrashic; midrashim (pl.) General name given to explanations and expositions of biblical verses cited by the sages of the mishnaic and talmudic eras. These include the _halachic_ midrashim—expositions of Torah law using traditional

GLOSSARY   343

exegetical methods (as in the midrashic works *Mechilta, Torat Kohanim,* and *Sifri*); or non-legal teachings, called *aggadah,* including ethics, homilies, narratives, etc. (as in *Pirkei d'Rabbi Eliezer, Midrash Rabbah,* and *Midrash Tanchuma*). In a looser sense, the term "Midrash" also includes post-talmudic narratives and teachings.

Midrash Rabbah General name given to ten different collections of midrashim on the Five Books of Moses and five other biblical books (referred to as the "five scrolls"), based mostly on the teachings of talmudic sages from the Land of Israel from the 3rd and 4th centuries. The ten works are: *Bereishit Rabbah* on the book of Genesis; *Shemot Rabbah* on Exodus; *Vayikra Rabbah* on Leviticus; *Bamidbar Rabbah* on Numbers; *Devarim Rabbah* on Deuteronomy; *Esther Rabbah* on the book of Esther; *Shir ha-Shirim Rabbah* on Song of Songs; *Ruth Rabbah* of the book of Ruth; *Eichah Rabati* on Lamentations; and *Kohelet Rabbah* on Ecclesiastes. The collections vary widely in date of compilation (between approximately the 3rd and 12th centuries) and their treatment of the source material, some parts being a running commentary on the biblical narrative while others consist of lengthy discourses on particular verses.

Midrash Tanchuma A midrash on the Five Books of Moses, collected from the sermons of Rabbi Tanchuma bar Aba (though quoting numerous other talmudic sages as well). Composed early-to mid-4th century; Israel.

Mikveh Lit., "pool." A ritual bathing pool used for the immersion of people, utensils, and other objects, as part of their transition to ritual purity.

Minchah Lit., "gift" and "offering." The afternoon prayer service.

Minhag; minhagim (pl.) "Custom." A traditional practice or ritual that, while not mandated by Torah law, is considered integral to religious life and Jewish identity.

Miriam Elder sister of Moses. A prophetess and leader during the Egyptian exile and in the period following the Exodus.

Mishkan "Dwelling place." The portable sanctuary (also called the "Tabernacle") built by the children of Israel to accompany them in their journeys in the desert, which served as the "dwelling" for the divine presence in the Israelite camp. The *mishkan* was the forerunner of the Holy Temple in Jerusalem.

Mishnah; mishnaic The Mishnah is the basic summary text of the laws of the Torah, as redacted toward the end of the 2nd century by Rabbi Judah HaNassi. It is the first officially written text of any part of the "Oral Torah" which had hitherto been passed down orally from teacher to disciple. The Talmud is structured as commentaries on the Mishnah.

Mishnah Berurah Code of Jewish laws compiled by Rabbi Israel Meir Kagan (he is also known as "Chafetz Chaim"), 1838–1933, Radun, Belarus.

Mishnaic Era Approximately 1st century BCE to 2nd century CE; see entry for Mishnah.

Mishneh Torah 14-volume codification of *halachah*, covering all areas of Torah law, composed by Maimonides (Rabbi Moses ben Maimon, c. 1135–1204, Spain, Morocco, and Egypt).

Mitzvah; mitzvot (pl.) Lit., "commandment." A good deed or religious precept; more specifically, one of the Torah's 613 divine commandments, or of the seven ordinances enacted by the rabbis. In chassidic literature the word *mitzvah* is also seen as related to the Aramaic word *tzavta*, "attachment," indicating that a *mitzvah* creates a bond between G-d who commands and the person who performs it.

Modeh Ani "I offer thanks..." A short prayer recited immediately upon waking.

Mordechai Mid-4th century BCE, Persia and Israel. Jewish leader at the time of the miracle of Purim and a member of the "Great Assembly" of sages and prophets that led the people of Israel during the return to the Holy Land at the start of the Second Temple Era. See entries for *Purim* and *Esther*.

Mordechai on Talmud Commentary on Talmud, by Rabbi Mordechai ben Hillel Ashkenazi (d. 1298; Nuremburg, Germany).

Moses 1393–1273 BCE. First leader of the Jewish nation and the greatest prophet in Jewish tradition. Moses took the Israelites out of Egypt, performed numerous miracles for them (including the ten plagues brought upon Egypt, the splitting of the sea, extracting water from a rock, and bringing down the *manna*), received the Torah from G-d and taught it to the people, and led the children of Israel for 40 years as they journeyed through the wilderness.

Moshiach Lit., "anointed one." One of the thirteen principles of the Jewish faith is that G-d will send a leader and redeemer to return the dispersed people of Israel to their homeland; rebuild the Holy Temple; and usher in a messianic era of universal peace, wisdom, and perfection, as foretold in the Five Books of Moses (e.g., Numbers 24 and Deuteronomy 30) and extensively prophesied by Isaiah, Ezekiel, Zechariah, and virtually all the prophets of Israel. In the words of Maimonides, "In that time there will be no hunger or war, no jealousy or rivalry. For the good will be plentiful, and all delicacies available as dust. The entire occupation of the world will be only to know G-d... as it is written (Isaiah 11:9): 'For the earth shall be filled with the knowledge of G-d, as the waters cover the sea.'"

Mount Sinai See entry for *Sinai*.

Musaf; musafim (pl.). Lit., "addition." Additional offerings brought in the Holy Temple on special days (Shabbat, *Rosh Chodesh*, the festivals, etc.). Also refers to an additional prayer service recited nowadays on those occasions.

Mussar Torah teachings that address the goals of refining the human character and

GLOSSARY   345

developing moral and ethical perfection. Also refers to the movement, devoted to the above aims, founded by Rabbi Israel Salanter (1810–1883; Lithuania, Germany, and Russia).

N

Nachal Yitzchak Work by Rabbi Isaac Elchanan Spector, 1817–1896, Belarus and Lithuania.

Nachmanides Rabbi Moses ben Nachman, c. 1195–1270, Spain and Israel. Recognized as a leading authority in all areas of Torah, Nachmanides is the author of influential works of talmudic analysis, Torah law, Jewish philosophy, and kabbalah, as well as an in-depth commentary on the Five Books of Moses.

Nathan, Rabbi Mishnaic sage of the mid-2nd century, Israel. Compiler of *Avot d'Rabbi Nathan*, expositions on the teachings quoted in *Ethics of the Fathers*.

Nazir A person who takes a vow to abstain from wine, not to cut his or her hair, and other self-imposed restrictions. See Numbers 6.

Nebuchadnezzar Babylonian emperor who destroyed the first Holy Temple and exiled the Jewish people in 423 BCE.

Niddah Lit., "removed." A state of ritual impurity brought about by uterine bleeding, or a woman in this state. Physical contact between husband and wife is suspended until the woman counts seven "clean days" free of bleeding and immerses in a *mikveh* (immersion pool). Also, the name of a tractate of the Mishnah that discusses these laws.

Ninth of Av See *Tishah B'Av*

Nissan First month of the Jewish calendar, approximately March–April. Also the seventh month, counting from Tishrei. The Torah, in Exodus 12, declares *Nissan*—the month of the Exodus and of Israel's birth as a people—the "first of the months of the year"; on the other hand, the first of *Tishrei*, the anniversary of the creation of Adam and Eve, is observed as Rosh Hashanah, "head of the year." Thus, the Jewish calendar effectively has two "heads" or beginnings: *Tishrei,* marking the beginning of the natural year; and *Nissan,* marking the beginning of the miraculous year. The holiday Passover, marking the liberation of the Jewish people from Egyptian slavery, begins on the 15th of *Nissan*. See pp. 1–12 of this volume. Also see infographic "The Jewish Calendar" on pp. 316–317.

O

Ohr HaChaim Commentary on the Bible, by Rabbi Chaim ibn Attar, 1696–1743, Morocco and Jerusalem.

Ohr HaTorah A multivolume series of discourses of chassidic teaching by Rabbi Menachem Mendel of Lubavitch (1789–1866).

Omer Lit., "sheaf." A measure of volume for grain or flour, used in biblical and talmudic times, equal to approximately 43 ounces. Also refers to a meal offering, consisting of this amount of barley flour, which was brought in the Holy Temple on the second day of Passover and inaugurated the 49-day "counting of the *omer*" culminating in the festival of Shavuot.

Orach Chaim Lit., "Way of life." The first of the four sections of *Shulchan Aruch* (Code of Jewish Law). The *Orach Chaim* section includes the laws of prayer, of frequently performed *mitzvot* such as *tzitzit* and *tefilin*, and the laws of Shabbat and the Jewish festivals.

Oral Torah Collective name for the entire body of interpretation, exposition, and commentary that is part of the Torah's "chain of transmission" from Moses onward, in contrast to the Written Torah canonized by Moses and the later prophets. Originally the Oral Torah was in fact oral, handed down from teacher to disciple without being officially put in writing. That changed when Rabbi Judah HaNassi —foreseeing the expansion of the Jewish diaspora and the end of a single, centralized *sanhedrin* (the council of sages which served as the highest authority on Torah law in each generation) to preserve the oral tradition—redacted the Mishnah in approximately 189 CE. The process was repeated some 300 years later when Rav Ashi and Ravina redacted the Talmud in the 5th century. In the centuries since, the Torah sages of each generation wrote and published their commentaries, responsa, and codifications of Torah law as their contributions to the constantly evolving Oral Torah.

P

Parashah; parashat; parashiot (pl.) Lit., "passage" or "chapter." A portion of the Bible as divided according to the annual Torah-reading cycle. Can also refer to a biblical section discussing a single topic, marked off in the Torah scroll by an empty space before and after it.

Pardes; Pardes Rimonim Fundamental work of kabbalah, by Rabbi Moshe Cordovero, 1522–1570, Safed, Israel.

Passover Heb., *Pesach.* A seven-day festival (eight days outside the Holy Land) beginning on the 15th day of the Jewish month of Nissan, commemorating the Exodus from Egypt. See volume III of this series, pp. 23–93.

Passover offering Heb., *korban pesach.* A yearling lamb or kid, brought as an offering on the eve of Passover in the Holy Temple and eaten on Passover night during the *seder* feast.

GLOSSARY   347

Penei David See entry for *Chida.*

Pesach Sheini Lit., "Second Passover." Occurring on the 14th of *Iyar,* one month after
the regular Passover, the "second Passover" was an opportunity to observe the
mitzvah of bringing and eating the Passover offering for those who were unable
to do so in its proper time on *Nissan* 14. See volume III of this series, pp. 113 ff.

Pesikta Rabbati Midrash on the Torah readings and *haftarot* for special Shabbats
throughout the year, composed in the Land of Israel around the 5th-6th centuries
by an otherwise unknown Rav Kahana.

Pilpul The sharp, mind-bending logic that describes certain aspects of talmudic
dialectic.

Pri Eitz Chaim Kabbalistic work by Rabbi Chaim Vital (1543-1620).

Psalms Biblical book of religious poetry arranged by King David.

Purim Lit., "lots" (Persian or Akkadian). A holiday celebrated on the 14th day of
the Jewish month of *Adar* (or on the 15th of *Adar* in ancient walled cities, notably
Jerusalem), commemorating the salvation of the Jews of the Persian empire from
annihilation at the hands of the prime minister Haman, who had cast lots to determine an auspicious date for that purpose. The biblical book of Esther, which
tells the story, is read twice during the holiday. Other observances include feasting and drinking, giving alms to the poor, and sending gifts of food to friends. See
volume II of this series, pp. 229-275.

R

Raavad Rabbi Abraham ben David, c. 1120-1198, Nimes and Posquieres (Vauvert),
France. Prominent Torah scholar and kabbalist. He disagreed with many of Maimonides' legal conclusions in *Mishneh Torah,* and his critical glosses on it are included in most editions of that work.

Rabbi Lit., "my master" or "my great one." Traditional honorific for Torah teachers
and leaders, particularly those upon whom the authority to decide matters of Torah law has been conferred.

Radak Rabbi David Kimchi, c. 1160-1235, Narbonne, France. A foremost authority
on Hebrew philology, and the author of a classic commentary on the Bible.

Radbaz Rabbi David ibn Zimra, c. 1470-1580, Egypt and Israel.

Ran Rabbi Nissim ben Reuben Gerondi, d. 1376, Barcelona, Spain. A leading authority on Torah law and an important voice of Jewish philosophy.

Rasha Sinner or wicked person.

Rashba Rabbi Solomon ben Aderet, 1235-1310, Barcelona, Spain.

Rashi Rabbi Solomon Yitzchaki, 1040-1105, Troyes, France. Foremost of the biblical elucidators, Rashi's commentary on Torah is a first point of reference for school-child and scholar alike.

Rav Lit. "master" or "great one." A variant of the title Rabbi (see entry above). With the sages of the talmudic era, "Rabbi" is used to denote the sages of the Mishnah and later sages who lived and taught in the Land of Israel, whereas "Rav" denotes the sages of Babylon. When applied to post-talmudic sages, the two forms are used interchangeably. (The title "Rav," without a name following it, can also refer to the 3rd century talmudic sage Rav Aba bar Aivu.)

Rava c. 280-352, Mechoza, Babylonia. A prominent talmudic sage quoted on virtually every page of the Babylonian Talmud, and whose debates on matters of Torah law with his colleague Abayei are classics of talmudic dialectic.

Rebbe A variant of the title "Rabbi." Generally used to refer to chassidic leaders. "The Rebbe" without qualification commonly refers to the Lubavitcher Rebbe, Rabbi Menachem Mendel Schneerson (1902-1994).

Rebbe, The See entry for *Lubavitcher Rebbe, The.*

Redemption, The See entry for *Moshiach.*

Rehoboam Son of King Solomon; reigned 797-780 BCE. Upon his ascension to the throne the people of Israel split into two kingdoms: the southern kingdom of Judea, which remained faithful to the House of David and Solomon; and the northern kingdom of Israel, which elected Jeroboam ben Nebat as their king.

Reish Lakish Rabbi Shimon ben Lakish, c. 190-280, Tiberias, Israel. A talmudic sage quoted often in both Talmuds and the Midrashim. Originally a gladiator and bandit, he was "discovered" and introduced to Torah by the talmudic sage Rabbi Jochanan, whose sister he married.

Rema Rabbi Moses Isserlis, c. 1525-1572, Krakow, Poland. Author of glosses on *Shulchan Aruch.*

Rephidim One of the 42 encampments of the children of Israel in their journeys through the desert.

Responsa Latin plural of *responsum*, "answer." A body of written decisions and rulings given by *halachic* scholars in response to questions addressed to them.

Rif Rabbi Isaac al-Fasi, 1013-1103, Morocco and Spain. Author of an early work of *halachah* (Torah law) written as a digest of the Talmud and including commentary by the *geonim*, which served as the basis for many subsequent *halachic* works.

Rosh Rabbi Asher ben Yechiel, c. 1250-1327, Germany and Spain. His commentary on the Talmud, discussing the legal rulings to be extracted from its discussions, is a foundational work of Torah law.

Rosh Chodesh Lit., "head of the month." The day or days which mark the start of a new month on the Jewish calendar. The first day of each month is observed as

GLOSSARY   349

Rosh Chodesh. When a month has 30 days (the Jewish month can have 29 or 30 days), the last day of the month also serves as the first of two *Rosh Chodesh* days for the following month. See infographic "The Jewish Calendar" on pp. 316–317 of this book.

Rosh Dovid See entry for *Chida.*

Rosh Hashanah Lit., "head of the year." The solemn New Year holiday, observed on the 1st and 2nd days of the Jewish month of *Tishrei.* Major themes of the holiday are our reacceptance of G-d's sovereignty over the universe and ourselves, and G-d's judgment and determination of the fate of all people for the coming year. See volume II of this series, pp. 1–31.

Ruth One of the books of the Bible, which tells the story of Ruth, a Moabite princess who converted to Judaism and, after the death of her husband, loyally followed her impoverished mother-in-law Naomi to the Land of Israel. Ruth's controversial marriage to the Judean leader Boaz produced a child, Obed, who was the grand-father of King David.

S

Saadiah Gaon, Rabbi c. 882–942, Egypt, Israel, and Babylonia. Author of the first comprehensive description of the Jewish belief system, written in Judeo-Arabic, the vernacular of his day, and translated into Hebrew as *Emunot ve-Dei'ot* ("Beliefs and Opinions").

Samuel 929–877 BCE, Ramah and Shiloh, Israel. One of the greatest of the prophets, and the last of the line of the Judges. Samuel anointed Saul as the first Israelite king, and then, after G-d revoked Saul's kingship because of disobedience, he anointed King David. He wrote the first part of the biblical book of Samuel (the rest was completed by the prophets of the next generation), which records the events of his lifetime and of Saul's and David's reigns; in medieval times it was divided into two books, I Samuel and II Samuel. Samuel also authored the biblical books of Judges and Ruth.

Sanctuary, The See entry for *Mishkan.*

Sanhedrin High court of Torah law. When unqualified, this term refers to the "great *sanhedrin*," consisting of 71 (later 72) members, the highest legislative and judiciary authority in Judaism, with original jurisdiction over matters of national policy such as war, as well as serving as a court of last resort for issues undecided by the lower courts ("small *sanhedrins,*" consisting of 23 members). Its heads were called the *nassi* ("prince") and *av beit din* ("father of the court"), respectively. Under Roman rule its powers gradually eroded, and, starting in the 4th century, it ceased to exist.

Schneerson, Rabbi Yosef Yitzchak 1880-1950, Russia and the U.S. Sixth "rebbe" or leader of the Chabad-Lubavitch branch of chassidism.

Schneur Zalman of Liadi, Rabbi 1745-1812. Founder of the Chabad branch of chassidism.

Second Tablets See *Tablets of the Covenant.*

Second Temple See *Holy Temple.*

Second Temple Era 353 BCE to 69 CE, the period during which the second Holy Temple stood in Jerusalem.

Seder Lit., "order." The step-by-step procedure for the meal on the first night of Passover. It includes the recital of the Passover *Haggadah* and the eating of *matzah* and bitter herbs. Outside of the Holy Land, the *seder* is held a second time on the second night of Passover.

Seder hishtalshelut Lit., "order of evolution." The chain of *sefirot,* processes, and "worlds" (i.e., realms of reality) by which G-d generates and relates to creation, as described at length in the works of kabbalah. See the essay *The Evolution of Time* in volume I of this series, pp. 3-19.

Sefat Emet Collective name given to the prolific works of Rabbi Yehudah Aryeh Leib Alter (1847-1905), the second rebbe of the Ger branch of chassidism. His discourses on the weekly Torah readings and the festivals have gained popularity and renown as classics of chassidic literature.

Sefer HaBahir Kabbalistic work, attributed to the mishnaic sage Rabbi Nechunyah ben Hakanah (1st century, Israel).

Sefer HaChinuch Compilation of the 613 *mitzvot* (divine commandments) of the Torah, each with a summary of its possible rationales and the basic laws applicable to it. Composed in 13th-century Barcelona, Spain by an unknown author.

Sefer HaMaamarim Lit. "book of discourses." Can refer to any of a number of collections of discourses of chassidic teaching authored and/or delivered by the rebbes of Chabad-Lubavitch. This title is usually followed by a number representing the Jewish year in which they were written or delivered (e.g., *Sefer HaMaamarim 5565,* which includes discourses delivered by Rabbi Schneur Zalman of Liadi in the Jewish year 5565 [1804-1805]).

Sefer HaSichot A 10-volume collection of essays adapted from the talks of the Lubavitcher Rebbe (Rabbi Menachem Mendel Schneerson, 1902-1994) and edited by him during the years 1987 to 1992. Each volume is followed by a number representing the Jewish year in which the talks were delivered (e.g., *Sefer HaSichot 5748* includes talks from September of 1987 to September of 1988).

Sefer Yetzirah An early work of kabbalah attributed to the patriarch Abraham.

Sefirah; sefirot (pl.) In kabbalistic literature, the term for the divine attributes or

GLOSSARY

351

emanations which G-d manifested to create the world and relate to His creations. The term *sefirah* (lit. "counting") is also used to refer to the "counting of the *omer*" between Passover and Shavuot.

Selichot Lit., "forgivenesses." Special prayers recited during the week preceding Rosh Hashanah, on fast days, or on other penitential occasions. On the night following the Shabbat before Rosh Hashanah, this prayer service is held just after midnight.

Sforno Commentary on the Bible, by Rabbi Obadiah Sforno, c. 1475-1550, Rome and Bologna, Italy.

Shaar HaPesukim Kabbalistic work containing the teachings of Ari (Rabbi Isaac Luria, 1534-1572).

Shaarei Orah A work by Rabbi DovBer of Lubavitch (1773-1827).

Shabbat Lit., "cessation" and "rest." The weekly day of rest observed on the seventh day of the week (i.e., Saturday) in remembrance that "six days G-d created the heavens and the earth... and He rested on the seventh day" (Exodus 20:11). See volume I of this series, pp. 73 ff.

Shach Commentary on the *Shulchan Aruch* by Rabbi Shabetai HaKohen, 1622-1663, Lithuania and Bohemia.

Shaloh Rabbi Isaiah Horowitz, c. 1560-1630, Poland, Austria, Germany, and Israel. Served as rabbi of numerous leading communities in Europe (including Dubna, Frankfurt am Mein, and Prague), and later in Jerusalem, Safed, and Tiberias. Author of *Shenei Luchot ha-Berit*, an encyclopedic work blending talmudic discourse, Torah law, kabbalah, biblical commentary, and ethics. Both the work and the author are commonly referred to as "Shaloh," an acronym for the work's title.

Shalom DovBer of Lubavitch, Rabbi 1860-1920. The fifth rebbe or leader of Chabad-Lubavitch. Also known by the acronym "Rashab."

Shamash Lit., "servant." The beadle (caretaker) of synagogue or other religious institution. Also the name of the candle that is used to kindle the Chanukah lights and is then positioned above them in the *menorah*.

Shammai First century BCE, Jerusalem, Israel. A mishnaic sage who served as vice-president of the *sanhedrin*. In questions of Torah law Shammai tended toward the stricter view, as did his disciples (known as the "House of Shammai"), in contrast to the opinions of his colleague Hillel and his disciples.

Shavuot Lit., "weeks." A one-day festival (two days outside of Israel) commemorating the giving of the Torah on Mount Sinai. Shavuot occurs on the 6th (and 7th) of the Jewish month of *Sivan*, but strictly speaking is defined as the day after the completion of the seven-week "counting of the *omer*" beginning on the second night of Passover.

352　　　　INSIDE TIME

Shechinah Lit., "indwelling." The manifestation of the divine presence in this world; equated in kabbalistic and chassidic literature with G-d's feminine manifestation.

She'erit Yaakov Commentary on Torah by Rabbi Israel Jacob Algazi, 1680–1756, Safed, Israel.

Shema Lit., "hear." The Jewish creed of belief in G-d, also including the fundamental precepts of love of G-d, awe for G-d, Torah study, tefilin, mezuzah, tzitzit, and remembering the Exodus from Egypt. It consists of three passages from the Torah (Deuteronomy 6:4–9 and 11:13–21, and Numbers 15:37–41), opening with the declaration, "Hear O Israel, G-d is our G-d, G-d is one." The Shema is recited in the morning and evening prayers, and before retiring for the night. Its first two passages are inscribed on the parchment scrolls placed inside tefilin and mezuzot.

Shemini Atzeret Lit., "eighth [day] of ingathering" or "eighth [day] of retention." A one-day festival (observed for two days outside of the Land of Israel) that immediately follows the seven-day festival of Sukkot. See volume II of this series, p. 125 ff.

Shemittah; shemittot (pl.) Lit., "suspension." A biblically mandated sabbatical year, occurring once every seven years, during which all agricultural work on the land ceases, indentured servants are freed, and personal debts are suspended.

Shetei Yadot 17th-century work by Rabbi Abraham Chizkuni.

Sheva berachot Lit., "seven blessings." The blessings recited under the chupah (wedding canopy) as part of the marriage ceremony. The term is also used for the week of festivities following the wedding, during which these blessings are repeated.

Shevat Eleventh month of the Jewish calendar, or the fifth month counting from Tishrei. (For the significance of the two different systems for numbering the months of the Jewish year, see entry for Nissan). Approximately January–February. The 15th of Shevat (Tu BiShevat) is the "New Year for Trees." Also see infographic "The Jewish Calendar" on pp. 316–317 of this book.

Shimon bar Yochai, Rabbi Second century; Israel. A disciple of Rabbi Akiva and a key figure in the transmission of the Torah's "inner" or esoteric dimension. Rabbi Shimon bar Yochai's mystical teachings are recorded in the Zohar, the most important text of kabbalah.

Shimon ben Gamliel, Rabbi Also called "Rabban Shimon ben Gamliel" ("Rabban" being a title given to the president of the sanhedrin). A mishnaic sage of the mid-2nd century who lived in Shefar'am, Israel. Can also refer to his grandfather and namesake, who was killed during or after the Roman siege of Jerusalem in 69 CE.

Shitah Mekubetzet Talmudic-halachic work by Rabbi Betzalel Ashkenazi, c. 1520–1592, Israel.

GLOSSARY   353

Shmuel of Lubavitch, Rabbi 1834-1882. The fourth rebbe or leader of Chabad-Lubavitch. Also known by the acronym "Maharash."

Shofar The horn of a ram or other animal, sounded on Rosh Hashanah and at the close of Yom Kippur, and by custom also throughout the month of *Elul*. The symbolisms of the *shofar* are numerous and varied, including: the reminiscence of the ram "tangled in the bush by its horns" during the Binding of Isaac (Genesis 22:13), the *shofar* sounded at Sinai (Exodus 19), and that of Moshiach (Isaiah 27:13, et al.). It also represents a child's primal cry, and the trumpets sounded at a royal coronation.

Shulchan Aruch Lit., "set table." The code of Torah law composed by Rabbi Yosef Caro (1488-1575) as a digest of his encyclopedic work *Beit Yosef*, with glosses added by Rema (Rabbi Moses Isserlis, 1525-1572). The *Shulchan Aruch* and its commentaries form the basis for virtually all subsequent deliberations of Torah law.

Shulchan Aruch HaRav Code of Torah law, authored by Rabbi Schneur Zalman of Liadi (1745-1812).

Siddur The Jewish prayer book. Its basic framework was developed by the sages of the Great Assembly, and was later reshaped under the leadership of Rabban Gamliel, with additional prayers being added by various authorities from then until contemporary times. It includes selections from the Bible (particularly the book of Psalms), praise of G-d, requests for personal and national needs, and much else, and has been the subject of hundreds of commentaries spanning all genres of Jewish thought.

Siddur HaRav Prayer book that includes rulings on the laws of prayer and other laws compiled by Rabbi Schneur Zalman of Liadi (1745-1812).

Siddur Im D'ach Prayer book with commentary in the form of discourses of chassidic teaching by Rabbi Schneur Zalman of Liadi (1745-1812).

Sifri Midrash on the biblical books of Numbers and Deuteronomy, from the school of Rabbi Shimon bar Yochai (2nd century; Israel).

Simcha Bunim of Peshischa, Rabbi Chassidic leader, c. 1765-1827, Przysucha, Poland.

Simchat Torah Lit., "rejoicing of the Torah." A festival on which the annual Torah-reading cycle is concluded and recommenced, and celebrated with great joy, singing, and the *hakafot* procession and dancing with the Torah scrolls. Outside of the Land of Israel, Simchat Torah is observed on *Tishrei* 23, the second day of Shemini Atzeret; In Israel, it is observed on the first (and only) day of Shemini Atzeret, on *Tishrei* 22. See volume II of this series, pp. 125 ff.

Simeon The second of the twelve sons of Jacob. Also refers to the Israelite tribe descendant from him.

Sinai; Sinaitic Pertaining to the giving of the Torah on Mount Sinai, as related in Exodus 19-20 and 24.

Sivan Third month of the Jewish calendar, or the ninth month counting from Tishrei. (For the significance of the two systems for month numbering, see entry for *Nissan.*) Approximately May–June. The festival of Shavuot is on the 6th of this month. Also see infographic "The Jewish Calendar" on pp. 316-317 of this book.

Solomon, King 849-797 BCE; Jerusalem, Israel. Son and successor of King David, and builder of the first Holy Temple in Jerusalem. Regarded as "the wisest of all men," the wisdom of Solomon is contained in the biblical books of Proverbs, Song of Songs, and Ecclesiastes. Under Solomon's reign the people of Israel flourished as never before, both materially and spiritually.

Song of Songs Biblical book composed by King Solomon (849-797 BCE). Its form is a poetic dialogue between a shepherdess and her beloved, describing their mutual love and desire for each other through all the vicissitudes of their relationship. Classical Jewish tradition sees this as an extended allegory on the various phases of the relationship between G-d and the people of Israel throughout history.

Spies, The The twelve spies sent by Moses to scout the Holy Land, whose negative report delayed the Israelites' entrance into the land by 40 years, as related in Numbers 13-14.

Sukkah Lit., "shed." A hut of temporary construction with a roof-covering of branches, in which the Torah (Leviticus 23:39-43) commands to dwell for the duration of the Sukkot festival, to commemorate the divine protection of the children of Israel during their forty-year trek in the desert.

Sukkot A seven-day festival, beginning on the 15th of the Jewish month of Tishrei. The festival takes its name from the temporary dwelling, called a *sukkah* ("shed"), in which the Torah (Leviticus 23:39-43) instructs to dwell during this period, commemorating the divine protection of the children of Israel during their forty-year trek in the desert on their way to the Promised Land. Sukkot is noted for its special joy, coming in the wake of the solemn "days of awe" of Rosh Hashanah and Yom Kippur in the first half of the month. Another of its observances is the daily taking and waving of the "four kinds" (citron, palm branch, myrtles, and willows). See volume II of this series, pp. 77 ff.

T

Tablets of the Covenant Heb., *luchot ha'berit.* Also called "the tablets of testimony" (*luchot ha'eidut*). The two stone tablets on which G-d inscribed the Ten Commandments and which Moses brought down from Mount Sinai. The tablets were kept in a specially built "ark" in the innermost chamber of the Holy Temple (the

GLOSSARY   355

"Holy of Holies"). There were actually two sets of tablets, as the first were broken by Moses when he witnessed the people of Israel worshipping the Golden Calf; when G-d forgave Israel's sin, He instructed Moses to carve a second set of tablets (see account in Exodus 32–34).

Talmud; talmudic The most important work of Judaism after the Bible, the Talmud is a multivolume compilation of teachings and deliberations by hundreds of sages over a period of close to 300 years, from the 3rd through 5th centuries. The Talmud follows the format of the Mishnah's six "orders" and 63 "tractates" (with the addition of 14 "minor tractates"), and is structured in the form of legal expositions on the Mishnah and other mishnaic-era teachings (called *baraitot*), along with non-legal teachings (called *aggadah*) including ethical aphorisms, homilies, stories, and narratives. Much of the Talmud is written in Aramaic, which was the spoken language of the Jewish community at the time. The terms "Talmud" and "talmudic" are also used in the more general sense to include the Mishnah and *baraitot* along with the Talmudic commentary and discussion, and other works by the sages of the mishnaic and talmudic eras (also called midrashim).

Tammuz Fourth month of the Jewish calendar, or the tenth month counting from Tishrei. (For the significance of the two different systems for numbering the months of the Jewish year, see entry for Nissan.) Approximately June–July. The "Three Weeks" of mourning for the destruction of the Holy Temple begin with a fast day on the 17th of this month, commemorating Moses' shattering of the Tablets, the Roman penetration of Jerusalem, and various other calamities. Also see infographic "The Jewish Calendar" on pp. 316–317 of this book.

Tanchuma See entry for Midrash Tanchuma.

Tanya A work by Rabbi Schneur Zalman of Liadi (1745–1812) in which he presents the fundamental doctrines of the Chabad branch of chassidism.

Targum Collective name for various Aramaic translations of the Bible.

Taz Halachic work by Rabbi David Segal (1586–1667, Poland), composed as a commentary on the Shulchan Aruch.

Tefach; tefachim (pl.) A biblical measurement, equal to the width of a closed fist (approx. 3–4 inches).

Tefilin Lit., "prayer accessories." Small leather cubes, dyed black and containing parchment scrolls inscribed with the Shema and other biblical passages, worn on the arm and head of adult men during weekday morning prayers. (See Exodus 13:9 and 13:16, and Deuteronomy 6:8 and 11:18.)

Ten Commandments Ten fundamental divine commandments which G-d spoke before the assembled people of Israel at the giving of the Torah at Mount Sinai. The Ten Commandments are: belief in G-d; the prohibition to worship idols; the prohibition to take G-d's name in vain; observing the Shabbat; honoring one's parents; and the prohibitions of murder, adultery, theft, testifying falsely, and coveting another's property.

Ten Days of *Teshuvah* The first ten days of the Jewish year (*Tishrei* 1–10), which begin with the two-day holiday of Rosh Hashanah and culminate in Yom Kippur. See volume II of this series, pp. 33 ff.

Tereifah Lit., "torn." An otherwise kosher animal or bird that is nonviable—whether because of injury, disease, congenital malformation, or improper slaughtering—and whose meat is therefore prohibited by the Torah for Jewish consumption. In common parlance, *tereifah* (or a syncopated form, *treif*) means any nonkosher food.

Teshuvah Lit., "return." Repentance, seen in Jewish literature as a return to G-d and to one's true essence.

Tevet Tenth month of the Jewish calendar, or the fourth month counting from Tishrei. (For the significance of the two different systems for numbering the months of the Jewish year, see entry for *Nissan*). Approximately December–January. Also see infographic "The Jewish Calendar" on pp. 316–317 of this book.

Thirteen Principles, The The thirteen principles of the Jewish faith, as formulated by the 12th-century sage Maimonides. The thirteen principles are: 1) belief in the existence of G-d; 2) the oneness of G-d; 3) the non-corporeality of G-d; 4) the eternity of G-d, and that G-d preexists all other existences; 5) the imperative to worship and obey G-d exclusively; 6) that G-d communicates to man through prophecy; 7) belief in the prophecy of Moses; 8) the divinity of the Torah; 9) the integrity of both the Written Torah and the Oral Torah; 10) G-d's knowledge of and providence over all human actions; 11) that G-d rewards those who obey His commandments and punishes those who transgress them; 12) to believe in and anticipate the coming of Moshiach; 13) the future resurrection of the dead in the messianic age.

Three Weeks, The A three-week period, beginning on the 17th of the month of Tammuz and ending on the 9th of Av, mourning the destruction of the Holy Temple in Jerusalem. See volume III of this series, pp. 207 ff.

Tikkunei Zohar Addenda to the kabbalistic work *Zohar*.

Tishah B'Av "The ninth of Av." The ninth day of the Jewish month of Av, observed as a day of fasting and mourning commemorating the destruction on this date of both the first and second Holy Temples in Jerusalem, as well as various other calamities in Jewish history. See volume III of this series, pp. 207 ff.

Tishrei Month of the Jewish calendar, approximately September–October. Counting from Nissan (which the Torah designates as the "first of the months of the year")

GLOSSARY   357

it is the seventh month, and is referred to in the Torah as such. However, it is also
regarded as the beginning of the year, as the 1st of *Tishrei* is the anniversary of the
creation of the first man and woman, Adam and Eve. *Tishrei* is a month replete
with festivals: Its first two days are celebrated as Rosh Hashanah, followed later
in the month by the solemn day of Yom Kippur and the joyous festivals of Sukkot
and Simchat Torah. Also see infographic "The Jewish Calendar" on pp. 316-317 of
this book.

Torah Lit., "teaching" and "instruction." In the narrow sense, the term refers to the
Five Books of Moses. In its broader sense, the term refers to the entire body of
Jewish teaching deriving from the divine communication received by Moses at
Mount Sinai and handed down and expounded upon through the generations.

Torah Ohr A book of discourses of chassidic teaching, by Rabbi Schneur Zalman of
Liadi (1745-1812).

Torah-reading cycle See entry for *Annual Torah-reading cycle*.

Torat Chesed *Halachic* responsa by Rabbi Schneur Zalman Fradkin of Lublin
(1830-1902).

Torat Kohanim A midrash on the biblical book of Leviticus, compiled in 2nd-cen-
tury Israel.

Tosafot Collective name given to commentaries on the Talmud by dozens of sages
who lived in Western Europe in the 12th and 13th centuries.

Tosefta A collection of supplementary teachings by mishnaic sages, published as addenda to the Talmud.

Tu BiShevat The 15th of the Jewish month of *Shevat*, observed as the "New Year for
Trees." See volume II of this series, pp. 215 ff.

Tur Important *halachic* work, upon which the *Shulchan Aruch* is based and whose
structure it follows. Compiled by Rabbi Yaakov ben Asher, c. 1270-1345, Germany and Spain.

Turnus Rufus Roman military commander and governor of the Holy Land in the
2nd century CE.

Tzaddik; tzaddikim (pl.) Perfectly righteous person.

Tzemach Tzedek A collection of responsa on Torah law and talmudic commentary
by the third rebbe of Chabad-Lubavitch, Rabbi Menachem Mendel of Lubavitch
(1789-1866). Also used as a reference to Rabbi Menachem Mendel himself.

Tzitzit Lit., "fringes." An arrangement of knotted strings, mandated by the Torah
(Numbers 15:37-40) to be attached to garments of four or more corners as a re-
minder to fulfill the 613 commandments (*mitzvot*) of the Torah.

V

Vital, Rabbi Chaim Safed kabbalist, 1543–1620. A disciple of Ari, and the one entrusted by him with recording his teachings.

V'kachah 5637 A series of discourses of chassidic teaching, by Rabbi Shmuel of Lubavitch (1834–1882), authored and delivered in the Jewish year 5637 (1876–1877).

W

World to Come Heb., *olam haba.* Can refer to the afterlife in which each individual soul receives its reward, or to the collective resurrection of the dead which will take place in the era of Moshiach.

Written Torah The 24 books of the Jewish Bible. Also called *Tanach*, which is an acronym for its three components: 1) *Torah*—the Five Books of Moses; 2) *Neviim* or "Prophets;" and 3) *Ketuvim*—"Scriptures." These are referred to as the "Written Torah," in contrast to the Oral Torah—the explanations and expositions of the Written Torah which were handed down through the generations and not officially committed to writing until the mishnaic era. The final format of the Written Torah was set by the prophets and sages of the "Great Assembly" under the leadership of Ezra in the 4th century BCE. In some contexts, the term "Written Torah" refers more narrowly to the Five Books of Moses only.

Y

Yaavetz Rabbi Jacob Emden, 1698–1776, Altona, Germany. *Yaavetz* is an acronym for his Hebrew name and patronymic, "Yaakov ben Tzvi."

Yahrtzeit Yiddish for "time of year." The anniversary of a person's passing on the Jewish calendar.

Yalkut Reuveni Anthology of kabbalistic teachings compiled by Rabbi Abraham Reuben ha-Cohen Sofer (d. 1673; Prague).

Yalkut Shimoni Comprehensive anthology of early midrashim on the Bible, compiled in the 12th or 13th century by Rabbi Shimon ha-Darshan of Frankfurt am Mein, Germany.

Yerucham, Rabbeinu 14th century *halachist* Rabbi Yerucham ben Meshulam, who lived in France and Spain.

Yishai Hebrew for Jesse, the father of King David.

Yishmael, Rabbi Mishnaic sage Rabbi Yishmael ben Elisha; d. circa 130 CE; Kefar Aziz, Israel. A colleague of Rabbi Akiva.

Yom Kippur Lit., "day of atonement." The holiest day on the Jewish calendar,

GLOSSARY

occurring on the 10th of *Tishrei* and culminating the "Ten Days of *Teshuvah*." A solemn day of fasting and prayer, devoted to repentance and return to G-d. See volume II of this series, pp. 33 ff.

Yom tov Lit., "good day." A festival day on the Jewish calendar, particularly those days on which work is forbidden (though the term is also used more broadly for any festive day or occasion).

Yom Tov Shel Rosh Hashanah 5666 A series of discourses of chassidic teaching, by Rabbi Shalom DovBer of Lubavitch (1860–1920), authored and delivered in the Jewish years 5666 to 5668 (1905 to 1908).

Yoreh De'ah "Instructor of knowledge." The second of the four sections of *Shulchan Aruch* (code of Jewish law). *Yoreh De'ah* codifies ritual laws requiring the expertise of a rabbi, such as the kosher dietary laws.

Yosef, Rav d. 323; Pumbedita, Babylonia. A central figure of the Babylonian Talmud. Although he suffered from blindness, the Talmud characterizes him as a "Sinai," possessing a tremendous breadth of Torah knowledge. He headed the Torah academy of Pumbedita (one of the flagship institutions of Babylonian Jewry), where his disciples included Abayei and Rava.

Yossei, Rabbi Mishnaic sage Rabbi Yossei bar Chalafta, mid-2nd century, Sepphoris, Israel.

Yovel See Jubilee.

Z

Zebulun One of the twelve sons of Jacob. Also refers to the Israelite tribe descendant from him.

Zedekiah The last Judean king of the First Temple Era; reigned 434–423 BCE.

Zohar The fundamental work of kabbalah. Contains the esoteric teachings of Rabbi Shimon bar Yochai and his disciples, in the form of a series of discourses on the Five Books of Moses.

Zohar Chadash Portions of the kabbalistic work *Zohar* that came to light after the work's initial publication in the late 13th century.

INDEX

NOTE: This index references all three volumes of *Inside Time*. The letter indicates the volume number, followed by the page number. Thus: "a167" indicates volume 1, page 167; "c88" indicates volume 3, page 88; etc.

A

Aaron a167; a174; c2; c4; c88; c126; c156; c161; c220; c222–223; c226; c233

Abayei c144; c146

Abraham a61; a67; a143; a153; b3; b92; a94; c71; c159; c174; c202; c287–288

Acharon Shel Pesach see: Eighth day of Passover

Achashveirosh, King b208; b230; b254; b259

Acronyms a8; b165; b195; b208; c31; c298–299; c302; c305

Action see: Deed

Actuality see: Potential vs. actual

Adam a142; b2; b8; b10; b22; b23–24; b224; c7

Adar (month) b243–244; b267; b273; c316–317

Adon Olam (prayer) a121

Afikoman c25; c34; c43; c54; c55; c77

Afternoon prayer see: *Minchah*

Agriculture a190–192; c306–308; c312–313

Ahasuerus
see: Achashveirosh, King

Akeidat Yitzchak (biblical commentary by Rabbi Yitzchak Arama) a3
also see: Binding of Isaac

Akiva, Rabbi a95; a104; c130; c132–137

Al hanissim (prayer) b164; b168–169

Alef (letter) b40

Altar (in the Holy Temple) b95; b120; b213; c51; c244; c277; c283; c288

Alter Rebbe see: Schneur Zalman of Liadi, Rabbi

Amidah (prayer) a47; a123; a201

Aminadab a153

Amram c166

Ananei hakavod see: Clouds of glory

Angels a23; b34; b74; b241; c40; c177–183

Animal kingdom see Four kingdoms

Animal soul b46; b48; b60–61; b222–223; c100; c153; c196

Annual Torah-reading cycle see Torah-reading cycle

Apple b3; b152; c25

Arama, Rabbi Yitzchak see *Akeidat Yitzchak*

Aravah (willow) b88; b92–93; b111; b114–124
also see: Four kinds

Ari (Rabbi Isaac Luria) a52; a121; b66; c73; c90; c139; c233; c299

Ark (in the Holy Temple) b61; b213; c224; c236; c239; c240

Artist a100

Arvit see *Maariv*

Asaf c246–247

Asarah b'Tevet see: Tenth of *Tevet*

INDEX   361

Asceticism; self-denial c74–79
Asham see: Guilt-offering
Ashi, Rav c250
Attachment to G-d see: *Deveikut*
Attributes of the soul see: *Sefirot*
Atzvut see: Sadness
Autumn a190; b145; c296
Av (month) a177; c249; c274; c279–284; c316–317
Av 1 see: First day of *Av*
Av 9 see: Tishah B'Av
Avot see: Ethics of the Fathers
Avudraham, Rabbi David c83
Awe of G-d b274–275; c147
Ax c277; c282–283

B

Baal Shem Tov, Rabbi Israel a28; a31; a33; a42; a121; a208; a213; b114; b116–117; c69; c92; c139
Baal Teshuvah b51–55; b67–68; b94; b144–147; c12; c120–125; c243
  also see: *Teshuvah*
Babylonians b213; c208 ; c216; c254; c256
Baitusim c104
Bal tashchit see: *Lo tashchit*
Balaam's donkey a139
Bar Kochba rebellion c276
Bar mitzra (law of the neighboring field) c177–186
Bar mitzvah c124
Barley a190; a191–192; b222–223; c100; c153; c196
Beauty c285; c289
Bechayei a232; b60; c251
Beinoni (the "intermediate" person) c83–85; c290
Benjamin, Tribe of c276; c282

Berachah see: Blessing on food
Bet (letter) b40
Betar c276; c282
Betrothal see: *Kidushin*
Betulah see: Virgo
Bikurim (first fruits) c153; c193; c195; c197; c199–200
Binding of Isaac b2–3
Birkat haTorah see: Blessing on the Torah
Birth of the moon see: New moon
Birthday a182–183; b244; c6
Bitachon see: Trust in G-d
Bitter herbs see: *Maror*
Bittul (halachic "nullification" of a prohibited substance) c62
Bittul (self-abnegation) a155–156; b54–55; b74; c122–123; c160–161; c224; c229–233
Blessing on food b100
Blessing on the Torah c160
Blood c37–38
Blood, Plague of c36; c37
Boaz a153
Body, the b72–75; b181; b207–213; b233–234
  also see: Physicality
Bon, Rabbi c250
Boots b83; b112
Bow & arrows c130; c138–143
Brain b5–7
Bread b222; c76–78; c306–307; c312–313
  also see: Leaven
Breaking of the Tablets see: Broken Tablets
Brit milah see: Circumcision
Broken Tablets b37–43; b141; c208; c216; c299
Brotherhood b88; b92–93

Burial c276–277; c282
Burning bush b139; c71; c96; c157
Business b19–20; b266; c178–179;
c309

C

Calendar, the Jewish aII; a38–45;
a150; a151; a184–189; a190; a195–
202; a203–204; a208–218; b6;
b137–147; c4–12; c15–16; c101–102;
c277–279; c316–317
Career c31
also see: Earning a living
Caro, Rabbi Joseph b273
Carrying from one domain to
another (on Shabbat) a95–105
Chafetz Chaim a60; c69
Chaim ibn Attar, Rabbi see: *Ohr
HaChaim*
Chametz see: Leaven
Chanah (mother of Samuel) b25;
b29–31
Chananiah ben Akavia, Rabbi c123
Change a10–11; a77–78; a99–102;
a181–182; a188; a195–202; a210;
b90; c35–36
Chanukah a187; a227; b163–203;
b233–234; b241–242; c306
Chanukah *gelt* b165
Chanukah lights b164; b170; b173–
179; b183; b191; b193; b194–203
Charity a28; a113–114; b109; c305
also see: *Matanot l'evyonim*
Charoset c25
Chassidism a187–188; c5
Chatat see: Guilt-offering
Chavah see: Eve
Chazakah (legal status quo) a210–
212; a218

Cherubim see: *Keruvim*
Chesed (*sefirah*/attribute of) a7; a79;
c39; c103; c287
Cheshvan (month) a188; b155–162;
c316–317
Cheshvan 7 see: Seventh of *Cheshvan*
Children c42–43; c285; c289
Chinuch see: Education and *Sefer
HaChinuch*
Choice see Free choice and Chosen
people
Chol HaMoed (intermediate days of
the festivals) c306
Cholent c268–270
Chosen people b243–244; c39–41;
c45; c156; c201–206
also see: Jewish identity
Chronology (in Torah) c117; c126
Chumrot see: Stringency
Chupah (wedding canopy) c293
Circle a82–85; c4–5
Circumcision a132; b259; b263–265;
c37; c40–41; c174–175
Circumference a83–85
Cities of refuge c298–300
Citron see: *Etrog*
Clothing c237–238
Clouds of glory b78
Code of Torah law see: *Shulchan
Aruch*
Coercion b47; b248; b251
Commitment see: *Kabalat ol*
Communication technologies a3–5
Community b92–93; b106–113;
c47–52
Compromise b190–192
Concubine at Gibeah c276
Constraint see: Limitation
Converts (to Judaism) a231; b250;
c124

INDEX 363

Cordovero, Rabbi Moshe a10-11
Coronation see: Divine kingship
Counting of the *omer* a133; b138;
 b140; c25; c29; c57; c64-65; c68;
 c95-112; c130; c153; c157; c191;
 c193; c195-197; c198-200
Covenant between the parts c71
Creation a6-9; a11; a12; a20-22;
 a31-37; a89-92; a121-123; a213;
 b8-16; b40; b53; b116-117; b159;
 c7; c9; c120; c291
 also see: Six days of creation
Creation *ex nihilo* ("from nothing")
 a31; a3:
Custom b123; b151-153

D

Daat (knowledge; awareness;
 experience) a120; a123-124;
 b224-225
Dairy c153
Dancing b248-150; c285
Daniel c234
Darkness a64-65; a155; a156; a204-
 206; b173-179
Darkness, Plague of c37; c72; c203
Daughters of Jerusalem c285;
 c289-290
Daughters of Tzelafchad see:
 Tzelafchad's daughters
David ibn Zimra, Rabbi see: Radbaz
David, King a67; a151; a153; a156;
 a161; c87; c138; c142-143; c264
Day a57-72
Dayeinu (Passover song) c82
Days of Awe b34-35; b79; b275;
 c296; c304
 also see: Rosh Hashanah; Yom
 Kippur; and Ten Days of *Teshuvah*
Days of the week a79; a80; b66

Death a62; a182-183; b46; b243-244;
 c116; c135-136; c139-140
 also see: *Yahrtzeit*
Debate (in Torah) b90-91; c124;
 c158-159; c192
Deborah c87
Deed a90-91; a144-147; b89; b91-92;
 b210; b225-226; c289
Depression c214
Desire b208;
 also see: Will
Destruction of the Temple a135;
 a153; a177; a229-230; b213;
 c77-78; c208; c215-216; c234-237;
 c239-240; c242-243; c244-252;
 c253-261; c280
Deveikut (attachment to G-d) a68;
 b62; b68; b131; b207-213; c144-
 149; c254; c293-294
Dew a117
Diaspora a214-218
Dice see: Lottery
Differentiation a119-126
Diminution of the moon a154-155;
 a160-166
Dira betachtonim see Dwelling for
 G-d in the physical world
Disguise b231
Diversity a124; b90-91; b112; b117;
 c133; c158-159; c167
Divine attributes see: *Sefirot*
Divine kingship b2-3; b7; b10;
 b21-24; b70-71; b101; c278-279;
 c306; c312-313
 also see: *Malchut*
Divine omnipotence c262-263; c264
Divine presence a135; b30; b93; b162;
 b213; b249; c2; c199; c240; c242;
 c280
 also see: Dwelling for G-d in the
 physical world

Divine providence a208; a227; b266; c73

Divine retribution see: Punishment

Divisiveness c282

Divorce b47; c292

Doorway b175; c37

Doughnuts b165

Dov Ber of Mezheritch, Rabbi a8; c79; c263

DovBer of Lubavitch, Rabbi b44; b255

Dreams a71; c267

Dreidel b165

Drunkenness see: Inebriation

Dwelling for G-d in the physical world a27; b28-29; b50; b91-92; b158-162; b209-211; c11; c41; c183-186; c195; c200; c280; c309

E

Earning a living a111-118; c144-149

Eating see: Food

Eber c159

Ecclesiastes a77; a145; a185; a227; b42; c139; c243; c304

Echo c175-176

Education b191-192

Effort see Struggle

Ego; selfhood b54-55; b74-75; b210; b212; b239; c62-70; c122-123
also see: Individuality and *Bittul*

Egypt b140; c29; c36-37; c54; c65-66; c91; c178; c202; c213; c260

Eidut see: Witnesses and Testimonial *mitzvot*

Eight (number) a127; a131-134; a138; b178-179

Eighth day of Passover c26; c66-70; c91-93

Eiruv (Shabbat) a17-18; a95-105

El Al (airline) a37

Elazar ben Azariah, Rabbi c76

Elazar ben Durdaia b57; c120-121

Elazar, Rabbi (son of Rabbi Shimon bar Yochai) c134

Eli b25; b29-30

Eliezer (Abraham's servant) c174

Eliezer, Rabbi c4; c10; c192

Elijah the Prophet c25; c192

Elul (month) a177; a219-221; b37; b39; b43; b158; c5; c295-313; c316-317

Elul 25 b8; b11-13

Engagement c292

Engraving a146-147

Esau b244; c39

Essence, the a42

Esther, Book of b202; b231; b235-238; b242; b249

Esther, Queen b207-208; b230; b235-239; b257

Ethics of the Fathers a3; a49; a139; a145-146; b98; b193; b266; c30; c48; c50; c75; c146; c148; c236; c241; c305

Etrog (citron) a182; b87; b90; b103-105; b110; b111
also see: Four kinds

Euphrates River b157; b162

Eve b224

Evening prayer see: *Maariv*

Evidence a167-168; a170

Evil b41; b53-54

Evil inclination c179; c186

Exile see *Galut*

Exodus, the a186; b94; b196; c2; c7-10; c13-14; c24; c28; c34; c41; c50; c53-57; c82; c87; c91; c99-100; c156; c191; c253; c278

INDEX   365

Ezekiel a232; b44; b46; c37; c38; c50
Ezra a135; c249

F

Faith b217-219; c38; c53-61; c89-90;
  c203
Farming see Agriculture
Fasting & fast days b34; b70; b71;
  b72-75; b257; c179; c209; c215-219
Fast of Esther b231; b257
Fast of Gedaliah c216
Fast of the Firstborn c25; c38
Fear of G-d see Awe of G-d
Feast of Moshiach see Moshiach,
  Meal of
Feet b103; b126; b136;
Femininity see Women & femininity
Festivals (of the Jewish calendar)
  a29-30; a38-45; b259; b262-263;
  c17-18 c204-205
  also see Second day of the
  festivals
Field a190-192; c304-313
Fifteenth (of the month) see Full
  moon
Fifteenth of *Av* a158; c273-290
Fifteenth of *Shevat* see Tu BiShevat
Fifth child, the c45-46
Fifty (number) a133-134
Figs b224-225
Final redemption see Redemption
First creation see Time as the first
  creation
First day of *Av* c209
First day of *Sivan* c155-161
First of the month see Rosh Chodesh
  and New moon
First Tablets see Tablets of the
  Covenant and Broken Tablets

First Temple c239-240
  also see Holy Temple
Firstborn of Egypt c19-20; c37
Flavor see Taste
Flexibility a228
Flood, the a142
Food b72-73; b109; c76
  also see Blessing on food
Forty-nine gates of depravity c64-65
Forty-two journeys (of the children
  of Israel) a232
Four children (Passover) c43-46
Four Cups c25; c54; c58
Four expressions of redemption
  c54-55
Four kinds (Sukkot) b78; b86-94;
  b98; b103-104; b106-108; b110-
  113; b118-120
Four kingdoms b14-16; b57
Four questions c25; c42-43
Four Sons see Four Children
Free choice b8-9; b22; b247-253;
  c202; c204
Freedom b139-140; c28-33; c42-43;
  c54; c91-93; c157
Friday a211
  also see Sixth day (of creation)
Fruit b219-220
Full moon a152-153; a157-158; b101;
  b144; c274; c277-284
Future a178; a213; c92-93
  also see Morning

G

Galut (exile) a134-138; a145; a216;
  a225-233; b96-97; b177; b184;
  b213; c29; c71-79; c89; c128; c198-
  200; c208; c212-213; c242-243;
  c251-252; c253-261; c262-267;

c268–271; c280
also see: Diaspora

Gamliel, Rabban c71; c146

Gavra **vs.** *cheftza* (person vs. object)
a24–30

G-d see: Unity of G-d; Divine
kingship; Divine omnipotence;
Divine presence; and Divine
providence

G-dly soul b222–223
also see: Soul, the and Animal soul

Gebrokts see: Matzah *sheruyah*

Gedaliah ben Achikam c216

Gematria (numerical value of the
Hebrew letters) b12

Gevurah (*sefirah* /attribute of) a79;
c38; c39; c103

Giver-recipient relationship a162–
166; a184–189; c301–303

Giving of the Torah a51; a54; a143;
a187; b38; b42; b143; b149; b247–
263; c8; c25–26; c28–29; c45; c57;
c96; c152; c155–161; c164–165;
c166; c171–176; c178–179; c189–
191; c193–196; c198; c222; c253;
c293; c299

Goal see: Means & end

Gold c224–225

Golden Calf b37–43; b141; b149;
c208; c216; c220–233; c299

Good & evil b53–54; b224;
b243–244

Grace after Meals a85; a94; a105;
a118; a128; c69; c218; c277

Great Assembly b108; c28

Greatness a162–166

Greek (language) c220–221
also see: Hellenism

Guide for the Perplexed a32; a60;
b264

Guilt-offering b44; b46–48

H

Habit c237

Hadas (myrtle) b88; b111;
also see: Four kinds

Haftarah (reading from the Prophets)
a156; c69; c92; c209; c256

Haggadah (Passover) c43; c53; c55;
c71; c83; c91; c266

Hakafot b126–127; b148–150;
b151–153

Halachah (Torah law) a17; a110;
b42; b99; b195; b201; b267–268;
c59; c119; c124; c141; c170; c177;
c221–222; c228–229; c245

Hallel a47; b164; b196; b242

Haman b230; b240; b241; b242;
b243; b244; b247; b254; b259;
b266

Hamantash b231

Hannah see: Chanah

Hanukkah see: Chanukah

Harmony see: Peace

Hashgachah peratit see: Divine
providence

Hasidism see: Chassidism

Hasmoneans b164; b167; b168; b169;
b174; b188

Havah see: Eve

Havdalah a119–126

Hayom Yom a70; a125; a145; b46; c76

Head b5–7; c7

Hellenism b169–170; b174; b184–
187; b233; c4
also see: Greek

Herod c248; c249

Hezron a153

High priest see: *Kohen gadol*

INDEX

Hillel a24; a219; a222-223; b194-203; c47-50; c137; c206; c220-221; c227-233

Hillel II a215-216

Hillel of Paritch, Rabbi c257

Hirduf see: Nerium oleander

History see: Jewish history

Holiness a25-27; a66; a70; a101-102; a125; a129-131; a171; a212; b74; c173; c205-206; c225; c304; c308-313

also see: Sparks of holiness

Holy Land a23; a134-138; a215; a217; a218; b216; c127; c202; c275-276

Holy of Holies b59-60; c236; c239-243; c254

Holy Temple a135-138; a143; a229; b122; b157; b162; b212; c87; c143; c198-199; c208; c234-234; c239-243; c276; c280; c281

also see: Temple service; Second Temple; and Destruction of the Temple

Home b83-84; b210; c79; c184-185; c237

also see: Dwelling for G-d in the physical world

Honey b3; b152; b221

Horowitz, Rabbi Isaiah see: Shaloh

Hoshana Rabbah (seventh day of Sukkot) b114; b121-124

House of Hillel see: Hillel

House of Shammai see: Shammai

Humanity; human being a191-192; b2; b8-16; b22; b23; b40-41; b84; b197-203; b222-223; c7-8; c47; c164; c168; c188; c192; c248; c258; c288

Hypocrisy b226

Hypothesis (in Torah) a23

I

Idolatry c38; c178; c222-233; c291

Individuality c47-51; c167; c237-238

Inebriation b231; b241-242; b263; b266-271

Infinity a121; a131; c30-33; c160; c164

Initiative see: Personal initiative

Inner will see: Will

Innerness see: *Penimiyut*

Inspiration a185; c98-108

Instantaneousness b57-58; b147; c120-121

Intellect & rationality b15; b90-91; 185-187; b242-246; b262; b267-271; c40-41; c133; c145; c158-161; c187; c257-261

also see: Subconscious

Intermediary a141-142

Internalization see: *Penimiyut*

International date line c102

Intuition b151-153

Iron c282-283

Isaac a67; a153; b2; b92; b94; c159

Isaac Luria, Rabbi see: Ari

Isaiah a86; a105; a110; a124; a132; a162; a229; b34; b65; b95; b96; c26; c45; c52; c53; c56; c69; c87; c92; c139; c145; c194; c213; c215; c217; c234; c235; c249; c250; c256-257; c287; c291

Iskafia (self-conquest) c75-76

Israel see: Jewish identity and Holy Land

Israel, Land of see: Holy Land

Issachar, Tribe of a191

Isserles, Rabbi Moshe see: Rema

Iyar (month) c111-112; c316-317

Iyov see: Job

J

Jacob a62; a67; a153; a161; b92; b94; b244; c8; c39; c71; c74; c159; c266

Jeremiah b56; b82; b207; b255; c52; c56; c89; c209; c212; c245; c247; c249; c253; c256

Jeroboam ben Nebat c276

Jerusalem c208; c249; c276; c285
also see: Siege of Jerusalem

Jerusalem Talmud a55; a120–124; a138; a143; a177; a201; a216; b114; b122; b174; b196–197; c49; c75; c140; c191; c221; c250; c281

Jesse (Yishai; father of King David) a153; c250

Jewish history a153–154; c8; c83; c86–87; c198–200; c270

Jewish identity a53; a124–125; b47; b66; b92; b110; b148–150; b243–246; b250–252; b259–265; c7–9; c12; c28; c38; c45–46; c50; c155–156; c203; c277; c287

Job (biblical book) a223; b46; b72; b171; b244; c84; c258

Jochanan ben Zakkai, Rabbi a114

Jocheved c166

Jonathan (son of Saul) a151; a156; c138; c142–143

Jordan River c18

Joseph a226

Joshua a135; c87

Joshua ben Chanania, Rabbi b96; c4; c10; c192

Joshua ben Eilah, King c276

Joshua ben Levi, Rabbi b135; b138

Joshua, Book of b42

Joshua, Rabbi see: Joshua ben Chanania, Rabbi

Josiah, King c239; c241

Joy b34; b78–79; b101–102; b108–110; b144; b223–224; b262–263; b266–267; b272–275

Jubilee a132–38

Judah a153

Judah ben Beteira, Rabbi c35; c41

Judah HaNassi, Rabbi b57; b65; b69; c120; c123; c215; c217; c218–219

Judah Loew of Prague, Rabbi see: Maharal

Junctures in time a207–233

Justice, Divine attribute of see: *Gevurah*

K

Kabalat ol (obedience to G-d) a172–174; b71; b98–105; b187; b188–189; c53–61
also see: *Merkavah*

Kabbalah c130; c138–142

Karpas c31

Ke'arah see: Seder plate

Keli Yakar a132

Kennedy Airport a37

Keriat yam suf see: Splitting of the Sea

Keruvim (the "cherubim" in the Holy Temple) b213; c224–225; c253–255; c260–261

Ketoret ("incense" burned in the Holy Temple) b59–62

Ketubah (marriage contract) c253

Kiddush a30

Kiddush hachodesh see: Sanctification of the New Month

Kidushin (betrothal) c286; c291–294

Kings; kingship see Divine kingship

Kinot c209

Kislev (month) a187; a188; c316–317

Kitever, Rabbi Gershon a213
Kittel b34
Knowledge of G-d c264
Ko ("like this") b11-13
Kodesh hakadoshim see: Holy of Holies
Kohelet see: Ecclesiastes
Kohen; kohanim (priest) a53; c156; c161; c166
Kohen gadol (high priest) b59; b61; b167; b241; b243
Kol nidrei (prayer) b34
Korach a139
Korban pesach see: Passover offering
Korbanot (animal and meal offerings brought in the Holy Temple) a48-49; a151; a169; b48; b60; c48-50; c205-206
also see: Temple service
Kosher a120; b255; c153

L

Lag BaOmer c129-149
Lamb c19; c40
Lamentations (biblical book) b56; c209; c212; c247; c253
Lamp b180-181
Land & sea c80-85
Land of Israel see: Holy Land
Laser beam c170
Latkes b164
Law see: Halachah
Leap year a193-206
Learning b89; c259-260; c274
also see: Torah, the
Leaven c24; c58; c62-70; c119-120; c121-123
Lecha dodi (prayer) c285

Lechem mishneh (double bread) a109; c55
Leo (constellation) c249
Levi Yitzchak of Berditchev, Rabbi c234-235; c237-238
Levites a53; a191; c86; c159; c166
Life b46
Light a203-206; a218; b53; b170; b173-176
also see: Sunlight
Limitation; constraint b140; c29; c91; c170; c188; c212-213; c288
Lineage c285; c289
Lion c249
Lo tashchit (prohibition to destroy something of value) c245-247
Loft (second floor) b175
Lottery b230; b240-246
Love a7; b44; b52; b131; b151-152; b207-208; b244; b253; c39; c103; c132-137; c257-261; c286-290; c301-302
Lubavitch, town of c296
Lubavitcher Rebbe see: Rebbe, The
Luchot see: Tablets of the Covenant
Lulav (palm frond) b87-88; b90-91; b111
also see: Four kinds
Lunar cycle a150; a151-159; a169; a188; a193-206; c17; c277-278
also see: New moon; Full moon; *Rosh Chodesh*; and Month
Luria, Rabbi Isaac see: Ari
Luxury c71-79

M

Maariv (evening prayer) a67; b34
Maaser; maaserot see: Tithes
Maccabees see: Hasmoneans

Machloket see: Debate (in Torah)

Maharal a23; c28

Maimonides a24; a31; a42–45; a67–68; a83; a121; a168; a201; a231; b45; b47; b60; b73; b109; b115; b150; b260; b264; b268; c31; c49; c63; c103; c174–175; c248; c251; c300
also see: *Mishneh Torah* and *Guide for the Perplexed*

Majority a120; b170; c3; c124; c192; c221–222; c228; c232

Malachi a21; b244; c39

Malchut (*sefirah*/attribute of) a7; a50; a55; a71; a79; a84
also see: Divine kingship

Mankind see: Humanity

Manna a106–118; a139

Marcheshvan see: *Cheshvan*

Maror (bitter herbs) b86; b94; c25; c34; c71; c76–78; c91

Marriage a52; a127; b145–146; b151; b207–208; c187–188; c253–255; c275–276; c286–287; c291–294
also see: Matchmaking; Engagement; *Kidushin*; *Nissu'in*; *Sheva berachot*

Masculinity see: Men & masculinity

Masei (Torah reading) a227–233

Matanot l'evyonim (gifts to the poor on Purim) b231; b235; b242; b253

Matchmaking b270–271; b274; c285

Material world see: Physicality

Matityahu see: Hasmoneans

Matot (Torah reading) a227–233

Matta Mechasia (Babylonian city) c250

Matter see: Physicality

Matzah b86; b94; c25; c34; c53–61; c71; c76–78; c91; c120; c122

Matzah *sheruyah* ("soaked matzah") c66–70

Meal of Moshiach see: Moshiach, Meal of

Means & end c31–33; c148–149

Meat c76–78

Meditation a68; c287

Megillah see: Esther, Book of

Mehadrin (doing more than is obligatory) b191
also see: Stringency

Mehalech ("goer") a155

Melachah (constructive work) a97–105; c246; c305–311
also see: Work and Thirty-nine works

Memory c91

Men & masculinity a50–56; b237; b261–262; c301

Menachem Mendel of Lubavitch, Rabbi a217; a218; b255

Menorah (in the Holy Temple) b164; b167–168; b173–179; b183
also see: Chanukah lights

Merirut see: Sadness

Merkavah (divine "chariot") c266

Mesirat nefesh (self-sacrifice) b188–189; b264–265

Messiah see: Moshiach

Messianic era see: Moshiach, Era of

Metaphor a13–15; c264–265

Midnight c34–36; c39–41

Midrash b42

Mikeitz (Torah reading) a226

Minchah (afternoon prayer) a67; b34

Mind see: Intellect & rationality; Brain; and Mind & heart

Mind & heart a36; c167–168; c257–261

Mineral kingdom see Four kingdoms

Minhag see: Custom
Minyan b93
Miracles a47; b188–189; b245; c6–12;
c15–21; c41; c189; c236
Miriam c18; c86; c88–89
Miriam's well see: Well of Miriam
Mishkan see: Tabernacle, the
Mishlei see: Proverbs
Mishloach manot (sending food-
portions on Purim) b231; b235;
b242; b253
Mishnah a42; a44; a54
Mishneh Torah a32; a43–45; a67;
a124; a125; a129; a138; a140; a168;
a231; b47; b65; b66; b71; b73; b82;
b100; b107; b108; b109; b115; b121;
b122; b175; b190; b223; b268; c31;
c49; c103; c166; c177; c180; c181;
c185; c217; c225; c239; c244; c245;
c246; c248; c251
Mitzrayim see: Egypt
Mitzvah; mitzvot a24–27; a44;
a144–147; a172–173; a200–201;
b9–10; b67; b82–85; b89; b151–153;
b173; b181–183; b210; c9; c38; c40;
c111–112; c184; c194; c204; c208;
c229–230; c286–287
also see: Rabbinically-ordained
mitzvot and Noahide *mitzvot*
Mitzvah mide'oreita (biblical
commandment) a138; c77–78;
c103
Mitzvah, instrument of a28–29;
b9–10; b83; c229–230
Mitzvah, object of a24–27; c173–174;
c225
Mitzvot assei see: Positive
commandments
Mitzvot lo taaseh see: Prohibitions

Mitzvot, women's obligation of
a50–56
Mo'adim (the festivals of the Jewish
calendar) a38–45; a46–47; a48–49
Modeh ani (prayer) a70–72
Molad halevanah see: New moon
Moment, the a31–37; a213–214;
b57–58
also see: Instantaneousness
Month a149–178; a196–197; c7;
c16–18; c277–279
Moon a60; a143; a151–159; a160–166;
a167–174; a196; a198; a199; a203–
206; c277
also see: Lunar cycle; New moon;
Full moon; and Diminution of the
moon
Morality a119; b9; b16
Mordechai b230; b235–237; b241;
b256; b259; b266
Morning a63; a70–72
Morning prayer see: *Shacharit*
Moses a51; a167; a174; a182; a220;
a231; b12; b37; b38; b39; b42; b43;
b45; b137; b243–244; c2; c13; c24;
c28–29; c36; c40; c51; c71; c72;
c87; c115–116; c117; c126; c147;
c155; c156; c157; c160; c166; c171;
c172; c173; c178; c180; c181; c183;
c220; c222; c223–224; c226; c249;
c260; c264; c281; c296; c299–300
Moses' staff a139
Moshiach (the messiah) a177; c140;
c143; c210; c249; c250–252; c266–
267; c286
Moshiach, era of a85–88; a89; a94;
a105; a127; a128; a129; a132;
a143–147; a232; c26; c52; c69; c87;
c90; c92–93; c191; c217–219; c280;

c283–284; c291; c293–294
also see: World to Come
Moshiach, meal of c69; c92–93
Motion; movement a77–78
Mourning a127–128; c130
Mud b184–187; c82–85
Murder (in the spiritual sense) c300
Musaf (prayer) a111; b5; b34; b72;
c242; c255
Music see: Song; music
Myrtle see: *Hadas*
Mysticism see: *Kabbalah*

N

Nachmanides a47; a85; a125; a128;
a142–143; b73; b208; b221; c54;
c75; c240; c251
Nahshon a153
Nassi c2
Nathan, Rabbi c192
Nature; natural order a130; b45;
b238; b245; b249; b254–258;
c8–12; c20–21; c41; c120; c189
Nazir c74–75
Ne'ilah (prayer) b34; b35
Nebuchadnezzar b245; c215; c239;
c244–245; c249
Negative commandments see:
Prohibitions (*mitzvot*)
Neighbor c177
Nerium oleander b88; b92
Neurology see: Brain
New moon a151–153; a167–174; 177;
a196; a215; c2; c278
also see: *Rosh Chodesh*
New year for chassidism see:
Nineteenth of *Kislev*
New year for trees see: Tu BiShevat
Nidcheh see: Postponed fast day

Niddah (menstruating woman) a127
Night a62–63; a65–69; b173–179;
c274
Nightfall a139–140; b173–179
Nile River c31
Nine Days, the c209
Nineteenth of *Kislev* a187–188; c5
Ninth of *Av* see: Tishah B'Av
Nissan (month) a157; a184; a186;
a196–197; b94; b137; c1–12; c13–14;
c146; c278; c316–317
Nissu'in (full marriage) c286;
c291–294
Nitzutzei kedushah see: Sparks of
holiness
Noahide *mitzvot* a231
Numerology see *Gematria*

O

Obed a153
Obedience see *Kabalat ol*
Object, the a24–27
Ocean see: Land & sea
Ohr HaChaim a232; c281
Oil b181–182; b187; b188–189; b226;
b233–234
Oleander see: *Nerium oleander*
Olive a225; b226
Omer (biblical measure) a106; c100
Omer offering c98; c100; c101; c103;
c196; c198–199
also see: Counting of the *omer*
One (number) c167–168; c187
Oral Torah a54; a65; b42; b86–87;
b97; b102; b199; b201–203; c104;
c175; c191–192
Order of Evolution see *Seder
hishtalshelut*
Outer will see: Will

INDEX 373

Outreach c45-46; c136-137; c194
Ownership b106-108; b113

P

Palm frond see: *Lulav*
Parable see: Metaphor
Parashah see: Torah-reading cycle
Parnasah see: Earning a living
Passover a157; a186; a190; a191; a196;
  b94; b135; b144; c6; c23-93
Passover offering b86; b94; c19; c25;
  c34; c37-38; c40; c43; c47-52;
  c71; c76-78; c115; c121; c124; c127
Past, the a34; a213; b262; c91
Peace a77; a81; a86-87; b227;
  c166-170
Penimiyut (innerness; integrity)
  a222; b133-134; b139-140; b144;
  b233-234; c56
Perez a153
Perfection a86; a136-138; a181-183;
  b90; b112; b227; c70; c103; c104-
  108; c289
Perpetual creation (doctrine of)
  a31-37; a70; c262-263
Personal initiative a184-189; a195-
  202; c98-108; c287-288; c302-303
Pesach Sheini c113-128
Peshitut see: Simplicity
Pharaoh c20; c28; c31; c36; c37; c54;
  c80; c178
Philosophy b45
Physicality a8; a25-27; a68; a204-
  206; b28; b72-75; b92; b158-162;
  b207-213; b233-234; b235-239;
  b241-242; 244-246; c74-79;
  c125; c134-135; c171-176; c182;
  c184-186; c217-218; c224-225;
  c228-231; c308; c312-313

Pi a83
Pirkei Avot see: Ethics of the Fathers
Plague of the Firstborn c19-20; c25;
  c34; c36-37
Pleasure a99; a110; a115; b100; b207-
  208; b212-213; c75; c76-78
  also see: Desire
Pluralism c132-137; c158-161;
  c162-165
Point (geometry) a82-83; c35
Pomegranates b225-226
Positive & negative c291-294
Positive commandments (*mitzvot*)
  a50; a54; b49; c122; c230;
  c291-292
Postponed fast day c215-219
Potato pancakes see: *Latkes*
Potential vs. actual b196-201; c223
Poverty a164; c25; c53; c55; c57-58;
  c76-79; c290
Prayer a49; a66-69; a201; b25-31;
  b210; c86; c287; c305
Present see: Moment, the
Priests see: *Kohen; kohanim*
Private domain (Shabbat) a95-105
Prohibitions (*mitzvot*) a50; a54;
  b49-54; c75; c122; c221; c229;
  c291-292
Prophecy b12; b44; b45-46; b249
Proverbs b44; b86; b88; b173; b180;
  b226; b272-274; c148; c166; c181;
  c203
Psalms a44; a50; a67; a69; a157;
  a164; a195; b10; b12; b22; b23; b34;
  b37; b41; b56; b66; b75; b99; b101;
  b117; b151; b167; b184-185; b222;
  b227; b244; b266; b272; b273;
  b275; c20; c33; c63; c83; c86; c87;
  c172; c181; c212; c242; c249; c267;
  c268; c279; c306

Ptolemy, King c220; c226; c227

Public domain (Shabbat) a95-105

Punishment (for sin) b44-46; c37-38; c39; c260

Pur see: Lottery

Purim a157-158; a187; b169; b202-203; b229-271; c6; c306

Purim Katan b272-275

Pushka (charity box) a28

Q

Quality vs. quantity b57-58

Quorum see: *Minyan*

R

Rabbeinu Bechayei see: Bechayei

Rabbeinu Yerucham see: Yerucham, Rabbeinu

Rabbinically-ordained *mitzvot* a138; a187; b152-153; b176; b201-203; c67-68; c77-78; c103; c198-199; c216

Rachel c89

Radak a31

Radbaz c35

Radio a4-5

Radius a83-85

Rain a117; a184-189; b157

Rainbow a139; c140

Ram a153

Rasha (sinner; wicked person) b46; c43-44; c83-84; c290; c300

Rashab see Shalom DovBer of Lubavitch, Rabbi

Rashba a36-37; a142

Rashbi see: Shimon bar Yochai, Rabbi

Rashi a20; a21-22; a23; a49; a54; a80; a100; a108; a115; a120; a131;

a135; a138; a167; a182; a196; a222; a225; b31; b37; b38; b41; b56; b94; b100; b111; b130; b139; b184; b185; b197; b207; b224; b236; b248; c9; c32; c34-35; c38; c44; c53; c74; c105; c126; c127; c155; c156; c158; c159; c179; c180; c183; c220; c222; c253; c254; c289; c309

Rationality see: Intellect & rationality

Rava b266

Real estate c180; c182

Reality a83-85; b196-198; b212; c162-163; c266-267; c291

Reason see: Intellect & rationality

Rebbe, The aII-III; a35-37; a208; c266-267; c292

Rebbi see: Judah HaNassi, Rabbi

Recipient see: Giver-recipient relationship

Red Heifer a146

Red Sea, splitting of see: Splitting of the Sea

Redemption c8; c44; c45; c54-55; c86-90; c92-93; c203; c210; c213; c251-252; c274; c278

also see: Moshiach, era of; Four expressions of redemption; and Yearning for redemption

Regret c262-265

Rehoboam (Judean king) a153

Reish Lakish a161

Relationships c187-188; c253-261; c291-294; c301-303

also see: Marriage and Giver-recipient relationship

Rema (Rabbi Moshe Isserles) b273

Repentance see *Teshuvah*

Rephidim c158; c161

Rest a80-88; a130-131

INDEX   375

Restraint c103
Reward a144-147; c39; c72
Righteous person see *Tzaddik*
Ritual impurity a127; b190; b196–
 197; b200; c115
Ritual slaughter see: *Shechitah*
Rome; Romans c134; c172; c208;
 c215; c216; c256; c276; c280; c282
Roots b217-219
Rosh Chodesh ("head of the month")
 a156; a161; a167-174; a214; a219–
 221; b7; c278; c305
 also see Lunar cycle; Full
 moon; and *Shabbat mevarachim*
 hachodesh
Rosh Hashanah a110; a111; a157;
 a187; a212-217; b1-31; b34; b65–
 66; b70-71; b101; c2; c5-8; c278
Russia see: Soviet Union

S

Saadiah Gaon, Rabbi a21; a31; a108;
 c251
Sabbatical year a129
 also see: *Shemittah* cycle
Sadducees b95; b97-98; b102-104
Sadness c63; c214
Salmon (son of Nahshon) a153
Samuel a161; b30-31
Sanctification of the New Month
 a22-30; a150; a167-174; a198;
 a215-216
Sanctuary, the see: Tabernacle, the
Sanhedrin a150; a169-171; a198;
 a215-216; b122; b133; b237; c49;
 c102
Saul, King c142-143
Schneerson, Rabbi Menachem
 Mendel see: Rebbe, The

Schneerson, Rabbi Yosef Yitzchak
 a35-37; a225; c114; c116; c296
Schneur Zalman of Liadi, Rabbi
 a21; a33; a34; a68; a121; a125; a182;
 a187; a225; b13; b25; b46; b48;
 b60; b129; b161; b255; c11; c59;
 c67; c75-76; c83; c145; c147; c251;
 c267; c275; c306
 also see: *Tanya*
School of Hillel see: Hillel
School of Shammai see: Shammai
Science c189
Scroll of Esther see: Esther, Book of
Sea see: Land & sea
Sea of Reeds see: Splitting of the Sea
Seasons a179-192; a196; b90
Second day of *Sivan* c155-156
Second day of the festivals a214-218;
 b133; b136; c67-68; c92; c120; c205
Second Passover see: *Pesach Sheini*
Second Tablets see Tablets of the
 Covenant and Broken Tablets
Second Temple a135-138; b213; c239;
 c240-242
 also see: Holy Temple
Seder (Passover) a24; a157; a211;
 a86; b196; c25; c31; c34; c42-43;
 c45-46; c52; c53-61; c71-79; c82;
 c92; c100; c278
Seder hishtalshelut a3-19; a213; b161
Seder plate c25; c53; c55; c77
Seeds b219-220; b225
Sefer HaBahir c278
Sefer HaChinuch a46; a47
Sefer Yetzirah b150; b272
Sefirat haomer see: Counting of the
 omer
Sefirot (kabbalah) a78-79; a128-129;
 b140; b227; c39-40; c65; c68; c96;
 c102-103; c120; c257

Self-abnegation see *Bittul*

Self-denial see: Asceticism

Selfhood see: Ego and *Bittul*

Selichot (prayer) b25–26; c297

Septuagint, the c220–221; c225–227

Seudat Moshiach see: Moshiach, Meal of

Seven (number) a77–88; a127–129; b178; b227; c119–120

Seven fruits (of the Holy Land) b216; b221–227;

Seven Noahide laws see: Noahide *mitzvot*

Seven of consolation (*haftarot*) c256–259; c296

Seventeenth of *Tammuz* b37; b39; b42–43; c208–209; c215; c220–233; c256; c280; c299

Seventh day of Passover c6; c80; c87; c92

also see: Splitting of the sea

Seventh of *Cheshvan* b157; b161–162

Seventy (number) b227

Seventy languages c220–221

Sforno, Rabbi Ovadiah a20; a31; c54

Shabbat a74; a77–88; a89–94; a95–105; a106–118; a124–126; a127–131; a211; a214; a219–224; b7; b114; b122–123; c16; c18–19; c48–49; c104–105; c178; c181; c216; 218–219; c246; c305; c307; c309–311

Shabbat candles a110; b173; b177–178

Shabbat Chazon c234–238

Shabbat HaGadol c2–3; c15–21

Shabbat meals a109–110; c216

Shabbat mevarachim hachodesh (the Shabbat before *Rosh Chodesh*) a175–178

Shabbat Shirah c88

Shacharit (morning prayer) a67; b34

Sha-dai (divine name) a8

Shadchan (matchmaker) b270–271

also see: Matchmaking

Shaloh a10–11; a32; a226–227; b45; b73; b208; c64

Shalom DovBer of Lubavitch, Rabbi a145; b255; c5

Shamash (servant candle) b193

Shamir (worm) a139

Shammai a219; a222–223; a194–199; c206; c220–222; c228–233

Shankbone see: *Zeroa*

Shavuot a133; a190; a192; b42; b136–137; b139–140; b144; b149–150; c17; c25; c29; c64; c68; c96; c101–102; c152–206

Shechinah see: Divine presence

Shechitah (ritual slaughter) a120

Sheloshah d'puru'nita see: Three of rebuke

Shem (son of Noah) c159

Shema, the a67

Shemini Atzeret a132; a217; b79; b125–147

Shemittah cycle a74; a128; a132–138; b216

also see: Sabbatical year

Sheva berachot (marriage benedictions and celebration) a127; c293

Shevet; Shevatim see: Tribes of Israel

Shevi'i shel pesach see: Seventh day of Passover

Shiloah Spring b96

Shiloh b29; c245

Shimon bar Yochai, Rabbi c130; c132–136; c138–132; c144–149; c251

Shimon ben Gamliel, Rabban c275; c277

INDEX   377

Shirat hayam see: Song at the sea
Shiva d'nechemta see: Seven of
  consolation
Shivah (week of mourning) a127
Shivah Asar b'Tammuz see:
  Seventeenth of *Tammuz*
Shlomo ben Aderet, Rabbi see:
  Rashba
Shmuel Munkes, Rabbi b25-26
Shofar a157; b2-3; b17-18; b70; b71;
  b101; b114; b122-123; c212-213;
  c279; c296
Shtei halechem see: Two loaves
Shulchan Aruch (code of Torah law)
  a53; a97; b81-82; b100; b107;
  b133-134; b148; b233; b263; b268;
  b272-273; c3; c34; c58; c59; c68;
  c133; c136; c177; c180-181; c185;
  c216; c219; c248; c250; c274
Shulchan Aruch HaRav a108; a110-
  111; a216; b107; c15; c18; c20; c67;
  c69; c77; c103; c200; c206; c245
Shushan b230; 254
Siege of Jerusalem b213; c215; c256;
  c280
Simchat beit hashoeivah see: Water-
  drawing celebrations
Simchat Torah a225; b126-127; b133-
  134; b135-147; b148-150; b151-153
Simon, Rabbi b114; b122
Simplicity b114-124
Sin b2; b3; b41; b44-56; b67; b141-
  143; c118; c124; c214; c242; c300
Sin'at chinam see: Divisiveness
Sinai see: Giving of the Torah
Sivan (month) c166; c316-317
Sivan 1 see: First day of *Sivan*
Sivan 2 see: Second day of *Sivan*
Sivan 12 see: Twelfth of *Sivan*
Six (number) a83-85

Six days of creation a78-85; c10; c16
Sixteenth (of the month) a151-159
Sixteenth of *Tammuz* c222-223;
  c226; c232-233
Sixth day (of creation) b8
Sleep a60; a62-63; a71; b17-18
Smallness a160-166
Soil a191; b185
Solar seasons see: Seasons
Solar year see: Year
Solomon, King a13-14; a143; a153;
  b45; b86-94; b207; b225; c87;
  c148; c239; c240; c249; c253
Song at the sea c86-90; c92
Song of Songs b207; b225; c87; c239;
  c253; c301-302; c305
Song; music c86-87
Soul, the b46-48; b68; b71; b180-
  183; b209; c32; c73; c84; c181; c286
  also see: *Sefirot*; Spirituality; and
  Animal soul
Sovereignty see: Divine kingship
Soviet Union a35-36
Space c236; c294
Spacetime a82
Sparks of holiness (kabbalah)
  a231-232; b49-52; c73-74; c149;
  c270-271
Speech a89-92; a120-123
Sphere see: Circle
Spies, the c209; c216; c275; c281
Spiritual space a9
Spiritual time a10-11
Spirituality a7; a8; a204-205; a212;
  a223; b72; b74; b158-159; b167-
  172; b211; b233-234; b241; c172;
  c174; c179; c182; c304-313
Splitting of the Sea b11; c8; c24; c54;
  c80-85; c87
  also see: Song at the sea

Spring a190; a196–197; b145–147; c13–14

Stricture see: Limitation; constraint

Stringency (in Torah law) c228–233 also see: *Mehadrin*

Struggle a77; a145–147; a222; b90; b226; c84–85

Subconscious a71–72; a93–94; c80–82; c234–235

Sufganiot see: Doughnuts

Sukkah b35; b78; b81–85; b106–108; b112–113; b131–134

Sukkot (festival of) a157; a190; a217; b77–124; b130; b135; b143–144; b157; b161; b162; c279

Summer a184–189; b138; b140–141

Sun a60; a143; a154; a160; a161; a163; a184–187; a196; a198; a199; a204

Sunday a219–224

Sunlight a184–187; a204–206

Synagogue c248–250

Syria c172

Syrian-Greeks see: Hellenists

T

Tabernacle, the a127; a132; c2; c224–225; c308–310

Tablets of the Covenant a139; a146–147; b37–43; b61; b141–142; b149–150; c240; c286; c299

Tachanun (prayer) c3

Talmud a54

Talmud (citations from)

Berachot a30; a60; a67–68; a89; a132; a228; b18; b41; b46; b51; b56; b66; b68; b72–73; b98; b100; b200; b223; b225; c4; c11; c72–73; c77; c116; c124; c147; c158; c161; c178; c300; c311

Shabbat a47; a62; a64; a95; a98; a109; a114; a140; a145; b9; b88; b94; b111; b167–172; b173; b175; b188–189; b191; b194–195; b247–248; b255; c18; c51; c134–135; c137; c144–145; c146; c155c166; c178–179; c181; c190; c201; c220; c307; c309

Eruvin a85; a139; a144; b91; b223; b233; c124; c288

Pesachim a142; a225; a231; b175; b176; b190; b196–197; c19–20; c77; c115; c119–120; c122; c123; c126; c162–163; c270

Yoma a117; a137; b44; b51–52; b60; b62; b68; b84; b186; b213; c109; c159; c171; c236; c239–240; c253–254

Sukkah a151; b82; b87–88; b95–96; b106; b121–122; b132; b133–134; c262

Beitzah a110–111; a219; a222; c206

Rosh Hashanah a30; a43; a157; a182; a213; b65; b275; c4; c5; c6; c10; c279

Taanit a117; a228; b43; b157; b207; b267; c216; c253; c275; c285; c287

Megillah a197; a222; b207–208; b236; b240; b243–244; b254; b256; b259–260; b263; b266; b268; b273–274; c215; c217; c234

Chagigah a8; b90; c205; c241

Yevamot a125; a210; a211; c75; c133; c134; c184

Nedarim b42; c58; c75; c160; c290

Sotah a52; b46; b48; b190; b233; c90; c100; c196; c220–221; c281; c300

INDEX   379

Gittin a139
Kidushin a53; b16; b58; b84; b200;
   c75; c292
Bava Metzia c106; c177; c180;
   c135; c192
Bava Batra a114; c248; c250; c254
Sanhedrin a85; a89; a128; a228;
   b22; b93; b142; b157-162; c73;
   c74-75; c92; c181; c203; c223;
   c236; c251
Makot a54; c305
Shevuot b65; b69
Avodah Zarah b57-58; b81-82;
   c120-121
Eiduyot c232
Sofrim c227
Sefer Torah c220
Menachot a52; c103; c104-105
Chulin a66; a154; a160-161; a201;
   c74; c76; c80
Erchin a127; a135; c63; c122
Temurah c49
Tamid c218
Middot c283
Keilim c238
Nidah a64
Uktzin b197
also see: Ethics of the Fathers and
   Jerusalem Talmud
Tambourine c88
Tammuz 16 see: Sixteenth of
   Tammuz
Tammuz 17 see: Seventeenth of
   Tammuz
Tanya a25; a31; a33; a36; a54; a90;
   a98; a121-122; a125; a182; a223;
   b13; b16; b17; b28; b46; b50; b52;
   b60; b61; b72; b91; b93; b104;
   b146; b158; b161; b171; b189; b209;
   b222; c6; c11; c63; c83-85; c109;

   c136; c145; c147; c183; c185; c187;
   c195; c243; c266; c287; c290; c292
Tashlich b3
Taste c58-61; c69
Tea essence b129-130
Teacher & student c259-260
Tefilin b259; b265
Telegraph a3-4
Temple service a48-49; a66; b78;
   b95; b121; b190; b241-243; c25;
   c48; c64; c36; c205; c208; c215;
   c277; c282-283
   also see: Korbanot
Temple, the see: Holy Temple
Ten Commandments a54; b38; b40;
   b42; c8; c153; c176; c201; c240
   also see: Tablets of the Covenant
Ten days of *Teshuvah* b34; b43;
   b65-71; c300
Ten Plagues c20; c36-37; c54
Ten Utterances a3; a6; a31; a89-92;
   a121-123
Tenth of *Nissan* c18
Tenth of *Tevet* b206; b213; b215; b216
Teshuvah (return; repentance) a145;
   a187; b2; b7; b11; b34; b37-43;
   b44-56; b57-58; b59-64; b65-71;
   b141-147; c109; c116-125; c216;
   c296; c300
Testimonial *mitzvot* a44; b242
Tevet (month) b204-213; c316-317
Tevet 10 see: Tenth of Tevet
Third Temple c236; c240; c248-249
Thirteen attributes of mercy c300;
   c305
Thirty-nine works (Shabbat) a95-
   105; c246; c307-311
Thought a89-94; c10
Three (number) a210-212; a218;
   b91-92; c166-170; c187-190

Three of rebuke (*haftarot*) c256–259
Three Weeks, the a227; a229–230;
    a233; c207–271; c256–259; c280
Thursday a211
Tiferet (*sefirah*/attribute of) c166
Time a1–56; a58; a77–88; b5–6;
    c34–36; c109–110
Time as the first creation a11;
    a20–30
Timelessness a3–19; c35; c265
Tishah B'Av c208–210; c215–216;
    c219; c234; c239; c244; c250–252;
    c256; c280
Tishrei (month) a157; a184; a186;
    a187; a218; b79; b94; b101–102;
    b126; b137–138; b141; b144; b151–
    153; b157–158; c2; c4–12; c146;
    c278–279; c316–317
Tithes b216; c5
Toil see: Struggle
Tolerance c132–137
Tomorrow see: Morning and Future
Torah, the a201–202; b89; b142–143;
    b148–150; b198–201; b259; b261–
    262; c30; c32–33; c87; c117–118;
    c119; c134–135; c144–149; c152;
    c160; c163–165; c168–169; c177–
    186; c189–192; c193–200; c253;
    c291; c305
    also see: Giving of the Torah;
    Written Torah; Oral Torah;
    Tablets of the Covenant; and
    Halachah
Torah scroll b148–150
Torah-reading cycle a109; a225–227;
    b126; b135–137
Toughness 227–230; 233
Tranquility a144–147; b227
    also see: Rest
Translation c220–221; c225–227

Tree of Knowledge b224
Trees b217–220; b221
Tribes of Israel a53; a228–229;
    c275–276; c282
Trust in G-d a111–118
Truth a195; b91; c132–137; c162–165;
    c225
Tu BiShevat a157; a190; b215–227; c5
Tum'ah see: Ritual impurity
Tur a68; b100; b121; b268; c68; c133
Turnus Rufus a95; a104
Twelfth of *Sivan* c205
Twilight a139–147
Two (number) c167–168; c187–188;
    c291
Two loaves (Shavuot offering) c64;
    c153; c196–197
Two Tablets see: Tablets of the
    Covenant
Tzaddik (perfectly righteous person)
    a182; b18; b51–55; b58; b94; b110;
    b144–147; b227; c12; c74; c83–85;
    c120–125; c134; c233; c290; c300
Tzelafchad's daughters c117
Tzemach Tzedek see: Menachem
    Mendel of Lubavitch, Rabbi
Tzom Gedaliah see Fast of Gedaliah

U

U'netaneh tokef (prayer) b7
Ugliness c285; c289–290
Unity b106–113; b123–124; b131–134;
    c158–161; c166–169; c187–189; c282
Unity of G-d a32; a121–122; b55;
    b74–75; b115; b159; c220–233

V

Vayeishev (Torah reading) a226
Vayigash (Torah reading) a226

INDEX 381

Vegetable kingdom see: Four kingdoms
Vegetables c76-78
Vernal equinox a196; a198
Virgo (constellation) c303

W

Water b95-105
also see: Land & sea
Water-drawing celebrations (Sukkot) b78; b95-105; 109
Wealth a163-164; c71-74; c271
Wedding ring c292
Week a73-147; a139; a213; a220-221; c7; c15-21; c68; c101-108; c120
Weekly Torah-reading cycle see: Torah-reading cycle
Well of Miriam a139; c87
Wheat a192; b222-223;
Wick b181-183
Wicked child (Passover) c43-44
Will b17-24; b47; c265
Willow see: *Aravah*
Window b175
Wine b95; b97; b99; b102; b223-224; b230; b233-234; c57; c58; c60; c74
also see: Inebriation
Winter a184-189; b138-144; b204-213
Witnesses a167-170; a173-174
Women & femininity a50-56; b237; b261-262; c88-90; c285; c301-303
Woodcutting c277; c282-283
Words a120-123; c226
Work a74; a95-105; c30-31; c305-311
also see: Earning a living
World to Come a132; a144-147; a162-166; b72-75; c236

also see: Moshiach and Moshiach, Era of
Worship of the Golden Calf see: Golden Calf
Written Torah b86; b199; b201; c191

Y

Ya'aleh veyavo (prayer) c69
Yahrtzeit (anniversary of passing) a182-183; c130; c133; c135-136; c139-140
Yam suf see: Splitting of the Sea
Yamim Nora'im see: Days of Awe; Rosh Hashanah; Yom Kippur; and Ten Days of *Teshuvah*
Year a151; a179-192; a196; a203-206; a210; b189
Yearning for redemption c268-271
Yechidut a35
Yemei tashlumin ("fulfillment days" of the festival of Shavuot) c205-206
Yerucham, Rabbeinu c103; c199
Yetzirah (world of) a82; a213
also see: *Sefer Yetzirah*
Yichus see: Lineage
Yishmael, Rabbi c35; c41; c144
Yitzchaki, Rabbi Shlomo see: Rashi
Yom Kippur a111; a187; b5; b33-75; b141; b144; b241-243; b244-246; c6; c274; c275; c277; c285-286
Yom Tov sheni shel galuyot see: Second day of the festivals
Yosef, Rav c162-165

Z

Zebulun, Tribe of a191
Zedekiah (Judean king) a153
Zeh ("this") b11-13

Zemirot (Shabbat songs) a110
Zeroa ("shankbone" on *seder* plate)
   c25; c77
Zimum (refutation of witnesses) a168
Zodiac see: <u>Leo</u> and <u>Virgo</u>
Zohar a60; a61; a62; a84; a89; a115;
   a124; a141–142; a151; a174; b7;
   b10; b23; b62; b73; b131; b150;
   b227; b242; c38; c57; c64; c133;
   c138; c139; c140; c145–146; c181;
   c235; c248; c277–278
Zot Chanukah (the 8th day of
   Chanukah) b195–196